THE
ST. MARY'S
ST. MARY'S CITY, MARYLAND 20686

The Writer's Practical Rhetoric

Adrienne Robins
Department of English • Occidental College

The Writer's Practical Rhetoric

With a guest chapter on library use
by **Ann Waggoner** • Reference Librarian
California State University, Northridge

John Wiley & Sons
New York • Chichester • Brisbane • Toronto

Cover and book design by Laura C. Ierardi
Cover photo by LeBe/Alpha
Production Supervision by Rose Mary Hirsch

Copyright © 1980, by John Wiley & Sons, Inc.

All rights reserved. Published simultaneously in Canada.

Reproduction or translation of any part of
this work beyond that permitted by Sections
107 and 108 of the 1976 United States Copyright
Act without the permission of the copyright
owner is unlawful. Requests for permission
or further information should be addressed to
the Permissions Department, John Wiley & Sons.

Library of Congress Cataloging in Publication Data:

Robins, Adrienne.
   The writer's practical rhetoric.

   Includes indexes
   1. English language—Rhetoric. 2. English language—Grammar—1950-
      I. Waggoner, Ann, joint author.
II. Title
PE1408.R599   808'.042   79-19667
ISBN 0-471-03033-3

Printed in the United States of America

10 9 8 7 6 5 4 3 2 1

Preface

A friend of mine once told me this story:

> When I was first in college, I took a writing class. One of the first things I discovered in my composition class was that I had not been taught how to write in high school. I had written book reports and what I had thought were term papers (they weren't), but now something new was expected. Teachers called it a "paper." I would set out to write 500 words on the assigned topic, would try to put down my ideas on paper, but they never came out right. That term I did a lot of writing, but my papers improved very little because I kept making the same errors, over and over. I continued to get C's and found half-encouraging comments like "Your ideas are good, but your writing is undisciplined." It took me several more years to recognize that my problem was exactly what my teacher had suggested. In my writing there was no system. I never knew that I should have started with a broad idea, narrowed it, brought it into focus in a statement. No wonder I couldn't say anything well. Even worse, I know I was not the only person in my class without any idea of how to go about writing an essay. And the knowledge that I wasn't the only one probably made it possible for me to get through those years.

This person is now an English teacher, so it can be assumed that he now has a system that he feels quite comfortable with and that produces results, for him and his students. What cannot be assumed is that all his schoolmates found ways to improve their writing.

In fact, when I began teaching, I found that there were many students who, like my friend and his classmates, didn't know how to go about writing a paper. I also was convinced that writing skills could be taught, that insights could be channeled and clearly expressed by writers once they had some system at hand. These observations led me to survey the textbooks used in composition classes. Did they teach a system? Few cover even one system from beginning to end. Consequently, I have emphasized in this book a step-by-step process derived from the processes of successful writers. By following a plan, the writer can identify a purpose and a strategy at every stage of composing. The plan is not just a formula, however. Conscious writing is the key—the only way to become a good writer. Writers must listen to themselves, identify what they want to say, and check what flows onto paper to be sure it says what they mean. Through a process, call it a happy combination of nature and discipline, comes a direct, lively style, a worthwhile statement.

My approach is based on six principles.

1. Writing improves with frequent practice based on sound writing processes.
2. Writing is a process in which ideas arise spontaneously and must be judged, constantly and instantaneously.
3. The act of writing itself can generate ideas. Making a place for it in one's daily schedule stretches the mind, making it seek ideas to explore.
4. Not all writing, not even what is published, is necessarily good, and part of becoming a good writer is being critical of what one reads.
5. Writer's "block" can often be overcome by concentrating on a series of steps that lead to the final paper.
6. There is no one way to write. Different people require slightly different methods. The presentation of alternative reliable methods is important to the teaching of writing and the recognition of each person's uniqueness.

Keeping each of these points in mind, I have tried to design a practical book that is based on steps in a suggested system for writing. However, the chapters may be used in various sequences since they are independent.

Chapter 1 introduces some of the key considerations of college writers—what college writing is like, how a writer sounds, what approach writers take to their material, and how audience influences this approach. The last part of the chapter is an overview of the writing process taken up in the next seven chapters.

Chapter 2 poses various solutions to the problem, "What should I write about?" It quickly moves into a method of developing a topic into a thesis that will control the development of the essay.

Reinforcing the sense of purpose the writer defines in the preceding chapter, Chapter 3 describes the major patterns of organization writers use. This chapter also stimulates the imagination of the writer to entice the reader with appropriate and eye-catching beginnings and provocative endings that flow with the rest of the essay. Examples from students' essays provide realizable goals for the student writer.

Chapter 4 engages the writer in the outlining and reasoning process. Developing both scratch and formal outlines comes in here, with special emphasis on how to detect logical errors early in the essay writing process. It is at this stage, before the rough draft gets under way, that a series of easy-to-understand tests for logic may be applied.

Chapter 5 presents the paragraph, the basic structural block of the essay. The chapter shows structural similarities and differences between paragraphs and full essays and between journalistic paragraphs and those in college writing. Development of thoughtful, coherent paragraphs is emphasized through establishing clear boundaries for each paragraph and creating within each block careful play between coordination and subordination. Paragraph models are put into the framework of Christensen's "generative rhetoric."

Chapter 6 shows the writer how to direct emphasis and meaning through varied sentence structure, by combining related ideas, using deliberate marks of punctuation, and imitating the styles of established writers.

Chapter 7 encourages concrete and direct word choice, correct use of the dictionary, building a solid but natural vocabulary, avoiding wordiness, and recognizing levels of language appropriate to various audiences, purposes, and occasions. Strategies for vocabulary development and avoiding trite expressions or jargon are included.

Chapter 8 takes writers from the rough draft to the polished paper, offering a three-step method for identifying and correcting common writing flaws, among them deadwood, trite phrases, faulty repetition, and excessive reliance on "to be."

Chapter 9 is a comprehensive guide to library use written by Ann Wagonner, Reference Librarian at California State University, Northridge. Arranged by subject areas, the guide is easy to use. Its lively, conversational tone makes it appropriate for a one-sitting reading, but its design by subjects most students are familiar with makes the guide a handy reference as well.

Chapter 10 takes the writer through ten effective steps for writing a research paper. This chapter has been used for five years as the handout for the annual Term Paper Clinic at Occidental College. A sample complete research paper, annotated with helpful information, ends the chapter.

Chapter 11 explains and gives samples of various special assignments and writing tasks: journals, book reviews, annotated bibliographies, business letters and resumes, and scientific papers.

Chapter 12 is the "basics" section of the text with descriptions of the parts of speech, sentence structures, and dialects, followed by a brief discussion of common interdialectical and interlanguage confusions. A final section explains the principles of spelling and lists commonly misspelled words.

Chapter 13 explains how to correct common errors. Many writers will want to review the entire section, which is organized in a step-by-step process. Others will find the section a handy ready reference before and after their papers are graded. The chapter explains alternative practices for freeing writing of such prevalent errors as subject and verb disagreements, faulty predication, faulty pronoun reference and agreement, and so forth.

Chapter 14 is a comprehensive glossary of effective punctuation and mechanics. Effective examples for each rule are stressed and revisions for common weak or incorrect usages are suggested.

Chapter 15 is the usage guide, a glossary of commonly misused and confused expressions. Suggested reworkings for the entries are all in context. The glossary, written with the awareness that language is not static, also explains that certain usages are controversial.

Each step in the process is based on sound theories of teaching writing, and moreover, on the patterns of good thinking. Writing and thinking should not be separated, and presenting only the steps without showing writers the progress of their thinking could be of little more help than having no method. While there are no departures from the practical intent of this book—and there are not, therefore, lengthy discussions of theory—writers can see as they prewrite, write, and rewrite how good writing clarifies thought. This book, then, is no shortcut to the essay. Quite the contrary, it asks writers to slow down and examine the landscape. It invites them to experience their own writing processes.

I thank the following scholars in various fields who kindly advised or greatly influenced me in the preparation of the manuscript: Kenneth Oliver, Robert Noreen, Delores Lipscomb Anderson, and William Stryker in English; Bill Neblett in philosophy; David West in chemistry; Judy Anderson in psychology; Andrew Rolle in history; and Onofre Di Stephano in Spanish. I also thank Emmett Dingley for his helpful suggestions in the early stages of the manuscript and Jim Gray of the Bay Area Writing Project whose consultations during a workshop on the teaching of writing inspired me to make substantial change in the sentence chapter. If there is one book I am indebted to it is *Errors and Expectations* by Mina Shaughnessy. I thank my husband, Steven Robins of Antelope Valley College, for his invaluable encouragement and for the many hours of professional time he devoted to this project. I hope also that Steve Perine, Tom Gay, Arthur Vergara, and, especially, Clifford Mills of John Wiley and Sons realize that their many suggestions have been helpful.

Adrienne Robins

Contents

1 How Do You Write an Essay? 1
   Audience 2
   Modes of the Essay 7
   Point of View 12
   Development of Ideas 15
   Tone 19
   The Writing Process 24
      A Chronicle of One Student's Essay 26

2 What Should You Write About? 35
   Why Prewriting? 36
   Inventing the Subject 37
   Limiting the Subject 38
   Exploring the Subject 39
      Keeping a Writer's Notebook 39
      Brainstorming 42
      The Subject Chart 47
   Pinpointing the Limited Subject 48
   Developing a Thesis 50

3 How Should You Organize Your Ideas? 56
   Writing Good Introductions 57
      The Basic Patterns 58
      Effective Strategies for Introductions 59
      Ineffective Strategies for Introductions 62
   Writing Good Middles 67
      Process Order 67
      Chronological Order 68
      Spatial Order 68
      Classification Order 69
      Illustration Order 70
      Comparison Order 71
   Writing Good Conclusions 77
      Basic Patterns 78
      Effective Strategies for Conclusions 79
      Ineffective Strategies for Conclusions 83

4 Does Your Argument Make Sense? 85

Why Use an Outline? 85
Developing Your Outline 87
Checking for Logic 93
    Is My Thesis Reasonable? 95
    Does Each Support Defend My Thesis? 96
    Have I Proven My Thesis Step by Step? 99
    Are My Underlying Assumptions Clear? 99
    Are All My Points within Reason? 100
    Do the Abstractions Reveal My Meaning? 101
    Have I Acknowledged Opposing Viewpoints? 103
    Are My Causes and Effects Accurate? 104
    Do My Analogies Clarify My Points? 105
    Is My Thinking Free of Stereotypes? 106
    Is My Information Representative? 107
    Are the Sources of My Information Reliable? 107
    Do My Statistics Tell the Truth? 108

5 What Is the Shape of a Paragraph? 114

Paragraph and Essay 114
    Thesis Statement and Topic Sentence 115
What Makes Paragraphs Good? 116
    The Topic Sentence 116
    The Top Sentence 118
    Unity 119
    Coherence 121
Paragraph Development 124
    Dividing Paragraphs 127
    Sequencing of Sentences 128
    A Few Words About Using Paragraph Models 135

6 What Is a Good Sentence? 138

Following Patterns 139
Coordination 141
    Punctuation Pointers: Coordinating Conjunctions 141
    Punctuation Pointers: Series 142
Subordination 142
    Relative Pronoun Clause 143
Passive Voice versus Active Voice 144
Reordering sentences 146
Balance and Rhythm 147
    Sentence Length 147
    Parallelism 147
    Marks of Punctuation 148
    Directional Movement 149
Sentence Mimicry 154

7 What Is the Best Word? 158

Match Your Words 159
Levels of Language 160

The Feeling That Your Words Convey   164
Specific Trouble Spots   166
Avoid Triteness, Jargon, and Abstractions   169
Avoid Circumlocutions   173
Avoid Jargon and Slang   173
Avoid Abstractions and Generalities   175
Avoid Euphemisms   176
Avoid Sexist Language   177
Increase Your Active Vocabulary   180
Use the Dictionary and Thesaurus   181

8 What Makes Your Writing Polished?   189
Let Your Writing "Cool"   190
Check What You Have Written   191
Refine What You Have Written   192
Revision in Action—A Sample Essay   196

9 How Do You Use the Library?   219
Books   219
General Reference Works   224
Humanities   232
Social Sciences   240
Sciences   259

10 How Do You Write a Research Paper?   267
Ten Steps to Writing a Research Paper   268
  Step One: Choosing the Topic   268
  Step Two: Becoming Your Own Librarian   269
  Step Three: Getting Acquainted with Your Topic   270
  Step Four: Writing Bibliography Cards   271
Forms of Bibliography   272
  Step Five: Taking Notes on Cards   275
  Step Six: Devising a Thesis   281
  Step Seven: Constructing the Outline   281
  Step Eight: Writing the Rough Draft   282
Forms for Footnotes   288
  Step Nine: Revising the Draft   292
  Step Ten: Typing the Final Paper   292
Questions Often Asked about Research Papers   294
Sample Research Paper   297

11 What If You Want to Write Something Special?   326
Writing In-Class Essay Examinations   326
Evaluating Nonfiction   331
Writing Book Reviews on Nonfiction   337
Writing Resumes   338
Writing Annotated Bibliographies   341
Writing Scientific Reports   344

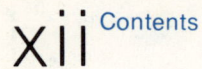

Writing An Observation Report   348
Writing Business Letters   353
Keeping a Journal   357

The Handbook   359

12 A Review of Grammar and Spelling   361
The Parts of Speech   361
Sentence Structure   371
Grammar, Dialect, and Language   380
Principles of Spelling   394

13 Correcting Common Errors   405
Adopting a Plan   405
How to Sift for Errors   406
  Step One: Do Your Subjects Agree With Their Verbs? Do Your Predicates Match Their Subjects?   406
  Step Two: Are There Any Sentence Fragments or Run-On Sentences?   416
  Step Three: Are All Your Verbs and Verbals Formed Accurately?   431
  Step Four: Do All Your Pronouns Fit Their References and Functions?   447
  Step Five: Is Your Syntax Correct?   406

14 A Glossary of Punctuation and Mechanics   472

15 A Glossary of Usage   529

Index   559

1

How Do You Write an Essay?

You have already done a lot of writing in your life. Very probably much of that writing has had a rather simple and immediate purpose. You wrote a letter to a friend, you dropped a note to your boss asking for next Friday off, or you wrote to the local department store to point up a mistake in your bill. In these instances of writing, your purpose was to get your point across to your reader quickly and clearly; and your writing probably flowed without much effort on your part.

The assignments that you will write for college classes (and later the more formal reports that you may need to write as a part of your job) differ from personal notes and letters. Unlike the matter of fact feeling of dashing off a note to a delivery person is the momentary confusion over beginning to write an essay. You begin to concern yourself with your purpose in writing and with your intended audience. However, your essay, just like your more informal everyday writing, must be designed to communicate your ideas directly and clearly.

One of the most obvious purposes for writing essays in your college classes is to give you the opportunity to sort out your thinking and formalize it. The fiction writer and essayist E. M. Forster once said, "How do I know what I think until I see what I say?" Formal writing gives you an opportunity to see what you say or think about a topic. Unlike conversation, in which thoughts whiz by unquestioned and unchallenged, the physical presence of a piece of writing summons you to look and think again. As you look back through your writing, you may realize that you have not carefully enough explained a concept or that you have not grouped your ideas in their most effective manner. Thus you rewrite and clarify your own thinking at the same time.

2 The Writer's Practical Rhetoric

FIGURE 1-1
The finished piece of pottery evolves from a step-by-step process as does the finished essay. (Photo by Steve Dierks.)

Writing is an intensely personal activity. You write from your own experiences—physical, emotional, intellectual, and spiritual. Your writing may be designed to share your experiences with your readers or even to convince them to accept some view. In every instance you will want to keep in mind two very important parts of the writing process: purpose and audience.

Many of the essays that you will write in college will focus on material studied in class. You may be asked to explain or to defend a topic discussed or an essay read. No matter what the assignment, you will first have to decide on your purpose and your audience. You must then design what you intend to say so that it will accomplish the intended purpose for that particular audience.

AUDIENCE

The people you speak with are your "audience," and those you write to may be called your "readers." In everyday writing and speaking,

How Do You Write an Essay?

you relate to a specific person or a certain group. To a great extent, what you say or write and how you do it depends on who is to receive your words. For example, when talking to your parents and when talking to your roommate, you might describe differently the party you went to last night. You would certainly explain your concept of marriage differently to a six-year-old and to another adult. In talking to members of your immediate family or friends, you might even use a different dialect (see p. 381) than in talking to your math professor. Although talking provides a more immediate audience than does writing, writing also has an audience. In writing, you would be just as likely to present the concept of love differently in a philosophy paper than in a psychology paper. Each way of relating material involves decisions about word choice, grammar, tone, and subject matter. And each has much to do with audience.

It is true that certain writing tasks have more clear-cut audiences than others. When you write a journal, for instance, you are writing only for yourself and can include pet phrases without explaining them, or you can leave out steps in a sequence of events because you know what you mean. When you write a personal letter to someone, you know exactly to whom you must appeal. You usually know something about the tastes and interests of the person, so you try to refer to them. You wouldn't try to use words far above or below the vocabulary of the individual you're writing to.

Of course, the teacher will read the paper, not to mention grade it, so he or she is part of the audience. But to assume that only your teacher is the audience would seem to defeat the purpose of the writing assignment. Writing the essay has exposed you to a body of information and ideas that have stimulated you to think in a new way. Your essay sets forth these ideas, clarifying them for you and for your reader. But if the gap between you and your reader is great, as it could be if your teacher were a specialist in some technical area of the same field, you could run into difficulty by trying not to communicate at your own level. Although teachers are not always specialists in the fields they assign papers on, they sometimes are. Therefore, teachers shouldn't be your only audience. The most practical decision, unless your teacher suggests otherwise, is to write to an audience of your peers. That is, write to those on your level: your classmates. Then you have a common ground, the coursework, to build on. You needn't talk up or down to them. You can assume they are a group of intelligent people who will be convinced by a logical argument, and who share some of the same interests and background. On this same level you will no doubt, to some degree, appeal to your teacher as well.

Here is an example of what kinds of decisions based on audience you might make if you were writing to your classmates. Suppose you were asked to write a paper on *The Great Gatsby* for your freshman

English class, and you know that all your classmates have read the book. It would be unnecessary to retell the plot of the novel. When you need to use the plot as an illustration for such an assignment, you need only mention some main event that will identify for your audience the part of the story you mean. You might say something like this: "The failure of Gatsby's dream of success is further illustrated by the fact that only Gatsby's father and the drunk from the library show up at Gatsby's funeral." You need not explain the scene in which the drunk appears earlier in the book, since your audience is already familiar with the plot of *The Great Gatsby*. Neither do you need to explain how Gatsby's father came to town or how Gatsby dies. On the other hand, you do need to discuss in detail the point you make about the dream of success. You need to point out the implications of what you have said about the failure of the American dream. The explanation may involve an interpretation of *why* the drunk appears at the graveyard, but your explanation should not require a plot summary.

This practice of constructing an audience in one's mind by appealing to a known group seems reasonable, but the question remains whether professional writers, not just students, do so as a matter of course. Skimming any popular magazine or technical journal will lead you to a "yes" answer. One way of evaluating to whom any magazine writer appeals is to study the advertisements in the magazine. Articles in any magazine are written for a certain sector of the public—those who would buy the magazine. Similarly, the manufacturers who advertise in the magazine want to sell their products to that audience. Professional ad writers, therefore, are supported by staffs of researchers who survey the likes, dislikes, interests, values, and buying habits of the public. Perhaps you have even participated in such a survey at some time in your life. With this information at hand, the ad writers see how they might sway the readers to buy their products.

Technical journals, too, have definite audiences. In most technical journals, specialized language that the ordinary layperson would not understand is used. Also, advertisements, if there are any, appeal to a specialized group that knows a great deal about the specifications and use of the equipment or materials needed for whatever field the journal is from. Unless a reader knows the field, he or she may find the articles and advertisements confusing. Some time, try to read part of an article in a journal from a field you have little experience with. Then, just for fun, pick up a fourth- or fifth-grade textbook. What is your response to reading matter obviously designed for a different audience than you? Confusion? Anger? Laughter?

You can often tell at least the audience's educational level and interests by taking note of several characteristics of the professional writing itself. Is the language very formal? Very informal? Do specialized terms abound? Are there many undefined terms or concepts that assume prior knowledge in the field? Does it seem that the readers and writer share certain unstated assumptions? Are the paragraphs long, like those in formal writing, or especially brief—just a few sentences—like those in popular magazines and newspapers? Are many of the sentences complicated? Even word length might be considered a mark of formality and of the audience's educational level, or at least of their concentration span. Finally, there actually may be direct references to the readers as in "Now listen, freshmen and sophomores" or "Perk up your ears, my fellow Americans." As a writer you can use these same techniques to appeal to your audience.

AN AUDIENCE SURVEY To employ these strategies effectively in your own writing, you will need to assess the character of your audience for a particular paper. One way to make such a judgment is to do an "audience survey" in which you ask yourself several key questions about the tastes, values, and experiences of your readers. Here are some guidelines for questions you might wish to ask.

- Why would the readers be interested in my essay?
- What is the average educational level of my readers?
- Do the readers have specialized knowledge in the field? How much?
- Will any of my evidence for the essay seem strange to the audience and thus require special explanation?
- Will the readers be likely to accept my main point? If not, what might they think instead?
- Are the readers generally of any one age, sex, or ethnic background? If not, what diversity should I keep in mind?

For a particular essay, you might think of even more specific questions that pertain to the assignment and help you to know your readers. You can see that asking yourself these kinds of questions will keep the concept of audience in the back of your mind as you write, helping you make decisions about what to include and what not to include in your essay.

The value of adapting your writing to a particular audience is evident at every stage of the writing process. Whenever you write, then, you should try to keep in mind the interests of your readers, how much expertise they have on the subject, and the occasion for which you are writing. (Is it formal or informal?) In other words, from the first step of writing—picking a subject—you will want to appeal to the group you have defined as readers in your "audience survey." Pick a subject that suits you both; then decide on a main point to focus the essay, making sure both you and the readers are likely to be interested in it. Then, as you select evidence for the body of the essay, consider what the readers already know, what they want to know, and what they

6 The Writer's Practical Rhetoric

need to know. Do they need elaboration on a given point to understand it? If in your essay you take a stand on a subject, you will want to recognize the possible opposing views held by your readers. Finally, throughout the paper, you will want your writing to sound readable to the audience.

This close connection with your readers should not confine you so that you write only to please your audience, as does the student in the "Peanuts" cartoon on this page. Writing, remember, should grow out of the relationship between the readers and the subject, the writer and the readers, and the writer and the subject. Otherwise, the writing will probably mean little to the readers or to the writer, even if it "sells," as it does in the cartoon. You can see how writing that communicates something important to the writer, in the writer's personal style, differs from writing made only of compromises to a reader—the writing that merely "sells." Good writers express themselves while appealing to their audiences.

FIGURE 1-2
(c United Feature Syndicate, Inc.)

EXERCISES

A. Explain how writing about the same topic for two different audiences would affect your subject matter. For example, if you were writing a paper on alcohol use on college campuses, how might the information be differently presented to a group of parents of prospective students and to the students themselves?

B. Your teacher is usually a member of your audience. Write a paragraph that discusses the advantages and disadvantages of having to appeal to your teacher as well as to a general audience when you write essays for classes. What special considerations about your subject are introduced when you must write for a particular teacher? Can they cause a moral conflict? Explain by giving an example.

MODES OF THE ESSAY

In college classes, particularly in composition classes, you will be asked to write *expository essays*. Expository means "to set forth or explain." The term *expository essays* is used in college to refer to non-fictional pieces of writing that center around a main point or idea, known as the thesis. In an expository essay, then, the writer appeals to an audience with the intention of their grasping his or her thesis. The overall manner or form adopted by a writer to carry out this intention is known as the *mode* of writing.

Expository essays are often said to be written in one of three *modes*: descriptive, narrative, or argumentative. But usually essays are not only one of the three. Most good writing requires a mixture of modes: a bit of narration to explain what happened and a short description of the setting of the action, a brief description of a problem and an argument as to why one solution would be better than another. The combination of modes is set by the writer's interpretation of a subject and the thesis, or purpose. Although the modes are often combined, to write an essay in one mode or another just for practice will help you learn the elements of good writing. And many college assignments are so formulated to provide experience in a particular mode.

DESCRIPTION Description conveys the significant physical or abstract qualities of a person, place, event, idea, or object. That is, if your intention is to tell what something is like, you are using *description*. You could describe the look on your brother's face the first time he tasted oatmeal in such detail that the audience feels they are there watching your brother. You could describe your school's cafeteria during lunch hour so that even the readers who have never been there get the picture: the rushing about, the noise, the team efforts of food service employees. But you can also describe ideas. You could describe, for instance, the melting pot theory or the idea of a ratio. Such a definition of a concept is description because it, too, explains what something is.

Good description is not merely a listing of details in random order, but a piecing together of details that combine to form a dominant impression or a generalization. For example, if you are describing your room, the dominant impression might be that it is a warm place. Some of the details contributing to the impression of warmth might include a cozy bed with two handmade quilts stretched across it, a poster of a family of bears with the caption "snuggle today," and a colorful oversized pillow collection—red, blue, and green—tossed on the floor. Most description relies on the senses, and good sensory details—sights, sounds, smells, tastes, textures—are what make description real to the reader. Of course, description of a more abstract type, the kind that explains an idea, would need to be just as detailed as physical descriptions. And all the details would have to contribute to the overall generalization about the idea. The following description of a laugh is from a student's essay.

> *Laughing is really a messy business. My jowls gyrate up and down at incredible rates, slapping against the bone. A strained open mouth stretches the face. My eyes cloud over with misty sweat from the forehead. My brow is unable to contain the sweat that mixes with tears and stings my foggy eyes. The rolls of my paunch rush like waves in a sea of jelly. Sweat surfaces profusely, causing my underclothes to cling to my body, now sticky. Saliva finally wells up and overflows above the lips, slowly sliding down my second chin in a sporadic dribble. A puddle forms on the shirt near the collar button. Stomach and lungs expanded to their limits, I gasp for air, but none comes. My face turns bright red—a plump tomato.*

The dominant impression of the passage is that laughing is messy. Each detail—the perspiration, the rushing rolls of the stomach, the saliva—is vividly messy. Of course the passage is disturbing because the details are unpalatable. Contributing to the picture are sensory details: hearing, seeing, and feeling.

Just as common in writing is the description of an idea or event. You may need to define a key word you use, or you may want to clarify an underlying concept in your discussion. Many descriptions, like the following one, start out with a generalization that is then developed through details and examples.

> *"Cloning" is a technique by which an organism or several organisms are produced without sexual reproduction. The resulting organisms are genetically identical to the original one. Clones are asexually produced by exchanging the nucleus from an unfertilized egg with the nucleus of one body cell from the original organism.*
>
> *Plant "slip" cuttings and bulbs are examples of this type of reproduction, and the human counterpart would be the much debated "test-tube baby." A clone is, then, a kind of branching off from a single parent, which is precisely what the originally Greek word means: a twig.*

The generalization is in the first sentence, which says that cloning is a type of asexual reproduction. Then the description becomes more

NARRATION

detailed, telling characteristics of the technique, giving a few examples, and mentioning the origin of the term.

Narration unfolds the sequence of occurrences that make up an event. It retells all the stages or steps of a happening, usually in detail so that the readers identify with what happened. Although they may never have experienced the narrated event, they are there. Narration differs from description in that it focuses more on *what happened* than on what the event was like. As a matter of fact, though, description and narration often travel together, the description expanding the narration or vice versa. Narration is sometimes confused with short story writing, but the two are actually quite different in the source of their materials—exposition, remember, is true, not made up. Here is a narrative paragraph from a student's essay.

> *The expected vertigo caused by the early morning transition from the subconscious to the conscious, similar to a small scale hangover, disappeared soon after I sat up in bed. I routinely dressed, slipping on my trousers, tugging at them to caterpillar them past my shoes. This compulsive idiosyncrasy of putting on my shoes before my trousers never failed. I reached for the crumpled mass, a slightly soiled T-shirt at the foot of my bed. It was my favorite, a vintage Farrah Fawcett-Majors, no less. I untangled the knotted shirt and thrust my head through the big hole. The problem now would be to negotiate my arms through the armholes. I suddenly felt like a fool in a straitjacket, but the feeling was entirely appropriate—I had even put the shirt on backwards. Yanking off the shirt in mock disgust, I chuckled to myself, but at the same time I sheepishly looked over my shoulder just to make sure I was indeed alone.*

Two things make the passage effective. First of all, most people have had an experience like the one the student writer details here. Second, the writer breaks down this sequence into minute steps, adding description along the way, mentioning details that anyone could relate to. Most people have awakened with a headache. Most people have a special routine for getting dressed in the morning. Most people have, in utter fatigue, put on a piece of clothing backwards. Most people have been embarrassed about someone watching them when they acted awkward.

ARGUMENTATION

Argumentation makes a specific persuasive statement—it takes a stand and defends it. The writer is trying to convince the audience to accept a certain viewpoint. There is always the possibility of taking the opposite stand of the one presented in an argumentative essay, and keeping this fact in mind, writers of argumentation anticipate contrary assertions and adequately answer objections to the argument. At the same time that they are going about presenting information to back up their ideas, they are certain not to give anyone the chance to say the ideas are narrowminded. An argumentative essay requires especial attention to logic (see Chapter 4). Can you see how the following excerpt from an argumentative essay differs from the description and the narration?

> *Safety is another major advantage solar energy has over other energy sources. Coal, oil, and gas are very explosive materials. Newspapers frequently carry stories of people injured or killed by explosions caused by these three items. Another dangerous energy source is nuclear energy. It is only a matter of time before a major disaster occurs because there is no protection from the potential damages caused on the nuclear sites if an earthquake, for instance, would hit. Thousands of people could be killed because we do not have adequate controls yet. Solar collectors, on the other hand, contain no materials that could explode. They also produce no waste materials that could be dangerous.*

The argumentative passage takes a stand—solar energy sources are safer than others. The writer then supports the statement by asserting that other methods of producing energy are unsafe. Once the point is established, the writer shows how solar collectors have none of the disadvantages of other methods. Each point is made to support the original assertion about the comparative safety of solar collectors and other types of energy sources. No extraneous information is injected into the argumentation.

EXERCISES Directions: Identify the mode or modes of the passages below. Are they descriptive, narrative, or argumentative? Or are the modes mixed?

A. It was a time of action and achievement for the Forest Service under the direction of the headstrong Pinchot until 1909, when Roosevelt left office and William Taft became President. Taft, not concerned with the conservation crusade, brought about an inevitable conflict with Pinchot, who faced a reversal of principles and purposes with the newly headed government. Pinchot was soon dismissed from office for his efforts in a scandal he created when he objected to the "issuance to powerful economic interests of mineral claims, entitling them to exploit coal-rich public lands in Alaska."[15] Because of disagreements with the Secretary of the Interior, Richard A. Ballinger, Ballinger was dismissed from the Service, bringing about a new awareness and strength for reform of the national forests and their resources. Gifford Pinchot gave his energy and concern to the Service, and his efforts have made it one of the largest divisions of the Department of Agriculture today.

B. Golding and Robinson disagree on the subject of whether or not different levels of thought can be reached by everyone. Golding outlines three grades of thought of which only *grade three* is attainable by the majority of people. Persons of this rank contradict themselves and do not like their contradictions to be pointed out. *Grade two* thinking, involving the "detection of contradictions," can be reached by a significantly fewer number of people. *Grade one* thought is attainable by only a few gifted people. The author cites Einstein as an example. In his essay Robinson outlines four kinds of thought, some which relate to Golding's levels. Robinson's categories are called *reverie, practical decision making, rationalizing*, and *creative thought*. The first he believes accounts for how all mankind, high and low thinkers, are able to reason. The others, like Golding's, are more limited, with the level of *creative thought* paralleling Golding's highest level, *grade one* thinking.

C. Attitudes regarding sex role differentiation are reflected in the responses to a questionnaire distributed by Julie Edwards, a teacher in California. She found that parents of nursery school children at a private school divided their approval on factors affecting their children's sociability according to the sex of their child. Parents of girls answered that cooperation, malleability, and willingness to take directions were the preferred characteristics for a girl to develop. Assertiveness and the tendency to quarrel were designated as undesirable character traits. Boys, on the other hand, were supposed to be independent, assertive, and inquisitive; being timid or fearful was generally considered unmanly.[9]

D. In many cases, advertisers hope to sell more than just their products. Considering an advertisement for a weekend in Las Vegas, the average consumer is buying a lot more than the trip. He is getting (in his own mind) that smiling blonde in a bikini and two big nights. The female consumer of Virginia Slims cigarettes is buying more than a smoke. She is getting the image of the liberated woman. People buy products for many emotional reasons, and advertisers play on the unconscious insecurities and needs of the consumers. It is not unusual for someone to purchase a product because of its strong emotional appeal, despite its quality. Because this kind of coy advertising is in wide use across the country, the buyer must be especially aware not to be swindled by it, not to buy something that he does not need or really want just because the advertisement is convincing in some hidden way.

E. Amphibolic reactions are sensitive to the levels of specific metabolites. Many catabolic pathways produce essential biosynthetic starting materials. If these catabolic pathways were entirely shut down, by high energy levels, then the biosynthetic pathways would also shut down. Therefore, it is necessary to have more than one method of regulation of amphibolic reactions. Specific metabolites that are indicative of the levels of biosynthetic starting materials act as this other method of regulation.

F. If a student gets special permission to take his or her final examinations either later or earlier than other students, given certain circumstances, he or she will do a better job on them. The reason for this improved performance is that the student is able to devote his or her full attention to concentrating on one subject. He or she will be able to retain facts more easily and clearly because there will be no others competing for attention. He or she can sit down and take the test without having to worry about taking another final right after that one. After taking the first final, a student is often shoved right into taking others, and this arrangement causes unnecessary pressure. When the finals are split up, the student can study for one at a time, as he or she should be able to do.

POINT OF VIEW

Whatever mode or modes your essay includes, your discussion will be written from a certain *point of view*. That is, the ideas you describe, narrate, or argue will be seen from one or another vantage point, from the viewpoint of someone with particular ideas and values. If you are talking about the problems of unemployed youth, you would be wise to analyze for yourself from whose viewpoint you are making statements—from the view of the unemployed, the social workers, or the taxpayers? Point of view should remain consistent within the discussion of a subject, unless you intend in one essay to discuss various points of view, and that intention is made clear by the wording of the introduction to the essay. Usually, essays that take up several points of view are doing so to provide comparisons of them.

Is your point of view influenced by the points of view of others around you? How can you settle on a point of view for an essay? All these questions will seem to find their answers the more you write and the more you consciously think about exactly what it is you are trying to say in any given essay.

Point of view is an indication of how subjectively or objectively your subject is treated. When writing from your own point of view, you will probably want to use the informal pronoun "I" for all necessary references to yourself. Calling yourself *I* and then later calling yourself *the writer of this paper* would be inconsistent and confusing to your reader. Similarly, speaking of *people* to mean a general group and then referring to the same group as *you* would throw the reader back and forth between a rather objective point of view and a very personal one. Any shift in perspective should be automatically suspect. Each time you switch your discussion from one level of familiarity to another you are slightly altering your relationship to the subject, the stance or vantage point from which you perceive and present ideas. Note how in the following paragraph the writer confuses the reader by losing track of the point of view that should have been maintained.

> *Most words, when not used with slang intent, have the same meaning in both black and white lexicons. For example, the word* cold *has a common definition to all people. If I were to say "It is very cold outside," most people would know I would be referring to the weather. On the other hand, if I were to use it with slang intent and comment, "Man, that remark is cold," there would be no mistake by blacks that the remark is uncalled for. In the slang of whites, however, the comment might have been interpreted as meaning something has been said cold,* without preparation. *The word* nasty *can be seen in the same light. When you use it without slang intent, it has a common dictionary meaning. However, if you were to hear a black person say that a particular person is* nasty, *you would know he or she is not referring to cleanliness. On the contrary, that person is very desirable.*

If the writer were to correct the inconsistent point of view, the passage would look like this.

> *Most words, when not used with slang intent, have the same meaning in both black and white lexicons. For example, the word* cold *has a common definition to all people. If I were to say, "It is very cold outside," most people would know I would be referring to the weather. On the other hand, if I were to use it with slang intent and comment, "Man, that remark is cold," there would be no mistake by blacks that the remark is uncalled for. In the slang of whites, however, the comment might have been interpreted as meaning something has been said cold,* without preparation. *The word* nasty *can be seen in the same light. When I use it without slang intent, it has a common dictionary meaning. However, if I were to hear a black person say that a particular person is* nasty, *I would know he or she is not referring to cleanliness. On the contrary, that person is very desirable.*

14 The Writer's Practical Rhetoric

EXERCISES Directions: Identify the confusing shifts in point of view that occur in the passages below. How might you correct them?

A. There is no justification for anybody's saying that we are not funny people. One need only tune in the programs of such radio personalities as Hudson and Landry, Bill Balance, or Dick Whittington—all of whom are very popular and more than a little comic—to hear America laughing. Or turn on a television at any time. If you do, you will be likely to hear and see newscasters cracking jokes, game show guests and contestants laughing and goofing around, and countless situation comedies, all depicting happy, joking Americans. I even find it impossible to keep from laughing at our laughing: we are so funny when we are having fun. No, you can't say we don't have our joke or two.

B. Why shouldn't you marry a woman or man whom you have never met? Really, there is no good reason why two complete strangers should not marry each other, why husband and wife should not be introduced to each other at the altar. After all, one never knows another person inside and out, completely, down to the deepest, most repressed and vile secret in that other person's mind. Even if you marry someone you have known for twenty years, so much about that person will remain unknown. Often, those feelings that are most strong in us are those we are not willing to share with others. This being the case, why should one suppose that there is much value in getting to know a partner before you enter a marriage?

C. The dirt on antiques is really the dust of memories. Although I cannot afford to buy antiques (we used to call the stuff junk and think nothing of it), I love to wander through shops, sniffing the old, dusty, moist air and remembering how life was when all this was new and I was young. Anyone old enough to have been around in the 1940s will remember the tiger bamboo furniture that was so cheap then (ten dollars for a new, two-level side table), and he or she will marvel at the enormous price now paid for this same type of table, even though it is now worn out and dirty. It makes you realize just how much simpler life was then, how many problems seemed slighter because you had to worry only about ten dollars, not one hundred.

D. People get a lot out of owning a pet. It doesn't really matter whether the pet is a dog, a cat, a lizard, or a goldfish. What matters is that you get a chance to watch something natural, an animal, as it eats and sleeps, plays and fights. You can see how we humans might have behaved when we were less civilized than we are now. It's also possible to see what animals do now and how it is like what we do. In a sense, I get a lot out of owning my cute little cat because she helps me realize that I am an animal in many ways.

How Do You Write an Essay? 15

FIGURE 1-3
(Photo by Steven Robins.)

Directions: From the point of view of one of the following people, write a paragraph describing the scene in Figure 1-3.

| A police officer | A photographer | A mugger |
| A politician | A social worker | A five-year-old child |

Then write a second paragraph, this time from the point of view of a different person on the list. How do the different points of view in your paragraphs cause you to emphasize different details in the photograph? Would the daughter of the man on the bench be likely to agree with either of your descriptions?

DEVELOPMENT OF IDEAS

The point of view from which any writer perceives the subject influences him or her to develop a central idea or thesis. An essay is never just a stringing together of facts. Instead, it narrows a subject area to a limited subject, to some point that makes a statement about a subject, that adds an "aboutness" to it. The subject *dogs* becomes the limited subject *the value of affection training for show dogs* and *city life* becomes *the need for organized activities for urban youth*. The point is developed and expanded in the paper; information and ideas are selected for the essay because they develop the point an essay is making, not just because they are interesting.

Evidence is needed for an essay. Opinion alone or bright ideas that do not back up the thesis, no matter how sincere they may be, are inappropriate and best saved for a journal, a letter to a friend, or a different paper that develops them. Even the most heartfelt ideas must bear examination and development. In college, unfortunately, you will have very few assignments that call for your feelings alone. Note how the short paper below seems full of such incidental remarks and how the essay does not hold together because it fails to develop any one point, skipping around in four or five directions, spending so little time on each point under consideration that the reader comes away from the paper with very little understanding of the value of a degree.

A DEGREE

Why is getting a degree a very important thing in our lives? There are many reasons.

The first of these reasons is that a degree can get you respect. People admire an educated individual. They believe he has something to say and they listen to him. A degree is a piece of paper that symbolizes you have completed X number of years of college, and there are many different degrees but four are commonly known. They are the A. A., B.A., M.A., and Ph.D. Once you have a degree of some kind you are able to compete in society.

At any level a degree makes life a little easier than not having one. It also makes you a lot richer. The higher the degree, the more money people have to pay for your services.

People respect those with degrees and think they can ask them all sorts of questions about whatever they need to know. Actually, they may have too much respect, but that doesn't hurt anyone really. If you don't get a degree, you are only hurting yourself because in this day and age anybody can get into a college if he wants to.

You can get more from college than a degree. The second important reason is that a degree can make a family's life more enjoyable. Do not misunderstand me. A degree does not make happy families. That is between the individuals. What I mean is with it you and your family can buy the things you need or want. And in order to survive in this world today, you must have some kind of degree.

There are other reasons to go to college too as we all know. I will not explain them here. But the degree, the sheepskin, is what counts in most people's eyes. It is what will get you a job and make people like you. So why not play the game instead of giving up halfway?

The main impression the reader comes away with is that the paper lacks direction and development. The writer starts out asking why a degree is an important part of life and, without establishing if there is any significant difference between the two, soon switches to the importance of going to college. There are unsubstantiated statements, including "people admire an educated individual," and "once you have a degree, you can compete in society." This writer needs to elaborate on these points so that the reader knows just what he or she means by them and how they relate to the overall importance of having a degree. Many good ideas, sincere and even analytical questions, are raised in the paper, but none is explored in detail. The last paragraph gives a hint of organization to the ideas and shows that the writer has some definite value judgments in mind—that getting a degree is a "game" and it is worth playing for the rewards it brings. Now what the reader really wants to know is how each of those rewards (many of which the writer hints at in the paper—respect, economic gain) come about and why they are worthwhile. Although this first essay is not well written and could not serve as the final draft, it could have served to sort the writer's ideas on the subject before he or she began to write the real paper. It is, instead, preparation for writing the paper, a way of collecting ideas. The writer of the essay on page 16, only after scratching down these thoughts, was ready to come to a thesis and write a real essay. Drawing the best ideas from the preparatory writing, the student composed a paper that looked like the better developed essay below. Note how some of the ideas in the original essay were thrown out because they do not fit the point the writer is trying to make. Note too how the repetition has been removed, and in its place is careful development with examples of each main point.

The introduction cites the opposing view and clearly sets forth the writer's thesis.

A DEGREE (REVISED)

Most educated people realize that the degree is only a symbol of a person's having attended college for some number of years. It certainly does not show all that a person has learned or that a person is any smarter than somebody who does not have his degree. Nevertheless, to survive in society a person really needs a degree. In the eyes of society, of employees, parents, and even friends, having a degree means that a person is respectable, intelligent, and a social elite. Therefore, in the long run staying in college until one has some sort of degree to show for his effort is worthwhile.

A person with a degree generally does better when applying for jobs than a person without the degree. Employers would rather hire someone who has gone to college, first of all, because he or she usually considers college graduates to be very disciplined. The college graduate has studied for a certain number of years, which is a task that requires dedication and hard work. Someone without a degree, even

The second paragraph deals with the value of a degree in the job market.

if he or she has gone to college, appears either to be a drifter or to have no special dedication. Otherwise, the person would have completed the course of his or her education. An individual with a degree is automatically considered more intelligent than one without a degree because in college all one does is learn. The person not in college may never even have read a book all the way through. On the other hand, the college graduate is almost guaranteed to have learned about a variety of subjects. They have, in fact, studied a major field which they should know extremely well, and, in many cases, a job may require that specific knowledge. A degree tends to weigh more than even the practical knowledge of somebody already trained to do the exact job.

The third paragraph discusses parental pressure and why parents want their children to have degrees.

Parents want their children to have degrees. They encourage their kids to get degrees for many of the same reasons that employers think degrees are important. In addition to these reasons, parents may want their children to have what they themselves were denied. Thus the uneducated parents find it very important that the children get more education than they did. Somehow they think it raises their own state. If a child only starts to go to college but does not finish, the parent feels cheated. There is no degree to show what the child is learning. The degree to most parents is the proof, in their own minds, that they have brought up their children right. And for the educated parent a degree in their children's hands is equally important. Either the children must get as much schooling as the parents did, or they must surpass their parents. Education is for many parents a status symbol and for a child of theirs not to possess the degree is shameful. Or at least it is disappointing. They judge people, their respectability and intelligence, by the letters behind their names. Being naturally intelligent or reading all the time does not count for much without a degree.

The fourth paragraph shows how peer pressure motivates people to get degrees.

Even a person's own friends could not help absorbing some of the cultural conditioning, and they can alienate those without degrees from their social group. People who married right out of high school usually belong to different social groups than the ones who went to college. "Where did you get your degree?" is a common question in certain social circles. Any who did not may feel uncomfortable among those who have degrees, and they often wind up acting apologetic for themselves. There is a type of experience in college that separates the two groups—the pressures are very different. The values that result are also different, and that is why college graduates value learning and books whereas nongraduated people value more "real life" things like families and struggling for money.

The difference in experience makes the college graduate different from the nongraduate, but it does not make either group better. College friends often fail to realize this point and can be especially unfair to the person who has dropped out of school—the person they think is not quite on their elite level.

Even if a person realizes that the degree itself is only a piece of paper, playing the game of getting it influences other people to respect and accept him or her, and at the same time the person getting the degree can learn by going to school. A person might as well get a degree because he pleases himself and others at the same time, which makes life a lot easier for him in the long run when it comes to getting jobs and recognition.

The conclusion deals with the implications of the essay—getting a degree is a game worth playing.

To be sure, there are errors in the revised essay: the second paragraph has a pronoun disagreement, and the third paragraph uses the too informal "kids" instead of "children." Many of the sentences are wordy. The logic is sometimes weak. Sexist language flaws much of the essay. Nevertheless, these errors are minor when taking into account the improvement in the organization and development of the paper. Even if the readers disagree with the ideas presented, they have to give the writer credit for developing most of the points well.

TONE

Tone is the writer's attitude about the subject. Tone should be watched for consistency and appropriateness at every step of writing since it shows feelings toward the subject—whether the writer is serious, humorous, or indifferent, whether the essay sounds formal or informal, straightforward or subtle and cunning, comical or somber. The word choice, type of evidence, and the structure of each paragraph and sentence can, for different reasons, affect tone. At different times a writer may want to experiment with each type of tone, but in most of the writing done for term papers and essays that discuss the subject matter of your classes, the goal is serious tone, neither too formal nor too informal. Most of the words will be in the vocabulary of an educated reader, the evidence will be drawn from reliable sources and tested, and the paragraphs and sentences will be well developed, longer than those characteristic of an article in a popular magazine.

Certain problems with tone can arise in writing, especially when a writer deals with a subject about which he or she tends to become impassioned, one way or the other. One of the basic rules of writing essays is to avoid panicked emotionalism or sarcasm. In the passage below, the writer loses control of feelings, relying on hysterical judgments instead of on solid evidence. How might you suggest to the writer that the passage be rewritten to make it more objective?

Violence in the cinema is very dangerous. It motivates people in the worst possible ways. Violence seduces children more than adults into

> *its horrible grips. And these are the very children who will be tomorrow's adults and leaders. How can we let this lawlessness continue? If children go on being corrupted by movies our future will be unavoidable misery. The only way to prevent our fate is to either clean up the violence in the cinema or to completely do away with war and crime movies. What will happen to your life and mine if crime takes over?*

The writer of the preceding passage becomes hysterical about the subject and uses an array of highly emotional words—"the worst possible ways," "seduces," "its horrible grips," "lawlessness," and so forth. The ideas are often vague (how are we to "clean up the violence in the cinema"?) and stated too dogmatically (we must either do one thing or the other).

When you are very involved with a particular political or social cause and find yourself writing an essay on it, take a deep breath and a step back from your intense involvement. The danger otherwise is that you could begin to sound as if you are preaching in a tone that only alienates your readers. If you allow yourself to think that you can pressure others into accepting your view, you are forgetting that the mode of persuasive writing is based on logical argument. The passage below shows the ineffective preaching tone that a student has slipped into for his conclusion to a paper on what he believes to be the good life. If you were to discuss with this student what he or she might do to remove the preaching tone, what would you say?

> *We always want to explain, express everything, to verbalize instead of being absorbed in thought. Some feelings are too full, too deep to be expressed. We are too wordy, let silence be thy guide. Many times our individuality makes us stand apart from what is close to us. We become very objective about the things around us, instead of just absorbing them. We have a deep tendency to advocate the logos doctrine too readily. We subject our experience to the intellect, instead of to the heart. We become too analytical, individualistic, intellectual; instead we should be more spiritually individualistic, socially group minded, intuitive, totalizing, etc.*

The writer is too close to the material. The immediate evidence of this fact is the use of first person in a kind of sermonizing way. The writer wants to show people the ills of their ways and to convert them. Instead, it would be better to see the subject more as a reporter would. The writer also should try to make concrete some of the abstractions and try to give examples of what he or she means by "our individuality makes us stand apart from what is close to us." Presently, this statement is hard to understand. He or she should remove old-fashioned language like "let silence by thy guide" and replace it with a statement instead of a command. Finally, the writer should remove the "etc." at the end of the passage and instead explain what is meant.

Yet another kind of emotionalism to be avoided is flowery writing, writing that seems inflated and false. Treating your subject with sensitivity does not call for exaggerating your feelings. For instance, it is a bit much to say that your mother *wept piteously* instead of that she *cried* or that you *chanced to set your gaze on the sky and its billows of radiant and varied colors* instead of you *looked at the sunset*, or even at the *colorful sunset*. This overly poetic tone, often called "purple prose," can be confusing and offensive. Note in the following passage that all but the first sentence is bogged down with a flowery perception of the subject, a perception that seems insincere and ineffective.

> *It was a simply beautiful day in the Rockies. Early the sun peered over the ominous high black ridge and stirred me from my sleep with its filtered rays of warmth. Sun was entreating me to relinquish my cozy bedroll and venture into the vast daylight that beckoned me onward to become a part of the beauteous world of morning. The oh so fragrant essence of the forest, the chirping of God's winged creatures, and even the movements of the tiniest insects all told me that my day had begun.*

The same passage might have been written as below, directly and still with feeling, giving more concrete and less ethereal details, making it more effective.

> *It was a beautiful day in the Rockies. Early the warm sun appeared above the black ridge and awakened me, inviting me to leave my bedroll and face the morning. The strong pine scent emanating from the surrounding forest, the birds' chirping, and the busy movement of insects on the ground next to my resting place all told me that my day had begun.*

An ironic tone may be created deliberately by mixing formal vocabulary with slang or by writing about a common subject (like frying an egg) in a very inflated, formal way. In either case it would be clear that the tone was deliberately mixed because the author intended to be humorous. The cartoon on page 22 is funny because of the mixture of tone. Normally a wedding ceremony is a solemn occasion, but take a look at the clergyman's choice of words.

FIGURE 1-4
"Dearly beloved, we are gathered here . . . to join this gal and this guy in holy matrimony."

It is best for the writer of academic papers to stick to a consistent tone. A tone that is formal mixed with a tone that is informal would confuse readers about the writer's attitude on the subject, making it unclear how they are to piece together the ideas in the essay. Moreover, a close look at unintentional mixed tone always shows it to sound unnatural. Most writers can look back over what they are writing and judge whether it sounds natural or suddenly shifts to a pretentious voice. An adjustment needs to be made if the writing sounds uneven and unnatural in spots. Take a look at the mixed tone in the following passage. What would you suggest that the writer do to even out the passage?

> *I love to walk through the city. It makes me feel exuberant and free. The pushing and shoving and honking of the cars as they zoom down the street or argue their way down congested boulevards points out how hassle free I am when not in an automobile. I am a high-spirited kid among arguing so-called "mature adults" and I get where I want to go just as well as they do but without having to feel uptight. I certainly am not a victim of that well-known modern malady: angst. If I time my stride just right, as I'm able to do, I can avoid all red lights and walk jubilantly past those poor sufferers who must sit in their gas-guzzling death traps stopped in a close order outside the pedestrian walk. And there is one other benefit to walking through the city. While cars eat up their owners' money in gas bills (ha, ha)*

How Do You Write an Essay? 23

> *I find change and even an occasional greenback on my lovely, free pavement.*

EXERCISES   Directions: Describe the tone of each passage below. Is it ironic or serious, light or comical? Is it informal and subjective or formal and objective? What specifically contributes to the tone of each?

A. Certain government actions have helped reduce the number of cigarettes smoked. In 1970, Congress passed the Public Health Cigarette Smoking Act, which prohibited cigarette commercials on television or radio after January 2, 1971. It has long been suspected that cigarette advertising serves two purposes. First, it definitely helps develop brand loyalties, and it emphasizes the differences between basically similar tobacco products. In addition, as it has been mentioned by many market development and research groups, cigarette advertising encourages young people to take up smoking in the first place, and this is the reason the government has sought to control cigarette advertising. Television presented smoking as part of a way of life most young people found attractive and exciting. Physical appeal, success in school, and financial success were some of the positive attributes of the smokers pictured in name-brand cigarette advertising.

B. Few people have ever been spared the feeling of total frustration one experiences when the lead of a pencil breaks. This frustration is matched only by that which one may experience when he is unable to locate a pencil sharpener at such times. A person may find a rock, a knife, fingernails, or even teeth to be adequate substitutes. Imagination must come into play at such moments of great despair. For instance, what if the world had only one way to shape a pencil point—the pencil sharpener? Suppose then that the production of the devices had to come to a sudden halt because of a drastic reallocation of resources that had taken place. Within a short time there would be no pencil sharpeners available, except to the very rich on the black market, and people would be forced to switch to pens. With the psychological problems caused by not being able to erase, unless people were to lug around a chalk board, many would find their imaginations running wild in their quest for replacements for pencil sharpeners.

Directions: In the passages below correct any tone that would be inappropriate to a college essay.

A. Colleges must alter their dorm facilities to accommodate students who want to live in coed rooms. Residents pay rent for their living quarters on campus; and the current regulation, which must have been made up by someone with a brain the size of a green pea, is a ripoff. Students should be treated as adults and allowed to live however and with whomever they choose for companionship. No normal person intends any harm by living with someone of his own choosing. Justice is often envisioned as the goddess Libra who balances all good and evil. Like Justice, the heads of colleges must achieve an equal amount of consideration for students, and not just give themselves all the credit for having the brains and power to judge the morals of others. In other words, it's time the higher-ups started to consider the opinions and rights of the individual adult student!

B. Every politician should be able to be trusted. His or her morals should guide his or her platform. Ultimately, politicians are responsible to their own consciences. But how can politicians go around preaching honesty in government and committing little crimes like enforcing laws for everyone but themselves? And what about tax evasion—how many politicians who talk about honesty are really crooks when it comes to their own taxes? The fact is that few politicians show pure honesty, and we shouldn't so readily believe those who come on so strong for openness and honesty. At the same time we must not fall for the good, honest senator trick; we must demand true honesty and not accept the omnipresent corruption that is slowly seeping into the veins of federal government.

THE WRITING PROCESS

Considerations of mode, tone, and point of view lie in the back of the mind during the writing process. More immediate concerns are the structure of the essay, as well as such incidentals as accurate spelling and punctuation, and good choice of words. Knowing mechanics well saves you a lot of time spent in correcting errors when you revise. But when you write the essay and plan to write it, try not to become preoccupied with these less important considerations and instead try to concentrate on the steps you can use to achieve a good thesis, support and flow. Good writing, although it adheres to the standards of written English, is first well reasoned, honest, and purposeful, qualities any writer needs practice to develop.

Because you cannot be expected to know how to write effective essays without understanding how to achieve the necessary qualities, writing classes and writing textbooks emphasize a system you can practice whenever you write. There are basic guidelines for essay composing that writers commonly agree on. Most successful writers divide their task into three broad stages: prewriting, writing, and rewriting.

Prewriting is very important to good writing. It provides the time to develop and cast away a number of possible topics and theses until you settle on the one that feels right for you and then to map out your paper before sitting down to write it out. Actually setting aside time

How Do You Write an Essay? 25

FIGURE 1-5
The potter cuts away a chunk of clay from the block as the writer trims off a limited subject from a subject area. (Photo by Steve Dierks.)

for this stage gives you a chance to engage yourself in a dialogue of choices, a process that can make a big difference in the next step, the writing of the rough draft. The entire paper has already been planned in the prewriting stage, and in the writing stage you can lend your ear to such concerns as word choice, sentence and paragraph development, and flow. Finally, the rewriting stage gives you a chance to polish up words, sentences, grammar, punctuation, and spelling.

Some subjects seem to have a built-in natural order that develops as you write. But to most people, having a pattern such as the one above is necessary in order to avoid writing essays with practically no form. Using this process gives your essays direction as you write and assures a finished product with a clear beginning, middle, and ending. Each person naturally develops individual habits the more he or she writes. There is no one way to write, and there is no one set of guidelines that cannot be adjusted for a good reason. But the overall pattern offers structure for beginners or for those who wish to improve the clarity of their presentation.

Now, just how do these stages work? You can get a sense of their effectiveness by reading over the following sample essay, in all its various stages, and by putting yourself in the writer's place. Try to concentrate on how each stage contributes towards the whole and towards the final version of the essay.

26 The Writer's Practical Rhetoric

A CHRONICLE OF ONE STUDENT'S ESSAY

Write Freely

Given the assignment to write a short paper on anything about the subject *college*, the writer first jotted down some notes. Speeding along as fast as the ideas occurred to her, trying to record them, she jotted down notes on what her family thinks of education, on the use of a diploma, on trades compared to professions—whatever she could think of. The point of writing down whatever comes to mind is to force a confrontation with the subject, to put down as many ideas in as short a time as possible, no matter how unrefined the thoughts may seem. In this prewriting exercise, called *automatic writing*, the writer need not discriminate among ideas—just get them down, even if they seem irrelevant. You can see that the prewriting below is far from a perfect piece of writing, but still it is good because it helped the writer to come up with an idea for an essay. Prewriting is for you and is rarely read by anyone else, so you can be free to say just what you are thinking at the moment. After reading through the prewriting below, you may wish to try an automatic writing on your own.

COLLEGE

Education is something my family always expected from its children. In my growing up years there was always talk of going to college, value of education, etc. My brothers & sisters & I all went to at least some college. Why did they dropped out? I wonder if I will "make it/ finish." My parents put a lot of pressure on me to do so, but in the end it will be my own decision—not their's and we will all have to accept that. What can I say. I can't think of anything I can't think of anything I can't The idea of "making it" really is important to me, but what do I mean by it? Wouldn't I be just as happy in some business type job as in a profession? Maybe it would be easier to get ahead if I didn't waste so much time learning things I don't need in college. Is making it (i.e., going to college and getting a diploma) outdated in a way? Of course it is valuable to go to school for learning new things, and I like to learn (I get a kick out of little bits of knowledge and I like to read). I can't see what I will do with what I have studied, though. I mean who needs to know the names of the phyla after the test is over? How can such knowledge apply to my life once I am out of the protected shell of college? I will have to pay back all my loans and what will I have for all the expense—a piece of paper. Maybe I should become a woman plumber instead. What can I say.

Limit the Subject

From the automatic writing, the student decided on a limited subject: the changing value of a college education.

How Do You Write an Essay?

Devise the Thesis

The student's next step was to develop a thesis statement. She systematically devised the point she wished to make and checked over the final statement to assure that it said what she had set out to say.

Develop the Thesis

> *Subject: College education*
> *Limited subject from the automatic writing: The changing value of a college education*
> *Question: Are the time, effort, and skyrocketing costs of a college education worth what college brings it graduates?*
> *Thesis: While college is still certainly valuable for its enrichment qualities alone, these hardly seem sufficient when one considers the time, effort, and money spent by the average student.*

Write a Scratch Outline

Then the student wrote a scratch outline. Because the subject was not involved and the student felt very familiar with the ideas for the paper, she did not write out a formal outline. A set of basic notes was enough to keep her writing in the order she wished to present her ideas.

> *Thesis: While college is still certainly valuable for its enrichment qualities alone, these hardly seem sufficient when one considers the time, effort, and particularly the money spent by the average student.*
> *Getting a good job*
> *Devaluation of degrees*
> *Effort*
> *Time*
> *Money*
> *College should offer more training for the real world.*

Write the Rough Draft

Using the scratch outline to map her course, the student wrote out one draft of the essay. As she wrote, it only seemed natural to cross out and rephrase several expressions, but mainly she concentrated on getting down her ideas.

Revise the Rough Draft

Once the rough draft was complete, the student set it aside for a day and worked on other classwork. The next day when she came back to the essay she felt more able to criticize her work than she had been the day before when she felt so saturated with this particular paper that she thought it was nearly perfect. Now she found many words, phrases, and sentences she would change as well as several spelling errors, grammatical errors, and sexist language.

The rough draft along with revisions is reproduced on the next few pages. The typed portion of the paper is the first draft. Any cross-outs and written-in words are either changes the student made as she wrote the rough draft or changes she made after that draft, during the revision stage. The final typed essay, as the student handed it in, incorporates all these changes.

The Value of College

For years most people ~~who went to college~~ went to college in order to prepare for their future careers in the outside world. Some people went to college just for the status afforded the college graduate, and a few went simply for personal enrichment. However In more recent years, ~~some changes~~ the coming of specialization and high inflation have ~~have occurred in society which~~ altered the role of a college education in people's lives. ~~college situation~~. People ~~They~~ are now beginning to question whether the traditional liberal arts college education holds enough value to be continued on in its present form. While college is still certainly valuable for its enrichment qualities alone, these hardly seem sufficient when one considers the time, effort, and particularly the money spent ~~sky-rocketing costs that are expended~~ by the average ~~college~~ student.

A college degree no longer guarantees a good job as a great many graduates are learning ~~the hard way~~--to their dismay. In many cases, a college degree does not guarantee any kind of a job. Frequently, the person with a year or so at an appropriate trade school or community college is better off facing the limitations of the job market. ~~real world out there (the job market)~~ than the person who has spent four years in college getting a liberal arts

degree. Most of these trade schools produce graduates
easily well paid jobs. a community college offers training for many paraprofessional jobs, a market
who find work easily. Their jobs pay more, to boot. The
with a high employment rate.
average college graduate is turned loose on the job
He or she cannot even do simple office procedures.
market with no skill or experience.

Thinking, as unfortunate as it may be to say so, is
There has also been a widespread devaluation of college
not a very salable skill. Even jobs that require
degrees. For people going after an occupation which does
degrees are not open to all people with B.A. degrees;
demand college first, the too real fact is that a B.A.
employers just do not value B.A. degrees as highly as they
degree and even an M.A. degree mean nothing anymore in
value experience or skills. Furthermore, in certain
certain fields such as business administration and some
fields in which degrees are required a B.A. is not enough.
of the sciences. If a student is interested in a business
and plans to use
administration major today with a view toward using this
because of the specialization of today's businessmen and scientists and the stringent requirements of these fields,
degree in the future, this student must realize that he or she
should at least get a Masters Degree, and frequently
sufficient
even this is not sufficient. Our culture has become
increasingly specialized. In most cases, college has
its
retained it's importance for future careers only for the

student who wishes to specialize and endure many addition-
for   attend
al years of work, or to the student who wishes to take
Someone with a Bachelor's Degree frequently
on medical or law school. For the same reasons that its
has more trouble finding a job than someone without a degree
employable value has decreased, the status of college has
because most employers do not want to risk hiring someone who is likely to become bored or who is only
also decreased. planning to stay until he or she earns enough to go back to school.

~~A student entering college today must be willing to~~
The average student spends five years before he or she graduates.
put in at least four years of hard work. College is
with the coursework alone taking
serious concentration and dedicated study
undeniably a struggle from beginning to end, and there is
The student, always
striving for good grades, must
persevere through the anxiety of tests
usually the pressure of competition added to the task. Exams,
and papers. He or she must write papers on subjects that are
not especially interesting, memorize thousands of new words and
read hundreds of books. Living conditions are not always the best either.
¶ The cost of college today is also a problem. Although the
than others
state schools are less expensive, the average education
at a university or private school totals at approximately
twenty thousand dollars
~~$20,000~~ for four years. Most students must pay at least a
sizeable portion of that figure, and the rest is taken
care of through student loans which must be paid back by
the student after graduation, these loans frequently running
expense
into the thousands of dollars. Then, after all ~~of~~ this,
cannot
the graduate ~~can't~~ find work without additional schooling
The whole cycle of expenses has to continue creating
seemingly unsurmountable debts.
of some kind. ¶ While college is undeniably important if

we are to live in an interesting and informed society,
definite
college should also offer something more ~~definate~~ in the
graduating students.
form of a successful career for ~~the future~~.

Type the Final Draft

After the student reviewed all the changes and felt sure that they made her paper sound just as she wanted it to sound, she went ahead and typed up the final draft. Even as she typed in all the revisions that had so improved her presentation, she considered other changes and incorporated a few that added to the flow of the final essay. She added a whole new sentence, for instance, to the beginning of the fourth paragraph. It is usual for a writer to add finishing touches to the essay as he or she types it up, and by no means should you feel that it is too late to make minor changes. Note that the final product presented on the next few pages has a few penciled-in corrections on it. If, when proofreading the final draft, a few typing errors should come to your attention, as they did in this student's case, it is perfectly acceptable to pencil in corrections. Most readers would rather see a few pencil marks than read an incorrect copy. However, if many corrections had been needed, the student would have retyped the paper; a sloppy paper should always be retyped, even if doing so takes a little longer than you have planned.

The Value of College Today

For years most people went to college in order to prepare for their future careers in the outside world. Some people went to college just for the status afforded the college graduate, and a few went simply for personal enrichment. However, in more recent years, the coming of specialization and high inflation have altered the role of a college education in people's lives. People are now beginning to question whether the traditional liberal arts college education holds enough value to be continued in its present form. While college is still certainly valuable for its enrichment qualities alone, these hardly seem sufficient when one considers the time, effort, and particularly the money spent by the average student.

A college degree, first of all, no longer guarantees a good job as a great many graduates are learning--to their dismay. In many cases, a college degree does not guarantee any kind of a job. Frequently, the person with a year or so at an appropriate trade school or community college is better off facing the limitations of the job market than the person who has spent four years in college getting a liberal arts degree. Most trade schools graduate people who can easily find well-paid jobs. A community college offers training for many para-professional jobs, a market with a high employment rate. ~~On the other hand,~~ The average college graduate is turned loose on the job market with no skill or experience. He or she cannot even do simple office procedures, in many cases. The ability to think, as unfortunate as it may be to say so, is not a very salable skill. Even jobs that require degrees are not open to all people with their B.A.; employers just do not value B.A. degrees as highly as they value experience and skills.

Furthermore, in certain fields in which degrees are required, a B.A. is not enough. If a student is interested in a business administration major today and plans to use this degree in the future, this student must realize that because of the specialization of today's business people and scientists and the stringent requirements of these fields, he or she should get a Master's Degree at least, and frequently even this is not sufficient. In most cases, college has retained its importance for future careers only for the student who wishes to specialize and endure many additional years of work, or for the student who wishes to attend medical or law school. Someone with a Bachelor's Degree alone may have more trouble finding a job than someone without a degree, because most employers do not want to risk hiring someone who is likely to become bored or who is only planning to stay until he or she earns enough to go back to school.

Aside from the considerations of what one will do with his or her life after college, there are questions as to the value of all the work involved in actually getting the

degree. The average student spends five years before he or she graduates. Every student entering college today must be willing to put in at least four years of hard work. College is undeniably a struggle from beginning to end, with the coursework alone taking serious concentration and dedicated study, and there is usually the pressure of competition added to the task. The student, always striving for good grades, must constantly push himself through the anxiety of tests, exams, and papers. He or she must write papers on subjects that are not especially interesting, memorize thousands of new words, and read hundreds of books. Living conditions, either in dorms or in low-cost housing, are not always the best. Ultimately, the tensions of college life and the financial conditions of the average student must be considered part of earning the degree.

The cost of college today is, in itself, a problem. Although the state schools are less expensive than others, the average education at a university or private school totals approximately twenty thousand dollars for four years. Most students must pay at least a sizeable portion of that figure, and the rest is taken care of through student loans ~~which~~ *that* must be paid back by the student after graduation, these loans frequently running into the thousands of dollars. Then, after all this expense, the graduate cannot find work without additional schooling of some kind. The whole cycle of expenses has to continue, creating

---

seemingly unsurmountable debts.

While college is undeniably important if we are to live in an interesting and informed society, colleges should also offer something more definite in the form of a successful career for graduating students.

Note that the main changes made during typing were of two kinds:

The adding of transitional words and sentences
The refining of words and phrases

Proofread After she had typed the paper, the writer read it over and made pencil corrections. Since none of the corrections were extensive, she did not have to retype any pages.

By using a step-by-step process to write your essays, you will be able to perfect each stage of the writing, making the final essay your best possible effort. There are several specific things a good writer needs to know about the individual steps, so each step is taken up in depth in the following chapters.

2
What Should You Write About?

Many writers have some trouble getting started with their writing. When asked what they plan to write about, they answer that they need more time to think. They may not realize that a good way to resolve their confusion is to take a pen in hand and think the subject through on paper, right away. There is no need for you as a writer to fear the tyrannical white page if you become familiar with a few structured ways to sort out your thoughts. Soon you will find yourself able to arrive, rather simply, at an interesting and sufficiently limited topic for a paper.

Few people can sit down at a desk or a typewriter without first putting off the task for a few hours—there's always the laundry to wash or drawers to clean out or some very important checks to write for bills that have been sitting around for several months. Did you ever notice how hungry you get the minute you think of sitting down to write? The fact is that writing often frightens people because it requires so much integration of feelings and ideas, so much personal evaluation, so much commitment to a subject. Writing cannot be merely a mechanical skill—it engages the whole person.

This involvement is certainly the same reason that many writers have felt revitalized after finishing a particularly good piece of written expression. Eldridge Cleaver remarked that he began to write to "save himself." Cleaver, who was in jail at the time, found that by writing he was able to reaffirm his personal worth and to discover an inner life beyond the depression and oppressiveness of the prison world.

Certainly, most of us are not as isolated as Cleaver, nor as demoralized. Every day we express many feelings and thoughts verbally. As a result, we are so used to dropping ideas and attitudes in casual conversation that we feel alarmed by the permanence and concreteness of the written word. We feel that once our ideas are expressed on paper we cannot eradicate them or alter them even slightly; and we fear that once down on paper, our ideas are not the only things judged—worse, we ourselves are being personally evaluated.

Thus, either we do not write until we have formulated our ideas with a degree of precision, or we get so tense in our alarm over a required written assignment, that we can temporarily block the flow and spontaneity of our thoughts. What all professional writers know—and what you too should remember if you tend to feel blocked—is that writing an essay for a class assignment is the second step of the process.

WHY PREWRITING?

The first step should be merely the scratches and scrawls of a working mind: a valuable if imperfect beginning. At this point, your thoughts need not be polished, or even clear. Just keep your mind rolling. You should no more begin with such rigid expectations of yourself in writing than you would, for instance, if you were buying a car. You wouldn't just drive home in the first one you saw; you'd consider the various levels of quality, options, safety records, engineering. In fact, you might write a list of comparisons so that you wouldn't forget about any one important advantage or disadvantage. For the car buyer, the first step is to record raw ideas, sort through them, and adjust them. This step is important for the writer, too.

As you recall from Chapter 1, the step before writing is prewriting: everything you put down on paper before you actually write out a draft of the paper. The following steps are all part of prewriting.

Inventing the subject: in this step you pick a general subject area that interests you.

Limiting the subject: in this step you explore the limits and the possible options that your subject offers; then you settle on one focused subject.

Writing a thesis: in this step you develop the limited subject into an assertion that will direct your whole essay.

Outlining the paper: in this step you create a set of detailed notes that you can use as a map for writing out the first draft of the paper.

How each writer goes about the steps involved in prewriting is largely a matter of personal taste. For example, you may find, after trying several methods of inventing and exploring subjects, that one method sticks with you—you feel at home with it. Because the technique works well for you, you use it whenever you write, over and over. Or the methods you use may depend on how familiar you are with the subject of an assigned paper, or on the amount of time you have to spend on an essay.

Whatever method of prewriting you use, you will save yourself much time and worry in the long run. There are two good reasons for this: you will have the chance to look over your options and select a topic you want to write on, and you will feel in control of your presentation so that you will not be faced with the discovery when writing page seven of your paper that on page six there are three irrelevant ideas and that on page four there are five more ideas that belong to page one. Essays written without recorded preparation are likely to be diffuse, unfocused, underdeveloped, boring, and illogical despite all your efforts to think your topic through before beginning to write. As you saw in Chapter 1 with the essay called "A Degree," the chances are that the essay handed in without prewriting would serve as a good example of prewriting, but not of the final product.

You can view prewriting as a written conversation with yourself rather than as a formal writing assignment. It is free writing in the early stages, without any demands for proper grammar or spelling. As long as you can decipher what you have put down, it will be perfect. Prewriting is also generative and positive—it can help you see how many ideas you really do have, how many views you can come up with that give an interesting slant on your topic.

INVENTING THE SUBJECT

It's fine to say you should find an interesting general subject and it is a good first step, but how do you begin? Where do good topics come from? You can begin by writing rough notes, really just words and phrases, as they strike you. The specific sources of these ideas are various: personal experiences, reading experiences, experiences of people you know, discussions with friends, television watching, class discussions and lectures, searching indexes in the library (See Chapter 9), suggestions from teachers and friends, daily casual reading of newspapers and magazines, and so forth. To invent a general subject for a paper, you only need to tap your recent experiences or responses to what you have read, seen, discussed, and heard. Everyone has experienced many things that are valuable sources of ideas for essays. One possible way to approach all these experiences at once is to write a list of ideas and events that have angered or delighted you over the past few weeks. You might even divide a sheet of paper in half and let your mind roam free on this topic:

ANGRY	DELIGHTED
TV movies—"Wide Screams"	*Got an A on chemistry midterm*
Dorm curfews	*Read "Allegory of the Cave"—*
Lack of social activity on campus	*liked the idea of truth*
4 students dropped Speech 101	*Dodgers won*
	Linda got a medical school interview

Now, this list may not at first appear to offer many possible topics, but it actually does. The writer of the list could single out the most annoying qualities of TV movies or just write on "Wide Screams." She or he could write about the dropout rate in speech courses, the competition on chemistry tests, the Dodgers, or medical school interviews. These topics are at least possibilities, starting points. If the assignment were slightly more restricted, of course, the student would have had to find a general subject within the restrictions. Still, an "angry and delighted" chart would work; still, the subjects could come from the same sources.

LIMITING THE SUBJECT

When you are given an assignment to write an essay of 500 words, you are expected to limit your subject to an appropriate size for the paper. It is true that you could, in effect, write in a few pages on any topic, and encyclopedias do just that. Turn to the entry on China, and you find only a few pages. But you can see that the kind of information in encyclopedias is far less specific than that required in most college papers. Even if your assignment is to write a paper of about fifteen pages, you probably need to limit the original conception of your topic. As you research or explore your own ideas, you will repeatedly find reason to narrow your subject. You can't elaborate on all the points of nuclear energy in five pages, but you may be able to discuss the role of one person in the situation or how his or her role led to a certain event. You cannot write about education for the handicapped in ten pages, except in a very general way—whole volumes are devoted to the subject. However, you can discuss the need to teach both lipreading and sign language to young deaf children.

You may wonder if it is possible to limit your subject too much. The fact is most college writers have little difficulty settling on a subject that is broad enough—rather, they struggle to cut down the scope of their topics to manageable size. A good college essay usually says a lot about a few things, not a little about many things. If you do prewriting every time you write, you should be able to limit your subject systematically and adequately. Generally, you need not worry about cutting your subject up too small. Writers who feel that they have limited their topics too much (and as a consequence have little to say) have more likely failed to expand adequately on the separate subdivisions of a good limited subject. As you become acquainted with the writer's notebook, brainstorming, and the subject graph, you will feel more comfortable settling on a limited topic.

EXPLORING THE SUBJECT

Writers have found certain prewriting techniques especially helpful in identifying limited subjects. The techniques explained here have structures, but they are very flexible. They aim only at getting you to explore the limits of your subject and helping you to determine what view and which parts of your broad topic you are most committed to investigating and writing about. Naturally, this process will be somewhat different for each individual. You may find that you use one pattern exclusively because it works best for you or that you concoct a version of your own by combining the prewriting techniques explained in this chapter. Try each pattern and suit yourself.

KEEPING A WRITER'S NOTEBOOK

The writer's notebook is a source book of collected insights and a testing ground for ideas: an entry may provide you with a general subject, but more important, it can free you to express your important feelings about an idea. However, before you try this technique, it's important to know the differences between this sort of notebook and a diary, so that you avoid making entries that will not help you. Perhaps at some time in your life you have kept a daily record of events—a diary. Different in purpose is the writer's notebook, in which you record only *special* perceptions that might serve as the *core statements of essays*. These insights may arise out of the particular way in which you view something that has happened to you during the day, from your response to some book, or simply from an unsummoned idea that pops into your head.

The most satisfying part of maintaining a writer's notebook is that it becomes a record of how your perceptions change and grow over a time. When you begin to read a novel, for instance, you may identify with a certain situation between two lovers in the book, but by the middle of the work you may find that the characters act in predictable and unrealistic ways that make the writing cheap and sentimental. The series of entries in your writer's notebook could provide you with specific critical points that you might turn into an essay on the shallowness of character development. In a writer's notebook your first impressions often combine to become a generalization about the work you are dealing with or the aspect of your life you are exploring. These generalizations are at the heart of all essays. The writer's notebook

40 The Writer's Practical Rhetoric

FIGURE 2-1
The potter wedges the clay, getting the feel of it, just as the writer allows his or her mind to penetrate and become comfortable with a topic. (Photo by Steve Dierks.)

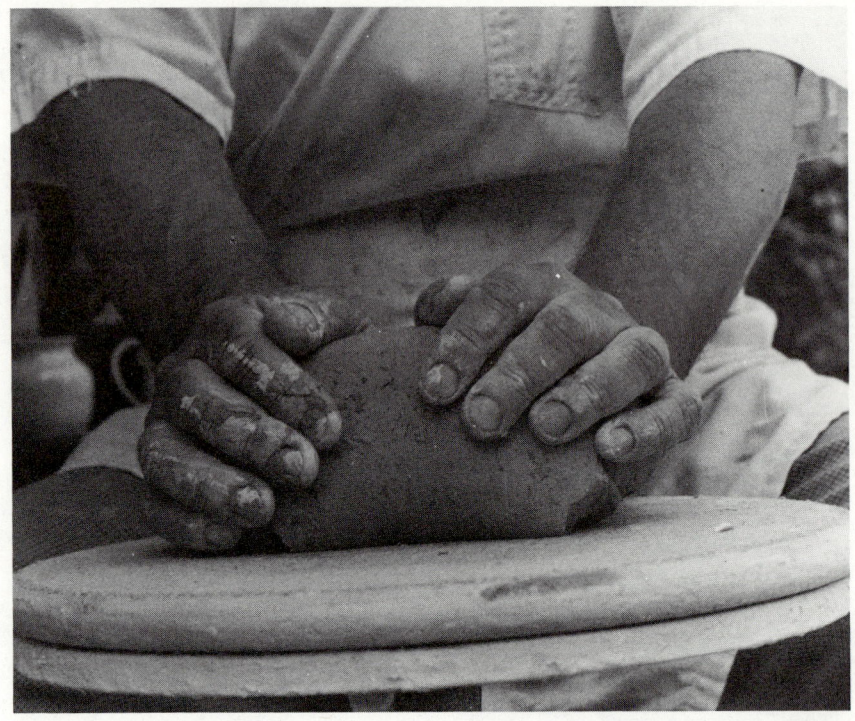

serves a dual purpose in prewriting: helping you to hold onto the ideas that flow so quickly through your mind and helping you to explore those ideas beyond their rough beginnings as they become more developed and more clearly formed thoughts.

Many professional writers keep a notebook of this type. In fact, the term *writer's notebook* has been borrowed from the title of W. Somerset Maugham's journals. What follows is a sample from a student's notebook. You will notice many writing errors, but these you will recall, do not matter in prewriting, which is done only to collect ideas. Notice also that the three entries are cumulative, each showing different thinking patterns that eventually lead to the generalization (in the third entry). What essay topics might this student have developed from this germinal idea?

NO. 1

I was babysitting yesterday and Jon and Eli were particularly wild. It really made me wonder whether I ever want to have children of my own. I mean, if anyone were to ask me of course I'd say yes, but I really don't know. Jon was playing with his toy gun and Eli came in and grabbed it away from him saying that it wasn't his toy anymore. This really made Jon frantic; his whole face reddened and he howled over and over, "Give me my gun." Meanwhile Eli stood there and laughed at Jon calling him a baby in a very mean way. I tried to reason with Jon and I asked him why he took the toy. He wouldn't answer me. I felt totally in the power of these two monsters. Finally, I decided that the only thing to do was to scream louder than they could, so I did. Silence. It actually angered me that I had to resort to this. It makes me wonder if that is how a parent has to be and if the relationship between adults and children has to be defined as "might makes right." Do those kids just provoke their parents to the point of yelling louder than their kids? Is the only sort of communication that is possible on this level? Maybe I'm idealistic but I also want to be the kind of parent who can sit down and reason with my children about why they do things. In psychology class we read Dialogues with Mothers *by Bruno Bettelheim and the main point of the book was that parents should treat their children as people. The question is how do you get your kids to act like the people you want to treat them as?*

NO. 2

Maybe I was a little too hard on Jon and Eli yesterday. I should have been angrier with their parents. Maybe they have taught the kids to act this way by the model they set in their own relations. Now that I think about it I have been Mr. Rodder degrade and yell at Mrs. Rodder right in my presence. In fact, he seems to get a thrill out of her cowering to him when others are around. Usually it is about something he wants and she does not want. She kind of "charms" him and just when it seems to work he screams at her. "Don't try to decide things that are my decisions, etc." He gets loud and obnoxious and she gets quiet. Anyway, I was just noticing the games between adults and how much they resemble the way little kids respond to authority—the kind that carries a big stick. My own father was always this way. He would hold things inside and just when we thought we were getting our own way, he would howl at us and threaten to whip us. Then we would fall right into line. Now I can't stand people who treat their kids like this and I can't stand to hear a lot of yelling or fighting between people. The relationship between people, it seems, should rest on a different kind of authority than one of physical might.

> **NO. 3**
>
> *This thing about parents' power & childrens' power really bugs me. So, what is the kind of authority that I respect in people? I don't respect policemen who club or bully to keep order, but I do respect those who carry out their duties peacefully. But that—Never mind, I don't respect teachers who use the power of grades to threaten students into working hard. But I do like teachers who maintain their authority because they are knowledgable in their subject. What other authority figures are there? Bosses. I don't like bosses who treat you as slaves. Good bosses treat you as an important part of their business operation, no less a person for being a secretary than they are for being an executive. Respect for the individual is important and expertise in the area of authority—I guess these can be summed up as more rational or intellectual aspects of authority. They are the more important and more liveable ones for me. I guess that gets back to what Bettelheim was saying in a way. Don't treat your kids as if they are "little people" but as real people with thoughts and feelings of their own. If they see that you treat all people this way, maybe they will return that respect to you.*

BRAINSTORMING The process of freely associating ideas in prewriting is called *brainstorming*. This technique takes a lot less time than a writer's notebook. To brainstorm, as the word suggests, is to write down everything that comes into your mind—words, phrases, or sentences. You usually begin with some stimulus (a word, a film, a photograph, a painting, etc.) and, writing as your mind works, come up with a list of related thoughts. The very act of writing under pressure without a set structure produces new ideas. There are two slightly different approaches to brainstorming: *automatic writing* and *word lists*. Remember that in neither case should you concern yourself with grammar and spelling. Never go back to cross out a word or think twice of what to say.

Automatic Writing *Automatic writing* is particularly useful when you feel blocked on a given subject. It provides a good way to get started on writing because, as in the writer's notebook, grammar and structure don't matter. The technique of automatic writing is to write as fast as possible, without stopping, for some prescribed time limit—say, five minutes. You're given a subject and you write, in complete sentences or phrases, whatever comes into your head. Don't lift your pen from the paper. If your mind is blank, write "I can't think of anything to say . . . I can't think of anything to say . . ." until a different thought replaces that one. After completing the automatic writing, examine each line closely for

What Should You Write About?

interesting ideas on which you might like to write. There is no question that automatic writing is not the world's greatest writing, but for prewriting it is fine. Here is an example. Another example is on page 26.

> *Television—What can I say about t.v.—it's all been said before. I can't think of anything. I can't think of any—Television is a waste of time for anyone who is trying to lead an intellectual lifestyle. Commercials are insults to anyone with a brain in their head. They are merely sexual exploitations having little to do with the products they are supposedly selling, you are buying beautiful sleek bodies and not a car or a lovely sexy smile and not toothpaste, etc. Also the level of programming. I once read is aimed at an audience with a ninth grade education. What am I going to college for? I can't think of any—How can a college student learn from the low level mentality projected in t.v. the vocab. simple-minded—jokes, slapstick. Even controversial shows like "All in the Family" or "Maude" are so pat (stereotyped), don't challenge the watcher at all. All the t.v. viewer is is a viewer—he has only to sit back and watch and never think. On shows where he supposedly has to think its only the most dumb kind of mental exertion—who done it sort of thing—besides most of these shows are just set to some sort of boring formula that a six year old could figure out. It'd be frightening to realize that every day we talk and communicate with people who know the Jack in the Box commercials by heart and the soap opera plots and all their details but they don't know how to read anything complex or what I would call intelligent. What can I have in common with these guys? It's not that I'm an elitist. But its scary to think that they are running our government—it's a mass homogenized society.*

Then make a list like the following one of the interesting subjects. You may be able to arrive at even more limited subjects from yours than this writer did.

> *Mass homogenization of people by t.v.*
> *Formulas of t.v. adventure shows*
> *Educational level of average t.v. audience*
> *How t.v. commercials reflect the audience*
> *Sexual implications in t.v. commercials*
> *Stereotyping in the controversial t.v. shows*
> *Rigid differences between t.v. watchers and nonwatchers.*

If you felt a need to further narrow these subjects, you could do an automatic writing on each one of them, finally selecting the best ideas. This expanding, limiting, and selecting process will eventually lead to a topic sufficiently limited for an essay.

Word Lists

Word lists are another type of brainstorming. When you have an idea for a paper or think of some subject that interests you and you are wondering whether it is worth pursuing, you might try the word list technique. Many people prefer this technique to automatic writing because it is not timed and because it requires only listing key words. The first step in writing a word list is to write a column of at least twenty to thirty words quickly, without stopping if possible, and without hesitating to select the most appropriate word. One student's word list on the Aemrican jail system looked like this:

Jobs	Killers
"Cures"	Suicide
Punishment	Bitterness
Cruelty—guards	Macho
Life terms	Rehabilitation
Money gets you off	Initiation
Probation arrangement	"Time"
Condition of cells	Toilets
Social hierarchy	Showers
Homosexuality	Theft
Public defenders	Drugs
Rapists	Smuggling
Murderers	Plan future crime
Dehumanization	No real behavior change
Loss of privacy	Underdogs
Loss of hope	Muggings
Crowded	Bugs
Church	Rats
School	Beds on floor
Occupational therapy	Recidivism

The next step is to review your list to cross out any word that repeats another. Here the writer could cross out *killers* and leave *murderers* and could delete *jobs* in favor of *occupational therapy*. Step three is to go down the list and to group similar ideas. This is often a very subjective process that begins to direct you toward the main point of your paper. Another student might have grouped the same words in a different way to achieve a different set of ideas. No one way is right—it's entirely up to the writer. Here is a possible grouping for the words in the list.

What Should You Write About?

Crime Within	**Punishment**	**Jail Sentences**
Drugs	Cruelty—guards	Life terms
Muggings	Social hierarchy	Money gets you off
Macho	Initiation	Public defenders
Future crime plans		Probation
Rapists		arrangement
Murderers		"Time"
Suicide		

Condition of Cells	**Psychological Adjustment**	**Rehabilitation**
Crowded	Loss of privacy	"Cures"
Beds on floor	Social hierarchy	Church
Bugs	Initiation	School
Rats	Underdogs	Occupational therapy
Toilets	Loss of hope	No real behavior
Showers	Bitterness	change
	Suicide	Recidivism

Note how the writer has developed a category to cover each main idea. He or she found labels in the word list—or else made them up, as with "Crime within Jail" and "Jail Sentences." From the pattern that emerges from the word list, you are able to tell at a glance on which subjects you have the most material. Although both interest and sufficient knowledge are not always present, it is easy enough to know when you are sufficiently interested in a subject or merely know so much about it that it bores you. After completing the word list and the grouping, you can select one or two word groups, the most interesting ones, as a list of potential limited subjects.

THE SUBJECT CHART The most structured and most graphic of the prewriting techniques for limiting the subject is the subject chart. To draw up a subject chart, begin at the middle of a clean sheet of paper. Draw a circle and write your broad subject in it.

FIGURE 2-2

(ADVERTISING)

Then, turning the subject over in your mind, ask yourself what aspects of the subject you can name. Remember, you want to look at some interesting, and possibly controversial aspects of your subject. For example, if your subject is advertising, you might break it down according to different kinds of advertising: television, radio, magazine, and so forth.

FIGURE 2-3

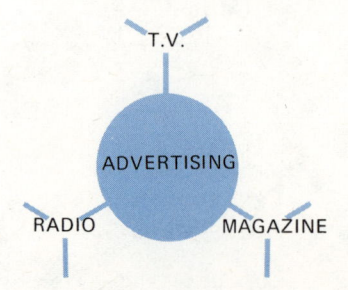

```
         T.V.
          |
      ( ADVERTISING )
       /          \
   RADIO         MAGAZINE
```

You might ask yourself next what smaller units you can break down each of the second-level topics into. You might decide on categories such as cosmetics, cigarettes, clothing, and notions. Or preferably you might approach controversial issues, such as the ethics of cigarette commercials being taken off television, how radio commercials suggest subliminally, and the rights of sponsors to dictate content on television. Topics like these really add focus to your subject.

FIGURE 2-4

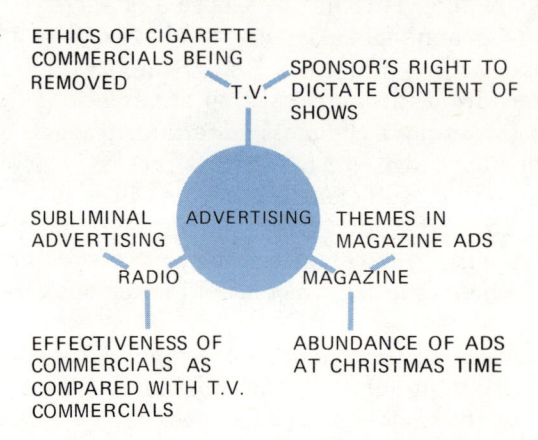

```
ETHICS OF CIGARETTE
COMMERCIALS BEING         SPONSOR'S RIGHT TO
REMOVED          T.V.     DICTATE CONTENT OF
                           SHOWS

    SUBLIMINAL     ADVERTISING    THEMES IN
    ADVERTISING                   MAGAZINE ADS

              RADIO         MAGAZINE

    EFFECTIVENESS OF        ABUNDANCE OF ADS
    COMMERCIALS AS          AT CHRISTMAS TIME
    COMPARED WITH T.V.
    COMMERCIALS
```

You could, then, in turn break down further each of the second-level topics. The point of this exercise is to allow you to subdivide your subject into many of its focused categories, presenting all your ideas for paper topics in a logical order. You can see on page 47 how one student has used this method to draw up a rather extensive subject chart on "animals." After drawing up the chart you can pick potential topics for a very short or detailed paper from the circle farthest from the center of your subject chart. The progression of general to specific topics might serve you well when you need to settle on a topic; the more general the assignment is intended to be, the closer your topic probably will be to the center of the subject chart.

What Should You Write About?

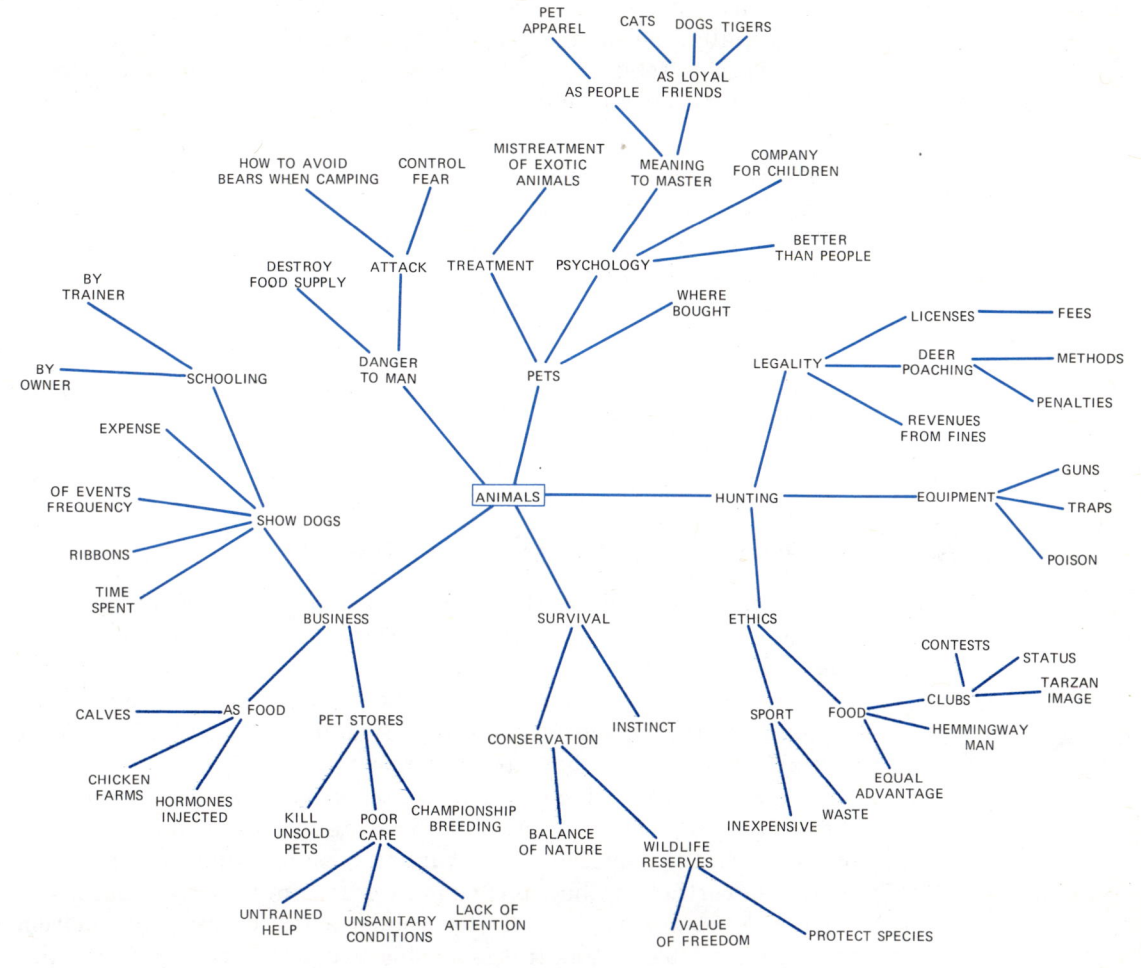

FIGURE 2-5 Subject Chart.

The preceding subject chart is very well developed and, no doubt, took quite some time to complete. Your charts need not always be so developed. You may include certain categories that you do not wish to explore, so you leave them far less developed than others. You may quickly decide on a variety of interesting topics and feel no need to expand the chart as completely as the one shown here. Nevertheless, the complete chart above offers several possible limited topics. Here are a few.

If you trace some of the topics out on the chart, you can see how the writer's mind worked, focusing the topic more and more. For example, the topic "unsanitary conditions in pet shops" is one good possibility for a short essay. The broad subject of animals was broken down to animals as a business, then to pet stores, which was further subdivided. Finally, the subdivisions of pet stores led to the limited subject. Other possible topics for a three-to-five-page essay might have been derived from the same chart.

- Mistreatment of exotic pets
- How wildlife reserves protect species
- The image of the hunter who joins a club
- Cats as loyal friends
- A fair definition of "poaching" deer

Trace out the development of each to see how the writer focused the very broad subject of animals.

PINPOINTING THE LIMITED SUBJECT

Once you have explored the limits of the general subject in which you're interested, you are ready to decide which aspect of the subject you wish to write about. From your exploring, you have various choices. This decision should be made with a few things in mind. Who is your audience? What information is available on your subject? What sort of interest do you have in the subject?

You can evaluate which of your limited subjects would sustain your interest. Remember, you are going to devote some time and quite a bit of energy to the subject, so you want it to be one that is meaningful to you. Nevertheless, the topic, no matter how interesting, must invite further development. In order for you to investigate it, information must be available to you. If it is a subject requiring research, but also very current (you heard about it on the news two days ago), you may or may not experience difficulty finding up-to-date information in the library (see Chapter 9). You should find out before you go a step further.

The same goes for a topic requiring no library research. Do you know enough about it to expand it into a good paper? Are you full of good ideas at this point? Then, of course, there is the matter of whether your audience (the teacher and your classmates) will find the limited subject interesting, valuable, and appropriate to the assignment (see Chapter 1). Whatever limited subject you select should be appealing from the vantage points of writer, subject, and audience. The appropriate limited subject for a paper would fall, ideally, where these considerations meet.

What Should You Write About? 49

FIGURE 2-6

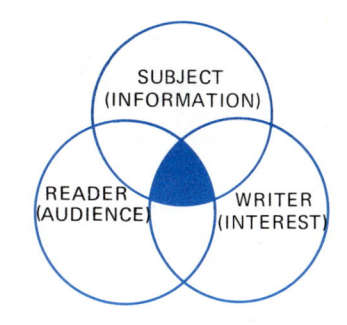

[Venn diagram: three overlapping circles labeled SUBJECT (INFORMATION), READER (AUDIENCE), WRITER (INTEREST)]

EXERCISES
A. Write a paragraph discussing whether you believe it easier to write about subjects that are interesting to you than subjects that you have no opinion about. Is it possible to develop an interest in any subject? Offer one example from your personal experience as concrete support of your opinion on the matter.
B. Keep a writer's notebook of your reactions to classes and readings for two weeks. Before you write each new entry, read the one before it. After the two weeks are up, sift through the notebook and make a list of ten possible topics for essays.
C. Make a subject chart on one of the following topics and identify three limited subjects for essays from the chart.
Violence
Morality
The family
D. Write a word list on one of the subjects below.
Sports
Teachers
Women's Liberation
E. Develop a four-minute automatic writing on this subject: the value of first impressions.
F. Deliberately pick a very broad subject and write a page-long essay about it. What characteristics stand out about the information?
G. Look up China in the encyclopedia. How long is the article? Why do you suppose an author of encyclopedia articles can write on broad subjects in such a short space? Can you think of any other types of writing that does the same thing?
H. Spend five minutes doing an automatic writing about a movie you have seen recently. How many topics for essays can you derive?
I. Write a word list on the subject of responsibility. Derive four possible essay topics from your efforts.
J. Select any object you would like to examine and look at it for ten minutes without writing anything down. Next write for ten min-

utes (try not to stop) any associations that occur to you. Can you think of anything to compare the object to which will clarify for your reader what it looks like, feels like? Did this sort of "meditation" suggest any issues to your mind? For instance, did studying a lake suggest the issue of pollution? Might your ten-minute writing sample serve as the beginnings of an essay?

K. Write a writer's notebook entry on the subject of materialism. Can you derive any topics for essays?

DEVELOPING A THESIS

Since writing ought to be a series of promises to the reader and responses to those promises, the first part of your essay should include a thesis: a sentence or group of sentences that presents what the essay sets out to prove, define, describe, or illustrate. The chances are that you do not have the point of your paper clear in your own mind if, early in the paper, you cannot commit yourself to a concise statement of it. Papers without focus lose the readers' interest. After all, no one wants to listen to others who don't even know what they want to say.

Your thesis should be stated concisely and directly—it should prepare the readers in a few words for what is to come. Compare these two thesis statements for a simple informative essay.

> The purpose of this paper is to explore the three types of humor in existence since Elizabethan times.
>
> Since Elizabethan times, comedies have been designated as three types: romantic, critical, and rogue.

In the first example, the words "the purpose of this paper is" are monotonous. Your readers are likely to be disturbed by them. Why tell the readers that a paper has a purpose? Don't they expect that? Is it necessary to tell readers that they have a "paper" in front of them? What exactly are the "three types of humor"? Just what is meant by "explore"? What methods will the writer use to explore them—philosophical, sociological, historical? Will he or she classify, compare, set in chronological order (see Chapter 3)? The readers do not get enough clues in the first thesis.

Effective thesis statements have three parts that you should learn to recognize. First of all, because the thesis is a complete sentence, it has a subject and a predicate. Naturally the predicate part of the sentence makes a statement about the subject. The predicate part also contains the third part you should look for: the controlling idea. The controlling idea indicates your main idea for support and it is always a clue to the development of the essay. A clear controlling idea is crucial to the thesis because it shows the readers what to expect in the

What Should You Write About? 51

FIGURE 2-7
The potter centers the clay as the writer finds the central impression he or she wishes to make. (Photo by Steve Dierks.)

body of the paper and commits the writer to the information that supports the main point. The controlling idea says for you, "Here is what evidence supports my point."

Thesis   Smoking in public buildings should be outlawed because inhaled smoke is dangerous to the health of all people and often offensive to nonsmokers.

The subject is *smoking*. The predicate part is *should be outlawed because inhaled smoke is dangerous to the health of all people and often offensive to nonsmokers* and the controlling idea is *dangerous to the health of all people and often offensive to nonsmokers*. You can see that while this information tells the readers a great deal, it avoids the obviousness of statements of intention.

Making the thesis no longer than one complete sentence is usually not too difficult, but there may be times when, for clarity, you will need more than one sentence. Your goal is to state your main idea as directly and clearly as possible. Therefore, when you can fit the point into a sentence you should do so. The following steps will help you write a direct one-sentence thesis.

As you progress through the steps, you are getting closer and closer to developing the whole thesis. In the final step, you add up the work in the previous steps and create the thesis. Try not to digress or take shortcuts at first when following the steps—always remember in each step to write out your subject completely, for it is an integral part of the final step and should not be lost.

1. *Name your limited subject.* Assume for a moment you are assigned a five-page essay on the subject of nutrition. You can write about anything within that broad subject. Having completed the word association, you decide to write about fad diets. But you realize that, though *fad diets* is more limited than the very general area of nutrition, it may not be limited enough for a short paper. Therefore, you ask yourself which facet of fad diets you are interested in, and you come up with a controversial topic: *the value of the Stillman diet.* Step one consists of checking the scope of your limited topic against the requirement of the assignment and coming up with a definite limited topic.

    STEP ONE: the Stillman diet and its problems

2. *Ask a question about the limited subject.* Here you focus on what you want to investigate in your paper. Devising an interesting question, you can see that, in effect, you are adding a predicate or "aboutness" to the limited subject. On the subject of the problems with the Stillman diet, you might ask, "Is the Stillman diet advisable for the typical college student?" You may be interested in this question because you or a friend has tried, or is thinking of trying, the diet. Step two consists in stating the question you wish to look into.

    STEP TWO: Is the Stillman diet advisable for the typical college student?

3. *Revise your question into a statement.* Usually, this step is just a matter of changing the form of the question you made up in the previous step. Since a thesis for an essay is an assertion, not a question, you do not want to leave your idea in question form. You can see, then, that this step may involve answering the question posed in step two. To answer the question about the diet, you have to take a stand. Suppose you decide that the diet is not recommended. Your resulting statement would be all that is required for step three.

    STEP THREE: The Stillman diet is inadvisable for the typical college student.

Now, check the predicate part to make sure that it says what you want to say. Then, go on to the next step.

4. *Add a group of words in which you summarize your key supporting ideas.* You may be able to use words such as "because," "by," or "in that" to introduce the controlling idea, linking it to the rest of the sentence. In step four you are listing your key supporting ideas, each of which will be taken up in your paper. For the paper on the Stillman diet a clause introduced by "because" might serve best.

   STEP FOUR: because it is inconvenient, not healthful, and provides only temporary weight loss.

5. *Recognize the opposition.* If your topic is controversial (as is the Stillman diet topic), you will remember from Chapter 1 that it is sound argumentative practice to state your opponents' claims. There may be members of your audience who would disagree with you. Assume there are. A good place to insert these claims is in an "although" clause at the beginning of your assertion, or, if the claim is long, in a complete sentence preceding the thesis. Ask yourself what someone who would defend the Stillman diet would say, and recognize the validity of that person's argument by placing that idea right in your thesis, where your reader can get a fair view of the issue.

   STEP FIVE: although the Stillman diet does provide quick weight loss

6. *Combine the last three steps in the following order: step five, step three, and step four.* Now, as a finishing touch, polish up any wordiness or awkwardness in the thesis sentence.

   STEP SIX: Although the Stillman diet does help people lose weight quickly, this method is inadvisable for the typical college student because it is impractical, is nutritionally unsound, and provides only temporary weight loss.

In polishing up the sentence, you might call the diet "this method" and replace "inconvenient and expensive" with the less wordy "impractical." Also, "not healthful" could be improved to "nutritionally unsound." An "is" should also be added to the middle reason to make all the elements in the controlling idea parallel. At this point, too, if you find the controlling idea forms an unwieldy list that overwhelms the reader, try to condense it by using fewer words.

Now you have a thesis with three parts:

Subject—Stillman diet
Predicate—is inadvisable for the typical college student because it

is impractical, is nutritionally unsound, and provides only temporary weight loss

Controlling idea—is impractical
                 is nutritionally unsound
                 provides only temporary weight loss

The key to developing a good thesis, as you can see, is learning how to ask a good question and then turning that question into a statement. After practicing the six steps to an effective thesis for a while, you will probably find yourself able to compose good thesis statements just by asking a question and stating a complete answer to it. The answer will be the thesis. It is worth noting that you have many opportunities during the day to practice the development of a good thesis statement; you don't have to wait until a paper is due. As you walk out of a lecture with the ideas fresh in your mind, ask yourself the central question of the lecture and then turn it into a statement that sums up the whole lecture. You will not only be reinforcing the classwork in your own mind, a good study habit, but also will be practicing the most crucial step in effective writing: forming a thesis.

EXERCISES Directions: The following four theses are appropriate to different length essays because of their various levels of specificity. Rate the specificity of the theses from *least* to *most* specific.

A. Capital punishment should be discontinued because it is inhumane and without value to society.
B. Capital punishment should be discontinued because it is inhumane and because it does not deter criminals from committing crimes.
C. Hanging as capital punishment should be discontinued because it is inhumane.
D. Capital punishment should be discontinued because it denies those punished the rights guaranteed by the Constitution.

Directions: For three of the following questions write two theses, one which is appropriate for a two- or three-page essay and one better suited to a ten-page essay.

A. What is wrong with the President's energy program?
B. Why is Catholicism undergoing changes in its stand on abortion?
C. In what way has the increase in minority graduates from colleges and universities affected racial relations in urban areas?
D. In what way is Transactional Analysis an outgrowth of modern social movements?
E. Why do most political scientists interested in modern Germany argue that another Hitler would have little success now in assuming control of the West German government?

What Should You Write About? 55

Directions: Practice the thesis steps for three of the following topics. Your efforts should yield possible thesis statements for each of the topics you select.

A. Conflict between nations' energy needs and the conservation of natural resources.
B. The ethics of fishing with electrical devices.
C. The value of growing plants at home.
D. The overcrowded judicial system.
E. Movement in national entertainment from interest in books to interest in films.

Directions: For the following theses, identify the controlling idea and suggest at least one likely supporting idea.

A. The design of most modern suburban developments encourages social interaction among neighbors.
B. The alarmingly great increase in dog and cat populations makes necessary the mandatory sterilization of all pets found straying.
C. Modern law—the result of a nation's unrealistic attempts to be humane, to understand the psychology of criminal behavior, and to attack the cause of antisocial acts rather than to punish the actors—has resulted in a system of "justice" by which criminals are protected against punishment for their crimes so that they can go out and commit more illegal acts.
D. Natural disasters, more than wars and habitual propagandizing, have the effect of solidifying national interests and involving people in the concerns of others.

Directions: Which of the following are good thesis statements for a five-page essay?

A. Another Arab-Israeli war will eventually be started if the United States does not force both sides to accept a settlement that is practical.
B. Antique collecting is popular because it allows collectors to feel that they can regain the past and postpone the change and uncertainty of the future.
C. Artistic creations are invariably the products of deeply felt longing and an immature sense of self-worth.
D. The peacock, a recurring image in Flannery O'Connor's stories, functions as a gauge of spirituality.
E. Air travel has become more convenient since the early days of commercial flight.
F. Peasant revolutions that are run by social or intellectual elites will not result in improved living conditions for the masses.

3

How Should You Organize Your Ideas?

You have an idea you wish to communicate, but first you need to give some serious thought to the organization of that idea. In order to do so, you will want to picture in your mind the format of a finished essay. You don't have to decide about the particulars of yours yet, but you should recognize that a clearly defined beginning, middle, and ending characterizes good writing.

The introduction and conclusion of your essay, although proportionately not as large as the middle, are certainly important to the worth of the total project. The introduction serves much like the display window at a department store to suggest to your readers what is inside. It gives your readers an indication of your subject and of your attitude toward it (see discussion of *tone* in Chapter 1). If the beginning is not interestingly written, they may not read any further or, at best, read with very little attention and interest. The middle is, of course, extremely important because it supports the thesis—it is the "body" of the essay. Since much of your readers' satisfaction comes from fulfillment of their expectations, you must attempt to organize the middle of the essay in a plan that will let them see answers to their questions and that will let them follow your thinking step by step. The conclusion, for some writers the most difficult part of the essay to write well, rounds out the discussion of your topic in an interesting manner and gives your reader a feeling of completion.

Writing good introductions and conclusions is a skill that you will develop a "feel" for with practice. Although they may come to you more easily at some times than at others, introductions and conclusions, not having a prescribed form, have to be thought out for each paper individually and therefore can be time consuming. Many writers find that writing the introduction and conclusion in conjunction with one another saves time and produces the needed originality. Written at the same time, the beginning and ending balance each other. There is no one length for a beginning or an ending. You have to use good judgment on the matter by considering the length of the essay, the complexity of the thesis, and the familiarity of the readers with the point you are making.

WRITING GOOD INTRODUCTIONS

The introduction to an essay accomplishes three things in a relatively small space. (1) It sets the tone of the paper, be it humorous, satiric, serious, or prophetic. (2) It also engages the readers, making them want to read on. (3) Most importantly, it states the main point of the essay, the thesis. For a short paper, one having only three to five pages, the introduction may be only one brief paragraph. However, longer essays such as research papers sometimes require much background information before the major proposition can be stated. For papers such as these, often ten pages or more, the introduction may include several paragraphs and can run as long as one-fifth of the essay.

Many people think that they should write the introduction to an essay first. Yet the opening is often the hardest part of the paper to write. It is difficult for most people to focus the beginning of the paper from just a thesis statement or even from an outline of the body of the essay. The act of writing the body of the paper from the outline makes you think and clarify exactly what you want to say; and it is not until you have written the body of the paper that you usually feel completely comfortable with your material, in many cases.

Staring at a blank paper and worrying about how to begin will most likely lead to stiff writing, and you probably will need to rewrite the introduction later anyway. Instead of facing what has been called "the tyranny of the blank page," why not try the following process? You have already accomplished steps one and two.

STEP ONE: Invent and focus your subject (see Chapter 2).

STEP TWO: Develop a thesis statement (see Chapter 2).

STEP THREE: Set down an arrangement for the middle in notes (see pp. 67–74).

STEP FOUR: Write out your thesis statement as the first sentence of your rough draft.

STEP FIVE: Use your notes, or a fuller outline (see Chapter 4), as a guide to writing your middle.

STEP SIX: Now, return to the thesis and write the introduction (see pp. 59–64).

STEP SEVEN: Reread the whole rough draft and write a conclusion that grows out of the rest of the essay.

You will usually arrive at a good beginning before you write the final draft of the essay. Think about how to begin in your spare moments—when you take a break, while you eat dinner—for good ideas often come when you least expect them. Remember that the idea you decide to place before the thesis should be generated by the point in the thesis; in other words, it should clearly pave the way for the main part of the essay. The effective introductions explained in this chapter will help you accomplish this connection.

Equally important is the consistency of tone in the introduction and the rest of the essay. So keep tone in mind, too. Because certain ways of introducing an essay are more dramatic than others, you have to be careful that the one you pick matches, in other words is not lighter than the tone you expect to convey in the rest of the paper. Before you settle on a dramatic opening, you should consider the point you are making—how serious you want to sound. It is quite possible that a straightforward opening would be as suitable or even better than a dramatic one. Each essay should be judged separately. For example, if your essay explores the psychological trauma of dying, it would be inappropriate to use the theme song of "M*A*S*H," which says, "Suicide is painless/it brings on many changes," to begin your paper. Similarly, for an economics paper on the inaccuracies in a very technical report on inflation, you would not be starting out with the appropriate tone if you gave a personal anecdote about the horrors of inflation in your life. In either example, the use of background, a significant statistic, or just the thesis would be more effective than a dramatic example.

THE BASIC PATTERNS One of two basic patterns effectively introduces most essays. The first is the thesis paragraph. In very short essays of three to five pages, you may wish to have your thesis sentence stand as the thesis paragraph. This method is direct. It is very helpful for saving time during in-class essays. But to many readers, the short one-sentence opening is too abrupt. A second type of thesis paragraph is the thesis sentence followed by several sentences that elaborate on it. A third type of thesis paragraph is one in which the thesis statement is not one sentence but is made up of several sentences that add up to the main point of the paper. Unless the thesis is very complicated, however, and the point would be missed by condensing all the information in it, you should probably restrict the thesis to one sentence, as Chapter 2 suggests. You can see from the following example that the second kind of thesis paragraph provides a clean statement of the point of the paper.

> Wines are classified into three major kinds: dry, sweet, and sparkling. Each type has distinctive characteristics resulting from a specific production method. Within each of the major classifications are many distinct variations due to the blending of different kinds of grapes and the production secrets of the manufacturer.

The first sentence gives the thesis. The writer is going to classify the types of wine. The following sentences expand that point, showing that there are subcategories of the three main types.

Starting right off with the thesis, however, can be too abrupt a start for some papers. Therefore, many writers use a second kind of basic pattern for certain essays. In this pattern, a few sentences of lead-in prepare the way for the reader. The content of the lead-in should always be interesting to the audience and should add something to the understanding of the thesis, which normally follows it in the same paragraph. The lead-in is, in some cases, more general than the thesis, but in others it draws on a specific detail that might have been included elsewhere in the paper but that has been reserved instead for the introduction. The following introduction includes a lead-in.

> Biology's increasing sophistication has been accompanied by an expanding of its uses and its power. Through the practical applications of biological knowledge, human beings have gained a great amount of control over their lives. They can, for instance, now manipulate the environment, change their life-styles, and alter themselves permanently both mentally and physically. Beyond the awe most people feel of these accomplishments, there must be questioning of the uses of this knowledge. Other issues must be raised than whether something can or cannot be done. The question is whether some of it should be done and if scientists should restrict their research and experimentation if the morality of a particular part of their work is questionable. Scientists must be forced to face up to the moral and ethical implications of future research and experimentation.

The introduction moves from general background on applications of biology (the lead-in) to the specific statement in the thesis about the moral consequences of scientific freedom.

EFFECTIVE STRATEGIES FOR INTRODUCTIONS

1. Make a clean statement of the thesis.

   > Despite the harmful side effects of using birth control pills, the benefits of the pill, when weighed against the risks of the pill and other forms of contraception, indicate the young woman who needs effective contraception is wise to use it.

2. Explain your personal interest or involvement with the subject.

Between the ages of ten and nineteen, I was a television addict. There was rarely a free moment when I did not have the set on. And, come to think of it, there were busy moments when I had it on too—cooking dinner, washing my hair, getting dressed. Of course, being cured, I now wonder how I ever watched so often, or more accurately, I have wondered for a year, now, what made me addicted to television. According to many psychologists who have studied the television habits of children, the television addict shares many of the problems of those with other common forms of addiction, such as excessive drinking and overeating.

3. Explain the divisions and proportions of your topic.

After living in a small town for five years, I am a changed person from the typical alienated urban person I once was. Many qualities of small town life have contributed to these changes, which I view as favorable. The key influences on my life here have been political, cultural, and social. But the social influences have been most telling. Small-town life has shown me the human need for solidarity with one's neighbors and the personal value of viewing myself as an integral part of a town.

4. Offer some important background.

The social and economic conditions in England during the sixteenth century influenced Sir Thomas More to develop his theory of punishment. Farmers had been forced from their homes to roam the countryside because their lands were needed for grazing. They wandered until their funds were depleted; without jobs, they then had no alternative for survival but stealing. The state tried to deter these vagabonds by inflicting a death penalty—hanging—as punishment for theft. It felt obligated to destroy the very thieves it had produced. More, however, suggested an approach which, although it required a restructuring of the economic system, was far more practical and humane.

5. Tell a dramatic or amusing anecdote about your topic.

An eighteen-year-old girl goes to the chemistry laboratory of her college, mixes together a few chemicals, and drinks the solution. She is dead on arrival at the community hospital. A twenty-year-old man who attends a prominent East Coast college returns to the dormitory from a late party and slits his wrists. He is found dead in his room on the following morning. These horrifying events occur more often than we would like to think. The number of youthful suicides has almost doubled in the last ten years. A number of psychologists are currently investigating the kinds of personalities that fall victim to this behavior and how much the pressures of college life play a role in the tragedies.

6. Offer a startling but reliable fact or statistic that pertains to your topic.

In the past decade, the average price of hamburger has risen from fifty-one to more than two dollars a pound. Other meats have shown even greater price jumps. As a result of this high inflation and an increased awareness of proper dietary habits, many American families are decreasing the amounts of meat in their diet and substituting more healthful but less costly vegetables or vegetable products.

7. Make an analogy that would interest your reader.

Picture a man who plans to move to a foreign town. He imagines that by studying a street map he can learn all about the place. The man is obviously naive. No doubt, the information he has absorbed from the map will help him when he actually arrives at the town, for he will have at least a "book" knowledge of the street layout. But far more than this characterizes a town. The man certainly cannot "know" the landscape, the architecture, or the attitudes of the people until he lives there. Biology students are in a similar situation when they study only textbooks. Although they can learn a certain amount from written descriptions and diagrams, to "know" biology students must actually work with organisms. Laboratory work is therefore a very important experience for the biology student because it provides the active and practical scientific investigation "book" learning alone cannot give.

8. Begin with a quotation that supports or contradicts your main point. Be careful to connect the quotation to your ideas.

"In a culture in which the marketing orientation prevails, and in which material success is the outstanding value, there is little reason to be surprised," says Erich Fromm, "that human love relations follow the same pattern of exchange which governs the commodity and the labor market." This comment from *The Art of Loving* couldn't be more true in 1980. People draw up lists of qualities desired in their future mates and go "shopping" at meetings for singles. Naturally, their perfect lovers have their own lists, so matches become a sort of trade-off. Computerized dating services, thriving in every part of the United States, are based on a materialistic view of love.

9. Contrast or explain the views of two or more people.

Joan Didion in "Some Dreamers of the Golden Dream" indicts the suburban life style as being a dead end, where love affairs end in disappointment and betrayal and marriages in collection of double indemnity. Phyllis McGinley, on the other hand, sings the praises of the surburban regularity, the surburban freedoms in "Suburbia of Thee I Sing." Of course, both views are extreme, and the truth lies between the two, at least according to my own experiences.

10. Ask a question that leads into your thesis.

> Is daydreaming worthwhile or is it a waste of time? Two psychologists at a major United States university who have been studying the brain waves of daydreamers for four years, have concluded that there is a positive correlation between the amount of daydreaming one does and one's mental capacity for creativity.

11. Cite your opposition and refute it.

> It may be that too many of our foods are nutritionally depleted by refining, but Adelle Davis's statement that we all need vitamin and mineral supplements daily to prevent malnutrition and other diseases is misleading. In fact, the intake of vitamin and mineral supplements should be watched carefully by a physician because, in excess, they can cause more health problems than Ms. Davis claims they can solve.

INEFFECTIVE STRATEGIES FOR INTRODUCTIONS

1. Avoid beginning your paper with a complaint or an apology.

> After spending three hours reading Masters' chapter on "overpopulation," I have concluded that I am no more informed on the subject than the average person in the street. There really isn't much to say about this subject that has not been said before.

This kind of opening strikes against you right away. It gives your readers the impression that you have nothing to say about the subject and causes them to question the value of reading on.

2. Avoid beginning your paper with information that is too general, obvious, or irrelevant.

> Advertising is an important part of American life. The American Dream, which has been a part of our lives since immigrants from Europe poured into this country expecting to see streets paved with gold, is alive in today's advertising.

This type of introduction is either irrelevant to the thesis or too general to be of importance to the reader. In the preceding example, the statement that advertising is part of American life does not link up with the point about the American Dream. The readers could easily become confused about the direction of the essay.

3. Avoid beginning with too obvious a statement.

> Slavery was one of the main issues of the Civil War.

This kind of beginning not only offends your readers but causes them to worry about your authority on the subject. They may utter under their breath, "So, what else is new?" Here there are two major flaws. First, you are offering a generalization that is too broad for a paper on master–slave relationships. Second, you are making a very, very obvious statement. The idea is far too basic—everyone already knows it, so leave it out.

4. Avoid beginning your paper with a literal question that you answer in the next sentence.

> What are the symptoms of diabetes? The symptoms of diabetes are extreme thirst, sudden weight change, and frequent urination.

This type of introduction is repetitive. Leave out the question and state the answer instead. In the preceding example, a question such as "Why are the symptoms of diabetes often overlooked?" might work better.

5. Avoid starting out with a dictionary definition.

> "Hearing" as defined in *Webster's New Collegiate Dictionary* is "the process, function, or power of perceiving sound; the special sense by which noise and tones are received as stimuli."* Hearing requires no voluntary thought. Because the process is involuntary, it goes on all the time, and people and other animals always hear what goes on around them. But listening is quite a different thing. It requires voluntary thought; when people listen, they analyze what they hear. While people hear many things, they sort out what is important or interesting and listen only to those things.

A dictionary definition proposes a stiff and uninteresting opening for a paper. Also, most readers consider the device trite. Many times the dictionary definition is not at all helpful to the readers because it is general or worded very formally and, in most cases, abbreviated. Your own words would flow more naturally and fit the context of your discussion much better than words from the dictionary. In the preceding example, the dictionary definition is not useful to the readers because it is very broad, formal, and out of the context of the discussion about voluntary and involuntary listening and hearing.

6. Avoid beginning with an introduction that merely repeats the assignment.

> The two essays I will be comparing and contrasting for this paper are "I Become a Student" by Lincoln Steffens on page 81 and "The Marks of an Educated Man" by Alan Simpson on page 117. The underlying theme in

---

* By permission from Webster's *New Collegiate Dictionary* © 1979 by G. & C. Merriam Co., publishers of the Merriam-Webster Dictionaries.

both of these essays is the struggle to get an education and to succeed in a profession. Both writers discuss the value of education, the difficulty of getting one in a university, and the true meaning of a liberal arts education.

This sort of introduction is boring and unnecessary. When an assignment is made, there is an understanding between the students and the teacher that it will be carried out, so there is no need to make any reference to it in the essay. The essay should stand on its own. In the preceding example, had the student left off the first sentence and placed the names of the two authors and the titles of their essays in the second sentence, the introductory paragraph would have been greatly improved.

7. Avoid introducing your paper with an obvious platitude.

> Today in modern America there are issues that are similar yet quite different once the issue has been analyzed. The role of women is a good example.

Platitudes are unimaginative and not very meaningful, so do not utter them as if they were profound. Avoid them in all writing. In the introduction they are especially harmful to your relationship with your reader, however, because the reader is likely to put the essay aside, deciding that it has nothing much to say. In the preceding example, the first sentence doesn't say anything. Whoever reads this beginning will probably mutter an annoyed, "So what?"

8. Avoid starting your essay with a reference to the title.

> As the title of this paper indicates, this essay is about the needs of senior citizens. They are a much ignored minority. In actuality, senior citizens could contribute a great deal to the communities they live in. If community leaders would only give senior citizens a chance, senior citizens could make valuable contributions, which at the same time would fulfill their own individual, social, and financial needs.

Because, technically, the title of the essay is not part of the essay, it should not be referred to in the introduction. The reader would normally expect that the title refers to the point of the paper, so why bother to say so? Readers are only put off by such comments. In the preceding example, the writer should have offered some interesting background on the current roles of senior citizens, or if the tone would have permitted, given an anecdote from the life of a typical senior citizen.

EXERCISES   A. Read an article in a popular magazine. What makes the introduction effective or ineffective? Is there a lead-in introduction?

B. What advantages are there to placing the thesis at the end of an introduction? Disadvantages?

C. What is your reaction to speakers or writers who start out their presentations with *"Webster's Dictionary* defines . . ."?

D. Read the introductions below from students' essays. What specifically makes them poor beginnings? How might they be improved?

1. The curiosity of human beings and the desire to find new experiences led me to my first job. Human beings are reasoning animals, and thus their minds must be constantly stimulated by new ideas and experiences. I became interested in cars at a very early age, probably because my father was a motor racing driver. Three summers ago I decided to work at his motor servicing center, and that job taught me a great deal about my ability to work closely with people who are different from me.

2. *Webster's New Collegiate Dictionary* defines "educate" as "to provide schooling for." After going to high school for four years, I guess I must admit to being educated, but I still do not feel that I am as prepared for college as I should have been. The area the high schools should work harder at developing in their students is basic skills.

3. Punishing bad behavior will usually lead to a decrease in that behavior. If a little boy is constantly pulling his cat's tail, and he is reprimanded each time, he will be likely to leave the cat alone. Although in certain cases punishment will not work and is not in order, today's parents should keep in mind that mild punishment actually shows children affection and values.

4. Many similarities and differences can be found between European and American celebrations. What are some of the similarities between the European celebration of Christmas and the American celebration? Some of the main similarities include the festive atmosphere, the sharing of gifts, and the eating of special goodies.

E. Which types of introductions might best appeal to the groups of people named for each of the following thesis statements? Why?

1. People living in the inner city should form renters' unions to protect themselves from infringements of their rights by absentee landlords and to inform themselves of their responsibilities.
    (a) A group of suburban housewives
    (b) A group of people from an inner-city neighborhood

2. Legalized gambling in our state offers more advantages than disadvantages.
    (a) A group of businessmen
    (b) A group of homemakers

3. No matter how much money a family has to spend, planning a budget for a vacation will ultimately save time, money, and anxiety.
   (a) Families
   (b) Members of a singles' tour group

F. Go to a dictionary of quotations or other source and find appropriate quotations that could be used as lead-ins for two of the following assertions.

1. Colleges should offer more vocational training than they now do.

2. Living in the wilderness for a summer taught me a great deal about myself.

3. Selfishness can be either constructive or destructive.

4. Grading should be abolished in college.

G. How would you characterize the writer's attitude toward the subject based on the following introduction? Does the writer intend to be serious, sarcastic, humorous? What tone might readers expect in the essay?

Spider webs are more often messes than messages, and a rodent's streamside burrow hasn't all the accessories of a comfortable home. Yet when children are read imaginative books that unrealistically portray animal life, they believe what they hear. They would be better off if they stopped wasting time on kid's stories and developed some healthy fears; spider webs are often sticky and the makers unfriendly, sometimes even dangerous.

H. For each of the following introductions, excerpted from professional essays, try to identify the strategy. Is it successful? Do you want to read on?

1. You can get a hint concerning the higher purposes of communication by looking at the word itself. "Communication" is much more closely related to the word "community" than it is to any of the instruments of communication which man has created, such as language, radio, and pictorial or dramatic art. This point suggests that you will miss the deeper meaning of communication if you allow yourself to think only of the machinery of communication. You might get a further hint if you really examine the meaning of the word "community."

   Lyle L. Miller and Alice Z. Seeman, "Concepts of Communication," Guidebook for Prospective Teachers.

2. The six-year-old child who succeeds in repairing his broken bicycle bell has a creative experience, New York University psychologist Morris I. Stein is fond of pointing out, but no one would claim that the repaired

bell constitutes a "creative product" in the generally accepted meaning of the term.

It is possible, in other words, to differentiate roughly between individual creativity and social creativity. If you have an idea, it may be creative in comparison to all the other ideas you have ever had, which certainly represents individual creativity, or it may be creative in comparison to all the ideas everyone has ever had; this represents social creativity of the highest order.

Helen Rowan,
"How to Produce an Idea," IBM Corporation Magazine.*

3. Scientists, above all, are supposed to be honest. Politicians and advertising copywriters are expected to distort facts, but if a scientist falsifies a single record, he commits an unforgiveable crime. Yet the sad fact is that the history of science teems with cases of outright fakery and instances of scientists who saw their data only through the distorting lenses of passionately held beliefs.

Martin Gardner,
"Great Fakes of Science," Esquire.†

WRITING GOOD MIDDLES

Most professional writers make use of basic organizational patterns common to essay writing: process, chronological, spatial, classification, illustration, and comparison. An entire essay, especially if it is short, may be structured around just one of these patterns. Longer essays usually use a combination of patterns but with a definite emphasis upon one.

PROCESS ORDER Process order is structured around the steps necessary to do something. This order is most appropriate for narrative or descriptive writing (see Chapter 1), but it is also used in many other instances. The "how to do it" essay is a process essay that develops its points in the exact sequence necessary for accomplishing the activity.

Sequence is the most important item in the process paper. Your task is to arrange your material in the proper order so that the sequence is exact; then you must provide appropriate connections between the parts so that your reader will see the movement from step to step and the logical connection between the steps. Here is an example of notes for a process essay.

---

* Reproduced by permission from *Think* magazine, published by IBM. Copyright 1962 by International Business Machines Corporation.

† Martin Gardner's introduction to the article "Great Fakes of Science" originally appeared in the October 1977 issue of *Esquire*.

Preparing a wall for painting is an important task that must be carefully done if the finished paint job is to be attractive and permanent.

STEP 1: Clean the wall of any grease or oil marks.

STEP 2: Use a scraper to remove any peeling paint or plaster.

STEP 3: Patch and sand any cracks.

STEP 4: Wipe entire wall once with dust cloth to remove all particles before painting.

CHRONOLOGICAL ORDER Your topic may lend itself to a chronological or time-ordered treatment. You might be describing the time stages required for giving an account of a historical event, or explaining the development of some theory of belief. Here is an example of notes for a chronological essay.

Thesis Chemical warfare, the morality of which should be questioned, has actually been practiced in wars throughout history.

Use of Greek fire in ancient times

Use of poison gas in trenches during World War I

Flame throwers and atomic bombs in World War II

SPATIAL ORDER Arranging the body paragraphs of the essay according to the way space is used may be most appropriate. For instance, when you discuss the ravages of a hurricane, it might be effective to trace the destruction from the point along the coast where the hurricane first hit, further inland through the city, to the farms nestled in the valley. Spatial patterns are like maps, whether they be charting the course over land, through a painting, from one end of a car to the other, or from a person's feet to forehead. But there must be a defined pattern such as left to right or near to far in you scheme. Such spatial patterns need not be merely descriptive either. For instance, a paper on cars that traces the spatial arrangement from rear fender to front fender may discuss not so much the appearance of the automotive parts as the function of each part in relation to the whole mechanism. Although spatially treated subjects are frequently descriptive, many analytic topics can be arranged effectively according to their physical space. Your notes for a spatial essay might look like the following ones.

Thesis Although my basement study, converted from a laundry room, could never be called fancy, it is the perfect place for me when I want to spend an evening studying.

Ceilings and floors practically soundproof

Door that closes

How Should You Organize Your Ideas? 69

Next to door is orange crate file cabinet

Wall adjacent and to left has school desk and chair

On top of crate next to desk are portable typewriter, lamp, and supply box

On wall to left of desk is a brick and board bookshelf

Against the fourth wall are refreshments—coffee pot and sink

CLASSIFICATION ORDER

Classification is dividing and labeling the various parts of a subject into logical classes or groups. This method of organizing is often used to explain or define a term or concept, but the arrangement is appropriate to any subject that can be broken down into types. To classify a subject, you simply need to ask yourself, "What are the broad types?" Classifying is an everyday process. Restaurants have smoking and nonsmoking sections. You identify yourself as a member of a college class: freshman, sophomore, junior, senior. You view yourself and others as part of the above-thirties group or part of the below-thirties group. You rarely think about these common sorts of classification, but when you do, you realize that the act of classifying provides a definite order to your thinking process.

Everyday experience with classifying makes the method relatively easy. For instance, if you want to classify the types of movies that are made, you might come up with the following groups.

Documentary: made to present facts

Esthetic: made to create beauty

Exploitative: made to use the media for the purpose of sensationalism

The preceding classification of movies is effective because it upholds the three requirements of a good classification.

1. The parts must be divided by a single principle.
2. The parts must be parallel.
3. The parts should add up to the whole subject.

When you choose to classify something, you should first settle on a rationale for the grouping. In the example of the movies, the rationale is the underlying reason for the movie. Each group represents a reason. None of the groups—documentary, esthetic, or exploitative—overlaps with the others. For instance, a single movie cannot be both esthetic and exploitative according to the given definition. The classifications are also parallel grammatically: each is described by an adjective. Finally, the total of the three groups covers all possible rationales for making movies. No film could be conceived that would not fit into one of the three groups. The following notes would be useful in writing the classification of movies.

Thesis Although some films might be made for more than one purpose, the main intention for making a movie can fall into one of three categories: for documentary purposes, for esthetic value, or for exploitative purposes.

ILLUSTRATION ORDER Illustration is arrangement by use of examples. An illustrative essay, frequently assigned in college, is usually the simple thesis and support paper in which various points work independently to illustrate the thesis. A paper on the benefits of self-hypnosis could discuss, say, three separate benefits of hypnosis: the ability to cope with pressures at work, the acceptance of one's physical appearance, and the confidence needed to quit smoking. You need not arrange these points in any special order for them to make sense, for just about any sequence would be logical. You may, then, arrange the points to show the emphasis you intend. In most papers you will find that your evidence for one or another of your points is stronger than the evidence for others. In an illustrative format you can take advantage of that fact. One supporting point can be so moving or convincing that it heightens the effect of the idea that follows it, or it seems a perfect note to end on.

Here is a plan for achieving the most effective pattern of order in an illustrative paper. Try to begin the body of your paper with a relatively strong point, but not with the strongest. Then pose a point that is a bit weaker. Finally, let your reader have your strongest point. Readers feel most impressed when they finish your essay on a powerful note. The paper leaves them with something to think about, without doubts about your competence as a writer. From the start, the strength of your arrangement manipulates the reader to accept your authority. A good illustrative essay keeps the reader's attention through careful placement of emphatic points. Keeping emphatic order in mind, you might arrange your notes for an illustrative essay in the following way.

Thesis Self-hypnosis, a beneficial therapy for most people, taught me to relax and to accept myself better than I had.

Helped me understand that I could quit smoking

Helped me relax myself at work—reduced pressures

Helped me overcome self-consciousness about my looks

The decision made by each writer is based on an understanding of the points he or she wants to make and a guess about the audience's reception of them.

COMPARISON ORDER Drawing a comparison means showing the similarities and differences between two or more parts of a subject. If only the differences are pointed out, the essay contrasts rather than compares. Before a comparison or contrast can be made, there must be some basis for it, some similarity between the parts of the subject. For instance, the pictograph systems of ancient Sumeria and China might serve well as a subject for a comparison. Both are writing systems of ancient cultures. But there would not be much point in writing a serious comparison of the physical exertion of watching television and that of playing racquetball. All you could say is that the activities are completely different, that one requires no exertion and the other a great deal of exertion. Your essay would probably turn out to be a one-sided discussion of playing racquetball. A significant point must arise from a comparison, and it is thus useless to compare thoughts, concepts, or things that have nothing significant in common. A sound thesis must come from the comparison, and the paper should not have very little to say about one point and a great deal to say about another. The comparison may show only similarities, only differences, or a combination of the two, but all pertinent parts of the subject should be discussed. The comparative essay may be structured in one of three ways: alternating between the parts of the subject, dividing the subject, or combining the two patterns.

ALTERNATING Alternating comparisons draw together similarities, show differences, or show both point by point. When specific comparisons come readily to mind, the alternating format, which makes for an easily read and coherent essay, should be used. That is, you should attempt to single out specific points about the subject and compare the parts of the subject. For example, if you were comparing the mating behavior of two types of birds, you might isolate typical behavioral patterns of birds as your points for comparison (courtship dances, calls, physical changes) and then discuss those characteristics as they appear in the two types of birds you are examining. The final essay might alternate either whole paragraphs or sentences, depending on how much there is to say about each half of the subject for a particular point.

 Because in analytic writing you should draw comparisons clearly, not leave them for your reader to figure out, the note-taking stages are especially important. Why not make a list like the following one on birds as you think through the comparisons you might wish to include in the paper? The list tests each comparison and offers notes for your more detailed outline, which will most often simply follow the development of the list.

Characteristic Compared	**Nordic Pigeon**	**Southwest Robin**
Courtship dances	Three types: square, circle, triangle	Two types: straight line back and forth, circle
Number of calls	Around thirty different calls, one for mate selection	Only calls to select mate
Physical changes during nesting	Beak becomes dark brown when nesting	Color of feathers changes and beak remains the same when nesting

You can see that an essay developed from this list would include differences but would emphasize similarities between the mating and nesting habits of the two birds. Here is a possible thesis for the essay.

Thesis Although the Nordic pigeon and the southwest robin live in quite different climates, one warm and one polar, their mating habits are surprisingly similar in courtship and in nesting.

Divided A divided order compares one complete part of the subject to another complete part of the subject instead of treating both parts of the subject point by point. Divided comparisons, used widely in journalism, are most useful when the subject you are writing about does not break up neatly into specific subpoints. That is, you are making a statement about the overall similarity or difference between the parts of your subject. In such cases, it is easier to divide your information in half, if you have two items to compare, or in thirds if you have three. Then, in the conclusion of the essay, you can try to draw more specific comparisons. For instance, comparing the way teachers and police officers interact with the people they serve is a good subject for a paper, but one that does not break down into point-by-point analysis. Nevertheless, you almost instinctively feel a comparison there. You may think that many of the qualities of a good teacher are also those of a good police officer. The most effective way to make your statement might be to discuss the role of a police officer in the first half and that of a teacher in the second. In the conclusion, then, you could name the parallels that you have discovered.

This type of comparison seems very easy to write, but it fools a lot of people. Most important to the success of this structure, you may have guessed, are the strong thesis that makes an important connection between the compared items, and of course the detailed conclusion. The middle of the essay should also be closely geared to the controlling idea in the thesis (see p. 50). Each point you make in the paper must be there for a purpose. It is better not to talk about the home life of the police officer in one part and about the convenient schedules of teachers in the other unless you think that there is some logical connection between the points. If you exercise control over your material, keeping in sight that the purpose of the paper is to compare, you will avoid the snare of producing a vague, disconnected description of two things. Notes for a divided comparison usually look like those that follow.

Thesis Indian religions and Christian religions are both concerned with death and afterlife, but their perceptions of it are quite different.

Indian
- Positive view of afterlife
- State of perfection defined
- Stages of reaching perfection

Christian
- Predestination
- One chance to heaven or hell
- Purgatory
- Living on in heaven—perfection

Combining Patterns If you write essays longer than a few pages, you may wish to integrate the divided pattern with the alternating pattern. Many readers feel that alone the alternating format creates an undesirable Ping-Pong effect, but at the same time they do not like the lack of specific information in the divided pattern. They would prefer that comparative papers offer the variety of the combined form. Considerations of subject and audience and your own personal preferences will dictate your choice.

At the beginning of an essay in the combined format might be one or more points fixed in an alternating pattern, discussing a certain trait of one part of the subject, then describing that trait as it is present or not present in the other half of the subject. After the two parts of the subject have been treated in this way, the essay may develop into a divided structure in which various traits of one-half of the subject are treated together. In an essay structured like this one, the first section would naturally discuss specific points of comparison, but the second half would discuss general points. Of course, any combination of divided and alternating patterns can be effective if it suits the nature of the subject.

An example of an essay developed in the combined form might be a comparison of contemporary public high schools and an ideal public high school. Here is how the notes would look.

Thesis The contemporary public high school's programs and atmosphere are more regimented and limited than those of an ideal school.

Curriculum
    How many courses public high schools now offer
    How many courses an ideal high school would offer
Grading
    How courses are graded in public high schools now
    How evaluations would be made without grades in ideal schools
High schools
    Tensions
    Competitive athletics
    Standardized testing
Ideal schools
    Individualized instruction
    Movement education
    Self-paced studies
    Free atmosphere

You can see that the combined method is, by far, the most complex type of comparison. In the notes above, a point-by-point comparison is used to convey specific similarities, and then a divided comparison is used to give an overall impression of each school system.

Choosing the best arrangement for a paper is a creative and engaging task that will ultimately be worth any effort you put into the decision. You could have all the interesting content available on a subject, but if the content is not pieced together so that the reader can grasp it, the ideas are lost. The pattern you choose will make the writing yours, allowing you to convey just what you mean to say.

EXERCISES
A. Find an essay written by D. H. Lawrence, George Orwell, H. L. Mencken, or Eldridge Cleaver in the library and identify the pattern or patterns used to organize the essay.
B. In the following essay, the student uses primarily a chronological arrangement. Might the author have made the same point by using a different pattern of organization? Why?

The Phenomenon of Death

When I was a child there was never any reason to think about death. I knew what it was, knew man was not immortal and I didn't have any fears. Then one day, unexpectedly, a man who I loved was erased from my life. He was my maternal grandfather, and I can never forget the day he died.

It was the second night of Chanuka in the year of 1965. We were just getting ready to open our presents when the telephone rang. Suddenly, I heard my mother screaming and crying. I was extremely horrified to hear her in such a state, so I too began to cry. I had sensed something was dreadfully wrong but had no idea what it was. Within a short time, I found my mother, father, and sister at my side. With a quivering voice and tears in her eyes, my mother said, "Dad isn't with us anymore." I began to cry and we all embraced for a few minutes. We began the long drive to San Diego about a half hour later because we wanted to be with my maternal grandmother in her time of need.

During the drive and for weeks thereafter a whole world of thoughts and confusion opened up for me. No matter how hard I tried to think things out, I couldn't accept the fact that my grandfather was gone forever. I became very inquisitive and asked my parents so many questions with the idea in mind to possibly acquire an understanding of the death of my grandfather in particular

and of death in general. What happens to the soul? Does he live in another world? Does he know we will always love him? My parents tried to answer. I was still not satisfied because there was so much more I had to think about than they could respond to. Within a week of the time he died, I found myself feeling angry toward grandpa for no longer being near me, for abandoning me. As the youngest grandchild in the family, I had the least number of years in which to love and be with my grandfather. I felt cheated and wanted him to come back to me. For a while my faith in God diminished to the point that I blocked all religious beliefs from my mind. What good was religion? I couldn't see why God would deprive such a fine man of the happiest years of his life, when he could enjoy his children and the material things he had worked so hard for all his life. These thoughts and others plagued me for years after my grandfather's death.

Now nine years have passed since grandpa died. I have begun to think more about the strange phenomenon of death. No longer do I question death, as I did when I was a child, but I realize that the confusion I felt right after my grandfather's death is a confusion that will always be on my mind--the living cannot know what death really is, not in all its strange aspects. I now can actually accept the possibility of my own death, that at some point my time will come. But accepting that death happens to everyone, I still have not overcome the sorrow of that occasion nine years ago enough to live without a fear of my last moments.

Perhaps when I am older and have put more of my life into a fixed perspective, I will be able to face the subject of death with a bit less diffidence. I wonder how my grandfather felt.

C. Write a miniessay about a piece of art or a place. Open with a description by spatial arrangement in the first paragraph and then in another paragraph or two analyze the artwork or scene through illustration.

D. Write a brief divided comparison of how a certain quality that two of your friends have is manifest differently in each of them. Make the first paragraph your thesis. Devote the next paragraph to one friend and another separate paragraph to the other friend. Then, in the conclusion draw together the similarities and differences.

E. Explain how two particular patterns of development—process, chronological order, classification, comparison, or illustration—might suit each of the topics below; justify your answers.

Periods of architecture

Day-to-day life in a foreign country

Oral hygiene
The enjoyment of popular movies
F. If you were writing an essay with the thesis and supports given below, in what order would you place the supports to achieve the best emphasis? Why?

Thesis   As soon as someone borrows money from a friend, the relationship changes.

The lender may discover that he does not trust the friend who borrowed money as much as he thought he did.

The formal attitude of a business arrangement enters the relationship.

The borrower might resent the authority of the lender and the subordinate position he automatically is forced into.

G. Draw a comparison chart for an essay on the subject of television. Focus the topic and develop a thesis that interests you before doing the chart.
H. Write notes for a chronological process essay on one of the following topics:
An event that changed your thinking on some matter of personal importance
The best way to ask for (or refuse) a date
The emotional changes a person experiences between the fifteenth and eighteenth years
I. Develop notes for a comparative essay on a topic of your choice. Is the thesis most adaptative to supports arranged in a divided, alternating, or combined pattern?
J. Read an essay in a magazine and write a one-paragraph analysis of the pattern or patterns of development used in the essay.
K. Be as specific as possible about which pattern of organization might best suit the topics below.
Similarities and differences between ice cream and frozen yogurt
Advantages of living in the city instead of in a small town
The diverse duties of a congressman
The dreams of a child and the dreams of an adult
The failure of youthful marriages
L. Write a question that you think one of your teachers might ask on an essay assignment. Choose some topic you have just been studying in one of your classes. What patterns might you use in writing the essay based on the question? Why?

WRITING GOOD CONCLUSIONS

The conclusion conveys a sense of completion to your readers, reinforces your central point, and ties together the different parts of the paper. Therefore, most of the time your papers will benefit from a conclusion. But every paper does not require a sophisticated one. If you have written an essay, especially a brief one that seems complete, you probably would not add a formal conclusion. But every essay should have a smooth and finished feeling about it; it should never just come to a halt. Similarly, a conclusion should not just be tacked on to whatever point comes last in the paper. Unless the paper is arranged in a logical order and each point fully developed to the advantage of the thesis, the end of the paper will seem abrupt, no matter how you conclude. Therefore, for the best possible ending, with or without a conclusion, the body of the essay itself has to be well formed. You will want to evaluate whether each essay you write requires a conclusion. One clue is length. Very short papers with complete thesis statements that set out the controlling ideas specifically and with clear paragraph divisions may seem boring if a summary conclusion is added. However, if you have something to add, even to a short paper, and you think that the idea naturally grows out of the previous discussion, the conclusion is probably effective.

The best way to write a conclusion is to reread your paper before you compose the ending. This process will freshen your awareness of the points in the essay and allow you to fit your conclusion to your purpose. Having a good idea of what you have written can help you avoid tacking on a mechanical and unenthusiastic ending that seems to say, "Let's get this assignment over with."

Just how long should your conclusion be? In a short paper of no more than five pages, a single paragraph can suffice; in a longer essay, you might want to write up to a whole page. Unless the essay is quite lengthy, you probably do not want to write much more than a page conclusion because you then risk digressing from your main subject; you may, in effect, find yourself beginning a new essay. One way of judging the length of the conclusion is to make it proportionate with the introduction.

Exactly what you will say at the end of the paper will depend on such things as your original purpose, your sense of what your audience expects, and the quantity and variety of information brought together in the essay. Keep in mind two hints when you choose a strategy for writing a particular conclusion:

You want your audience to be stimulated by the conclusion.

You want your paper to seem complete.

BASIC PATTERNS

One of two basic patterns is suitable for most conclusions: the summary or the lead-out. In the summary, you simply restate the thesis in other words or summarize your main points. Whether you need only one sentence, a group of sentences, or several paragraphs will depend on the complexity of the point. Summaries, however, often seem forced and unnecessary. They should be avoided in most short papers and used only in others when a restatement or summary contributes to your audience's understanding of the paper as a whole.

The other basic pattern, which is more imaginative, is the lead-out. This pattern begins with a point that acts as a transition between the body of the paper and an interesting related idea, anecdote, quotation, analogy, or question. The main point of using the lead-out pattern is to make a connection between your thesis and some other idea that will stimulate the readers to continue to think about the paper after they have finished reading it. Whether the information in the lead-out conclusion is arranged from the general to the specific or the specific to the general depends on how general or specific your related idea is compared to your essay's main point.

An example of a typical lead-out conclusion from an essay follows. The thesis of the essay is that using leisure time well is an important ingredient in everyone's life. This student explains various productive ways of using leisure time and shows the need for leisure. After tying up the main points in the essay, the student continues with an implication of what has been discussed in the paper.

> Leisure time, then, is more than just time with nothing to do. In fact, there are many things to be done during this so-called free time. There are no set rules, of course, for what qualifies as leisure because what might be leisure for one person, might not be for another. In any case, leisure is never what one considers "work." For instance, many people would consider a game of tennis to be leisure, but to the professional tennis player, it would be work. The tennis player would probably find leisure in something else. The many ways to spend leisure time are up to each person to discover, and they all share the same rewards: a healthy, clear mind and a strong, refreshed body.

The student draws on the suggestions from the essay and mentions what they all have in common in the last sentence. You can feel how the paragraph gradually leads out of the body of the essay and deals generally with the value of leisure for each person.

EFFECTIVE STRATEGIES FOR CONCLUSIONS

1. Restate the thesis in new words.
   An essay with the thesis "The Stanford Binet Intelligence Examination, comprehensive grade point averages, and comprehensive examinations are not reliable for analyzing a student's ability" used the following restatement of the thesis as the conclusion to the paper.

   > Test scores and intelligence tests should not be the sole basis for judging a student's work because they are often inaccurate and misleading.

2. Summarize the main points of the essay.

An essay with the thesis "Simulation models can be used effectively to teach students how to apply physics concepts they are taught in class" included the following summary of the main ideas as the conclusion.

Computer simulation opens up a new dimension in education. Students have often gained a lot of information from textbooks, but they seldom have the chance to do anything with it. By using simulation exercises, students can gain insight into a problem by making it possible for them to experiment and to see the consequences of their actions very quickly. The computer also imposes a strong discipline on students, forcing them to analyze a problem logically, while it frees them from a great deal of time-consuming computation. Their theories can be put into practice, and valued experience can be gained in a fast, safe, and inexpensive way.

3. Give an anecdote that drives home your point.
   An essay with the thesis "If people would only look around them and look closely at themselves, they would find subtle traces of sexism and racism" included the following anecdotal conclusion.

The belief that women's endeavors are not to be taken quite as seriously as men's is obviously all too common today. A month ago, despite my research, I was not convinced of this point. I decided to look around me at my friends, and what I found was startling. Here is just one example of a typical pattern that seems innocent enough but is nonetheless insidious. I went to a party at a close friend's house, where I heard the following discussion going on between two highly educated young professors—supposedly "liberal" people. The first said that his wife and he were moving to Oregon because he had been offered a one-year job at a small college there. The other said that he was surprised to hear the news because the man's wife had a stable job here and that with the Oregon opportunity being so temporary, there seemed little reason for her to give up what she was doing. Responding quickly, seemingly intuitively, the first man said, "What does that matter? A wife usually goes wherever her husband works." Perhaps even more distressing was that the other man agreed wholeheartedly after a moment of thought.

4. Offer an analogy that reinforces your main point.
   An essay on "the blend of inspiration and knowledge needed by the poet" had the following conclusion.

Writing poetry, then, takes more than imagination. It takes some knowledge of form. You could no more expect someone to write a good poem solely on the basis of inspiration than you could expect someone to build a house because he or she had a good idea for one. Of course, you realize that building a house is a technical matter. The builder needs to know the subtle interworkings of the materials at every phase of the process. So too, poets are deliberate about what they build with words, and they must work from a broad foundation of knowledge.

5. Add a final quotation that sums up your point well.
   An essay on "the benefits of taking the birth control pill" included the following conclusion, which sums up in someone else's words what the student means. See page 59 for the introduction to this same essay.

While it can still be argued that there is a health risk associated with use of the pill, the risk is declining. Also, the pill is the most accurate form of contraception available to a young woman today. However, the decision on whether the pill or something else would be best for an individual is entirely up to that person, and personal pros and cons must be considered. At the same time, every woman making the decision should keep in mind the words of Royal College of General Practitioners in Great Britain, the doctors who have done the most thorough study of contraceptives ever conducted: "The estimated risk at the present time of using the pill is one that a properly informed woman would be happy to take."

6. Ask a final question.
   An essay on "the need for intercultural education" used a final question that asks the readers to evaluate their own educations and those of their friends.

A blend of respect, empathy, and acceptance of other cultures than one's own is perhaps the most important quality of the liberally educated person. Most would agree philosophically with the content of that statement. However, how are we to be assured that educated people actually use these values in their daily living?

7. Suggest possible solutions, alternatives, or policies.
   An essay with the thesis "Japanese women have been granted equality with men both politically and economically, but the reality of a Japanese woman's daily life places her in a submissive, not equal, role" included a conclusion with a possible solution.

Although Japanese women have equal political and economic rights, the gap between constitutional rights and present-day attitudes has not decreased much since the last world war. Thus the stereotype of the submissive female is strongly felt. It is important for the Japanese people to realize that being granted rights is quite different from changing attitudes, and those who believe in equal rights will have to fight for them by educating Japanese people about the role of women in every facet of social, political, and business life. Current conditions should not be accepted, for until the stereotyped woman is ejected from the minds of Japanese people, there can not be male/female equality. And passively believing that the constitution will take care of the thinking of the people will only serve to invalidate the efforts of those who do want equality. Education, then, provides one possible solution to the problem of widespread naivete and ignorance.

8. Predict the outcome of a situation or warn the readers of possible effects of a situation under discussion in the essay.

An essay on "the inadequate tests for new drugs before they are placed on the market" ended with a warning.

> Not all drugs, then, are tested as well as they could be, and even those that are placed through rigorous tests may be shown to produce side effects as long as a decade after they are used. Unless more stringent testing is demanded of drug companies, and research for ten-year studies is required, we will continue to be victimized, as more and more drugs come into public use.

9. Reminder of the context of your argument.

Reminding the reader of the larger problem from which you extracted your argument drives home the importance of your ideas. Placing your ideas in perspective shows that your point develops one of the many directions implied by the consequence of your topic. In this kind of conclusion you explain the relationship between the problem at hand and other related problems. Be careful not to get off the track and onto a new subject. The sample research paper on page 321 ends by placing the problem of garbage disposal into the broader issue of pollution and relating waste pollution to other types of pollution.

10. Reference to the introduction.

Bringing your argument full circle gives the readers a satisfied feeling, a sense that the point of the essay has been brought around to its natural completion with all the loose ends tied up neatly. If you have, for instance, begun the essay with an anecdote that leads into the thesis, you might conclude by referring to the anecdote, noting how much it reflects your conclusions on the matter under discussion. If you have begun the essay with a question or have from the start posed a problem, the most appropriate conclusion might include a quick reference to the question or problem and a direct statement of your answer or a possible solution.

An essay that begins with several quotations from a survey by Hirsch on "the one quality that characterizes a good marriage" had the thesis that a successful marriage requires a lot more than just love. In the conclusion the writer returns to the quotations noted in the introduction of the essay and uses them to tie up the paper.

> Love is not enough, it would seem, to sustain a relationship. Hirsch is accurate in his findings, then, that many characteristics, not one—and certainly not just love—keep a relationship going. With love the relationship is set in force: with "friendship" and "security" and "shared values" the relationship keeps spinning.

INEFFECTIVE STRATEGIES FOR CONCLUSIONS

1. Avoid conclusions that telegraph what they are:

   In conclusion . . .

   This one is permissible in a formal speech, but in an essay such overt signals are obtrusive.

   This paper has attempted to show that . . .

   Any reader knows that the point of a paper is to show something.

   My paper has discussed . . .

   The readers say, "We know, we know."

2. Avoid conclusions that open up a whole new topic.
   Your conclusion should tie up your ideas and may possibly offer an implication of them, but you should not introduce any points that are far removed from the discussion in the body of the essay and that would be, in effect, the theses of new essays. Because you do not have the space for elaboration on new ideas in the conclusion, any related thoughts you present must be able to be understood by your readers without expanding on them. For instance, if the essay you have written shows that legalized gambling in Atlantic City, New Jersey, has saved that city from financial disaster, you should not conclude with a statement such as the following: "Atlantic City is bound to become a powerful political force in this country within the next ten years." Practically a whole new paper would be needed to substantiate that point, and there is no information in the body of the essay that logically leads the readers to the conclusion. A better conclusion might be derived from one of the other strategies: perhaps an analogy with another dying city that has picked itself up would work.
3. Avoid conclusions that apologize.
   Apologies are inappropriate conclusions because they diminish the authority of the writer. Readers should have confidence in the writer. Therefore, apologizing for a lack of information, for a rushed presentation, or for poor typing undermines the effectiveness of the essay.
4. Avoid conclusions that offer platitudes or panaceas.
   Pat answers to complicated problems and trite overgeneralizing should be avoided in all writing, as is mentioned in Chapter 7. In the conclusion, if you slip in a cliched thought, your readers will probably think the writing insincere. A conclusion should be tailored to the point of each paper you write. Tacking on an obviously held belief or a sweeping generalization to cover the end of your

essay is ineffective; it does not deal honestly with the material in the paper and comes to terms with nothing, instead substituting indiscriminately something that could fit any number of essays. Thus the conclusion is valueless. For an example of what to avoid, take a look at the following conclusion from a paper on the dangers of nuclear power plants.

> The country ought to look into this problem seriously because it represents a threat to the American way.

Here is another.

> But we're all human, aren't we? What will the future bring?

Of course, neither conclusion means very much and both should be avoided.

EXERCISES

A. How might the conclusion of a twenty-page essay differ in length from the conclusion of a three-page essay?

B. What is wrong with the conclusions below? Rewrite each of them so that it is effective.

1. In conclusion, the only way of thinking in which we are not concerned with ourselves is "creative thinking." This way of thinking might enable us to learn. At least we should admit the value of objective thinking so that we might be able to separate our own opinions and prejudices from the evidence before us.

2. This essay has attempted to show the insignificance of Corben's argument that water shortages are inevitable.

3. Marx's definition of a rebel is as valid as any other definition, in my opinion.

C. Take the conclusion from an essay you have already written and rewrite it using a different strategy.

D. Describe some of the ways you might create a transition between the body of the essay and the conclusion. To answer this question, you may wish to review some of the discussion on transitions on page 122. Is there anything special you would have to keep in mind if developing a transition between the body and the conclusion?

E. Read an article in a popular magazine. How does it end? Is the strategy for the conclusion effective? Why?

4

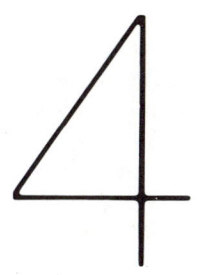

Does Your Argument Make Sense?

Now you have finished putting together some rough notes and decided on an order of arrangement. Your next task is to expand and evaluate the ideas in the notes so that they can be used as a guide for writing the paper. Some writers feel that notes such as those described in Chapter 3 are enough of a guide to write the essay. They use them as a "scratch outline," filling in a great deal more information about each point as they write the paper. However, using just a scratch outline has definite limitations since it is very general. It does not give you a chance to evaluate your ideas in all their complexity before you proceed to the rough draft. Therefore, unless your subject is quite simple or you know it very well, the only cases in which a scratch outline serves well, you usually need a more comprehensive type of outline.

WHY USE AN OUTLINE?

Writing a full outline, made up of either sentences or phrases that show the step-by-step development of your supporting points, may be the best way to test your evidence and to select those points that effectively support your thesis. By outlining the body of the paper fully before you write the first draft, you can ensure that your essay will be convincing and well developed.

An outline makes it easy for you to judge the material you have gathered because it allows you to order your ideas clearly according to the arrangement you have decided upon. You can then quickly see whether your evidence is as concrete as you first thought. You may find that you need to search out some more information, or you may discover that some of the information already gathered is not needed. In either case, preparing an outline can save you much time and trouble because it is much easier to detect any faults your argument may have by looking at an outline before you begin writing than it is by reading through a completed first draft.

The two types of full outlines that offer writers the most help are the topic outline and the sentence outline. The first part of this chapter is devoted to them. Actually, topic outlines and sentence outlines are very similar. The only difference between them is the form of the entries made in each. In the topic outline, main ideas expressed in a few words or even a single word are used as entries. In the sentence outline, each entry is a complete sentence. Were a sentence outline to be rearranged into paragraph form, your essay would be almost complete. The topic outline, however, obviously requires a great deal of filling in to become a full essay. Which type of outline to use, or whether to use a combination of the two, is up to the individual writer. Some writers feel that the sentence outline is too restrictive, whereas others feel that the topic outline is too relaxed. Many writers choose the type of outline that works best for each particular paper, preferring a sentence outline for those subjects that are abstract or complex and a topic outline for subjects that are more straightforward. Once you have learned the basic forms for these outlines, you will be in a position to choose the type that works best for you.

THE CONVENTIONS OF OUTLINING

The conventions of outlining are very easy to remember. To begin with, a typical outline might look like this:

Thesis: _____

I. _____
   A. _____
   B. _____
      1. _____
         a. _____
         b. _____
      2. _____
   C. _____
      1. _____
      2. _____

II. _____
   A. _____
      1. _____
      2. _____
         a. _____
         b. _____
   B. _____

The numerals and letters that head each entry stand for a general to specific progression of ideas in the entries themselves. For instance, roman numeral entries are the most general. Capital letter entries are more specific than roman numeral entries. Arabic numeral entries are more specific than capital letter entries. Small letter entries are more specific than arabic numeral entries. Furthermore, there must be at least two parts for each division of an outline. If there is a roman numeral I, there must be a roman numeral II; an A requires at least a B, a 1 a 2, and so on.

Three other conventions are usually kept in mind by careful outliners. All letters or numbers that serve as headings are followed by periods. Also, each entry begins with a capital letter. Finally, each entry in a sentence outline takes a period at the end, but in the topic outline the entry takes no punctuation at the end.

DEVELOPING YOUR OUTLINE

When you are ready to develop your outline, write out your thesis statement at the top of a piece of paper. The thesis will stand out so that you can check your outline of the body of the paper against it. The clearer the thesis statement is, the easier the development of the outline will be. At this point, it is a good idea to set down all your roman numeral entries. Perhaps the easiest way to write them down is to put each on a separate piece of paper so that you have plenty of room to develop ideas under each. Place each of your main supports for your thesis under the heading of a roman numeral. Remember, you are outlining the body of the paper, so do not include any ideas you may have for an introduction or conclusion. Naturally, the introduction and conclusion do not back up the thesis, but are, instead, at least as general as the thesis. Therefore, it's best to leave them out of the outline altogether.

When you have made all your roman numeral entries, check them over to ensure that they indeed prove your point. Have you left anything out or included anything unnecessary? Once you are satisfied with all the roman numeral entries, go back to roman numeral I. Under it, list the supports for your first main point. These will be your capital letter entries: A, B, C, and so forth. As you list your supports, look them over. Have your included everything you wish to? If so, it is now time to develop them, beginning with the first. List all the points about A that you want to discuss. These will be your arabic numeral entries: 1, 2, 3, and so forth. Then go on to list the points under those entries, if you have any, heading them with small letters. Although your outline can be subdivided even further, you should seldom need to go beyond small-letter entries. If you wish to go further, however, the process is the same. Subsequent entries would be made first by arabic numerals enclosed in parentheses and then by small letters enclosed in parentheses.

REQUIREMENTS OF A GOOD OUTLINE

Setting down your ideas in outline form is basically a process of carefully arranging your general and specific ideas in a logical sequence. The completed outline provides you with a clear picture of how your essay will develop. For the plan to be effective, however, you should keep three important ideas in mind as you develop your outline.

1. The Development of Your Outline Should Progress Logically

The thoughts presented in your outline should flow smoothly. One idea should clearly lead to the next, and each subdivision should logically expand the entry it is under. Therefore, you should watch what you are saying and make sure that when you promise something, you deliver it. For instance, suppose you are writing a paper on Strindberg, and your entry for capital letter A is "The three stages of Strindberg's plays." What you are in fact promising is a chronological arrangement of these stages.

    A. The three stages of Strindberg's plays
        1. The early plays
        2. The middle plays
        3. The late plays

Although you might decide that the reverse order is more suited to your discussion, some sort of chronological order is needed. If there is logical progression in your outline and you follow the outline, your paper should be logical, and the development of your thesis will be easy to follow.

2. Your Entries Should Be Parallel in Their Generality

Also important to an effective outline is parallel levels of generality. More simply stated, all of the supports for your thesis should be similar in their complexity. Roman numeral III should not be any more specific than roman numeral I or II. Similarly, all of the capital letter entries under a roman numeral should be similar in their complexity. The same is true for arabic numerals, small letters, and so on. The best way to ensure that your entries are parallel in their generality is to make them parallel grammatically. Wording similar by the entries of like scope helps you to keep your thoughts parallel. Although not an infallible rule, this practice at least keeps you thinking on the same track for each entry on the same level. Let's look at another example of a portion of an outline.

    B. Cities of the United States where aluminum is recycled
        1. Southern cities
        2. Western cities

3. Northern cities
4. Eastern cities

Notice that all the arabic numeral entries are phrased in a similar way. Suppose, instead, that one of the entries were worded differently—say, the entry for 2 were "Cities of more than 50,000." Or suppose the entry for 1 were "St. Louis." Either of the entries just mentioned would cause problems because it is not consistent with the other entries. The others treat geographical areas, so the entry treating the sizes of cities or the entry naming a particular city is out of place. Because the entries differ in their levels of generality, they would probably create difficulties when you begin to write the paper; the lack of parallelism shows a shift in thinking that would distract the reader. Even before you start to write, however, you should notice the difference in phrasing, alerting you to the potential problem and the need to restructure what you are saying.

3. Your Outline Should Be Balanced

As you develop your outline, you should make sure that you have about the same amount of information for each point you wish to make. You do not want your paper to be lopsided. One of the big advantages of an outline is that you can detect lack of balance before you begin to write the paper. If, for instance, you have seventeen entries under capital letter B, but only two under C, you probably need to reconsider the entries. Perhaps you have made two entries under B that are similar and should be combined. Maybe you have included an idea or two that really aren't very important and could be left out. It could be that your B category needs to be divided into two or more divisions. On the other hand, you might not have enough material for C to develop it fully. In that case, you should do some more research and rethinking before coming back to your outline. It is true that each part of the outline need not and should not contain the exact number of entries, but preparing an outline with a measure of balance will help you to ensure that your essay is adequately developed. An unbalanced essay is sketchy and generally unconvincing.

THE COMPLETED OUTLINE

Here are two versions of an outline a student developed for a research paper. The first version is not effective. There are flaws in logical progression, in levels of generality, and in balance. In the second version these errors have been corrected. Both versions have been annotated, the first to point out the flaws and the second to show you how the student corrected them.

Faulty Outline

Thesis Since 1947 both laypeople and scientists have engaged in an important controversy about the existence of unidentified flying objects.

A through D have various levels of generality.

The development of B lacks logical progression.

I. Since 1947 there have been many famous reports of UFO sightings.
   A. 1947, Kenneth Arnold
      1. Arnold's statement
      2. Newspaper's description
   B. After 1947 reports increased
      1. Everyone saw UFO's
      2. Many pranks
         a. Eat at Joe's
         b. Set up pictures
   C. Exeter
      1. Norman Muscarello's story
      2. Police reports
      3. Exeter townspeople's stories of similar sightings
   D. The hills
      1. Abduction by astronauts
      2. Dr. Benjamin Simon's report
      3. Spaceship psychotherapy

The capital letters under II and III lack balance of details. Need more details.

II. Details of sightings vary, but certain patterns occur frequently.
   A. Shapes
   B. Colors
   C. Electromagnetic effects
   D. Movement

III. Cynical interest by official agencies
   A. Report on reaction to Mt. Rainier
   B. Project Blue Book
   C. University of Colorado *Scientific Study of Unidentified Flying Objects*
   D. Formation of support organizations
      1. APRO
      2. NICAP

The capital letters under IV lack balance. Needs more details.

IV. Explanations for UFO's
   A. Unscheduled flights in an area
   B. Weather conditions
   C. Electrical corona
   D. Insufficient data
   E. Unknown cases still existing

The conclusion of the paper should not be part of the outline.

V. Value of continuing investigations
   A. Diminished fear of space exploration
   B. If theory of UFO's accepted, human's role in universe upset—will change

Corrected Outline

Thesis   Since 1947 both laypeople and scientists have engaged in an important controversy about the existence of unidentified flying objects.

    I. Famous reports since 1947
       A. Kenneth Arnold's experience
          1. Arnold's statement
          2. Newspaper's description
       B. Norman Muscarello's experience
          1. Muscarello's story
          2. Exeter townspeople's stories of similar sightings
          3. Police reports
       C. Dr. Benjamin Simon's experience
          1. Abduction of Simon by astronauts
          2. Spaceship psychotherapy
          3. Holes in Simon's report
   II. Patterns that reoccur in reports
       A. Shapes
          1. Saucerlike
          2. Cigar shape
          3. Pointed ovals
       B. Colors
          1. Green
          2. Blue
          3. White
       C. Electromagnetic effects
       D. Movement
          1. Jumping in air
          2. Floating
          3. Spinning
  III. Cynical interest by official agencies
       A. Report on reaction to Mt. Rainier
       B. Project Blue Book
          1. Duration of study
          2. Findings
       C. University of Colorado *Scientific Study of Unidentified Flying Objects*
       D. Formation of support organizations
          1. APRO
          2. NICAP
  IV. Typical scientific explanations of UFO's
       A. Human error
          1. Unscheduled flights in an area
          2. Conclusions from insufficient data
       B. Natural conditions

Margin notes:
- A through C are now parallel because they have one pattern of arrangement. B is logical.
- A through D are now balanced and elaborated through the analysis of sightings.
- (Official reaction)
- (Scientific reaction) IV and V have been expanded and logically subdivided.

                1. Weather conditions
                2. Electrical corona
                3. Previously undiscovered heavenly bodies

(Nonscientific reaction)
The conclusion has been deleted.

   V. Typical nonscientific justification that UFO's exist
      A. Lack of scientific explanation for 2 to 3 percent of sightings
      B. Lack of scientific explanation for people and vessels who suddenly disappear
      C. Presence of Biblical explanations
      D. Presence of aerial landing strips

EXERCISES   A. Make the unparallel entries of the following process outline parallel.

Baking a Cake

Thesis   Baking a cake is a four-step process.

    I. Preparation
       A. Preheat the oven
       B. Setting up ingredients
       C. Utensils used
       D. Grease the pan
   II. Mix
      A. Sugar and butter to be creamed
      B. Eggs added
      C. Other liquid ingredients
      D. Vanilla
  III. Baking
      A. Check oven temperature
      B. Pour batter into greased pans
      C. Bake for fifty minutes
      D. Remove after cake springs back when touched
      E. Let cool
  IV. Clean up kitchen

B. Arrange each of the following groups of words according to their most general to most specific entries.

I.	II.
Ironing	Foreign languages
Sewing	Spanish
Embroidery	Dialects
Household chores	College requirements
Cooking	Italian
Cleaning house	Latin
Washing windows	
Gourmet cooking	
Sweeping the floor	

Does Your Argument Make Sense? 93

C. An excerpt from an outline for a research paper appears below. Restructure any parts of the outline that need improvement in parallel development, balance, or progression.

Illegal Aliens in the United States

Thesis Although the illegal entry of Mexican aliens into the United States has brought many problems to this country, illegal aliens remain unstopped by police because they have devised deceptive methods of entry.

I. Problems caused by illegal aliens
   A. Take jobs from Americans
      1. Lower pay scales than Americans
      2. Availability of aliens
      3. Broad range of skills
   B. A drain on American economy
      1. Give birth to dependent children
      2. Increase hospital rolls
      3. Send money out of country to be spent
      4. Welfare—100 million dollars per year
      5. Use public schools but pay no taxes
      6. Use police, fire, and sanitation services
   C. Bring communicable diseases into United States
      1. Tend to avoid health officials—deportation fear
      2. Communicate with barrio people who pass on the diseases
II. Methods of illegal entry

CHECKING FOR LOGIC

A completed outline will now help you check the logic of your ideas and later serve as a guide to writing the paper. You will notice that the reasoning in your outline takes two main forms: *inductive* and *deductive*.

When separate bits of evidence add up in your mind to a generalization, your reasoning is inductive. Here is an everyday example of inductive reasoning. Suppose that you are driving down the street not far from your home when you smell smoke in the air. Then you see four fire trucks coming down the street with their sirens off. The firefighters appear weary and disheveled. Although the traffic in the area is slowly easing up, it is more congested than usually. The bits of information seem to add up. You inductively conclude that the firefighters have just put out a fire in your neighborhood. And were you to relate the incident to someone by first stating your generalization and then giving the eivdence that led to it, your reasoning would still be inductive. The type of inductive reasoning that might appear in a paper is perhaps a little less obvious, but it still follows the pattern of relating several events or ideas to create a generalization. The inductive paragraph below is from a student's essay on getting a job. The generalization is noted by brackets and the bits of evidence are numbered.

Generalization

> As I waited for my interview to begin, I looked around the office, [only to find that the business was poorly managed.][1] Clerks were sitting around and chatting.[2] I noticed stacks of unopened mail on one desk, and the "in progress" box of the organizer of another desk was stacked so high that orders were sliding over the desk in a huge avalanche of paperwork.[3] When I walked into the office of the company's manager, I heard her secretary say that someone from a company they do business with just called to complain about "the number of simple mistakes in one order."[4] Worse yet, I saw a check ledger open on a chair by the door, with a few checks falling on the floor.

When the evidence brings about a generalization, as it did in the preceding paragraph, the pattern is inductive. But when a generalization is applied to a specific instance, the pattern of reasoning is deductive. You may, for instance, have a generalization—all ground beef sold in Minnesota by law must have no more than 20 percent fat. Assuming that you live in Minnesota and have just bought a pound of ground beef there, you may deduce from this generalization that your pound of ground beef contains no more than 20 percent fat. In the following passage from an essay, a student uses deductive reasoning. The generalization is noted in brackets.

Generalization

> [According to the school district's charter, all people are entitled to equal opportunities to be educated.] Therefore, people who are in a class for slow learners should have the materials suited to slow learners. No one would deny students in regular classes the textbooks, supplies, and specialized teachers needed to help them learn, and no one should deny slow learners these things either. It should not be assumed that because they cannot benefit from the books already owned by the schools that they cannot benefit from books, nor should it be assumed that slow learners are not worth spending the money on.

We usually think without thinking about how we do it. But in writing, it is important to check the patterns developed in the mind because, even if they are perfect inductive or deductive thinking patterns, the statements derived from them can be untrue. Keeping a couple of criteria in mind, however, will help you to check your own ideas easily so that you can be sure they are both reasonable and true.

First, if your evidence is true and all the pertinent evidence has been included, your inductive generalization is true. Now, think back to the example about the fire. If you had to apply the first criterion, you would come away questioning the truth of the generalization that the firefighters had just finished putting out a fire in the neighborhood. Perhaps the smell of smoke had some other origin—a fireplace or a pile of burning leaves, for instance. Maybe the firefighters were returning to a neighborhood fire station after squelching a fire in another area. The traffic jam possibly was caused by something other than a fire. All this evidence would have to be looked into before the generalization could be true.

Second, there is a test for true deductions. If the generalization is true and all the apsects of the generalization fit the specific application of it, the deduced point is also true. Looking back to the example about ground beef, you can see a potential problem. If the store in which the ground beef was purchased adheres to the law, there is no problem, and the deduction is correct. But what if the store does not obey the law? From time to time such flagrant ignorance or disobedience of the law does occur, and the possibility must be considered by the writer.

Before using your completed outline to write your paper, you should check it over to make sure that the presentation of your ideas, whether arranged in deductive or inductive patterns, is true and valid.

A good way to evaluate your statements is to ask yourself the following questions.

1. Is My Thesis Reasonable?

Your paper cannot be logical unless the thesis is reasonable. First, make sure your assertion is not, in itself, so obvious that it is not worth expanding. What people already take for granted should not be the basis of your paper because it would not interest you or your reader. Nor would there be any purpose in writing a paper on an obvious point.

You need to check the wording of the thesis next. The thesis should always be expressed moderately. Even though the statement contains your opinion, you want to express it in an unemotional way. In doing so, you should make a special effort to avoid all-inclusiveness, often tipped off by expressions such as the following: *all, every, always*, and *must*. Remember, if there is even one exception to any point you make, moderation is in order. Instead of being so unrestrained, use words such as *many, some, often*, and *could*. The following examples show how you might wish to reword some of the all-inclusive statements that have slipped into the thesis.

> Ineffective: Students *always* derive more from living on campus than at home during their first year in college because a campus offers activities and contacts with people who share their interests.

Ineffective: *Students* derive more from living on campus than at home during their first year in college because a campus offers activities and *constant* contacts with people who share their interests.

Effective: *Many* students derive more from living on campus than at home during their first year in college because a campus offers activities and *frequent* contacts with people who share their interests.

2. Does Each Support Defend My Thesis?

Any support that does not defend the thesis or clarify some point needed to defend the thesis should be thrown out. As you check your outline, you should be on the lookout for three major types of support problems: supports that merely restate your thesis, supports that contradict your thesis or another support, and supports that extend beyond the scope of your thesis instead of defending it. Making this mistake is often called circular reasoning because it gets you nowhere. Notice how the problem occurs in the following outline.

Thesis Bicycle paths should be provided in all major cities to help reduce pollution.

  I. Bicycle paths would encourage more people to ride bicycles instead of drive cars.

  II. Bicycle paths would be a part of an effort to reduce pollution levels.

The first support is good. Point II, however, merely restates the thesis. Instead, it should give another example of *how* bicycle paths could help reduce pollution. Let's look at one more example of circular reasoning in an outline.

Thesis Life in the ghetto teaches young children to survive by using their wits to size up and handle social situations.

  I. Learning to get respect from peers

  II. Learning how to get what they need from their families

  III. Learning how to deal with police and bill collectors

  IV. Analyzing social situations to help them survive

In this example, the first three points are effective. The fourth, however, merely repeats the thesis. The fact that it is more general than the other supports is a good clue that it does not belong.

Avoid making any statements in your outline that contradict other statements you have made. Such contradictions are most likely to occur in the subpoints of your outline. Therefore, besides checking the subpoints against their main points and the main points against the thesis, you should check all your subpoints against each other. One slip can make the entire proof of your thesis shaky. In the complete outline that follows, the contradictory statements are noted in the margin. As you read through the outline, check the points that contradict one another.

Thesis Although old people can be demanding and emotionally taxing, their families should try to avoid hospitalizing them just to leave them in institutions until they die, and instead the families should keep them at home where they can die with dignity.

I. What is wrong with hospitals, why patients do not die with dignity
   A. Hospitalized patient feels abandoned
      1. After certain point in illness family tends to avoid the patient
      2. Patient still has a great need to be near people but cannot do so   *[Contradicts II B 4]*
      3. Family often stops perceiving patient as alive
   B. Hospitalized patient feels like a nonperson
      1. Often bedridden or so bored stays in bed
      2. Nobody for patient to take care, not even self
      3. Feels helpless and useless
   C. Hospitalized patient becomes resigned to death and cannot really accept it
      1. Almost impossible to get any aged person to accept growing old and dying   *[Contradicts II A 5]*
      2. Builds resentment because separated from family—what's the use?   *[Contradicts II A 5]*
      3. How much can any family do, not always a matter of environment

II. Why dying at home is favored
   A. Family can do specific things to make patient a part of family again
      1. Influence patient to live in the present
      2. Influence patient to identify with household
      3. Influence patient to accept medical care in a loving environment
      4. Can provide healthy interaction with a variety of people
      5. Help patient to accept death when temporarily happy
      6. Can at least try to influence patient to feel part of family, though does not always work—extremely hard   *[Contradicts I C 1]*

B. Improvement in family's morale despite the hard times
  1. Less resentment because the patient is more agreeable
  2. More understanding about aging and death for whole family—even children
  3. Less guilt about putting the patient away in a "home"
  4. Possibly less worry because the patient is right there with them

Contradicts I A I

Avoid statements that extend beyond the scope of your thesis by making sure that each support adheres to what you are trying to prove. You should not draw implications from the thesis statement, or from any other statement for that matter, before it has been fully explained and supported. If you wish to include such implications, reserve them for your conclusion. In the following outline, two of the supports are appropriate, but the other two extend too far beyond the thesis.

Thesis Vocational education programs will continue to succeed because they are more practical than liberal arts programs, are open to anyone, and provide a variety of opportunities for people who once thought they had none.

I. More practical than liberal arts
  A. Emphasize skills, not ideas
  B. We live in a time when skills producing more job offers than ideas
  C. Good opportunity for someone who already has a liberal arts education and wants something else
II. Open to anyone
  A. Anyone who is eighteen years old or older and applies for the program gets in
  B. No educational prerequisites
  C. No cutoff age
III. Success of vocational education may eventually diminish the interest in liberal arts programs
IV. Success of vocational programs will call for tremendous expansion in the programs
  A. New programs to fit the needs of the future
  B. Expansion of current programs
  C. Government funds to be increased for purpose of expansion

The first two roman numeral entries bear out the controlling idea of the thesis statement. The last two, however, expand on the assertion in the thesis rather than support it. They assume that the thesis has already been borne out. Only in the conclusion of the essay is there room for the sort of speculation that goes on in points III and IV. The wording of points III and IV should give you a clue that something is wrong. They are not grammatically parallel with points I and II. You might also have noticed that although the first two supports are based on the first two parts of the controlling idea of the thesis, the third part, that vocational educational programs "provide a variety of opportunities for people who once thought they had none," is not treated at all. It should be included in place of the unacceptable supports.

3. Have I Proven My Thesis Step by Step?

Although you have looked over each level of your outline as you completed it to make sure that your ideas are adequately presented and supported, you should make a final check of your finished outline. Have you included all the points necessary to logically prove your thesis? As you look at your points, you should keep in mind that it is usually not necessary to include absolutely every step in your proof. Those steps that your audience could reasonably be expected to take for granted or assumptions that are well known and generally accepted should be left out. Otherwise, you run the risk of making your paper tedious. For instance, were you writing an essay about the value of exercise and a proper diet during middle age, you might say that a fifteen-minute walk each day is good exercise for a busy middle-aged person. You might go on to mention that walking is an effective way to improve the circulation and maintain muscle tone. However, it should not be necessary for you to explain that people who do not get enough exercise probably have poor circulation and muscle tone. The statement would most likely be assumed by your audience from your other points. To mention it would therefore be unnecessary and possibly boring.

You must be careful, however, to make sure that the steps you feel are obvious will also be obvious to your readers. For an example look at the following sentence.

> The ratings for the television special on the life of Malcolm X must have been very high as very few people were in class on the night of the program.

A reader would not automatically make a connection between high absences and high ratings. Therefore, you need to say that because the show was on television at the same time that the class was held and because many people stayed at home to watch the show, class attendance was low. Furthermore, if your class attendance was any indication that just as many people stayed home from other planned events, there must have been considerable interest in the program, enough to cause the ratings to be high. If you provide the links in your thought process whenever you think your audience might be confused, they will never ask, "What's the connection?"

4. Are My Underlying Assumptions Clear?

Many of the statements people make are based on various assumptions. In writing, you must deal with assumptions carefully. As is mentioned in the preceding section on step-by-step reasoning, if the audience accepts these assumptions as obvious, you do not need to state them. However, any other assumptions must be substantiated in your outline so that they will be handled properly in the essay. Certain assumptions behind your statements may be firmly held opinions of yours, but you must realize that your readers may not hold the same views. Therefore, if there is any possibility that your assumptions might not be clear to your readers, you should state them, and prove them if necessary, before you make any assertions based on them. You can see why two problems could arise if you did not clarify your underlying assumptions. First, your readers may miss your point because they do not understand how you arrived at it, and second, even if they could infer what you mean, they might so disagree with what you imply that they would refuse to read on. On the other hand, if you clearly state the assumption and support it, they are more likely to see the point your way. For instance, suppose you wrote the following statement.

> Because he is innovative, E. E. Cummings is a great poet.

If you look closely at the sentence, you will realize that it implies a value judgment that is not explained or supported. The opinion that the sentence contains is that innovation is good. If you did not believe innovation is good, you could not say that it determines greatness, which is essentially what you are saying in the sentence about E. E. Cummings. Now, this point about the value of innovation is certainly one on which there is controversy. Since your readers might not share your opinion, you should state it and support it. Then you can apply the generalization to E. E. Cummings. As a result you would have a well-developed deductive argument (see p. 94). Let's look at another example.

> Destroying a nearly extinct flower to put up a power plant where the flower is growing is immoral and uncalled for.

If you write this statement, your underlying assumption is that the preservation of nature, symbolized by the flower, is moral. Some of your readers, however, might take exception to your opinion, believing that putting up power plants is perfectly moral because they serve humanity. They would therefore be likely to discount your argument because you did not clarify what is moral about preserving nature. Unless you clarify your underlying assumption, you do not give them the chance to see your side so that they might reconsider their own.

5. Are All My Points within Reason?

Have you ever noticed that a person may be socially undesirable—a car thief, for instance—yet still be an honest and caring parent? Most people are not either angelic or devilish, happy or unhappy, energetic or lazy. Instead, they generally fall into categories somewhere between the extremes. The same is true of ideas. Because there is usually more than one explanation for a problem and more than one way to see an issue, you should avoid making statements that are either-or judgments. A dogmatic stand can undermine the proof of your thesis. For instance, in a paper on the possibility of socialized medicine in the United States, a student might write that we can have either socialized medicine and communism or our present system and democracy, but not socialized medicine and democracy. Such a statement is not within reason; it sets up two extremes and connects them with the word *or*. Most readers would realize that the alternatives are not so rigidly opposed and that some sort of coexistence is possible. Furthermore, those who think in either-or patterns tend to press the panic button immediately. Their language becomes overly emotional and the readers tend to discredit what they have to say. Notice the unfortunate effects of the following statements.

> First of all, taxes *must go down, or everyone will starve*.
>
> It is a fact that if we stop employing undocumented workers in the United States, *the majority of our large industries will go bankrupt*.
>
> Urban renewal also should be *halted unless we want to say goodbye to the neighborhood as a community*.

Such exaggerated assertions are difficult to defend. At best they oversimplify the intended point, and at worst they falsify it. As you check over your outline, make sure that you have considered your points from as many angles as possible so that the ones you present are reasonable.

6. Do the Abstractions Reveal My Meaning?

An abstraction is a quality or concept that does not directly correspond with any physical object. However, abstractions may be illustrated by concrete or specific examples. You cannot conjure up in your mind a picture of "rage," the abstraction itself, although you could certainly think of an instance in which you were enraged. You might see the look on your face at the moment or picture the circumstances surrounding your anger, but those pictures are not "rage." "Love," "reality," "freedom," "beautiful," "forthright," and "absurd" are a few of the abstract words common in college essays. Nothing is wrong with using such words; in fact, they are usually necessary in all but the simplest discussions. But logical problems can occur if your readers do not have the same definition of the abstractions as you do or if you have not settled on one meaning for an abstraction. Suppose you had thought roughly the following: "People flocked to the stadium from all over the country to show their support of the new environmental protection law. It was a beautiful event for the good of all life on earth." And suppose in your outline you organized these ideas this way:

II. The occasion was the passing of the first environmental laws.
    A. People flocked here from all over country for beautiful event
    B. Event was for good of all life

Now, with these abstractions, "beautiful" event and the "good" of all "life," it might be hard for your readers to see exactly what you mean. To one reader a "beautiful" event may be one that runs smoothly. To another it may mean one in an attractive physical setting. To you it may mean one that brought people together for a worthwhile common cause. The same is true of "good"; what exactly is the "good"? And how exactly is "life" meant—with deep philosophical implications or literally? The confusion over definitions might well give your readers a different idea than you had intended.

If you do find abstractions in your outline, you can quickly determine whether the context of the abstraction causes the word to mean only one possible thing. If so, you probably do not have to define it. Also, if you are writing to a particular audience who shares your definitions, the abstractions will probably be clear enough. However, if an abstraction does require clarification, you can take one of three courses: replace the abstraction with concrete words, replace the abstraction with specifics, or keep the abstraction but explain it so that you and your audience know the definition you are using for it.

There is a subtle distinction between concrete words and specific words. Concrete language is often more specific than the language in abstractions, but that's not what makes it concrete. The quality of concreteness belongs to language that directly corresponds to physical objects and is expressed through the senses. "As warm as a motor revving up," "icy," and "blinding light" are all concrete images. Thus, the abstraction "beautiful" as in "a beautiful day" might be relieved by describing the day with the more concrete words "sunny and crisp." The abstraction "beautiful" in the preceding example about the environmental laws, however, does not refer to a physical quality. The problem, in fact, with all three abstractions in the outline at the top of this page is that the abstractions are too general for the context. They are so general that they do not reveal your meaning. The event might have been more precisely described as "support of a worthwhile common cause." The abstraction "good" might have been replaced with the more specific "to promote the continuance" and "life" with "plant and animal life." You can see that the revisions are more specific than the original.

Original

II. The occasion was the passing of the first environmental laws
   A. People flocked here from all over country for beautiful event
   B. Event for good of all life

Revision

II. The occasion was the passing of the first environmental laws
   A. People flocked here from all over country for support of worthwhile common cause
   B. Event was to promote continuance of all plant and animal life

Frequently, the unqualified use of abstract words is accompanied by highly emotional language. Such a combination, of course, is no substitute for reason and destroys the consistency of tone (see p. 19) that good writers strive for. But emotional language and abstractions are all around us in the advertising we read and the political rhetoric we hear. Worse, the combination seems to convince some people. You can see how members of an audience might attach whatever personal meaning they want to abstractions; they can, in essence, hear what they want to hear rather than listen closely to what is said. And the emotionalism in the language seems to carry it. For example, in the sentence, "The justice, humanity, and natural greatness of the American people is never to be denied," there are three abstractions composing the main part of the sentence. Each is emotionally charged, not to mention excessive (note the use of "never" and the strong word "denied"). What does the writer or speaker really mean? Is he or she merely playing a trick on the audience, intending only to move the emotions? It's hard to tell for sure.

In a well-known essay, "Politics and the English Language," George Orwell points out that language can be used in many ways to hide rather than reveal the writer's true meaning. But trickery is not the goal of the college writer, who does all he or she can to explain, as honestly and clearly as possible, what is on his or her mind. College writing appeals, furthermore, to a rational audience, and few in that group would settle for straight emotionalism. Therefore, it is unfair to the readers and inappropriate for the writer to use abstractions and emotionalism in place of reason. Cautious writers remove both kinds of language as soon as it crops up in the prewriting.

7. Have I Acknowledged Opposing Viewpoints?

Either-or thinking (see p. 101) often goes along with a failure to recognize the views of the opposition. You should be aware of ideas concerning your topic that disagree with your own. In Chapter 2 citing the claims of the opposition was mentioned in developing the thesis. But if the claims are important, you should also remember to discuss them in the body of the essay. Therefore, they belong in your outline. Deliberately leaving out mention of opposing viewpoints is likely to cause your readers to think that you are not familiar enough with your subject to fully defend your ideas.

If upon examining opposing ideas you do find weaknesses in your own argument, you should not be afraid to adjust it and even to alter your thesis. Your efforts up to this point will not have been wasted because you will have gained a greater insight into your topic from which to build a new paper. More often, however, you will feel that the opposing ideas are wrong, and you can refute them in your essay. You may find, too, that while you do not agree with some of the opposing ideas, others are worth considering. In this case, your paper may be structured so that although you point out the value of certain opposing viewpoints, you demonstrate the equal or greater value of your own thesis. Notice how more than one view is treated in the outline on page 91. Whole sections of the outline are devoted to each to each of the viewpoints. Frequently, opposing statements are found in subordinate clauses in the actual paper because, as you will see in Chapter 7, such structures deemphasize the points contained in them. You would want to emphasize your point and deemphasize your opposition's in most cases. Here are some statements from students' essays. Notice how they effectively treat opposing viewpoints.

> Despite the difficulties involved, many single, working mothers find jobs outside the home very rewarding.
>
> Although most gangs participate in actions that put the members at odds with society, many values are learned that reinforce community identity and help the members to survive hardships.

When checking over your outline, make sure you have accounted, in some way, for the opposition.

8. Are My Causes and Effects Accurate?

A cause is something that brings about a result. An effect is something that is directly produced by an action or agent. Many papers you will write will contain causes and effects, signaled by a variety of expressions including "because of," "due to," "the reason for," and "the result of." When you name the causes of an effect or the effects of a cause, you should keep in mind that only certain information can qualify as a cause or an effect. First, that one event preceded another is not enough reason to believe that the first caused the second, even though causes do always precede effects. Surely, if it rains just before an earthquake, the rain did not cause the quake. Even though a man or woman takes vitamin C for the first time on the morning of the same day he or she contracts a miserable cold, the vitamin did not cause the cold. This connecting of mere coincidences, which is the reasoning that pervades superstition, is not appropriate for college papers.

There is, however, an easy test for sound cause-and-effect reasoning. In true causal relationships, you should be able to say what links the cause to the effect. The *why* of the connection is important. For instance, you might say your father's dedication was the main reason for his success as a teacher. In giving this cause you are basing the relationship between dedication and success on more than just the sequence in which the two occurred. True, the dedication came before the success, but also you realize that people generally believe dedication pays off, bringing good results, and the result or effect in his case was success. You can justify the connection on the basis of other similar relationships you have recognized in the past. Your experience, then, helps you to recognize true cause-and-effect relationships.

Also, be careful not to conclude, just because you have found one cause for an effect or vice versa, that the cause or effect is the only one.

Be aware that most effects do not have only one cause, and most causes have more than one effect. To make sure you include the important information in your paper, try to search out all relevant causes for an effect and effects for a cause. In researching them, you may discover a host of causes and effects, some more significant than others. Even though you should have thought about many causes and effects, when it actually comes to including them in your outline, you should not list all of them. Select those that are pertinent to the point at hand. Most likely you will need to deal only with the important or "primary" causes and effects. Nevertheless, be sure to show in your choice of words that there are other unmentioned causes or effects. For instance, you may say "one cause" or "an effect" instead of using the too-inclusive "the cause" or "the effect." Let's return, now to the example of your father. You realize, of course, that other causes—his understanding nature, his ability to communicate well, his grasp of his subject—contributed to his success as a teacher. Thus, you will notice that the example above does not attempt to imply that dedication was the only cause; it appropriately says "the main reason."

9. Do My Analogies Clarify My Points?

An analogy is a comparison of two like ideas, events, or situations. Using an analogy can be helpful in explaining a point, so analogies are frequently used for clarification. In these cases, an idea that might otherwise be strange to your readers can click in their minds if you can describe it in terms of a similar, familiar situation. But you must be very cautious if you plan to use an analogy to prove a point because most ideas or situations that are analogous also have distinctive differences. Thus, by going about proving one point through reasoning out the analogy to it, you may dangerously ignore important differences between the original and the analogous points. The differences may throw off your reasoning.

If, for instance, you were to argue in an essay that moderators on television news programs should not make their personal views known because moderators need to maintain an image of objectivity, and if you wanted to drive the point home by providing an analogy, you might compare moderators with judges, who should also remain impartial. Despite the similarity, the analogy actually clouds the issue instead of clarifying it. You certainly cannot claim that the purpose of objectivity for the two is the same. If, assuming moderators are no different than judges, you defend the point about moderators by accounting for all the reasons a judge would need to remain objective during a trial, you have been illogical. Instead, before you use an analogy, you should pick out any differences between the point you have in mind and the analogy. Then examine the differences to see if they are significant enough to undermine your point. If the differences are not relevant to the point, the analogy will probably be effective.

10. Is My Thinking Free of Stereotypes?

The technical term *stereotype* refers to metal plates used by printers to reproduce many exact copies. Thinking can also be stereotyped in the sense of applying the same fixed notion about something to all the members of a particular group and not allowing for individual differences. Thus, inherent in stereotyping is the belief that all members of a group are exact copies of one another, who will act predictably. Some familiar stereotypes include the all-brawn, no-brain athlete; the dumb, sexy female; and the money-hungry physician. Other stereotypes are more subtle and perhaps for that reason more insidious: the lazy welfare recipient, the downtrodden minority person, or the old maid.

No matter how subtle, stereotypes are inaccurate and trite. Although some members of a given group may seem to fit their stereotype, not all, or even most, do. Yet stereotyped thinking plunges forward and takes a lot for granted. That is, people who stereotype others may observe one characteristic of the stereotype and incorrectly assume that all the other characteristics automatically fit the person. For instance, a person who thinks in stereotypes would see an athletic male student and assume the rest—that he is stupid, acts like a stud, and is more concerned with games and muscles than with academics. Unfortunately, any hint of the stereotype seems to reinforce it. Quite the contrary, the individual young man may be both physically active and highly academic.

You can see that the underlying assumption of any stereotype is either-or thinking: people are one way or another. People would be more accurate to evaluate their own stereotypes. They should look for exceptions to the "rule." If there is one intelligent athlete, one non-materialistic physician, the stereotype cannot hold since it assumes all athletes to be alike, all physicians to be the same. Like the cliches discussed in Chapter 7, stereotypes reveal a failure to evaluate on the part of those who use them. Passive and automatic acceptance of them is far too easy. Any hint of stereotyping therefore should be removed from your outline and replaced with thoughtful examination of your subject.

11. Is My Information Representative?

Your information should be as representative as possible. Representative statements are typical and true; they are quite different from stereotypes. Be careful not to cite an exceptional case as if it were typical. That is, one example of something is not usually enough upon which to make a generalization. The instance could be the exception to the rule. If, for instance, you were writing an essay about the abuses of prescription drugs, you might discuss the seeming casualness with which some doctors administer powerful prescriptions. To cite an instance in which a friend of yours went to the college doctor for sore muscles and came home with five prescriptions for symptoms from anxiety to cold sores would be a poor example because the case is certainly not usual. Most doctors do not treat any symptoms that they have not verified. And to assume they do from this example would be unreasonable. Attempting to sensationalize your argument by offering extremes and exceptional examples can only undermine the effectiveness of your point. Even if you found a second example, you would have to look further, into more cases, to be sure that the information is representative. Otherwise the rare incidence of the problem would probably require your abandoning the point altogether.

12. Are the Sources of My Information Reliable?

Whether the sources you use are reliable should be a constant concern, and they should be checked once more after you have written the outline. If your outline contains information from questionable sources, your paper will be weak. First, make sure each source is respectable in your field. Two good ways to check are to see if it is mentioned in lectures and discussions and to check if it is on bibliographies at the ends of articles or in books you have used. Perhaps you can also ask your teacher's opinion of those sources you are not sure about.

Sometimes it is helpful to check the publisher of the source. The information you need is on the reverse side of the title page. Is the source published by a well-known publisher? This information is not always helpful, but if you are using a source that has other questionable characteristics—sensationalism, conflicting information, weak use of statistical information (see p. 230)—and it is published by an unknown company, you have a bit of evidence that the source is not very reliable. Of course, some small presses publish high quality work, and the presence of an unknown publisher's name on the reverse of the title page is not, in itself, enough to incriminate a source.

Another consideration may be the date of publication. If you are writing about a current topic or one about which there is currently a great deal of discussion, you should try to get the most recent information on it. However, if your topic is, for example, campus riots in the 1960s, it would be more important to find sources written at the time of the riots. Of course, recent articles on the subject might well be enlightening also. The value of turning to primary sources, the actual accounts of what happened at the time or the original works, is worth considering. Have you relied only on secondary sources, that which has been written about the primary sources, in your outline? If so, perhaps you should take a good look at the primary sources and make sure that you still want to use the secondary ones instead. Since you have not yet written your paper, you are not locked into using the material in your present outline, or you could, perhaps, expand that material.

One last point worth considering about the reliability of your sources is whether you have used sufficiently sophisticated sources. You might want to use current technical journals in the field you are studying. They are usually more up to date and they go into a lot more detail than would, say, a general textbook in the same field. But your thesis will determine the level of the needed sources. For some papers the general materials might well be more desirable than the specific ones.

A problem that enters any discussion of reliability is that there can be major discrepancies between reports in widely distributed newspapers and reports in smaller periodicals. For example, were you to read about the same incident in *The New York Times* and in *The Village Voice*, your information could differ. The *Voice*, for instance, might be willing to include more sensational coverage that the *Times* might choose to suppress or might never discover. Statistics might even vary. The decision as to which is the more reliable source is complicated and depends on the nature of the information needed. In your outline, the best way to deal with conflicting information is to report the conflict to your readers, and not to suppress the information or change it to suit your point.

13. Do My Statistics Tell the Truth?

Statistics, even when taken from reliable sources, must be used carefully and accurately. Otherwise, they may be misleading, poor evidence. One point to keep in mind is that most statistics are based on samples. Samples refer to the number of certain people who have responded to the survey. Whenever you use a statistic as proof, you should evaluate the size of the sample and find out who was polled. For instance, a statistic that reveals that 50 percent of those polled in a company voted to fire a certain officer of the company may at first seem alarming, until you learn that two people out of hundreds in the company voted on the decision. If the total sampling is unrepresentative of the group, the statistics can mean very little. Similarly, if 500 questionnaires are circulated at random on a campus to determine the physical educational needs of students, but if only 100 of the 500 students respond to the survey, very little information can be concluded from the limited and unrepresentative sample.

Statistics that are averages can also be misleading. Let's say that over a ten-year period the average score of high school seniors on a math test was 62 percent. There are two reasons you would have to be very careful about using this information. First of all, the word *average* may mean that some students scored a hundred while others scored only, say, 18 percent. That is, you should understand the range of statistics as well as the averages. Also significant is that the test was given over a ten-year period. You would at least need to know the averages for each year in order to use information from any one year. You might otherwise discuss averages for those ten years as if they were true of each year. To further establish that the scores have dipped severely because in 1968 the average score was 78 percent and in 1977 the average score was only 59 percent would be poor reasoning. Perhaps 1968 was an atypical year, and usually the scores were around 60 percent. To show a trend you must know the scores from all the years, and the trend must be based on the consistent changes in the scores. Do not let the seemingly factual quality of statistics in your outline convince you until you have closely examined them.

In this chapter each question is presented separately so that you can know what to look for, but when you check your outline, you may well find that the reasoning flaws overlap. There is no reason to be concerned about their appearing together so long as you can identify them and correct them. As you read through the sample theses and supports listed below, you will recognize the coincidence of the reasoning flaws. The questions you should ask and the concerns you should have about each weak point are explained in the margin. After you read through these examples, go back to the questions in the second part of the chapter to review them if any of the points still seem a bit fuzzy to you.

Example 1.

Thesis The federal government must ban big cars to lessen air polution in major cities.

Reliable Source?
I. My mechanic says that big cars use more gas, and consequently emit more fumes than little cars.

Any Opposition?
II. Big cars are unnecessary because small cars can move people just as well.

Does This Defend the Thesis?
III. Rapid transit systems would eliminate the need for most cars, big and small.

Within Reason
IV. If big cars are not banned, exhaust fumes will blanket the cities, ruining everyone's health.

Example 2

Thesis	Capital punishment, which is really a moral issue although most people do not view it that way, should be considered unconstitutional.
Underlying Assumption?	I. Even the meanest murderer or rapist is a human being.
Does This Defend the Thesis?	II. Capital punishment is not even an effective deterrent because criminals still commit crimes even after other human beings are slaughtered like pigs in gas chambers and on the gallows.
Restates the Thesis?	III. The constitution does not really allow capital punishment.
Underlying Assumption?	IV. There is always the chance that convicted criminals might be innocent of the crime, or that they might honestly repent and become kind, creative individuals.
Circular Reasoning and Emotional Language?	V. If we act immorally and demand an eye for an eye, what hope is there for society?

Example 3

Thesis	College classes should be ungraded because grading is arbitrary.
Underlying Assumption?	I. Teachers are human and can favor certain students.
Underlying Assumption?	II. There are differences in opinion about right and wrong answers.
Within Reason?	III. There is a variety of different grading procedures—grades not standardized.

Example 4

Thesis	College students today do not have the basic skills or attitudes needed to survive in college because they have watched too much television, have not learned fundamentals of mathematics, and are lacking the motivation of former generations.
Faulty Cause and Effect? Within Reason?	I. Television has caused illiteracy.
Within Reason?	II. Calculators have done away with the need to learn simple math.
Stereotyping? Within Reason?	III. Students are trained to be passive by liberal school systems that do everything for them.
Is This Evidence Representative? Reliable Source?	IV. According to *Parents Today* magazine many parents claim that they do not think children should have to study things that will not help them in living.
EXERCISES	Directions: Read through the sample thesis statements below and the main supports. Identify the logical flaws in any of the supports that are poorly reasoned out.

A. Every home, whether it is a house or a one-room apartment, should have plants in it.
   1. Plants add warmth to drab modern buildings and old run-down ones.
   2. Taking care of plants is a hobby.
   3. Watching the growth of a favorite plant helps a person to understand and find contact with the simple majesty of life.
   4. Many plants are beautiful, as beautiful as fine art, and plants are never cheap imitations like the artwork found in most homes.
B. The best way to travel short distances is on a bicycle.
   1. Cars move too fast and are dangerous if one tries to look around at the beauty of nature and architecture.
   2. Most accidents occur with cars, not bicycles.
   3. Driving a car as opposed to riding a bicycle is like skimming a book instead of studying each word.
   4. Bicycle racks let one carry groceries home on a bike.
   5. Modern bicycles are precise, well-crafted instruments that demand only a little physical effort.
C. Although my parents wanted me to be a doctor, I knew that I could not become one.
   1. I have no interest in science—I prefer to believe in personal magic.
   2. I am not interested in charging high fees and getting rich so I can buy an estate and big cars.
   3. A lot of medical students never complete school, internship, and residency.
   4. An article in a recent news magazine said that doctors have the highest percentage of drug addiction of any profession.
D. Inflation over the past five years has made the college students who get money only through their own work live in poverty.
   1. Food costs have doubled.
   2. Entertainment at the best theaters has nearly doubled.
   3. Transportation is going up everyday.
   4. Suddenly a student realizes he or she has to choose between getting textbooks and doing well in school or eating a healthful diet and not getting sick.
   5. The average rent for a student's apartment at my school is $190 a month.
   6. In 1967 the same apartment rented for half the price.
   7. It is not even worth going to school if you have to live in the slums.

Directions: The outline below is fraught with logical flaws of one kind or another. Identify as many of them as you can. Also note what you would consider to be poor form.

The Dangers of Drinking Milk

Thesis Drinking milk is not healthful for everyone, as the slogan would have people believe, and mothers should be aware of the dangers of including milk in very many meals.

  I. False advertising by the Milk Producers Board
      A. Board is being sued for the slogan "milk has something for everybody"
      B. Only interested in money, not people's health
 II. Allergies to milk
      A. Skin rashes
      B. Stomach upsets
      C. Acne
      D. Ulcers
      E. Running noses
III. Other side effects caused by indigestible lactose
      A. People need an enzyme (lactase) to break down lactose into two digestible sugars
      B. Babies born with high levels of lactase
      C. In adults lactose increases acidity in digestive system
          1. Causes ulcers
          2. Causes stomach pains
          3. Causes diarrhea
          4. Causes death in some cases
 IV. Nutritional value overrated
      A. Poor source of iron, which can cause anemia
      B. Mothers who give babies milk during the day are causing iron deficiency anemia
          1. Babies lose appetite for other more nutritious foods
      C. Milk is high in cholesterol and leads to heart failure or arterosclerosis

Directions: Name two problems with the outline below from a student's research paper. How might the student go about rethinking the subject in order to construct a logical argument?

Stop Smoking Right Now

Thesis Cigarette smoking should be banned from public places.
  I. Threat to the environment
      A. Link between smoking and cancer
      B. Nicotine is addictive
      C. The air can become polluted with smoke
 II. Experiments demonstrate the danger of smoking
      A. Damage to bodily tissues
      B. Masochism of smokers

       C. Rats in the same cage as smoke suffered heart failure
       D. Must we experiment on humans before we call it quits?
III. Cigarette advertising a bad influence
       A. Strong advertising campaigns
       B. Millions of dollars spent on cigarette ads
       C. People in cigarette ads are always happy
       D. The average person in a cigarette ad is young and virile
IV. A ban on cigarette smoking in public is needed
       A. Too many deaths relate to smoking
       B. Smart people will kick the habit if told to do it
       C. Most smokers realize they are doing the wrong thing
       D. No one really needs to smoke

5
What Is the Shape of a Paragraph?

Have you ever wondered where to begin or to end your paragraphs? Why paragraphs were important in essay writing? How to organize your thoughts in the proper sequence for a paragraph? The answers to these and other questions often asked by student writers are not so difficult when you see the paragraph as a miniature unit of composition designed to fit into the total pattern of the essay.

Three types of paragraphs are most common in essay writing. The introductory paragraph often has an attention-getting lead-in and contains the thesis. The middle paragraphs each clarify one or another part of the controlling idea in the thesis. The concluding paragraphs may relate a summary of the points in the essay and add to that summary an implication derived from your argument.

PARAGRAPH AND ESSAY

Introductory and concluding paragraphs were discussed in Chapter 3. This chapter is concerned with the structure of body paragraphs. A striking similarity exists between a body paragraph and an essay—a similarity that can make learning to write a bit easier than you would at first suppose. In fact, some scholars in the field of writing feel that

FIGURE 5-1
The potter gives the pot shape, pulling up the sides from the base, as the writer shapes an argument through paragraphs that build on an outline. (Photo by Steve Dierks.)

if you can master the structure of the paragraph, you can write a good essay and vice versa. You can see why if you take a look at the shape of each.

Essay

Introduction—thesis
    Support
    Support
    Support
Conclusion

Paragraph

Topic or top sentence
    Support
    Support
    Support
Transition or concluding comment

THESIS STATEMENT AND TOPIC SENTENCE The thesis statement and the paragraph topic sentence perform the same function: they are primary focal points for the readers. Each serves as the place where writers commit themselves to their material, for the paragraph or essay, by clearly setting out the point.

SUPPORTS Supports for the paragraph and essay serve the same purpose. Because of this, paragraph supports may be arranged in the same ways as the body of an essay (see pp. 67–74). Usually, however, it is not necessary to compose your paragraphs according to strict arrangements, since they develop intuitively, depending on what you need to say to explain whatever point you are making.

CONCLUSION Writing a conclusion for a paragraph is a bit more difficult than writing one for an essay because the paragraph's requires more subtle choice of words; however, the concepts are parallel. Whereas the essay may have several sentences of summarized information in its conclusion, the paragraph may end with a lighter, less obvious, concluding comment, or it may wind up with a transition leading into the next support.

WHAT MAKES PARAGRAPHS GOOD?

Your body paragraphs will have four characteristics: a main idea expressed in a topic sentence, or a top sentence that begins the sequence of ideas; unity of purpose; coherence, or flow, from one sentence to the next; and adequate development through explanations and examples.

THE TOPIC SENTENCE It is not necessary to fit a topic sentence into every paragraph; topic sentences that set forth exactly what you want to say in the paragraph are more suitable for some paragraphs than for others. To make the point of a paragraph clear, however, you may wish to control the ideas in it and your readers' perception of the ideas by including a topic sentence. When you do, it is important to create topic sentences that will not be too general to support your thesis. In just one paragraph you should be able to handle what you have promised. You want your topic sentence to be specific enough so that, in turn, your supports for the topic sentences will offer essential details, and as a whole the paragraph will drive home part of the controlling idea of the thesis.

Not every paragraph is written at the same level of generality, so there is no one rule for how specific a topic sentence should be. As you write, you will develop skill in using your thesis sentence as a guide to how specific a topic sentence should be. Here are a few examples of the relative levels of generality between a thesis and a topic sentence for the same paper.

Possible Thesis Sentences

T.V. shows are more controversial than ever this year.

Possible Topic Sentences

This season several television shows are permitting "daring language" on the air.

Vitamin E has been acclaimed the miracle drug of the 1970s.

Most of the dreams of a child around the age of five, according to many psychologists, are wish-fulfillment dreams.

By studying Latin, one can gain a better awareness of the workings of the English language.

People can aid the healing of skin injuries and erase scars by applying E right from the capsule.

Freud maintained that a child at the age of five is "id" driven and thus often "gets his way" in his dreams when he has frustrated and repressed a desire for something during the day.

Many of the words a college student should know are based on Latin roots.

Practice developing topic sentences on several topics; only by trying your hand at it will you become aware of the specificity required at the topic level. This part of paragraph writing will come relatively easily to you if you have formed good, parallel entries on your outline (see p. 88), with each subdivision being more specific than the one that it follows.

Your topic sentence has two parts: the subject and the predicate. Just as the controlling idea in the thesis statement contains the key words showing the content of the essay, the predicate of the topic sentence is the key to the entire paragraph. The predicate includes the verb and any words that follow it. In topic sentence 2 above, the predicate is *can aid the healing of skin injuries and erase scars by applying E right from the capsule*. The writer will therefore tell how scars can be erased and sores healed. Here is another topic sentence with the predicate underlined.

Joe Kemp <u>has achieved a great deal for such a young man.</u>

The predicate promises the reader that some of Joe Kemp's achievements will be explained. You can see that it is very important to write precisely in the topic sentence and to present a predicate about which you will have something to say.

If you decide to write a topic sentence, you need to decide also where it might best be placed in the paragraph. Some writers like to place topic sentences first where the sentence really stands out. But topic sentences may work just as well anywhere in the paragraph as long as the paragraph remains focused on the central idea in the predicate. For instance, some writers like to bring in the topic sentence after an introductory sentence or two. The introductory sentences might be a pertinent analogy, a transition from the previous paragraph, or information needed for a full understanding of the topic sentence. In the following beginning of a paragraph, an analogy opens the paragraph, and the topic sentence (in brackets) comes next.

> When the Santa Ana winds blow in Southern California, it is as if the gods have loosed their rage. [The winds cause massive destruction and evoke in people their most vitriolic humors.] Trees fall. People rush about with frayed tempers. Fires spread unchecked throughout the Southland.

Placing the topic sentence at the end of the paragraph can have the effect of building up your ideas to a climax. The climactic topic sentence lends an air of surprise or finality to your paragraph. This technique of reserving the main idea of the paragraph is not one you would want to use very often because it would then appear gimmicky rather than logical and sincere. But there might occur to you some idea which would function best placed at the end of your paragraph. For instance, if you were writing a paper on the technique of flashbacks in Alfred Hitchcock's film *Marnie*, you might open a paragraph with a description of a flashback and a detailed explanation of the technique, only then concluding the paragraph with the topic sentence. Another type of paragraph that works effectively with the climactic topic sentence lists a number of examples, only clarifying the connection between them in the final sentence, the topic sentence, of the paragraph.

> A woman with a master's degree in English finds a job at a salesclerk in a large department store after a six-month search in trying to find a position in her field. She earns $500 a month. A man with a double B. A. in philosophy and history accepts a $600-a-month position as a beginning file clerk for an insurance company. Thousands of others, college graduates, register for unemployment; in their desperate quest for work, they are repeatedly turned away because their education is counted as a strike against them. College no longer brings the rewards, financial or professional, that it once promised. ["Overqualified and underpaid" describes the average college graduate in the United States.]

THE TOP SENTENCE

Topic sentences can lend considerable clarity to paragraphs, making them easy to read and keeping you on the track. A more difficult type of paragraph to write, but one that sounds less mechanical, does not come right out and state a topic sentence. Nonetheless, the paragraph is organized around an unstated central idea or has as its first or second sentence the beginning to a sequence of thoughts that is played out in the rest of the paragraph. In such cases, this first sentence is simply called the "top" sentence. Here is an example.

> The market around the corner had an advertisement in the window for a stock clerk. It said, "Full-time, reliable, experienced stock clerk needed." I knew I needed to work more hours. At my present job, money ran out every

week by Wednesday. Although I had never been a stock clerk before, I knew the work was something I could learn because I had worked for the past four years part time as a salesperson in a bakery. For sure, that job was more challenging than being a stock clerk, which really didn't sound too hard, the more I got to thinking about it. It probably required a lot of organization—that's me, always organized. Also, the advertisement said "reliable"—somehow I'm always the one everybody counts on to get the job done. Except for the part about "experienced" that job was mine.

UNITY

The ideas in a paragraph should all point toward the same statement or idea. Unity—the consistency of ideas—should come automatically if you have organized the paper with a clear thesis and outline. Still, you should be sure not to include extraneous information or ideas in a paragraph. You are trying to convey something definite. Digressions, as interesting as they may seem, will confuse your readers. Avoid them. In a well-handled paragraph every point relates to the predicate of the topic sentence or to the intention you set forth, even if there is no topic sentence.

Here is an example of a paragraph that lacks unity. The sentences that throw off the paragraph do not stick to the point of the predicate in the topic sentence. They take up a side issue. Most likely, the point of them, the relationships between parents and children and the lack of reinforcement at home, would belong in this essay. But it belongs in a separate paragraph. The writer could have improved the paragraph by taking out these sentences, which do not flow with the established sequence of ideas.

Not Appropriate to Topic Sentence

The letter grades of D and F should not be recorded on elementary school children's report cards. First of all, students who are doing poorly feel bad enough without being reminded of the fact that they have failed. The child may identify very strongly with the grade on the card, responding with "I am a D" or with "I am worth an F—in other words, nothing." Actually, the grade only represents the student's work in the class, not the whole person; but that fact is hard to get across, especially to a person with low self-esteem. Low self-esteem is a serious problem among elementary age children. They often feel that they are not capable of learning at all, partly because their home environment does not support them. Education is often not very important to their parents, and thus what the children are doing in school receives no reinforcement in their homelife. The result is that the children begin to feel as if they have split personalities, one personality at school and one at home. They begin to wonder whether they belong anywhere or if they should worry very much if they do poorly in school. What are the expectations others have of them? Another problem with the grade of D or F is that it does not tell the child very much. A student who is doing so poorly as to receive a D needs individual attention that is specifically directed at his or her academic problems. The overall evaluation of D acts merely as negative reinforcement, causing his or her failure instincts to come out and set this person in the path of continued failures.

EXERCISES   A. Write a possible topic sentence for each of the following groups of details. Underline the predicate in the topic sentence.

(a)
- He is bulky and muscular.
- He never listens to anyone.
- His sentences are short, abrupt, and insinuating.
- He drinks too much.
- He doesn't trust people.
- He thinks people do not like him.

(b)
- There always are interesting discussions in classrooms, hallways, and dormitories.
- There are many opportunities to meet people from different cultures.
- One can experiment with a new life-style.
- Going to college gives many people the first opportunity to take responsibility for their lives.

(c)
- Snow covers Wisconsin for two-thirds of the year.
- It is difficult to buy fresh vegetables there in the winter.
- Travel is not easy during the winter in Wisconsin.
- Temperatures get so low that walls of the houses can crack, and car engines must be warmed with electrical devices.

B. The following paragraph from a student's paper appears to have no topic sentence. Devise a topic sentence that will work and underline the predicate.

It is necessary to make the rights and privileges of being Americans known to the Chinese people here in Los Angeles' Chinatown. It is also important to inform the general public of the problems confronting the Chinese community. There should be development of facilities in the areas of employment, physical and mental health, education, housing, and recreation. The city should establish a day care center. An old age home and a youth community center should be available in Chinatown. On the job training should be provided for new immigrants through vocational guidance centers. Bilingual education should be the method used in the schools of Chinatown.

C. Discuss the photograph below by writing one detailed paragraph with any of the following topic sentences.
A tower is a piece of art.
A tower is a symbol of our technological society.
A tower would make a unique house.
A tower can look eerie in the early morning hours.

What is the Shape of a Paragraph? 121

FIGURE 5-2
(Photo by Steven Robins.)

COHERENCE At both the essay and the paragraph level, coherence means the ability of the writing to stick together and at the same time to flow. Two devices help you to tie your sentences and paragraphs together gracefully: *natural order* and *word choice*. Using the most natural order for your subject is usually intuitive, so don't strain for coherence; instead, arrange your paper in the order that is the most logical and easiest to understand. Here are a few tips. It is important always to state the background before you make the points based on that background. And never place step three of a process before step two (unless you are using reverse order on purpose). In nonanalytic papers use chronological or process arrangements whenever appropriate because they automatically provide smooth shifts between ideas. Remember: you want to be understood, and you want your reader to be able to anticipate the order of the ideas in your essay.

Your choice of words also keeps your ideas flowing. Repetition of a key word that reinforces the controlling idea or the use of a synonym for a key idea within the essay or paragraph reminds the reader of a main point. But be very careful to select the right words when you use this technique. Below are two paragraphs, one that effectively uses repetition of a key word and synonyms, and another that tediously repeats and repeats and repeats.

> Paragraph 1
> The real American *Dream* is the *fantasy* that we can be as unmarked as those models in magazines, movies, and television commercials *appear* to be. This *quest* of the modern American woman is never realized, however, for *unerasable* are the *wrinkles,* the *blemishes*, and *scars* of aging. These are the *wrinkles* that cannot be *removed* with magical creams. These are the *blemishes* that must heal slowly and cannot be *prevented* with layers of pomades and packs and gels. These are the *scars* that come from living, and no "beauty plan" can cause them not to happen. But the *dream* perpetuates the great *cover-up.*

Note how the synonyms and repeated words tie the paragraph together.

> Paragraph 2
> Most Americans would find the life-styles of Hell's Angels repugnant. The Hell's Angels seem to engage in the most distasteful activities. They engage in communal sex orgies that would humiliate a "normal" American. The Hell's Angels engage in more aggressively violent activities than most people. The Hell's Angels fight with other Hell's Angels as often as they threaten or attack others. The bodies of the Hell's Angeles and the clothes of the Hell's Angels seem dirty, their dirty hair is matted, and the stench exuded from a gang of Hell's Angels would repulse most "normal" Americans. The Hell's Angels disdain the stable life that most Americans work to achieve.

You can see that the writer practically hits the readers over the head with repetition of "Hell's Angels," "most Americans," and that dead verb "engage." None of these words is significant to the point about life-styles, and thus such repetition breaks down the flow of the paragraph rather than lends coherence.

Transitions

Another way to control flow in your essay is by using transitions. These are connective words with three functions: to point out an addition to what has been said, to signal a contrast or a concession to the opposition, or to show a result. Here is a list of transitions you might want to select from.

> Addition or Expansion: moreover, furthermore, finally, last, first, also, in fact, for instance, in particular, in addition, besides, another, actually.
>
> Contrast or concession: yet, though, nevertheless, despite this, but, however, although, on the other hand, on the contrary, still, whereas, otherwise, now, in the past, instead, the truth is.

Results: thus, in any case, finally, therefore, hence, on the whole, in other words, as a result, then, predictably, now, all in all.

This list should be helpful when you're writing, but keep something in mind when you use it. Because a paragraph is brief, transitions can stick out awkwardly, defeating their purpose, unless you place and choose them cautiously. You don't want them to seem merely mechanical. This problem, which is not as common in the essay as in the paragraph, can be avoided without too much trouble. Here's how.

First, never weigh down a paragraph with too many transitions; use a variety of methods for coherence. Don't forget that a logical sequence of ideas or natural repetition of a key word can do the same trick. It is easy to tell if you have overdone it with transitions if you read what you have written aloud. If there are too many, they will call attention to themselves rather than keep the essay moving. Second, try not to place the transitions in the same position in each sentence. Many people fall into a habit of making the transition the first word of the sentence; they consequently fail to write interesting, varied sentences. Try, instead to insert the transition after the first word—or include it in the middle or at the end of a sentence to achieve a less blatant link between ideas. Then, too, you should, as always in writing, avoid the obvious. Don't use the same transition over and over. And avoid "to begin with" and "in conclusion" at the beginning and conclusion of your essay, for these say outright to the reader, "Hey, you dummy—this is the beginning (or ending), get it?"

Note how effectively transitions are used in the following paragraph from a student's essay.

Though it may sound strange, working in the dishroom at the college cafeteria has improved my study habits. *First* of all, this experience has shows me how to be a more organized worker. *Actually,* I used to pretend, *in the past,* that I was organized. *But the truth is* that I could never find what I was looking for. I stacked up in a corner of my room all of my papers, mail, books, anything that came into my hands. *Now, instead,* I have established a filing system for each of my classes and extracurricular activities. In the dishroom, since I have to work fast, I must keep my stacks of dishes perfectly in order. The dishroom has *also* taught me to be a doer, not a procrastinator. There one job gets done at a time, before the worker moves on to the next. I have used this method in studying during the last six months, and it has made a difference in my grades. *Another* habit I have carried over from the dishroom is careful scheduling. *Now,* I plan my homework according to the class test schedule—no more cramming for me. It's surprising how parallel the work in the dishroom is with homework, and it's a pleasure to find myself with such expeditious study habits.

EXERCISE Here is a paragraph from *Science and Human Values* by J. Bronowski. Identify the transitional words and phrases.

The discoveries of science, the works of art are explorations—more, are explosions, of a hidden likeness. The discoverer or the artist presents in them two aspects of nature and fuses them into one. This is the act of creation, in which an original thought is born, and it is the same act in original science and original art. But it is not therefore the monopoly of the man who wrote the poem or who made the discovery. On the contrary, I believe this view of the creative act to be right because it alone gives a meaning to the act of appreciation. The poem or the discovery exists in two moments of vision: the moment of appreciation as much as that of creation; for the appreciator must see the movement, wake to the echo which was started in the creation of the work. In the moment of appreciation we live again the moment when the creator saw and held the hidden likeness. When a simile takes us aback and persuades us together, when we find a juxtaposition in a picture both odd and intriguing, when a theory is at once fresh and convincing, we do not merely nod over someone else's work. We re-enact the creative act, and we ourselves make the discovery again. At bottom, there is no unifying likeness there until we too have seized it, we too have made it for ourselves.

B. The following excerpt from a student's essay does not hold together. Provide transitions for the passage so that it will flow better.

Christianity became popular in Japan because of the wave of Westernization. The Meiji Restoration aimed to make Japan into a modern country in order to seek equality with the West in the eyes of the rest of the world. The international world of the nineteenth century was completely dominated by the West. Since the Western countries believed themselves to be culturally superior to the East, the Japanese assumed that they had no chance to be considered equal unless they adopted Western ways. The adoption of many superficial aspects of Western culture was encouraged by the government. The people started to practice the Western style of life, adopting whatever they could of Western clothing, hairstyles, and eating habits. Western dress was prescribed for all court and official ceremonies in 1872. In 1873 the ban on Christianity was removed.

PARAGRAPH
DEVELOPMENT

The paragraph techniques in this chapter should help you expand and support each of your ideas within fully developed paragraphs. One of the most common flaws in college writing is inadequate development of paragraphs. A reader's eye can pick up this problem immediately because the paragraphs look too short. The presence of many paragraph breaks on a page is called overdifferentiation of paragraphs. It is true that overdifferentiated paragraphs are found often in print; journalists and advertisers often write paragraphs of just one, two, or three sentences. Does this fact mean that some professional writers do not accept the principles of paragraphing discussed in this chapter? Yes and no.

Your paragraphs will be longer, in most cases, than those found in newspapers, magazines, and even textbooks. The audience of a news article is not as homogeneous as that of your essays for college, so the writers must appeal to a broad group, not only insofar as interests are concerned but also in relation to education and experience. Within the group of readers are various educational levels and attention spans. In order to accommodate the various readers, most copy writers try to keep their material fairly simple and brief. In newspapers and magazines, too, the layout is often in columns, and brief paragraphs look attractive on the printed page. Advertisers and textbook writers often use short paragraphs to set off important material for emphasis. So do journalists. The point is that overdifferentiated paragraphing in these cases is deliberate and effective.

You would see, however, if you combined several of the paragraphs from a news item into one, that they would probably work into unified and coherent units that fit the standards of regular college essays. It's not that journalists have left out any elements of good paragraphs. They simply have broken up their paragraphs into smaller logical units in order to suit the needs of their audience. Doing so suits their purpose. For an example, evaluate the paragraphing in the following article from *Prevention Magazine*. You can see that the paragraphs are not just one or two sentences, but they are still much briefer than you would want any of yours to be unless you had a specific reason for cutting them short. Take a look at how you might logically combine the paragraphs from the following article to make them look more like those in expository essays for college.

Sugar, the Hidden Persuader*

Does our lust for sweetness make us all
so many dancing bears in the circus of processed food?

What happens in your mind just before you decide to reach for a candy bar or a dish of ice cream? Have you freely made a simple selection, or have you been manipulated at levels below your conscious awareness?

The latter possibility may actually be the case. For the pursuit of sugar can become an addiction that reshapes people's behavior. That's the argument advanced by Dr. Michael Cantor, assistant professor of psychology at Columbia University, and Richard J. Eichler in the April, 1977,

---

* "Sugar, the Hidden Persuader." Reprinted by special permission from October 1977 issue of Prevention Magazine, Emmans, Pa. Copyright 1977 by Rodale Press.

issue of *CHEMTECH*.

"Everyone knows that sweet things taste good," the authors state, "but few realize another important function that they have: sweetness is a supernormal reinforcer of behavior." According to this line of reasoning, a person placed in a situation where more positive forms of reinforcement or gratification such as love or high income are not forthcoming, may turn to sugar again and again. "In other words, 'sweetness' has come to be a substitute for that which is positive, that which is pursued.

"Some people compulsively eat large quantities of sweets and other foods in times of 'stress,'" Dr. Cantor and Eichler point out. "When they are lonely, when work is going badly, when there are family problems, or when their sex life is not up to par— in general when the probability of reinforcement is low—that is the time for a cookie, candy, cake or ice cream 'binge.'"

The result is a virtual addiction to sugar on a national scale, with processors adding sweeteners to everything from canned soup to salad dressings to boost sales. "Per capita consumption in the United States is a third of a pound of sweeteners per day," the authors report. "Sweets, like opiates, are immediate, supernormal reinforcers. Perhaps most tellingly, demand for both substances is relatively inelastic; despite a fourfold increase in the price of sucrose in 1974, per capita consumption of sweeteners fell only three percent."

In one study, laboratory rats made dependent on alcohol could only be weaned away from their habit by offering them a sugar water or saccharin solution instead. "Only a sweet taste could compete with the alcohol dependence," the authors note. Yet, "In choosing the sweet taste, over ethanol [alcohol], animals had convulsions, sacrificed calories and, in the case of saccharin preference, faced death from malnutrition . . . can it not be concluded that these animals gave up one 'addiction' for another?"

No wonder Dr. Cantor, and Eichler conclude that with sugar, "The Technologist and policymaker have in their hands a supernormal reinforcer that can be used to control the behavior of people just as surely as the circus trainer has the wherewithal to control the behavior of his dancing bears."

One logical rearrangement of the paragraphs might be to combine the first and second paragraph into one and to combine the third and fourth into one, leaving the others as they are. The first paragraph, as the article now stands, includes the lead-in device (see Chapter 3). The next paragraph in the current article gives the thesis. Certainly, these could work together as a typical introductory paragraph. The next (third) paragraph introduces the idea of sweets as positive reinforcers. The fourth paragraph exemplifies that idea, so in most essays the two would belong together. In each of the paragraphs following these, one idea is taken up and followed through. Although each point could be further developed, if information were needed and available, the combined paragraphs would work well. The last paragraph is brief, as is common for a conclusion. Other combinations could be made and new topic sentences drawn up for them. But you can see that basically the paragraphs hang together as they are when they are combined. Breaking them up may serve the readers, and at the same time it does not hinder the development of ideas, at least for this kind of journalism.

Dividing Paragraphs   You may have guessed that the paragraphs you will be writing for most essays will be, on the average, a third or a half page, typed and double spaced. This is by no means an ironclad rule—it could not be expected to govern the length of every paragraph you write—it is only a guideline so that your paragraphs are not grossly underdeveloped. One source of poor development is overgeneralizing your ideas. You already know that you cannot discuss, in more than a very general way, the duties of a high-school math teacher in a single paragraph, but you could handle in one detailed paragraph which classroom audiovisual aids are used by the math teacher in an algebra class. So the first step in good development is framing a topic you can say something about for each paragraph. Then develop your paragraph to the point that it covers your topic sentence, or fulfills your intention, one point after the other without leaving any blanks.

Essentially, begin a new paragraph where it is logical to do so as you write from your outline or notes. Sometimes you may find that covering the point of a paragraph takes three entries about the point, producing a paragraph of about nine sentences. Other entries may take only one sentence each. Also, you may have more entries for one point than for another. Paragraphing is rarely predictable from the outline alone. You need to start writing, letting your ideas flow, from the ideas suggested in the outline before you can decide exactly where to divide paragraphs. And sometimes even then changes are needed. You may well go back over your rough draft, in fact, to change your paragraph divisions. The structure of the paper and of the paragraph, of course, help you generate ideas along the way, but you should be careful not to allow yourself to be so fixed into a prescription that your writing loses its sparkle, in focusing on technique. Good writers are flexible so that their writing doesn't become mechanical, repetitious, or lifeless.

BUILDING PARAGRAPHS

Avoiding repetitiousness and at the same time covering the point thoroughly seems to require a delicate balance of examples and elaboration every step of the way. Some writers struggle to develop their ideas but, because they fail to imagine themselves communicating with readers, they cannot get very far. Do the readers expect elaboration on a point? Do the readers need to know exactly what is meant by a key term in the paragraph? These are important questions. By familiarizing yourself with the way in which the logic of successful paragraphs takes your readers into account, and by trying to use these logical sequences, adapting them to your personal writing style, you will find answers.

SEQUENCING OF SENTENCES

A paragraph contains only two kinds of sequences. You can analyze your paragraphs from sentence to sentence as you build them, making sure they are logical. A very good method of analyzing paragraphs is based on the discovery of Francis Christensen that both paragraphs and sentences in modern American writing seem to be "cumulative." That is, they begin with a base to which the rest of the sentence or the rest of the paragraph is added. What is added to the base can be viewed as a sequence of related ideas that detail, expand, and emphasize what is set forth in the first part. Christensen described these two sequences as either "coordination" or "subordination."

Coordination Emphasizes at the Same Level of Generality

T. S.	My room is cheerful
Adds detail (subordinates first sentence)	The wallpaper is a gay lavender.
Adds emphasis (at same level)	Colorful posters decorate the walls with happy messages.
Adds emphasis (at same level)	The room gets a lot of sunlight.

Subordination Adds Detail and Complexity at a More Specific Level of Generality

T. S.	My room is cheerful.
Adds detail (at more specific level)	The wallpaper is a gay lavender.
Adds still more detail (at more specific level)	It's the color of a carefree summer day.

In the preceding example, the two ideas at the same level—"The wallpaper is a gay lavender" and "Colorful posters decorate the walls with happy messages"—are coordinate. They reinforce the idea of cheerfulness, and both are as general. However, in the subordinate example, "The wallpaper is a gay lavender" subordinates, or takes a step further, the idea in the first sentence. Also, "It's the color of a carefree summer day" takes further the idea about the gay lavender wallpaper, so it is subordinate to the second sentence.

Infinite combinations of coordination and subordination are possible. A certain combination will result from your thinking through a specific topic as you write. You will subordinate when you feel your readers need further explanation or more details; you will coordinate when you feel your readers need another example to reinforce a point you have just explained. Every sentence you add to the topic or top sentence should fit into one of the two sequences, and you can determine just what to write next by keeping your readers' needs in mind, then subordinating or coordinating as needed.

Sometimes coordination will dominate the paragraph; sometimes subordination will.

Coordinate Sequence
T.S.   My apartment is disorderly around midterms.
    I simply cannot take the time to straighten up the place.
        Books are stacked up on tables, on top of cabinets, and even on the floor—wherever I last read them or set them.
        Also, the kitchen table generally has notebook paper, pens, clips, and used staples spread across it, leftovers from the papers I've been writing or the notes I've been recopying.
        My bed remains unmade each morning as I dash out of the house barely in time to make it to class after only a few hours sleep.
        The kitchen sink is half full of dishes when I wake up because by the time I get to bed I'm too sleepy to wash them.
        Worst of all, the trash is lined up in three or four bags next to the kitchen door.

(COORDINATION)

Subordinate Sequence
T.S.   Cartoons, which are geared mostly toward children, contain some of the most violent scenes imaginable.
    Nevertheless, because of the homorous framework these shows fit into, most viewers accept the violence without really questioning the effects it is having on children.
        In effect, this type of shows says that violence is acceptable and even funny.
            Krazy Kat can hit everyone in sight on the head with a brick, and children think such behavior is heroic and funny.
                If these behaviors are imitated both in play and in real-life situations, as studies claim they are, children are confusing the rewards of constructive behavior with the punishment for destructive behavior.
                    Beating a neighbor's child over the head should not for a moment, even in a child's fantasy world, be considered acceptable or joking behavior.

Most often, however, you will need to mix coordination with subordination, as is done in the following models. These models show you how to use the two kinds of sequences to build some common types of paragraphs. At times when you feel stuck writing a paragraph, you may want to imitate the following models, sentence by sentence, for your own paragraphs, using your own content. Otherwise, you may wish only to study these paragraphs to reinforce your understanding of how coordination and subordination can help you build paragraphs.

EXPLAINING AN IDEA: A MODEL

Suppose that you are writing a two- or three-page essay on "death as a business" for a sociology class and that you have narrowed it down to a descriptive essay about a recent trip to Forest Lawn Mortuary. Your thesis is that Forest Lawn is a cemetery in name only because it is designed more for the living than for the dead. The major outline divisions of your essay look like this:

I. Scenic park and playground
II. Cultural center for religion and the arts
III. Tourist attraction

You could certainly work each of these points into a well-developed paragraph by explaining which points of interest cater to the "life trade." By showing your readers three or four examples of how Forest Lawn is a recreation park and playground and then showing how people use the park areas for these activities, you could compose a very adequate paragraph on the subject of I. This sort of paragraph would demonstrate automatic unity and coherence because you would stick to your "place built more for the living than for the dead," and would follow up that concept by a logical progression of examples and expansions on those examples. Along these lines, you need only follow a few steps to develop your paragraphs into unified and coherent units with adequate coordination and subordination to bear out your ideas. If you adhere to the general formula explained here, you need not worry about slipping from your main idea nor fear that you have left out connective links.

Step One

Write a clear, precise topic sentence. At this level you take only one of your supports from the controlling idea of your thesis statement or one of the major subdivisions of your outline and make it into a sentence with a subject and predicate.

| Subject | Predicate |

Forest Lawn is a scenic park and playground.

What your reader now expects to learn is how Forest Lawn is a parkland. To fulfill this topic sentence you must stick to it—not go off on tangents about the financial success of Forest Lawn, the members of the board of directors, or descriptions of grave sites. Instead, follow up on the areas used by visitors for recreation and perhaps discuss the suitability of the site as a scenic park.

Step Two:
Subordinate

Return to the predicate of the topic sentence to see what might need further explanation. Which terms or concepts are still a bit fuzzy to your reader? For instance, why do you consider Forest Lawn "scenic"? Is this one of Forest Lawn's advertising promotions, or do you feel that this is the best way to describe the place? Perhaps here you might compare Forest Lawn with another park that is more familiar to your reader.

> Some Californians visit Forest Lawn regularly, and they insist that going to Forest Lawn is no different from spending a pleasant day among the rolling hills of Griffith Park, except that the Memorial Park is quieter.

Step Three:
Subordinate

Exemplify the predicate. In this paragraph either show one manner in which people use the park or explain something about the park that makes it attractive.

> Forest Lawn offers a lovely 480 acres on which to enjoy many activities.

Step Four:
Subordinate

Exemplify or expand on your example. In this case you might say something further about the expansive park.

> Acres of rolling green provide the perfect place for lovers to stroll and talk, or for children to play.

Step Five:
Coordinate

Emphasize with a second main support. Be sure to bring up another facet from the predicate.

> The advertisers of Forest Lawn actually encourage people to come to the park to enjoy themselves.

Step Six:
Subordinate

Explain or expand on the second support. Stick to the predicate.

> In the family section of a local newspaper, an article recommends that families come to spend the day at the park.

Step Seven:
Subordinate

Expand again or conclude with an interesting remark or lead-out transitional sentence.

> Perhaps this Californian habit of playing or loving beside dead people appears a bit irreverent at first; but the idea is catching on, apparently, since thousands of people visit Forest Lawn every year for pleasure.

Instead of this concluding remark, you might have alluded to the next section—on how Forest Lawn is also a cultural and religious center.

> People may hike around one morning on the manicured slopes, and they may plan to spend the afternoons visiting some of the art exhibits of the park.

DESCRIBING
A PROCESS:
A MODEL

For paragraphs in which you describe a method or the history of an event, you may wish to begin with the first step or earliest event or with the final step and last event explaining step to step whatever you are describing. You will want to derive the order of supports in the paragraph from your outline. For instance, if your paragraph is to describe the old-fashioned technique of baking bread, part of your outline might look like this:

A. Topic Sentence: Old-fashioned breadmaking is not difficult—it does, however, require that one follow the steps in the recipe very closely.
   1. Preparing dry ingredients
   2. Combining dry with wet ingredients
   3. Kneading
   4. Dough rising
   5. Baking
   6. Finishing touches

It would be easy to write a sentence or two on each entry, listing the steps involved in each part of the process.

In order to describe the process, try to concentrate on one step or event and to develop consecutive substeps of that event or step. Writing a process paragraph is much like reconstructing a story for a friend who knows nothing of the event you are describing. You must pay close attention to detail and chronological order of events, making sure that each time a new step is introduced, the readers are adequately prepared for it by the information you have already given.

First, state, if you wish, your topic sentence to direct the reader's attention. Next, state your first event or step and then elaborate on it. You are subordinating. Third, state the second step (coordinating it with the first step) and then elaborate on it, again subordinating. Continue in this fashion, each time taking the process a step further than the one before it. When you have developed all of the steps in a process paragraph, you may well have a sequence that is entirely coordinate or, if you have elaborated on the steps along the way, you will have a mixture of subordination and coordination. If you have a mixture of the two, make sure that the elaborations in the paragraph fulfill the promise put forth in the topic sentence, if you have given one. For example, if you have said that homemade bread is an "easy six-step process," make sure you have not only explained all six steps but demonstrated how easy the steps are.

One student's process paragraph follows. The levels of subordination and coordination are shown through the indentations.

To polish a good pair of leather shoes, use applicators and buffing techniques properly.
   Not any old rag around the house will do, though many people think so.
      The rag must, first of all, be clean.

What is the Shape of a Paragraph? 133

When you are applying the polish, the first step, use a soft muslin cloth, which you can probably find if you look among the rags for a piece of an old sheet.
Dab on the polish and then with the soft muslin rag smooth the polish on the shoes in circular motions.
Cover all the leather on the outside of the shoe.
After the polish is on (don't spare it), use a soft-bristled brush to work in the polish and bring out the shine.
A boar-bristle brush is best for this step.
Use sweeping motions and maintain the lines of the shoes: sweep across in the front, and on the sides use a lengthwise sweep.
The step most people ignore comes next; take a clean piece of terry cloth and, applying pressure, buff shoes to a brilliant shine.
That's the shine that will have been worth all your work.

DESCRIBING HOW SOMETHING LOOKS: A MODEL

Suppose you were to describe the architecture of a building or the peaceful atmosphere of your favorite scene. The best way might be to begin in the upper left-hand corner or boundary and move to the lower right corner; or you might begin at some other place. The key to writing this sort of physical description is that you base the movement in the paragraph on relationships between the parts of the object you are describing. In this kind of paragraph, when a topic sentence is present, it usually sets physical boundaries, and the rest of the paragraph discusses what lies within the boundaries. Your sequence could be quite similar to that of the paragraph about Forest Lawn on page 130.

You have quite a bit of latitude in arranging your ideas, but the coordination and subordination sequences will still be the basis for the arrangement. For example, you may want to open the paragraph with the most lovely part of the scene and move to sections you're less excited about. Perhaps you want to start with the section that shows the brightest color or demonstrates the most haphazard pattern. Nevertheless, as you move from part to part of the scene, you will be coordinating ideas. Most likely, you will also be subordinating as you detail what some of the parts look like. Here is a paragraph from Golding's "Thinking As A Hobby."* You'll notice that it has a top sentence, not a topic sentence. As you read through the paragraph, study the levels of subordination and coordination as they have been indented for you.

I must have been an unsatisfactory child for grownups to deal with.
    I remember how incomprehensible they appeared to me at first, but not, of course, how I appeared to them.
        It was the headmaster of my grammar school who first brought the subject of thinking before me, though neither in the way nor with the result he intended.
            He had some statuettes in his study.

They stood on a high cupboard behind his desk.
One was of a lady wearing nothing but a bath towel.
She seemed frozen in an eternal panic lest the bath towel slip down any farther; and since she had no arms, she was in an unfortunate position to pull the towel up again.
Next to her, crouched the statuette of a leopard, ready to spring down at the top drawer of a filing cabinet labeled A–AH.
My innocence interpreted this as the victim's last, despairing cry.
Beyond the leopard was a naked, muscular gentleman, who sat, looking down, with his chin on his fist and his elbow on his knee.
He seemed utterly miserable.

COMPARING THINGS OR IDEAS: A MODEL

Writing a paragraph in which you describe and discuss the similarities and differences between two or more things may be the most common college assignment. You might use the following process to build such a paragraph.

Step One

Set forth what exactly you wish to compare in a clear topic sentence derived from the controlling idea of your thesis. Remember that the predicate of the topic sentence focuses the rest of the paragraph. Suppose you are comparing the ideas of two writers on the subject of "what makes someone truly educated." Your first sentence might look like this.

> Both Lincoln Steffens and Alan Simpson, in their articles on education, believe that to be educated in the true sense of the word means to be actively skeptical and intellectually aggressive.

Step Two: Subordinate

Explain what you mean by offering an example. If the predicate seems clear, you want to begin to develop your first point, first about Steffens.

> Steffens states that "everything in the world remains to be done or done over," that "everything is still in the air waiting to be researched and rewritten."

Step Three: Subordinate

Explain your first main idea. Your readers will want to know the relationship between the quotation and the point of the paragraph. What makes someone truly educated? Therefore, you need to expand, add detail to, the second sentence.

> He implies that no real student just sits back and absorbs what he or she is taught.

Step Four: Subordinate

Expand on the explanation. Still, it's not entirely clear how you are backing up the predicate of the topic sentence. The readers will be interested in what a student does with the learning other than "absorb."

---

* "Thinking as a Hobby." Permission to reprint granted by *Travel Magazine,* Inc., Floral Park, N.Y.

The application of what he or she is learning is important, and the student should recognize that this learning can be demonstrated only by upgrading something he or she learns about.

Step Five: Coordinate

Now that the first point is clear, the second part of the point in the predicate comes forth.

In agreement with this view, Simpson talks about looking deeper, past the "sham."

Step Six: Subordinate

Explain the second point: "What does it mean?" The readers wonder.

One should be able, according to Simpson—and Steffens would agree—to listen to and detect a false argument, to assess its inaccuracy.

Step Seven: Subordinate

Expand on the point. The readers would want you to take this last point a step further. What's the difference between a "sham" and a fact? What does the real student do that the less involved student fails to do?

According to Simpson, taking notes from a lecturer and accepting tradition is a sham, but to argue with the lecturer or to challenge the tradition is a sign of education.

Step Eight: Subordinate

Directly compare by expanding the last point. Now that the points of each writer are clear, show the similarity.

This can be compared to Steffen's demand that the educated revise the intellectual world.

Step Nine: Subordinate

Expand the last point, one notch more, and wind up the paragraph. The readers need a key concept to take away from the paragraph and to remember.

The key word for both writers seems to be "action."

A FEW WORDS ABOUT USING PARAGRAPH MODELS

The models in this chapter are guides. Many good thoughts are in your head, no doubt, but you must get them down on paper in the clearest and most expressive manner possible. You want to communicate, but the transference from your mind to the paper causes some problems. Here is where models and a conscious effort to use coordination and subordination can help. They suggest ways for you to put down your thoughts and remind you of ideas you might otherwise have forgotten to include for the readers. Models can help you fulfill your commitment as a writer because in most paragraphs you will want to make a promise to the reader in the opening sentences and spend the rest of the paragraphs fulfilling the promise through sufficient logical support. Each model does just that.

Models are flexible and allow for you to express your own personal style through your various choices: to use or not to use a topic sentence, what type of coherence devices you select, how long your paragraphs will be. These will be the marks of your unique style.

136 The Writer's Practical Rhetoric

EXERCISES A. Place the sentences in this paragraph in the best possible order, and add transitions.

Thieves, though, can get into any place they wish to enter, no matter what safeguards there may be.

I am certain I would protect my family and myself if someone entered my house, and that is all there is to the matter.

I would use any weapon I could.

Because I care for my family, I try always to protect them as well as I am able.

My house is equipped with dead bolts on the door and locks on all windows.

We have a trained dog who barks at any strangers who come to the house.

And often thieves have knives and guns with them when they burglarize homes.

They can, despite what everyone would hope, pick locks and trick even the most loyal dogs.

It would grieve me terribly to see my little girl hurt by a burglar.

B. Describe the pattern or patterns of the following paragraphs. Select two of the paragraphs. Explain the subordinate and coordinate sequences in them by writing out the paragraphs in the indented form.

(a)

Just as the opportunity must be seized in economics, it must be seized in politics. For example, in 1974 there were many political opportunities which were taken by those who were ready. In the United States, the Democrats took advantage of the Watergate scandal and the fall of President Nixon to attain a landslide victory in Congress. In Ethiopia the young military officers overthrew the aging Emperor Haile Selassie and his advisors. A spy scandal in West Germany allowed Helmut Schmidt to capture the opportunity to succeed Willy Brandt as Chancellor. (From a student's paper.)

(b)

The loud speaker in the East Los Angeles Stadium screamed first call for the Bee won hundred yard dash. I put my warm up shoes on and began to jog my warm up laps. In the middle of my warm up, the speaker again cried out second call for the one hundred yard dash. I hurried and put on my new track shoes that my mother had purchased the day before and walked slowly over to the starting line. I looked at the now nine empty lanes and wondered which lane would be filled by the one who was really best. For months I had worked to get where I stood now, and in about ten seconds or less my worries and possibly my dreams would come true. (From a student's paper.)

(c)

Not only industrial production is ruled by the principle of continuous and limitless acceleration. The educational system has the same criterion: the more college graduates, the better. The same in sports: every new record is looked upon as progress. Even the attitude toward the weather seems to be determined by the same principle. It is emphasized that this is "the hottest day in the decade," or the coldest, as the case may be, and I suppose some people are comforted for the inconvenience by the proud feeling that they are witnesses to the record temperature. One could go on endlessly giving examples of the concept that consistant increase of quantity constitutes the goal of our life; in fact, that it is what is meant by "progress."

Erich Fromm, from The Revolution of Hope, *p. 37.*

C. Name four or five details that might support each of the following possible topic sentences.
  (a) A garage at a gas station is not a comforting place to spend the afternoon.
  (b) Old books are for holding and touching and looking at, not just for reading.
  (c) New cars are not built to last for many years.
  (d) Animals have some of the same physical expressions as do humans.
  (e) A simple, rustic cabin near a pine forest surrounding a small lake is a relaxing location for a summer holiday.

D. Name at least three details that might support each of the following potential topic sentences and suggest which of the models on pages 130 to 133 might be an appropriate pattern of development for those details.
  (a) Just as clothes affect an individual's personality, so it is true that furniture determines the character of a dwelling.
  (b) People in markets exercise little concern for others.
  (c) The money spent enforcing antidrug laws could be used to improve other more important conditions, especially in the inner city.

E. Write a spatially arranged one-paragraph description of the building in the accompanying photograph. The topic sentence of the paragraph should convey on overall, dominant impression you derive from the picture.

FIGURE 5-3
(Photo by Steven Robins.)

6

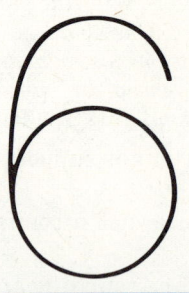

What Is a Good Sentence?

Most of the time you probably don't stop to think about individual sentences and their structure when you write or read. Yet flowing, meaningful sentences are the mark of a mature writing style. Learning to develop such sentences is surprisingly easy and enjoyable. You need to practice two methods: sentence combining and sentence mimicry, both aimed at giving your sentences a professional flair.

"A subject and a verb combined to form a complete thought" is the traditional definition of the sentence; but what makes the difference between a mediocre sentence and an effective one can be the amount of conscious sentence combining practiced in the revision stage. When additions are made to basic sentences, the sentences take on more texture. For example, both of these sentence groups say the same thing, but what is the difference in their effects on the reader?

> John is a librarian. As a librarian, he is very efficient. John is also an organizer of events. These events are for the college extracurricular programs.

> John, who is a very efficient librarian, is also an excellent organizer of extracurricular events for the college.

Notice that combining the individual sentences in the first group into one coherent thought has de-emphasized certain sentences in order to explain basically who John is and what his involvement is with the college's extracurricular activities. Also, observe how much smoother the second sentence sounds when read aloud, whereas the first group of sentences produces a disjointed, choppy effect.

FIGURE 6-1
The potter evens out the rough lines in his pot as the writer smooths out rough spots in sentences, adding flow, balance, and rhythm. (Photo by Steve Dierks.)

Had you wanted to emphasize that John is an excellent librarian, you might have combined the sentences in this way:

> John, who is a successful organizer of extra-curricular events for the college, is also an excellent librarian.

There is a real pleasure and sense of creativity to be derived from experimenting with different sentence patterns because the great variety in these patterns promises multiple possibilities for expressing any idea. When you begin to juggle the order within your sentences, to experiment with various connective words, or to place emphasis in a variety of positions with various punctuation, it dawns on you that you have the power to convince through your strategies at the sentence level as well as through the content of your argument. You realize that your writing works for you.

FOLLOWING PATTERNS

Sentences can be combined quite naturally most of the time by simple imitation of the sentence patterns of other writers. The sentence patterns used by good writers can be categorized into a few basic structures, which can be built by using five devices: coordination, subordination, active or passive voice, reordering, and balance and rhythm.

Even if you might never compose sentences as choppy as the first group illustrated on page 138, you can enhance your natural skills with language and add precision and variety to your statements by practicing revision of your sentences, a process that makes you conscious of the impact behind your words, one that is guaranteed to improve your writing. Notice how many ways the following short sentences can be combined—and these are only a few of the ways!

Components

Anna studied for the grammar test for five hours.

Anna knew the parts of speech by heart.

                                                but
                                                so

Results

Anna studied for the grammar test for five hours, and she knew the parts of speech by heart.

Because Anna had studied for the grammar test for five hours, she knew the parts of speech by heart.

Though Anna knew the parts of speech by heart, she studied for the grammar test for five hours.

Either Anna studied for the grammar test for five hours, or she knew the parts of speech by heart.

Anna, who studied for the grammar test for five hours, knew the parts of speech by heart.

After studying for the grammar test for five hours, Anna knew the parts of speech by heart.

Anna, who knew the parts of speech by heart, studied for the grammar test for five hours.

Having studied for the grammar test for five hours, Anna knew the parts of speech by heart.

To know the parts of speech by heart, Anna studied for the grammar test for five hours.

And certainly there are a number of other possibilities, each demonstrating a slightly different emphasis, a different rhythm, a different relationship between the key ideas.

You may be saying to yourself, "I won't even be able to get out the first word if I have to think which pattern to use all the time!" You would be justified in feeling this way. The clue here is always to rephrase your sentences during the revision stage of your paper. First, write your rough draft as you usually would and then look that draft over with your attention focused on the sentence structure. Simply look at consecutive sentences to see whether by combining, inverting, or embedding parts of them you can clarify the relationships between the ideas in those sentences. See whether you can direct the concentration of your reader to the idea that you most want to emphasize.

COORDINATION

Coordination implies the setting up of a balance; and when you balance your sentences, you are really making the decision to emphasize equally the sentence parts that are positioned on both sides of a coordinating conjunction (and, for, so, but, or, nor, yet, either ... or, neither ... nor, both ... and, not only ... but also). Looking back at the sentences on page 140, you find

> Anna had studied for the grammar test for five hours, and she knew the parts of speech by heart.

The use of the coordinating conjunction *and* in this case signals that *Anna had studied for five hours* is equally important to the fact that *she knew the parts of speech by heart*. The writer wants neither of the statements to be more important than the other. Below are some other examples of coordination.

1. *And* signals an addition: I am tired of you, and I am sick of your shenanigans!

2. *But* indicates a contrast: Jules is a quiet person, but that doesn't mean he has no feelings.

3. *So* indicates a result: English teachers are always emphasizing the importance of good grammar in everyday speech, so in class I am careful to think before I speak.

4. *Yet* and *but* function similarly: The United States is supposedly a free country with "equality and justice for all," yet many people have suffered persecution.

5. *Or* signals an alternative: Either the cat is sleeping, or he is causing trouble.

6. Any coordinating link takes a semicolon when the other commas in the clause might confuse or blur the separation between the main ideas: Woodrow Wilson was compelled to dispel any feelings of negative self-worth; and this, in part, explains his striving for power, achievement, and perfection.

PUNCTUATION POINTERS: COORDINATING CONJUNCTIONS

1. When a coordinating conjunction is used between what would otherwise be two complete sentences, a comma precedes the conjunction.
2. If the coordinating conjunction were removed, the coordination could be attained by the use of a semicolon.
3. A semicolon precedes the coordinating conjunction between what would otherwise be two complete sentences in which there are commas (6 above).

Another way to coordinate is to combine equally important elements from several sentences equally and put them together as a series within one sentence with a coordinating conjunction between the final two elements. The sentence

> Mary, Jane, and Anita are the best tennis players on campus.

is really composed of three ideas.

> Mary is one of the three best tennis players on campus.
> Jane is one of the three best tennis players on campus.
> Anita is one of the three best tennis players on campus.

PUNCTUATION POINTERS: SERIES

When punctuating a series of words, phrases, or clauses, it is most clear to place commas after all but the last element in the sequence. Note the components of the following coordinated sentences:

1. Love develops in three stages: attraction, infatuation, and settling in.
2. Bob did not go with the hikers, horseback riders, or swimmers who went to the mountains, for he preferred to stay at home.
3. Hann's naive, trite, and uninformed concept of the effects of technology on humaneness cannot be taken seriously.

Sentence 2 has two sets of coordination in it. First, there are the two main clauses—of equal emphasis and connected by *for: Bob did not go with the hikers, horseback riders, or swimmers who went to the mountains* and *he preferred to stay home.* Second, there is the series that includes *hikers* and *horseback riders* and *swimmers*, each of which is given equal importance, the coordinating conjunction being *or.*

It is very boring to read ideas connected only by simple coordination. (Think of someone who patches most of his or her speech patterns with *and* or *but.*) You should use coordination precisely and sparingly, for there are many other more sophisticated sentence patterns that point out the exact relationships between any two or three ideas that you may want to link.

SUBORDINATION

Subordination usually requires that one idea be less important than the others. If you are subordinate to your boss, you are dependent on him or her in a sense; if one clause is subordinated to another in your sentence, it is grammatically dependent on another and often it is less emphatic. Subordination, then, is a sentence pattern used when two ideas are *not* to be treated or understood as equal. The subordinated clause is added to a base, or independent, clause. Subordinate clauses may be seen as expansions on an independent clause or on a part of it.

To "tilt the balance" a bit to one side—to emphasize one idea and to subordinate the other—you simply add the appropriate subordinating conjunction: *because, since, whereas, although, when, where, after, before, as, so that, unless* (or others)—or a relative pronoun like *who, whose, which, what, whom, that*—to the sentence that you want to de-emphasize. Here is an example of this process:

Components:

There are many windows close to us.

We have a beautiful view of the city.

Results:

Since there are many windows close to us, we have a beautiful view of the city.

We have a beautiful view of the city since there are many windows close to us.

In some sentences, the meaning drastically changes if the emphasis pattern is reversed:

Components:

Margaret drank the warm coffee.

She felt better.

Results:

Margaret drank the warm coffee after she felt better.
(implies that she couldn't stand coffee while she was ill)

After she drank the warm coffee, Margaret felt better.
(implies the coffee was the cure)

or look at the difference between

Because she is beautiful, I love her.

and

Because I love her, she is beautiful.

RELATIVE PRONOUN CLAUSE Another way to subordinate is to place an idea that you want to de-emphasize in a relative pronoun clause. Simply remove repeated nouns and pronouns and attach *who, whose, which, what, whom,* or *that* to the idea. As in the placement of other modifiers, it is important to place the clause introduced by a relative pronoun next to the word it explains. Some sentences give less trouble than others.

John, who is the best runner on the team, is an above-average student.

Anna, who had studied for the grammar test for five hours, knew the parts of speech by heart.

But look at the confusion that is caused by a misplaced clause in this sentence:

Mrs. Jones gave her daughter a check for the sweater, which was quite large.

Does *which was quite large* refer to the sweater or the check? As the student has written it, it refers to the sweater; in fact, she meant it to describe the generous check. Still, this combining technique is easy to use. Suppose you want to join two sentences.

Components:

The sounds of all animals have common characteristics.

These characteristics meet the feeding and mating needs of the particular animal.

Results:

The sounds of all animals have common characteristics that meet the mating and feeding needs of the particular animal.

or

Components:

Lolita "shipwrecked" Humbert.

Lolita can be seen as a heartbreaker.

Results:

Lolita, who can be seen as a heartbreaker, "shipwrecked" Humbert.

For variety, make an appositive of a descriptive phrase. An appositive follows directly a noun or pronoun and renames it, as in the following:

Humboldt, a great and crazy poet, led a wonderful life.

Combine some of your sentences by leaving off the relative pronoun and verb. For example:

Sentence with relative pronoun clause:	John, who is a librarian, teaches X-90, which is a political science research class.
Sentence with appositive:	John, who is a librarian, teaches X-90, a political science research class.

X-90 is a political science research class, so the writer has chosen to omit the relative pronoun (*which*) and verb (*is*) and to place the phrases in apposition. For variety, the writer has maintained the relative pronoun (*who*) in the first part of the sentence.

PASSIVE VOICE VERSUS ACTIVE VOICE

Verbs in the active voice say what the subject is doing. Verbs in the passive voice say what is being done to the subject.

```
                     Active
            Subject     Verb
Passive: Smith was elected treasurer because he is honest.
```

Whether you choose to write a sentence in active or passive voice depends on whether you want to emphasize the doer of the action or the receiver of the action in the sentence. However, you may be cautioned by a wary science or history instructor to avoid the passive construction altogether. History and science are disciplines that emphasize the *doer*. Unless you deliberately use the passive voice to achieve an objective stance (for example, to avoid an inessential use of *I*) and to emphasize the *thing done* rather than the *doer*, use the active voice. This advice does not mean to suggest that the passive voice is any less effective than the active voice; in some instances, it is even more effective. Note the difference in the emphases in these two sentences:

```
                              Receiver
                    Active      of
         Doer       Verb       Action
Active: Copernicus shocked the world of science when he asserted that man
        was not the center of the universe.

         Receiver
           of              Passive
         Action            Verb         Doer
Passive: The world of science was shocked by Copernicus when he asserted
         that man was not the center of the universe.
```

Both sentences say approximately the same thing, but the active voice emphasizes *who did the shocking*, whereas the passive voice construction emphasizes *who was shocked*.

Be careful not to overuse the passive voice; it is generally more direct to say, "Three gaily dressed, costumed men told the tale," than to say, "The tale was told by three gaily dressed, costumed men." However, if you find the subject of the sentence relatively unimportant, you can feel free to revise the sentence using the passive voice. Vague and indefinite subjects such as, in some cases, *someone* or *people* weaken the sentence. The passive voice is then preferable.

Weak: People believe that open-mindedness is the highest virtue.
Better: It is believed that open-mindedness is the highest virtue.
Weak: The writer wrote the book in 1909.
Better: The book was written in 1909.
Weak: Someone explained the rules to me before I began.
Better: The rules were explained to me before I began.

It is extremely important to keep in mind that the use of the passive voice is simply another way for you to direct your emphasis. It is neither all good nor all bad—use it for appropriate occasions, and do not find yourself adhering to inflexible rules either way.

REORDERING SENTENCES

Many phrases or clauses can be rearranged so that your sentences are *varied* and *focused*. A simple case is when you have two sentence parts such as

> Because Anna had studied for the grammar test for five hours,/she knew the parts of speech by heart.

Suppose you already have several sentences beginning with the word *because* (or with a similar subordinate clause up front). An easy way to achieve variety is to *reverse* the order of the clauses or to move a phrase to a different part of the sentence.

> Anna knew the parts of speech by heart because she had studied for the grammar test for five hours.

Here is another example:

> This book gives to the Chicano a detailed view of the power and technology that he once possessed.

The phrase *to the Chicano* can be placed in front of the sentence without changing the meaning, and the alteration will add variety to a paragraph that opens too many sentences with *This book* or a similar construction.

The following sentence has four phrases that might be rearranged to add sentence variety.

> As a team we always lectured on Thursday in Mosher Hall.

The best way to tell whether phrases or clauses can be rearranged more successfully is to try the sentence parts in a number of positions, noting changes in the meaning of the sentence.

Certain sentence parts cannot be rearranged coherently because the phrase in question must be placed next to the word it modifies. Usually, by reading your sentence aloud, you can determine whether the new arrangement works. The flaw in sentence structure illustrated below is very common, and at times it can be not only misleading but also very funny.

> *Before engaging in a love affair*, Philomela is told that her sister died.

Since the italicized phrase applies to Philomela, it must be placed next to her name. A variation might be

> Philomela, *before engaging in a love affair*, is told that her sister died.

But the following placement of modifiers is confusing:

> Philomela is told of her sister's death *before engaging in a love affair*.

It is unclear to whom the love affair belongs: is it Philomela's or her sister's?

BALANCE AND RHYTHM

Well-combined sentences sound pleasant when read aloud partly because we intuitively listen for certain rhythms—signaled by marks of punctuation, by directional movement, by parallelisms, and by sentence length.

SENTENCE LENGTH There is no single length of sentence that you should strive for. Average length among professional writers is about twenty words, but one of the things that make for effective writing is variety in sentence length. The most emphatic presentations are those in which there are a few long sentences and then, suddenly, a short one:

> As this essential creativity is continually suppressed, it is stifled and a powerfully destructive and repressive force grows up in its place. Further stifling the women's creativity, emotional stability, and ability to communicate, this destructive force leaves the women with little effective means of self-expression. [Their most important tie to the world around them is severed.] With the lines of communication destroyed, the force has nearly full reign in the women, causing the repression, destruction, and isolation in their lives, and closing the doors to fulfillment of their basic human needs . . .

Strive for balance and rhythm; variety in sentence length and shifts between coordination and subordination add to the readability of sentences.

PARALLELISM When used properly and not to excess, coordination achieves balance and rhythm through parallelism or uniformity of word and phrase formation. In *I came, I saw, I conquered*, each group of words is parallel, for each is made up of a subject and verb. Notice the parallelism in the following examples:

> My reservation in this matter is due [to my inability] to understand your demands and [to my fear] of the consequences were I to agree.
>
> In the key role of the play, Harriet performed with [grace], [precision], and [sensitivity].
>
> When I get an idea for a poem, I want [to leap into the air], [to scream at the moon], [to grab history by its collar and shake it].

To maintain parallelism in this sort of coordination, you must use the same part of speech (noun, verb, etc.) for each element in the series.

Not parallel: I was happy, energetic, and wanted to leap over fences.
Parallel: I was happy and energetic, and I wanted to leap over fences.
Parallel: Happy and energetic, I wanted to leap over fences.
Parallel: I was happy, I was energetic, and I wanted to leap over fences.

MARKS OF PUNCTUATION   Your writing can also be improved by the deliberate placement of dashes and semicolons. Both of these forms of punctuation can make your sentences rhythmic, balanced, and emphatic.

The Dash   Dashes show special emphases: interruptions, parenthetical comments, initial or final focus, and illustrative series. To set off a part of a sentence with dashes is to call attention to it. Often, the same phrases set off by dashes could be separated from the rest of the sentence by commas or parentheses, but with less attention directed to them. An example of each use follows; read the sentences aloud and observe the rhythm and emphasis in each sentence.

PARENTHETICAL

Even in Europe, the great strings of beachfront hotels along the Costa del Sol and at Palma de Mallorca have been influenced strongly—and not always happily—by Miami Beach architecture and design.

Esquire, December 1975

FINAL FOCUS

It's everywhere in the spring—love.

INITIAL FOCUS

Big-city life—I have to admit that I love it.

The study of great books is essential to human understanding—an understanding that today appears to be on the wane.

INTERRUPTIONS

He replied, "Of course—I mean, of course *not*—why would I do a thing like that?"

SERIES WRAP-UP

Equal pay for equal work, respect for individuality, recognition in the job market—that's what women want.

The Semicolon   The semicolon is used as a symbol of equivalency to show that the parts of the sentence separated by the semicolon are to be equally emphasized. Two independent clauses separated by a semicolon, therefore, are coordinated. As perhaps its most important function, the semicolon serves to relate the thoughts in two clauses. The writer might be showing one of three things about the relationship by using a semicolon: (1) that the independent clauses are equal and separate but are linked to one idea; (2) that although the clauses could stand alone, the second amplifies the first; or (3) that the second directly contrasts the first.

EQUIVALENCE

Joseph walked to school every day in spite of nasty weather; most of his friends thought he was foolish.

Note that the emphasis would remain the same even if the order of the ideas were reversed.

AMPLIFICATION

Helen White was the girl all the boys in Winesburg sought; she was beautiful, rich, and intelligent.

CONTRAST

Anyone can rewrite a paper; not everyone can rewrite a paper well.

Situated between independent clauses, the semicolon signals a link between complete thoughts. The rhythm is less fluid and slightly more formal than it is with the coordinating conjunctions; for variety, however, and in moderation, they may be used interchangeably. (Note the use of the semicolon in the preceding sentence.)

Be careful not to place complete independent clauses together without either a coordinating conjunction or a semicolon.

DIRECTIONAL MOVEMENT

Which pattern of movement—*backwards* or *forwards*—you choose for your sentences also affectsthe rhythm and meaning. Vary the rhythm and focus of your sentences by varying the direction. Periodic sentences move forwards (towards the period), and cumulative sentences move backwards (toward the first word of the sentence). The reader's attention is drawn towards the period or towards the first part of the sentence.

Periodic (Forward)

Before I had time to refuse, [he had slammed his foot on the accelerator].

Cumulative (Backward)

[She drunkenly made her way across the room], knocking her hips into tables as she moved, swinging her arms in weird contortions, and singing "Blue Moon" as loudly as she could.

Whether you select backward movement, as in the second example, or forward movement, as in the first example, is simply a decision about effect: the rhythmic, almost poetic sway of the cumulative sentence seems to fit the subject matter in the second sentence. In fact, the frequency of cumulative sentences in modern essays should encourage you to write them. They so resemble the natural flow of thought that they are often more easily incorporated into a rough draft than periodic sentences, which tend to be assembled from simple sentences during the revision stage.

Cumulative sentences may be developed in much the same way as the paragraphs discussed in Chapter 5. That is, effective cumulative sentences are a logical sequence of clauses and phrases built through coordination and subordination. The particular point of the sentence will, naturally, dictate how you develop it, being that certain points require more expansion than others. You might try numbering as you indent your sentence parts to keep track as you write. The base clause, always first in the cumulative sentence, is number 1. The next phrase or clause can be numbered 2 if it expands on (subordinates) the base, or it may be a 1, merely a restatement of the first phrase (any two phrases saying the same thing have the same number and are coordinate). The next may be another two if it expands on the base (subordinate to the first clause and coordinate with the second) or a 3 if it expands on (subordinates) the preceding clause and so on. Note the numbering of the sentences below.

1. He was vigorously telling old war stories to the women at the bar,
    2. his arms flashing about as if to keep his enemies at a distance, [an example of 1]
    2. his smile wide [an example of 1]
        3. turning to a snicker now and then. [an expansion of 2]

1. She was an outgoing young woman,
    2. with a deep-pitched voice [an expansion on 1]
        3. that bellowed when she spoke to strangers, [an expansion on 2]
            4. especially to men. [an expansion on 3]

1. The non-smoker has every right to breathe clean air,
    2. not the smoke-polluted air one finds everywhere these days, [an expansion on 1]
        3. in school, [an example of 2]
        3. in restaurants, [an example of 2]
        3. in elevators, and [an example of 2]
        3. even in doctors' offices. [an example of 2]

1. Christmas is a very festive time of the year in my family,
    2. full of surprises and love. [an expansion on 1]

Cumulative sentences are pleasurable to write, with the sense of immediacy they allow, for once the base clause has been written, further details can be added more or less as they occur to you.

Remember, however, that most writers mix patterns of movement as a device to achieve varied stylistic effects. In fact, do not forget the value of short sentences, especially when you want to emphasize a point or pose a climactic remark. Use longer sentences to amplify the shorter ones. Keep your purpose and your audience in mind as you develop sentence strategies. Don't forget you are communicating to an audience.

EXERCISES   A. Combine each group of sentence components in at least two ways and explain your purpose.
1. (a) My father had worked for an automobile firm since he came to California in the middle 1940s.
   (b) In about 1953 he decided to go to work for himself.
   (c) He chose to be a landscape gardener.
2. (a) When my father had worked for someone else his income was about forty-five hundred a year.
   (b) In 1955 his yearly income had risen to twenty-five thousand.
3. (a) Being sick was second nature for me.
   (b) Trips to and from the hospital were a matter of course.
4. (a) The nurses explained to me why I couldn't move and what they were going to do to help me.
   (b) However, I was still very upset.
5. (a) A married couple must show an interest in each other's hobbies.
   (b) If they don't, one or the other may go astray to find someone to share his or her "happy times" with.
6. (a) Big money can involve international struggles.
   (b) Bringing together several successful people can also mean a fusion of egos.
7. (a) Distribution can be the independent's worst enemy.
   (b) In the financing stage of a picture, a distribution deal can be a major factor.
8. (a) There are no windows close to us.
   (b) The only view we have is four ugly walls.
9. (a) I find that in most businesses the owners get carried away with profitmaking.
   (b) I have never seen a guideline that dictates or even suggests the amount of profit one piece of equipment should make.
10. (a) Some native Americans were nomadic hunters who followed the buffalo.
    (b) Some were primarily farmers who tended peach orchards or raised corn and melons in the fertile river valleys.

B. Combine the sentences in each group below in different ways, each time subordinating different elements.
1. Dr. Albert Norras is wanted by the F.B.I.
   He is a Communist.
   Dr. Norras is a leader of an occult revolutionary group.
   He is usually the guest speaker at the radical assembly open meeting.
2. I would not stop reading over my uncle's shoulder.
   My uncle became annoyed.
   My uncle threw the newspaper into the fire.
3. The building on the corner lot is for sale.
   The lot is in a good location.
   The lot is right in the middle of a busy business district.
4. My roommate makes sounds.
   I like my roommate.
   The sounds are strange.
   The sounds are much like primitive mating calls.
5. Sunland Oil Corporation reported high earnings.
   Sunland Oil Company is a subsidiary of Amalgamated Resources.
6. John ate heavily at the Thanksgiving dinner.
   The Thanksgiving dinner was bountiful.
   John cannot control himself.
7. Produce prices rose sharply.
   There was a frost in the valley.
   The truck drivers were striking.
8. Having to tell your best friend that your friendship is over is difficult.
   You still care for that person.
   You know that he or she is a dishonest backstabber.

C. Change the active constructions below to passive forms. Describe the difference in meaning or emphasis. When would the active form be more desirable? The passive form?
1. The president made an error which the company had to pay for no matter how it was explained away.
2. People believe that love is felt only by people.
3. Only a small number of immigrants survived the long months of hiding until someone secured their passage from Russia to the United States.
4. The industrial elites were controlling the economic shoestrings of the nation by 1900.
5. The necessary equipment for the magic act arrived on time, but the magician somehow did not agree to use it.

D. Change these passive constructions to active forms. Describe the difference in emphasis between the passive and active versions of

each sentence. When would passive form be most desirable? Active form?
1. The wine was spoiled by someone.
2. As a result of their outstanding efforts in a variety of fields, the fraternity of scholars was awarded a special citation.
3. Much more can be said in favor of forced busing than can be said against it.
4. The company's earnings were assessed by the tax commissioner and they were found to be substantial.
5. Ugly, festering wounds are often found on the bodies of young antelopes.
6. On October 22, 1962 the United States was informed by President Kennedy that the Soviet Union had begun to build missile bases in Cuba.
7. On the television show, the Jeffersons are portrayed as a black family who have climbed their way up the social ladder and can lend an occasional hand to those less fortunate than they are, but the Jeffersons otherwise give the audience a very poor impression of black people.
8. That the world and its people were created by one Almighty God who is supreme is believed by the Aoholi tribesmen.

E. Identify the structures by numbering each of the cumulative sentences below.
1. *It is the vast darkness of a cavern's mouth, the cavern of anterior darkness whence issues the stream of consciousness.*   D. H. Lawrence
2. *The pear tree across the road opposite was now in full and frosty bloom, the twigs and branches springing not outward from the limbs but standing motionless and perpendicular above the horizontal boughs like the separate and upstreaming hair of a drowned woman sleeping upon the uttermost floor of the windless and tideless sea.*
    William Faulkner
3. *He was walking ahead of me along Fifth Avenue in his alert, aggressive way, his hands out a little from his body as if to fight off interference, his head moving sharply here and there, adapting itself to his restless eyes.*   F. Scott Fitzgerald
4. *The literature of our society dealing with imprisonment and capital punishment is extensive, including contributions by Tolstoy, Camus, Dostoyevsky, and Sartre.*   Theodore Roszak
5. *Yet, as I said before, nonviolence has the power of moral suasion, which makes it possible to solicit help from many white and liberal summer soldiers, who would otherwise shrink rapidly from the cause.*
    J. Oliver Killens
6. *Your fingers must do the releasing, on their own, remotely, like the opening of a flower.*   Lewis Thomas
7. *Those last days! There were so many religions in conflict, each ready to save the world with its own dogma, each perfectly intolerant of the other.*   E. B. White

8. *"Feeling" as I am using it here covers much more than it does in the technical vocabulary of psychology, where it denotes only pleasure and displeasure, or even in the shifting limits of ordinary discourse, where it sometimes means sensation (as when one says a paralyzed limb has no feeling in it), sometimes sensibility (as we speak of hurting someone's feelings), sometimes emotion (e.g., as a situation is said to harrow your feelings, or to evoke tender feeling), or a directed emotional attitude (we say we feel strongly* about *something), or even our general mental or physical condition, feeling well or ill, blue or a bit above ourselves.* Suzanne K. Langer
9. *October 7 began as a commonplace enough day, one of those days that sets the teeth on edge with its tedium, its small frustrations.*
Joan Didion
10. *At first I thought it was another party, a wild rout that had resolved itself into "hide-and-seek" or "sardines-in-the-box" with all the house thrown open to the game.* F. Scott Fitzgerald

SENTENCE MIMICRY

Even with several devices for building sentences clearly in mind, you may feel that you haven't quite found your own style. One very effective way of experimenting with various styles and of broadening your store of sentence patterns is to mimic the style of other good writers, writers you respect. Not all good sentences, not even most, arise out of sentence combining during revision. Getting a selection of sentence patterns into your head gives you structures to write from. The best place to find these patterns is in your reading. The process is simple and enjoyable: pick out sentence structures that you like from the work of professional writers and mimic their patterns, replacing their words and ideas with your own. In order to assure that you can pick out their patterns accurately, you have to be able to do three things.

1. Identify the *base clause*.
2. Identify the *additions*.
3. Identify the connections between the descriptive parts of the sentence and what they describe.

Suppose you have the following sentence.

Pattern One: Every child deserves love.

The sentence is only a *base clause*. The clause is made up of a doer (every child), a verb (deserves), and a thing done (love). You could imitate the sentence by substituting in those same positions other words which would convey different ideas in the same way.

Mimicry of Pattern One: [Many children like bugs.]

Children is the doer, *like* the verb, and *bugs* the thing done. Take a look at the other mimicries below, noting the form.

[Most cats climb drapes.]

[Some gardeners do landscaping.]

[Every politician needs support.]

The next pattern is a bit more complicated.

Pattern Two: Despite what a son or daughter has done to disappoint his or her parents, every child deserves love and understanding.

The base clause is [*every child deserves love and understanding*.] The base is the same as is the base in the first pattern except that now there is a phrase *love and understanding* serving as the thing done. Also, there is one addition—in this case a subordinate clause, its purpose to tell to what extent *every child deserves*. The addition is *Despite what a son or daughter has done to disappoint his or her parents*. Thus the pattern to imitate is the following:

Addition: *Despite what a son or daughter has done to disappoint his or her parents*, [Base: every child deserves love and understanding.]

An imitation of the *base* might be:

[Many gardeners do landscaping and general maintenance.]

An imitation of the *addition* might be:

Although some do not advertise all their services.

The completed imitation would be: *Although some do not advertise all their services, many gardeners do landscaping and general maintenance*. Below are other mimicries of the same pattern.

Because votes are not easy to get, every politician needs support and recognition.

Unless they have been declawed, most cats climb drapes and furniture legs.

Perhaps these patterns seem too easy. You probably use such structures all the time without consciously mimicking them, without giving the bases and additions much thought. However, far more complicated patterns, found in the writing of your favorite authors, can be analyzed and mimicked in the same way. Below are examples of more complex patterns.

Pattern Three: Although many potted plants thrive in indirect sunlight, a few, including the pothos, can survive in dimly lit environments.

The base clause is [*a few can survive in dimly lit environments.*] The base clause is interrupted by the phrase *including the pothos*, which describes the word *few*. The additions are *including the pothos* and *Although many potted plants thrive in indirect sunlight* (describing *can survive*). Thus the pattern to mimic is the following:

Although many potted plants thrive in indirect sunlight, [a few,] *including the pothos,* [can survive in dimly lit environments.]

In the imitation a *base* is needed.

> [Some individuals can read at a speed of 3000 words a minute.]

Two *additions* are required, one beginning with an *-ing* word:

> *including high school and college students*

and one with a subordinating conjunction (see p. 143).

> *Although many students today are slow readers*

The mimicked sentence would then result in *Although many students today are slow readers, some individuals, including high school and college students, can read at a speed of three thousand words a minute.* Below are other mimicries of the same pattern.

> *Despite all the cultural conditioning by the media, some men, including young ones, realize that being a "he-man" is not the best role to play.*
>
> *Until someone warns them, swarms of teenagers, meaning many of our friends, will mindlessly follow the dictates laid open to them by fanatics.*
>
> *Because women are entering the workforce at twice the rate of men, feminist organizations, bringing large numbers of qualified executives into the business world, are evening out employee rolls for most large companies.*

Another pattern might be cumulative.

> Pattern Four: Working at the wine bottling plant bored me after only two weeks, drove me to counting the minutes left to the day, days filled the small talk, about as meaningful as the incessant droning of the label machine, which I was stationed in front of.

The base clause comes first [*Working at the wine bottling plant bored me.*] There are five additions, each expanding on the one before it (see p. 150). A mimicry of the base might be [*Telling my mother that I wanted to drop out of school for a term made me feel small.*] The next phrase tells "when" about *made feel almost immediately*. The second addition takes a past tense verb: *caused me to reevaluate my reasons*. The third addition repeats the last word of the second: [*reasons that were perhaps irrational*]. The fourth addition describes the preceding addition: *not in line with my usual decisions*. The last addition describes the last word of the fourth addition, and it begins with *which* (*who* might have been substituted, had the sentence called for its use): *which always had to pass rigorous logical tests*.

The mimicry would then be

> *Telling my mother that I wanted to drop out of school for a term made me feel small almost immediately, caused me to re-evaluate my reasons, reasons that were perhaps irrational, not in line with my usual decisions, which always had to pass rigorous logical tests.*

Whole paragraphs can be mimicked in the same fashion as the sentences above. You will be surprised how smoothly some flow from your pen. Others may require that you stop to analyze the structures. Sometimes the structures will be familiar and the mimicry will serve only to remind you to use them when you write, but other times the mimicry will cause you to compose sentences that you might never have tried or conceived. An additional benefit, knowing how to disassemble a sentence to analyze its meaning, helps you to read complicated passages with ease.

EXERCISES Directions: Mimic the sentences below, using your own ideas.

1. *Knowledge is always a matter of whole experience, what St. Paul calls knowing in full, and never a matter of mental conception really.*
   D. H. Lawrence
2. *The Oedipus Complex was a household word, the incest motive a commonplace of tea-table chat.*   *D. H. Lawrence*
3. *One of them, a young dog hound without judgment yet, bayed once, and they ran for a few feet on what seemed to be a trail. Then they stopped, looking back at the men, eager enough, not baffled, merely questioning, as if asking, "Now what?" Then they rushed back to the colt, where Boon still astride it, slashed at them with a belt.*   *W. Faulkner*
4. *When they reached the end of the lane they could see the moon, almost full, tremendous and pale and still lightless in the sky from which day had not quite gone.*   *W. Faulkner*
5. *A sure sign of distress: telephone numbers stormed through my head—area codes, digits. I must telephone someone.*   *Saul Bellow*
6. *Some statements are meant to pass, some to echo.*   *Saul Bellow*
7. *Business, sure of its own transcendent powers, got us all to interpret life through its practices.*   *Saul Bellow*
8. *I try to feel proud, but in my heart I know that it was fear of what his friends might do to me that kept me silent, and not the code of the street.*
   Norman Podhoretz
9. *My son—who is no genius, just an alive young mind—is learning plumbing, electricity, auto mechanics, the joys of sharing.*   *Judson Jerome*
10. *It was an immense crowd, two thousand at the least and growing every minute.*   *George Orwell*

7

What Is the Best Word?

A reporter, apparently expecting an intensely sophisticated response, once asked the novelist Ernest Hemingway what was the single most difficult task he had as a writer. After some careful thought, Hemingway replied that the most difficult task was "finding the right word." It sounds simple enough, but selecting the absolutely right word to convey the exact meaning you intend for a specific situation is no easy task.

Writing, after all, is made up of words. If the words you select do not project the meaning that you intend for your readers, your effort at communicating is lost. If the words call undue attention to themselves, they may detract from your message. Words must be selected carefully to fit your meaning, to serve the purpose of your communication, and to convey your ideas effectively to the minds of your readers.

Compare the two sentences below. Which gives you a better idea of what happened?

That boy was thoroughly obnoxious.

That obnoxious boy was striking his older brother with a broom handle and cursing him.

The second sentence not only offers more details, it uses a more energetic verb. The verb in the first sentence is *was*—very dull compared to the more concrete action verb *was striking*. Note in the sentences below a similar "dull verb" problem and the solution to it.

He *is* an advocate of conservation in any form.

He *advocates* conservation in any form.

When you find too many *to be* verbs in your writing, substitute action verbs. The chances are that your revised sentences will be more concise and will display more energy. However, this example of the importance of word choice is only one of the many little changes that you can make to energize your writing. It is true that most of the corrections in word selection will come about, as did those above, by substituting various words in your sentences. Nevertheless, you can take a few major steps to use words more effectively *the first time* you write so that there will be fewer changes to make later on.

MATCH YOUR WORDS

Be natural. Many students feel that when they write they must "sound academic" and inevitably they present language that sounds just like the lectures they most hate: stuffy, wordy, excessively formal. Big words *can* sound impressive, but good lecturers and writers do not stupefy their audiences with them. Their lectures are designed to suit a purpose, and the words are impressive only if chosen with care and used precisely. An excessively formal student paper sounds just as insincere and stiff as a stuffy lecture. For that matter, any piece of writing that is unnecessarily formal is drudgery to read.

The best level of language to use comprises a selection of words that would flow naturally in a typical intellectual, friendly discussion with a classmate. A good way to make sure that you have kept your reader in mind is to read your essay aloud. Does your writing sound like you

FIGURE 7-1
(Here is an example of how confusing words can be. Reprinted by permission of United Press International.)

IT'S LUCKY THEY DIDN'T SAY 'SHOTS'

RIO DE JANEIRO (UPI)—An unidentified man in Machado, Minas Gerais state, bought a pistol Friday and went to police to get a license for it, according to press dispatches.

Police told him he needed to bring in his identification and three photographs.

The man returned Saturday with his documents and a front and two side views—of the pistol.

do? Is your writing clear? If the paper discusses a highly technical subject and many new terms must be used to convey your material, listen to see if you have defined them carefully for the reader. You can follow a simple rule: be yourself. If a phrase you have written doesn't sound like you, revise it.

EXERCISES

A. In the passage below you will find italicized examples of stiff writing. Suggest alternative words and phrases.

Coal is an *underutilized resource* whereas oil and gas have of late *attained a most adscititious interest* in the import market of the United States *of America*. In 1973 the United States imported 8.1 million barrels of oil per day. Today we accept as much as 9.5 million every day. To *augment* the current oil importation would be *undiscerning*. Not only does our *trade equilibrium sustain many failings*, but the supplies can be easily *placed in a state of arrest* that would threaten our national security. Anyone familiar with the Arab oil embargo that occurred in 1973 *would concur readily on this matter*. In order to lessen our *vulnerable status regarding* economic and political blackmail, America must strive for an energy independence, *a status that could be attained*.

B. In the passage below correct any wordiness and stiff expressions so that the passage will be more readable. Read the passage aloud to hear the problem areas. Note that the excessive formality of the writing causes the passage to sound humorous, whereas the writer intended it to be serious.

Left-handed people are a persecuted minority in our society. From the time they reach for their Pablum with the "wrong hand" the idea is infixed in their craniums solidly: right is right; left is wrong. A trifle later, when they advance to the lowest level of educational endeavor, they are firmly admonished that they should not use their left digits to learn penmanship. When they also travail to handle a scissors for the purpose of producing a string of paper dolls, they are described with jeers as having clutched the instrument in the very reverse of the normal manner. This humiliation continues into adulthood. The laughter and scoffing affect different left-handed individuals in different ways. Amid all the embarrassment there is one who is willing to ignore the fuss. In the same room there may be another left-handed person who succumbs to social pressure and uses his right hand in public.

LEVELS OF LANGUAGE

Good writing is natural and consistent. Appropriate word choice is primarily a matter of recognizing and choosing from the various levels of usage. Language can be divided, for the purpose of discussion, into three levels: cultivated, casual, and familiar, with cultivated being the most formal, made up largely of words most people do not hear every day, casual being the middle range of words heard and used every day, and familiar being the least formal, including slang and colloquial expressions. The everyday or casual word *home*, then, has its cultivated counterpart, *domicile*, and its familiar counterpart, *pad*. The casual word *alcohol* or *liquor* has its cultivated form, *intoxicant*, and its familiar form, *booze*. The casual expression *children* has its familiar form, *kids*.

The range of usage from cultivated to casual to familiar is illustrated on the following bar graph. Most of the writing and speaking encountered in college level work is cultivated or casual, although some interaction with friends is undoubtedly at the familiar level. Interestingly enough, studies have shown that the more educated a person becomes, the more he or she communicates at the cultivated and casual levels, and the less he or she uses the familiar level. The level of any usage is neither right nor wrong in itself, but different levels fit different purposes. As you study the graph, think about most of your communication and on which level it occurs.

Try to figure out representative words that you would use in specific instances and classify them according to the three levels. For instance, in a formal business letter you might refer to *inner fortitude*, but in your letters to your family you would probably write *inner strength*. And in a conversation with friends you might even say *guts*.

FIGURE 7-2

	Cultivated	Casual	Familiar
Letter to mother		Man	Guy
Conversation with friends		To bother	To hassle
Personal essay	Intoxicated	Drunk	High
Article in local newspaper	Vagrant	Tramp	Bum
Public speech	Mawkish	Sentimental	
Business letter	Penultimate	Next to last	
Scholarly article	Hackneyed	Trite	
Research paper	Despondency	Depression	

EXERCISES

A. List ten words in your everyday vocabulary and try to identify more formal and less formal synonyms (words that mean about the same thing).

B. Write a short dialogue between you and your parents or you and your employer on the subject of profanity in public. Can you detect different levels of language usage in the dialogue? What does the

level of a person's language say about his or her personality?
C. Analyze the level of language in two advertisements, one from a technical journal and one from a popular magazine. What does the level of the language tell you about the subscribers to the periodical?
D. Note the inconsistency in language levels in this passage from a student's research paper. What should the student have done to make her language more acceptable?

> The Romans not only imbibed spirits of alcohol when sacrifices were proffered unto the gods, but on great occasions they also had the tendency to "tie one on." On these great occasions and for public entertainment, in ceremonious fashion, the wine was mixed with water so that the people who partook could return home uninebriated. It was common for people to get loaded, though, to the point that they would consume as much as seven gallons of wine during the festivities. The Romans believed that wine was a very spiritual drink and there was nothing wrong with getting snockered, not morally, anyway. Pliny, a Roman writer, once pointed out something that Romans who drank to excess probably believed: "Wine refreshes the stomach, sharpens the appetite, and conduces to slumber." Thus Romans drank heartily with no reservations, physical or mental.

E. Identify the predominant level of language usage (cultivated, casual, familiar) in each of the passages below. Which words, in particular, clearly show the level you have indicated?

1. *Pastimes occur in social and temporal matrices of varying degrees of complexity, and hence vary in complexity. However, if we use the transaction as the unit of social intercourse, we can dissect out of appropriate situations an entity which may be called a simple pastime. This may be defined as a series of semi-ritualistic, simple, complementary transactions arranged around a single field of material, whose primary object is to structure an interval of time. The beginning and end of the interval are typically signaled by procedures or rituals. The transactions are adaptively programmed so that each party will obtain the maximum gains or advantages during the interval. The better his adaptation, the more he will get out of it.*

    Eric Berne, Games People play.*

2. *At issue is one of the most religiously held beliefs about the nature of alcoholism and the alcoholic: that alcoholism is an incurable disease for which the only solution (as opposed to cure) is to abstain forever from any drinking. This idea pushed most dogmatically by Alcoholics Anonymous, but also subscribed to by a large number of physicians and researchers*

---

*From *Games People Play* by Eric Berne. Copyright © 1964 by Eric Berne. Reprinted by permission of Random House, Inc.

in the United States, claims that alcoholism is, in fact, a disease or, to put it slightly differently, the alcoholic has some sort of chemical deficiency in his or her body which prevents him or her from ever being able to drink without becoming immediately involved in drinking behavior and alcoholic binges.

Arthur Stickgold, "Alcoholism" A.A. vs. Rand,"
Los Angeles Free Press, October 29, 1976.*

3. *We were stuck a whole day in the Suez Canal. A steamer ahead of us ran aground, and had to discharge cargo. Then we passed Sunday at Port Said, which is a hole such as words won't express. Today we are just halfway between Sicily and Corsica. Tomorrow afternoon we hope to reach Marseilles, and by Sunday (11th) we should get to Paris. After four months' steady travel, and fifteen thousand miles of ocean, I ought to be glad to get anywhere; but I don't really feel puffed by the prospect. Our voyage since leaving Brisbane has been so charming that I am spoiled. Never a day when the weather was not fair, and generally quite exquisite; a sea almost motionless for ten thousand miles; constant change, and most of the time near strange and fascinating lands; for the first time in my life I have learned what an ideal journey is. Luckily there is no other like it, and can't be. If there were, I should start on it as soon as I could get my teeth put in order. As there is not, I must first get LaFarge comfortably started for home, and then I will read my letters, and think what next. On reaching Marseilles I shall mail this letter at once so that you may know of my safe arrival. At Paris I shall get something from you, no doubt, and then will start fresh. Love to you all.*

Henry Adams, Letter to a Niece, Oct. 8th, 1891.*

4. *In regard to the supposed substandard language of lower-class Negroes, schooled investigators are just beginning to recognize that Negro speech is not a dialect of English at all but rather part of a language system unto itself which differs from "standard" English in everything but vocabulary. Probably originating from an African Portugese Creole language, New World Negro dialects developed through a substitution of the vocabularies of the speech of the dominant culture in the places the slaves were deposited (Whinnom). In the United States, rather than viewing the various types of Negro speech as different dialectal corruptions of English, it is more meaningful to view them as one creole language, whole unto itself, which has been progressively gravitating toward the regional English dialects with which it has come into contact (William Stewart). This English creole is not a language* manque *but a communications system which is as fully developed as any other language. Only by an unfortunate historical accident has it accrued the vocabulary of English, and therefore appeared to many observers as an English dialect. What this means for*

---

*L. A. Free Press, Arthur Stickgold, "Alcoholism: A.A. vs. Rand." By permission of the editor.

*From Letters to a Niece by Henry Adams. Reprinted by permission of Houghton Mufflin Company. Copyright 1920.

FIGURE 7-3
The potter settles on a tool from his collection as the writer decides to use a particular word for a certain purpose and effect. (Photo by Steve Dierks.)

> teachers is that they must learn to deal with the teaching of Standard English as if it were a different language, but one in which most (but not all, by any means) of the vocabulary is the same.
>
> Roger Abrahams, Positively Black.*

THE FEELING THAT YOUR WORDS CONVEY

Even if you manage to select language that is both appropriate in level to your topic and natural for you, you haven't limited your choices enough to be sure the words you pick are the best ones. If the writing is natural, it will be easily read, but another important consideration is the *feeling* attached to those words. Not only is the definition of your words a matter of concern for you, but also you must know the implications of the words.

Words have both *denotation* and *connotation*. The *denotation* is the literal definition of the word: the denotation of the word *orphan* is "a child, one or both of whose parents are dead." The *connotation* of a word is the attitude or feeling generated by the word. *Orphan* implies loss, emptiness, lovelessness, and general unhappiness—it is negative in connotation. Although the dictionary usually gives only the denotation, it sometimes offers a clue to connotation; for example, under the entry for *nigger*, most dictionaries would say that the word is

---

*From *Positively Black* by Roger Abrahams. Reprinted by permission of the author. Copyright 1970.

"offensive." But for less apparently negative and positive connotations, a dictionary is of little help. For example, under the entry for *materialism* the dictionary offers the following definition: "a theory that physical matter is the only or fundamental reality and that all being and processes and phenomena can be explained as manifestations or results of matter."* Thus *Webster's New Collegiate Dictionary* tells us that materialism is a theory having certain tenets. If you say that your roommate is materialistic, however, you are conveying more than a description of a theory; your comment holds an inherent criticism.

When you write—especially if you are using new words—it is important to use the right connotation of each word. A man would not walk up to his date and tell her that her perfume has an exotic odor. *Odor* is more neutral than a word like *stench*, but still slightly negative; *fragrance*, though, carries a positive connotation.

EXERCISES
A. Suppose you were writing an essay on divorce and the trauma associated with separation. You want to write the sentence, "Divorce may be so frightening an experience because of the finality it represents that the couple may avoid the experience altogether and settle for separation." You also want to substitute something for the word "*experience*," which has occurred too many times in your essay anyway. You open your book of synonyms to the entry for *experience* and find the following list of substitutes: adventure, escapade, lark, ordeal, tribulation, trial. Does any of these words suit the sentence? Analyze the denotations and connotations of each substitute and base your decision on your analysis.

B. The context always coincides with the *feeling* of your words. In the sentences below, show how the context helps to clarify the connotative meaning of the words. Why would a word with a different connotation be inappropriate?
   1. A Sanitation Officer is a county employee like any other and deserves the respect of people on his route. (Compare "*garbage man*.")
   2. Gay Liberationists are lobbying at the Capital in order to gain the rights promised to all people in the Constitution. (Compare "*homosexuals*.")
   3. The defendant was judged not responsible for the crime since he was temporarily insane. (Compare "*crazy*.")
   4. Her clumsy girlfriend broke the antique china cup. (Compare "*awkward*.")
   5. About 45 percent of the students entering the University of California at Berkeley must take a basic English class. (Compare "*remedial*.")

*By permission. From *Webster's New Collegiate Dictionary* © by G. and C. Merriam Co., publishers of the Merriam-Webster Dictionaries.

6. Though some clothing appears to be of good quality, it is very cheaply made. (Compare "*inexpensively*.")

C. Discuss the various connotations that would be conveyed if each of the following words were inserted into the blank: *gullibility, innocence, naivete*.

The girl's _____ about sexual matters surprised everyone in her therapy group.

D. What is the difference in *denotation* in the following pairs of words? In *connotation*?
1. Aggressive-pushy
2. Reserved-repressed
3. Liberal-permissive
4. Stocky-obese
5. Elderly-aged
6. Wealthy-rich
7. Dogma-doctrine
8. Request-demand
9. Debt-loan
10. Agreement-compromise
11. Smart-intelligent
12. Independent-alienated
13. Nonviolence-passive resistance
14. Disinterested-apathetic
15. Prostitute-whore
16. House-home
17. Extensive-exhaustive
18. Long-voluminous
19. Employment-job
20. Reuse-recycle

SPECIFIC TROUBLE SPOTS

Certain little words cause big problems. Here are some practical suggestions about their use.

USE OF I
Many students struggle with the problem of how to refer to themselves in their papers. Should they use *I*? The answer depends on what is emphasized in the sentence and on what the purpose of the paper is. Some writing, including personal essays, descriptive essays, diaries, letters, and other informal assignments, is rather relaxed, and you should use *I* to refer to yourself in these. To do otherwise would be indirect and unnatural. In the sentences below (from a student's personal essay), the use of *I* seems the natural choice.

> In spite of the fact that I have lived in a large city all of my life, I have always yearned to be part of a community. I found such a group when I moved to a small town in Wisconsin to attend college. There I was not only a part of the college community, but also a part of the town where I served on the Miners' Council and various conservation committees.

Had the student used the more impersonal *one* or the expression *the writer* to refer to herself or himself, this passage would have lost its energy, its intimacy. In this paper the writer wants to show the reader his or her personal response to being in a community; the *I* is appropriate.

The use of *I* should be avoided, however, if the focus of the sentence does not *need* to be the writer. Unnecessary reference to yourself only misleads the reader about the content of the passage. Instead of focusing on the *I*, bring forward the real subject of your sentence. Note the difference in emphasis in the following sentences.

Poor Use of I *I* think that the beach is most beautiful in the winter when the sand is damp and musty and the sky is hazy.

Real Subject Forward *The beach* is most beautiful in winter when the sand is damp and musty and the sky is hazy.

There is no need for the writer's presence in the statement. The reader assumes that all assertions not attributed to another source are statements made by the writer, ones that the writer will then support.

USE OF ONE *One* is less personal than *I* and more general. But tedious repetition of *one* can wear on the nerves.

> Whenever one tries to correct one's own writing, one finds oneself in a difficult position.

Contemporary usage calls for the simple use of *I* over *one*, when you intend to refer to yourself alone. *One* or *the writer of this essay* can get very stuffy; on the other hand, unnecessary reference to yourself makes your writing disagreeable in another way. Be as direct as you can in your choice of pronouns, always weighing the relative importance of each questionable pronoun.

EXERCISES Directions: Note the differences in emphasis in the three passages below. When would each be appropriate? Which is the most formal and objective?

  A. One may stay up all night to study for a physics test, but if he or she studies the wrong material, he or she will score poorly on the test. Unfortunately, effort is not a good basis for the grade.

  B. Even if I stay up all night to study for a physics test, if I study the wrong material, I will score poorly on the exam. Unfortunately, my effort is not the basis for my grades.

C. Studying all night for a physics test will not help unless the right material is studied. Unfortunately, effort is not the basis for grades.

USE OF YOU

Another stickler is the use of *you*. In friendly conversations people often use *you* to mean *people*. "You get up and the first thing on your mind is coffee," they say. Who is the *you*? It clearly includes the speaker, but it is also a more general reference, probably to the audience. To use *you* in this general sense may be too informal for essays written in college. Unless you are deliberately addressing the reader, you may wish to avoid the generalized use of *you*.*

Try to use *people* instead, or write whatever word you really mean by the general term. Is it politicians, blacks, modern homemakers—to whom are you referring? Another possibility is of course to use the more formal *one*. Whenever the *you* is not essential to the meaning of the sentence, omit it and bring forward the real subject.

Too Informal *You* attend college assuming *you* can get a good job when *you* graduate, but that is not always the case.

Formal *Students* attend college assuming that *they* can get good jobs when *they* graduate, but that is not always the case.

Too Informal When *you* try to define Existentialism, *you* realize that there are no definite tenets *you* can outline.

Formal Because Existentialism has no definite tenets, *it* is hard to define.

Too Informal *Don't think* [literally "don't *you* think"] that the government in any way waived the responsibilities of the Puritans.

Formal The government did not, in any way, waive the responsibilities of the Puritans.

EXERCISES

Directions: Make the following sentences formal enough to include in an essay written for one of your classes.

A. When you realize how little research has been done on alcoholism, you begin to question the dogma that organizations like AA hand out.

B. When you do psychology experiments, you learn a great deal about people.

C. You should find a quiet place to study if you want to improve your concentration.

D. Because you know that relaxation is important, you should try to

*In this book, *you* is employed to keep a conversational tone. The reader is being addressed.

relax as much as possible every moment. If you do the correct exercises, you will relax.
E. Having a noisy roommate makes you want to live off campus.
F. Growing up in a gang atmosphere makes you feel that you always have to be ready to crush the next guy because if you don't, he might step on you.
G. It is not until you study literature for a couple of years that you realize novels are about the real feelings and thoughts of people. Before that, you tend to think that anything in fiction is nothing more than a story.
H. Learning about your body through movement education helps you to gain coordination and physical confidence.
I. As a woman, you want to be attractive by male standards, yet you do not want to be looked at as a sex object.
J. When you realize that men have dominated, and may always dominate, women who have attained quasi-executive positions, it makes you sick.

USE OF CONTRACTIONS

Contractions, such as *don't* for *do not*, lend an informal quality to writing. They are not necessarily to be avoided altogether in the essays you write, but their overuse should be checked since they affect the tone of your writing (see Chapter 1). Some writers feel that contractions should not be used in formal papers, but many contemporary writers use contractions without their interfering with tone. Even the book reviews and the editorials in newspapers now contain contractions, once considered too informal. In fact, there are times it would seem most natural to use a contracted form. For instance, suppose you wrote the following sentence: *Isn't it unfair to a dog to lock it up all day in an apartment?* The sentence would sound less natural if the contraction were replaced with "is it not."

AVOID TRITENESS, JARGON, AND ABSTRACTIONS

Speakers have little or no chance to go back and revise what they say, but writers are expected to polish their expression. The following passage from a student's paper shows too much resemblance to spoken English. It is very informal and includes, besides abstractions, many trite phrases.

> As you see, it is almost impossible to remain a Puritan. In other words, you become a little unbalanced from the strain of resisting it all. Every time you experience a little pleasure, you worry yourself sick that you've been living it up too much. So you say, "Forget this trip, man." You cool it considerably and wind up a real deadbeat. How can you keep a level head when everyone is watching you like a hawk night and day. You begin to hate society. But because you are a Puritan, you suppress your hatred, too.

A trite expression or cliche is a word or phrase that was once used as an effective image but has since lost its meaning through overuse. No one even thinks about the original "word picture" in any cliche. If words are to be important, they must communicate, and as a writer you should be especially concerned with saying what you mean with vivid, living words. For example, you should avoid expressions like "crowded in an elevator like sardines in a can" because what was once an effective comparison no longer communicates more than a vague sense of "crowdedness." You may argue that you know what someone means when he or she says this. The point is that it is not on account of the choice of words that you know what "like sardines in a can" means. You don't picture little fish all lined up and smothered in oil. Instead, your reaction is to the word *crowded*. Admittedly, if you had never heard the cliche before, it would seem clever.

It may sometimes be difficult to identify your own cliches. If you can't free your speech and writing of them, at least have an awareness of them and try whenever possible to avoid their use. Occasionally everyone uses a cliche without analyzing its staleness carefully enough. Your teachers can help you identify the ones you don't catch (either because at first they sound good to you or because you do not recognize the prefabricated sense they give your essays). Instead of feeling angry with your teachers for pointing out a cliche, use them as a resource to help you freshen up the language in your papers. No list could include all the cliches found in speech and writing, but below is a partial list that will help you recognize the types of cliches you might look out for.

Cliches

A heavy heart
As much chance as a snowball in hell
Avoid like the plague
Beat around the bush
Bite your tongue
Bored stiff
Bright and early
Budding genius
Clean as a whistle
Cracking up
Crystal clear
Deader than a doornail
Don't count your chickens
Draw to a close
Feast your eyes on that

Fits like a glove
Goal in life
Happy as a lark
Head over heels
Horse of a different color
In conclusion, come to the conclusion
It's a small world
Kill two birds with one stone
Last but not least
Like it grows on trees
Live and let live
Low blow
Mind over matter
More or less
My cup of tea

Nip in the bud	Sigh of relief
One in a million	Stiff upper lip
Pass the buck	That's life
Put your foot down	To be in his shoes
Reading between the lines	Too numerous to mention
Safe and sound	Without rhyme or reason
Short and sweet	Year in and year out

There are two good ways to revise your cliches once you identify them.

1. Rewrite the expression into direct, concrete words.
2. Make up a *new* phrase that conveys a specific word picture. Make sure that your audience can identify the implications of the expression you use.

Rewording an expression so that it is more direct is usually the best method. "Our boss *really saved the day* when he let us go home early on Christmas Eve" would become "All the employees appreciated the boss's generosity when he let us go home early on Christmas Eve." "Maria decided that it wasn't *worth eating her heart out* about her broken date for New Year's Eve" would become "Maria decided not to feel depressed about her broken date."

If you choose to be adventuresome and wish to make up an equivalent image to take the place of the worn-out one, be careful to avoid images that do not express just what you mean, even though they seem to sound good. If you wish to rewrite "His ideas were as stale as yesterday's news" and come up with "His ideas were as stale as Egypt," your image will not work. Although Egypt is ancient, it is not stale, and consequently no picture can be conveyed. You would be better off just saying that his ideas were "outdated" our even "stale," which is an image in itself. Always try to see the picture of what you are saying—your image will usually work if the picture comes through.

Also avoid writing mixed metaphors. A metaphor makes the informative—yet literally impossible—assertion that one thing is another thing. For example, "Love is a rose," "The heart is a lonely hunter," "Time is a sickle," and so on. Mixed metaphors are two or more word pictures that are inconsistent and therefore conflict. The result is that no picture can be formed in the reader's mind; or if one is formed, it doesn't make sense. If you write, "A diplomat, casting his line far into the troubled sea of his predecessors' blunders, is as courageous as a lion," you have created a mixed metaphor. A diplomat can be a lion. A diplomat can be a brave fisherman. But a lion cannot be a fisherman—and vice versa. Always check the logic of the word pictures you create before you conclude that the words "sound good" in your essay.

EXERCISES   A. Identify the cliches in the following passages.

1. Football tryouts are a blood-and-guts battle, a fight to the finish. Because football is so popular, there are never slim pickings when coaches hold their annual tryouts for the team. There are the brick-wall frontliners who block and push in all their splendor. Also, there appear the statuelike and blue-eyed quarterbacks who want to lead the team on to victory. Last but not least are the monkey-armed defensive backliners who are always on hand with their dreams of glory. Each of these prospective team members wages battles against the others. Competition is the name of the game. In the end only the cream of the crop is given a jersey.

2. I had not been in a classroom for around twenty years, and going back to college after what seemed an eternity was a trying experience. I must have been a sight for sore eyes the first day of class because I was worried sick for two whole days before. It was necessary to keep a stiff upper lip as I entered the door of Room 212 and found my way to a seat on the left at the back. But then my nerves flared up again. All around me sat young girls, nineteen years old at the most, and younger-looking boys. It was obvious to us all that I was no spring chicken, and the differences in our ages made me feel like last year's model. Even worse, the teacher was nearly young enough to be my daughter. Finally, two minutes before the class began, the door opened and three middle-aged ladies entered the room. They seemed to feel right at home as they informally greeted a number of the younger students. I gave a big sigh of relief, sat back in my chair and listened to a very enjoyable lecture about an old man named Robert Penn Warren.

B. Keep a list of your own and friends' cliches for a week. Try to record at least twenty of them.

C. Use four of the words on the cliche list below in sentences. Then revise those sentences so that they would be formal enough to include in an essay.

Part and parcel	Blessing in disguise
Broaden one's scope	Sooner or later
Root of the problem	More or less
Learning experience	Second home
Problem at hand	Rules and regulations
Give undivided attention	Above your head
Undisputed fact	

AVOID CIRCUMLOCUTIONS

Circumlocutions—language that travels "round about" and gets right back where it started from—should be cut from your writing. Circumlocutions are unconscious redundancies in word choice that show writers are not thinking carefully about the words they put together. Many circumlocutions have become cliches. Circumlocutions are automatic and consequently hard to spot. But they always have the same effect—they weaken your expression. In the list that follows, words could have been left out of each phrase, and the meaning of the expression would have been retained. After looking over the list presented here, make your own list drawn from your speaking and writing and the speaking and writing of those around you.

Which of the words on the list could be omitted without changing the meaning of the phrase?

Absolutely empty
A true fact
Circle around
Completely empty
Completely finished
Distort the meaning of
Final conclusion
If and when
In any shape or form
Living incarnation
One and the same
One-sided prejudice
Part and parcel
Period of time

Personal friend
Point in time
Regress back to
Reminisce about past experiences
Return again
Strangle to death
Sum total
Tail end
Totally absorbed in
Untrue lie
Ways and means
While at the same time

AVOID JARGON AND SLANG

JARGON Jargon is specialized language that has been adopted by people in certain fields (journalists, politicians, social scientists, etc.). Most areas of work and study use some sort of jargon. Jargon can function in your writing if you are exploring a subject that employs terms new to you that are essential to an understanding of the subject or are usual in any discussion of it. In this case, define all jargon so that it makes as much sense to your reader as it does to you. More often, however, jargon should be deleted from your writing whenever the same thought can be expressed in everyday language. Jargon tends to be long winded and redundant. Students often carry over jargon into other fields than the one for which it was intended and the word use consequently confuses the average reader.

The student who characterizes the narrator of a novel as "*id*-oriented" instead of saying that the character is "demanding of his wife" may be trapped by the jargon of the psychology industry. A writer who claims that people who "utilize all their potential tend to validate the learning process" is really just saying that students who study hard learn a lot. The student who writes that "attendance at the national convention of chiropractors topped out at 1500" is borrowing stock-market jargon to say that only 1500 people attended the convention, but if the reader is unfamiliar with the jargon used by stockbrokers, he or she can only guess at the meaning of that sentence. Substitute ordinary English for any unnecessary jargon you can find in your writing.

SLANG

Slang is a highly informal, nonstandard vocabulary—often jargon-like—that is used at times by speakers of all levels of education, although less frequently by educated ones. In your writing for college classes, slang is usually inappropriate (unless it is part of a quotation, is used deliberately to characterize someone's speaking habits, or is consciously employed for some definite and special effect). Some slang is derived from shortening words—*TV, photo, typo, taxi, phone*—and

FIGURE 7-4
"Take this clear and simple memo of mine and convert it into legalese so it will sound official." (Reprinted by permission of Newspaper Enterprise Association.)

other slang comes from specific "code language" from a field or subculture—*turn-on* (radio/television), *spaced out* (drug culture), *wiped out* (surfing). Other examples of slang are *joint* (place), *no sweat* (no bother), *chick* (girl), *stoned* (intoxicated by drugs or alcohol), *cold* (unfeeling), *heavy* (philosophical/intellectual), and *neat* (good or enjoyable). Slang is not incorrect or crude; it is simply too informal even in most personal and descriptive essays. Unless a teacher makes an assignment deliberately relaxed, use more formal guidelines for word choice.

One reason that slang is not acceptable in the essays you write is that in different societies and times it is always changing. A person can readily show his or her age by using slang from a past decade. Perhaps you have noticed this with your parents or with older friends. From subculture to subculture there is variance, too. For example, *a heavy rap* used to mean in the underworld *a long jail sentence* or *much blame*, but to most college students during the 1960s and early 1970s it meant *an involved and serious talk*. Only rarely does a slang meaning last in the vocabulary.

AVOID ABSTRACTIONS AND GENERALITIES

Many words convey a level of abstractness; they also are either specific or general. That is, you can name for any concept both more specific or concrete (see p. 102) and less specific or concrete meanings. In the sentence, "An organization is concerned about ecological matters," there are three rather abstract notions: *organization, concerned*, and *ecological matters*. Questions are raised in the reader's mind, "which organization?" "what do you mean by *concerned*?" and "what are ecological matters?" The writer seems to be avoiding direct statements. Often the puzzling abstraction is not conscious on the writer's part; nevertheless, he or she has been a bit careless. Use words that are as specific or as concrete as possible to convey precise ideas.

You could say that you like *poultry*; but if you are not referring to all kinds of poultry and, in fact, you mean only duck with orange sauce, you are obliged to let the cook know. Otherwise you might end up eating fried chicken wings. Certain words are usually too abstract and should be removed from your writing or else thoroughly explained. They include *facet* or *aspect* (both used in a very general sense to mean an *element*), *everything, nice, cute, the situation, the element*. But not all general terms constitute poor usage; they are only weak when your reader expects more specific information.

> Many aspects of his work as a fireman were dangerous. (Weak. *Aspect* means duties, which is more specific than *aspects* and actually suggests work: *Many of his duties as a fireman . . .*)

> The new information was presented as a fresh aspect of the defendant's case. (Acceptable. Aspect here means a view.)

When you can think only of a generality and you realize that you need something specific, check your book of synonyms, and perhaps you will find an entry that fits better.

Abstraction and generalization can weaken your evidence (see Chapter 4). In a paper with the thesis "Ghetto children are forced learn responsibility at an early age," a student cites a case history: "In the Brown family a female member looked after the six younger children every evening when the mother attended night classes to get her high school diploma." The case is rather vague, however, because so much of the impact depends on who the *female member* is. Is it a grandmother or is it a seven-year-old girl? Clearly, to be evidence in this essay, the person must be a child, but how young? If it were directly stated that a seven-year-old child was expected to care for six younger children, the information would certainly exemplify the extensive and responsible role played by the ghetto child. But with abstract and general language the connection is loose.

AVOID EUPHEMISMS

Euphemisms—seemingly polite ways of saying things that, put more plainly, might be unpleasant or offensive—should be avoided in essay writing. In expository writing this excessive politeness implies evasiveness and insincerity. To refer to a politician's death as the person's "meeting his maker" or "going to his reward" is hedging. To reveal in a news release that much "bedroom activity" occurs in off-campus fraternity houses is to hide behind respectability in word choice. If you are bold enough to expose sexual activity on campus, be mature enough to say the word *sex*. If you are writing a paper on legal prostitution in Nevada, don't call brothels "eros centers" or prostitutes "members of the oldest profession."

Just a moment of thought about the *manipulation* of *the truth* in euphemistic writing will explain why you should avoid it. Of course, you should not go to the other extreme—obscene or coarse language—in an effort to avoid euphemism. Use either cultivated or casual language, and do not assume that unpleasant ideas need to be padded with nice sayings in order to prevent shock.

EXERCISES Directions: Rephrase the euphemisms in the following sentences.
  A. The police officer noted that the man he had taken into custody was inclined to alcohol.
  B. If a man and woman are not willing to try new things, they may suffer a parting of the ways.
  C. The industry is not without fiscal instability.
  D. My father is not as young as he once was and cannot exercise so strenuously.

E. Her intention is to inspire the thought of a nuptial bond in a man of means.
F. Busing places culturally deprived students in better equipped high schools.
G. Because Harriet and I wished to speak in private, I suggested that Mark go outside for a bit of air.
H. He has been known to transgress the law.
I. He procured pleasures for the sailors who had reached port.
J. For centuries man's best friend has been a source of comfort and pleasure, a companion for hunters, and a protector of worldly goods.

AVOID SEXIST LANGUAGE

Unnecessary emphasis on sexual roles should be avoided, both in word choice and in thinking, with men and women treated as people, not as stereotyped members of one or the other sex, each with its place in the family and in the working world. Using *ladies and gentlemen* or *women and men*, each of which contains parallel expressions, is better than, for instance, using *ladies and men,* which does not contain parallel expressions since *ladies* connotes a type of behavior and *men* only a gender. In the examples you compose for essays it is inaccurate to assume that a woman must do the family's shopping and cooking and that a man must be the provider, or that the doctor mentioned in an anecdote or case study is a man. A secretary or nurse is not necessarily a woman, nor is an executive automatically a man. In like manner, all physical and emotional natures belong to all people—crying and experiencing heartbreak are no more natural for a woman than for a man, and possessing physical strength is no more natural for a man than for a woman. Both sexes, when depicted as human beings, have equal capacity for feeling and thinking, productivity and laziness, proficiency and inadequacy in everything they do.

Some commonly used expressions that indicate surprise at a woman's role of authority or make clear distinctions in the roles of men and women are offensive and to be avoided. A few of the most abusive expressions and suggested alternatives are listed below.

Avoid	**Use**
Gals, girls (referring to adults) ladies, the fair sex, coeds	Women
Lady or male as an adjective as in "the lady doctor" or "the male nurse"	Simply use the noun—doctor, nurse
My better half, the little lady, the wife	My wife

The suffix *ess* or *ette* added to a noun to designate the female, as in Jewess, poetess, heiress, suffragette	Jew, poet, heir, suffragist
Woman's libber	Feminist, member of the women's movement

Many words contain *man* but refer generally to all people. Because many people associate the word *man* with its reference to a person who is male, it is perhaps fairest to use alternative words when people of either gender are referred to in your writing. Of course, if a specific person is being described, it would be permissible to use the appropriate suffix, as in *policewoman* or *policeman*. In the sentences below substitutions have been made in an effort to avoid sexist language. Study each sentence until you understand why the change was needed and how the substitution improves the sentence.

Ineffective: *Manmade* lakes are not as exciting as natural ones to most *fishermen*.

Effective: *Artificial* lakes are not as exciting as natural ones to most *people who fish*.

Ineffective: The *manpower* needed to build bridges costs the taxpayers millions of dollars each year.

Effective: The *workforce* needed to build bridges costs the taxpayers millions of dollars each year.

Equally offensive are more subtle sexist usages of language. Take special care not to imply that the male in the family is always the decision maker and the wife and children his supplicants. For instance, do not unthinkingly write a sentence like this one: *Lionel Greer has decided to move his wife and children to a neighborhood that offers many more cultural advantages than where they currently live*. The implication is that Mr. Greer makes the decisions, not his whole family. Instead, convey your idea in this form: *The Greer family has decided to move to a neighborhood that offers many more cultural advantages than where they currently live*. Similarly, the ineffective *Mrs. Jordan's husband lets her take night classes at a local community college* offends the ears of those who believe that women are whole people, entitled to make their own decisions. Unless you are emphasizing the inequity in the couple's relationship, revise: *Mrs. Jordan takes night classes at a local community college*.

One of the most problematic uses of language is pronouns since English does not have a single pronoun to mean *he or she*. Until recently, the masculine forms of pronouns (he, his, him) have been used to stand for both sexes, and in the sentence *Everybody should be his own best friend, his* has supposedly meant that the *everybody* is either male or female. But usages such as these have been questioned for the same reason as the suffix *man*. Some writers have tried to dodge sexist language by using the pronoun *one* as in *One must work hard if one wants to get good grades*, but sometimes the result is a string of cumbersome *one's*, making sentences sound excessively formal. At the other extreme is the informal *you* as in *You must work hard if you want to get good grades*, a usage best saved for personal essays, letters, journals, and conversations. With neither of these alternatives presenting especially good solutions to the problem, the situation seems to call for the use of plurals whenever possible. In many instances, the singular pronoun can be avoided altogether by making the noun or pronoun it would refer to plural or by taking out the questionable pronoun.

Ineffective:	*A person* who loves to win will always be disappointed if *his* team loses.
Effective:	*People* who love to win will always be disappointed if *their* team loses.
Ineffective:	*One* must work hard if *he* wants to get good grades.
Effective:	One must work hard *to get* good grades.

The expressions *he or she, him or her*, and *hers or his*, used occasionally, effectively replace the sexist *his*, but overuse of these long phrases is repetitious. Some writers alternate *he* with *she*. You will even see combined forms such as the impossible to pronounce *s/he*, but because this abbreviation has not yet been adopted by most users of the language, most readers prefer other forms. It is not effective to use the plural pronoun *their* to modify a singular noun or pronoun. *They* and *their* are gaining some acceptance as singular pronouns and are already popular in speaking, it is true. However, this usage is not generally accepted yet, and therefore it is best avoided in writing where it is usually perceived as an error in agreement. Therefore, if you are writing a sentence with the word *anyone, everyone, somebody*, or *each*, and a pronoun is to refer to that word, you might stick with the singular, the expression *his or her*, just *his*, just *her* (alternating); or you might change the sentence so that the singular pronoun is not needed.

Ineffective:	*Everybody* in the room did *their* experiment correctly the first time.
Effective:	*Everybody* in the room did *his or her* experiment correctly the first time.
Effective:	*Everybody* in the room did *the experiment* correctly the first time.

There are many ways to avoid sexist language, and each writer has to decide which way suits a particular sentence. The first step to ridding your language of sexist implications is to look for them.

INCREASE YOUR ACTIVE VOCABULARY

We have at least two kinds of vocabularies. One is recognition—the one we use most when we read and listen. Although we recognize the words in this group, we do not know their exact meanings. All the words that we decipher from the sentences in which they appear are part of this recognition vocabulary. We usually do not use these words because, not knowing exactly how they work, we avoid them or they do not occur to us as we are writing. In contrast to our recognition vocabulary, our active vocabulary comprises all the words we readily use when we write and speak.

As a writer, try to turn much of your recognition vocabulary into active vocabulary. In order to make the switch, you must be certain to observe the context, connotation, and denotation of every word you intend to transfer. Here is one helpful method. First, identify words from your recognition vocabulary by noting words that recur in your reading. Write up an index card for each word you wish to transfer from recognition to active, including the following information.

- The word centered at the top of the card.
- A notation of the part of speech next to the word.
- The sentence in which you found the word.
- The definition of the word according to its context in the sentence.
- A sentence you write using the new word.

FIGURE 7-5
"That's right, Dad—I've graduated *summa cum laude*. What does that mean?" (Reprinted by permission of Glenn Bernhardt. *Wall Street Journal*.)

Here is how a typical index card would look:

FIGURE 7-6

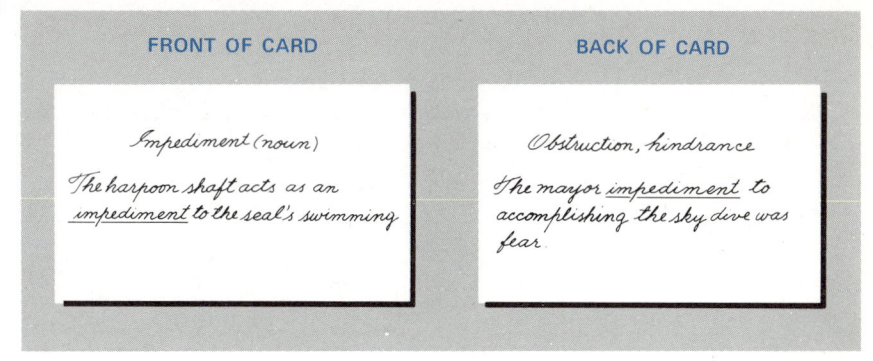

FRONT OF CARD

Impediment (noun)
The harpoon shaft acts as an impediment to the seal's swimming

BACK OF CARD

Obstruction, hindrance
The major impediment to accomplishing the sky dive was fear.

With a definition, the part of speech, and a sample context for the word, you can fully understand one meaning and one use of it. The word cannot become your own, however, unless you use it. Therefore, on the back of the card you should write a sentence of your own using the new word. Imitate the context you wrote down on the front of the card. The next step is to use the word whenever appropriate, making sure that you are adhering to the context you found the word in. If at some time you come across other uses of the same word, be sure to make up another card showing the new usage. You can, in this way, build up a variety of contextual clues for a single word; and in so doing you are increasing the number of potential ways that you might use the word.

USE THE DICTIONARY AND THESAURUS

Every student should own a college-level ("desk") dictionary. The dictionary can be very helpful provided that you know something about the usefulness of the one you select. College or desk dictionaries contain about 150,000 entries, among which you should be able to find most of the nontechnical words you will need to check during your undergraduate years. As a bonus, college dictionaries usually contain appendices on grammar, alphabetical lists of colleges and universities, and handy mathematical tables. By adding one of these books to your shelf, you are providing yourself with a small reference library, not just a book in which to check definitions and spelling. Any dictionary you choose will have invaluable information in its preface; read it to learn the symbols used, attitudes towards usage, order of definitions, pronunciation, syllabication, variant forms of words. Syllabication, pronunciation, and usage may vary slightly from dictionary to dictionary, but the minor differences are nothing to worry about. If you are really unsure about a matter of usage, it is best to check a dictionary of usage like Wilson Follet's, *Modern American Usage*; Bergen and Evans', *A Dictionary of Contemporary American Usage*; M. Bryant's, *Current American Usage: How Americans Say It and Write It*; or H. W. Fowler's, *Dictionary of Modern English Usage*. For most purposes, the desk dictionary will be adequate. Although entries in different dictionaries take slightly different forms, all contain much the same information as is shown in the following sample entry from *The American Heritage Dictionary*.*

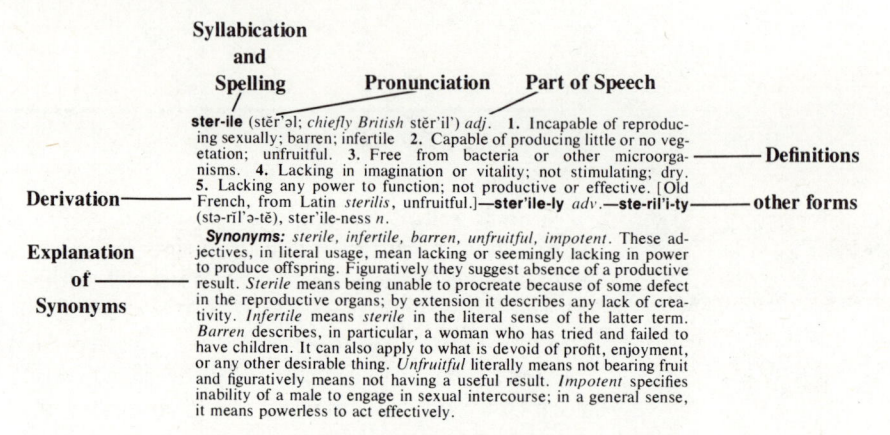

<pre>
                Syllabication
                    and
                 Spelling   Pronunciation   Part of Speech

              ster-ile (stĕr'əl; chiefly British stĕr'il') adj. 1. Incapable of reproduc-
              ing sexually; barren; infertile 2. Capable of producing little or no veg-
              etation; unfruitful. 3. Free from bacteria or other microorga-   —— Definitions
              nisms. 4. Lacking in imagination or vitality; not stimulating; dry.
              5. Lacking any power to function; not productive or effective. [Old
Derivation —— French, from Latin sterilis, unfruitful.] —ster'ile-ly adv. —ste-ril'i-ty —— other forms
              (stə-rĭl'ə-tē), ster'ile-ness n.
              Synonyms: sterile, infertile, barren, unfruitful, impotent. These ad-
Explanation   jectives, in literal usage, mean lacking or seemingly lacking in power
    of   to produce offspring. Figuratively they suggest absence of a productive
              result. Sterile means being unable to procreate because of some defect
 Synonyms   in the reproductive organs; by extension it describes any lack of crea-
              tivity. Infertile means sterile in the literal sense of the latter term.
              Barren describes, in particular, a woman who has tried and failed to
              have children. It can also apply to what is devoid of profit, enjoyment,
              or any other desirable thing. Unfruitful literally means not bearing fruit
              and figuratively means not having a useful result. Impotent specifies
              inability of a male to engage in sexual intercourse; in a general sense,
              it means powerless to act effectively.
</pre>

Syllabication   Check your dictionary whenever you cannot fit a complete word at the right-hand margin of your paper. All words should be hyphenated according to dictionary syllabication.

Spelling   The question "How can I look up a word I can't spell?" seems reasonable. Dictionaries can help you, though, if you have a basic picture of the word and are willing to persevere through trial and error. Sound out the word as best as you can and check the dictionary for that spelling. If you do not find it, substitute different vowels and check those spellings. Say you are trying to check the spelling of *sternum*, the technical word for breastbone. Your first guess is *stirnem*, but since you find no entry under that spelling, you try *sturnem*. Still no luck, so you try *sternem*, from which you locate the correct spelling of *sternum*. Many poor spellers like to have handy a wordbook containing a list of frequently misspelled words. However, this little rapid speller has no definitions, and you may find without realizing it a spelling that matches the one you have in mind but that means something different from the word you were checking. It is very important, therefore, whenever you check a spelling to read the definition of the word

---

* © 1969, 1970, 1971, 1973, 1975, 1976, Houghton Mifflin Company. Reprinted by permission from *The American Heritage Dictionary of the English Language*.

you settle on so that you can be sure you have located the correct word. If you consider yourself a poor speller, the guidelines beginning on page 394 of this book will be of interest to you.

Pronunciation It is very important to learn the pronunciation of new words so that you can use them comfortably. Some dictionaries offer British and American pronunciations when the two differ. Accent marks indicate which syllables should be stressed: The syllables marked by heavy accent marks should be emphasized. Pronunciation symbols are explained, in most dictionaries, on each page. If several pronunciations are given for a word, none is more correct than the others, nor is it preferable. Those listed are alternatives.

Part of Speech It makes a considerable difference whether a word is a verb, noun, adjective, or other part of speech if you want to use it well. Many words function as more than one part of speech but have slightly different meanings for each. For example, the word *stew* is both a noun and a verb; so is *advocate*. The part of speech is listed before the respective definition. One abbreviation that you will see pertains only to verbs. Verb intransitive (sometimes noted *v.i.* or *i.v.*) means that the verb does not take a direct object. Some verbs have both transitive (verb takes a direct object) and intransitive forms with slightly different meanings for each. Knowing whether a verb takes an object provides an important clue to the use of the word.

Definitions Different dictionaries place definitions in different order. *The American Heritage Dictionary* places them in order of "psychological understanding" to show how the various meanings of a word grow out of a central meaning. No one meaning is ever more *correct* than another, but some other dictionaries use an order based on most-common to least-common usage.

Derivation The derivation is usually placed in brackets. *The American Heritage Dictionary* also makes reference in this space to a special appendix of Indo-European roots that further explains the history of the word.

Variant Forms The spelling of other parts of speech—or other forms of the same part of speech—is given so that the base word may be adapted to your purpose.

Synonyms A list of words that have meanings close to the base word is often given. Because there are distinctions in the shades of meaning conveyed by synonyms, good dictionaries point out distinctions as well as the shared meaning of the words.

Usage Most dictionaries offer usage notes on controversial words. You may have heard somewhere that you shouldn't use *ain't*, because "*ain't* ain't in the dictionary." In fact, *ain't* is in the dictionary, but it is accompanied by usage notes. For an example of the usage notes see the excerpt below from *The American Heritage Dictionary*.*

> **ain't** (ănt). *Nonstandard.* Contraction of *am not.* Also extended in use to mean *are not, is not, has not,* and *have not.*
> **Usage:** *Ain't,* with few exceptions, is strongly condemned by the Usage Panel when it occurs in writing and speech that is not deliberately colloquial or that does not employ the contraction to provide humor, shock, or other special effect. The first person singular interrogative form *ain't I* (for *am I not* or *amn't I*), considered as a special case, has somewhat more acceptance than *ain't* employed with other pronouns or with nouns. (*Ain't I* has at least the virtue of agreement between *am* and *I*. With other pronouns, or nouns, *ain't* takes the place of *isn't* and *aren't* and sometimes of *hasn't* and *haven't*.) But *ain't I* is unacceptable in writing other than that which is deliberately colloquial, according to 99 per cent of the Panel, and unacceptable in speech to 84 per cent. The example *It ain't likely* is unacceptable to 99 per cent in both writing and speech. *Aren't I* (as a variant of the interrogative *ain't I*) is acceptable in writing to only 27 per cent of the Panel, but approved in speech by 60 per cent. Louis Kronenberger has this typical reaction: "A genteelism, and much worse than *ain't I.*"

USE OF THE THESAURUS

The thesaurus is a book of synonyms that can be very useful when you are writing and cannot think of just the right word to fill a slot or if you feel that your word choice is repetitious. A thesaurus is used to *remind* you of words you *already* know that do not flash into your mind at the times you need them. Do not pick out of the thesaurus words whose meanings you are not sure of (see p. 226 for a suggestion). Also pay careful attention to the *part of speech* of the words you select.

LEARNING THE ORIGINS OF WORDS TO EXPAND YOUR VOCABULARY

Affixes (prefixes and suffixes) are parts of words that can give you important clues to the meanings and accurate use of words. The roots in a word offer a basic meaning, the prefixes adjust the meaning, and the suffix tells you the part of speech—all this information can be observed at a glance once you train yourself to pick it out. Suppose you came across the word *recreant* in your reading. You could get a basic idea of its meaning from the root word *cre* from the Latin word *credere* meaning "to believe." Most easily distinguishable is the prefix *re* meaning "back" or "again." The suffix *ant* indicates a noun—the quality of something. Thus the word *recreant* means literally "one who takes back belief" and is used to describe an unfaithful person.

It is easy to see how learning roots and affixes can help you when you come upon an unfamiliar word in reading. But in order to make words stick in your head, more than a vague idea of word origins is needed. When you come upon an unfamiliar word, check its derivation in the dictionary. Take time to see the mechanics behind what makes the word work. What does the root mean? What are the prefixes and suffixes? How has the literal meaning been adapted through usage?

EXERCISES

A. Underline the cliches, euphemisms, and circumlocutions in the following sentences.
 1. At our last social gathering, we were packed like sardines, the

---

* © 1969, 1970, 1971, 1973, 1975, 1976, Houghton Mifflin Company. Reprinted by permission from *The American Heritage Dictionary of the English Language.*

band members performed to absolute perfection, but the beer keg, that receptacle of heavenly bliss, was bone dry.
2. It was the nostalgic homesick longing for my parents' sweet home that caused me to dream of the dear departed couple.
3. When Amalgamated Union officials were requested by the Senate committee to testify at the hearing, the officials made it perfectly clear that minor transgressions of the law in the world of business were part and parcel of daily operations.
4. The grease monkey claimed that unavoidably necessary changes of adjustment would inflate the bill.
5. The marks of time that were present on her face did not diminish her beauty.
6. The unfortunate shift in the quality of your schoolwork necessitates the unavoidable removal of you from these ivy-clad halls.
7. The two wrestlers butted against each other like rams who desire the favor of the exact same female.
8. I had totally completed my day's strivings when my boss, with a look that could turn one to stone, told me that I had not adequately cleaned the latrines to his satisfaction.
9. His unappetizing odor is the direct result of too few baths and an overactive perspiratory apparatus.
10. The titular head of the country, who wished to come to the point of the matter, responded to the reporters' probing investigation with the short and sweet announcement that he had no power to protect his land from foreign industrialists.

B. The following sentences are inconsistent because they contain a mixture of formal and familiar words. Replace the familiar diction with more appropriate word choice. Do you think that any of the formal diction is too formal for an essay you would write in class? How would you change the word choice, then?
1. "Redeeming social value" is a term so vague that it might permit the Bible to be established as obscene and *Hustler* magazine to be deemed great stuff.
2. I was very happy to learn that my professor is a very eminent Asian history hotshot.
3. The tactical peculiarities necessitated by battle in a desert territory rendered the Arab's martial experience and know-how of great worth.
4. Gregory's analysis of his team's hangups was impeded by overweening vanity and loyalty to his buddies.
5. I dig the part of *Hamlet* in which the prince speaks with a ghostly interlocutor, the dead King Hamlet, who fills the prince in on heretofore unknown facts.
6. The old hack writer was mad because his editor reviled each of his endeavors.

7. Hector was stating the usual complaints about his A− grades, and Professor Robins just took it all.
C. Change any familiar diction in the following sentences to more appropriate diction for a college paper.
1. She has an incredible ability to know just what others think of her.
2. Telling his supervisor how bombed out he had been the night before was not too bright, so he just kept cool about it.
3. Harry was a mean son of a gun. I mean, that guy was cold to his best friends at times.
4. Shoplifting has been on the rise in the past couple of years.
5. Drug addicts who shoplift will take long shots and will try for the quickest getaway.
6. So many salespeople are fond of lines that make the customer feel guilty.
7. The current economic scene resembles a flea market in India.
8. The mayor had to boogie in order to make it to the press conference on time because his last appointment was way across the city.
9. When the students in Introductory Sociology found a question about deviance on their final exam, they freaked out.
10. It's about time that psychologist stopped rewording Freud and started to get into and identify contemporary problems.
D. Correct any unnecessary references to the writer, inappropriate uses of "you," and excessive or unnatural uses of contractions in the following sentences.
1. If you think about it, as this writer certainly has done, you will see that the college needs a student newsletter that would be concerned, I hope, with the rights and responsibilities of students.
2. I think that politics should be kept out of the churches since religion has enough problems already, in my opinion, and people spend too much time worrying over mundane concerns.
3. You can imagine how utopian the world could've become if governments had begun to apprehend and work toward the finer goals of life.
4. Congress simply can't pass the bill because they're not convinced of its efficacy.
5. In my opinion there are too many cars on the freeways and too few people in their homes.
6. Having studied the rock formations in the nearby hills and read a few books on the subject, I think I can say with some truth that I fear a massive landslide in the near future.
7. The streets of Rome are dangerous places after dark, and you are in constant peril if you walk alone in that city.

E. Correct any errors in inconsistent word choice and connotations of words in the following sentences.
  1. During long months in which necessity prompted me to apply for unemployment compensation, I wrote many letters to the Corinth Press requesting an editorial position, until finally I was permitted to meet and to chat with the Press's chief editor.
  2. I investigated the figure of the tiny gal as she sidled by in her bikini.
  3. The company's assets are substantial and stable, but its stock report suggests a touch of foul play within the ranks of its officers.
  4. Let it be said that this war which was waged by nations that had histories of such conflagrations was the result of misunderstanding, stupidity, and money grabbing.
  5. Clifton Merkle was not only a philanthropist, but a man of means who praised brotherhood over the dollar.

F. Underline the jargon and circumlocutions in the following sentences. How could you write the same idea in more direct words?
  1. The consensus of opinion favors his retirement from office.
  2. The vase in the African Art Exhibit was elliptical in shape.
  3. At this late date, we are unable to effect a real understanding of what transpired during the administration of Nixon.
  4. She just needs a week's vacation to recover from the effects of her nasal coryza.
  5. After I had taken an affirmative stance on the controversy, I undertook a thorough investigation which revealed to me that my earlier stand was totally erroneous.
  6. The detrimental nature of the adding to food certain colorings and preservatives is evident to consumers in this day and age.
  7. In the estimation of the educational system, through the process of letter grade evaluation, he did not attain the highest possible level of achievement.
  8. Please inform me of the position of the time indicators on your watch.
  9. She took delight and pleasure in the cultivation of her practice of equestrian skills.
  10. After a careful search for evidence, it will become obvious to all that creativity is a requisite to our mental health.

G. Rewrite each of the sentences below, correcting any errors in diction. Explain in a sentence or two why you corrected each faulty word or phrase.
  1. The value of interfacing within the modern family often is not realized.
  2. I love the feeling that is the result of a breeze passing through my hair.

3. His jump shots were wise investments since he could outperform all other players from the periphery of the court, but his free throws brought no returns.
4. The dramatic moment of the evening occurred when Mr. Gilfarb became interested in his daughter's private affairs and demanded an explanation of her recent id orientation, the explanation of which served as the evening's denouement.
5. Whereas the party in question, the aforementioned Cecelia Jones, is no longer my friend, I cannot tell you where she is employed or where her living quarters are.
6. The tree outside her house is so beautiful that I would like to effect a transference of love from one object to the other, from Mabel to her tree.
7. The possibility of an increase in swing vote activity has had its resultant effect in a more liberal party platform.
8. The apparent fact that the man who is soon to assume the position of chairman is a member of a minority race has caused an unreasonable and unwarranted lessening of support among the company's financial backers.
9. When one finds it feasible to impose objectifying controls over a particular subject under investigation, there is greater possibility for valid test results.
10. When the mists of time are blown away, it will come to be seen that our fraternity is indivisible and has traits worthy of merit.

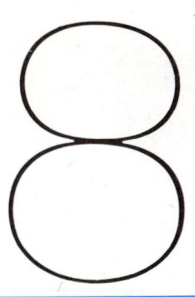

8
What Makes Your Writing Polished?

Good writing, even for most professional writers, seldom happens the first time a piece is developed. When you are preparing the initial draft of your essay, you are probably so concerned with proving or developing your ideas that you pay little attention to some of the finer points of writing. There is nothing wrong with this attitude; that is exactly what you should be doing during the first draft. If you want your essay to be more polished, more professional, you should then address yourself to the serious activity of revision.

Probably you have heard someone say that there is no good writing, only good rewriting. And probably you have wondered just why you had to rewrite something into which you have already invested so much time and thought. Carefully planned rewriting need not be a difficult task; in fact, it can be exciting to see just how you might improve what you have already done. If you approach the task correctly, you will almost certainly turn an ordinary piece of writing into something that is much more effective.

Revising your paper does not have to be a long, involved process. Just as your initial draft was written by following carefully designated steps, so there are structured steps that will aid you in revising. One of the most workable systems has three phases:

- Let your writing cool.
- Check what you have written.
- Refine what you have written.

FIGURE 8-1
The potter adds attractive last-minute touches as the writer refines the structure and texture of his or her essay. (Photo by Steve Dierks.)

If you use this system, you will find that you do not have to revise an essay five or six times to improve it.

LET YOUR WRITING "COOL"

Only when you are alert and able to concentrate fully on your words can you revise your writing effectively. Before you start, let your paper "cool." Set it aside—a day or two is ideal but even an hour or two will help—and try to forget about it. The time spent away from your writing will help to freshen your mind. You will then be able to return to the paper with "new eyes" and greater objectivity.

CHECK WHAT YOU HAVE WRITTEN

An important part of polishing is to make sure that the paper gives a clear and complete impression. Read your thesis sentence and identify the controlling idea. What type of arrangement does it promise: spatial, chronological, cause and effect, comparison? Is the arrangement promised the one you actually use? Does all of the information in the paper support the thesis, or do irrelevant ideas, no matter how interesting, somehow slip in?

To check the overall impression of what you have written, complete each of the following steps.

STEP ONE Read the introduction and ask yourself these questions.

1. Is there an attention-getting device? Is it effective?
2. Is the material in the introduction pertinent to the thesis?
3. Is the thesis controversial? If so, is the opposition cited and effectively dealt with?

STEP TWO Identify the topic sentence of each paragraph and put it to the following tests.

1. Does each topic sentence either support the thesis directly or further the case of a principal support of the thesis?
2. Do the topic sentences follow the order promised by the controlling idea of the thesis, or are there gaps in the development of the essay?

STEP THREE Read the conclusion and ask yourself the following questions.

1. Is the conclusion effective?
2. Does it leave the reader with something to think about?
3. Does the ending round out the essay, or does the essay come to an abrupt halt?

STEP FOUR Examine the title.

1. Is it short and eye catching?
2. Does it convey your main idea in an original way?

REFINE WHAT YOU HAVE WRITTEN

This phase takes you through a once-over reading of the essay and a spoken reading so that you can make what you have written clearer and less awkward.

EXAMINE YOUR SENTENCES

Let your eyes glide over the paper, paying particular attention to the sentence structure. Is passive voice used only where effective? Are the sentences of varied lengths and structures? If not, recombine the sentences as you learned in Chapter Six. Remember that a lack of sentence variety is likely to bore your readers.

REMOVE UNNECESSARY WORDS

Now, read the paper out loud. As you read, listen for ineffective word use—deadwood, pileups, overuse of "to be" verbs, and poor repetition. Also rewrite trite phrases and clarify transitions.

Deadwood

Deadwood is a word or phrase that serves no purpose. All deadwood should be removed from your writing. Writing full of deadwood seems heavy, and its weight can misdirect your meaning. Besides, it's boring. Some common examples of deadwood are phrases such as *the fact that, my point is,* and *the reason is*. Another kind of deadwood is sheer repetitiveness. The following sentences are examples of how deadwood should be removed from your writing.

> He was aware of the fact that many members of the upper class had rich parents.
>
> His associations   damaged
> ~~The fact that he associated~~ with members of the Mafia ~~proved damaging~~ to his testimony.
>
> ~~My point is that~~ we are isolated from any sort of real culture when we live on a college campus.
>
> ~~The fact is that~~ the majority of high school students in a large Eastern city voted for nongraded classes.

Pileups

The use of too many prepositional phrases is a major cause of wordiness. They have a tendency to pile up in sentences and bog down your writing. Phrases beginning with *of* as well as those starting with *by, to,* and *on* are frequent trouble makers. As you read your paper aloud, see if you have used any unnecessary prepositional phrases. Some, such as *in terms of, of the fact,* and *in regard to,* seldom add to the effect of your writing and might simply be deleted. If a sentence is still wordy, you can remove other prepositional phrases in either of two ways. You can often convert the noun of the prepositional phrase to a verb. This process streamlines the sentence, making it more concise and readable.

Original: By morning, most of the prisoners in the camp had undergone the process *of interrogation by a group of government agents*.
Revised: By morning, *government agents had interrogated* most of the prisoners in the camp.

You can instead convert the noun of a prepositional phrase to an adjective. This change is a particularly effective way to eliminate *of* phrases.

Original: The needs *of the students for cultural activities* were not met by my high school because the budget *of the school* was too small.
Revised: The *students' cultural* needs were not met by my high school because the *school's* budget was too small.

The following are examples of some of the ways sentences can be revised to eliminate pileups.

consumer-action
One member of the committee ~~of consumers~~ from ~~the state of~~ New Jersey admitted that consumer groups were not able to help about 45 percent of the people who brought complaints to them.

Two of the magicians in the Kansas City Hilton's "Forty-Niner's Club" in the cocktail lounge ~~of the Hilton~~ gave my friend a magic lesson.

The final act, which has as its highlight the murder of the king, the remarriage of the queen, and the suicide of the prince, ~~is one of excitement for~~ excites the audience.

"To Be" Verbs

"To be" verb forms lead to deadwood and pileups and in themselves have little spunk. Overuse of "to be" forms can make your writing tedious. Instead of writing *is* or *are*, try to use more descriptive verbs as often as possible. Note how the following sentences have been revised.

designs
She ~~is a designer~~ of dresses for actresses.

~~There are many people to whom~~ Political involvement is a way of life for many people.

shows
The need for companionship ~~is quite apparent~~ in her behavior.

students are often confused
~~There is a prevailing confusion among many students of~~ Literature about the differences between a narrator and an author.

Rewrite Trite Phrases State more directly any cliches you can identify as you read along. After all, anybody can use a cliche, and readers will expect that your essay be more than a pastiche of worn words. (See pp. 169–171 for a full discussion of cliches.)

Repetition of Words Check your paper for the unnecessary repetition of words. Such repetition can ruin the flow of your paper and cause your readers to lose interest. Look at what it does to the following paragraph.

> Natives are usually prejudiced against immigrants. The natives think the immigrants are a danger to society and they do not think they can be trusted. They think the immigrants are spies infringing on their traditions and politics. Furthermore, the immigrants become thought of as lower-class people, possibly because the natives have stereotyped images of them. In fact, the stereotyping may be the root of much of the anti-immigrant thinking.

Awkward isn't it? Now see how much better the paragraph sounds without the unnecessary repetition.

> Natives are usually prejudiced against immigrants, considering them untrustworthy and dangerous to society. Immigrants seem to be spies infringing on the native traditions and politics. Furthermore, natives perceive the immigrants as lower-class people, possibly because the natives know only their own stereotypes and have no idea what the standard of living of the other people actually is. In fact, the stereotyping may be the root of much of the anti-immigrant thinking.

CHECK FOR TRANSITIONS Look for transitions between the sentences and between the paragraphs of your paper. Remember that readers will need to be helped along from point to point in your paper. (See pp. 121–123 for a complete discussion of transitions.)

Using the three-stage revision process is quick and profitable. Your strategy would be something like this:

Stage One
LET YOUR WRITING COOL
   Set aside your essay.
     Stage Two
      CHECK WHAT YOU HAVE WRITTEN
        Evaluate the introduction.
        Look at the topic sentences.
        Evaluate the conclusion.
        Examine the title.

Stage Three
REFINE WHAT YOU HAVE WRITTEN
   Check the sentence variety.
   Eliminate deadwood and pileups.
   Omit excessive "to be" verbs.
   Rewrite trite phrases.
   Make sure your words are not repetitive.
   Check for transitions between ideas.

EXERCISES   A. Remove or revise any wordiness or unnecessary repetition in the following sentences taken from students' essays.
1. Mrs. Elan lives a difficult and hard life.
2. Many women wish that they could be more recognized and visible in society.
3. My mother's reaction to the loud noise of the siren and the sudden movement of the car, which was making a right turn, happened simultaneously.
4. Despite the wide variation in their labor market potential which shows they have skills for performing a variety of jobs, a large proportion of criminal offenders are faced with employment problems and are actively in need of help.
5. Writing to one's congressman has a minimal effect on changing laws.
6. Prior to commitment to state prisons, most criminal offenders have jobs that involve them in a variety of labor type of vocational experience.
7. When my aunt makes her last and final departure through the door of our house we will miss her.
8. Pinball machines can have a hypnotizing type of effect on people.
9. The fact that some ex-criminals cannot adapt to the real world can be attributed to the basic fact that the cultures in which they have been living have been of the emotionally nonsupportive nature.
10. The inmate's training needs should take first precedence over the utilization of the inmate's potential skills and talents in terms of the prison's needs for staff.
11. But not only do white women often not fit the model of beauty shown on television and in magazines, but women from other racial backgrounds do not either.
12. The main problem with school is academics versus social life, basically not which is of more importance but which has a more attractive force to draw the student.

B. Evaluate the following passive constructions and convert any sentences that should emphasize the doer of the action into active constructions.
   1. In the United States, nearly 75 percent of waste materials could be converted into energy.
   2. *A Farewell to Arms* was written by Ernest Hemingway.
   3. An analysis of the story was assigned by the teacher.
   4. Next year a freeway to Simi Valley will be opened if the voters demand it.
   5. Since the topic had not been thoroughly researched by the student, he could not have written a very good essay.
   6. A book entitled *Topics for the Restless* was studied by everyone in the grammar class.
   7. Emotion-packed speeches were delivered by three members of the Senate.
   8. Was it right that a New York woman and her three small children were refused medical treatment last year by a doctor who did not feel they could pay for fees?
   9. Thirteen of the most popular students on campus were nominated for campus offices.
   10. The puppy was given to Arnold by his aunt last Christmas.

REVISION IN ACTION—A SAMPLE ESSAY

To get an idea just how you would make revisions as you read along, look at the sample essay on the next few pages. It is a rough draft of an essay on skepticism about research on extrasensory perception. Here is how the writer revised this essay. First, she set it aside to "cool"; a day later she turned to her essay with her eye on making it the best paper she had ever written. She had enjoyed the research and wanted to convey what she had learned. You can tell which changes she made on the draft by looking at the notes on the page next to the essay. Any changes she made during the second stage of revision, Check What You Have Written, are noted in the left-hand column. Any changes she made in the third stage of revision, Refine the Expression, are explained in the right-hand column. The final draft of the essay with all the changes incorporated follows the marked-up version of the rough draft. The final draft is the one the writer handed in to her English teacher.

By revising, the writer has clarified her own grasp of the subject; she has put her research into a structure that contributes to the thesis she wishes to defend, and she has polished her use of words to suit her purpose and meanings. Although by the time she had finished the revision, even she could not say that the essay was perfect (and she did decide to change a few things while typing), she felt that the revision was an improvement—that it said basically what she had set out to say, in the least possible words and in an interesting way. She was ready to receive criticism from a reader.

As you read through the following rough draft, pretend that it is your own essay. Can you detect any other weak spots that the writer missed? How would you change the paper, were it your own?

CHECK WHAT YOU HAVE WRITTEN

(1-14) The first part of the introductory paragraph gives important background information about studies of E.S.P. leading to a thesis sentence that explores the skeptical reactions to these studies.

(14-19) The thesis clearly states the assertion: "Most nonbelievers see E.S.P. only as a theory and refuse to consider its existence as a fact even when presented with scientific evidence."
The controlling ideas are
A. To nonbelievers, E.S.P. is unreal;
B. They feel that science cannot accommodate it.

REFINE WHAT YOU HAVE WRITTEN

(1) Remove deadwood.

(3-4) Change pileups.
Be direct.

(13-14) Make passive sentences active.

EXTRASENSORY PERCEPTION AND SKEPTICISM

1   Extrasensory perception ~~can be defined as~~ *is* a

2   process in which knowledge is gained without the

3   use of the senses. The first controlled *attempts* ~~experiments~~

4   ~~directed toward proving~~ *to prove* the existence of E.S.P. took

5   place in the 1930's at Duke University. These

6   experiments were widely criticized by scientists who

7   claimed that the tests were unsound and based on

8   unacceptable presuppositions. More rigorous methods

9   were adopted at Duke and in laboratories all over the

10 country and research continued. However, despite the

11 interest of numerous scientists and the results of

12 experiments conducted over the last twenty years,

13 *many psychologists* ~~E.S.P. continues~~ continue to be ~~met with~~ skeptical ~~skepticism by many~~

14 *about E.S.P.* ~~psychologists.~~ While some claim that extrasensory

15 perception is unreal, others argue that science can

16 not accommodate the phenomenon. Most nonbelievers

17 see E.S.P. only as a theory and refuse to consider

18 its existence as fact even when presented with

19 scientific evidence.

CHECK WHAT YOU HAVE WRITTEN

(1-3) Good topic sentence—E.S.P. does not "make sense." This supports the thesis, that psychologists do not believe that E.S.P. is real.

REFINE WHAT YOU HAVE WRITTEN

(6-7) Use the present tense to relate stories and for consistency.

(12) Give pronouns clear references.
(12) Include transitions.

Many skeptics refuse to accept extrasensory perception on the grounds that it does not "make sense." Dr. C.E.M. Hansel, a well-known critic of extrasensory perception, cites an interview with D.O. Hebb, Professor of Psychology at McGill University, to express this view. Hebb states that he can not accept E.S.P. "for a moment" because his "external criteria of physics and physiology" do not coincide with the evidence reported.[1] Here, Hebb admits to being prejudiced against the argument that E.S.P. exists. Understandably, there have been arguments with Hebb's viewpoint. For example, the English author Aldous Huxley commented on Hebb's statements, "That a man of science should allow a prejudice to outweigh evidence seems strange enough. It is even stranger to find a psychologist rejecting a psychological discovery simply because it cannot be explained."[2]

[1] C.E.M. Hansel, *E.S.P.: A Scientific Evaluation* (New York: Charles Scribner's Sons, 1966), p.6.

[2] Ibid.

The Writers Practical Rhetoric

CHECK WHAT YOU HAVE WRITTEN

(1) Good transition—"Another angle...."
(1–6) Good topic sentence—science would have to change to accept E.S.P. It supports the controlling idea that non-believers feel that science cannot accomodate the phenomenon.

REFINE WHAT YOU HAVE WRITTEN

(1) Liven up "to be" verbs.

(4) Remove deadwood—"proven fact" is unnecessary repetition.

(6–7) Rewrite trite phrases.

(7) Remove deadwood.

(10) Rewrite trite phrases.

(12–14) Remove deadwood.

(15) Remove deadwood.

(16) Rewrite trite phrases.

(17) Change prepositional phrases that pile up.

1   Another angle that ~~seems to be~~ *persists* persistent in
2   the skeptics' arguments against the existence of
3   E.S.P. is that parapsychologists are trying to
4   force the critics to accept ~~that~~ E.S.P. ~~is proven~~ *as*
5   fact and change the rest of science to include the
6   phenomenon. These skeptics ~~were than more hard to~~
7   ~~bend on the issue when it came to accepting~~ *refused to accept* the
8   results of carefully conducted laboratory experiments,
9   mainly because the tests have not been repeatable.
10 This problem has ~~been a major bone of contention~~ *disturbed psychologists*
11 ever since the tests were first administered;
12 however, parapsychologists will argue that ~~aspects~~ *they*
13 ~~are involved which can influence the scores on~~
14 ~~tests and~~ can account for the variance in results
15 during each repetition. ~~In my opinion,~~ A close
16 *analysis* ~~inspection~~ of the work of parapsychologists is
17 imperative to ~~make a just evaluation of~~ *evaluate fairly* the
18 possibility of extrasensory perception. If the
19 parapsychologists' claims are justified, they will

204 The Writers Practical Rhetoric

CHECK WHAT YOU HAVE WRITTEN

REFINE WHAT YOU HAVE WRITTEN

(1–2) Change prepositional phrases that pile up.

(2–3) Combine related sentences for fluency and variety.

(6) Remove deadwood.

(7) Remove deadwood.

(11) Remove deadwood.

(16–17) Rewrite trite expressions.

1 require a complete revision of contemporary scientific thought.

2 ~~of scientific investigation. These revisions can be~~

3 comparable to ~~those~~ that made necessary in biology by

4 Darwin and in physics by Einstein.[3] The skeptics

5 still maintain that it is important to understand

6 ~~the very nature of~~ how conventional experimental

7 methods can yield results leading to ~~very highly~~

8 erroneous conclusions.

9   Some people, even after they have studied the

10 evidence for E.S.P., will insist that E.S.P. does

11 not occur ~~at all~~ and that all the alleged testimony

12 for it is based on nothing more than superstition,

13 imagination, coincidence, bad memory, or faulty

14 observation on the part of highly emotional or

15 unstable individuals. These skeptics listen to the

16 stories told by people who have experienced ~~one~~ a

17 form ~~or another~~ of E.S.P. and then claim that

[3] Ibid., p. 8.

206 The Writers Practical Rhetoric

CHECK WHAT YOU HAVE WRITTEN

REFINE WHAT YOU HAVE WRITTEN

(1–2) Change noun pile-ups and remove deadwood.

(3) Rewrite trite expressions.

(4) Give all paragraphs clear and relevant topic sentences. The new topic sentence expands on the typical response of skeptics from the previous paragraph.

(6–8) Combine related sentences for fluency and variety.
(6) Remove deadwood.
(7–8) Remove deadwood.

(10) Include transitions.

(11) Include transitions.

(13) Include transitions.

(14–15) Remove deadwood.

(17) Remove deadwood.

the person ~~did not in actual fact experience this manifestation of extrasensory perception, but rather came upon~~ the experience by chance. ~~it out of the blue.~~ Many skeptics will place the label "coincidence" on any case study for E.S.P. and some will even accuse of fraud people who relate stories of personal E.S.P. experiences. A typical case study is ~~For example,~~ the story ~~is told~~ of a ~~certain~~ woman who lived in a boarding house and was accused of stealing a lost watch. As ~~She described the incident~~ explained to Dr. Louisa Rhine at Duke University, ~~It is apparent that~~ she was ostracized by the others in the rooming house and she even had begun to feel guilty. As a result of this anxiety, ~~S~~she kept repeating over and over to herself, "Where is that watch?" A week of these questions had gone by when she dreamed that the watch was wedged between the leg of the bathtub and the wall. To her surprise ~~T~~the woman found the watch right in the place she had dreamed it to be.[4] Most ~~Because of the fact that someone did not believe in E.S.P,~~ skeptics ~~he~~ would consider the dream and the finding of the lost item a coincidence ~~for the simple reason that~~ because there

[4] Louisa Rhine, E.S.P. in Life and Lab (London: MacMillan, 1967), p. 70.

208 The Writers Practical Rhetoric

CHECK WHAT YOU HAVE WRITTEN

REFINE WHAT YOU HAVE WRITTEN

(1) Remove deadwood.

(3–8) Combine related sentences for fluency and variety.
(3–4) Remove deadwood.

(5) Remove deadwood.

(7–8) Remove deadwood.

(8) Rewrite trite expressions.

(9–10) Remove deadwood.

(10–15) Combine related sentences for fluency and variety.
(10–13) Remove deadwood.

(14) Rule out excessive negatives and rewrite trite phrases.
(15) Remove deadwood.

(16) Avoid obvious signals in concluding.
(16–19) Remove irrelevant ideas or new subject of discussion from conclusions.

is no ~~concrete~~ evidence ~~which would convince him~~ of any relationship between the dream and the finding of the watch. Some skeptics might even ~~go to such an extent as to~~ claim that the dream did not occur ~~in actuality~~ but that the woman had actually stolen the watch and had made up the whole story to relieve herself of the blame; though ~~It should be added, however, that very~~ few skeptics would offer such an extreme analysis. ~~go to such great lengths.~~ ~~Though most skeptics share some of the beliefs mentioned above.~~ Not all skeptics are as closed minded, however, ~~as some of the people cited in these examples which have been set forth to identify the main currents in skeptical views of E.S.P.~~ and a few ~~It is a fact that some skeptics~~ can cast aside their antagonisms upon learning ~~in light of~~ new scientific evidence ~~presented to them.~~

~~In conclusion, experimental~~ work is no longer ~~directed toward attempting to prove the existence of extrasensory perception or towards trying to convince people who are unconvinceable.~~ E.S.P., it is true,

210 The Writers Practical Rhetoric

CHECK WHAT YOU HAVE WRITTEN

REFINE WHAT YOU HAVE WRITTEN

(1) Remove deadwood.

(2) Vary word choice and avoid unnecessary repetition.

(3–4) Any statement made in the essay automatically belongs to the writer of the essay; consequently, for the writer to mention the fact is unnecessary and improper.

(3) Remove deadwood—"and expand." "Continue," in this case, implies expand.

(5–7) A good conclusion to an essay which discusses an ongoing controversy is a suggestion about the future. Note the moderation of the suggestion through the use of "perhaps."

(5) Rewrite trite phrases. (In this case the words were deleted.)

1 has not achieved a status of acceptance by "official
2 science." Yet even without official acceptance, E.S.P.
3 research will continue and expand and it is hoped by
4 many including the writer of this treatise that soon
5 a major breakthrough will occur in which E.S.P. will
6 be able to be more fully studied--its operational
7 mechanism discovered.

1.

Extrasensory Perception and Skepticism

    Extrasensory perception is a process in which knowledge is gained without the use of the senses. The first controlled attempts to prove the existence of E.S.P. took place in the 1930's at Duke University. These experiments were widely criticized by scientists who claimed that the tests were unsound and based on unacceptable presuppositions. More rigorous methods were adopted, at Duke and in laboratories all over the country, and research continued. However, despite the interest of numerous scientists and the results of experiments conducted over the last twenty years, many psychologists continue to be skeptical about E.S.P. While some claim that extrasensory perception is unreal, others argue that science can not accommodate the phenomenon. Most nonbelievers see E.S.P. only as a theory and refuse to consider its existence as fact even when presented with scientific evidence.

    Many skeptics refuse to accept extrasensory perception on the grounds that it does not "make sense." Dr. C.E.M. Hansel, a well-known critic of extrasensory perception, cites an interview with D.O. Hebb, Professor of Psychology at McGill University, to express this view. Hebb states that he can not accept E.S.P. "for a moment" because his "external criteria of physics and physiology" do not coincide with the evidence reported.[1] Here, Hebb admits to being prejudiced against the argument that E.S.P.

2.

exists. Understandably, there have been arguments with Hebb's viewpoint. For example, the English author Aldous Huxley commented on Hebb's statement, "That a man of science should allow a prejudice to outweigh evidence seems strange enough. It is even stranger to find a psychologist rejecting a psychological discovery simply because it cannot be explained."[2]

Another angle that persists in the skeptics' arguments against the existence of E.S.P. is that parapsychologists are trying to force the critics to accept E.S.P. as fact and change the rest of science to include the phenomenon. These skeptics refuse to accept the results of carefully conducted laboratory experiments, mainly because the tests have not been repeatable. This problem has disturbed psychologists ever since the tests were first administered; however, parapsychologists will argue that they can account for the variance in results during each repetition. A close analysis of the work of parapsychologists is imperative to evaluate fairly the possibility of extrasensory perception. If the parapsychologists' claims are justified, they will require a complete revision of contemporary scientific thought comparable to that made necessary in biology by Darwin and in physics by Einstein.[3] The skeptics still maintain that it is important to understand how conventional experimental methods can yield results leading to erroneous conclusions.

3.

Some people, even after they have studied the evidence for E.S.P., will insist that E.S.P. does not occur and that all the alleged testimony for it is based on nothing more than superstition, imagination, coincidence, bad memory, or faulty observation on the part of highly emotional or unstable individuals. These skeptics listen to the stories told by people who have experienced a form of E.S.P. and then claim that the people came upon the experience by chance.

Many skeptics will place the label "coincidence" on any case study for E.S.P., and some will even accuse of fraud people who relate stories of personal E.S.P. experiences. A typical case study is the story of a woman who lived in a boarding house and was accused of stealing a lost watch. As she explained to Dr. Louisa Rhine at Duke University, she was ostracized by the others in the rooming house and even had begun to feel guilty. As a result of this anxiety, she kept repeating over and over to herself, "Where is that watch?" A week of these questions had gone by when she dreamed that the watch was wedged between the leg of the bathtub and the wall. To her surprise, the woman found the watch right in the place she had dreamed it to be.[4] Most skeptics would consider the dream and the finding of the lost item a coincidence because there is no evidence of any relationship between the dream and the finding of the watch. Some skeptics might even claim that the dream did not occur but that the woman had actually stolen the watch

4.

and had made up the whole story to relieve herself of the blame, though few skeptics would offer such an extreme analysis. Not all skeptics are closed minded, however, and a few can cast aside their antagonisms upon learning new scientific evidence.

    E.S.P., it is true, has not been accepted by "official science." Yet even without official sanction, research will continue. Perhaps someday E.S.P. will be able to be more fully studied--its operational mechanism discovered.

Notes

[1] C.E.M. Hansel, E.S.P.: A Scientific Evaluation (New York: Charles Scribner's Sons, 1966), p. 6.

[2] Ibid.

[3] Ibid, p. 8.

[4] Louisa Rhine, E.S.P. in Life and Lab (London: MacMillan, 1967), p. 70.

It is a good assumption that your rough draft is just that—rough. Critical revision develops that rough vision into a fully expanded and polished statement. Really, then, good writing is usually only good revision. Very few persons can set down what they want to say, as they wish to express it, the first time around. The point of revising is to *look again* at what you've created, checking to see whether you have conveyed to your reader just what you set out to say. Revision is usually the natural follow-up to the rough draft, the point at which you give your approval before the final presentation to your reader.

Most often you will revise before handing in the essay, and that will be that. You will receive the paper back with comments and an evaluation so that next time you write a paper you may take into account some general suggestions. But sometimes there is an opportunity to rewrite, after the paper has been handed in. After the teacher has evaluated your paper or after you and a classmate have gone over the essay together (a good way to do so is to read out loud to a partner), you may be called upon to revise the essay based on the comments of a reader. This assignment may, for a moment, stump you—all those markings on the paper you have already tried to perfect may make your previous efforts appear less fruitful than you had expected.

But there is a better way of interpreting these comments. The second revision makes you even more aware of the expectations of your reader, and the resulting essay will naturally be clearer than the first. All writers find it very difficult to guess exactly all the readers' responses. Writing alone in your room is equivalent to having a one-way conversation. Thus it is only after sharing your thoughts with someone that you can fully test your effectiveness as a writer. So it is important to look upon your readers' comments positively and to see the required changes as a challenge in communicating what really matters to you.

As you revise you may wish to refer to the list, Twenty-five Questions for the Writer, inside the front cover. The questions will perhaps offer clues to some of the concerns of your reader, indicating where you might find helpful suggestions for revising.

EXERCISES Directions: Refine the writing in each of the paragraphs below by using the steps you learned in the chapter.

   A. Flying in a modern jet is ten times safer than traveling in planes of the mid-1950s. Over the years, airplanes have become sturdier and engines not only much more powerful but also much more reliable. Manufacturers of airplanes as well as airlines are spending millions of dollars on the development of better instruments and warning devices onboard to insure greater safety. Radar used today has been made better or improved to give a clearer picture. A number of important and significant warning devices have been introduced. One such device sounds an alarm if proper wing flaps are not extended on takeoff. Another flashes a red light, which is a warning signal, sounds a whooping alarm, which can be heard, and plays a recording with a voice that orders, "Pull up, pull up" if the pilot is flying into a mountainside or into a tower on ground without his knowing it. The introduction of the most modern planes and devices has made air travel of this day and age one of the safest means of transportation of people.

B. In *The Great Gatsby* Tom Buchanan and his wife Daisy represent the established rich who have never needed to work in order to attain their needs as well as a position of wealth and status. In contrast to Gatsby, the Buchanans own an elegant Georgian colonial-style mansion type of house in East Egg which is the other side of West Egg on the opposite side. The vanity of their lives is pointed out by Fitzgerald as Fitzgerald shows the sensitivities and responsibilities which the Buchanans lack. As a result of their inherited wealth, they never have had to struggle or suffer so they tend to live their lives without any specific purpose or directional objective. They are in the habit of wandering, for instance, whenever they wish—to New York—to London—back to East Egg or even to France. Without the existence of goals in their lives they have become preoccupied with themselves and have led hedonistic lives, in my opinion.

9

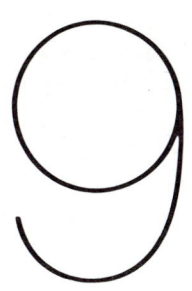

How Do You Use the Library?

You are bombarded with information daily, not just from the printed word, but from radio, television, film, newspapers, and personal communications. How do you know if this information is correct? How can you find out more about it? The answers probably lie somewhere among the many thousands of books, periodicals, and government documents published each year. It has been said that true education is not so much knowing large quantities of facts and information as it is knowing how to find the facts and information you need quickly and efficiently. You can acquire this skill by learning how to use libraries effectively.

Libraries bring order to the chaos of publications by specific systems of classification, storage, and retrieval. They can help you find out just about anything you want to know, from how to raise goats to how to find a summer job. You can even delve into more theoretical areas such as the causes of the Vietnam war. Although this chapter is intended to be read as a whole, you will probably want to refer to particular reference tools when you choose a topic for your research paper.

BOOKS

THE CARD CATALOG

Books are probably the first things you expect to find when you enter a library. Don't be intimidated by the seemingly endless rows of books you first see. Finding the exact book you want is actually quite easy. Most American libraries arrange their books by assigning call numbers from either the Dewey Decimal System or the Library of Congress

System (LC). You don't need to worry about the intricacies of these systems. They are simply letter by letter or number by number methods of putting books in a logical order. Here are brief outlines of both systems:

Library of Congress System (LC)

A	General
B	Philosophy, Religion
C	History
D	Foreign History and Topography
E-F	American History
G	Geography, Anthropology
H	Social Sciences
J	Political Science
K	Law
L	Education
M	Music
N	Fine Arts
P	Language and Literature
Q	Science
R	Medicine
S	Agriculture; Plant and Animal Industry
T	Technology
U	Military Science
V	Naval Science
Z	Bibliography and Library Sciences

Dewey Decimal Classification

000	General works
100	Philosophy
200	Religion
300	Social Sciences
400	Philology
500	Pure Science
600	Technology
700	The Arts
800	Literature
900	Geography, Biography, History

In most libraries, the card catalog lets you use three tools for looking up a book—the author, the title, and the subject. Usually, if you are looking for a particular book, you will look under the author's name (last name first, of course). Sometimes you may not know the author's name or be sure of the exact spelling. In these cases, you can look directly under the title. Finally, you can look up a book under the subject or subjects with which it deals.

Suppose you are asked to write a paper on "Violence in the media" or "World War I cartoons" and know of no books on the subject. You will quickly realize how useful the subject catalog can be. Sometimes, however, you will find what seems to be a credibility gap between the subject headings you have in mind and the headings actually used in the card catalog. Who would ever suspect that books on World War I cartoons would be listed in the card catalog under the heading *European War, 1914–1918—Humor, Caricatures, etc.*? How do you bridge this gap? Well, libraries also have systems for assigning subject headings to books. Those who use LC call numbers use the *Library of Congress Subject Heading Guide* (8th ed., 1975, with semiannual supplements), and most who use Dewey call numbers use the Sears' *List of Subject Headings* (10th ed., 1972).

Consulting either the LC or the Sears guides can help you find the headings you want in three ways. To begin with, you will find cross-references. If you look in the *LC Guide* under the heading "Literature and War," you will be referred to the heading *War and Literature*. Secondly, you will find under most of the headings that *are* used (indicated by dark black print in the subject heading guide) a list of "see also" references. These will give you ideas for alternate ways to approach your topic. As an example, in the *LC Guide*, you can find the following:

Socialism

    sa Collective settlements
          Dialectical materialism
          Old-age pensions
          Utopias
    x   Marxism
          Social democracy
    xx Sociology
          Collectivism

The *sa* stands for "see also." The *x* means that the heading is one that is not used in the card catalog, and the *xx* is similar to a "see also" reference, except that the headings here are usually broader and more general than the heading you have looked up.

Finally, to help you narrow down a topic to the specific area you are interested in, many useful subheadings are listed. For instance, under the broad heading *Plants*, it may be helpful to know of the following subheadings: *Identification, Nutrition, Reproduction,* and *Water requirements*. Books about how to teach a particular subject use the subheading *Study and teaching* under that subject as in *Political Science—Study and teaching*. Children's books on a subject, come under the subheading *Juvenile Literature*, for example, *Porpoises—Juvenile literature*. The subheadings *History* and *Bibliography* appear under almost every subject in the guides. Often you may encounter sub-subheadings. How's this for a really long one? *United States—History—Civil War, 1861–65—Personal narratives—Confederate side*. As you can see, this heading really does zero in on a specific area of the topic. The point here is that you do not need to settle for the subject heading *Middle Ages* if what you really want is a children's book on the history of the Middle Ages. *Middle Ages—History—Juvenile literature* will take you much closer to what you are looking for.

You will also need to learn the peculiarities of alphabetizing and filing in the card catalog. Every library has its own eccentricities, but most of them follow a few basic rules. The order of arrangement in the card catalog when the same word appears as an author's name, as a subject, and as the first word of a title is illustrated by the following example:

Love, John L. (author's name)
Love—Quotations, maxims, etc. (subject heading)
Love and beauty (title of book)

The articles, "a," "an," and "the," as well as similar articles in foreign languages, are ignored in filing. Numerals and abbreviations are filed as if they were spelled out ("15" and "54" would be filed as "fifteen" and "fifty-four," "Mr." and "Dr." would be filed as "mister" and "doctor"). German umlauts (ü and ö) are filed as if spelled "ue" and "oe." Once you have these rules down pat, you should be off to a good start. If you have any problems, however, don't hesitate to ask the librarian at the reference desk for assistance.

Once you have found the heading you need, it's time to go to the card catalog. When you find the entries for the books you want, copy down the entire call number, the author, and the title for each one. Most libraries provide maps, directories, or handouts to help you find where various call numbers are located. Still, you may not find a book in its proper place on the shelf. Persistence, you will discover, is one of the keys to successful library use. Circulation departments (where you check books out) maintain lists of missing books and books that have been checked out. If a book you want is not on either of these lists, they will usually begin a search procedure and notify you when the book is located.

BEYOND YOUR LOCAL LIBRARY

The card catalog will help you to find books in your own college library, but you need not be limited by local resources. The Library of Congress in Washington, D. C., has a copy of almost every book every published in the United States plus a great many of those published in foreign countries. They publish a card catalog in book form of what they have. So if you want to find additional works by a certain author or more books on a certain subject, look in the *Catalog of Books Represented by Library of Congress Printed Cards Issued to July 31, 1952*. This catalog (usually referred to as the LC catalog), along with its supplements, lists all the books in the Library of Congress up to 1952. In 1953, the catalog became known as the *National Union Catalog* and, in addition to listing books, began listing the other libraries in the United States in which the books may also be found. Supplements are published regularly so that the catalog is always complete to within three or four months of the time you use it. You can look up books in the LC catalogs by author or subject, but not by title.

Another tool that can help you find the books you need is the *Bibliographic Index*, which since 1937 indexes by subject the book-length bibliographies as well as the brief bibliographies that have appeared at the end of books or journal articles.

Now, how can you get hold of all these reference sources you have just found out about if your library doesn't have them? First, check the other libraries in your town or immediate area. You can often obtain borrowing privileges at public libraries or those of neighboring universities. Next, consider Interlibrary Loan, a procedure by which your library can borrow a book for you from another library. Many libraries are trying to cope with decreasing budgets and increases in the number of books published by expanding their inter-library loan programs. Be sure to ask at your library's Reference Desk about this service.

Finally, you may find a particular book so interesting or valuable for your research that you want to buy it. To see if it is available for purchase, look in *Books in Print* (1948–) or *Subject Guide to Books in Print* (1957–), annual author, title, and subject indexes to all of the books currently in print in the United States. Here you may obtain the correct author, title, publisher, date of publication, and price and then order the book on your own or through a bookstore.

EXERCISES

A. Answer the following questions about your library.
 1. Is the card catalog divided into author-title and subject sections or not?

2. Are books cataloged by the Library of Congress System or the Dewey Decimal System?
3. Are the bookstacks open, or must you ask for a book you want at the circulation desk?
4. What special areas, such as a microfilm room or special collections, does your library have?

B. For each of the following topics, find and list five useful subject headings from the subject heading guide your library uses. Use the supplements if necessary.

Evolution   Mental healing
Energy conservation Sex in literature
Capital punishment

C. By consulting the *Bibliographic Index*, find out if a bibliography already exists on any of the topics in exercise B.
D. Compile a minibibliography of your own, listing at least ten books on one of the above topics. If your library does not have enough books, consult the LC catalogs or *Books in Print*.
E. Look up a book in which you are interested, copy the catalog card onto a piece of paper, and identify all of the parts.

GENERAL REFERENCE WORKS

Reference books are valuable tools for finding specific bits of information about a subject or locating sources for in-depth information quickly and efficiently. Every library has a special area where they are kept. You should never hesitate to ask the librarian at the reference desk for any help or advice you may need. In this section, indexes and fact-books of a general nature will be discussed. Those relating to specific areas of study will be covered in later sections.

When approaching a particular reference book for the first time, you should ask yourself several questions. What does the book set out to do? What limitations in such areas as time span, geography, or nationality does it have? What kinds of indexes—subject, author, or title—does it have? How accurate and reliable is it? Some of these questions will be dealt with in this chapter, and others can be answered by scanning the introduction to the book itself. Almost any question you might have, however, can be answered by looking in *A Guide to Reference Books* (9th ed., 1976), compiled by Eugene P. Sheehy, which gives detailed information on just about every reference work you might want to use.

ENCYCLOPEDIAS AND DICTIONARIES

Usually, before beginning to search for books, articles, and documents, you will want to more clearly define what your topic is all about. Is it so broad that the information available will be overwhelming, or is it so narrow that you will be frustrated in your search for any information at all? Can it conveniently be broken down into smaller components? A general encyclopedia is an excellent tool for answering these questions. For years, the *Encyclopedia Britannica* has been considered one of the best English-language encyclopedias. The ninth and eleventh editions, which are especially well regarded, have long, signed articles by specialists in their fields, bibliographies at the end of many of the articles, and detailed indexes. With the publication of the fifteenth edition, the format of the encyclopedia was changed and there are now three sections: the *Propedia* (a one-volume outline of knowledge), the *Micropedia* (a ten-volume set of short articles), and the *Macropedia* (a nineteen-volume set of long, detailed articles). Although the fifteenth edition does contain more brief factual information and biographical articles, the lack of a detailed subject index and the sometimes confusing three-part arrangement cause many people to prefer the earlier editions.

The *Encyclopedia Americana* is authoritative and reliable. It is particularly good on American cities and towns. To get a thorough perspective on a topic, you might find it helpful to read the articles from both the *Americana* and the *Britannica* as well as one from a specialized encyclopedia appropriate to the particular field of study. Say you were doing research on the ancient city of Pompeii. Under "Pompeii" in the *Encyclopedia Americana* are photographs, three pages of text, and a bibliography. The *Britannica* includes diagrams and maps rather than photographs and offers a slightly longer text. A specialized subject encyclopedia, the *Encyclopedia of World Art*, which will be introduced later, scatters its references to Pompeii throughout most of its thirteen volumes, giving a total of about ten pages of information along with numerous maps and color plates.

In the process of reading encyclopedia articles, you may run across unfamiliar words, or words you recognize used in unfamiliar ways. A dictionary should help here. Dictionaries can be far from dull. A storm of controversy greeted the publication of *Webster's Third New International Dictionary of the English Language*, unabridged, in 1961. It was caused, in part, because of the omission of proper names, but mainly because many people disliked the fact that the dictionary reflected changing speech habits in which new words are coined and old ones fall into disuse. The purpose of *Webster's Third*, however, is to show how the majority of educated people talk, not how someone wishes they would talk.

Offering more direct guidance to traditional usage, *Webster's New International Dictionary of the English Language*, unabridged (2nd ed., 1934, rev. 1961) is still a highly respected dictionary. If you are unsure which to use, compare definitions from the two dictionaries, as well as from another recent unabridged dictionary such as the *Random House Dictionary of the English Language* (1966).

Many words and phrases currently used are not yet considered to be generally accepted by word experts. To look up expressions like "outfox," "bite the bullet," or "party pooper," you will have to check in a dictionary of nonstandard usage such as Wentworth and Flexner's *Dictionary of American Slang* (1960). Similarly, there are some words that are no longer in common use. Sometimes you may want to find one of these, or see what a word actually meant in the past, or even trace the history of a word, say through the eighteenth and nineteenth centuries. The *Oxford English Dictionary* (1933, with supplements), regarded by many as the grandparent of all dictionaries, comes in thirteen volumes and can tell you more about most words than you will probably ever need to know.

To add interest and variety to your writing, try using a dictionary that lists synonyms and related words. *Roget's International Thesaurus* (3rd ed., 1962) or *Webster's Collegiate Thesaurus* (1976) can be very helpful.

A quotations dictionary such as *Bartlett's Familiar Quotations* (14th ed., 1968) or *Evans' Dictionary of Quotations* (1968)—both of which index memorable quotes from prose and poetry by author, first line, and subject—can also help you to add color and emphasis to a point you are making. For example, an argument you are presenting against civil disorder might be enhanced by Lincoln's statement, "There is no grievance that is a fit object of redress by mob law."

Now that you have a clearer perspective on your subject, perhaps by breaking it down into more workable components and defining any unfamiliar terms, you are ready to begin searching for sources that deal with your topic in greater depth.

ESSAY AND GENERAL LITERATURE INDEX

Often, instead of being a monograph on one subject, a book will consist of a collection of essays, speeches, historical articles, or similar short pieces. One of these may be just the thing you need to back up an important point. How do you find it? Actually, it's quite easy. Suppose you are doing a paper on student rebellion in the 1960s. There is an essay entitled "Permanent Campus Revolution?" in *Humanistic Frontiers in American Education*, edited by R. P. Fairfield, that could be very useful. The card catalog, however, lists only the main title of the book, not every essay included inside. You could scan the table of contents, if you were lucky enough to find the book in the first place. Luckily, there is a better way. Look in the *Essay and General Literature Index*. Beginning in 1900, this reference work indexes materials appearing in about 300 anthologies annually by author, subject, and title. The entry for the essay you are interested in looks like this:

"College students—United States—Political activities"
Dixon, J. P. Permanent campus revolution? *In* Fairfield, R. P., ed.
Humanistic frontiers in American education, pp. 261–68.

Once you have discovered the sources, all you have to do is check the card catalog to find out if your library has the book you want.

BOOK REVIEWS

Normally, you will want the sources you use for a paper to be the best ones possible. Since there is a great deal of material available on most subjects, you don't want to waste your time reading an inaccurate or superficial book. It is sometimes wise, therefore, to first evaluate a book for accuracy and thoroughness. If you are unfamiliar with the subject of executive power, for example, you may wonder whether or not the book *President and Congress; Power and Policy*, by L. Fisher (1972), will be a good source of information. The easiest way to find out is to read some reviews of the book.

Book reviews appear in almost every newspaper and magazine. To find the reviews you want quickly, use a reference tool such as the *Book Review Digest*. Beginning in 1905, this work annually compiles book reviews from about seventy-five periodicals and newspapers and arranges them by author. There is also a title and subject index in the back of each volume. You need to know two things to use this tool—the year the book was published and the correct spelling of the author's name.

The entries include brief summaries of each review and the name of the periodical or newspaper where the review may be found along with the volume, page number, and date. In addition, you are given the number of words in each review. This is a helpful clue in deciding which reviews will be the most valuable for you to search out.

A reference tool with slightly broader coverage is *Book Review Index* (1966–). In it, however, summaries of the reviews are not included. A newcomer, *Current Book Review Citations*, is even better for books published from 1976 on, since it indexes the book reviews that are listed in many major periodical indexes. One caution when searching for reviews: if you don't find one under the year a book was published, look at the following year or years. Reviewers, like college students, sometimes fall behind in their writing schedules.

PERIODICALS AND THEIR INDEXES

Most of the reviews you will find appear in periodicals, which are especially valuable sources of current information or information on specific subjects. Don't let yourself be confused by the terminology. Some instructors insist on referring to them as journals, others as periodicals, still others as magazines, and libraries often call them serials. All of these terms refer to publications, such as *Saturday Review*, *Sports Illustrated*, or *American Journal of Sociology*, that appear regularly (two, four, twelve, or more times a year) for an indefinite period. Libraries vary widely in how they list and shelve periodicals. Many maintain a separate list of periodical titles, and most have a periodicals room where current, unbound issues are kept. They are sometimes arranged by call number, sometimes alphabetically by title. Ask at the reference desk which system your library uses. In most cases, however, old issues are bound into annual volumes. A useful guide, *Ulrich's International Periodicals Directory*, annually lists every periodical currently being published in the world. The periodicals are grouped by subject so that you can conveniently scan the titles available in the field you are interested in. There is also a comprehensive title index at the end.

A problem you may face with periodicals is that you may not know which title, volume, or pages you need. You simply know that you need information about a specific topic. This is where the periodical indexes come in. The most general, and the most widely used, is the *Readers' Guide to Periodical Literature*. Along with its predecessor, *Poole's Index, Readers' Guide* indexes the article in about 150 magazines by subject and author from 1802 to the present. It is published monthly. The magazines included are, for the most part, popular, general interest magazines such as *Time, New Yorker, Organic Gardening and Farming,* and *Scientific American*. Thus, the index is a good reference tool for finding articles on newsworthy events, current or historical, and popular or controversial topics. It also indexes film and theater reviews. As with the card catalog, you have to approach the subject headings in the *Readers' Guide* in an adventurous frame of mind. For example, movie reviews are found under the heading *Moving picture plays—Criticisms, plots, etc.—Single works*. Articles on busing were for years listed under the roundabout heading *School children—Transportation for integration*. Volumes of the *Readers' Guide* are cumulated annually, and, as in any periodical index, the extent of your search should be determined by your topic.

When you look under a subject heading, such as "Mulching," in the *Readers' Guide*, you will find a citation, or reference, to a periodical article which always gives the following information:

a

Canary Islanders mulch with volcanic ash.

b   c d

A. Halperin. il Org Gard and Farm
17:52 O '72

e f g

  a   title of article
  b   author (if there is one given)
  c   illustrations. Here you may also find "por" (portrait), "bibliog" (bibliography), or other informative notes.
  d   title of the periodical (usually abbreviated).
      A list of abbreviations is found at the front of each issue of most periodical indexes.
  e   volume number
  f   page number or numbers
  g   date of the periodical

There are over 100 periodical indexes, covering many fields of study, currently being published. Most of them use a similar form for their citations. Many specific periodical indexes will be mentioned in later sections.

NEWSPAPERS AND THEIR INDEXES   Newspapers are also a valuable source of information. The best directory of U. S. newspapers is the *Ayer Director of Publications*, which lists the newspapers by state and city and has a title index at the end. Many libraries keep older issues of newspapers on microfilm, as they are readily available and much more usable in this form. However, it's very difficult to make use of microfilm without an index. That's why well-indexed newspapers tend to be the ones that are well used. The prime example is *The New York Times*, which is indexed from 1851 to the present. In the index, which is cumulated annually, you may look under a subject or person's name and find the titles of articles, often with an abstract or summary, and the date, the page number, and even the column number. This enables you to turn quickly to the point you want on the reel of microfilm. Researchers looking for a name or a fact often need go no further than the index. Someone wanting to know the U. S. budget for 1974, for example, could find the amount ($277.8 billion) under the heading *United States—Finances—Budget* in the 1974 index. Thus, in addition to being a guide to *The New York Times, The New York Times Index for the Published News* is an important reference tool in its own right. For a more detailed indexing of international news stories, the *London Times Index* (1790–) has long been a major resource.

BIOGRAPHIES   Sometimes the subject of your research may be a person rather than a topic. You can, of course, look up his or her name in the subject card catalog to see if a book-length biography exists. Relatively few people, however, have entire books written about them, so you must often rely on brief sketches, periodical articles, or news stories. The best place to begin, particularly if you are not sure of the period or the nationality of your subject, is the *Biography Index*. Beginning in 1947, this work indexes biographical sketches of persons from all occupations, geographical areas, and periods that have appeared in over 1500 magazines, newspapers, and biographical dictionaries. It is published by the same company that publishes the *Readers' Guide*, so the citations are in the same convenient form. An interesting feature of this index is the classification at the back of each volume of all the persons referred to in it by occupation. Thus, if you are assigned a biographical report on a sociologist or an arsonist and no names spring immediately to your mind, you may get some ideas from the *Biography Index*. If your subject is a living American, you may find a new reference tool, the *Biographical Dictionaries Master Index* (1975/76–), very useful. It is a personal name index to the biographical sketches that appear in more than fifty current biography collections, including the "Who's Who" references.

GOVERNMENT DOCUMENTS

Government documents are published on almost every conceivable subject. Therefore, they are introduced here as general reference tools rather than under a specific discipline. Although government publications are often thought of as simply transcripts of hearings, reports of congressional committees, bills introduced in Congress, and laws passed, looking through the 1975 *Monthly Catalog of United States Government Publications* you can find such titles as "Bilingual/Bicultural Education, Privilege or Right?", "Windows and People, Psychological Reaction to Environments With and Without Windows," and "Geological and Geomagnetic Background Noise in Two Areas of the North Atlantic." So, no matter what your research topic is, a look at the *Monthly Catalog* can be very fruitful. The catalog, which lists all the publications of the U. S. government, has an annually cumulated subject index. Title and author indexes have been included since 1974. Recently a cumulated subject index covering 1900–1971 was published. Using this index can save your having to look through year after year of annual indexes.

FACTBOOKS AND STATISTICS

After you have located the books, articles, or documents you need for your topic, you may find that you want some hard facts and figures to back up the points you wish to make. Perhaps the most basic type of factbook is a good almanac such as the *World Almanac*. An amazing variety of facts and figures, everything from U. S. pollution control expenditures to a list of the duckpin bowling champions, is packed into its more than 900 pages. In addition, most general encyclopedias publish yearbooks, which are useful records of each year's progress and events. You may assess, for example, trends in fashion and dress or the most important events in some country, such as China, during a particular year. *Facts on File* is another annual publication that summarizes the news events of each year in chronological order. It has a detailed subject index at the end of each volume.

It seems that almost everything today is measured in one way or another, and people usually tend to be impressed by numbers. You may therefore want to use some statistics to reinforce certain aspects of your research. But a word of caution. When using statistics, you should always do the following:

- Check the date carefully. Are you sure that the statistics you want to use are not too old for your purposes?
- Check the size of the sample. Is it large enough to reveal a meaningful trend?
- Check out the source. How reliable and authoritative is it?
- Check the size of the number you use. Is it thousands, millions, or maybe even billions? You should always read the notes at the top of the table carefully to find out how many zeros to add to the number given in the table.

Keeping these points in mind, a detailed digest of U. S. statistics may be found in *Statistical Abstracts of the United States*, published annually since 1878. In it, summary tables of statistical surveys made by the government on a wide variety of subjects, from mortgages to museums, are presented in a concise, readable form. For international statistics, look in the *United Nations Statistical Yearbook*, which began publication in 1948. If you are writing a paper about the current rise in coffee prices, for instance, it might be helpful to see the table outlining the world production of coffee, nation by nation, for the past fifteen years.

Statistical Abstracts or the *United National Statistical Yearbook* may not contain statistics on the subject you are interested in. It is possible that there are none, but before assuming this, check in *Statistics Sources* by Wasserman and Paskar. In this work, under all kinds of subject headings, from "Fish meal" to "Poland—Museums," are listed other sources in which to look for statistical information.

EXERCISES
A. Find out the following information about your library.
 1. Where is the reference desk located?
 2. Is the reference collection arranged by call numbers or are the reference works grouped together by subject?
 3. Is all of the collection in the reference room, or are some of the reference tools in other areas or on other floors?
 4. Where are government documents collected?
 5. Where are current newspapers and periodicals kept?
B. Choose one of the following topics and compare the articles on it from the *Encyclopedia Americana* and *Encyclopedia Britannica*. List the similarities and the differences. Do you think one is more informative than the other? Why?

 Television   Peking, China   Muscles
 Cincinnati, Ohio Michaelangelo

C. Assume you are doing a research paper on one of the above topics. Choose a period of two years and list the citations on your topic (a maximum of ten) from the *Readers' Guide*.
D. Using the same time period as for exercise C, check *The New York Times Index* and list a citation, if there is one, appearing there on your topic. If there is not a citation, check for one of the other topics in exercise C. Explain all the parts of the citation.
E. Locate and list a citation to a biographical article on one of the following:

 Ronald Ziegler   Tom Wolfe
 O. J. Simpson   Marian Anderson
 Mike Nichols

F. Find a citation to a review of one of the following books:

 Walden Two   *All the President's Men*
 The Greening of America *One Flew over the Cuckoo's Nest*

G. Choose one of the following subjects and describe the procedure (search strategy) you would use in finding information about it. List the steps you would take in order. Describe how you might narrow down the topic as you progress.

   Television censorship   Marijuana
   Solar energy   Euthanasia
   Organic gardening

HUMANITIES

People have varying ideas about which areas of study should be included in the humanities. The dictionary definition even includes history and mathematics. Generally, however, the humanities are thought of as comprising the creative arts (such as literature), the speculative arts (such as philosophy), and the performing arts (such as theater). This section will deal with art, language, literature, music, philosophy, religion, and the performing arts, all of which are considered as the areas of the humanities by the majority of colleges and universities.

With the increase of interdisciplinary studies and the complex character of most contemporary problems, it is often difficult to decide to which field your topic is most closely related. For example, if your topic is "The Influence of the Computer on the Arts" you will want to consider art, music, and literature (as well as computer science). A good interdisciplinary periodical index for the humanities is the *Humanities Index* (1974–), which was formerly part of the *Social Sciences and Humanities Index* (1916–1973). In it, under the headings "Arts and computers" and "Computers in literature" you will find several articles on your topic:

   Poets, birds, snow, kites and the computer.
   A. Layzer, Arts in Soc 11:351 Sum-Fall '74

As you can see, the citations are arranged like those in the *Readers' Guide*, but the *Humanities Index* covers a different set of periodicals. They are usually considered to be more scholarly and research oriented. A similar index is the *British Humanities Index* (1962–), which indexes periodicals published in Great Britain.

ART

When you begin research in a specific subject area, you will often find it helpful to first analyze what types of information you will be concerned with in that particular field. Research in art, for example, usually involves the following four aspects of the subject:

- Periods, movements, or types of art.
- Particular artists.
- Reproductions of artists' works.
- Critical opinions of artists' works.

Suppose you are interested in a general topic in art, "Impressionist painting." The *Encyclopedia of World Art*, which comes in fifteen volumes, has a long article with twenty-five color plates. From it, you may get the names of a few major artists in this school, and hopefully, some idea of how you might narrow down your topic.

Perhaps you decide that you are most interested in the artist Claude Monet. You would then go on to the second part of your research—finding out more about the artist. After checking in the subject catalog to find any book-length biographies, your next resource should be the *Index to Artistic Biography*, which refers to biographical articles in one or more of sixty-four different sources.

Your next step may be to look at reproductions of Monet's work. You might want to select a few to concentrate on in your paper. If there is a book-length collection of an artist's work, you will find it listed in the card catalog under the artist's name—an artist is the "author" of paintings just as a novelist is the author of books. Often, however, the works are scattered through various collections of reproductions. To locate them, you must use an index such as the Munros' *Index to Reproductions of European Paintings* (1956) a guide to pictures in more than 300 books, or their *Index to Reproductions of American Paintings* (1948, suppl. 1964), covering about 800 books. These works have been updated by Thomson's *Art Reproduction in Books* (1974).

After looking at reproductions of Monet's work, you may decide to focus on his series paintings in which he painted particular subjects, such as cathedrals and water scenes, during different times of the day. For critical opinions and discussions, your best source would be the *Art Index* (1929–), organized exactly as the *Readers' Guide*, but indexing different journals. Since Monet lived during the nineteenth century, you may want to begin your search with the first volume (1930–1933) of the index and work up to the present in order to find the greatest number of articles. You may find additional biographical information about Monet, more articles on "Impressionist painting," or other reproductions included in the journal articles. The following is a typical citation:

Monet's series. J. Elderfield. Art int 18:28–9
N '74 il: Houses of Parliament—effect of fog;
Waterloo bridge—cloudy weather (col)

Art Bibliographies Modern (1973– ; formerly *LOMA*: *Literature on Modern Art*, 1969–1971) is another index to articles in art journals. It also includes exhibit and museum catalogs and some books. Its chief advantage is that it includes brief abstracts or summaries of the material indexed. Its limitation is that it covers only "modern" art and artists, which to its editors means beginning in 1800.

Now, after finding and reading books and articles on Monet, you may have run across some terms, such as "pointillism," or contemporaries of Monet's, Sisley or Pissaro, for example, that you are not familiar with. To find out something about them, you should consult a good art dictionary, such as the *Oxford Companion to Art* (1970). A more recent, and very entertaining, dictionary is Walker's *Glossary of Art, Architecture and Design Since 1945* (1973). In it you may find out about terms such as "food art" or "lost sculptures" and groups such as the "Hairy Who" or the "Los Angeles Fine Arts Squad." A handy reference book for miscellaneous information is the *American Art Directory*, which is published annually. It lists art schools, art museums, leading art journals, and contemporary American artists. Finally, if your major field is art, you should consult Ehresman's *Fine Arts: A Bibliographic Guide* (1975), which is an up-to-date guide to doing research in this field.

MUSIC

In music, you may want to investigate a general subject such as "types of musical instruments," a musician or composer such as Woody Guthrie, or a particular musical work such as Beethoven's Ninth Symphony. For most general topics, particularly in classical music, *Grove's Dictionary of Music and Musicians* (1954), which comes in nine volumes, is the best place to begin. Under the heading "Instruments," for example, you will find a twenty-page discussion of the different types of musical instruments with numerous illustrations, a bibliography, and a complete list of musical instruments at the end. Long biographical articles on composers and musicians are included, and for major composers a useful list of compositions is appended. Suppose you are asked to listen to Haydn's Military Symphony. By looking in *Grove's*, you will find that this is his *Symphony No. 100 in G Major*, the title under which it is most likely to be classified in library collections. A more up-to-date source with briefer articles is the one-volume *Oxford Companion to Music* (1970). Although biographical articles may be found in both of the previous sources, the standard biographical work for musicians is *Baker's Biographical Dictionary of Musicians*. The almost 7000 entries cover all periods and nationalities. Again, the emphasis of this work is classical.

For information about persons or groups in recent, nonclassical music, you may refer to Feather's *New Edition of the Encyclopedia of Jazz*, the *Encyclopedia of Country, Folk and Western Music* (1969) or Roxon's *Rock Encyclopedia* (1969). However, these works do not include long articles on subjects in modern popular music, such as folk rock or reggae. For a general topic of this kind, you must refer to the *Music Index*, which has indexed music journals since 1949. Unfortunately, this index is about five years behind in publishing its cumulated volumes, so for recent years you must look through every monthly issue, one by one.

Now let's look at a particular topic. If you have chosen Woody Guthrie, you will not find him in *Grove's*; it is a little too staid for his type of music. You may, however, find book-length biographies of Woody Guthrie in the card catalog, biographical sketches in encyclopedias such as *Encyclopedia of Country, Folk, and Western Music,* or articles about him and his songs through the *Music Index.* Remember, also, to consider the interdisciplinary nature of this and many other topics. You may want to look in the subject card catalog under headings such as *Depressions—1929—U.S.* You might also look in issues of the *Readers' Guide* during the 1930s to see what the popular magazines were saying about him then or in more recent issues for reviews on the film, *Bound for Glory,* based on his life.

Research in music often includes listening to music. Records and cassettes can therefore become a part of your investigation. Find out what your library has and what the borrowing policies are. If you want to evaluate recent recordings of a particular work or by a particular artist or group, check *Records in Review* (1955–), an annual publication that includes lengthy reviews of classical records by respected music critics. For popular music, look in the *Annual Index to Popular Music Record Reviews,* which indexes reviews from over sixty magazines, including *Rolling Stone.* For example, you might want to find a review of an album called *The Greatest Songs of Woody Guthrie.* In the 1972 index, six reviews are listed under *Guthrie, Woody—Greatest Songs of Woody Guthrie* in the following form.

Journal of American Folklore. Oct/Dec, 1972 p. 402 100w. 3

Given are the name of the journal, the date, the page number, the number of words in the review, and a rating. The rating is based on a scale from zero to five, with zero indicating a poor recording and five a superb one.

Finally, for the music major, *Music Reference and Research Materials,* by Vincent Duckles, is a complete guide to research in music.

LANGUAGES

When studying languages, you will usually be either attempting to master the grammar and vocabulary of a particular language or doing research on a general topic in linguistics or the history of language. If you are learning a language, it should be helpful for you to know some of the important card catalog subject headings. For vocabulary, the headings *English language—Dictionaries—Spanish* (or French, German, etc.) can come in handy. For grammar, you might look under the language you are studying with its various subheadings. Examples are: *Spanish language—Grammar—Orthography—Pronunciation.* If you are studying about language, one of the best sources for finding periodical articles on a general topic, such as "speech therapy," is *Language and Language Behavior Abstracts* (1967–). The cumulated subject indexes for each year will refer you to the abstract numbers for that year. Under the abstract number, you will find citations to periodical articles, as in the following example.

7401719
Bennett, Clinton W. A four-and-a half year old as a teacher of her hearing-impaired sister: a case study. Journal of comm dis, 1973, 6(2), 67–75.

For more articles on the history and development of language, check in the "Linguistics" section (Part III) of the *MLA International Bibliography*, which has been published since 1921. The articles are arranged by language and by topic (etymology, morphology, phonology, etc.) within the language. You can also use the *Humanities Index*, which indexes many of the most common and generally available language journals.

LITERATURE

Your research in literature may involve general topics such as "novels of the working class," specific authors such as John Steinbeck, or specific works of literature such as *The Grapes of Wrath*. For finding brief background material on general topics, brief biographies of authors, or summaries of major literary works, you should first look in a one-volume encyclopedia such as the *Oxford Companion to American Literature*. Oxford also publishes encyclopedias of English, German, French, and Canadian literature. If you are interested in drama, check the *McGraw-Hill Encyclopedia of World Drama* (1972), which includes general topics, brief biographies of dramatists, and brief critiques of plays as literature. For briefer definitions of words and phrases, such as "propaganda novel," "pathos," or "octave," there are several literary dictionaries. Holman's *A Handbook to Literature* (3rd ed., 1972) is one example.

For a more extensive history of American literature, turn to the two-volume *Literary History of the United States* (3rd ed., 1963). The first volume traces movements, influences, and major literary figures from Cotton Mather to Norman Mailer. The second volume is a bibliography of further sources. The British counterpart, even more famous, is the fifteen volume *Cambridge History of English Literature*. Chapters written by specialists cover literature from the earliest times to the ends of the nineteenth century. This work also includes good bibliographies.

After you have established the scope of the topic you have selected and have defined any terms associated with it, you may want to find out more about a particular author, say John Steinbeck. The first thing to do is check the card catalog for a book-length biography. Next, you might refer to a new reference book, the *Index to Literary Biography* (1975). This tool eliminates the guesswork of deciding which biographical dictionary to look in. It indexes biographical sketches from fifty different reference sources.

You may decide at this point that your final topic will be "The Grapes of Wrath: Propaganda or Art?" For critical articles on a particular novel or writer, a valuable source is the *MLA International Bibliography*, an annual publication indexing journal articles and books on the writers of all countries. The articles are grouped by nationality, within nationality by century, and within century under the writers' names, listed alphabetically. Thus, for your topic, you would look for *American Literature—Twentieth Century—Steinbeck, John*. In the citations, the abbreviations of periodical titles are particularly cryptic, so it's a good idea to double check the list at the front of each volume. A sample citation is:

> Trachtenberg, Stanley. "John Steinbeck: The Fate of Protest,"
> NDQ 41, ii:5–11.

Notice that the title of this article does not correspond exactly with your topic, but you should usually follow up even those articles whose titles seem only slightly related. The article itself could easily turn out to be very useful.

A periodical index that does not cover as many journals as the *MLA International Bibliography*, but which does include abstracts of all the articles it indexes is *Abstracts of English Studies* (1958–). An abstract can be especially helpful. As you can discover the gist of an article through the abstract, irrelevant articles can be eliminated without actually having to search them out.

A quick way to arrive at critiques of specific novels, poems, plays, or short stories is through using a one-volume index to criticism. The names of some of these handy tools are *Poetry Explication* (1962, with supplements), *Twentieth Century Short Story Explication* (1967, with supplements), *The American Novel* (1961), *English Novel Explication* (1973, with supplements), *The Continental Novel* (1968), and *Drama Criticism* (1966, with supplements). All of the citations are arranged by author and specific work. The drawbacks are that they are less up to date than the indexes that come out every year and they do not cover as many sources or list as many citations.

Finally, you will often want to find the actual works of literature. Novels are not much of a problem, as they are listed in the card catalog under the author's name, but what about plays, poetry, and short stories that are often scattered throughout various collections? You may have to consult the *Play Index* (1949–), *Granger's Index to Poetry* (6th ed., 1973), or the *Short Story Index* (1953–). All are author, title, and subject indexes to works that appear in collections.

To learn more about reference sources for literature, there are several good guides, one of which is Patterson's *Literary Research Guide* (1976).

PERFORMING ARTS "Performance" may be considered common to all the areas so far discussed in this section. Dramas and novels can become plays or films, a gallery exhibition of an artist's works is a "performance," and, of course, the chief communication of music is through performance. A reference work that deals with this aspect of the humanities is the

Guide to the Performing Arts (1957–). It annually indexes over forty publications, mostly periodicals, dealing with opera, dance, film, theater, radio and television, magic, and the circus. You may look under a person's name or a subject heading, in this case "Nudity in the theater," and find a citation such as this.

Nudity in the Arts: the Dancer and His Body.
W. Terry. il AD 10:3, 32–37, Jl '68

The main disadvantage of this index is that it is rather slow in coming out. The last published volume was in 1968. A more recent index is the *Film Literature Index* (1973–), an author-subject index to about 300 international film periodicals.

Reviews of films, plays, TV shows, art exhibits, or concerts may be located through such standard reference tools as the *Readers' Guide* or newspaper indexes. In addition, the *New York Times* puts out two series—*New York Times Theater Reviews* (covering 1870–) and the *New York Times Film Reviews* (covering 1913–)—which collect, print, and index all of their film and theater reviews. Each set is indexed by title, personal name (including those of actors and actresses reviewed), and production companies. The big advantage of these sources is that they are one-step reference tools.

There are several good, one-volume encyclopedias that concentrate on the performing arts. These include the *Oxford Companion to the Theatre* (3rd ed., 1967), the *Oxford Companion to Film* (1976), and *The Filmgoer's Companion* (4th ed., 1974), a biographical dictionary with numerous illustrations.

RELIGION AND PHILOSOPHY

These two areas of the humanities are combined, both because the terms sometimes overlap and because some of the reference books you will want to use cover the subjects together. Fortunately, there are several encyclopedias to start you on your way. You may want to begin your research by looking in the *Encyclopedia of Philosophy*, in eight volumes. It provides brief biographies of philosophers from Artistotle to Rousseau, overviews of the philosophies of subjects ranging from "tragedy" to "the social contract," and brief philosophical interpretations of concepts such as "ugliness" and "society." Another very interesting encyclopedia, which best fits in this section, is the *Dictionary of the History of Ideas*. In it, topics like "Wisdom of the Fool," "Witchcraft," "Heresy in the Middle Ages," and "Theories of Beauty Since the Mid-Nineteenth Century," are examined and put in their historical perspective.

The *Encyclopedia of Religion and Ethics* (1951, twelve volumes) is the most comprehensive source for information about religions and ethical systems from all ages and places. The long, detailed articles have very good bibliographies at the end. It is, however, a bit out of date when it comes to modern religious movements. More recent is the *New Schaff-Herzog Encyclopedia of Religious Knowledge* (1966), an updating of an older work. It is particularly good for Biblical theology and history. The *Encyclopedia Judaica* (1972) gives detailed information on Jewish customs and is an especially good source for finding out about minor Jewish figures, both biblical and contemporary. Finally, the *New Catholic Encyclopedia* (1967) thoroughly examines matters pertaining to the history, teachings, and activities of the Roman Catholic Church. Particularly useful are its biographies of all the saints, as their names have a way of coming up in many other fields of study.

For specific or up-to-date information on religious or philosophical questions and people, there are three useful periodical indexes. The *Index to Religious Periodical Literature (1949–52–)* is an author and subject index to over 100 journals. The following is a sample citation under the heading "Seminarians, Women."

> Women in the ministry; Southern theological students join liberation forces. J. J. Griffin, Chr Cent 91:855–7 S18 '74

The *Catholic Periodical and Literature Index* (1930–) concentrates on Catholic periodicals and books. It is indexed by author and subject. The *Philosopher's Index* (1967–) is an author and subject index covering international journals. It also includes abstracts.

If you are studying the Bible, a concordance, or word index to Biblical quotations, will be most helpful. *Nelson's Complete Concordance of the Revised Standard Version Bible* (1957), compiled by computer, is very thorough and reliable. Be sure, however, that the edition of the Bible you are using is the one specified by the concordance. Otherwise, it will do you little good, as different words are used in the different editions.

EXERCISES

A. List the relevant subject headings you could use to look for sources for two of the topics below in the card catalog.
   - The Computer and the Arts
   - The Hero in the 20th Century American Novel
   - Reasons for the Current Popularity of Eastern Mystical Religions
   - Popular Music and the Drug Culture

B. Look up "Buddhism" in four different encyclopedias. Evaluate and compare the articles you find. Which do you think would be the best starting point if you were assigned to write on this topic. Why?

C. List five works by each of the following authors. Which source or sources of information did you use?
   - B. Traven
   - George Eliot
   - Sylvia Plath
   - Nikki Giovanni
   - Eugene O'Neill

D. Prepare a minibibliography of five articles about one of the following persons. Which sources did you use?
   David Bowie   Henri Toulouse-Lautrec
   Karl Barth   Saul Bellow
E. Locate and give the citation for a biographical sketch or article on each of the following artists:
   Mies Van der Rohe
   Giotto
   Barbara Hepworth.
F. Identify briefly the following people and musical terms. Name your source of information.
   Counterpoint   Hautboys
   Gustav Holst   Carter Family
   Princess Ida   Shelly Manne
G. Identify briefly the following terms in art. Name your source of information.
   Pantograph   Palenque
   Romanesque   Elgin marbles
   Etching
H. Identify briefly the following terms in literature. Name your source of information.
   Problem novel   Archetype
   Foot   Theatre of the Absurd
   Morality play
I. Choose one of the following subjects and describe the procedure (search strategy) you would use in finding information about it. List in order the steps you would take. You should also describe how you might narrow down the topic as you progress. Don't forget about the reference tools covered in the section "General Reference Works," as they may be of use here.
   War Protest Music
   Impressionist Art in 19th Century France
   Reasons for the Current Increase in Church Membership
   The Poetry of T. S. Eliot

SOCIAL SCIENCES

In the humanities, you can usually count on a novel having only one title, a musical piece only one composer, and a work of art only one artist. Similarly, in the physical sciences, the names of plants, animals, and chemical compounds remain fairly constant. But in the social sciences things are different. New words and concepts are coined frequently, and there are sometimes many names for the same thing. Occasionally, you won't even be certain in what field your topic belongs because subjects in the social sciences have a way of spilling over into one another. Is a topic like "The Effects on the Child of the One-Parent

Family" in psychology, sociology, or education? In this case, you can probably find useful information under all three.

A very well-written and comprehensive reference work that can give you a good background or overview of most social science topics is the *International Encyclopedia of the Social Sciences*, in fifteen volumes with an index. Long, signed articles by specialists will give you a thorough background on such broad topics as "sleep" or "human rights" as well as clear definitions of more specific terms such as "homeostasis" or "sequential analysis." Recent research is presented in every field and an extensive bibliography of further sources is given at the end of each article. This reference tool should be considered as a starting point for any research you may wish to do on a topic in the social sciences.

Two interdisciplinary periodical indexes are also good starting points. The *Social Sciences Index* (1974–; formerly the *Social Sciences and Humanities Index*, 1916–1973) use broad subject headings such as "War and Society," "Language and Culture," and "Government and the Press." For a paper on the "energy crisis," you could look under the heading "Power Resources" and find articles from economic, environmental, and sociological journals:

> As the West sinks slowly into the sun.
> B. Commoner. Bus & Soc R no. 14:46–7 Sum '75
>
> Behavioral analysis of peaking in residential electrical energy consumers.
> R. Kohlenberg and others. J App Behav Anal 9:13–18 Spr. '76

The citations take the same form as those in the *Readers' Guide*. Again, remember to look in the front for a list of abbreviations.

Another periodical index, particularly good for economics, sociology, and government, is the *Public Affairs Information Services (PAIS)*. *PAIS* is the only index that includes pamphlets, government documents, and books along with periodical articles. Libraries usually have pamphlet collections, which are good sources for current, specific information. If your library does not have the pamphlet you are interested in, you can always order a copy. Many are free or very inexpensive.

A unique reference tool that you may find more useful in upper-division courses is the *Social Sciences Citation Index*. Suppose you are doing research in an area where subject headings seem hard to pin down or where little information seems to be available. You need not despair. As long as you know of one person who has written articles on the subject you are interested in, then the *Social Sciences Citation Index* can be a starting point. By looking in the "citations" section of the index under your author's name, you can find a list of articles he or she has written and a list of other people who have cited or referred to the work in articles of their own. This discovery can begin a chain reaction. Articles that refer to an article about your topic may themselves have relevant material that you can use.

Finding out about various groups is often necessary for research in the social sciences. You may want to find out when the Teamster's Union was founded or its current membership, the names of some professional organizations in psychology, or what exactly the Burlap and Jute Association does. The *Encyclopedia of Associations* gives a brief description of more than 16,000 organizations in the United States and Canada. They are grouped by subject, but are indexed by name of association and location.

For information about people as individuals, *American Men and Women of Science, Social and Behavioral Sciences* is an excellent source for contemporary figures. Indexes by occupation and birthplace are included at the end, so if, for example, you need to write a biographical sketch of a recreation leader, and few people can think of one offhand, you have it made.

ANTHROPOLOGY

Anthropology and its closely allied subject, archeology, are fascinating. Who has not heard of Margaret Mead and her study of *Coming of Age in Samoa* or Dr. Leakey's discovery of primitive human skeletal remains in Africa? These discoveries came from the investigation of *primary sources* (firsthand reports or records of phenomena as they happen), in these cases living with the Samoans and digging in Africa. You probably won't have the time or the inclination to live with a primitive tribe or to participate in a "dig" for your research paper, so you will have to rely on secondary sources (interpretations of or commentaries on events, usually seen through the perspective of time). These may be less glamorous, but they can still yield interesting topics.

A good place to start looking for information is the *Annual Review of Anthropology*, a collection of bibliographic essays (sources listed in essay form) on current subjects in the field. A typical essay is "New Directions in Ecology and Ecological Anthropology." As usual, the *International Encyclopedia of the Social Sciences* will also provide a good background on almost any topic.

Periodical indexing for anthropology is, unfortunately, relatively new on the scene. *Abstracts in Anthropology* began in 1970 and indexes periodicals in archeology, ethnology, and linguistics, with author and subject indexes published annually. Looking under the heading "Ecology" in 1975, you could find:

Galston, Arthur W. "Bios: the Ungreening of South Vietnam," *Natural History*. 1974, 83(6):10–12.

Folklore, which is a part of anthropology, is covered by *Abstracts of Folklore Studies* (1963–). It indexes are also cumulated annually. The *International Bibliography of Social and Cultural Anthropology* (1955–)

is a comprehensive listing of books, pamphlets, and periodical articles in the field, but many of the entries are not in English, which can be a drawback. The author and subject indexes, however, are given in *both* English and French. Once again, the *Social Sciences Index* and the *Humanities Index* can give you many relevant articles from the more common periodicals.

You can look up terms in anthropology in Winick's *Dictionary of Anthropology*, which is comprehensive but a bit old, or in Davies' *Dictionary of Anthropology* (1972), which is more up to date but also briefer. Jobes' *Dictionary of Mythology, Folklore, and Symbol*, in three volumes, is a handy key for checking out the significance of certain rites or objects in various cultures.

Finally, the best source, although a brief one, for current information on living anthropologists is the *International Directory of Anthropologists* (5th ed., 1975).

BUSINESS AND ECONOMICS

Topics for most beginning research papers in business or economics are usually fairly specific. You may want to take a look at the advertising of a certain product such as breakfast cereals, do a profile on a particular company such as General Motors, or investigate a particular economic problem such as the controversy over free international trade versus high tariffs for imported goods to protect the American manufacturer.

The best place to begin searching for current specific topics is a periodical or newspaper index. The *Business Periodicals Index* (1958–) is a subject index to about 170 business periodicals. It is put out by the same company that publishes the *Readers' Guide*, so the citations are in the same form. If you are writing on "Methods of Advertising Breakfast Cereals," you may want to look under the subject heading *Cereals, Prepared—Advertising*, where you would find the following citation:

> Big ad spending a prime target in FTC's cereal industry case. P. L. Gordon. Adv Age 47:3 Mr 29, '76

More general periodical indexes, such as the *Public Affairs Information Service (PAIS)* and the *Reader's Guide*, may also have articles on this topic.

Another useful index for basic research in business is the *Wall Street Journal Index* (1958–). Many libraries have back issues of the *Wall Street Journal* on microfilm. The index is divided into two sections: corporate news, listed under the names of specific corporations, and general news, listed by subject headings. For example, if you are interested in Quaker Oats, you can find the following citation in the 1974 volume of the index:

> Probably won't be able to achieve traditional rate of earnings growth in near future, R. D. Stuart, president, told shareholders' meeting. 11/14 25:3

Here you are given not just the title, but also an indication of the contents of the article, the date, the page number, and the column number.

Instead of finding bits of information here and there, you may want to locate a summary of the information about a corporation all in one place. If you only want such information as the yearly profits, number of employees, or the name of the president of a company, you can check in one of several one-volume directories such as *Poor's Register of Corporations, Directors, and Executives*, which is published annually. If a more complete overview or background is necessary, Standard and Poor's *Corporation Records*, seven volumes of brief histories and financial information about large U. S. corporations, is the best place to look. In the *Directory of Intercorporate Ownership* (subtitled *Who Owns Whom in America*), you can find a complete list of the subsidiaries and affiliates of all the large companies in the United States.

Sometimes you will want facts about an industry as a whole. What kinds of profits did the cereal industry make last year? What is the per capita consumption of ready-to-eat cereals? Of courese, you can always look under the name of the industry in the *Business Periodical Index* but, for quick facts, *Standard and Poor's Industry Surveys*, updated periodically, analyzes the leading industries with charts, figures, and brief essays.

Suppose you run into trouble in your search because you don't understand certain concepts, such as "international trade controls," "business cycles," or "inflation." Since there is no general encyclopedia for business, the best thing to do is to turn to the *International Encyclopedia of the Social Sciences*, which has excellent articles on all of these terms. For briefer definitions of words and phrases like "managed currency," "Federal Home Loan Bank Act," or "Commodity Exchange Commission," the *McGraw-Hill Dictionary of Modern Banking and Finance* covers many of the terms used in general business.

Current biographies are well covered by *Who's Who in Finance and Industry*, published every two years. In addition to U. S. business executives, it also includes biographies of the executives of the 1,000 largest corporations in the world.

If you need a particular kind of information in the field of business not covered by the sources mentioned so far, turn to the *Encyclopedia of Business Information Sources*, a detailed two-volume listing of thousands of business-related subjects with references to the publications, organizations, and directories where this information can be found.

EDUCATION

Information in the field of education is well indexed and documented. Once you have decided on a manageable topic, you should have little trouble finding what you will need. It is often difficult, however, to know how much information is actually available on a given topic so, as usual, you should begin with a specialized encyclopedia.

If you are interested in "tests," for example, a look at the index to the *Encyclopedia of Education Research* will refer you to many additional subject headings—admissions tests, aptitude tests, achievement tests, and marks. Suppose you decide that "marks" is the closest to what you want. Under the heading "Marks and Marking Systems" the encyclopedia offers a seven-page article, with a bibliography of other books and articles at the end, describing different systems and reviewing recent research. In the ten-volume *Encyclopedia of Education*, if you look under "Marks" you will be referred to "Grading Systems." There you will find a four-page article with a briefer bibliography. This encyclopedia concentrates on defining and describing subjects rather than on surveying recent research.

You may discover that you will need to define some terms and concepts. For example, you may run across terms such as "mark-sensing," "relative mark," "class mark," or "admissible mark." All perfectly common English words, but what do they mean in this context? You can find the definitions for these terms in Good's *Dictionary of Education* (1973). It has 681 pages of very small print, so you can be pretty sure of finding the word you're looking for.

Perhaps you have decided to evaluate the pass/fail grading system in a paper. *Pass/fail grading system* is an LC subject heading, so you can find some books on the subject. You can also look under the more general heading *Grading and marking (Students)* and find certain books that may have sections on the pass/fail system. Remember to also look in the *Essay and General Literature Index*, which indexes essays and sections of books. However, since this is a fairly recent and specific topic, you will probably find that periodical articles are the best sources of information.

In the *Education Index* (1929–), an author-subject index to leading periodicals in education, if you look under "Pass/fail grading system," you will be referred to "Marking systems." A sample citation under this heading is:

Pass/fail grading: an unsuccess story.
J. C. Quann. Coll & Univ 49:230–5 Spr '74

The citations follow the same form as those in the *Readers' Guide*.

Now for a different kind of index. The U.S. government, through HEW, established the Educational Resources Information Center (referred to as ERIC). Its purpose is to collect, index, and publish on microfiche (microfilm on separate sheets rather than on reels) previously unpublished information such as conference reports, state government documents, and work done on government grants. To use ERIC, you should start with the *Thesaurus of ERIC Descriptors*, which functions as a subject heading guide to the indexing terms that are used. Under "Marking" you will be referred to "Grading," where you can find the following list.

GRADING
nt Pass-Fail Grading
     Credit—No Credit Grading
rt Achievement Rating
     Summative Evaluation

The abbreviations function as "see also" references—"nt" stands for narrower term and "rt" stands for related term—to lead you to other subject headings. After writing down the subject headings you think might be helpful, you should go to the index itself.

The index to ERIC comes in two parts. First there is the *ERIC Educational Documents Index* (1966–), bound in red. It gives you a title and a number referring you to the entry in the *ERIC Educational Documents Abstracts* (1966–), bound in blue, for the same year. For instance, looking under the subject heading "Pass-Fail Grading" in the red volume for 1974, you will find this entry:

H-P-F Grading System in Graduate Education
ED 083 187

The "ED" stands for "ERIC document." In the blue volume, you will discover that this title refers to a five-page paper presented by Robert Thayer at the annual meeting of the Western Psychological Association. You will also find a one-paragraph abstract of the paper. If you feel that the document contains some information that might be useful and you wish to read all of it, ask whether your library has the ERIC microfiche collection. If it does not, and you are starting your research well in advance, you can order most of the documents directly from ERIC in either xeroxed or microfiche form.

If you come across a person in your reading whom you want to learn more about, there are several biographical directories. *Leaders in Education* (1974), a standard "who's who" type of publication, gives for each person listed the birthplace and date, education, employment, publications, awards, and honors. *American Men and Women of Science, Social and Behavioral Sciences* and *Biography Index* would also be good places to look.

GEOGRAPHY

The first things people usually associate with geography are maps, so let's begin by talking about some good atlases. After all, if you are going to study geography, you will have to have a general idea of the lay of the land and be able to locate features such as towns, rivers, and mountains.

The *Times Atlas of the World* (1955–59) is a good basic reference work, very authoritative and detailed, giving as many place names as can be squeezed onto the maps without sacrificing legibility. There are five volumes, each covering a different section of the world. Since this atlas was published between 1955 and 1959, you may occasionally need something more up to date to keep up with changing political boundaries. One of several recent and attractive world atlases is the *Hammond Medallion World Atlas* (1971). Among its many special features are historical maps and an "Environment and Life" section. For maps of the United States, you should look at the excellent *National Atlas of the United States of America*, published by the U.S. Geological Survey in 1970. This atlas was in the works for more than twenty years, and the planning shows in the great accuracy and detail of its 765 maps, which give economic, cultural, and historical as well as physical features.

Historical geography, which emphasizes the historical processes of physical and cultural evolution, could be discussed with either history or geography. It is included here because it does rely on maps and atlases. Shepherd's *Historical Atlas*, now in its ninth edition, is the standard and most often used historical atlas. In it, you can find many interesting maps such as "The West Indies and Central America, 1492–1525" or "London, 1200–1600."

If you need a very specialized or detailed map that you have been unable to find, the American Geographical Society of New York publishes the *Index to Maps in Books and Periodicals*. Entries are alphabetical by subject and geographical-political division.

Most atlases include indexes to geographical features such as cities, towns, and mountains. For more detailed information about a particular place, a gazeteer, or dictionary of places, is the source to use. *The Columbia Lippincott Gazeteer of the World* (1962) gives location, altitude, trade, resources, and population (with the date of the census from which figures were taken) for over 130,000 geographical areas.

The most specific periodical index for the field of geography is *Geographical Abstracts* (1966–). The fragmentation in this work is so great that only a specialist could always know under which category a particular topic would fall. The abstracts are divided into parts:

A—Landforms and the Quaternary (the Pleistocene era)
B—Biogeography and Climatology
C—Economic Geography
D—Social and Historical Geography
E—Sedimentology
F—Regional and Community Planning

Each part has its own annual subject and author indexes. Thankfully, there is also an annual index that covers all of the parts together, so you don't have to guess which one to look in. This index deserves some special attention. It is what is called a Keyword-in-Context (KWIC) index. This means that each article is indexed under every word in the title that is considered a significant, or key, word. For example, the title "Food and Population in Historical Perspective" could be found in the index under "Food" as well as the following ways:

Population in historical perspective = Food and
Historical perspective = Food and population in

Another source of articles, books, pamphlets, and government publication is the American Geographical Society of New York's *Current Geographical Publications* (1938–). Its indexes are arranged by author, subject, and region.

A good dictionary for defining such terms as "quaternary" and "sedimentology" (the classification and interpretation of rock terms) is *A Dictionary of Basic Geography* (1970), designed for the beginning student.

For further informational sources, several research guides like Durrenberger's *Geographical Research and Writing* (1971) are available.

HISTORY

The study of history involves people, specific events, and general trends or movements. Usually, you will want to begin your research with a brief, rather general description of the area in which you are interested. Therefore, historical dictionaries and encyclopedias will often be the first reference tools you will need. There are so many of these that it is often difficult to decide which one to use. Only a few of the best ones will be mentioned here, but you can consult your library card catalog under the subject heading *U.S.* (or *Great Britain, France, Russia,* etc.)—*History—Dictionaries and Encyclopedias* to find others. You can also browse through the reference collection in your library or consult Poulton's *Historian's Handbook*, which offers a complete survey of historical reference tools for the student and beginning researcher.

The *Dictionary of American History* (1976), in seven volumes, is a good example of a thorough, up-to-date, and quick reference source. For instance, you can look under the Spanish-American War and find a brief summary of the causes, effects, names of important people involved, and dates as well as a bibliography of further sources at the end. For world history, Langer's *New Illustrated Encyclopedia of World History* is a good source. It is arranged chronologically and has a detailed index at the end.

For an overview of historical events or eras, the best place to begin is with one of the multivolume Cambridge series. The *Cambridge Ancient History*, the *Cambridge Medieval History*, and the *Cambridge Modern History* all present essays, written by specialists, offering chronological summaries of the important events in history. Bibliographies of further sources are also included.

If you are interested in the Spanish-American War, you might want to find out more about one of the people involved, Admiral George Dewey. The standard source for pretwentieth-century American biographies is *Dictionary of American Biography (DAB)*. The signed articles are well written and usually include a long bibliography of further sources. Under "Dewey, George" there is a seven-page article with a bibliography of six further sources. The DAB does publish supplements for notable twentieth-century figures but, for very recent or less famous people, you may have to turn to the *Biography Index* or one of the *Who's Who* books.

The British counterpart of the *DAB* is the *Dictionary of National Biography (DNB)* which is, of course, larger since it has more years to cover. Supplements bring it up to 1950. For international biographies, the *McGraw-Hill Encyclopedia of World Biography*, in twelve volumes, is a good recent reference tool that includes portraits, photographs, illustrations, and bibliographies of further sources.

When doing research, particularly in history, most of the sources you will use will be of two general kinds: primary and secondary. Primary sources are reports or records of an event as it happens. For instance, suppose that after reading about Dewey you decide that you want to focus on the Philippine Campaign. Your primary sources in this case might be articles from the *New York Times* during the first half of 1898, when this campaign was taking place. There might also be articles in the magazines of the period, possibly written by reporters who were in the actual area. These sources can be found through the supplements to *Poole's Index to Periodical Literature* for the years of the war. Another type of primary source is available in the very useful reference tool *Documents of American History*. In it you can find documents ranging from the first charter of Virginia in 1606 to President Kennedy's proclamation calling for the removal of Soviet weapons from Cuba in 1962.

Secondary sources are interpretations of or commentaries on events, usually as seen through the perspective of time. An indispensable secondary source for American history is the two-volume *Harvard Guide to American History*. In it, the best books, articles, government documents, and other materials on American history are listed by broad subject areas. There is a detailed subject index at the end. Looking under "Spanish-American War" in the index, you will be given several sources and referred to the headings "Philippine Campaign" and "Cuban Campaign" and to biographies of Dewey.

A broader reference tool is *Writings on American History* (1948–), published annually and designed to include every book and article of value in the study of American history. The big advantage of this reference is its comprehensive coverage. The disadvantages are that it is a little slow in coming out, and you might be overwhelmed by the amount of material, finding it difficult to select the best sources. The British counterpart, *Writings on British History*, is also extremely comprehensive, but it is even slower in coming out. The latest volume covers materials written between 1952 and 1954.

For up-to-date international indexing of periodical articles, you should go, as usual, to the *Social Sciences Index* and the *Humanities*

Index. A more specific tool is *Historical Abstracts*. This reference source, which began in 1955, indexes and summarizes articles on history covering the period 1775 to 1945. After 1964, America seceded, so to speak, and the United States and Canada are now covered in an index of their own, *America: History and Life* (1964–). Beginning in 1971, *Historical Abstracts* comes in two parts: *Modern History Abstracts, 1775–1914* and *Twentieth-Century Abstracts*. Where, then, would you look for recent articles on the Philippine Campaign or the Spanish-American War? Actually, you might find sources in either *Historical Abstracts (Modern History Abstracts, 1775–1914)* or *America: History and Life*, since both the campaign and the war were international issues. All of these abstracts are arranged in broad subject categories and have author and subject indexes at the end.

MINORITY AND ETHNIC STUDIES

Areas such as Afro-American studies, Chicano studies, and women's studies are relatively new and are interdisciplinary by nature. Afro-American studies, for example, can include art, literature, politics, history, music, and many other subjects. The Library of Congress, through its subject headings, and publishers of reference books are acknowledging the presence of minority studies by setting up special headings and reference tools for these studies.

For years, all information about Afro-Americans was entered under the heading "Negro." However, with the eighth edition of its supplement to the *LC Subject Heading Guide*, the Library of Congress has changed all headings that used to begin with "Negro" to "Afro-American." Of course, for libraries, changing thousands of cards in the card catalog is an expensive and time-consuming task, so the changeover may not yet be complete in your library. Similarly, information on Mexican-Americans used to be found under the heading "Mexicans in the United States." Now the heading "Mexican-Americans" is used. American Indians are still found under "Indians of North America." The more recent term, "Native Americans," has not yet found its way into the subject heading guide. "Women's Liberation Movement" is a standard heading in the subject heading guide.

Of all the minority and ethnic studies, Afro-American studies, in one form or another, has been around the longest. For brief factual articles and biographical sketches, there are two good sources. The *Negro Almanac*, now in its third edition (1976), covers a wide range of topics in the social sciences and has subject and name indexes and bibliographies. The multivolume *Afro-American Encyclopedia* covers topics ranging from a comprehensive list of African tribes to the "Birmingham, Alabama, Movement." Another useful quick-reference source that also covers a large number of other minority groups is

Burke's *Civil Rights: A Current Guide to the People, Organizations, and Events* (1974).

For books and articles, the most comprehensive reference tool is the *Dictionary Catalog* of the Schomberg Negro History and Literature Collection at the New York Public Library. This is one of the best collection of Afro-American books, articles, and other materials in the United States, and supplements are published to include the new additions to the collection. Beginning in 1960, the *Index to Periodical Articles By and About Negroes* provides detailed coverage of periodical articles, but it is very slow in coming out. A new index, *Black Information Index* (1970–) will, it is hoped, be kept more up to date. Many of the periodicals indexed in these two sources are also covered by the *Readers' Guide* and the *Social Sciences Index* but, by using these specific indexes, you can zero in on your topic more readily and avoid having to weed out irrelevant material.

Who's Who Among Black Americans (1975/76–) provides good coverage for contemporary blacks. An older publication, *Who's Who in Colored America*, begun in 1927, is the best source for information about persons living earlier in this century.

The *Reference Encyclopedia of the American Indian* is the best source for obtaining a good background on the tribes, customs, and other factual information about native Americans. A new reference source, *Index to Literature on the American Indian* (1970–) covers periodicals and some books on both current topics and Native American history.

No periodical index has been put together yet for Mexican-American studies, but several good bibliographies exist. Among them are Meier and Rivera's *Bibliography for Chicano History* (1972) and *A Comprehensive Chicano Bibliography, 1960–1972*, by Talbot and Cruz, which includes articles and government documents as well as books. For other reference sources on Mexican-Americans, look at *Ethnic Information Sources of the United States*, which lists reference books, pamphlets, organizations, agencies, and media sources for many different minority groups, including Mexican-Americans. Blacks and Native Americans are not included in this reference work, as the editor felt that these groups were well covered elsewhere.

Women's Studies Abstracts (1972–) has proven a valuable guide for locating pertinent information on women from periodicals, books, and pamphlets. As with all publications of abstracts, you have to use the subject index first and then turn to the abstract (or summary) section for the citation. For biographies of women, you may use any of the standard biography sources already covered. There is also a reference source that covers some relatively minor and otherwise undocumented figures. *Notable American Women, 1607–1950* is fascinating to read.

It reveals an unexpected number of both active and activist women from 1607 on. Most of the women included are not listed in the *Dictionary of American Biography*.

Since minority studies is a relatively new area, as you can see from the publication dates of most of the works mentioned, there is not yet the variety of reference tools that you can find in other fields of the social sciences. This is gradually changing, however, so you should be on the lookout for new information sources as they appear.

PSYCHOLOGY

The study of psychology can involve technical terms and concepts that the average layperson may not be familiar with. Lulled by the popular approach to psychology of such magazines as *Psychology Today*, you may plunge into an article such as "Dream Interpretation" and run into terms like "psychotropic effects" and "ego modalities" that you do not understand. For a few definitions to help clear things up, you can turn to the excellent *International Encyclopedia of the Social Sciences*, already mentioned, or to the more specific *Encyclopedia of Psychology* (1972). This three-volume set contains about 5,000 brief entries, including a few biographical references. More technical terms, over 13,000 in fact, are included in *A Comprehensive Dictionary of Psychological and Psychoanalytical Terms: A Guide to Usage*. The most up-to-date source is the *Psychological Almanac: A Handbook for Students* (1973). In it you can learn, for example, that "psychotropic" refers to something that affects the mind, such as a tranquilizer.

Once you have located some reference aid to bolster your confidence, you should narrow your subject to a workable topic about which there is enough information. One way is to scan a recent issue of the *Social Sciences Index* to see what some of the current subject headings are. You can find many articles in well-known psychology journals through this index, and they can provide a good starting place for your research. For example, you may decide to write on "Nightmares." By looking under the more general heading "Dreams," you can find the following citations:

[Nightmares:]
etiological, theoretical, and behavioral treatment considerations.
S. N. Haynes and D. K. Mooney. bibl Psychol Rec 25:225–35 Spr '75

For more detailed or technical articles and write-ups of experiments dealing with your topic, the place to look is *Psychological Abstracts* (1927–   ). The abstracts are arranged by broad subject areas, and there are author and subject indexes for each six-month period. Cumulated indexes are published occasionally; the latest cumulation covers the period 1974 to 1976. Subject headings are not too specific in *Psychological Abstracts*, so you may want to consult the *Thesaurus of Psychological Index Terms*, a subject heading guide, before beginning.

For the topic "Nightmares," you can, however, look directly under that heading and find the following:

diagnosis and treatment, disturbed sleep 5774

This refers you to the following citation:

5774 Kales, Anthony and Joyce.
Sleep disorders: recent findings in the diagnosis and treatment of disturbed sleep. New Eng J Med 1974 (Feb) vol. 290 (9) 498–499.
(abstract)

If your topic could fall in the area of psychoanalysis, and many topics in psychology can, another specific index to check in is the *Index to Psychoanalytical Writings* (1956–), which covers books, journal articles, and reviews. You can look under the heading "Nightmares" and find a reference to the book *Dreams and Nightmares* (1954) by J. A. Hadfield. Here you may think, "But I could find books through the card catalog." True, but an index such as this covers many books that your library probably doesn't have. Thus, it is a good way for you to find out about the existence of books beyond your local library.

Before going to that trouble, however, it would probably be a good idea to find out how useful or authoritative a particular book will be. Psychology has a special reference tool for book reviews: the *Mental Health Book Review Index* (1956–). To use it, follow the same steps as you would for finding any other book review. Find out the title, author, and the year the book was published and then look in the index under that year as well as several later years in order to catch any late reviews.

Biographies of contemporary psychologists are covered in the American Psychological Association's *Biographical Directory*, published every three years. Addresses, specialties, degrees, and employment history are given for its members. Important figures in the field who are no longer living may be located through one of the encyclopedias or in the *Biography Index*.

If you find that you need still more information, Bell's *Guide to Library Research in Psychology* is an excellent handbook for locating library sources and doing a research paper in this field. Finally, psychology is one of the subjects with its own ideas about bibliography and footnote formats. The APA puts out the *Publication Manual of the American Psychological Association* (1967), and you will probably want to consult it when doing a paper for a psychology class.

POLITICAL SCIENCE In political science as in any other area, one of the first things to do when beginning your research is to narrow down your topic and identify possibly useful headings. Suppose you are interested in electoral systems. Looking in the LC guide to subject headings, which is always a good place to start, you will find the following:

Elections
sa Ballot
Campaign funds
Presidents—U.S.—Election
Women—Suffrage

There are also many more "see also" references and subdivisions, which should give you some ideas for ways to narrow down your topic. Let's say you decide on "Campaign Funds" as a topic. You might want to take a look at the old standby, the *International Encyclopedia of the Social Sciences*, which probably sounds quite familiar to you by now. There are over 100 different articles in the area of political science. Looking under "Campaign Funds," you would be referred to the heading "Political Financing," where you would find a six-page article. Don't forget to use the bibliography at the end as a guide to further sources. If you need a dictionary to define any specific terms you may have encountered, good examples are Laquer's *Dictionary of Politics* (1971) and the *Dictionary of American Politics* (2nd ed., 1968).

After reading encyclopedia articles, always remembering to make use of any bibliographies at the end, you can return to the card catalog with your subject headings and look for books. Next, you will probably want to check the periodical indexes in the field. The major index for political science is *International Political Science Abstracts* (1951–). It selectively indexes over 1,000 journals in many languages, but the abstracts themselves are in either English or French. Under *Elections—U.S.A—Campaign Organization* you can find the following:

Kayden. The political campaign as an organization. Publ. Pol. 21 (2), Spr 1973: 263–280.
(abstract)

You may notice that in many of the series of abstracts the elements of the citations are presented in a slightly different order than they are in the more common periodical indexes. Still, the basic ingredients are all there: the title of the periodical, the volume, the date, and the page numbers. The *International Bibliography of Political Science* (1953–) goes one step further and lists books, pamphlets, and government documents as well as periodical articles.

If, so far, you have come up with only foreign language articles or periodicals that your library doesn't have, don't forget the interdisciplinary indexes mentioned at the beginning of the social sciences section. The *Social Science Index* and the *Public Affairs Information Service* index numerous political science publications.

Let's go back even farther, to the section on general reference tools. What could be more pertinent for research in political science than government documents? For example, in 1974 the government held hearings on the campaign practices and finances of the 1972 presidential campaign. These could be very useful for a paper on campaign funding.

Political science involves more than theory or history. It is also the study of the ongoing processes of particular governments. A handy reference book for American government is the *Guide to the Congress of the United States* (1971). It begins with a brief glossary of congressional terms and then goes on to discuss the history, powers, responsibilities, and committees of Congress. An appendix at the end includes, among other things, a biographical index to all the members of Congress from 1789 to 1971. A detailed table of contents and an index can help you to locate specific information quickly. Another useful guide is the *U.S. Government Organization Manual*. New developments seem to occur in government almost every day. This publication, updated annually, is a convenient way to keep track of them. If you would like to know the names of certain officials in the Defense Department, for example, or how the department is structured, you will find complete information in this manual.

The most detailed day-to-day record of what is going on in Congress is the *Congressional Record*. It includes every word that is spoken on the floor, plus a number that aren't. These voluminous records are indexed frequently, and a final index is prepared at the end of each session, so you don't have to wade through thousands of pages looking for a particular speech by a particular member of Congress.

You may not need such a detailed record, however. To keep up with recent developments, such as campaign contributions during a recent election, there are always the *Readers' Guide*, current to within about a month, and the *New York Times Index*, current to within about two months. A more specific source for information about Congress is the *Congressional Quarterly Weekly Report*, often referred to as *CQ*. If you ever wonder what Congress did to earn its keep during a particular week, just pick up the issue of *CQ* for that week and you will get a relatively good summary. It also includes a few feature articles on pending legislation.

The same company publishes the *Congressional Quarterly Almanac*, a yearly summary of legislative action and important events in American government. One of the most useful sections is a record of all roll-call votes taken in the House and Senate. You can find out how your congressman or congresswoman voted on key issues and see how well the votes coincide with campaign promises. Also included are transcripts of presidential messages and speeches and an analysis of the presidency. Another reference source, again by the same publisher, gives you long-term information. It is *Congress and the Nation* (1945–), which is organized at four-year intervals so that you can get a good idea of the developments during a particular presidential term.

You now know how to find out the voting records of Congress, but what about the voting of the nation as a whole? *America Votes*, published every two years since 1956, gives presidential, congressional, gubernatorial, and senatorial results for both primary and general elections, with a county-by-county breakdown of the voting. You might sometimes want a breakdown of the voting in state elections, also. There is no reference book that gives this information, but you can often find it by looking at the issue of a major newspaper in your state for the day after elections were held.

Finally, a biographical directory for American politics, which includes local as well as national personalities, is *Who's Who in American Politics (1967/68–)*, published every two years.

International relations are another important element of political science. You should know how to find information about the relations between one nation and another in the card catalog. The basic pattern subject headings you will want is "Country"—"Foreign Relations"—"Country." Thus a book on U.S.-Cuban relations would be found under *U.S.—Foreign Relations—Cuba*. If you wish to know more about the government of Cuba, one of the best starting points is the *Europa Yearbook (1946–)*. This source gives information about the forms of government and the major officials for nations throughout the world as well as for a selection of international organizations. It also lists major newspapers, languages, and religions and gives statistics on population, finance, trade, production, and so forth. For biographies of international figures, the *International Yearbook and Stateman's Who's Who (1953–)* includes leaders in religion, commerce, industry, and government.

Finally, a well-organized, annotated guide to still more reference tools for students is Holler's *The Information Sources of Political Science (1971)*.

SOCIOLOGY

Sociology deals with the different types of groups and structures into which people are born or are socialized. It also studies how people may transform these groups or structures. A helpful source to begin with is *Current Sociology (1958–)*. Published quarterly, each issue contains a trend report, with a supporting bibliography, on some area in sociology. This publication is a good place to get some ideas for a possible topic for research in the area.

Although there are specific reference tools for sociology, most of the topics in the field are interdisciplinary. Psychology and education are but two of the areas that are often related to sociology. Therefore, it is a good idea to remember the reference works mentioned in the introduction to this section on the social sciences. Many of them can be very helpful in your research in sociology.

Sociology has both its theoretical and its practical aspects. You could choose a thoeretical topic such as "Crowd Behavior," or you might be interested in the more practical aspects of social work, such as those involved in "Family Counseling." Suppose you decide to investigate "Crowd Behavior." Looking in the *International Encyclopedia of the Social Sciences* under "Crowds," you will be referred to "Collective

Behavior," "Mass Phenomena," "Queues," and the biography of LeBon. All of these articles probably have a bibliography at the end, so you will be off to a good start if you read them and follow up the references. You can find additional books in the card catalog under the subject heading *"Crowds."* For periodical articles, a standard reference tool for sociology is *Sociological Abstracts* (1953–), which indexes over 500 journals. This work can be a little confusing to use at first, since sometimes the index volume is bound and published separately and sometimes it's included with the abstracts. The abstracts are published at irregular intervals, but each year does have its own index. Therefore, you simply have to persist until you find the index for the year you want. You can also look in *Psychological Abstracts* and find citations you want, in this case under "Collective Behavior."

Should you choose a more practical topic oriented toward social work, such as "Family Counseling," the *Encyclopedia of Social Work*, which emphasizes the professional practice of social work and welfare institutions, would be a good place to begin. Two abstracting services cover this area specifically. *Abstracts for Social Workers* (1965–) indexes over 200 journals, and *Human Resources Abstracts* (1966–), formerly called *Poverty and Human Resources Abstracts*, indexes periodical articles, books, pamphlets, and agency reports. It emphasizes research and action programs, legislative and community developments, and policy trends. The subject headings are very general. For instance, under "Family" you will find the following citation:

Bernstein, Blanche and William Meezan.
The Impact of Welfare on Family Stability. N.Y.:
New School for Social Research.
June 1972. 124 p.

If you are investigating a particular state or city and want to get an idea of the services available, the *National Directory of Private Social Agencies* (1964–) can provide valuable information. It is divided into two parts. Part one is classified by services offered, such as homes for the delinquent or drug rehabilitation programs. Part two is a list of agencies arranged by state and city. It is published in a loose-leaf binder so that it can be updated constantly. Also, don't forget another source that may come in handy, the *Encyclopedia of Associations*.

Much of the information in sociology comes from questionnaires and interviews. In fact, most theses and dissertations in sociology are expected to include firsthand information or observations in addition to information gained through searching the literature. Although you may not conduct any personal investigations for a beginning research paper, you should keep the importance of primary sources in mind. You should also be aware of the card catalog subject headings— *"Questionnaires"* and *"Social Surveys"*—under which you can find books about these information-gathering processes.

Sociology is developing a jargon all its own. This is especially true as the use of statistical methods in research becomes more and more widespread. You may find that a dictionary, such as Hoult's *Dictionary of Modern Sociology* (1969), which provides examples of how to use most terms, is helpful for understanding current usage.

Finally, Pauline Bart's *Student Sociologist's Handbook* can be a useful aid for finding further sources of information. It includes an introduction to library research as well as a guide to writing research papers involving actual fieldwork.

EXERCISES
A. List three or more subject headings in your library's card catalog relevant to the topic of the education of Afro-Americans in the United States.
B. List three or more subject headings in your library's card catalog relevant to the subject of Mexican-American migrant labor in the United States.
C. Briefly describe the following historical terms or events and give your sources of information.
  Federal Emergency Relief Administration
  Webster-Hayne Debate
  Espionage Act of 1917
  Treaty of Berlin
  Sack of Rome
D. Give citations for four periodical articles on U.S.-Brazilian relations. What sources did you use?
E. Make a minibibliography, including two primary and four secondary sources, on the assassination of President Kennedy.
F. Write a one-paragraph profile on one of the following corporations. Include what you think to be the most important facts about it. What sources did you use?
  General Motors   Heublein
  Pet Foods, Inc.   Revlon
G. Locate by state or province and country the following places:
  Carignan   Pickle Crow
  Golden Hinde   Roxbury
  Narbada River
What source or sources did you use?
H. Look up "psychoanalysis" in three different encyclopedias. Which do you think provides the best starting point for a paper and why?
I. Locate biographical sketches for the following persons and list the sources you used.
  B. F. Skinner   W. E. B. Dubois
  George Murdock   Leonid Breznev
  Ann Hutchinson

J. Outline a search strategy for one of the following topics. You may use any sources you wish, either from this section or from previous sections.
>   The Future of Marriage as an Institution
>   The "Open Classroom": Its Place in Education
>   Geographical Environment and its Psychological Effects
>   The Mayas in Mexico: History and Architecture
>   The Image of Women in the Media

SCIENCES

Until you begin to take courses above the introductory level in one of the sciences, the topics you will want to research will be, for the most part, rather nontechnical. They will usually deal with areas of general interest, such as pollution problems, the environment, alternative sources of energy, or the current furor over experiments on recombining DNA molecules. However, most of the indexes, abstracts, and handbooks for specific sciences are quite technical. Therefore, much of this section will be concerned with the many reference tools that are useful for the sciences in general.

Let's begin, as usual, by considering a sample topic: solar energy. Many people are interested in this subject. After all, it is supposed to solve many of our future energy problems. As you begin, however, you may not know much about how solar energy works or how feasible it is. Is it expensive? Could it work in such cities as Portland, Oregon, where the annual average rainfall is quite high? A good starting point for any research in the sciences is the *McGraw-Hill Encyclopedia of Science and Technology* (1971, in fifteen volumes). It has well-written articles designed for the nonspecialist on many broad scientific topics. It also is illustrated and well indexed, and most of its articles have bibliographies.

You may decide, after reading and following up some of the bibliographic references, that you want to limit your topic to "The Feasibility of Using Solar Energy for Heating Individual Homes." Books can certainly provide additional background information. Going to the card catalog, you will find the headings *"Solar energy"* and *"Architecture, domestic"* to be particularly useful. However, science is an area in which many new developments occur every day. Therefore, most important scientific material is first published in journals. To learn of the latest developments in applications of solar energy, you should go to the periodical indexes.

For nonspecialist subjects, a good place to look is in the *Readers' Guide*. It indexes such popular journals as *Scientific American, Science,* and *Science News,* which offer scientific articles of interest to the general public. There are three other indexes with broad coverage in the sciences. *General Science Index* (1978–) is a new subject and author index that is designed to give a more thorough coverage of popular science periodicals than does the *Readers' Guide*. It's published by the same company, so the format and citations are the same. *The Applied Science and Technology Index* (1913–) covers periodicals in such fields as automation, engineering, earth sciences, and transportation. Many of the articles include applications of these fields to energy and the environment. Under "Solar heating," for instance, you can find the following citation:

> House of copper plugs into the sun. il diag
> Mod Metals 31:47–8 My '75

The *Biological and Agricultural Index* (1946–) covers many major biological periodicals. The articles indexed are generally concerned with applying scientific principles to the areas of home economics and farming. Nevertheless, you might find the following citation under "Solar heating" useful:

> Sun helps heat farrowing house. M. Hall il
> Crops and Soils 26:11–15 Je '74

The environment is a very popular and important subject that makes use of the knowledge in many fields of science, including biology, engineering, physics, and chemisty. A reference tool that concentrates on U.S. information in this area is *Environment Abstracts* (1971–). It covers periodical articles, technical reports, and conference proceedings. In addition, each issue contains a review article on the environmental movement for the previous year. The work lists environmental bills that are currently before Congress or pollution control officials. The annual index to the abstracts, *Environment Index*, is published separately.

A great deal of good information on topics in the sciences can be found through the *Monthly Catalog*. For instance, on the subject of solar energy, the Energy Research and Development Administration published the "National Plan for Solar Heating and Cooling (Residential and Commercial Applications)" in 1975. NASA alone puts out hundreds of technical reports yearly. In addition, the government holds numerous hearings each year, with testimony by experts, on many subjects of general scientific interest, from cyclamates to nuclear testing.

Another index, which is a bit more specialized but still has applications for the sciences in general, is *Pollution Abstracts* (1970–). Articles, books, and technical reports on all aspects of pollution—air, water, land, and noise—are covered. Your library may not have some of the technical reports you might find in this reference tool. Also, the index, of the Keyword-in-Context variety, can be a little confusing at first. However, since this is the major international service for pollution information, it's a good source to know about. For your paper on solar energy, you might want to use an article on how other types of heating systems can cause pollution.

The *Social Sciences Citation Index* was briefly discussed in the social sciences section. Its counterpart in the physical sciences is the *Science Citation Index (SCI)*. To review briefly what these indexes do, let's suppose that you read an article by R. E. Hartle on solar heating in which he discusses a particular scientific technique or theory that you are interested in. You may want to find some other articles about the same technique or theory, but it is difficult to figure out what subject headings to check under. Using the *SCI*, you would look in the "Citation" section under Hartle, R. E., to find the entry for his article. Under this, there will be a list of other articles that have cited or referred to this article.

For biographies of living scientists, *American Men and Women of Science*, now in its thirteenth edition, is the best source. It provides an index by discipline. For scientists no longer living, the *Dictionary of Scientific Biography* covers all places and periods of history. The articles are by specialists and have bibliographies of further sources.

Scientific books are particularly hard to evaluate if you're not familiar with the subject, and often they are not covered by *Book Review Digest* or *Book Review Index*. Fortunately, there is the *Technical Book Review Index* (1935–), which covers reviews of books in the pure and life sciences as well as in technology. The entries are arranged by the author of the book being reviewed, and brief quotes from each review are included.

APPLIED SCIENCES

In this section, the sciences are divided into three broad categories: the applied sciences, the biological sciences, and the physical sciences. For each of these areas, you should know about at least a few of the major specialized reference tools. When actually doing your research, however, the categories are seldom separated so neatly. Don't be surprised, therefore, if you find that you want to use reference works from all three categories for one topic. Let's begin with the applied sciences, which include such fields as engineering, home economics, agriculture, and computer science. Here, the basic principles of the more theoretical sciences—physics, chemistry, mathematics, and biology—are applied to everyday problems.

One field that is well documented is engineering. The *Engineering Index* (1884–), which now includes abstracts, is among the oldest of the periodical indexes. It also covers books, reports, and lists of patents on all aspects of engineering. You must know something about your subject when you approach this index. The entries are arranged under main subject headings and subheadings with only an author index. There are many cross-references, however, so without too much trouble you can usually find your way to the heading you want. For the topic of solar energy, the heading "Solar Energy" *is* used, and under it you can find a citation such as the following:

Countdown for Solar Energy
   (abstract)
Halacy, D. S. Jr. Energies v. 1 n 1 Mar 1975 p 7–9.

In this citation, the title is given first, then the abstract, and then the author, the name of the periodical, the volume, date, and page numbers. Abstracting services often vary in how they arrange their citations, but once you know what elements are necessary in a citation, you can easily sort them out.

You may run across some puzzling terms as you do your research in engineering. What, for instance, is a "phase-advancer"? Is it something out of "Star Trek"? Are "fillets" some kind of fish? To answer questions like these, a reference tool such as the *Engineering Encyclopedia* (3rd ed., 1963) can come in very handy. Finally, an interesting dictionary, designed for the layperson and useful in a practical sense as well as for research, is *The Way Things Work* (1967). This two-volume reference includes explanations, with detailed diagrams, on subjects ranging from nuclear reactors to toasters.

The field of home economics has several good basic indexes. Two of these are *World Textile Abstracts* (1969–) and *Nutrition Abstracts and Reviews* (1931–). A third, *Food Science and Technology Abstracts* (1969–), deals with such consumer-oriented topics as food additives and packaging.

Should you choose a topic dealing with foods or nutrition, there are two helpful quick-reference books you might want to take a look at. *Food Values of Portions Commonly Used*, now in its twelfth edition, gives the amounts of vitamins, minerals, protein, fat, and other substances in just about everything one might conceivably eat, from Fig Newtons to armadillo meat. The *CRC Handbook of Food Additives* (2nd ed., 1972) consists of essays, with bibliographes, on topics like "Starch in the Food Industry" and "Non-nutritive Sweeteners." This reference work, by the way, can often be a good source of ideas for a topic.

Although computer science is the newest technology on the scene, it is one that is already changing our lives. A good place to start your research on this subject is with some useful card catalog headings. The subject heading guide divides computing machines into two groups. Pre-1945 models are entered under "Calculating machines" and those coming after 1945 are entered under "Computers."

"Computers" also has some interesting subheadings, such as "Moral and religious aspects," "Caricatures and cartoons," and "Vocational guidance." Some other headings you might want to consult are "Programming languages (electronic computers)" and "Computer programs." For a helpful introduction to the field as well as a source for finding the meaning of new terms, the *Computer Dictionary and Handbook* is a good reference tool. Finally, *Computer Abstracts* (1966–) provides an international index of periodicals, government documents, books, and technical reports in the field. These abstracts will be the most useful if you are researching fairly technical aspects of computer science. For more general topics, such as the effect of the computer on an individual's right to privacy, a better source might be the *Social Sciences Index* or the *Humanities Index*.

BIOLOGICAL SCIENCES

Since the recognition, description, and classification of plant and animal life is basic to the study of biology, it is important to know which tool can help you to do these things. *Grzimek's Animal Life Encyclopedia*, in thirteen volumes, is an excellent reference tool. It gives the physiological, evolutionary, and behavioral characteristics of animal life all over the world and has numerous illustrations, many of them in color. The animals are arranged by broad classifications, but each volume has a detailed index by both common and scientific names. For plants there is the recently published *Hortus Third: A Concise Dictionary of Plants Cultivated in the United States and Canada* (1976). It is arranged by scientific names, but it also has an index of common names. For brief definitions of terms like "symbiosis"—associations between unlike kinds of organisms—a work such as *The Encyclopedia of the Biological Sciences*, in its second edition, is a good source.

A rather overwhelming reference tool, but one that is indispensable for research in biology, is *Biological Abstracts* (1926–). A thick volume of abstracts appears every month, and a three-volume index comes at the end of each year. Fifteen large volumes per year—now that's a space problem for a library! *Biological Abstracts* has many different kinds of indexes. Most useful are the author index, good if you know the name of a particular researcher whose work you are interested in, and the subject index, called BASIC (Biological Abstracts Subjects in Context). This is a fancy name for a Keywood-in-Context index, which many of the other abstracting services also use. The index is printed by computer, which makes the size of the letters uniform and thus a bit hard to read. Many of the citations are technical, but such titles as "Criteria for the Diagnosis of Human Alcoholism" and "Crane Populations in a North Florida Sandhill" sound quite readable. In any case, the abstracts are certainly worth looking at.

The main indexing tool for medicine, *Index Medicus* (1960–), occasionally overlaps with *Biological Abstracts* in areas concerning the human body and how it works. *Index Medicus*, however, emphasizes the practice of medicine and medical research. It also includes such social concerns of doctors as malpractice insurance. *Index Medicus* is international in coverage. It indexes only periodical articles by both author and subject. The first volume for each year includes a subject heading guide for the headings to be used during that year. Many of the subject headings have "see also" references. A sample citation under the heading "Natural childbirth" is:

> (Supportive hypnotic technics as a proposed development in obstetrical psychoprophylaxis). Mosconi, G. Minerva Med 65:209–13, 20 Jan 74 (Ita)

The parentheses indicate that the title is translated into English, and the notation "(Ita)" means that the article itself is in Italian. To avoid such language problems in beginning research, you are probably better off using the *Abridged Index Medicus* (1970–), which your library is also more likely to have. It indexes about 100 selected English language periodicals.

Now, look again at the citation from *Index Medicus*: what does "psychoprophylaxis" mean? According to *Stedman's Medical Dictionary*, a comprehensive and reliable source in its twenty-third edition, psychoprophylaxis is "Psychotherapy directed toward . . . the maintenance of mental health." Another quick-reference work that deals more specifically with diseases and their treatments is the *Merck Manual of Diagnosis and Therapy* (12th ed., 1972). Diseases and their symptoms are grouped according to type, and a list of prescription drugs is included in the back along with an index. This book is useful for informational and research purposes, but don't try to use it for diagnosing your own illnesses as you would use *The Way Things Work* to try to fix your toaster. Finally, you can also find information about many topics involving health through such indexes as *Nutrition Abstracts and Reviews* and *Pollution Abstracts*.

PHYSICAL SCIENCES

The *McGraw-Hill Encyclopedia of Science and Technology* is the best starting point for your research in the fields of chemistry, physics, mathematics, or geology. There are also a number of good specialized dictionaries. Miall and Sharp's *A New Dictionary of Chemistry*, in its fourth edition, includes brief, understandable definitions of general terms and some biographical articles. Gray's *New Dictionary of Physics* (1975) gives brief definitions, many with illustrations, as well as tables and lists such as "Radioactive and Stable Isotopes" or "Nobel Prize Winners in Physics." Glenn James' *Mathematics Dictionary* (1976) has many brief biographical articles in addition to definitions of mathematical terms. A guide to pronunciation is also included. If you are embarrassed to use the word "cyclosymmetry" in public because you don't know how to pronounce it, here's help. Finally, there is Gary's *Glossary of Geology* (1972). This reference tool emphasizes the current or preferred meanings of geological terms in North American usage. These dictionaries are among the best and most recent. To locate others that your library may have, look in the card catalog under the name of the field, as in *Chemistry—Dictionaries and encyclopedias*.

For those who major in chemistry, physics, or mathematics, there are two indispensable reference works: the *Handbook of Chemistry and Physics* and the *Handbook of Mathematics*. Thousands of pages long, they are crammed full of tables, lists, formulas, charts, and other good quick-reference information, and both are frequently updated.

When it comes to periodical indexes, *Chemical Abstracts* (1907–) is one of the most thorough of them all. It provides worldwide coverage of books, periodicals, patent descriptions, dissertations, government documents, and more. *Chemical Abstracts* appears weekly and offers semiannual indexes by author, subject, patent, and formula. If you are interested in a particular chemical compound, you can use the formula index to find out all the ways it has been synthesized and marketed.

Science Abstracts. Section A: *Physics Abstracts* (1898–) is also worldwide and covers a variety of materials. *Mathematics Reviews* (1940–) indexes books and periodicals. Its citations are arranged by broad groups of subjects rather than alphabetically.

The *Bibliography of North American Geology* (1931–) is about five years behind in its publications, but it is still the most comprehensive source of information for geology of North America. Each volume, normally published annually, consists of a bibliography of books, articles, and government documents on geology and has a detailed index. The *Bibliography and Index of Geology* (1933–) covers literature of the world in the earth sciences. Author and subject indexes are cumulated annually. Geology often tends to intersect with other disciplines, such as archaeology and geography. Therefore, when pursuing the topic "Fossil Discoveries in Rock Formations in Nebraska," don't forget also to check *Geographical Abstracts* and *Abstracts in Anthropology*.

You may find, in the course of your research, that you would like to know of some additional reference works covering the sciences. For more detailed information on what is available, check Lasworth's *Reference Sources in Science and Technology* (1972). This book is also a good guide on how to conduct searches of the literature of all the sciences.

EXERCISES A. Find relevant card catalog subject headings for the following broad topics.
    The History of Science
    Moral Aspects of Science
    Human Factors Engineering
    Space Exploration

B. Briefly identify the following terms and give your sources of information.
   - gyrocompass
   - herbarium
   - quark
   - Gause's law
   - black hole
C. Locate a biographical sketch of the following individuals, list their field of study, and name your source of information.
   - Robert Oppenheimer
   - Henry Gray
   - Joseph Priestly
   - Linus Pauling
D. Give citations for four articles on "Food Additives" or "Problems of Solid Waste Disposal" and name your sources of information.
E. Give citations for four articles on "Organ Transplants" or "Euthanasia" and name your sources of information.
F. Outline a search strategy for one of the following topics. You may make use of reference tools from any of the sections of the chapter.
   - Prediction of Earthquakes
   - Legalizing Laetrile
   - Saving Vanishing Species
   - Nuclear Power as a Source of Energy
   - Hydroponic Gardening

10
How Do You Write a Research Paper?

Carefully researching a subject can be one of the most exciting and rewarding activities of your college program. When you research a topic, you become a specialist on that subject. You read extensively what has been written by others, evaluating ideas and comparing and contrasting them; then you synthesize them to develop your own learned opinion. Research writing makes use of all the skills that you have learned for specific writing tasks: effective introductions, clear organization, logical reasoning, and effective expression.

To master research writing, you need to focus attention on three specific new skills:

- Finding and using necessary information.
- Integrating the ideas of others into your own arguments.
- Documenting the sources of your information.

A research paper should not simply be the stringing together of the ideas of others. You will use your organizational skills and your awareness of logic to go a step further than your sources. You will revise the structure of their arguments, add a new idea to their explanation or concept, or reconcile two seemingly opposite views. You will attempt to support some opinion—thesis—of your own by fusing your own ideas with what has been written by others about the same subject.

Writing the research paper need not be a fightening task. The project may be longer than most of your college essays, but you will undoubtedly be given more time to complete it. Having a plan for your work will make the entire process go smoothly. Over the years, most experienced researchers have arrived at the same time-saving approach—a simple, ten-step method. The first five steps prepare you to write, and the remaining five steps help you to write your documented essay. Before you begin, however, you should have available a few indispensible materials. You can probably pick them up at your school's student store. Make it a practice to keep these items, along with your copy of the *Writer's Practical Rhetoric,* with you while you are researching.

3" × 5" index cards   A red pen or pencil
4" × 6" index cards   Scratch paper
A pen or pencil

TEN STEPS TO WRITING A RESEARCH PAPER

STEP ONE: CHOOSING THE TOPIC

Because you are going to invest a lot of time and energy into your research project, the topic is especially important. In many instances, your instructor may assign a specific topic. If this is done, you have little choice, but most instructors will permit or even welcome a slight refocusing of a topic when it is supported by interesting critical thinking.

In some of your classes, the instructor may present a suggested list of several topics from which you are to make a choice. If this is done, do not simply select the first idea that attracts your attention. It may be one with which you would soon become bored, or it may be one on which you would have difficulty finding all the necessary information. Examine all the topics. Try to consider how you might go about developing each of them. When you find one that seems especially interesting and worthwhile, do a bit of preliminary checking in the library to determine whether the basic sources you will need are available.

In some classes, the instructor may require a research paper but permit you to select your own topic. This is the most exciting of all research papers, because you can define a subject that particularly interests you. Suppose you are in a psychology class and your teacher asks you to write a paper on "anything you are interested in." If a topic doesn't flash into your mind, go back and do some of the prewriting exercises suggested on pages 37–49. An automatic writing or a word list should help you to get started. If you have been keeping a journal, refer to some of the entries to see if you can find an interesting and workable subject there. Choosing a good research topic does not necessarily mean finding something that has a lot written about it. Many times you will have to research around a topic in order to find the most useful information. Exciting and original topics often

How Do You Write a Research Paper?

come to mind by combining two completely different interests. Let's say that you are interested in child psychology and in sports. Perhaps you can combine these into a study of the effect that watching violent sports has on children. In this case, if there is not material directly available on the subject, you can research the topics individually and, by putting your information together, draw a conclusion.

STEP TWO: BECOMING YOUR OWN LIBRARIAN

The next step takes you to the library. Topics for term papers usually evolve from general ideas broken down into specific areas. Thus you may start with a general idea that you are interested in the subject of "population problems" and end up looking for specifics such as statistics on the birth rate in the United States in 1977. The many information resources of the library are fully discussed in Chapter 9. It is the strategy of searching for information that concerns us here. A strategy is outlined on the following flowchart.

FIGURE 10-1

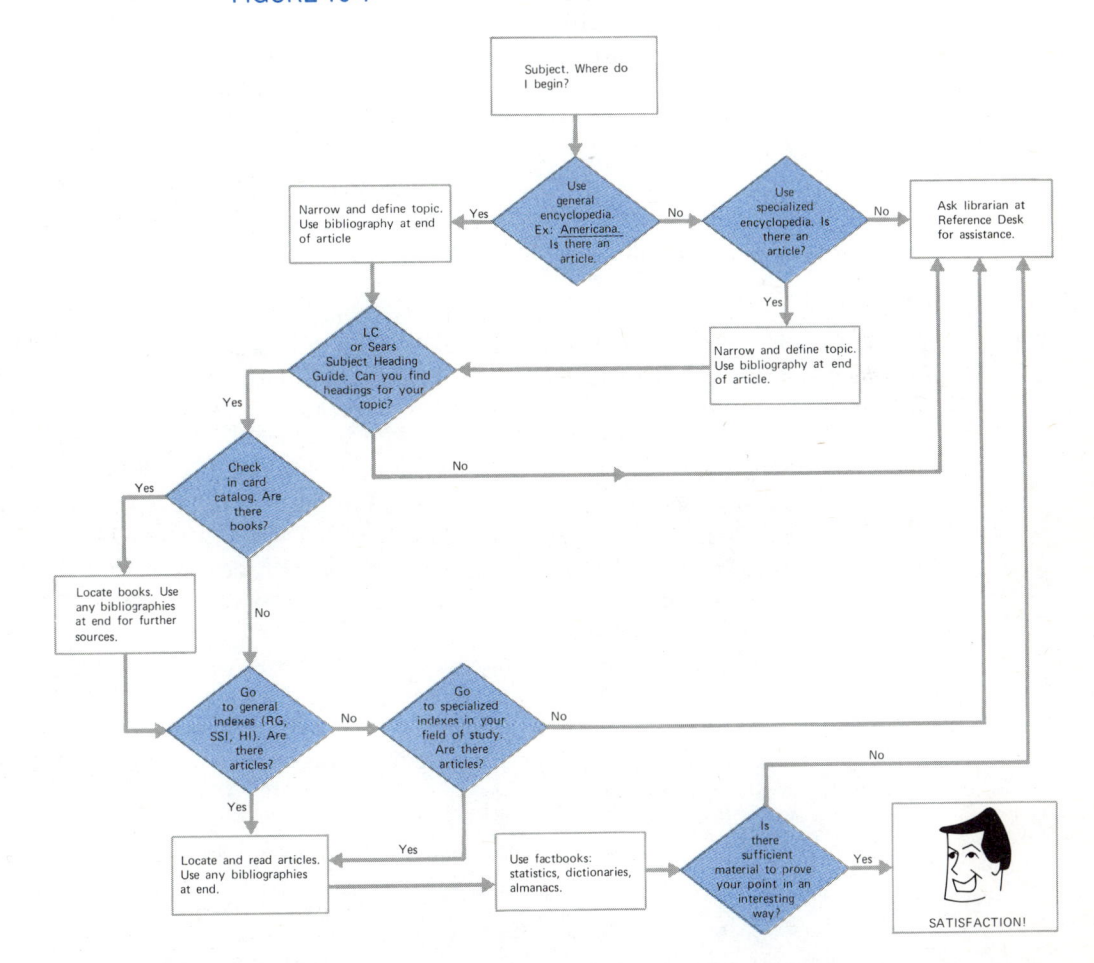

The first phase of the strategy for finding material is to get background material on your topic or an overview of it. For this you will want to use a basic reference tool such as a general or subject encyclopedia. Usually, you will also want to make use of the bibliography of further sources found at the end of most encyclopedia articles.

At this point, you may have found some aspects of your topic that interest you. These should be translated into subject headings that will make it easy for you to find books on each subject in the card catalog. Now you are ready to go on to the second phase of your strategy, consulting the LC or Sears Subject Heading Guide and then looking in the card catalog. Many of the books you find will probably have bibliographies at the end, similar to those for the encyclopedia articles, and documents. This method is sometimes referred to as "snowballing." From your beginning point, you are directed to a few sources that, in turn, will guide you to more sources. Before you know it, you will have enough material for your paper, maybe even too much.

You will probably still want to go on to the third phase of the strategy. Here you will consult specific reference tools such as periodical indexes and abstracts, newspaper indexes, dictionaries, and factbooks. Periodical and newspaper indexes, which are published frequently, can update and supplement the sources you may have found through bibliographies. Dictionaries and factbooks can supply the specifics needed to give your paper interest and authority. After your general search, you will want to return to Chapter 9 for suggestions on researching your specific subject.

STEP THREE: GETTING ACQUAINTED WITH YOUR TOPIC

At this point you have selected a subject and have found a few promising books and periodicals. Skim their indexes, tables of contents, and subtitles. Now sit down and quickly read through the ones that seem most important. You do not want to take notes yet. In this step you are still searching out the limits of your topic. You are not yet compiling information for your paper. Instead, read to find some specific area of the general subject that you might like to develop into a thesis for your paper. Only after reading four or five sources will you want to take pen in hand as you think. Remember, however, that the sooner you commit yourself to a preliminary thesis, the more time you can save for your intensive research.

Based on your reading, write down three or four possible thesis statements. Pick the most interesting and list three or four subtopics for it. For example, if your topic is the relationship between fashion consciousness and liberation among contemporary women, you might write the following:

Thesis In advertising, fashion-conscious women can find the image of the woman they imagine themselves to be.

A. The liberated woman

B. The man pleaser
C. The mother

Your thesis in this step does not have to be polished. In fact, you don't want it to be. Your final thesis should evolve as you take notes with the subtopics in mind. The last but most important part of Step Three is to check over your sources to see if you have enough to do a good job of researching. Many times you will want to go back to the card catalog and indexes to find more specific materials. Note that useful suggestions for further reading often come at the ends of the chapters or articles you have been skimming in this step. Step Three helps you to accomplish three things:

It orients you to the background of your subject.
It directs you to a preliminary thesis.
It leads you to sources for further research.

STEP FOUR: WRITING BIBLIOGRAPHY CARDS

A bibliography is simply a list of books, articles, essays, reviews, or other sources of information. In Step Four, you put together the working bibliography for your paper using 3″ × 5″ index cards. As you search for information about your thesis, make up a separate card for every source that promises to offer useful material. Each of your bibliography cards should contain all the information shown on the following sample.

FIGURE 10-2

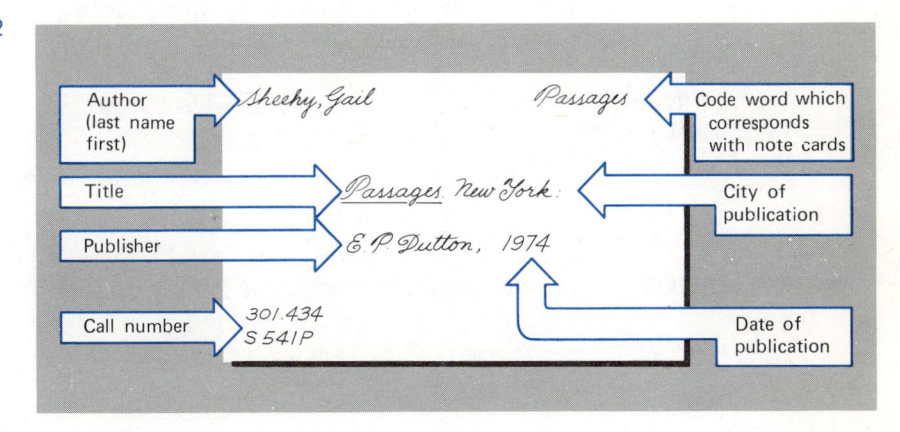

Author (last name first)	Sheehy, Gail	Passages	Code word which corresponds with note cards
Title	Passages New York:	City of publication
Publisher	E. P. Dutton, 1974	
Call number	301.434 S 541P	Date of publication

The information about each source—author, title, city of publication, publisher, date of publication—should be placed on the card in a particular order. The form used should be the same as that you will use when you prepare your final bibliography during Step Ten. You will save time then if you get all the necessary information as well as every comma and period in the right place now. Various library resources require different bibliographic formats. For example, a book with one author has a different format than does a news article or a book with an editor. Unless your teacher specifies the use of a particular form for your bibliography, use the standard format for the various types of sources. The following sample entries are based on the 1977 edition of the *MLA Handbook*.

FORMS FOR BIBLIOGRAPHY

A BOOK BY ONE AUTHOR

Anaya, Rodulfo A. Bless Me, Ultima. Berkeley, California: Tonatiuh International, Inc., 1972.

The simplest form for an entry is the book by one author.

A BOOK BY MORE THAN ONE AUTHOR

Wagner, Kenneth A., Paul C. Bailey, and Glenn H. Campbell. Under Seige. New York: Abelard-Schuman Ltd., 1973.

Invert only the first author's name and place "and" between the last two names.

A BOOK WITH AN EDITOR

Literary History of the United States. Ed. Robert E. Spiller. New York: The MacMillan Company, 1955.

For more than one editor, place "and" between the names of the last two editors.

For an article in a collection by an editor, use the special form for an essay in a collection.

A BOOK IN A SECOND OR LATER EDITION

Richter, Gisela M. The Sculpture and Sculptors of The Greeks. Rev. 2nd ed. New Haven, Connecticut: Yale University, 1965.

A TRANSLATION

Freud, Sigmund. Moses and Monotheism. Trans. Katherine Jones. New York: Vintage Books, 1967.

A BOOK OF MORE THAN ONE VOLUME

Hitchcock, Henry Russell. Early Victorian Architecture in Britain. 2 vols. New Haven, Connecticut: Yale University Press, 1954.

List number of volumes after the title.

A GOVERNMENT DOCUMENT OR A PAMPHLET PUBLISHED BY AN ASSOCIATION

    League of Women Voters. Recycle. League of Women Voters,

        Education Fund, No. 132, 1972.

The key here is to give as much information as possible to identify the publication. If an author or city is stated, place it in the usual position.

AN ESSAY, STORY, OR CHAPTER IN A BOOK OR ANY SELECTION FROM A CASEBOOK

    Boyle, Kay. "His Idea of a Mother." In Images of Woman

        in literature. Ed. Mary Ann Ferguson. 2nd ed.

        Boston: Houghton Mifflin Company, 1977, pp. 119-125.

Omit the number of the edition if the book is a first edition. Give the inclusive page numbers of the article, chapter, or selection using the abbreviation pp. for "pages."

    Flanagan, John T. "Hemingway's Debt to Sherwood Anderson."

        In Winesburg, Ohio: Text and Criticism. Ed. John H.

        Ferres. New York: The Viking Press, 1969, pp.482-

        487.

A NEWSPAPER ARTICLE

    Mink, Randy. "Rainy Day Pastime in New York." Los Angeles

        Times, Final Ed., 18 Jan. 1976, p. 6, cols. 1-3.

If no author is given, begin the entry with the title of the article and alphabetize by the first letter of the first word in the title in the final bibliography. Give inclusive column numbers, if possible, using the abbreviation cols. for "columns."

A MAGAZINE ARTICLE OR A JOURNAL ARTICLE

    "Turning Trash into Energy." U.S. News and World Report,

        20 Oct. 1975, pp.67-68.

Begin the entry with the title if no author is given. Include the complete page numbers of the article after the abbreviation pp., which stands for "pages."

    Netherby, S. "Cleaning Up Our Act." Field and Stream,

        April 1976, p. 96.

Begin the entry with the author's name if it is given.

Drone, H.B. and Michael H. Langley. "Juvenile Justice:

Reneging on a Sociolegal Obligation." <u>Social Service

Review</u>, 47 (1973), 561-70.

When the volume number appears in an entry, pp. is omitted.

AN ENCYCLOPEDIA ARTICLE

Crabtree, Arthur Payne. "Adult Basic Education."

<u>The Encyclopedia of Education</u>.

Niemeyer, Robert. "Dog Racing." <u>Encyclopedia Americana</u>.

1976 ed.

When several editions of an encyclopedia have come out, indicate which one you have used either by the date of publication or by the number of the edition.

Webb, Byron H. "Dairying and Dairy Products."

<u>Encyclopedia Britannica: Macropaedia</u>. 15th ed.

To find the author's name in the *Encyclopaedia Britannica,* note the initials at the end of the article you have read and check the last sixth of the Outline of Knowledge, where you will find a list entitled "Initials of Contributors and Consultants." Place the author's full name in the entry.

A MAGAZINE INTERVIEW

"You Can't Destroy This Movement." Interview with Jessie

Bernard, sociologist and author. <u>U.S. News and

World Report</u>, 8 Dec. 1975, pp. 71-74.

A PERSONAL INTERVIEW

Gaz, James. Personal interview. 28 March 1977.

A BOOK REVIEW

Russin, Joseph M. Rev. of <u>The Voices of Guns</u>, by Vin

McLellan and S.S. Paul Avery. <u>N.Y. Times Book Review</u>,

27 Feb. 1977, pp. 5, 14.

Begin the entry with the author of the review, but be careful to include as well the author(s) of the book being reviewed. Begin with the word "review" if no author is given for the book review. A comma is placed between the page numbers when an article is continued on a nonconsecutive page.

When you have completed your working bibliography, keep the cards you have filled out in two stacks. Each stack should have a rubber band around it. Reserve one stack for the sources you have already located and the other for those you have yet to find. The cards are easy to switch from one stack to the other as you find the sources you need and, by keeping them separate, you can tell at a glance how well your search is going. Some teachers may want you to hand in an annotated bibliography (see pages 341–344), either with your paper or sometime before the paper itself is due. As you skim each source, describe it briefly on its bibliography card. When you have finished your search, you will have almost completed your annotated bibliography as well.

STEP FIVE: TAKING NOTES ON CARDS

As you begin Step Five, you have already accomplished quite a bit. In Step Three, you have skimmed through several books or periodicals on your subject. You have developed a tentative thesis statement—which you will probably want to modify several times before you have written the final draft of your paper. You also have identified three or four subtopics of your thesis. Finally, in Step Four, you have gathered together your working bibliography. Now, using this bibliography, your tentative thesis, and its subtopics, you are ready to extract the information you need for your paper from the sources you have found.

It is a good idea to use subtopic headings on your note cards to help keep all your related ideas together. The more notes you take, the more important it is to use subtopic headings. If you have fifty note cards, for instance, and they are not identified by subtopics, you will have to read through all fifty cards each time you look for evidence to back up one of the subpoints of your thesis.

Notetaking is probably the most crucial step in preparing to write your research paper. Naturally, it is necessary to understand a passage before you can take notes on it. Try to take notes only on information that is going to be useful as you develop your thesis. Not all the material you read will be important to your thesis or its subtopics. Be selective but, on the other hand, be sure to write down anything that might be valuable. You will not want to use all your notes in your final paper, yet you cannot tell until your essay begins to take form just which and how much information you will need.

The three techniques used in notetaking include *paraphrasing, summarizing*, and *quoting*. At times, you will want to use combinations of quoting and paraphrasing or summarizing.

Paraphrasing is putting an author's ideas into your own words while keeping the length about the same as that of the original passage. It is usually used when the style of the passage is notable and would lose something if severely shortened.

Summarizing is greatly condensing a passage using all your own words.

Quoting is copying word for word a complete passage, or sometimes even a single significant word or phrase, from someone's writing. Quotations must always be indicated by quotation marks around both ends of the copied material. But quotation marks are not all you need. In the final paper a footnote number must be placed at the end of the idea taken from the source and the footnote itself placed either at the bottom of the page or at the end of the paper.

Of course, not every word you take from a source needs quotation marks—certainly words like "is" or "these" could appear anywhere and should never be cited for themselves. But any specific word or phrase that is peculiar to an author's argument or style requires quotation marks and a footnote. If a writer calls the rising cost of coffee "a plot by the South American growers" and you wish to use the phrase, you must give credit for the specific words as well as for the idea. If an article in a magazine refers to community colleges as "havens" for older adults returning to the education world and you wish to use the word, give the writer credit.

Quoting should be held to a minimum. A paper full of quotations jolts the reader, who must constantly adjust to many writing styles even in the same paragraph. It also tends to show a lack of originality. Most of your notes should be summaries of what you have read. Summarizing material forces you to consider the essence of what you read so that you can compare your ideas with those of others who have written on the subject. You may wish to quote a few words that sum up especially important ideas but, whenever possible, quotations should be integrated into your own sentences, not set off as separate sentences. Your resulting sentences containing the quotations should be smooth and grammatical. Students who only copy quoted passages onto their note cards often experience difficulty when writing their papers because the ideas from the sources have not been assimilated into their theses. When this happens, it seems especially difficult to meaningfully alter the words from the sources, and the writing in the final essays is frequently less original than it could be. In short, you do not want to be trapped into using the words of others in your final essay when your own would be better.

Sample Notetaking Methods

Let's say that you are writing a paper on the changing values about motherhood among different age groups of American women. You come across the following passage in a book:

> Great leaps of the last fifteen years in technology and ideology have given us the brand new "contracepted woman" and a profound feminism, followed by antimotherhood books and even antifertility rites. The revolt against automatic motherhood has spread to all classes. In a 1973 survey by Daniel Yankelovich, only 35% of college women and an astoundingly low 50% of noncollege women agreed to the proposition that "having children is a very important value." How much of this is their heads talking? Career counselors say that young women students today may know that motherhood is no longer

a lifetime career, but they still cannot feel that way about it.

The thrall of motherhood has subsided very little among girls from 15 to 19. The birthrate plummeted by one-third in the 1960's for girls between 20 and 24. Yet married teen-age girls continued to turn out babies at an amazing and almost consistent rate over the same period. And nearly half the brides in this age group are rushed to the altar by shotgun.

From Passages, by Gail Sheehy*

After recognizing that this is an important selection to cite in your paper, you must decide whether to paraphrase, summarize, or quote. You may wish to use a combination. Perhaps you will summarize but include in quotation marks some of the key phrases, like "motherhood is no longer a lifetime career" or "they still cannot feel that way." Here are some sample notes based on the selection from *Passages* for you to use as models.

PARAPHRASE

Technological development and advances in ideology over the last fifteen years have offered up a strong feminism which has been succeeded by movements against fertility and motherhood. The contraceptive-protected female has emerged to make her choice about motherhood. The new woman has arrived in all social classes. A study by Yankelovich in 1973 showed only 35% of college women and merely 50% of noncollege women in the U.S. believing that having children was important in their lives. But these results have been criticized as having been polled of women who have intellectualized their feelings.

Among the 15 to 19 age group many women still want to have babies. The 1960's showed a sharp decrease in the number of girls between 20 and 24 wanting to have babies. Married teenagers remained the same in their desire to reproduce, though. Almost 50% of teenage brides were found to have been in a position of having to get married because of pregnancy.

SUMMARY

Over the last 15 years, in our technological age, women between the ages of 20 and 24 from all social classes and educational backgrounds have shifted to the belief that bearing children is not a very important part of their lives. However, younger teenage girls, according to evidence from a study in the 60's, continue to want and bear children. Some critics have described the attitude shift in older women as mere intellectualizing.

QUOTATION

"The birth rate plummeted by one-third in the 1960's for girls between 20 and 24. Yet married teen-age girls continued to turn out babies at an amazing and almost consistent rate over the same period."

---

* From *Passages* by Gail Sheehy. Copyright 1974, 1976. Reprinted by permission of E. P. Dutton.

EXERCISES   A. Paraphrase the following passages:

1. *But to the Indian there was no such thing as emptiness in the world. There was no object around him that was not alive with spirit, and earth and tree and stone and the wide scope of the heaven were tenanted with numberless supernaturals and the wandering souls of the dead. And it was only in the solitude of remote places and in the sheltering silence of the night that the voices of these spirits might be heard.*
   Margot Astrov, American Indian Prose and Poetry

2. *The superficial adoption of his culture by the African is what the European notices with pride, and is the yardstick by which he measures the African's progress towards civilization. He has been all too unaware of the more significant changes. The fact, for instance, that an urban life not only entirely disrupts the traditional family life of the African, but destroys all the practical economic and political ties that are of any significance to him, resulting in moral and spiritual degeneration. He is also naively unaware of the tremendous intensity of feeling generated by social segregation. The European, particularly in eastern, central and southern Africa thinks of African hostility and opposition as being founded entirely in political causes. He is so obsessed by the notion that the African wants political equality and equality of economic opportunity, thus challenging white political and economic supremacy, that he has failed to see that a great proportion of the real hostility, the real bitterness and hatred, springs from other causes, trivial to the Europeans but of deepest significance to the African.*
   Colin M. Turnbull, The Lonely African

B. Summarize each of the following passages.

1. *There are as many different "sub-fields" within bioethics as there are applications of biology; however, those which arouse the greatest emotional response inevitably occupy the largest segments of public consciousness. Recently, genetic ethics has evolved into a significant subfield within bioethics. Cloning, genetic engineering and gene transplants are fascinating biological procedures and have elicited much public interest. They were first introduced to us in the realm of science fiction, but now have a basis in reality. Although such genetic procedures have yet to be performed upon human beings, genetic counseling is an accepted medical practice.*

   Genetic counseling evolved in response to the perception that genetic disease is a serious health problem. According to the National Genetics Foundations, fifteen million Americans have a genetic problem of one sort or another. One out of every 250 newborn babies has a genetic disorder. One out of every five hospital admissions of infants or children occurs because of a genetic or genetically-related problem. Concern about genetic disease has also been stimulated by continuing discoveries of a "genetic predisposition" in many illnesses without previous genetic as-

sociations. There is a crucial predisposing factor in some forms of heart disease, cancer, ulcers, and schizophrenia.

Erlaine Bello, "Bioethics and Genetic Counseling"

2. *In the early part of this century, mosquitoes got so bad in New Jersey that farmers were unable to farm and industry around Newark had to shut down temporarily on several occasions. To combat the "New Jersey Terror," the state established the first U.S. mosquito control program. They sprayed millions of gallons of undiluted diesel oil on the waters of coastal marshes in amounts of 20 gallons or more an acre. The oil damaged aquatic and plant life, but it killed mosquitoes and brought the Terror under control. Encouraged by these results, other states, including Florida, adopted similar programs. Today, there are some 350 organized mosquito control districts active in the U.S. Altogether, they spend some $50 million a year to kill mosquitoes.*

   But the mosquito has continued to fight back. In 1922, two million people caught dengue fever in Gulf Coast states. In 1933, mosquitoes killed 200 Missourians by infecting them with St. Louis encephalitis.

   Then, in the 1940s, the world was handed a new weapon so miraculously effective against mosquitoes that some authorities boldly predicted victory in man's battle with the bug. The wonder-weapon was DDT. Dusted, sprayed, or fogged, DDT meant death to both adult and larval mosquitoes.

William Shelton, "Winning the Battle of the Bug"*

Mechanics for Note Cards

The mechanics of notetaking come easily with a little practice. Note cards are better than full-sized sheets of paper or notebooks because the cards are easier to shuffle and to keep neat. Many students like to use 4" × 6" index cards for notes. The larger cards can be quickly distinguished from the 3" × 5" bibliography cards, and they have more space. The following suggestions should prove helpful as you write your note cards.

1. Write only on one side of a card so that you do not lose material.
2. On each card, take notes on only one subtopic from only one source and indicate the subtopic at the top center of the card.
3. When you quote directly, circle the quotation marks in red ink to remind yourself that the words came from someone else. This practice will protect you from unintentional plagiarism.
4. Write the page number of your source and the abbreviated reference that corresponds with your bibliography card.
5. Make sure that all quotations are copied accurately—double-check the spelling, the punctuation, and the number of words in each

---

* From "Winning the Battle of the Bug." Reprinted with permission of Exxon Company, U.S.A.

quotation. If you find an obvious mistake in spelling or punctuation in your source, you should leave the error in the quoted passage. However, if the error will distract the reader, write [*sic*] after the word in question. It is a sign to your reader that the error is in the text and not in your copying.

Example: The Mayor said he "couldn't recieve [*sic*] the honor without blushing."[2]

Study the sample note cards on the short passage cited next. Make sure that each of your note cards includes all the essential information written on the sample cards.

> Witness the following: Dr. Jay Schamberg, a noted Philadelphia dermatologist, reported an epidemic of teenage syphilis that was spread one evening by young people engaging in a common kissing game. Should Spin-the-Bottle now be outlawed? Should the kids who played the game be stripped forever of their label as "nice" kids? Or should some better rational thinking prevail?
>
> The point is that there is a difference between "sin" and disease, between morality and treatment. "Sin" is a theological concept which is widely divergent between peoples of varying faiths; disease is a physical fact requiring positive treatment. Yet the myth insidiously links the two together: Be "nice" and you should feel ashamed—so ashamed that you will never tell anyone you have it.

FIGURE 10-3

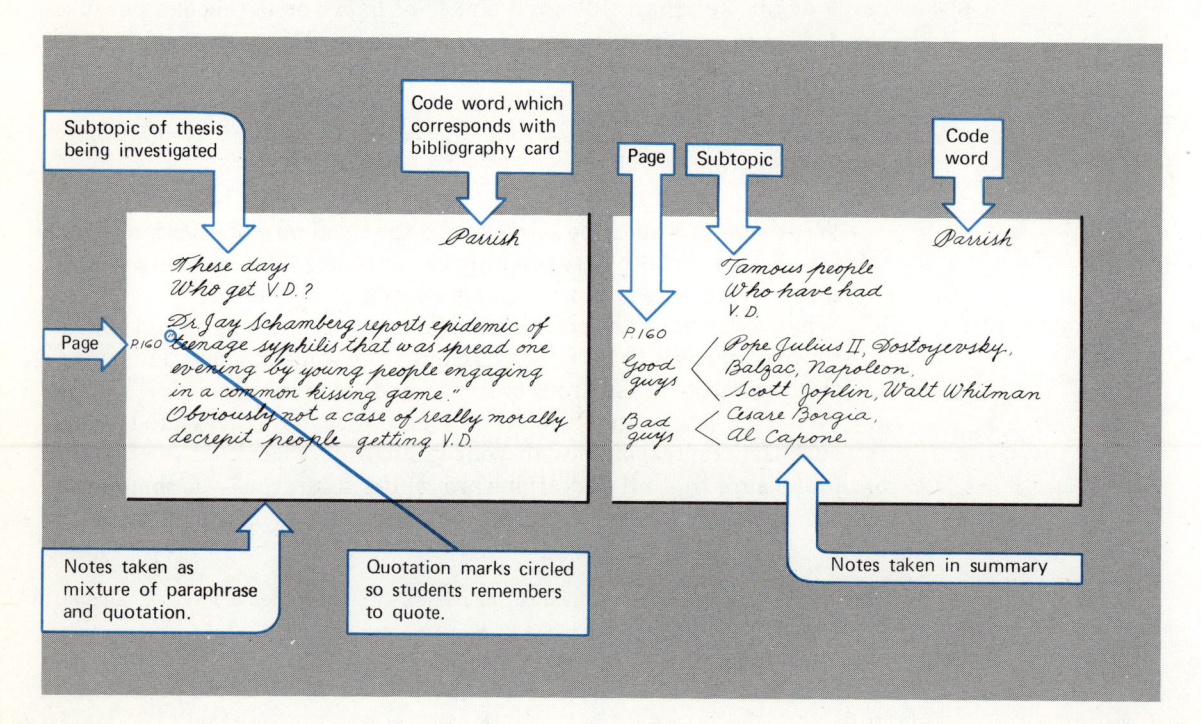

The VD epidemic will not decrease until we have successfully destroyed the myth. Anyone can and may get VD. *It is a disease just like TB is a disease, or rheumatic fever, or diabetes. No more, no less. Happily, it responds to treatment much better than many other "acceptable" diseases.*

Only poor misguided people get VD? Then to the list we would have to add Pope Julius II, Fyodor Dostoyevsky, Honore de Balzac, Napoleon, Scott Joplin, and Walt Whitman. They all had it. Of course, we would also have to list Cesare Borgia and Al Capone. Clearly, VD is not a respecter of position and/or accomplishment.*

STEP SIX: DEVISING A THESIS

By the time you have taken notes from all your sources, you have probably adjusted your thesis several times. You may have realized that a slightly different angle on your subject would be more defensible or that there was a great deal of information on an important point you had not included at first. In Step Six you are actually working on your thesis, revising and polishing it before setting it into your paper. You may want to get the thesis in form by using the steps for a good thesis on page 52. Your subtopics may be tailor-made for the new thesis, but probably you will want to adjust them, too.

Remember that a good thesis statement covers all the material to be placed in the paper. (See Chapter 2 for a more complete discussion of theses.) It should be clearly, concisely, and interestingly stated. Even in an informative paper in which you do not take a stand on an issue, you should include a summary type of thesis. A statement of intention is usually too dry and general.

> In this paper I will attempt to show how the reproductive cycle of toads functions. (Ineffective)

A summary statement is far more effective.

> The reproductive cycle of toads has three main stages. (Effective)

Most readers do not need the fact that they have a paper in front of their noses called to their attention. From the assertive tone of a good thesis, any reader should be able to identify it as the statement of structure in the essay. There is no need to resort to the obvious tags of the intention statement.

STEP SEVEN: CONSTRUCTING THE OUTLINE

Outlining is the step in which you clear a path for using your note cards. Before you begin working on the paper itself, write a detailed topic or sentence outline of what you plan to say. Your outline should be broken down to at least the Arabic numeral state (1, 2, 3, 4) to make sure that you have developed enough details. It is particularly important to wrestle with this step when writing a research paper, since these assignments are usually longer than unresearched ones. A tendency to digress is very common. If you find that you have this

---

* From "VD for the Millions." October 1972 *Future*, the official publication of the U.S. Jaycees. By permission of the editor.

problem, use your outline to help keep track of your thesis. For a thorough review of how to construct an outline, turn to pages 86–92. Finally, since many teachers will ask you to turn in your outline, usually placed after the title page of the final draft, you should make sure that it is clear, accurate, and neat.

STEP EIGHT: WRITING THE ROUGH DRAFT

All the following parts of a paper are the same for the research paper as for other types of essays. You may wish to review these sections of the book if you feel unsure of any of them.

Introductions—pages 57–64

Arrangement of Middle Paragraphs—pages 67–74

Paragraph Structure—pages 114–123

Conclusions—pages 77–84

Avoiding Plagiarism

Plagiarism means passing off information you have learned from a source as your own. It is dishonest if done deliberately. But plagiarism is more than simply copying someone else's words. It can also occur because of paraphrasing improperly or combining sources incorrectly. Avoid plagiarism by making sure of the following.

1. All notes should be carefully marked with source references and page numbers.
2. All quotations should be identified by quotations marks. If you type your paper use the quotation mark symbol on your typewriter, not the apostrophe, which is only used for a quotation within a quotation.
3. A paper should be centered on your own ideas. Never string together the ideas from a number of sources and call the result your research paper.

The two best ways to prevent yourself from slipping into plagiarism are to learn all the forms it can take and to document your paper meticulously.

When to Document

You already know that it is necessary to cite any sources from which you quote and many of those from which you borrow ideas. The general rule for knowing when to document is that every direct quotation and any idea that is not common knowledge must be identified and footnoted. The only thing that is difficult about this rule is determining what material is considered to be common knowledge.

Common knowledge does not mean, as many people think at first, only what everyone on the street knows, although that may indeed be included. Instead, it refers to what most authorities on the subject you are studying consider to be general information known by most of the writers in the field. General information is "common" enough not to need a reference. For example, the fact that preservatives are added to prepared foods would be hard to pin down to one source and is thus considered to be common knowledge.

The opposite of common knowledge is specific knowledge, the unique view of a particular writer on the subject under study. Specific knowledge is always documented. For example, the statement that the absorption of sodium nitrate, a preservative added to bacon and ham, can cause cancer in humans offers specific information and includes an opinion. It must, therefore, be footnoted.

The most reliable way of testing whether a bit of information is common knowledge is to survey what you have read on a subject. If seven out of ten writers mention the same bit of information, you can assume that it is common knowledge.

When to Quote

Paraphrasing and quoting should be used sparingly. Excessive quoting makes for a poor research paper because the style of the writing will vary so frequently. The reader may, after a while, begin to feel lost. For the most part you should summarize or, if the passage is brief and the style is noteworthy, paraphrase. There are only three instances when quotations should be used.

1. Quote when citing a well-known quotation. You would not want to reword "to be or not to be."
2. Quote when presenting evidence about a particular style or choice of words. In this case, the actual words should be your evidence. For example, if you are doing a study of Faulkner's narrative style, you would quote his writing, not paraphrase it. Similarly, if you are writing a mathematics paper in which you must use a certain equation as evidence, quote the equation directly.
3. Quote when presenting an idea most concisely and effectively requires the use of someone else's words. In some instance, you might wish to quote ideas that are so radical or controversial that your audience needs to see the exact words in order to accept their existence. The direct quote assures your reader that you have not misinterpreted the statement or removed it from the correct context. However, be sure of yourself as a writer—use your own words as much as possible and fit the key words from your sources into your own sentences.

How to Quote Short Passages

Short passages can be inserted into your paper to add firm support. It is very important, however, for you to lead up to all quotations and comment on their reason for being in your essay. Quotations should never be "stuck into" your paper as in the following example:

> Many birds are taught to repeat complicated phrases and sentences which sound remarkably like human speech. "One bird was in the habit of saying 'Hey, who's that guy in back of you with the big, black axe?' The bird's voice was enough to frighten anyone who was brave enough to enter the closet where the bird cage rested on a wooden pedestal."[3]

When the quotation begins, the reader, not being prepared to hear from a different writer, gets lost. The preceding passage could have been more smoothly handled in the following way:

> Many birds are taught to repeat complicated phrases and sentences which sound remarkably like human speech. A leading American ornithologist has described a humorous anecdote in which a Myna bird was trained to repeat. "Hey, who's that guy in back of you with the big, black axe?" As the story goes, the bird's voice frightened anyone "brave enough to enter the closet where the bird cage rested on a wooden pedestal."[3]

You should always lead your reader along and give warning when the style is about to shift. Also, extracting the key words from your sources and integrating these quotations into your own ideas makes your paper far more original. Here are a few examples of nicely integrated quotations from some students' research papers.

> Allen characterizes the role of the Coolidge Administration in foreign affairs as "making little effort to persuade the American people that they were not happily isolated."[6]

> During the period flanked by two "limited wars"—the Spanish American and the Korean—the United States is labeled by Allen as "a reluctant world power.[3]

> "Pushed by events," says Allen, Americans "resisted the idea" of greater involvement with "distasteful world politics," but "had no choice"; according to the personal accounts of some Americans, they were stripped of will.[5]

How to Quote Long Passages

At times you will want to include a longer quotation in your paper. Just as with short quotations, you should lead up to a long quotation. In addition, you should use a special form if the quotation is four or more lines. Long quotations should follow these guidelines:

1. Block off the quotation, single-spacing the direct quotation and double-spacing the quotation from the rest of your paper.
2. Indent five spaces from the left margin of your paper.
3. Omit quotation marks at the beginning and end of the quoted material; block citations are used only for direct quotations as the form signals word-for-word copying.
4. Do not double-indent for a one-paragraph quotation, but indent ten spaces for new paragraphs in quotations of two or more paragraphs.

The following is an example of the use of a long quotation in a student's paper.

The use of insecticides on our food crops even in the 1960's was disturbing to environmentalists for good reason. According to Rachel Carson far too many arsenic compounds were used, compounds which have been known to be killers:

PROSE OF MORE THAN FOUR LINES

Despite the competition of a constant stream of new chemicals issuing from the laboratories, arsenic compounds are still liberally used, both as insecticides (as mentioned above) and as weed killers, where they usually take the chemical form of sodium arsenite. The history of their use is not reassuring. As roadside sprays, they have cost many a farmer his cow and killed uncounted numbers of wild creatures. As aquatic weed killers in lakes and reservoirs they have made public waters unsuitable for drinking or even for swimming. As a spray applied to potato fields to destroy the vines they have taken a toll of human and nonhuman life.[5]

Quoting Poetry One or two lines of poetry can be included in your text. They should be enclosed by quotation marks, with the separation between lines indicated by a slash (/). Longer quotations from poems should be separated from your text in a block style and centered on the page. To separate the passage from the text of your paper, double-space before and after it and single-space the passage itself. Again, no quotation marks are used at the beginning or the end of a blocked quotation.

VERSE INCLUDED IN THE TEXT

Many writers allude to cats as mysterious creatures of the night or morning. Frost compares the fog to a cat, for instance: "The Fog comes/ on little cat feet."

VERSE BLOCKED FROM THE TEXT

Poe's "Annabel Lee" is a tribute to the intensity of childhood love:

> But our love it was stronger by far than the love
> Of those who were older than we—
> Of many far wiser than we;
> And neither the angels in heaven above,
> Nor the demons down under the sea,
> Can ever dissever my soul from the soul
> Of the beautiful Annabel Lee.[6]

Omissions from Direct Quotations You should only omit part of a quotation without filling in your own words if what remains can stand by itself and still make sense. An ellipsis (three periods, each followed by a space) should be placed where the omission occurs. Usually, no ellipsis is used if the omission comes at the beginning of a quotation. If the omission comes at the end of your sentence, use four periods with no space between the last word and the first period.

PART OF A SENTENCE

Three men . . . walked into the cafe, and four men left . . . at the same time.

There is no point in calling sports-lovers fanatics. . . . They are . . . advocates of a cause.

To show the deletion of a line or more of poetry or a paragraph or more of prose in a blocked quotation, use an entire line of widely spaced periods.

A LINE OR A PARAGRAPH

WHAT WERE THEY WATCHING?

He'd rise early, he'd leave when the birds sang;
down to the office he'd go without a lark.
She'd rise later, she'd drink coffee slowly,
then plug in the vacuum and collect old dust.
. . . .
They never grumbled, living together,
or hoped for some way quicker to pass their time;
when repeat shows stared like sore memories,
their eyes often wavered, glanced down toward
  the floor.

Punctuation Guides for Quoting

1. When including a quotation in one of your own sentences, punctuate as your sentence requires. Do not place a comma between your sentence and the quotation unless the sentence would call for it anyway. Check the comma rules beginning in Chapter 14.
2. Use a colon to introduce lists and passages you have mentioned in the lead-in. Remember that a colon signals an equivalence between two statements. For a more thorough explanation of the use of the colon, see Chapter 14.
3. You may wish to circle all quotation marks and footnote numbers in your rough draft to remind you to type them in the final draft.

EXERCISES

Directions: Evaluate the use of quoted material in the following excerpts from student essays. Suggest revisions for poorly quoted material.

A. The easiest type of shoplifter to identify is the kleptomaniac, who often has no economic reason to steal. Cleveland police Lt. Frank Corrigan said, "A lot of the poor shoplift because they're poor and can't afford to buy much. But just as many affluent or middle class people shoplift."
B. Men have never been content to live in a world they cannot understand, so societies have invented religions and promoted investigations of the earth in order to gain that understanding which

brings contentment. According to Dr. George Kernalie, "The religious impulse is a reflection of man's need of security," for "man must always know why disasters occur, why death is inevitable, and why rain falls on some days and not on others," even though "man cannot [do] anything to alter these unavoidable facts of life." A gas station attendant I once spoke to informed me that "To know is to control," by which he meant that there is comfort in knowledge, although knowledge may not bring the power to act. One might add, also, that to control is to comfort, for one controls oneself, and so can comfort oneself. This is what W. O. Malid seems to be implying in his fine book which he calls *Nature's Abandoned Children,* which I suggest to all of you. In fact, all of the books I read said that man has the inherent itch to discover how things work, that man is not satisfied until he can discover the secret of the atom and the composition of the moon's crust. As B. Q. White cogently said, "We all want to know who the murderer is, and what was his motive."

How to Footnote

The main purpose of footnoting is to provide your reader with a reference that can supply further information on a particular point you have made in your paper. One way of thinking about when to footnote is to ask yourself whether your reader could go to a particular source to learn more about the idea or information at hand. Your obligation as a writer is to lead your reader directly to the source, When in doubt, put in a footnote.

The form for footnotes is similar to the form for bibliography entries with slight differences in punctuation and arrangement (see p. 293). Footnotes are numbered, whereas bibliographies are arranged alphabetically. But because practically the same information is required for both, you may use the information on your bibliography cards to compose all your first footnote entries. Footnotes for a source you have already used have a shortened form (see p. 290). You will not have to go back to the original source because your note cards will supply the page references you need, and the corresponding bibliography cards will give you the necessary publishing information.

Writing footnotes is just a mechanical skill. There are two parts to a footnote, the number that appears in the text of your paper and the actual reference, which can be placed either at the bottom of the page on which the number appears or, in some instances, in a list at the end of the essay. The first time you refer to a source, you must give enough information to lead the reader to it. The standard format is easy to follow. Just imitate the sample forms and follow these rules.

1. Footnotes should be numbered consecutively throughout the paper.
2. Footnote numbers in the text of your essay come after the information being cited and, generally, after all the punctuation in your sentence.

3. Footnote numbers should be raised about half a space above the line you are writing on.
4. No parentheses or other punctuation is placed around footnote numbers.

FORMS FOR FOOTNOTES

A BOOK BY ONE AUTHOR

Rudolfo A. Anaya, <u>Bless Me, Ultima</u> (Berkeley, California: Tonatiuh International, 1972), p. 67.

A BOOK BY MORE THAN ONE AUTHOR

Kenneth A. Wagner, Paul C. Bailey, and Glenn H. Campbell, <u>Under Seige</u> (New York: Abelard-Schuman, 1973), p. 17.

A BOOK WITH AN EDITOR

<u>Literary History of the United States</u>, ed. Robert E. Spiller (New York: MacMillan, 1955), pp. 269-270.

For more than one editor, place "and" between the last two names.

A BOOK IN A SECOND OR LATER EDITION

Gisela M. Richter, <u>The Sculpture and Sculptors of The Greeks</u>, rev. 2nd ed. (New Haven: Yale University Press, 1965), p. 43.

A TRANSLATION

Sigmund Freud, <u>Moses and Monotheism</u>, trans. Katherine Jones (New York: Vintage Books, 1967), p. 174.

A BOOK OF MORE THAN ONE VOLUME

Henry Russell Hitchcock, <u>Early Victorian Architecture in Britain</u> (New Haven: Yale University Press, 1954), II, 65.

When a volume number is indicated, omit the abbreviation for the word "page" that normally precedes the page number.

A GOVERNMENT DOCUMENT OR A PAMPHLET PUBLISHED BY AN ASSOCIATION

League of Women Voters Education Fund, <u>Recycle</u>, No. 132 (1972).

AN ESSAY, STORY, OR CHAPTER IN A BOOK OR ANY SELECTION FROM A CASEBOOK

Kay Boyle, "His Idea of a Mother," in *Images of Women in Literature*, ed. Mary Ann Ferguson, 2nd ed. (Boston: Houghton Mifflin, 1977, pp. 121-122.

A NEWSPAPER ARTICLE

Randy Mink, "Rainy Day Pastime in New York," *Los Angeles Times*, 18 Jan. 1976, Final Ed. p. 6, col. 1.

It isn't necessary to give the edition of the paper, but it can be helpful, since sometimes articles run in one edition are not run in another one.

A MAGAZINE ARTICLE OR A JOURNAL ARTICLE

"Turning Trash into Energy," *U.S. News and World Report*, 20 Oct. 1975, pp. 67-68.

S. Netherby, "Cleaning Up Our Act," *Field and Stream*, April 1976, p. 96.

H.B. Drone and Michael H. Langley, "Juvenile Justice: Reneging on a Sociolegal Obligation," *Social Service Review*, 47 (1973), p. 563.

AN ENCYCLOPEDIA ARTICLE

Byron H. Webb, "Dairying and Dairy Products," *Encyclopedia Britannica: Macropaedia*, 15th ed. III.

ONE BOOK CITING ANOTHER

Harold Stearns, *Civilization in the United States* (1922), as quoted in William E. Leuchtenburg, *The Perils of Prosperity* (Chicago: University of Chicago Press, 1958), p. 151.

A MAGAZINE INTERVIEW

"You Can't Destroy This Movement," interview with Jessie Bernard, sociologist and author, *U.S. News and World Report*, 8 Dec. 1975, p. 72.

A PERSONAL INTERVIEW

Interview with James Gaz, President of the Gay liberation league for Human Rights, Los Angeles, March 28, 1977.

If you conduct a personal interview, try to identify it as fully as possible in the footnote. Information on the personality interviewed, city, date, and (occasionally) time are helpful.

A BOOK REVIEW

Joseph M. Russin, rev. of The Voices of Guns by Vin McLellan and Paul Avery, N.Y. Times Book Review, 27 (Feb. 1977), 5.

If review has no author begin entry with word "Rev."

SUBSEQUENT FOOTNOTES

You need to spell out all the footnote information only once for each source. Subsequent references to a source take shortened forms. Latin terms such as *loc. cit.* and *op. cit.* were previously used for this purpose. Except for *ibid.*, which is still generally used, these Latin forms are now outdated.

The usual reference to a book that has been cited in previous notes is

[9]Mondale, p. 34.

However, if there is more than one author with the same last name or if an author has contributed more than one source, a fuller reference is required for clarity.

[10]Richard Mondale, p. 30.

[11]Mondale, The Way Out, p. 28.

Even though Latin abbreviations are becoming less and less common in scholarly works, you may still come across them, particularly if you use older materials. *Consequently* you should know what they mean. The most often used abbreviations are the following:

op. cit.   located in the same source referred to in a recent note, but on a different page of that source.
loc. cit.   located in the same passages referred to in a recent note.
ibid.   located in the same source referred to in the previous note. When followed by a page number, it means the present reference is to a different page.

Other, less frequently used abbreviations include the following:

cf.	compare
et al.	and others, usually used to refer to several authors or editors of a book.
n.d.	no date
rev.	revised
viz.	consult for information
vol.	volume

SPECIAL TYPES OF FOOTNOTES

Parenthetical notes are notes placed right in the text of your essay. They are very useful whenever you have many references to the same source. In the first reference, which looks like any other footnote, fully cite the source and indicate to your reader that all future references to that source will be included in the text. Then simply place the title of the work and the page number in parentheses after the subsequent ideas you want to note the source of.

A First Reference for Intended Parenthetical Notes

```
    Kay Boyle, "His Idea of a Mother," in Images of

Women in Literature, ed. Mary Ann Ferguson, 2nd ed.

(Boston: Houghton Mifflin, 1977), p. 121.  Further references

to this work will be cited parenthetically in the text

as Images.
```

A Subsequent Reference with a Parenthetical Note in the Text

```
It is a surprise to the child that mothering

can be so pleasing.  He does not find it

odd that his cow can bring him such comfort.
```

(Images, p. 121).

Information footnotes are discussion footnotes. They introduce interesting information just on the periphery of your discussion or offer noteworthy background that would be cumbersome if fitted into your argument. The trick to wording informational footnotes is to be concise. Look at the informational footnote (number 17) in the sample research paper on page 319.

PLACEMENT OF FOOTNOTES

You may place the footnotes at the bottom of the pages on which the citations occur (be sure to leave enough room when you type the final draft) or in a list at the back of your paper, before the bibliography.

Technically, footnotes in a list at the back of a paper are "endnotes" and should be entitled "Notes." Your teacher may have a preference as to the placement of references. If he or she does not indicate a preference, it is much easier to place your footnotes in a list at the end of the paper. Doing so can save a lot of frustration when it comes to typing. Individual footnotes should be single-spaced, but you should double-space between each separate footnote if you have more than one on a page.

STEP NINE: REVISING THE DRAFT

After you have finished writing the rough draft of your paper, let it "cool." That is, put it aside for a day or two. If you don't have that much time, at least put it aside for a few hours. When you finish the first draft of your paper, you will probably feel saturated with material. Putting it aside, even for a short while, will help refresh your outlook. When you are ready to get back to it, use the same process you learned for polishing shorter essays (see Chapter 8). In addition, some students find it helps to have a friend look over their papers, simply because others provide needed objectivity. On the front cover of this book is a checklist you can use to help make sure that you cover all the strategic areas. These guidelines also indicate where in this book you can look if you find that you need advice on any of the checkpoints.

STEP TEN: TYPING THE FINAL PAPER

When you type or recopy your paper, be sure to go by the following rules of manuscript form unless your teacher suggests some alternate rules.

1. Double-space your typing (except for block quotations and footnotes) on good bond white paper of standard size (8½ × 11). The margins on all sides should be between 1 and 1½ inches. If your teacher accepts handwritten papers, write on every other line and follow all the other rules of the typewritten form (except for length—handwritten papers should have about twice as many pages.) All paragraphs should be indented five spaces.
2. Place the page number in the upper right-hand corner of the page, five lines down. Triple-space between the page number and your text.
3. One line above the center of the title page, type the title of the paper. Do not type the title of the paper again on the first page. No special punctuation, underlining, or quotation marks should be used unless part of your title would normally appear underlined or with quotation marks in the text of your paper.
4. A few corrections made after typing are all right. Be sure that you do them neatly. If your corrections cannot be made clearly right

over the typed error, place the correction in the space above the line. If there are more than three or four corrections on a page, or if any correction looks messy, you should retype the page.

5. If you are to hand in only the final copy of your paper, place one staple in the upper left-hand corner. Some teachers may prefer that you use a paper clip instead of a staple. If a teacher requests that you hand in your prewriting and rough drafts, it's a good idea to use a binder that can be purchased inexpensively in your college bookstore. Any note cards that must be handed in should be placed in the order in which they are used in the essay and sealed in an envelope.

6. Footnotes should be single-spaced. Double-space between the notes. If a note is typed at the bottom of the page, triple-space between the text and the first note. Indent the first line of a note five spaces. If a note continues onto the next page, do not triple-space from the text but type one solid line a space below the last line of the text and type the note on the next line. The line should begin at the left margin and extend about a third of the way across the page.

7. In the bibliography, indent the second line and any subsequent lines of the entry five spaces. Notice the difference between the bibliography form and the footnote form.

FIGURE 10-4

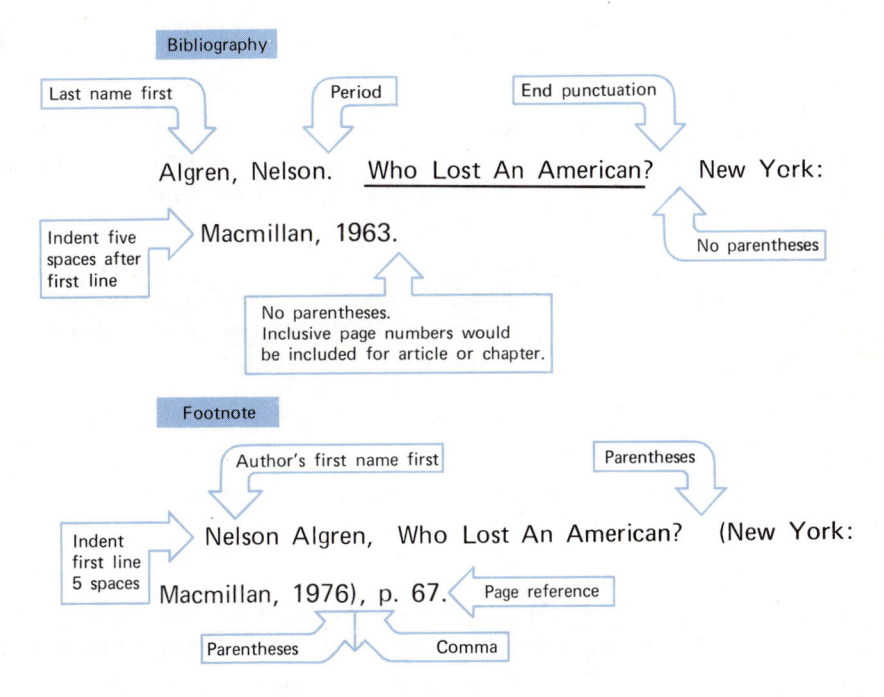

Bibliography

Last name first → Algren, Nelson. [Period] Who Lost An American? [End punctuation] New York: Macmillan, 1963.

Indent five spaces after first line

No parentheses. Inclusive page numbers would be included for article or chapter.

No parentheses

Footnote

Author's first name first → Nelson Algren, Who Lost An American? [Parentheses] (New York: Macmillan, 1976), p. 67.

Indent first line 5 spaces

Parentheses   Comma   Page reference

PROOFREADING Allow enough time to proofread your paper carefully. This last step is very important. Check your words carefully. Spell out loud the words you know you tend to misspell. If you have any doubts, look the word up in a dictionary. A teacher seeing a paper that has not been proofread, one that is spattered with spelling and typing errors, is likely to feel that the errors are evidence of a job done with little caring. Also, a paper full of careless errors is irritating to read. Many teachers will refuse to accept such a paper or will automatically award it a low grade.

QUESTIONS OFTEN ASKED ABOUT RESEARCH PAPERS

1. **Since I learned everything about the topic from what I have read, won't my whole paper need to be footnoted?**

No. First of all you will be organizing your essay around an original premise. Second, most of your topic sentences will be your own ideas and only your support for these ideas will, in most cases, need to be documented. Also, you will be commenting on any quotation that you include in the paper by using the "sandwich" method discussed in question 16.

2. **How long should my introduction be?**

The introduction in a research paper may be longer than in shorter essays. Do not delay stating your thesis for too long, however. In a ten-page paper, try to get your thesis in by the second page.

3. **What if I had a thought about my subject and it turns out that the same idea appears in one of the books I am researching. Do I have to give credit to someone else for something I too considered?**

You should give credit whenever an idea of your own occurs in one of your sources. However, if you wish to inform your readers that your idea came first, there is not reason why you shouldn't include an informational footnote such as the one below.

[1]My idea is shared by Calvin S. Hall, *A Primer of Freudian Psychology* (New York: World Publishing Co., 1954), p. 41.

4. **Was the footnote and bibliography form I learned in the past wrong? Why was it different from the form in this text?**

The main concern that scholars have with documentation is that it be consistent. Don't use a comma for one footnote in the same place that you use a period in another footnote. Generally, people in the humanities use the guidelines set by the *MLA Handbook*. Other disciplines may use other style sheets. For instance, the *Style Sheet of the American Psychological Association* is often used in the social sciences, and a special style sheet is used in the natural sciences. Unless your teacher asks you to use a specialized format, follow the guidelines in this book.

5. **Does every fact have to be footnoted?**

You should document all information that is not common knowledge. You need not, however, document material noted by most authorities in the field. If seven out of ten sources you read refer to the same information, you can assume that the point is common knowledge and needs no citation. But if a fact is quoted directly from a source or if you use information or opinions presented by a particular writer, you must document them.

6. **Should a bibliography include background reading or just the books cited in the paper?**

There is no one answer to this question. It depends on the situation and what your teacher asks for. If you do not wish to cite background materials, entitle your bibliography Works Cited or References.

7. **Do I need both a bibliography and footnotes in every research paper?**

The style sheet for the humanities does call for both. However, certain scientific style manuals call for shortened forms, which include all the bibliographical and footnote references on a page at the back of the paper. Formal research papers usually call for both footnotes and bibliographies. It's always best to check with your teacher on this question.

8. **Does it matter if I put my footnotes at the end of my paper or at the bottom of each page?**

Basically, where you put your footnotes is up to you, although your teacher may prefer one form over the other. Footnotes at the bottom of the pages are easier to check while reading. Notes at the end of the essay are much easier to type. Informational notes, however, are usually placed at the bottom of the page for convenience in reading. In these cases, they are indicated by an asterisk, not a number, in the text.

9. **How many note cards should I have?**

You should always have more notes than you need. Having twenty or thirty extra cards for a ten-page research paper is average. Be sure not to throw out your extra cards until you finish your essay—you can never tell when your paper will take an unexpected turn.

10. **If I am dealing with a controversial topic, do I have to present both sides of the controversy?**

When writing an essay on any controversial topic, you are obliged to present the opposition and to refute it if you wish to convince the reader of your stand. If you fail to cite the opposition, your reader may judge you as unknowledgeable in the field or feel that your views lack objectivity.

11. **How many footnotes should I have?**

This is a hard one to answer because there are not any real rules. You should footnote whenever necessary. Depending on your topic and the length and breadth of the essay, you will need more or fewer notes. You should not have too many footnotes, say twenty in four pages—this approach would normally indicate that not enough of the thinking in the essay is your own. On the other hand, too few footnotes might indicate that you did not do enough research.

12. **How many sources should I use?**

You should use a variety of different types of materials in any research project. Among them should be periodicals, general reference tools, and specialized books. Try to find the classics in the field and read them. In most cases your teacher can suggest primary sources on your subject. An example of a primary source on the study of dreams is Freud's *Interpretation of Dreams*. A secondary source on the same subject would be a discussion of Freud's book. The number of sources will vary with the project, but most teachers agree that two or three are not enough.

13. **When should I paraphrase and when should I quote?**

If a quotation is not essential (see the suggestions on p. 283), paraphrase the material. It will make your paper easier to read. Since it jolts the reader each time there is a change in the style of writing, unless the shift in style is deliberate or necessary, avoid quoting.

14. **How many words should a quotation have before I separate it from the body of my text?**

Four lines or more of prose and three lines or more of poetry should be placed in the block form of quotations.

15. **Do I need a thesis statement for a research paper?**

Yes. You always need an original direction for any essay, and that direction should be clearly set forth in a thesis statement at the beginning of the essay.

16. May I end paragraphs with direct quotations?

It is generally a poor practice to end paragraphs with direct quotations because they tend to just sit there rather than work for you. As a better strategy, lead up to all quotations, include the material, and then comment on it so that your reader knows why the quotation appears in the essay. For strategies to use in including quotations see page 283.

SAMPLE RESEARCH PAPER

On the following pages is a student's research paper which presents you with the correct form for most of the papers you will need to write in college. Each page to the left of the research paper contains explanations of the essay structure related to the numbering of the outline. You will also find notes on footnotes, bibliography, and format for presentation of the manuscript.

Arrange your final paper in the following order:

1. Title Page
2. Outline
3. Essay
4. Notes (if not typed at bottom of each page)
5. Bibliography

Garbage by Any Other Name

By

Dianne Cravens

English 101

June 10, 1977

Outline

Thesis: Modern science has identified the seriousness of the garbage problem and is experimenting with technologically and economically feasible methods of reducing the amount of waste in the United States.

I. Waste as a serious pollution problem
    A. Large quantities of waste from disposable items
        1. Paper discarded by Colonel Sanders
        2. Paper diapers thrown away by mothers
        3. Number of disposable items in a typical trash can
    B. Relationships between and effects of population and waste increase
        1. World has doubled thirty-one times
        2. In sixteen more doublings only one square yard per person left
        3. Human population expected to stop growing before sixteen doublings because of lack of natural resources

II. Methods of reducing amount of waste
    A. Recycling--steel, glass, aluminum, paper from trash
        1. Reprocessing less expensive than dumping
        2. Current recycling projects across the nation
    B. Bacterial digestion of waste--Texas project
    C. Trash burned to produce energy
        1. Successful in major cities--T.V.A.

       2. Flash process used.

       3. Less energy used in reprocessing than in processing new materials.

  D. Anerobic fermentation in dumps--methane

       1. Palos Verdes

       2. Hyperion Sewage Plant and Water Pollution Plant

       3. Production from cow manure.

       4. Limitations of methane and methanol

       5. Move toward methane economy.

  E. Clivus multrum--bathroom and kitchen wastes.

If your teacher requests that you not use a title page, type the title of the paper centered two inches from the top of the page. If you use a title page, however, do not repeat the title on the first page.

The student opens the paper by stating the problem and relevant background. Her humorous reference to the slogan, "Go west young man," implies that waste problems have always been caused by the same thing: the inability of human beings to do anything with their trash but dump it.

Transitional remark—"Today waste disposal is not so simple." The historical discussion ends. This is the point at which the student begins to state the overall large proportions of the current waste problem.

Footnotes 1 and 2 represent first references to two books that will be used throughout the paper.

- The first line of a footnote is indented five spaces.
- The second line comes out to the margin.

1.

  When our ancestors lived as nomads, the disposal of garbage was quite simple: they moved away when the stench became unbearable. As they forsook wandering for a more permanent society, they threw their garbage out the tent flap for the pigs and nature to recycle. The Greeks of the 5th century, B.C., were the first to use town dumps for the disposal of their refuse. These unsanitary landfills received, along with the usual garbage, unwanted babies and bastard sons.[1] During the days of the Roman Empire, the first toga-clad garbage man emerged. Garbage was tossed loose into the streets and the world's first "sanitary engineers" would lead their horse drawn carts down the street, scoop the garbage into their wagons, and deposit it in a neighborhood dump.

  But the collection and disposal of garbage occurred infrequently. In fact, littering was the most common form of garbage disposal until the 1700's and 1800's. Early America's response to pollution was manifest in the slogan, "Go West, young man." When the neighborhood became too littered with garbage, our predecessors simply loaded up their wagons and moved on.

  Today waste disposal is not so simple. The United States produces a total of 4.3 billion tons of waste material

---

[1] Katie Kelly, *Garbage: The History and Future of Garbage in America* (New York: Saturday Review Press, 1973), p. 16.

The student continues to explain the large proportions of the waste problem. She gives pertinent statistics that may interest the reader, but she does not elaborate at this point with specific information that should be saved for the body of the paper. At the end of her statement of the problem, the student delivers her thesis, science's solutions.

Thesis: Modern science has identified the seriousness of the problem and is experimenting with technologically and economically feasible methods of reducing the amount of waste in the United States.

I. Waste as a serious pollution problem.

    A. Large quantities of waste from disposable items.
The student discusses the values about disposability in our society, and how they are responsible for people's generating enough waste to produce a pollution problem. (The topic sentence is the student's own idea, and the evidence she offers is used to support her idea.)

Footnote 3 is a second (shortened) reference to the same source cited in footnote 2. Note that footnotes are numbered consecutively throughout the paper.

2.

per year from household, commercial, industrial, agricultural and mining sources.[2] The sheer magnitude of the trash we produce is staggering. We Americans, who consume thirty-five percent of the earth's raw materials, represent only six percent of the world's population, yet each of us contributes one ton of garbage per year. When one considers that half the population of the United States lives within fifty miles of either Atlantic or Pacific Coast, and that by the year 2000, it is predicted, seventy percent of the population will live on ten percent of the land, the disposal of the waste produced becomes a grave, costly problem.[3] The United States already lacks land on which to dump its garbage, and the overabundance of waste is a serious threat to our natural resources. But the picture is not entirely bleak. Modern science has identified the seriousness of the problem and is experimenting with technologically and economically feasible methods of reducing the amount of waste in the United States.

    Much of the waste produced is the result of our highly technological society in which disposableness is considered an important quality for most items produced. We throw away twenty million tons of waste paper, twenty-five million pounds of toothpaste tubes, forty-eight billion cans, twenty-six billion bottles and jars a year. Colonel

    [2]Kenneth Wagner, Paul C. Bailey, and Glenn H. Campbell, <u>Under Seige</u> (New York: Abelard-Schuman Ltd., 1973), p. 8.
    [3]Wagner, p. 9.

B. Relationships and effects of population and waste increase.

Footnote 4 is a reference to a source not previously mentioned.

Footnote 5 is a subsequent reference to footnote 1.

3.

Sanders alone disposes of twenty-two million foam polystyrene containers, thirty-one million paperboard buckets and 110 million chicken dinner boxes. U.S. babies have their diapers changed 15.6 billion times each year, and most of the changes are with disposable diapers. One machine alone can turn out 300 disposable diapers per minute[4], and all of those diapers eventually wind up in trash cans. Truly descriptive of our "waste-full" life style are the contents of a typical garbage can in America: fifty to sixty percent paper and packaging material, ten percent lawn and garden waste, nine percent organic food waste, 8.5 percent glass and ceramics, and 7.5 percent metal such as beer cans and soft drink cans. The remaining six percent is rags, rubber, leather and just plain dirt.[5]

As the population increases, the volume of each type of waste increases. At present the solid waste is increasing at twice the rate of our population.[6] The Population Reference Bureau estimates that the world has doubled itself thirty-one times since Adam and Eve. If it doubles sixteen more times, the Bureau figures that each of us will have one square yard available in which to eat, sleep, live, breathe, and pollute. However, the Bureau notes encouragingly that "the human population will stop growing long before sixteen more doublings or even eight more

[4] Wesley Marx, *Man and His Environment: Waste* (New York: Harper and Row, 1971), p. 9.

[5] Kelly, p. 9.

[6] Wagner, p. 9.

The student integrates a direct quotation into her own sentence. This material is quoted because of its controversial nature. In order to convince the reader of the severity of the statement and to retain its context, the writer quotes the key words rather than summarizing or paraphrasing.

- The footnote number is placed at the end of a sentence whenever possible.
- The key words of the quotation are set into the grammar of the student's sentence.

II. Methods of reducing amount of waste.

- Note the use of a transitional sentence—"Before we pollute ourselves...."

A. Recycling—steel, glass, aluminum, paper from trash.

Most of the information in this paragraph is knowledge that could be found in many books about trash recycling or in the advertisements of popular magazines. Because the material is common knowledge, the student does not footnote it. However, she does provide a reference for the statement about the revolutionary paving surface, since that point was made in only one of her books and a specific claim is made for it—it lasts four times longer than ordinary surfaces.

4.

not for sheer want of space but for want of food, water and other natural resources and possibly because of environmental pollution."[7]

  Before we reach the point of polluting ourselves out of existence, we can begin to use some of what we throw away. Scientists, industrialists and municipal officials believe it is technologically feasible to separate the components of the trash pile and to remake them into useful products. Markets for these recovered materials--steel, glass, aluminum and paper--do exist. In fact, some cities in the United States are separating their garbage and profiting from the sale of the recovered materials. This type of reprocessing has proven to be less expensive than dumping. A method that shows great promise is recycling, from beer cans to automobiles. The seven million junked cars a year that litter our countryside represent the raw materials that can go into next year's models. The tires, along with bottles and glass, can be ground up and added to paving materials, resulting in the creation of a surface that is crack resistant and lasts four times longer than present surfacing.[8] Goodyear has found a way to use discarded tires in producing new ones. The ground-up tires are mixed with oil and burned to create carbon black, a key ingredient in tires. In this way, one recycled tire produces one new tire.

 [7]Kelly, p. 48.
 [8]Wagner, p. 10.

Footnotes are provided for the statistics offered as evidence that companies are switching to recycled products.

Footnote 9 uses the Latin form, *Ibid.* to mean "in the same place." An alternate but less expedient form, in this case, would have been to repeat Wagner, p. 10.

Even though footnotes 10, 11, and 12 refer to sentences right after each other in the text, separate notes are needed to point out the different page numbers.

5.

All over the country large companies are switching to recycled paper, metal, and glass products. Western Kraft of Albany, Oregon, has since 1968 reclaimed enough paper and cardboard to fill a football field to a depth of 60 feet, 18,000 tons of material.[9] Twenty percent of the newspaper stock in the United States is being recycled with a savings of more than 200 million trees a year. New York City's Environmental Protection Administration has encouraged the city to use recycled paper by requiring in their purchasing specifications twenty percent recycled fibers in the bond paper used by the city and thirty percent recycled fibers in corrugated boxes. Other large companies such as Consolidated Edison of New York and Wells Fargo Bank of San Francisco recover and recycle tons of billing envelopes, ledger paper and other paper products used in their businesses.[10] Fifty-two to fifty-seven percent of our steel produced each year is recycled. In 1967 Reynolds opened the first aluminum recycling center which collected more than four million pounds of aluminum that first year. In 1971, nearly twenty-five million pounds of aluminum were collected.[11] In Los Angeles, the Glass Container Manufacturing Institute opened a recycling plant and in 1970 took in 1.5 million bottles a week. Now one hundred centers serve twenty-five states and collect 793 million bottles

[9] Ibid.

[10] Kelly, p. 119.

[11] Kelly, p. 123.

The student continues to offer examples of recycling programs. Because she recognizes that the last several sentences have included many figures and statements of fact, she ends the paragraph with one point of common knowledge and a summarizing statement.

A transition is made between information on recycling programs and information on chemically changing the trash that is dumped into useful products.

 B. Bacterial digestion of waste.

 C. Trash burned to produce energy.

- The information contained in these two paragraphs can be found in many books about this subject. Since the writer need not make specific footnote references, a reader who is interested in reading more about these topics would simply consult the bibliography at the end of this paper.
- The student comments on the information throughout the paragraph.

6.

and jars each year.[12] Movements against disposable glass containers and slogans printed on metal cans that remind consumers to recycle seem to have taken hold. People are recycling materials and are buying recycled goods.

Recycling can save large quantities of natural resources each year. Nevertheless, a mountain of garbage must be contended with in this disposable society. One method of garbage conversion under study is bacterial digestion waste. Biologists at Texas Technological Institute in Lubbock, Texas, are working on a process of converting garbage into a protein-rich food for cattle and possibly for humans. The process uses selected bacteria to digest the cellulose in newsprint, waste paper, weeds, feedlot waste and other throwaways into a usable protein. One thousand pounds of these bacteria can produce 100 trillion pounds of protein per day as compared to one pound of protein per day per steer.[13]

Trash is also being burned to produce energy. A program of burning trash for power generation is being used in St. Louis, Baltimore, New York, New Orleans and the Tennesse Valley Authority (T.V.A.). One of the Nation's largest power plants, the T.V.A. serves Kentucky, Tennesse, North Carolina and Alabama. Farther west, San Diego is perfecting a "flash process" turning garbage into pyrolytic oil which is burned to produce electrical energy.

[12]Kelly, p. 126.
[13]Kelly, p. 137.

D. Anerobic fermentation in dumps—methane.

A direct quotation is used to include information that the student feels is particularly well stated.

- The student leads up to the quotation with a reference to the source.
- The student comments on the quotation to show its value in her essay.

Footnote 14 is the first reference in this paper to the article by Nicholson.

7.

Riverside, California, is also piloting a program to convert garbage to gas which will fuel an internal combustion engine on an electrical generator.

The Environmental Protection Agency experts estimate that if all major metropolitan areas would burn their garbage, the United States could save many million barrels of oil a year. By reclaiming the marketable materials at the same time, these plants could provide considerable percentages of the nation's tin, iron, and aluminum. Additional barrels of oil would be saved by the reprocessing which takes less energy than the processing of raw materials. These experts further estimate that nearly seventy-five percent of our total garbage per year could be turned into energy. This potential solution to our waste problem--burning the trash--is noteworthy, for if we could reuse enough of our garbage, what would be left over may not represent such a problem.

In fact, what is dumped might provide a valuable starting material for the production of fuels. In a recent news article, methane has been acclaimed the potential solution to out energy problems: "For many a U.S. community, relief from natural gas shortages may be no further away than the local garbage dump."[14] Any city landfill dump can produce methane. A spinoff material from trash, methane gas, which is colorless, odorless and pollution free, can

[14]Tom Nicholson, James Bishop, and Peter Greenburg, "Methane Method," Newsweek, 20 Oct. 1975, p. 85.

The projects cited in the paragraph are mentioned in most sources on the subject, but only one source commented on the clean engines in the Santa Clara Plant. For this reason, the student has footnoted that point.

Footnote 15 is the first reference in this paper to the article by Lindsley.

8.

be used in the same way as natural gas for heating, cooking, and powering engines. Already some cities are using methane from landfills to fuel homes. One such landfill in Palos Verdes near Los Angeles is supplying energy to 3,500 homes in Rolling Hills. The Hyperion Sewage treatment plant in Los Angeles produces enough gas to power its twenty-four-horse-power engines. A Water Pollution Control Plant on the outskirts of Los Angeles in Carson powers its generators, pumps and boilers with methane gas it produces, and the excess is sold to a neighboring oil company. A Santa Clara-San Jose, California sewage treatment plant runs its engines on the methane gas produced in its plant. After fifteen years using the same oil, these companies are as clean as they were when they were new.[15]

Producing this methane gas from cow manure has been tested on some dairy farms. The process, called anaerobic fermentation, is the decompostion of organic matter in the absence of air in order to produce a gas sometimes called Biogas. The process is particularly appealing to dairy farmers since they could power their entire farms utilizing a readily available fuel. This form of methane derived from pig and chicken manure and sewage is promising though of limited usage in the automobile:

> It has been claimed that such methane can be used for powering automobiles, where it has an operational cost equivalent to a cost of $0.03 per gallon for gasoline. It is also

[15] E.F. Lindsley, "Methane From Waste," *Popular Science*, Dec. 1974, pp. 58-60.

A direct quotation of four or more lines is used. Quotations of this length are single-spaced and double-spaced from the text. The student chose to quote this material because it so directly takes a stand on a currently controversial issue. Thus she felt it to be valuable for its context and its style.

- No quotation marks are used at the beginning and end of the citation which is blocked off and single-spaced.
- The student leads up to the quotation with her own words.
- This quotation begins at the second sentence of the paragraph in the source. If the quotation came from the beginning of the paragraph in the source, the student would have indented the first line an additional 3 spaces (8 altogether).

The paragraph continues after the blocked-off quotation. If the student had gone on to a new topic, she would have begun a new paragraph.

The term "methane economy" belongs to Dr. Klass and must therefore be cited when the student uses it.

The student comments on the value of methane conversion from waste.

Footnote 16 is the first reference to the article by Reed and Lerner.

Footnote 17 contains commonly mentioned information, but the article cited offers an unusually detailed study of these conclusions as the informational footnote indicates. This footnote refers to a summary of material on pages 1299 to 1304.

9.

claimed that enough fuel could be made from
this source to meet all present fuel needs
in the United States, and that the use of
such a process would reduce by half the
problem of sewage and animal-waste disposal.
In experiments with cars and trucks
converted to use methane, the U.S. General
Services Administration has reported clean,
reliable operation. However, the type of
cylinder required to contain compressed
gaseous methane severely limits the amount
of fuel that can be carried. . . . Conversion
of the organic wastes to methanol rather
than methane would make this fuel source
much more practical.[16]

Methanol, a liquid alcohol, is a versatile fuel that can be made from natural gas, petroleum, oil, coal, shale, wood, or waste material. It can be added, up to fifteen percent, to automobile engines without altering them. Using this fuel, the car increases its performance, reduces engine emissions, and decreases fuel consumption.[17]

Most advocates of methane and methanol admit that "methane recovery has yet to be proved economically feasible on a large scale." Yet of the 146 billion tons of organic waste produced each year, if only 1.6 percent can be tapped, by 1990 our country could operate on a "methane economy," according to Dr. Donald Klass of the Institute of Gas Technology.[18] We will probably be too reluctant to hold fast to the sort of schedule proposed by Klass, but nevertheless we should recognize the valuable by-product that lies unused in our dumps. If programs

[16]T.B. Reed and R.M. Lerner, "Methanol: A Versatile Fuel for Immediate Use," <u>Science</u>, 28 Dec. 1973, p. 1302.

[17]Reed and Lerner, pp. 1299-1304. The detailed discussion of the molecular structures of methane and methanol offers strong evidence for these conclusions.

[18]Nicholson, p. 87.

E. Clivus Multrum—Bathroom and kitchen wastes.

Sample Note Card

> *Clivus Multrum*   "Where's the Loo?"
>
> p.67   Abby Rockefeller received Amer. rights to distribute organic toilets. Developed 30 yrs ago in Sweden. Kitchen and bathroom wastes go through series of chambers to slowly decompose. Around 4 yrs. later arrive at storage receptable as humus for use gardens. 95% waste carried away through vent pipe. All odor in form of CO_2 & H_2O. Costs $1300 for on-site installation.

Footnote 19 is the only reference to the article, "Where is the Loo?" Since the article is anonymous, the reference begins with the title. This footnote cites a summary of a short piece in a magazine.

10.

for the conversion of waste to methane could be funded, perhaps more economical methods of production could be discovered.

Probably the most unusual method of disposing of waste matter, and one that touches us all close to home, is the Clivus Multrum. This organic toilet disposal system was developed in Sweden and is being introduced into this country by Abby Rockefeller. The Clivus Multrum recycles kitchen and bathroom wastes without using water, chemicals, or any energy. As the waste matter descends through a series of chambers, it decomposes slowly. Two to four years later it emerges as an organic humus that can be used in the garden. A vent pipe carries away ninety-five percent of the waste matter in the form of water and carbon dioxide and leaves the system odorless. Although the system is expensive, $1,300 per unit, the advantage is on-site disposal rather than transporting our waste, thus keeping our rivers, streams and oceans clean.[19] Though not economically feasible for many now, perhaps the system can be made less expensively once it becomes more commonly used.

Only one form of pollution which threatens us today is waste. When we consider the other forms of pollution--noise pollution, water pollution, air pollution--it is easy to become overwhelmed by the magnitude of the

[19]"Where's the Loo?" _Atlantic_, April 1975, p. 67.

The conclusion of the student's essay explains some of the implications of her discussion. Waste pollution can be brought under control with enough money and research directed toward it. But she wonders what the relationship between this type of pollution is to other types.

11.

problems and to ask, "But what can I do?" Of course one person cannot solve the problem, but little by little something is being done by interested scientists and the public. Recycling and reuse programs have helped to slow the depletion of our precious natural resources; and programs to rid us of at least some of our garbage are either on the drawing board, in the experimental stage, or to some limited degree in use now. Each one of us can let political and governmental leaders know his or her wishes to increase funding for research and experimentation in this field. If we do not encourage them to pursue these avenues to solutions, we might all be buried one day in our own throw-aways.

Guidelines for the Bibliography

1. All items are alphabetized according to the last name of the author. The last name of the author comes first.
2. If no author is given, the title of the article or book (omit the, an, or a) is used for the alphabetical sequence.
3. The first line of a bibliography entry comes out to the margin but all subsequent lines are indented five spaces.
4. The inclusive page numbers are given for articles, chapters of books, and essays or stories.
5. Periods are used in bibliographies to separate main elements.
6. Two abbreviations should be used for page(s) (same in footnotes).
   p. means page.
   pp. means pages.

Bibiliography

Garvey, Gerald. *Energy, Ecology, Economy*. New York: W.W. Norton & Co., 1972.

Glysson, E.A. "Landfills." *American City and County*, January 1976, p. 64.

Hall, R.F. "Waste Not, Want Not. *Conservationist*, March 1976, p. 1.

Institute for Solid Wastes of American Public Works Association. *Municipal Refuse Disposal*. Chicago Public Administration Service, 1970.

Kelly, Katie. *Garbage: The History and Future of Garbage in America*. New York: Saturday Review Press, 1973.

League of Women Voters. *Recycle*. League of Women Voters Education Fund, No. 132, 1972.

Lindsley, E.F. "Methane from Waste." *Popular Science*, December 1974, pp. 58-60.

Marx, Wesley. *Man and His Environment: Waste*. New York: Harper & Row, 1971.

Nicholson, T. "Methane Method." *Newsweek*, 20 Oct. 1975, p. 85.

Reed, T.B., R.M. Lerner. "Methanol: A Versatile Fuel for Immediate Use." *Science*, 28 Dec. 1973. pp. 1299-1304.

Syring, E.M. "Realizing Recycling Potential." *Nation's Business*, February 1976, p. 68.

"T.V.A. Looks at Garbage Power." *American City and County*, April 1975, p. 99.

Wagner, Kenneth A., Paul C. Bailey, and Glenn H. Campbell. *Under Seige*. New York: Abelard-Schuman, 1973.

Wolff, A. "Mining the Auto Junkyard." *Science Digest*, February 1975, pp. 49-51.

11
What If You Want to Write Something Special?

Most of the writing assignments you will receive while you are a student, such as doing book reviews, preparing abstracts of articles, or answering in-class essay examinations, will use the writing skills you have already learned. But in addition, many of these assignments will require special formats. They are best approached by using the step-by-step processes explained in this chapter. The guidelines presented are those commonly and successfully used by most students. Certain teachers, however, may prefer variations of the formats given. For this reason, it's always a good idea to check with your teachers to see if they prefer a different format.

WRITING IN-CLASS ESSAY EXAMINATIONS

STUDYING FOR THE TEST

Usually, in-class essay examinations require some analysis, not just the memorization of a bunch of unrelated facts. It is therefore important to do more than just leaf through your notes the night before the test. Thinking of possible test questions can be a very fruitful way of spending your study time. After reviewing the chapters from the texts and your class notes, make up some questions your teacher might ask you to write on. Try to come up with questions that relate various facts to one another. You might base them on the following:

- Points that your teacher has emphasized in class.
- Points that "sum up" the meaning behind what you are studying.
- Points that relate the present information to that studied during previous weeks.
- Points that compare with or contrast to other points in the same chapters or units.

Without looking at the texts or your notes, think of a thesis sentence that responds to each question. For every thesis, outline in your head all the information you need to support it. When you have done this, then go back and look up any facts that you were unsure of or did not know. Naturally, the number of questions you should think of depends on the type and amount of material to be covered by the test. Keep at it until you yourself are satisfied. Just remember that knowing a lot of facts will not help you very much unless you also know how to use them.

Considering possible questions can help you in more ways than one. While trying to "psyche out" what may be on the test, you will also be learning the material and, more importantly, gaining an understanding of it. This preparation should lessen your anxiety about the examination. After all, you will be sure that you know how to answer some of the questions you might be asked. It should also make you confident that you can rearrange the information you have studied in any new combinations that might be required. Besides, you may be lucky and think of a question that actually *is* on the test.

APPROACHING THE TEST

Prewriting is important in all writing assignments, but it is especially necessary for in-class essays, during which you rarely have enough time to recopy. The secret to doing well on essay examinations is to BUDGET YOUR TIME carefully. Up to about one-third of the time allotted for the examination should be spent in prewriting. Save five or, at the most, ten minutes at the end for proofreading and correcting errors, and spend the remaining time actually writing.

For an exam that requires one essay to be written in an hour, allow fifteen to twenty minutes of preparation and prewriting. Some tests may include a passage that you are supposed to read; others may ask you to select your topic from two or more alternatives. Include the time needed for reading or for deciding on a topic in your prewriting allowance. As soon as you have devised your thesis and a scratch outline, get to work on the essay. You should spend about half an hour writing the essay, making sure to leave five or ten minutes to proofread. If the exam is longer than one hour, allow more time for writing the essay.

For an exam that requires several short essays, you may want to allot time for each according to its relative importance. Often the teacher indicates the importance of specific questions by mentioning the number of possible points awarded for each essay or the amount of time that should be spent on it. If not, you may need to estimate for yourself the relative importance of each question by gauging just how much will have to be written in order to answer it fully. Naturally, you would not want to spend forty minutes answering a rather limited question, only to find that you have left yourself only twenty minutes to answer two questions that demand greater probing. If you think all the questions will be scored equally, allow equal time for each answer. Spend the bulk of your time on writing out the answers to the questions, but still give five minutes or so to jotting down notes before you begin working on especially complex questions.

Remember, you should aim for only one draft during any timed essay examination.

WRITING THE TEST

Step One

The first step in writing an essay examination should always be to *read the question* carefully. What does it ask you to do? To find out exactly, underline the key words in the directions. These will give you clues as to:

The *arrangement* of your answer: discuss, analyze, criticize, tell, explain, trace, outline, cite evidence for, justify, clarify, exemplify, and so on.

The content of your answer: why, what, which, how, when, the effects of, the causes of, the value of, the significance of, the reasons for, and so forth.

Next, underline the key words dealing with the subject matter of the question. These will help to ensure that your answer includes all the aspects of the topic the question asks for. Take a look at the following test question.

Tell about the three effects of urbanization on Latin American politics during the industrial revolution.

The key words in the directions are

tell—the arrangement the question asks for.

three effects—the content the question asks for.

The key words about the subject matter are *urbanization on Latin American politics* during the *industrial revolution*.

Of course, not all questions are so easily underlined. Many are made up of several sentences. Check out the example below. All the key words are underlined. Notice that most of them occur in the last sentence.

<blockquote>
Ayn Rand's <u>conception</u> of the <u>value of selfishness</u> has met with considerable <u>criticism</u> not only <u>from socialist theorists</u> but from <u>conservatives</u> as well. <u>In light of these criticisms</u> and <u>contemporary international economic</u> and <u>political affairs</u>, discuss what you consider to be the <u>principal inaccuracies</u> in Rand's philosophy.
</blockquote>

Step Two   In Step Two, form a question from the key words you have underlined. If the test topic is already a one-sentence question, you will not need Step Two. However, for longer test questions, use all of the key words to compose a one-sentence question. Doing this will probably remind you of the steps for forming thesis statements explained in Chapter 2. Actually, the process is very much the same. From the limited subject defined by the key words, you compose a focused question that you will later phrase into a thesis. As an example, the preceding test topic might become the following question.

> In light of the criticisms of both socialist and conservative theorists, can the principal inaccuracies in Ayn Rand's conception of the value of selfishness be demonstrated through current international political and economic affairs?

Step Three   The third step is to turn the question formed from the key words into a thesis statement:

> In light of the criticisms of both socialist and conservative theorists, the principal inaccuracies in Ayn Rand's conception of the value of selfishness can be demonstrated through current political and economic affairs.

Step Four   Write the body of your essay in Step Four. You may be able to think the organization of the essay through in your head, or you may want to jot down a scratch outline. Begin writing by placing your thesis statement (arrived at in Step Three) as the first sentence. Then present your first point. After the first point is made, go on to the second. After the second, make the third. It's that simple to be organized.

The most important parts of an in-class essay are a strong and relevant thesis and good topic sentences with plenty of supporting examples. Transitions, while still important, are not as vital as in writing in which your time is not so limited. Most of the coherence of your essay will depend on appropriate paragraphing and a logical presentation of your ideas. Usually, the introduction should be pared down to a concise statement of your thesis, and your conclusion should be merely a quick summary.

Good in-class writing should always be concise. Answers that are "padded" are detectable right away because they contain vague, wordy sentences supported by only a few concrete examples or sometimes even contain irrelevant information. The following suggestions offer sound advice.

- Avoid digressions. Make sure everything you say clearly supports your thesis or one of the points proving it.
- Avoid unsupported generalizations. Make specific statements you can back up with examples and analysis of examples, and avoid relying only on feelings.

If you absolutely do not know the answer to a question on a test, blame your failure on inadequate studying, fate, or whatever seems likely and MOVE ON to the next question. There is no reason to waste time on what you don't know when you could be using the time to do an excellent job on another part of the exam. Nevertheless, if you know part of the answer to a question, do your best to present what you do know clearly. Many teachers will give partial credit for such answers, especially if they are well written.

Step Five Spend the last five minutes or so reading over what you have written and making any minor corrections you find necessary. Grammatical consistency, correct spelling, and proper mechanics are, of course, important, but occasional slips of the pen are usually judged less harshly in impromptu writing than in formal essays.

Well-written answers to in-class essay examinations look like and sound like any other essay you would write. The transitions may not be as smooth and the overall structure may seem more mechanical, but essentially there are no new writing skills that must be learned. All you have to do is remember to budget your time and respond directly to the question.

SHORT-ANSWER ESSAY EXAMINATIONS

Sometimes an essay examination will be made up of several short questions that ask you to define specific terms, to tell the function of characters in a literary work, or identify real people in history. To answer these questions, compose a well-developed paragraph for each one. Following the same five steps as you would for longer essay questions will ensure that your answers are complete.

EXERCISES

A. Underline the key words in the questions below and state how the contents of a good thesis sentence would reflect them.
1. Why is "The Love Song of J. Alfred Prufrock" an ironic poem?
2. Explain the medieval conception of the universe.
3. Trace the development of the medieval conception of the universe.
4. The conflict between Hebraism and Hellenism, as Matthew Arnold has defined these terms, is the great and basic conflict shaping the histories of art, of governments, and of religions. Analyze the actions of the principal American participants in the Cuban Missile Crisis as an example of this struggle. Ex-

plain which influence—the Hebrew or the Hellenic—offered the soundest course toward relieving tense conditions and securing peaceful relations with the Communist nations.
5. What is the relation of the statement "Good fences make good neighbors" to the central meaning of Frost's "Mending Wall"?
6. Describe the innovations in composition that appeared in paintings of the Italian Renaissance.
7. Many rumors are circulated about the spreading of mononucleosis. Name three ways in which the disease can be transmitted and three ways in which people falsely believe it to be passed on. How can the misinformation be accounted for?
8. Cardinal Newman's definition of liberal knowledge, which is knowledge gained through a liberal education, has long influenced the curriculum in colleges, but modern trends in education have bent toward a curriculum emphasizing practical applications of knowledge, an emphasis which often results in overspecialization. Contrast Newman's definition of liberal knowledge with the kind of knowledge obtainable through the curriculum of this college and assess the worth of each for the contemporary student.
9. Historically, what has been the role of the mother in the Chicano family? Is this role applicable today or is it outdated? Why?

B. Explain how a change in the key words in the directions for the following questions would change the structure of the essay you would write in response to the question.
1. Identify the significant events of anti-war protests that led to the United States' withdrawal from the Vietnam War, and explain the importance of each.
2. Why did the movement for racial equality become especially prominent among the white middle class during the sixties?
3. Porpoises were once land animals. Supposing Darwin's theories of evolution to be valid, calculate what the porpoise's adaptation for life in the sea explains about the environment?
4. In his essay, "How to Size Up a Man," David Reuben says that people are constantly exposing their deepest secrets through gestures and dress. Would Sigmund Freud have agreed with this view? Support your answers with pertinent case studies and the discussion of specific theories.

EVALUATING NONFICTION

Every day, people are required to make a number of evaluations. Friends tell you of the injustices they have suffered and expect you to take their side, but you evaluate their stories and try to determine for yourself which side is more supportable. Advertisers try to sell you a product and you must assess the reliability of their claims, and the media bombard you with editorialized news from which you must decipher the facts as objectively as possible before taking a stand. It is also important to examine and evaluate the nonfiction books and articles you read in college. Not everything in print is equally reliable. The argument set forth in one article may be well supported, but an argument in another article on the same subject may lack proper evidence or adequate discussion. Also, the bias of an author may interfere with the authenticity or completeness of the information presented. You should remember that all writers are capable of misevaluating information or of presenting it in ways that distort its meaning. In order to determine if a particular argument is sound, you must be able to look closely at what the author both says and implies. Then, when you do accept what a writer has to say, your acceptance is meaningful because it has come from critically analyzing what you have read. In order to feel comfortable making judgments about what you read, though, it is necessary for you to adopt a critical attitude. You must come to realize that there is nothing sacred about what is printed. Published books and articles may be well written or they may be poorly written. Don't be afraid to pass judgment. Then every time you read something, you should be able to assess the performance of the author and to support your evaluation.

Evaluating what you read, however, requires more than a vague sense that something appeals or does not appeal to you. Knowing something is more important than simply "feeling" it. Appeal based only on identification with an experience or agreement with an idea is not valid. The best thing to do is to appraise what you read using the standards normally expected of good writing. Then the "why" that gives your judgment support will be well thought out.

The "why" can be determined only after you have figured out for yourself "what" an essay intends to accomplish and "how" it proceeds. Understanding the thesis, the intended audience, the supports, and the conclusion of an essay or book is necessary for crystallizing your opinion. Finding this information and writing it down as you read something should aid you in evaluating it. The following step-by-step T.A.P.S. System offers the structure to help you *tap* the important material in whatever nonfiction you may read and also gives you the means to express a sound personal opinion. It can also help you to balance your emotional and intellectual responses to what you read.

THE T.A.P.S. SYSTEM

Before you start to read a piece of nonfiction, take out a clean piece of paper and set it up for a T.A.P.S. evaluation. The letters stand for what you should look for.

```
┌─────────────────────────────────────────┐
│                                         │
│     T.                                  │
│                                         │
│     A.                                  │
│                                         │
│     P.                                  │
│                                         │
│     S.                                  │
│                                         │
└─────────────────────────────────────────┘
```

Step One: T—Record the *Thesis* — As you read, keep alert for the author's thesis. This information usually occurs in the early part of what you are reading, although it may not be in the introduction. Note that while in your essays you try to state the thesis in one sentence, professional writers sometimes use a thesis made up of several sentences. Still you should be able to extract the writer's assertion and state it concisely.

Step Two: A—Identify the *Audience* — After looking at the level of the language and considering the attitudes expressed in the essay, decide what sort of reader the essay was written for. What is the age and educational background of the average reader of the piece? Can you conjecture about the values of the average reader? (This question is tricky. Do not assume that an attitude or value expressed in the essay is automatically shared by the reader. After all, the writer may be trying to change the reader's mind.) By identifying and assessing the audience, you can better judge whether the author has succeeded in presenting effective arguments. For example, has the writer used the best possible strategies for influencing the intended audience or has that audience been unnecessarily offended?

Step Three: P—Isolate and Record the *Points of Support* — In your own words, describe and enumerate the author's subtheses, the points used to support the major assertion. Ask yourself whether each supporting point directly furthers the thesis. Is each point well enough developed to be clear and convincing?

Step Four: S—Record *Suggested Insights* — As you read try to relate the author's ideas to your own experience, both personal and intellectual. The best form for recording these ideas is to make a list of questions. Aspects noted in this step may well become the core of essays or classroom discussions on what you have read. Try to record at least ten questions dealing with both form and content.

After you have completed your T.A.P.S., ask yourself whether or not you feel that the essay is a good one. You should be able to find material in your T.A.P.S. that would support your opinion if you were ever asked to defend it.

The following T.A.P.S. was written by a student. Look it over carefully to see how the system works. Perhaps you might even go to the library to find the essay, "Why I Want a Wife," but it isn't necessary to have the essay in order to understand the method for doing a T.A.P.S.

1.

T.A.P.S. on "Why I Want a Wife" by Judy Syfers

T.   Through implication (discussing women's needs), Syfers defines the typical male view of a wife. By asserting, rather shockingly, that everyone should have a wife (someone who caters to him or her), Syfers is attempting to force husbands to reassess their definitions of wives. Wives are not, as they seem to think, women who exist solely to satisfy their spouses' needs. Syfers offers her thesis in two ways: by the repetition of the line "I want a wife who will . . ." and by the line "My, God, who wouldn't want a wife?" What she is saying, in effect, is that people should realize that a spouse is a partner, not a slave.

A.   There are two main audiences for the essay: liberated women and liberated men. They are the ones who would assert along with Syfers that marriage is a partnership. A secondary audience is the male who is not liberated and who holds to the stereotype of the wife that Syfers is trying to dispel. Since Syfers treats the point of view of the typical wife, another secondary audience is the wife who is just beginning to get tired of being submissive to her husband but who is not yet truly liberated. Syfers' sarcastic tone shows that she is talking to all these groups, but she is directing her article more at the first two groups than at the others.

2.

P. 1. A wife is designated to perform certain duties so that her husband can be concerned only with earning a living (husband's need for economic independence). The wife often supports the husband while he is in school.

    While this point is interesting, and often true, Syfers forgets that often the favor is reciprocated later when the wife quits work.

2. A wife takes care of her husband's physical needs including food, keeping up the house, and so forth.

    Good point. Many husbands automatically expect this from their wives. The point supports Syfer's argument perfectly.

3. A wife takes care of "the details of social life"--babysitters, parties at home (plays hostess); still she gives husband freedom of having a night out with the boys.

    A weak point. Many husbands give their wives time off too. Syfers is being too sarcastic and one-sided about the matter. What about other "details of social life"--who decides to go to restaurants and movies, for instance?

3.

4. A wife is sensitive to her husband's sexual needs. This includes the responsibility for birth control, responsiveness, and being understanding about extramarital sexual involvements.

   I'll accept all but the last point. Culturally the woman is supposed to be "responsive" and even "understanding" but who says she is supposed to accept whatever the husband does? What are Syfers' sources of this information?

5. A wife assumes the responsibility for children in the event a husband wants a divorce.

   Laws are changing. Is Syfers correct? If so, she has a good point.

S. 1. Is woman trapped into this stereotype through her own ignorance? Does she want to neglect her own individuality?

   2. Is it possible that the role of "wife" is biologically determined? What about for animals other than humans?

   3. How can the book Fascinating Womanhood win so much favor in these times?

   4. Do any women really have wives in the sense Syfers means? Aren't all men and all women sometimes in this role? When a man is the "wife," what is the woman?

4.

5. Why do some men believe women don't have sex drives like they do?

6. Does a happy marriage depend upon one ~~of the~~ mates having less individuality?
7. Does having a role automatically mean that one is trapped and has no real sense of self? Do I have a set role in my relationship with Jim?
8. Do children's books convey these stereotypes of wife and husband?
9. Even if women are treated equally to their husbands, won't the relationship eventually define new roles for each partner? Will there be any difference?
10. Can an androgenous person (Jung) really survive in a role dominated society? Whom would she have to marry?
11. What are other stereotypical roles I have been affected by: the teacher, the nurse, the mother, the drunk, the student? Are these as dangerous?
12. Is it wrong for **a woman not to want** children-- biologically a mutation? Is it wrong for a woman to support a man?
13. Do all divorce laws favor the father?
14. Do more men divorce women or vice versa?

WRITING BOOK REVIEWS ON NONFICTION

Although book reviews, or "critical analyses" as some teachers label them, may be any length, they usually contain some of the same basic information.

- An attention-getting device to open (See p. 59).
- A statement about the problem or thesis presented in the book.
- A discussion of the perspective into which the thesis of the book fits, which might include a key passage.

- An evaluation of the form and content.
- An analysis of the importance of the book in relation to its field or to the course work you are studying.

One way to get a good perspective of what constitutes an effective book review is to read *The New York Times Review of Books*. Generally of high quality, the articles in it might present some structures that could be useful to you. Try to evaluate what makes a professional book review interesting and well thought out. Then see if you can incorporate those elements into your own reviews.

When writing book reviews, be careful to avoid the following.

- Do not use outside sources in your discussion of the concepts in the book.
- Do not quote from the book without clearly showing the importance of the quotation.

COMPARISON AND CONTRAST

Sometimes you will want to write a comparison of two books in review form. Reviews of this nature are similar in format to other book reviews. Be sure, however, to select books that have a strong basis for comparison or contrast. Handle a comparison and contrast in the following way.

- Give a clear statement of the thesis or hypothesis of each book. Are the theses similar or different?
- Place each thesis or hypothesis in perspective with other works on the subject.
- Devise your own thesis which states the comparison that the rest of your paper will make.
- If possible, use the alternating pattern (see p. 71) to compare or contrast the two books.
- Conclude with an evaluation of the two books in relation to your field of study. Is one superior in form or content? Why?

WRITING RÉSUMÉS

Most professions require that job applicants submit a résumé (or curriculum vitae) describing their personal and educational background, employment record, honors received, and extracurricular activities. Even if a job announcement does not ask for one, a well-composed résumé can often enhance your application. Résumés indicate professionalism and, in today's competitive job market, anything that makes an application more attractive is definitely worth the effort.

There are many convenient formats for résumés, but most of them share two qualities: they are brief and they are positive. A résumé should rarely exceed two pages and, except for one written by someone with several decades of employment history, can usually be handled in a single page. Your attitide is also important. A positive attitude is best shown by a careful selection of words. You should avoid giving any hint of insecurity about your ability to do the job for which you are applying. Seemingly small matters of word choice, such as using "single" over "divorced," can help to keep the prospective employer on your side. Furthermore, details that might be held against you can often be omitted. For instance, if you are an unusually short person, leave your height out of the personal information you give.

Although it would be ideal for both the prospective employee and the employer if a new résumé could be drawn up for each job application, doing so would be impractical. Aware of this, most employers will accept well-reproduced copies. The best ways to reproduce your résumé is to have it either photocopied or printed on offset. Because a résumé may have to serve for several similar job applications, be careful to keep the material specific enough to show your background but general enough to submit for different positions.

Still, in certain cases, it is necessary to prepare more than one résumé. Let's say you were applying for two types of jobs, one editing and the other teaching English at the high school level. It would be important to emphasize your writing skills and background in English for the editing job, but it would be more important to focus on your teaching skills and tutoring experience for the teaching job. Since your résumé is your first chance to convince an employer that you can handle the job you want, it should demonstrate competence in the particular type of employment you are seeking. Always keep in mind that, although employers do not expect you to draw up a special résumé for every job, the applicants with backgrounds closest to what is required by the positions will be the ones interviewed. Therefore, a new résumé should be written if you feel that it will better meet the job requirements than would your old résumé.

You should not be afraid to show some originality in your résumé. Do not follow the standard résumé format so doggedly that you put yourself in a bad light. Leave out information that you consider unnecessary and put other material in its place. Try to be flexible. Some career and placement centers suggest innovations such as including a photograph on a particularly short résumé or using brightly colored paper. Career counselors at most colleges are willing to look over the résumés of students in order to suggest revisions and various techniques for adding spark to your presentation. Do not hesitate to check whether your school offers this service.

Keeping the following hints in mind should help you in writing your résumé.

- Be positive in your choice of words.
- Be only as specific as necessary. For a particular position, do not

explain in detail what duties you had in the same capacity for another employer. For instance, if you were a teacher's aide, you would not want to list grading papers as part of your job. Instead, you would want to emphasize the broad range of your skills.
- Be informative and brief.
- Be original enough to show your personality.

Here is a sample standard résumé to provide you with guidelines for preparing your own.

```
                        RESUME


                                        July 24, 1980

Jenifer Johnson
3722 Maple Drive                    Telephone number--
Los Angeles, California   90014       (213) 259-3461


Available:  July 1980

Personal Data:  Date of Birth:
                     February 2, 1958
                Health:  Excellent


Education
     6/79 B.A. Degree, California State University,
          San Diego.  Major: history; minor: Spanish
     6/77 A.A. Degree, City College of New York
          New York City
     5/75 Graduated Nyack High School, Nyack, New York

Employment History
     9/78 to present   Student Assistant for Department
                       of History, California State
                       University, San Diego.  Duties
                       included typing and proctoring
                       examinations for members of the
                       department.
```

```
9/77 to 9/78    Counselor for Upward Bound, La Jolla
                California.  Tutored students in
                U.S. Government and U.S. History
                classes.  During summer lived in
                dormitories and counseled 12 students.

6/76 to 12/76   Tutor for RSVP Community Center,
                Newark, New Jersey.  Taught reading,
                math, and history to minority junior
                high school and high school students.
                Part time during school year, but
                full time during summer.  Volunteer
                work during school year.

6/75 to 9/75    Tour Guide at Disney World, Orlando
                Florida.  Duties included tours in
                English and in Spanish.
```

Special Honors and Interests
```
    Who's Who in American High Schools, 1975.
    Pan American Society Charter Member, 1974.
    Member of Alpha Epsilon Service Sorority.
    Vice President, Women's Self Defense League, 1977-78.
    Selected as intern candidate for the National Conven-
       tion of Teachers, 1978 and as member of liason
       committee on funding for programs that teach
       English as a Second Language.
    I enjoy classical music and can play the guitar and
       piano.  I also enjoy writing poetry and acting
       in drama.
```

References
```
    I will be glad to furnish references at your request.
```

WRITING ANNOTATED BIBLIOGRAPHIES

While doing some research, you may have discovered the usefulness of annotated bibliographies. Annotated bibliographies are simply final bibliographies that include summaries of the information contained in each source and evaluations of that information. The annotations, which are generally written in block form, may contain standard abbreviations and incomplete sentences, as long as the point gets across to the reader. Key quotations are also often included. When you are writing annotations, try to be as concise and informative as possible. The bibliography entries themselves follow the standard guidelines for bibliographies (see pp. 272–274).

Some teachers may ask you to include an annotated bibliography at the end of a research paper in place of the regular bibliography. Others may request that you prepare an annotated bibliography on a certain subject without actually writing a paper. In either case, the format of the sample annotated bibliography given here is appropriate. You should use these guidelines for any annotated bibliography you may be assigned unless your teacher prefers that you use an alternate form.

1.

Toward a Humanistic Society

Callahan, Daniel R. "Science and Ethics." American
   Scholar (Summer 1975), 439-456.

   A series of discussions on various subjects dealing with science and ethics. Based on a gathering of scientists, historians, theologians, and philosophers in Washington, D.C., during April of 1973; provocative questions are asked and answered. Such questions as "Can science provide the foundation of ethics?" and "Are there ethical limits in scientific discoveries?" were reaised. Religion of the future was discussed, along with how science has dealt with religion throughout history. This article includes interesting, argumentative dialogue. A good general overview on the standing of religion and its ethical impact on science.

Erlanger, Rachel. "The Making of a Heretic."
   Horizon, 17 (Autumn 1975), 54-61.

   Explicit account of Giordano Bruno, the 17th Century Dominican Friar who was convicted by the Catholic Church as an obstinate "heretic." A very detailed story of his life, his scientific

discoveries and thoughts, and his reasons for
condemning the Church. His famous discoveries
are explained. Shows how he influenced future
scientists by his contributions. Brief account of

2.

why the Catholic Church, through the force of
the Inquisitions, killed heretics like Bruno. Useful but limited because of focus on Bruno.

Gastonguay, Paul R. "Scientists and their Religious
   Beliefs." America, 130 (June 1974), 503-505.

   The personal opinion writings of one scientist.
He expresses his point of view on religion and
science. The author defends the role of scientists
by stating how scientists are discriminated against
and stereotyped. Claims scientists do believe in
God, but he also believes that the Catholic Church
should accept science as "a quest for more knowledge
and as an awareness of the unfolding of nature."

Gilkey, Langdon. Religion and the Scientific Future.
   New York: Harper & Row, 1970.

   Study of lectures given by Dr. Langdon Gilkey
at New York University in March of 1967.
Enlarged and slightly revised versions. The
influence of science on theology through a
philosophical view is well described in this book.
Religious dimensions in science are uniquely discussed.
Detailed examples of scientific information as related
to the Bible are explained; evolution, creation of
the universe, and scientific laws are discussed as
clashing concepts in the two views. Tends to
be rather detailed and technical.

3.

Hardy, Kenneth R. "Social Origins of American Scientists and Scholars." Science, 185 (August 1975), 497-550.

    This article consists mostly of survey statistics and graphs which give the distribution of scientists and scholars in the U.S. The results of the surveys deal mainly with religious, academic, and social interrelationships.

White, Edward A. Science and Religion in American Thought. Stanford: Stanford University Press, 1952.

    The impact of naturalism is used to analyze the positions of various American thinkers for whom the relationship of science and religion is a problem. The impact of Darwinism and the refinements of pragmatism are discussed. Each American thinker expresses and examines his own views on the relationships and conflicts of the two fields. Includes John W. Draper, Andrew D. White, John Fiske, William James, and John Dewey. Good overview on social-scientific theories.

WRITING SCIENTIFIC REPORTS

Much of the writing done for science classes is in the form of scientific reports. In these reports, which mainly convey data, clarity and good organization are especially important. Most authorities agree that scientific papers should deliver their data as plainly as possible, avoiding flamboyant style or poetic words. Still, the value of good and varied sentences should not be underestimated. After all, anything you write, regardless of its subject, should be readable. Scientific writing should not be made up of boring, one-idea, one-clause sentences, nor should it be a jumble of excessively complicated sentences. As in all your writing, you should use active verbs whenever possible in scientific essays. Give your writing punch, but avoid fussy touches.

Two types of scientific reports are most often assigned. Research reports are in-depth discussions of a term project. They are usually ten to twenty pages long. Laboratory reports, which are considerably shorter, are detailed discussions of an experiment. They are normally four to ten pages long.

RESEARCH REPORTS

Research reports should be carefully planned because they are usually long and complex. Most writers of scientific research papers, therefore, use a four-part structure with the following subtitles.

- Introduction
- Methods and Results
- Discussion
- Literature Cited

Introduction

In the introduction to your report, you should specify the scientific problem you are investigating and give a brief summary of any current related research. Probably, the simplest method to use in arranging this survey is to place the related research in chronological order. You may, however, wish to develop a different arrangement based on the ideas, procedures, or results shown in the literature or on some other logical principle. Next, state the method you used for your investigation and present the principal findings—all in summary. Since this statement serves as the thesis of your paper, it should not be put off too far into the text. In addition, be sure to define in your report any specialized language you may have used so that classmates on your level will be sure to understand what you write.

Methods and Results

Some teachers may want you to have a Methods section followed by a separate Results section, but others will prefer that you combine the two into one section. Whichever format you use (you will probably want to check this out with your instructor), you should generally present the methods or procedures you used to solve your scientific problem before you present the results. The methods should be explained so clearly and so thoroughly that another individual could repeat them almost exactly. You should start by describing all of the materials you used, being sure to include any important technical specifications. Then outline the procedures you followed step by step.

Your results, which are the most important data offered in your report, should be clearly, but briefly, stated. You do not want to interrupt your results by giving any analysis of them here. The next section is for that.

Discussion

The Discussion section is where you tell what your results mean. Just as you should not analyze your results in the Results section, you do not want to repeat your results in the Discussion section. Here you want to discuss, interpret, and analyze what you have discovered. You should give the implications of your findings and show how your work agrees or disagrees with previous studies in the field. You will also want to assess any inconsistencies or unresolved matters and indicate what directions future research might take. Suggestions for future work might include the ideas you would explore if you had more time. Keep in mind that information that suggests specific directions open to future research might inspire those who read your report to carry on the study or to investigate related problems. You should therefore present the ideas logically, making sure that you have evidence to back up the suggestions.

Literature Cited

The last section is where you cite the published sources you used in solving your scientific problem. Most teachers, and also those journals that publish scientific reports, prefer that you list only your primary sources. In addition, many fields, particularly those in the sciences, use specialized formats for footnotes and bibliographic entries. You should check to find out the forms that are the most appropriate for your report.

LABORATORY EXPERIMENT REPORTS

Many introductory science classes require reports on experiments. These reports usually follow the format of a report from a respected journal in the particular field of science you are studying. The form for the report that follows is based on that used in many chemistry journals. In writing up experiment reports, as in writing many types of papers, it is important to realize that your audience is not made up of specialists. That is, assume that they are hearing this information for the first time. You should conceive of your readers as your fellow science students. The typical experiment report follows a straightforward, seven-part format.

Abstract: The abstract is a specific summary of your experiment. You should try to keep it brief, no more than 250 words.

Title: The title of your report should be brief and informative.

Introduction: The introduction should include a summary of the historical development of the method you used in the experiment, a general description of the current method, possible comparisons with other models, and any limitations or advantages of the method you used.

Theory: The theory should be a few pages of discussion of the concepts that stand behind the method of your experiment. Included should be specific information about the chemistry and physics or other field of study relating to the particular experiment.

Experimental Techniques and Apparatus: The techniques section, also known as the methods section, is a detailed description of the process and the apparatuses used in the experiment. Be sure to give specific details, including the specific settings used to obtain your data.

Results and Discussion: The results section is a detailed discussion of what you found, how precise the results were, and any problems you encountered. Criticism of your method should be included. All calculated data should be presented along with any important graphs or plots.

References: On the last page of the report, references are listed alphabetically by the last name of the author. It is usual to include only the sources cited in the report. In the paper itself, references usually include the name of the author and copyright date enclosed in parentheses and placed right in the sentence where the information being cited is discussed. Your teachers may suggest an alternate form, so it is a good idea to check with them on the matter of notes and references. If they have no preference, use the form that you find in a respected journal in your field.

Keep in mind not only the way the seven steps are written up but also that directness is important to communication in technical writing. The writer of a report should use a simple style, free of complicated terminology and fancy sentence structure. You may wish to ask your teacher to show you an example of a good report written by a former student.

WRITING AN OBSERVATION REPORT

Some classes, especially those in the social sciences, require short reports based on original research, usually in the form of extensive observation or interviews. Often, you will be expected either to participate in whatever you are writing about or to find someone who has participated in it so that you can interview him or her. For instance, in order to write the sample report that appears on the following pages, the students actually joined a consciousness raising group. The amount of time you should spend just observing and taking notes will depend on your subject. After you have gathered enough material, you will normally write a report that presents and analyzes the observations. This paper, which is like any other essay, should show that you have been able to integrate your observations with your analyses. In the following report, the writer has done an especially good job of mixing the two. Whenever she describes the group's activities, she does so for the specific purpose of illuminating the social structure that underlies the functioning of the group.

1.

CR

    Once a week eight people meet in the lounge of a dormitory on a college campus. The three men and five women greet each other with friendly smiles, then sit on the floor. For the next one to two hours, they talk about love, fear, rejection, sexism, and racism as well as personal goals and abilities. Someone feels insecure; the group buoys him up with patience and understanding. Someone excitedly tells of a goal she has achieved; the group shares in her joy. The people aim for self-realization, sometimes experiencing anger and frustration instead, but more often resolving conflicts, both personal and interpersonal, by talking with others and trying to understand. They find that open communication and honesty can help. Eventually the people must leave and return to their studies and other activities at the college. The meeting is over and they merge back into the larger social system of school, leaving their small group behind.

Some leave together to go for coffee; others leave alone to do some more studying. These people are members of one of several Consciousness Raising (CR) groups at Occidental College. They feel that CR is an effective answer to some of their personal needs. But the CR group is a social system in which the individuals try to work towards a definite purpose, to maintain norms, and to benefit from outside influences as well as from those generated by the group.

2.

    The CR group is a small social system in itself. Each week, the group tries new and varying methods in an attempt to increase their consciousness and encourage effective communication among the members. Combined with the meetings, the group occasionally goes out together to a restaurant for coffee or to see a student play. These activities create a balance between functioning inside and functioning outside of it. Without the balance, a one-sidedness would enter the system, which could cause it to collapse because of a preoccupation with only one matter.

    The CR social system exists within the larger social system of Occidental. Its boundaries are formed by the physical meeting of the members and by the values, attitudes, and expectations that the members share. These boundaries keep the CR system separate and distinguishable from the larger system only when the people are together as a whole. Otherwise, it is difficult for an individual to pick out the eight people and say, "They belong to a subsystem within Oxy's system." For this reason, the system is best described as a "group." The group does not encompass all aspects of the members' lives, but it is a small social system with interesting individuals and joint activities that functions for its members.

3.

The functions of the group for its members can be divided into two categories: manifest and latent. One manifest function of the system as a whole is to act as an agent for enabling members to discover more about their own and other people's attitudes. Another manifest function is to raise the consciousness, the self-realization, of all involved. Comments by the group's members confirm the need for these functions: "I joined because I wanted to find out how other people are thinking now and see how it relates to what I think and feel in similar situations," stated Chuck. "I thought it would help me straighten out some of the thoughts I have about me and other people" was Melissa's comment. Juliet claimed she was "doing it for the benefit of others."

The second category, the latent function, is not as easy to discover. The members don't even recognize it themselves. Through observation and analysis, it becomes evident that many members desire the expanded social contacts, the feeling of belonging, that membership in a group can provide. Joining a group that they are already interested in hides this second function. When the group was formed, few of the members were associated with each other outside of the group's boundaries. Soon they began to identify themselves with each other inside the group and to acknowledge each other outside the group as well.

4.

The group then split into three subgroups who regularly saw each other outside the meetings. The formation of these subgroups is directly related to the desire for expanded social contacts. What better way can there be to achieve this end, be it conscious or not, than to join a group?

As with any group, however, the CR group has norms that the members are expected to follow. The members are expected to attend the meetings; to talk about experiences or important thoughts, not about trivia; to talk honestly; to be confidential about what is said so people will feel free to talk and no one will be hurt by the spread of a story; to listen to others when they are talking; and to allow everyone a chance to talk. The idea is to get a meaningful discussion going in which everyone can participate. While these norms appear easy enough to follow, there have been examples of deviance in the group, and the group has brought pressure to bear on the offender to correct his or her behavior.

When deviant behavior is evident, encouragement is given to the offender to return to the norm. This is most often done by the leader of the group rather than by the group as a whole, although the group supports the leader's actions. Two norms--honesty and confidentiality--have never been broken (or if they have been, they have never been discovered). The norm which has been broken the most often--attendance--is also the most lightly

5.

enforced, which most likely account for its being broken so often. It isn't the most important, but if no one comes, there obviously cannot be a meeting. Members who fail to make it to a meeting are questioned as to why they missed it and are then filled in on what they missed, "Well, Juliet, what happened to you last week? We did this. . . . and I'm sure you would have found it beneficial and fun had you been here." The reminder is subtle and given lightly but it is there.

If a discussion is tending toward trivia, the leader often will state that "it would be more productive if we were discussing a different topic," and will steer the conversation elsewhere. Sometime during the meeting, a person who isn't listening to the others will be asked to show more interest. If someone is monopolizing the meeting, the leader will try to apply the topic to the rest of the members in the hope of spreading the discussion out. Failing with this tactic, he or she will use a stronger approach: "Well, Jeff, this all extremely interesting, and I can see its importance, but I think it's time to move on to a new topic now to give others a chance to express their thoughts." Such reminders are usually all that is necessary. The reason there is no need for intense pressure can be seen when the roles of the various members of the group are examined.

Each member of the group has a distinct role. Catherine offers the worldly experience, Jeff is the advocate of alternate lifestyles, Sam is the poet who sums up everyone's feelings, Chuck is the great compromiser, Janice is

6.

the sympathizer, and Juliet express the attitudes of the elite. All these roles are important, but none of them is as important as the role of the "leader." The leader stands out to anyone visiting the group for the first time, but the others take a fair amount of observation to discover. Originally when the CR group was formed, Melissa was appointed the leader. Melissa, however, was unable to attend the first meeting, so she asked Lucy, the only person she knew in the group, to lead it for her that night. From then on Lucy was the leader. Melissa became Lucy's back-up.

She makes suggestions, but she always lets Lucy make the decisions. The rest of the members are also willing to let Lucy be the leader. Although they all contribute to the group, only Lucy is responsible for controlling the group. The other members, having roles of their own to fill, do not wish to fill two roles simultaneously in the same social system, so they support Lucy. She uses the authority this support gives her to guide the group and gently encourage any deviant members back to the norm. Having agreed upon her role, the rest of the group readily follows Lucy's guidance. Thus the group is able to maintain its norm with little effort.

Through the conscientiousness of the members, the CR group survives, a small social system within the larger system of the college. The group is aware of the need for influences outside the group's boundaries. They also constantly work to keep themselves aware of their set goals.

7.

Finally, they establish norms and see to it they are enforced to everyone's benefit by choosing a leader and supporting him or her.

WRITING BUSINESS LETTERS

Many occasions call for writing business letters—applying for jobs, appealing to your congressman to change an unjust law, bringing consumer complaints to the attention of companies, and asking for information from agencies. Of course, these are only a few examples of the typical business letters you may want to write. Technically, any letter addressed to people you do not know is a business letter. When composing a business letter, you should be as direct as possible and follow a standard form. At the same time, you should try to inject your personality into your writing. Also, you should try to avoid stock phrases like "enclosed please find" and "respectfully I remain" because they are stuffy. The following is an annotated sample business letter. The annotations indicate the correct forms, but notice that they can be varied to suit the needs of the particular letter you are writing.

Always type on 8-1/2 × 11 inch white paper, preferably of good bond. Center the letter on the page. Set the typewriter on single spacing with 1-1/2 inch margins. Type only on one side of the sheet.

STEP ONE Type your return address, single-spaced, at the upper right-hand margin. Type the date on the next line. If you are using a printed letterhead, space down a few lines from the printing and put only the date at the right-hand side of the page. You should not abbreviate.

STEP TWO Type the name of the person to whom you are writing, his or her title, and the address at the left-hand corner, two spaces below the date. This part of the letter is called the inside address.

STEP THREE Space down two lines at the left margin and type the opening followed by a colon. The person's title should be included. For example, you might write one of the following—Dear Ms. Johnson:, Dear Mr. Simpson:, or Dear Dr. Wing:. For the special abbreviations of clergy and high officials, check your desk dictionary. When writing to a special group or company of people you may write Dear Sirs: or To Whom It May Concern:, the second choice to avoid sexist implications. Or you may choose to leave out the opening and skip to the next step.

STEP FOUR Now you are ready to write the body of the letter. Space down two lines from the opening and begin the first paragraph at the left-hand margin. Continue to block (line up at the left margin) all new paragraphs. Space two lines between paragraphs for easy identification.

An alternate form for the body, used infrequently, is to indent each new paragraph five spaces and single-space the entire body of the letter without spacing between paragraphs.

Notice the structure of the letter of application on page 355

Paragraph one indicates the purpose of the letter.
Paragraph two quickly reinforces the résumé by pointing out important background.
Paragraph three discusses why the applicant wants the job.
Paragraph four encourages the employer to contact the applicant. The letter ends on a positive note.

STEP FIVE Double-space from the last line of the body and, lined up with the return address, type a closing followed by a comma. Here are a few examples.

Yours truly,	Very truly yours,
Sincerely,	Sincerely yours,

343 Mill Dale Lane
Meadowbrook, California   91325
February 13, 1977

Mr. Arthur Weinar
Personnel Director
Bay Area Regional Planning Commission
P.O. Box 702
San Francisco, California   94501

Dear Mr. Weinar:

I am writing in response to your Los Angeles Times advertisement for an Assistant to the Transportation Planner because I hope to become associated with a planning commission such as yours upon my graduation from college this June.

With my double major in urban studies and economics, I have approached urban planning from two perspectives. As for practical experience, I can offer my two summers during my sophomore and junior years when I worked as an assistant to James Soverign, a planner for an urban renewal project in the Denver area. My primary interest is in urban reconstruction, and I believe I can bring some innovative ideas to your projects.

The transportation needs of urban centers have been aggravated by financial cutbacks and the energy crisis. Despite these setbacks, I continue to be impressed with the programs implemented through your department. It would please me to be able to work with you.

Enclosed is a resume. After you have had a chance to evaluate my background, I hope you will contact me so that we may arrange a personal interview.

Sincerely yours,

Richard B. Albany

The Writers Practical Rhetoric

Considering the formality of the letter, pick the closing that feels the most natural and conveys your attitude.

STEP SIX Space four lines down and, lined up with the closing, type your name. It is usual to include your middle initial. If you have a title, type it a single space below your name.

STEP SEVEN If you have mentioned individuals' names and you want to call their attention to that fact, you will want to send them a copy of the letter. To record that you have sent out copies, write at the bottom left of the letter the names of the people you have sent them to.

Sincerely yours,

John C. Smith

cc: Mr. Tony Grant
     Ms. Linda Maruyama

It is not usually necessary to send copies to former employers mentioned in letters of application for employment. Do so only if you expect the company to contact them and you want to let them know.

STEP EIGHT Sign the letter in the space above your name.

SAMPLE ENVELOPE FOR BUSINESS LETTER

Blocked Return Address | Use proper U.S. Postal Service abbreviations | Place stamp neatly, right side up in corner

```
Mr. Richard B. Albany
343 Mill Dale Lane
Meadowbrook, CA   91325



                    Mr. Arthur Weinar
                    Personnel Director
                    Bay Area Regional Planning Commission
                    P.O. Box 702
                    San Francisco, CA   94501
```

Blocked Mailing Address (same as inside address on letter except abbreviate state)

A list of the standard abbreviations for states can be obtained from the post office in your community. These abbreviations are always two capital letters followed by no punctuation, three spaces, and then the five-number zip code

KEEPING A JOURNAL

A journal is more than a record of interesting events—it is also a way to examine ideas. Full of half-formed insights, spontaneous flights of imagination, and even first drafts of would-be essays, a journal records the development of your thoughts on various subjects. Usually you will include more than one entry on a subject, considering its different aspects, evaluating it, and changing your attitudes about it. Growth of insights and shifts in opinion are what a journal is all about. This growing process is what makes the difference between a journal and a diary. While material for a diary is descriptive or narrative, material for a journal includes analysis, reaching for significant questions and perceptions.

The form for journal entries is usually very free. Some writers like to separate entries by date, but many simply suit their moods. Even when a journal is assigned by your teacher, you should write it primarily for yourself. Grammar and structure can be looser than in other types of writing. In the rush of insights, spelling and other mechanics need not be a source of worry, though enough clarity to convey your ideas is expected. Remember that a journal should be a discussion with yourself rather than a polished essay.

Journals can be used in every sort of class for many purposes. In an English class, you might wish to keep a journal as you read a novel. One evening, your journal entry might deal with what you believe to be the major theme of the book thus far, even though by the time you read fifty pages more you may change your mind. You could then note in a second entry that your first perception of the theme of the novel was only a partial understanding of the theme found in later pages. Such reflections on former entries are what make good journals. Keeping a journal as you read can help to improve your interaction with books, a necessary step in becoming a good reader. Instead of just letting your eyes glide across the pages of a book and letting your thoughts escape you, record your impressions. Later, take the time to observe the changes in your thoughts. You will probably find that this process will give you valuable insights concerning both the book and yourself.

Both personal and intellectual satisfaction can be derived from journal writing while you study a certain subject or unit in class. A journal allows you to evaluate and explore ideas in a loose format. You might even want to examine subjects you do not like in order to try to understand why. Journals offer good preparation for class discussions, in-class essays, and papers. The medium is equally valuable for the shy person, who wants to "try out" ideas before taking the chance of presenting them in class, and the more extroverted student who simply hasn't had enough time to explore all the good ideas thought of during a regular class period. Journals are good, too, for recording those ideas that occur at odd hours, when you haven't the heart to wake up your roommate to join you in a meaty discussion. In fact, many a student has been known to sneak around a dark room in search of a pen and a flashlight in order to make a journal entry.

Most writers, during some point in their lives, have kept journals. They may have done so, in part, for the therapeutic value of putting words to paper. Expressing what you feel, especially in such an unrestricted format, can offer needed emotional release. Another reason to keep a journal is that journals preserve thoughts. Ideas that might otherwise have been lost are saved to be reassessed and maybe even expanded. Keeping a journal during a difficult or impressionable time of your life can yield great personal satisfaction later. You might, for example, keep a journal during your first week of college, for the nine months of pregnancy, or while traveling.

Along with all the advantages of preserving and exploring ideas, journals are also a good place to practice your writing. Experiment with new sentence structures and vocabulary until you get the feel of them. Dare to start a sentence with "And" just to see how it works. Write an intentional fragmentary sentence. Analyze your personal style. Does your writing sound like you? It should. Try to imitate writers you like; what deliberate sentence patterns can identify in their styles? You might even practice those structures that sometimes trouble you when you write essays. If a teacher marks an idiom or tense error, write some similar correct sentences in your journal and the constructions will soon feel natural. Finally, keeping a journal during summer vacations can be very worthwhile. In addition to the personal value, the writing practice can help you avoid that "rusty" feeling many students experience when faced with their first writing assignments in the fall.

There is a series of sample journal entries starting on page 40.

The Handbook

12

A Review of Grammar and Spelling

As you work on your own writing assignments, you will become increasingly aware that some things just do not sound right; certainly, too, there will be times when your instructor marks something on your paper as an error in usage or grammar.

You might be surprised to know that you do not need very sophisticated knowledge to write correctly. Actually, you probably need only some brushing up on a few important terms and principles with which you are already generally familiar.

THE PARTS OF SPEECH

Every word in every sentence is a part of speech. However, the same word does not always function as the same part of speech. For example, the word *piece* can serve as a noun, a verb, or an adjective. In one context the word may function as a different part of speech than it will in another context.

The *piece* of tape stuck to the envelope. (Noun)

He can *piece* a puzzle together in one afternoon. (Verb)

The *piece-meal* approach Diana used in teaching music confused everyone. (Adjective)

Let's look at another example. You must not assume that because a word is used as a noun, it cannot also be used as a verb. For instance, the word *silence* is usually thought of as a noun, but in the sentence—The police *silenced* the crowd—it is used as a verb. In order to analyze the part of speech of words you find in a particular sentence, you must be able to identfiy each of the eight parts of speech. Then you can determine which of them a word functions as.

NOUNS

Nouns* name persons, places, things, or ideas. They do a variety of things in sentences. Most nouns have different forms to show whether they are singular or plural

> Boy   Boys
> Fox   Foxes
> Love   Loves

Others, however, have the same form whether they are singular or plural.

> series   sheep   species

Nouns can also be made possessive.

> The boy's shirt
> The foxes' den
> The sheep's wool

Nouns are often preceded by the words *a, an,* and *the.* Be careful, however, not to be thrown off track by an intervening word.

> *A* wicker chair
> *An* inexpensive suit
> *The* Smiths' address

PRONOUNS

Another kind of word that sometimes functions in the same ways as a noun is the *pronoun.* Pronouns can stand for nouns. They help writers to avoid producing sentences full of repetition.

> Weak: Jim gave the gift to Jim's father.
> Effective: Jim gave the gift to *his* father.

The second version is a lot smoother.

All pronouns do not take the place of nouns, however. In the following sentences, the pronouns are not substitutes for nouns.

> Tomorrow is the third Monday of *this* month.
> *Anything* John does is okay with Mary.

This, in the first sentence, is a demonstrative pronoun. *Anything,* in the second sentence, is an indefinite pronoun.

A Review of Grammar and Spelling

The best way to become familiar with pronouns and their uses is to notice them in what you read and write. Here is a list of the main types of pronouns. For more information about the distinctive features of pronouns, turn to page 000.

Personal Pronouns

Personal pronouns take the place of nouns most frequently.

I	We	Me	Us
You	You	You	You
He, she, it	They	Her, him, it	Them

We want a more responsive governor.

The last event on the agenda was brought to *our* attention by *you*.

Relative Pronouns

Relative pronouns link subordinate clauses to other parts of a sentence (p. 000).

Who   Which   That   Whoever   Whose

The man *who* helped to fix my plumbing is coming to dinner

Interrogative Pronouns

Interrogative pronouns begin direct and indirect questions (p. 447).

Who   What   Which   Whom   Whose

Who will be unable to attend the baseball game?

Demonstrative Pronouns

Demonstrative pronouns point out what they refer to.

This	These	That	Those	Such
Any	Every			

These volunteers have donated over one hundred hours to the Heart Fund.

Indefinite Pronouns

Indefinite pronouns represent undefined or loosely defined numbers of things.

Few	Each	Anyone	Anybody	Somebody
Both	All	Another	Most	Many
Neither	Other	None	Such	Some
Several				

None of us could attend the lecture, so it was canceled.

Reflexive Pronouns

Intensive pronouns and reflexive pronouns refer to or stress the doer of the action in a sentence.

Myself	Yourself	Himself	Herself
Ourselves	Yourselves	Themselves	

He wrote the novel by *himself*.

I treated *myself* to a bubble bath.

VERBS

Verbs are words that indicate actions or states of being. Those that indicate actions are called action verbs; those that indicate states of being are called linking verbs. The term *verb* is used both for the particular part of speech and for its sentence part (also known as the simple predicate). But not every verb can be spotted easily. Remember that a word that looks like a noun *can* function as a verb. Some examples are *handcuff, sleep, dress,* and *snow*. All verbs have certain qualities, however, that make them stand apart from nouns.

Types of Verbs

There are four characteristics of verbs you should know about. First, there are two types of verbs: transitive and intransitive (noted as v.t. and v.i. in most dictionaries). These labels can help you to understand how to use a new word that happens to be a verb. An intransitive verb acts without needing any person or thing to act upon. A transitive verb, on the other hand, must act on something or someone in order to make sense. The verb *go*, for example, is intranstitive, but *convey* is transitive.

> We *go* to museums whenever we can. (You do not *go* something.)
>
> We *conveyed* our warmest wishes to Mary's mother. (You do *convey* something.)

It would make little sense to say or write *I convey*. The thought is not complete. Some verbs are transitive in one context and intransitive in another. An example is the word *run*. You can *run* things, such as vacuum cleaners or businesses. In either case the verb would be transitive. But what about the sentence—*I ran away?* Nothing is being run, and the verb is thus intransitive.

Verbs that indicate states of being are called linking verbs, and linking verbs are always intransitive. Most people choose to memorize the list of common linking verbs rather than try to recognize them by their function in sentences. The following list covers most that you will need to know.

To be	To act
To seem	To sound
To become	To remain
To appear	To feel
To look	To taste
	To smell

Tense and Number

Second, verbs show tense and number. Tense is the system that shows time. Number indicates whether the verb is singular or plural. The past and present are the two most basic tenses. The present tense is used to refer to things that *happen now*. The past is used to refer to things that *happened before*. But by no means is a writer restricted to these two forms. Helping verbs (such as *has* or *have, may* or *might, will, would, must, ought to, does* or *do,* and *be*) blend with these simple tenses to make verb phrases that can express many more time sequences than could be expressed by the past and present tenses alone.

All verbs have principal parts (you can find the principal parts of a verb immediately after each entry word in your dictionary). Once you can find the principal parts of a verb, you can conjugate the verb: that is, name all its forms in all tenses in both singular and plural. The principal parts are the first person singular in the present tense, the first person singular in the past tense, and the past participle (the form used with is, have, or has). The principal parts for the verb *talk* are *talk, talked, talked*. All writers use a variety of tenses. The tenses most commonly used and examples of them are listed below.

> Present: I *give* money to charities.
>
> Present Progressive: I *am giving* money to charities.
>
> Present Perfect: I *have given* money to charities.
>
> Past: I *gave* money to charities.
>
> Past Perfect: I *had given* money to charities.
>
> Future: I *will give* money to charities.
>
> > Tomorrow I *give* money to charities.
> >
> > I *am going to give* money to charities.
>
> Future Perfect: I *will have given* money to charities by then.

Voice

The third characteristic of verbs is that they have voice, either *active* or *passive*. In the active voice, the doer of the action usually comes first.

> Jim *ran* the mile.

In passive constructions, the does of the action either is not stated or is in a phrase beginning with *by*, and the verb includes a form of *to be* with the past participle of the verb: The mile was run by Jim. In the passive voice, the thing done is emphasized over the doer (see p. 144).

Mood

The final characteristic of verbs that will be important to you is *mood*. Verbs, in some instances, change their forms to show mood. The most common usages of mood convey the nature of an expression.

The indicative mood is used to make a statement.

> A small group of people at the rock concert *smoked* marijuana.
>
> or
>
> Did you *do* your homework?

The imperative mood is used to give a command. The understood subject of *do*, and *kiss* in the sentences below is *you*.

> *Do* your homework.
>
> *Kiss* me, you fool.

The subjunctive mood is used to convey a condition that is contrary to fact, or a suggestion or request introduced by a clause beginning with *that*.

If I *were* angry with you, I *would* not be so affectionate.

Our neighbors asked that we *be* considerate of them and not *let* our dog dig up their flowers.

The various rules for the use of subjunctives can be found on page 435.

ADJECTIVES Adjectives modify nouns or pronouns, adding meaning to them, limiting or specifying something about them. They tell which, what kind, or how many. The articles *a, an,* and *the* are special adjectives. The possessive pronouns (*my, your, his, her, its, our, their,* and so forth) are adjectives in many sentences. The same is true of other words: *which, these, this, those, any,* and *whatever* are some of them. The possessive forms of nouns are often adjectives; for example, in the sentence—The president's speech raised the consciousness of even the greatest cynic—the word *president's* acts as an adjective. *Greatest* is also an adjective.

Adjectives frequently come before their nouns as in the sentence above, but they may also follow the words they modify.

The *young* man, *intent* on his work, was *unable* to answer *my* request for directions to the *county* courthouse.

A mule is sometimes *reluctant* to move along the trail, and a person could be *stuck* for an hour in a *single* spot.

ADVERBS Adverbs modify verbs, adjectives, or other adverbs. They tell how, when, to what extent, or where.

They did *well* on their exam.
The adverb *well* modifies the verb *did* (How did they do?).

Mr. Logan is the *most* sincere person I have *ever* known.
The adverb *most* modifies the adjective *sincere* (How sincere?).
The adverb *ever* modifies the verb *have known* (When have you known?).

Even though English was not her native language, she was learning to speak it *very* well.
The adverb *very* modifies the adverb *well* (To what extent?). *Well* is an adverb because it modifies the verb *was learning* (How was she learning?).

It is a good idea to memorize that *not, too,* and *very* are always adverbs. You can see that they answer the question "to what extent?"

Many adverbs end in *ly*.

Hungrily   Hopefully   Hatefully

PREPOSITIONS Alone, many prepositions are hard to describe. For instance, if someone were to ask you what *for* means, you would probably have a hard time answering. There are various definitions for prepositions. One is that they are structure words that tie parts of sentences together. But they also contribute meaning to sentences. Think of how *before* or *after* or *under* or *over* have different meanings from each other and how often you use them to clarify what you are saying. Quite often prepositions show direction. However you choose to define the preposition, it is easy to spot. Read over the following list of prepositions and try to develop a "feel" for picking them out. There is no need to attempt to memorize the list because, first of all, not all the prepositions are included here. Second, this page will be handy whenever you wish to turn back to it to check a particular word.

About	By means of	Over
Above	But (meaning except)	Owing to
Across	Contrary to	Past
After	Down	Rather than
Ahead of	During	Save (meaning
Along	Due to	except)
Among	Except	Since
Apart from	For	Through
Around	For the sake of	To
As well as	From	Together with
Aside from	In	Toward
At	Inside	Towards
Because of	In terms of	Under
Before	Into	Underneath
Behind	Like (meaning	Until
Below	similar to)	Up
Beside	Near	Up at
Besides	Of	With
Between	Off	Within
Beyond	On	Without
By	Out of	With regard to
	Outside	

Prepositions always appear in prepositional phrases. The phrases are made up of the preposition and usually the closest noun or pronoun to the right of it along with all the noun or pronoun's modifiers. In two instances though, finding the whole phrase can be a bit tricky. Not a noun but a noun-like element may end the phrase as in *of what I mean* or in *for his smiling*. The second case is that in which the word *and* or *or* is used between two or more nouns or pronouns: *inside the Senate and the House.* Be careful to keep on the lookout for *and* and *or* so that you will remember to identify the whole prepositional phrase. You can be sure that any word on the list is a preposition in a particular sentence only if it has an object—the label given to the noun, pronoun, or noun-like element that ends or completes the phrase. In the following sentences, words that appear on the list of prepositions are not prepositions.

The party was *over.*	*Over* is an adjective here.
They searched the house *inside* and *outside.*	*Inside* and *outside* are adverbs here.
Thomas shut *off* the engine.	*Off* is part of the verb *shut off.*

In the following prepositional phrases, the objects are underlined.

Under the <u>auspices</u>	As well as <u>swimming</u> and <u>tennis</u>
Without <u>sympathy</u>	Beyond <u>what had been expected</u>

One last point about prepositions is that they sometimes come at the ends of sentences. Here they may seem to have no object when, in fact, there is an object somewhere in the sentence, if only you will take a minute to think through the meaning of the sentence. The reason that the preposition is split up from the object is that doing so makes the sentence sound more natural than keeping the preposition and object together. For example, read aloud the following sentences.

What is it for?

For what is it?

The first sentence sounds a little smoother than the second. You can see that the object of the preposition in the first sentence is still *what,* just as it is in the second sentence. The actual prepositional phrase is *for what.*

CONJUNCTIONS

Like prepositions, conjunctions join words or groups of words to express a relationship between them. Some of the same words, in fact—*but, for, after, before,* and *until*—are prepositions in certain sentences and conjunctions in others. Whether a particular word is one or the other depends on just which words it joins. Conjunctions are mere joiners of words and groups of words; they never take objects and they do not come at the ends of sentences. Of course, prepositions always have objects. This distinction is clear-cut:

        CONJ
I am hungry, *but* I can wait until lunchtime, I am sure.
                                                  PREP   OBJ
I was so hungry that I ate everything in the refrigerator *but* the last *piece* of American cheese.

There are two kinds of conjunctions: coordinating and subordinating. Coordinating conjunctions connect sentence parts that are grammatically equal—one does not need to depend on another. The following list includes all the coordinating conjunctions.

And	But	Nor	Or
For	Yet	So	

Correlative conjunctions that come in pairs are also coordinating.

Either . . . or	Neither . . . nor
Both . . . and	Not only . . . but also

Subordinating conjunctions introduce grammatically dependent clauses, connecting them and setting them up as modifiers to the main part of the sentence. The following list includes many of the subordinating conjunctions.

Because	In order to	As
Where	Whereas	Whether
Unless	Before	When
Since	Although	So that
After		

Let's take a look at how the coordinating and subordinating conjunctions in the sentences below connect words or groups of words.

COORD
Jim asked for some good advice, *and* he got it.

SUBORD
When Jim asked for some good advice, he got it.

Sometimes coordinating conjunctions start out complete sentences.

COORD
Jim did not ask anyone for advice. *But* he got it.

INTERJECTIONS

Interjections are grammatically independent words that usually convey emotion and seem "thrown into" the sentence, interrupting its flow. Adverbs, adjectives, and other parts of speech can serve as interjections on their own when used as exclamations—outbursts of emotion. The interjections in the following sentences are underlined.

During the revision stage a writer might discover that, <u>oh no</u>, too many sentences are splattered with "and's."

<u>Well</u>, the time has come to pay what is owed.

<u>Well!</u> Look who finally showed up.

I thought you would do well on your Spanish test, and you did. <u>Good!</u>

VERBALS Verbals are not, strictly speaking, a part of speech. Instead, they are a hybrid form of verbs and certain other parts of speech. There are three kinds of verbals: infinitives, gerunds, and participles.

Infinitives An infinitive is the base form of a verb. Infinitives are usually preceded by *to: to hope, to ski, to know, to be felt, to have been*. Infinitives may come with subjects, objects, and complements. Together the subject, object, infinitive, and any modifiers intervening are called an infinitive phrase.

Infinitives are not always preceded by *to*. The form of the base word (the one that does not have any special ending attached to indicate tense and number) is the strongest clue to finding these infinitives. Also, they are usually found after certain helping verbs.

Should *interest*   Will *pertain*   Did *show*

The italicized words in the following sentences are examples of infinitives without their *to* signposts.

Don't you dare *tell* the new owners of the house that it is infested with termites.

With his friends coming, he need not *play* the game alone.

Infinitives may look much like verbs. Both may have subjects and objects or complements. However, *infinitives never function as verbs*. The phrases act as nouns, adjectives, and adverbs.

Gerunds Gerunds end in *ing* and act as nouns. They can occur by themselves.

Loving him was like no other *loving*.
   The first *loving* acts as the subject of the sentence.
   The second *loving* acts as the object of the preposition *like*.
Running is my favorite form of exercise because I do not like competing with others.
   Running is the subject of the sentence.

Gerunds can also occur as the first word of gerund phrases.

Participles Participles act as adjectives. The present participle form, in most instances, looks like the verb with an *ing* ending added to it.

Verb	**Participle**
Go	Going
Say	Saying

As you can see, some participles look just like gerunds and can be distinguished only by their function in a sentence.

The past participle may be formed in two ways. The first way is by taking a special ending, usually *ed, en, t,* or *n.* Some examples of past participles with these endings are *played, broken, spent,* and *torn.* The second way a past participle is formed is by a change in a vowel. The usual pattern is illustrated by the following words.

Verb   **Participle**

Fling   Flung
Sing   Sung

SENTENCE STRUCTURE

As you may already know, not every combination of words can make a sentence. *Fence brown,* for instance, is not a sentence. Neither is *In conclusion* or *Running to the market.* For a string of words to be a sentence, the words must be specific parts of speech arranged in proper sequence, and the words, when read together, must make a complete thought.

The most basic form for a complete sentence has two parts, *subject* and *simple predicate.* You are already familiar with the parts of speech that function as these sentence parts: nouns, pronouns and groups of words can function as subjects, and verbs function as simple predicates. In the following sentences the simple predicates are underlined and the subjects are labeled with an S.

S
John <u>thinks</u>.
S
Dogs <u>bite</u>.
S   S
Books and movies <u>entertain</u>.

In the first sentence, *John,* a noun, functions as subject. *Thinks,* a verb, functions as the simple predicate. In the second sentence, *dogs* is subject and *bite* is the simple predicate. In the third sentence, *book* and *movies* are the subjects and *entertain* is the simple predicate. And of course each sentence is a complete thought.

You can look at this basic sentence structure in another way. In the examples above, the subject and simple predicate relate to each other in the same way. The subjects state what the sentences are about (someone named John, dogs, and books and movies), and the simple predicates say something about the subjects (John is someone who thinks, dogs have a tendency to bite, and books and movies are sources of entertainment).

SIMPLE SENTENCES

The subject/simple predicate structure is called a *simple sentence*. Either or both parts of the simple sentence may be compound: have more than one part. For instance, the following sentences have compound subjects and compound simple predicates. They are, though, still simple sentences.

John and Laurie think.

Dogs bite and bark.

The subject/simple predicate is just the bare structure on which a variety of different simple sentences can be built. Five simple sentence patterns can be built from the subject/simple predicate base. Each of the following sentences represents one of these five patterns.

1. Gloria loves milk.
2. She gave me the milk.
3. I was given the milk.
4. She is generous.
5. She is a friend.

The first sentence begins with subject and simple predicate, but a new part is added to them, a *direct object*. Direct objects are those parts of sentences to which subjects do something. Gloria does something to the milk—she gives it away. She might also have drunk the milk herself. But even if she had done so and the sentence were *Gloria drank the milk, milk* would still be the direct object because Gloria, the subject of the sentence, would have done something to the milk. The direct object receives the action of the simple predicate. In the following sentences, direct objects are italicized.

I brought the *cake*.

Grover ate *it*.

I spanked *him*.

Sentence 2—*She gave me the milk*—has a direct object: *milk*. It also has another sentence part, called an *indirect object*. Not all sentences with direct objects can have indirect objects, but all sentences with indirect objects must include direct objects that are either stated or implied. Indirect objects are the beneficiaries in sentences. When subjects give away, teach, offer, bring, or do some such action to direct objects, it is the indirect objects that receive the direct object. Sentence 2 then includes the indirect object, *me*, for it is the *me* in the sentence that gets the milk. You may find it helpful to remember that indirect objects must come before direct objects. In the following sentences, indirect objects are italicized.

Grover offered *me* the cake.

I gave *Grover* a hard time.

He told *me* the news.

Sharon told *me*.

In the last sentence the direct object—news, a story, or whatever it was that Sharon said—is implied. In the context within which this sentence would have been written, the direct object would be clear, even though implied.

Sentences 1 and 2 are both written in the active voice. That is, the subject of the sentence is doing the action. Gloria is loving and she is giving. Sentence 3, however, is written in the passive voice, and therefore the subject, *I*, does not do the giving. Instead, the subject receives what would be the direct object if the sentence were written in active voice: *Someone gave me the milk*. When the verb of a sentence with objects is in the passive voice, either of the potential objects becomes the subject of the passive construction. The remaining object is called the *retained object*. In sentence 3 *milk* is the retained object. Retained objects are italicized in the following sentences written in the passive voice.

We were given *high grades*.
   Active voice: Someone gave us high grades.

The were shown the *exhibit*.
   Active voice: Someone showed them the exhibit.

The team was awarded a *trophy*.
   Active voice: Someone awarded the team a trophy.

Sentence 4—*She is generous*—has neither a direct object nor an indirect one. Rather, it has a *predicate adjective*. Predicate adjectives are adjectives that follow the simple predicate and describe the subject. *Generous* describes the subject of the sentence and is the predicate adjective. Predicate adjectives in the following sentences are italicized.

Grover is *hungry*.

Professors are *smart*.

Lamb chops are *fatty*.

Hungry, smart, and *fatty* are all adjectives that describe their respective subjects.

Because predicate adjectives follow the simple predicate and can be said to "complete" it, they are called *complements*. When sentences include complements, the simple predicates always are linking verbs (*is, seems, appears,* and so forth), never an action verb (hit, run, sleep, and so forth). Another kind of complement is contained in the fifth sentence—*She is a friend*. Notice that *friend* is not an adjective describing the subject, but instead a noun that renames the subject. Nouns, pronouns, and groups of words that function as nouns are called *predicate nouns* when they follow the simple predicate and rename the subject. Predicate nouns are the second kind of complement.

Note the predicate nouns italicized in the following sentences.

Gloria is a *student*.

Antelope Valley College is an *institution*.

She is an *executive and a mother*.

Student, institution, and *executive and a mother* are all nouns that rename their respective subjects.

One last comment is needed regarding simple sentences. Thus far, in talking about predicates, simple predicates (verbs) and complements of simple predicates, or predicate adjectives and nouns, have been discussed. *Complete predicates* include the simple predicate and any predicate ajectives, predicate nouns, direct objects, or indirect objects that accompany the simple predicate. Complete predicates are italicized in the following sentences.

She *is an executive and a mother*.

Professors *seem smart and inquisitive*.

Mr. Muldare *wrote five books*.

She *gave me her last dime*.

Simple sentences are made up of subjects and complete predicates. If a sentence has only a subject and simple predicate—as in the sentence *John thinks*—then the simple predicate is considered to be the complete predicate, too.

CLAUSES

Clauses are any groups of words including both a subject and simple predicate. Thus we can say that simple sentences are also clauses. Not every clause, however, is a simple sentence. Those clauses that have been called simple sentences (i.e., clauses that are complete thoughts) are *main clauses*. Every sentence must include at least one main clause.

Sentences may also contain one or more *subordinate clauses,* clauses that are not complete thoughts. You can usually identify subordinate clauses by the words that begin them. Relative pronouns (who, which, that), relative adverbs (when, where, and so forth), and subordinating conjunctions (because, since, although, and so forth) indicate that the clauses following them are subordinate. Note the italicized subordinate clauses in the following sentences.

I went to the store *because I needed a steak*.

The boy *who served me* was quite young.

Although I kept quiet, I felt like singing.

Each of the subordinate clauses is an incomplete thought, one that needs the other part of the sentence, the main clause, in order to make sense.

Subordinate clauses can function as a noun would in a sentence. Subordinate clauses that function as nouns are called *noun clauses* and are often introduced by pronouns such as *who, whoever, what, which,* and *that.* Other words such as *why, whether,* and *how* may also begin noun clauses. Like nouns, noun clauses become part of another clause or group of words. Noun clauses, then, can function as subjects of main clauses, as objects, or in any other way that nouns function. The following sentences include noun clauses functioning as subjects of main clauses.

Whoever ate the cake was hungry.

What the book said was interesting.

You can see how easily, though, noun clauses might be made to function as direct objects.

I envy *whoever ate the cake.*

They discussed *what the book said.*

Mary knows *why I left.*

Noun clauses function as indirect objects in the following sentences.

I gave *whoever was hungry* the cake.

They told *whoever was listening* the story.

Noun clauses function as predicate nouns in the following sentences.

His friendship was *what I wanted.*

The question was *whether we would win or lose.*

Subordinate clauses can also function as adjectives and adverbs do. Those clauses that describe nouns or pronouns are said to be adjective clauses. Adjective clauses are usually introduced by relative pronouns (*who, that, which*), but they can also be introduced by relative adverbs (*where, when,* and so forth). It is important to remember that relative adverbs can introduce subordinate clauses that function either as nouns, adjectives, or adverbs. Consequently, you must determine the kind of subordinate clause you are faced with by noting its function in the sentence. The following italicized clauses are adjective clauses.

Home is the place *where I want to be.*
  The adjective clause describes *place.*

The student *who works hard* will succeed.
  The adjective clause describes *student.*

I lost the book *that you gave me.*
  The adjective clause describes *book.*

Adverb clauses are those subordinate clauses that act as adverbs do.

That is, they describe verbs, adjectives, or other adverbs. Adverb clauses are introduced by subordinating conjunctions that indicate time, purpose or reason, a condition or stipulation, or a conflict between information in the adverb clause and information in some other part of the sentence. Adverb clauses in the following sentences are italicized.

> I left *when I became tired.*
> The adverb clause describes the verb *left,* indicating a time.
>
> It will rain *if we go to the beach.*
> The adverb clause describes the verb *will rain,* indicating a stipulation.
>
> We were pleased *because we did well.*
> The adverb clause describes the adjective *pleased,* indicating a reason.
>
> *Although we were present,* we did not see you.
> The adverb clause describes the verb *did see* (*not* is an adverb). The adverb clause points out a conflict.

When subordinate clauses are adjective or adverb clauses, they describe some part of the sentence. Be describing, they change or *modify* that which they describe. You can easily see the difference between the sentence *The boy was my friend* and that same sentence with a modifying clause added: *The boy who punched me was my friend.* Parts of the sentences that function as adjectives or adverbs, describing other parts of sentences, are called *modifiers.*

You can see, then, that modifiers are often subordinate clauses. Modifiers may also be single words. For instance, *heavy* modifies *automobile* in the following sentence:

> She owns a *heavy* automobile.

The sentence could have been written with an adjective clause.

> She owns an automobile *that is heavy.*

PHRASES

The preceding sentence—She owns an automobile that is heavy—might also have been written like this:

> Her Ford is an automobile *with much weight.*

You will notice that *with much weight* is neither a single word, as is *heavy,* nor a clause, as is *that is heavy. With much weight* cannot be a clause because it does not have a subject and a predicate. Instead, it is a *phrase,* a group of words that seem related, that form a functioning unit within a sentence, yet do not include both a subject and a predicate.

Phrases can function in the same ways that nouns, adjectives, verbs and adverbs do. Note the functions of the phrases in the following sentences.

He is the chairman *of our committee.*
  The adjective phrase modifies *chairman.*

She lives *without a care.*
  The adverb phrase modifies *lives.*

Studying Latin has helped me write English.
  The noun phrase functions as the subject of the sentence.

Ms. Williams, *the club treasurer,* has been married for forty years.
  The noun phrase renames Ms. Williams, the subject of the sentence.

We enjoyed *working on our research papers.*
  The noun phrase functions as the direct object.

To lie in the sun is what I want to do.
  The noun phrase functions as the subject of the sentence.

Forgotten by his mother, the infant began crying.
  The adjective phrase modifies *infant.*

Wanting desperately to win, the coach played his best team.
  The adjective phrase modifies *coach.*

The lake was *too pretty to describe.*
  The adjective phrase *too pretty* modifies *lake.*
  The adverb phrase *to describe* modifies the adjective phrase.

Phrases may sometimes function independently, not fitting into the structure of the rest of the sentence. Such phrases, which do not modify any particular part of the sentences but modify the whole sentence in a general way, are called *absolute phrases.* In the following sentences, the absolute phrases are italicized.

The room being in a mess, I decided to leave for a while.
To take the last point first, this school was never known as a playground.
Time running out, there wasn't much we could do.

In all three examples, the absolute phrases modify entire sentences.

Often verbals—participles, gerunds, or infinitives—combine with other words to make *verbal phrases.* The three kinds of verbal phrases—participial phrases, gerund phrases, and infinitive phrases—function in sentences in the same ways that their verbal counterparts do.

Verbal Phrase	**Function**
Participial phrase	Adjective
Gerund phrase	Noun
Infinitive phrase	Noun, adjective, or adverb

Notice the types and the functions of the verbal phrases in the following sentences.

Leaving by the back door, he tripped on a loose floorboard.
  The participial phrase, begun with the participal *leaving,* modifies the subject of the sentence—*he*.

When we learned that Judy, *wanting some privacy,* had locked herself in the bathroom, we thought it best to let her stay there until she was ready to come out.
  The participial phrase, begun with the participal *wanting,* modifies the subject of the subordinate clause—*Judy*.

Thinking about vacation does not help me finish my papers.
  The gerund phrase, introduced by the gerund *thinking,* functions as the subject of the sentence.

Coach Kleinbaur loved *eating apples during halftime.*
  Here the gerund phrase functions as a direct object. And notice that within the gerund phrase is another phrase—*during halftime*—that modifies the gerund.

To enrich one's life is a worthy goal.
  The infinitive phrase, begun with the infinitive *to enrich,* functions as the subject of the sentence.

Right now I want *to rest quietly.*
  The infinitive phrase, begun with the infinitive *to rest,* functions as a direct object.

That is a book *to read again and again.*
  The infinitive phrase acts as an adjective, modifying *book*.

By the time we reached them, the opportunity *to strike fear in their hearts* had passed.
  The infinitive phrase acts as an adjective, modifying *opportunity*.

I always read *to discover motives of characters.*
  The infinitive phrase functions as an adverb, modifying the verb *read*.

I wish I were small enough *to wear children's sizes.*
  The infinitive phrase functions as an adverb, modifying the adverb *enough*.

Prepositional phrases function most often as adjectives or adverbs. You will remember that prepositional phrases include a preposition, an object (noun, pronoun, noun phrase, or noun clause), and any modifiers of the object.

```
prep.  adj.  obj.
  |     |    |
to the new store
```

Note the prepositional phrases in the following sentences and what they modify.

My goals *for the future* were not formed then.
  The prepositional phrase acts as an adjective, modifying *goals*.

We went *to the lighthouse.*
  The prepositional phrase acts as an adverb, modifying the verb *went*.

That man looks like a person *without a care.*
The prepositional phrase acts as an adjective, modifying *person.*

Friends are helpful *in times of distress.*
This sentence has two prepositional phrases. The first, *in times,* acts as an adverb, modifying the adjective *helpful. Of distress,* the second prepositional phrase, modifies *times,* the object of the first phrase, and acts as an adjective.

KINDS OF SENTENCES

As you know, a *simple sentence* is the subject/predicate structure, or a single main clause. The simple sentence is one of the four kinds of English sentences. By adding subordinate clauses or additional main clauses to the simple sentence, other kinds of sentences can be formed. Plainly stated, a sentence with one main clause and one or more subordinate clauses is called a *complex sentence.* A sentence with two or more main clauses is called a *compound sentence.* And a sentence with two main clauses and one or more subordinate clauses is called a *compound-complex sentence.* The number of phrases that a sentence has does not determine the kind (simple, compound, complex, compound-complex) of sentence it is. The function of subordinate clauses, too, does not determine the kind of sentences in which the subordinate clauses are found. Instead, it is only a matter of numbers: the number of main and subordinate clauses in particular sentences.

In the following sentences, main clauses are italicized and subordinate clauses are indicated by brackets.

1. *They spoke to the convocation.*
   Simple sentence
2. *They left* [when they were ready.]
   Complex sentence
3. [Although I waited at the station for an hour,] *I saw only strangers.*
   Complex sentence
4. [*Whoever wants to see the show*] *can go with us.*
   Complex sentence in which a subordinate clause functions as the subject of the main clause
5. *Alvina* [,who was really a sensible person,] *could not live* [as her parents did.]
   Complex sentence
6. *The horse* [that won the race] *was my father's favorite.*
   Complex sentence
7. *I waited at the station, but I only saw strangers.*
   Compound sentence
8. *I was there; he was elsewhere.*
   Compound sentence
9. [*That he was lonely*] *was no excuse,* and *I told him so.*
   Compound-complex sentence in which a subordinate clause functions as the subject of one main clause

Notice the manner in which clauses are joined. When, in a complex sentence, the subordinate clause follows the main clause (as in sentence 2), no comma is needed to separate one clause from the other. However, when the subordinate clause precedes the main clause in a complex sentence (as in sentence 3), a comma separates the two clauses. Of course, when the subordinate clause is part of the main clause (as in sentence 4 or sentence 9), no punctuation is needed to join the clauses.

An important distinction exists between the two ways that clauses interrupting main clauses are treated. When the subordinate clause is a nonessential modifier (as in sentence 5), commas set it apart from the main clause. When the subordinate clause is an essential modifier, no commas surround it (as in sentence 6). For definitions of essential and nonessential modifiers, see page 494.

The ways in which clauses in compound sentences are joined are easily understood and applied. If a coordinating conjunction joins the two main clauses of a compound sentence (as in sentence 7), a comma precedes the conjunction. If the two main clauses are not separated by a coordinating conjunction (as in sentence 8), a semicolon divides them. The same applies to main clauses in compound-complex sentences.

GRAMMAR, DIALECT, AND LANGUAGE

You have been unconsciously using grammar since you first began speaking in sentences. Since then, you have been creating complex, intelligent sentences without having to pay much attention to their grammar. You may think, "Oh, but I talk in such bad grammar all the time." Actually, you shouldn't assume this because you are probably talking quite effectively in a variety of grammars that suit the group with whom you're conversing and satisfy your purpose. Many people automatically associate the word "grammar" with correctness—good or bad grammar. But those who do may well be unaware of what grammar really is. A grammar is an underlying system used by a closely associated group of people who wish to communicate. Grammar includes word order, word endings, and word forms. As Kenneth Oliver puts it in his pamphlet, *A Sound Curriculum in English Grammar*, "Grammar is what distinguishes a sentence from a list of words randomly ordered." Thus grammar contributes to meaning.

Those who limit their discussion of the grammar in a statement to being only correct or incorrect fail to recognize that grammar must contribute meaning within a context. The context is usually the regional or social group of the speaker and the speaker's audience. Many people who are concerned with correctness in grammar are automatically, but inappropriately, using one standard to judge all communication. The standard commonly used is not based on whether a statement is grammatical (in the sense that it has a grammar), or even meaningful, but whether it conforms to standard English, which is one variety, or dialect, of English.

A dialect is a system for use of vocabulary, grammar, and pronunciation that occurs within a language. People who live in a certain region and who, in turn, belong to certain social groups within a region share certain habits of language. You yourself may have observed that certain sounds or expressions are typical of New Yorkers, Southerners, or Midwesterners, or you may speak a different dialect in your home than in school. Nobody speaks strictly standard English, although some dialects are more like standard English than others. Perhaps the most obvious signals that people speak a different dialect than yours are what appears to be their "strange" use of words and pronunciations. Roger Shuy, a prominent researcher in the study of dialects, compares the first impressions of one dialect speaker hearing another speaking a different dialect to an American going to England and finding that Londoners drive on "the wrong side of the road." Well, it may be a different side of the road, but it isn't the "wrong" side. Other dialects than one's own sound different and may even be momentarily confusing, but they are not inferior. A dialect is more than one person's idiosyncrasies of speaking; it is a recognized system.

Here are just a few of the many examples of regional and social dialects in the United States. First, vocabulary varies. In the North the same animal called a "polecat" in the South is called a "skunk." What is called a "bag" in the North is called a "sack" in the South and in regions between North and South (the Midland). Everywhere some people use the words "cottage cheese"; however, in the North it is also known as "Dutch cheese," in the South it is also known as "clabbercheese," and in the regions between is also known as "smearcase."

Pronunciation differences between dialects can be marked. Southerners would say bacon is *greazy,* but Northerners would say it is *greacy.* People in the Midwest might add an *r* to the middle of words such as *worsh* for wash or *gorsh* for gosh. A Southerner might pronounce the words "time" and "Tom" or "oil" and "all" almost the same way. Even within the broad regions of North, South, and Midwest states within the United States, there are pronunciation differences. You may have noticed that people in New England would say *cah* when other Northerners would say *car,* or *pahk* when other Northerners would say *park.* Social groups vary these pronunciations, also. For instance, certain social groups within the Midwest would be more likely to say *gorsh* than would others.

Grammar also varies. In the North people would be more likely to say "It's a quarter of (or *to*) five" than "It's a quarter 'till five," which is common in the Midwest. Likewise, in the North people often say, "I had four bushel apples," but in the South people often say, "I had four bushels apples." Certain social groups would be likely to say, "He Jim father," but others would be more likely to say, "He's Jim's father." Some regional and social dialects would say the past tense of "to dive" is "dove," and others would say it is "dived."

The differences between dialects of the same language do not usually undermine communication because dialects of a language tend to share basic features of the language. All dialects of English share these features (e.g., sentence patterns) that make them distinctively English. It is true, however, that some of the nuances may be lost among speakers of different dialects because of the combined specialized features of vocabulary, pronunciation, and grammar. Also, because there are so many factors contributing to the speech of two individuals, including levels of formality within the dialects, communication might be difficult. Even with the special flavor of the regional or social group, the dialects are, overall, similar enough to be mutually intelligible. Dialects differ from languages in this way. Even though languages can have common roots, they are not mutually intelligible because among languages not only do underlying grammatical systems differ, but vocabulary also differs. The languages, then, do not overlap, a fact that could create great barriers to communication. Therefore, it is unwise to perceive the distinctions among dialects of the same language in like manner to distinctions among languages. Other dialect speakers are not talking a language foreign to you. Learning other dialects than your own is much easier than learning a foreign language, and speakers of other dialects than your own are relatively easy to understand. The person who says, "Ain't" nobody care 'bout 'im" usually has no trouble understanding the person who says, "There isn't a soul who cares about him," and vice versa.

STANDARD ENGLISH

Standard English is the dialect used by members of the most prestigious groups in our society: lawyers, doctors, broadcasters, writers, politicians, and educators. It is a shared, public form of English used whenever and wherever speakers of many dialects come together. However, it should not be considered superior to other dialects because other dialects of English have their own sets of grammatical rules, are equally logical, and are equally expressive as the prestige dialect, although perhaps they appeal to a more limited audience.

Realistically, people should recognize the value and effectiveness of the many dialects of English, not see any one as the only proper or elegant way to communicate. (Certainly, those speaking in nonstandard [other that standard] dialects have been communicating.) Instead, people should try to view dialects in the context of varying social situations, also recognizing that within dialects there are varying levels of appropriateness.

In itself, whether a statement conforms to one dialect or another does not make it grammatical or ungrammatical. An ungrammatical statement in English would have to be one that did not conform to any dialectical patterns of English. "I bit into the apple green and hard" is not grammatical because it does not conform to the basic sentence patterns of English. "Green and hard" should come before apple; then it becomes meaningful in English.

Dialects other than the standard may be more appropriate in certain situations than standard English, and in other standard English is more appropriate than nonstandard English. Still, appropriateness is the issue, not the presence or absence of grammar, not correctness without a context. Using one dialect in one situation and another in another situation is often compared to dressing one way for one occasion and another way for a different one. The analogy works because dialects are often shifted back and forth as people find themselves in different social situations.

RECOGNIZING INTERFERENCE FROM NONSTANDARD DIALECTS

Americans grow up speaking various dialects of English, many with grammatical features that differ from standard English dialect. Because a great deal of shifting between dialects is required of those who use nonstandard dialects in their communities and standard dialect for writing and other school activities, both dialects must be constantly present in some people's minds. The result is that sometimes the dialects get mixed up. The person makes a perfectly logical analogy between the two dialects, but the idiosyncrasies of one dialect make the analogy imprecise. Most of a student's paper could conform to standard English, but the rest of it could be sprinkled with inconsistencies based on these poor analogies. These inconsistencies are considered "errors" by most careful readers. However, they are not careless mistakes. They may represent gaps in understanding how the standard dialect differs from the nonstandard dialect, the dialect closest to home. Because these errors usually come from unconscious combining of dialects, they are called "interference errors."

The first step for writers struggling with the problem of interference is to learn the major contrasts between their home dialect and the standard dialect. It is important to see both the overlapping grammatical features and the distinguishing grammatical features. Here the contrasts will be emphasized, since they are what most people tend to forget. Of course, understanding the source of interference between dialects is only the beginning. Meticulous dialect shifting comes with patience and practice.

Although it is impossible to classify or explain briefly all the variations within nonstandard dialects because of the variety offered by the speakers themselves and the different levels on which communication takes place, some generalizations can be useful. The following discussion includes many of the common interference errors found in students' papers. Not all of them apply to all dialects of Americans, but among them you should be able to find a few that apply to you.

CONTRASTS BETWEEN NONSTANDARD AND STANDARD GRAMMAR

Verbs

The most contrast occurs in the formation of verbs.

1. Some nonstandard dialects do not usually use the verb *is* and *are* in simple sentences, whereas standard dialect does.

   Nonstandard: She over there.
   Standard: She is over there

   Nonstandard uses have a special use for *is* and *are*: for emphasis.

   Nonstandard: She *is* hungry (emphasized).
   Standard: She hungry (not emphasized).

   Standard English does not make the distinction made in the two preceding sentences.

2. Many nonstandard dialects do not consistently add an *s* to the third person singular verb, but standard dialect always does in the indicative mood (see p. 365).

   Nonstandard: She do her best.
   Standard: She does her best.

   Nonstandard: She know him from last term.
   Standard: She knows him from last term.

3. Often, even when the forms of *to be* (is, are, was, were) are used in nonstandard dialects, they do not necessarily follow the subject-verb agreement rules that standard dialect follows.

   Nonstandard: They is on time.
   Nonstandard: They are on time.
   Standard: They are on time.

4. The verb *to be* has a special form in some nonstandard dialects. For instance, black English makes the distinction not present in standard English that the *be* added to a statement indicates that the action is habitual.

   Nonstandard: He be working
   Standard: He is usually working.

   These statements are different from the following, which do not indicate habit.

   Nonstandard: He working.
   Standard: He is working.

5. The past tense of irregular verbs is often different in nonstandard dialects than in standard dialects. The standard dialect forms are listed in the dictionary under the infinitive form of the verb. Also, the commonly confused verbs can be found listed on page 437.

Nonstandard:	They run down to the store a few minutes ago.
Standard:	They ran down to the store a few minutes ago.
Nonstandard:	She give me a "B."
Standard:	She gave me a "B."

6. Many nonstandard dialects do not end certain past tense regular verbs with *ed*. The same verbs in standard dialect do have an *ed* ending. In the nonstandard dialects, whether the *ed* is added is usually decided by sound. For this reason, verbs ending in *t* or *d* will take the *ed* ending, but others may not.

Nonstandard:	I ask him to tell me what happen.
Standard:	I asked him to tell me what happened.
Nonstandard:	He start this nonsense.
Standard:	He started this nonsense.

7. Many nonstandard dialects do not use a *to be* verb as part of the progressive verb and thus have only one signal for it (the *ing* ending) instead of two as in standard dialect (*to be* and the *ing* ending).

Nonstandard:	They telling the same story.
Standard:	They are telling the same story.

8. Many nonstandard dialects use one of two signals (have and the *ed* ending) for perfect verb tenses, but standard dialect uses both.

Nonstandard:	I have talk with you before.
Nonstandard:	I talked with you before.
Standard:	I have talked with you before.

9. Some nonstandard dialects use *get* or *got* to form the passive voice (see p. 365), but standard dialect uses a form of *to be*.

Nonstandard:	The young man got hurt by his friends.
Standard:	The young man was hurt by his friends.

In addition to the *got*, a nonstandard dialect may use the past tense form of the verb or may omit the *got* and use only the past tense form.

Nonstandard:	All the meat got ate by the hunters.
Nonstandard:	All the meat ate by the hunters.
Standard:	All the meat was eaten by the hunters.

Nouns 1. Some nonstandard dialects do not add *s* or *es* to form plural nouns, especially if the meaning is already clear from the context, but standard dialect always takes the *s* or *es* on regular nouns.

Nonstandard: twenty book
Standard: twenty books

Nonstandard: many desk
Standard: many desks

> Some nonstandard dialects add the *s* or *es* to what would already be considered plural forms of irregular nouns in standard dialect.

Nonstandard: the childrens
Standard: the children

2. Some nonstandard dialects do not use *'s* in forming the possessive and rely on context instead, but standard dialect requires the ending on the noun to show possession.

Nonstandard: Over there is Steve girl.
Standard: Over there is Steve's girl.

3. Nouns formed from verbs (verbals) often have the same form as the infinitive, but in standard dialect they take an *ing* ending.

Nonstandard: Arnetta thanked James for try to help.
Standard: Arnetta thanked James for trying to help.

Nonstandard: In the begin the class was easy.
Standard: In the beginning the class was easy.

Pronouns

1. In some nonstandard dialects *which* is the most common pronoun and it may be used in the same places that standard dialect uses which, that, or who. But standard dialect differentiates between the meanings of which (nonrestrictive—see p. 494), that (restrictive—see p. 494), and who (used only for people and animals, not things.)

Nonstandard: The motor belongs to the man which came into the station yesterday.
Standard: The motor belongs to the man who came into the station yesterday.
Standard (but less strictly formal):   The motor belongs to the man that came into the station yesterday.

2. In some nonstandard dialects the subjective or objective pronoun is used as a possessive pronoun. In standard dialect only possessive pronouns may be used.

Nonstandard: Yesterday was they big chance.
Standard: Yesterday was their big chance.

3. The same rules apply for reflexive pronouns as for possessives (see rule 2).

    Nonstandard: You just let youself go.

    Standard: You just let yourself go.

4. Some nonstandard dialects use a form such as *that there* or *these here*, where standard dialect would use only *that* or *those*.

    Nonstandard: That there book is old.

    Standard: That book is old.

5. Some nonstandard dialects use *them* where standard dialect uses *these* or *those*.

    Nonstandard: Them books weigh a ton.

    Standard: These books weigh a ton.

Adjectives and Adverbs

1. Nonstandard dialects may form adjectives by using the infinitive, whereas standard dialect adds an *ed* or *ing* ending.

    Nonstandard: They just love boil potatoes.

    Standard: They just love boiled potatoes.

    Nonstandard: I am use to hard work.

    Standard: I am used to hard work.

2. To show comparisons, some nonstandard dialects use two signals (the *er* or *est* ending and the word *more* or *most*), but standard dialect uses only one or the other of the signals.

    Nonstandard: He is the most fastest gun in the West.

    Standard: He is the fastest gun in the West.

3. The same rules apply for adverb comparisons as for adjective comparisons (see rule 2).

    Nonstandard: They talk more quicker in New York than in South Carolina.

    Nonstandard: They talk more quick in New York than in South Carolina.

    Standard: They talk more quickly in New York than in South Carolina.

4. In many nonstandard dialects the adjective form may also be used as an adverb. This rule applies to certain adjective forms used with action verbs (see p. 364) and to the word *good* used instead of *well*. In standard dialect the *ly* ending is most often used to distinguish adverbs from adjectives, and *well* is used as an adverb.

Nonstandard: They fix cars good.
Standard: They fix cars well.

Nonstandard: Run quiet in the corridor.
Standard: Run quietly in the corridor.

Conjunctions

Nonstandard dialects may use two signals (the word and the word plus) to show a connection between phrases or clauses, but standard dialects use only one.

Nonstandard: She drank three glasses of milk and plus a cup of tea.
Standard: She drank three glasses of milk and a cup of tea.

Negatives

Many nonstandard dialects use two signals for negatives (a *not* with the verb and a *no* modifying the noun), but standard dialect uses only one signal.

Nonstandard: Tom didn't want no money for it.
Standard: Tom didn't want any money for it.
Standard: Tom wanted no money for it.

Articles

Some nonstandard dialects do not make any distinction between the use of *a* and *an*, but standard dialect uses *an*, not *a*, before a word beginning with a vowel sound.

Nonstandard: A automatic transmission on a car is convenient.
Standard: An automatic transmission on a car is convenient.

RECOGNIZING INTERFERENCE BETWEEN LANGUAGES

The difference between standard English and another language can be great, more marked, of course, than the differences among various dialects of the same language. Many college students today have learned English as a second language. They may continue to speak their first language at home and in their community and English at school. But because languages differ so significantly in idioms, pronunciation, and grammar, strict translation from one to the other is rarely effective. With both languages available to the mind of the bilingual speaker, transference of some of the conventions of the first language into written English is quite common. Of course, these half-English constructions are considered errors by readers; they do not conform to the standards of written English. Sometimes the writers have used a perfectly logical structure in their first language, generalizing it to a principle of English, but the result is considered wrong. It is important to realize that this kind of error is not merely a careless mistake. The thought that has gone into the analogy between the two languages needs to be rechanneled into recognizing the contrasts in the two languages. Once aware of some basic contrasts, any writer can look out for cases in which they would be likely to occur. By reinforcing the distinctions between the languages through observation and practice, the writer learns to separate the languages.

All speakers of second languages could benefit from learning the contrasts between their first and second languages. In this section Spanish will be used to illustrate some of the kinds of contrasts that might be noted and reinforced. Of course, among college students who speak Spanish as a first language, there are many separate people from various ethnic backgrounds. The form of Spanish they speak reflects their social status and where they come from. They may have parents from Cuba, South America, Mexico, or Puerto Rico. Also, how much formal Spanish the students know and how often they speak it contribute to the frequency and kinds of interference from Spanish they will find in their written English. And the social level of the people with whom they most often communicate in Spanish will influence the vocabulary and grammar, the two most common types of interference from first languages. Despite the differences in the background of a particular speaker, some general contrasts and common interference errors are worth noting because they are the source of confusion in the English of many bilingual students.

Verbs

1. In Spanish questions do not include the emphatic *do*, but in English the *do* is needed at the beginning of many questions.

    Spanish: You see what I mean?
    English: Do you see what I mean?

2. In Spanish a final *d* on a word is not pronounced as distinctly as it is in English, so many speakers of Spanish tend not to hear the *ed* at the end of a past tense verb or past participle. Because English speakers commonly drop the sound, too, it is not reinforced in the Spanish speaker's listening. Thus, sometimes the *ed* is left off in error.

    Spanish speaker hears the following:

    I listen to him for the last time.

    In English the *ed* is needed on many verbs in the past tense:

    I listened to him for the last time.
    I have listened to him for the last time.

3. In Spanish contractions are not used, but in English the verb may be contracted. Therefore, many Spanish speakers avoid the use of contractions or may misspell them when they realize that they lend a conversational sound to writing and that the apostrophe goes where letters or a letter is left out. The best way to learn contractions is to memorize them and to notice whenever using them that the apostrophe replaces particular letters.

    Spanish: I am not home in the mornings.
    English: I am not home in the mornings.
    English: I'm not home in the mornings. (the apostrophe marks the missing *a* in *am*)

Nouns 1. In Spanish possessives of nouns are shown by a phrase beginning with *of*. In English this structure is not incorrect, but it may be excessively formal or awkward when something is possessed by a person. English uses an apostrophe and *s* (*'s*) to show possession. Because the structure is strange to speakers of Spanish, they may avoid it even though it would make their sentences more fluent; or they may have trouble placing the apostrophe, tending to leave it out. In standard English the apostrophe must be present and in the appropriate place to convey the writer's meaning. See page 476 for the rules.

Spanish: The house of Mary is very small.
English: Mary's house is very small.

2. In Spanish, nouns have gender (masculine and feminine) expressed in the noun endings, but in English noun endings are the same for most nouns. In English, too, plurals are formed without regard to gender: *s* or *es* is usually added to the singular form of the noun (see p. 407).

Spanish: los rios (indicates masculine by *o* ending)
English: the rivers (makes no reference to gender by *s* ending only)

Pronouns 1. In Spanish the pronoun is combined with the verb form and may otherwise be omitted in a sentence, but in English the pronoun is always used in addition to the proper verb form.

Spanish: The reason she did it is has nothing else.
English: The reason she did it is she has nothing else.

2. In Spanish a phrase beginning with *of* is used to show the possessive pronoun, but in English there are specific words that are used alone as the possessive pronouns (see p. 447).

Spanish: The book of her is on the table.
English: Her book is on the table.

3. In Spanish the relative pronouns *that*, *which*, *who*, and *whom* are all one word, *que*, but in English each of the words has a slightly different function.

Spanish: The man which sold me the radio is friendly.
English: The man who sold me the radio is friendly.

4. In Spanish the pronoun used in front of a question will often be *which*, but the corresponding question in English would require *what*.

Spanish: Which is your name?
English: What is your name?
English: Which is your name?

A Review of Grammar and Spelling

The last sentence would indicate that the name is one of many already mentioned. The use of *qual* in the Spanish sentence does not assume that the name has been mentioned.

Adjectives and Adverbs

1. In Spanish adjectives agree in number with their nouns, but in English the adjective form remains the same whether the noun is singular or plural.

   Spanish: in differents classes

   English: in different classes

2. In Spanish adjectives agree in gender with the nouns they modify, but in English noun endings do not show gender, so neither do their adjectives.

3. In Spanish only one word, *mucho*, is used to mean *much* and *many*, but in English the two words are used differently. *Much* is used in English to describe quantities, and *many* is used to describe items that could be counted.

   Spanish: A person who lives on county money has much problems in these days of high inflation.

   English: A person who lives on county money has many problems in these days of high inflation.

4. In Spanish adjectives are placed after the nouns they modify, but in English adjectives often precede nouns.

   Spanish: The house white looks beautiful.

   English: The white house looks beautiful.

Negatives

In Spanish two signals are used to show negatives, but in standard English only one is acceptable.

Spanish: She does not want nothing today.

English: She does not want anything today.

English: She wants nothing today.

Articles

1. There is no equivalent in Spanish for the article *an*. Many Spanish speakers therefore tend to use *a* all the time, not realizing that before a noun with a pronounced vowel *an*, not *a*, is used in English.

   Spanish: A amateur does something for the love of it.

   English: An amateur does something for the love of it.

2. In Spanish the article may be used with an adjective to form a noun, but in English the word *one* must be added to the phrase to achieve the same effect.

   Spanish: the ugly (meaning the one who is ugly)

   English: the ugly one

Spanish: the great
English: the great one

3. In Spanish an article is used before a generalized noun, but in English the article is usually not present.

Spanish: the humanity
English: humanity

Spanish: the love
English: love

Prepositions Prepositions are perhaps the stickiest problem for the Spanish speaker. The main reason is that many idioms in Spanish cannot translate directly into English because different prepositions are used. Unfortunately, the Spanish speaker must simply memorize or refer to a list of common English expressions that take prepositions. With practice and recognition of which phrases tend to be confusing, a writer can reduce the interference. Here is a common example of this kind of interference.

Spanish: I was married with Julio last May.
English: I was married to Julio last May.
English: Julio and I were married last May.

The following list of idiomatic expressions with prepositions shows the way prepositions should be used in the English expressions. Reading it over and practicing with the expressions can help many. It should also be used as a reference.

Idiomatic Expressions

Abstain *from* something
Abundance *of* something
Acceptable *to* someone
Access *to* someone or some place
Accuse someone *of* something
Acquaint *with* someone or something
Adapt *to* something
Adhere *to* something
Affection *for* someone
Afraid *of* something
Agree *to* something
Agree *with* someone about something
Amazed *at* something
Analogy *between* two things

Angry *at* something
Angry *with* someone
Apply *to* someone *for* something
Appropriate *to* something
Ashamed *of* something
Ask someone *for* something
Ask something *of* someone
Assure someone *of* something
At the top *of*
Attraction *to* or *toward* someone or something
Aversion *to* someone or something
Aware *of* someone or something
Because *of* something or someone

Blame someone *for* something
Call *on* someone
Call *to* someone
Capable *of* something
Certain *of* something
Characteristic *of* someone
Characterized *by* something
Communicate something *to* someone
Communicate *with* someone on something
Comparable *to* something
Complain *to* someone *about* something
Composed *of* something
Concerned *about* someone or something
Confess *to* someone or something
Confidence *in* someone or something
Confident *of* something
Conform *to* something
Congratulate someone *on* something
Conscious *of* something
Consistent *with* something
Consult *with* someone *about* or *on* something
Count *on* someone or something
Cure *for* something
Demand something *of* someone
Depend *on* someone or something
Destined *for* something
Die *from* a cause other than disease
Die *of* a disease
Disgusted *with* someone or something
Distrust *of* someone or something
Doubtful *of* someone or something
Dream *of* or *about* someone or something

Engaged *in* some activity
Engaged *to* someone
Equality *with* something
Escape *from* something
Excel *in* something
Exception *to* something
Explain something *to* someone
Faithful *to* someone or something
Failure *of* someone *in* something
Fall *in* love *with* someone
Fond *of* someone
For fear *of*
For the purpose *of*
For the sake *of*
Free *from* someone or something
Full *of* something
Guess *at* something
Hear *of* something
Hinder someone *from* doing something
Hint *at* something
Hope *for* something
In accordance *with*
In case *of*
In defense *of*
In favor *of*
Inform someone *of* something
In opposition *to*
In spite *of*
In the event *of*
Insist *on* something
Intent *on* something
Interested *in* someone or something
Interfere *with* someone
Introduce someone *to* someone else
Irrelevant *to* something
Knock *at* or *on* the door
Laugh *at* something or someone
Lecture *on* some subject
Listen *to* someone or something
Look *at* someone or something

Look *for* someone or something
Look *up* someone or something
Motive *for* something
Need *for* something
Opportunity *for* someone or something
Opposed *to* something or someone
Pity *for* someone
Prefer something *to* something else
Prejudice *against* someone or something
Previous *to* some event
Proficient *in* something
Protect someone *from* something
Quarrel *with* someone *over* or *about* something
Reason *for* something
Reason *with* someone *about* something
Recover *from* something (an illness)
Refrain *from* something
Regardless *of* something
Rely *on* someone or something
Reply *to* someone or something
Require something *of* someone
Research *in* a field
Reverence *for* someone or something
Run *into* debt
Similar *to* someone or something
Subscribe *to* something
Surrender *to* someone
Sympathy *with* or *for* someone or something
Take advantage *of* someone or something
Talk *over* something *with* someone
Thankful *for* something
Tired *of* something
Wait *for* someone or something
Wait *on* someone (customer)
With reference *to*
Work *for* something or someone

When in doubt as to the correct preposition to be used with a word, always consult your dictionary. Also, try to note how idioms are used in your readings and imitate them using the same context.

PRINCIPLES OF SPELLING

Correct spelling is another one of those writing conventions that your reader should be able to expect of you. Just as you are expected to use the commonly accepted practices for grammar, punctuation, and mechanics, so are you expected to use conventionally correct spelling. To do otherwise, either through error or simple carelessness, slows your reader and detracts from your message. In the time it takes your reader to realize that you meant *they're* and not *their*, he or she may have lost the flow of your thoughts.

For some spelling seems an easy task; for others it is always difficult. You know into which category you fit. Even those individuals who find spelling simple usually write with a dictionary close at hand to check words with which they may not be familiar. But if you fall into the latter group of those for whom spelling is always a problem, a review of some of the most effective ways of improving will be beneficial.

USE A DICTIONARY Disciplining yourself to check a dictionary whenever you have doubts about a spelling is one of the most important writing habits you can develop. Using the dictionary is the best way to check accurate spelling and, at the same time, make sure you have the right word. Always try to keep a dictionary next to you as you are writing and use it freely.

The rest of the guidelines presented in this chapter are designed to save you time by reducing the number of words you should have to look up. None of them, however, should be thought of as a substitute for using a dictionary.

LEARN TO CORRECT YOUR PRONUNCIATION Many people misspell words because they mispronounce them. Usually, the closer you come to pronouncing a word correctly, the closer you are to spelling it correctly. As you have already discovered, having some idea of how a word is pronounced is helpful when looking for that word in your dictionary. Therefore, it is very worthwhile to learn a few basic principles of correct pronunciation. These principles fall into three general categories: the letters themselves, the syllables, and the symbols for sound and stress.

Every letter is either a *vowel* or a *consonant*. The letters *a, e, i, o,* and *u* are always vowels. The letter *y* behaves less consistently. Sometimes it is a vowel, as in the word *sky*, and sometimes it is a consonant, as in the word *yes*. All the other letters are always consonants. Thus, in the word *placard*, there are two vowels—the two *a*'s—and five consonants—*p, l, c, r,* and *d*. Similarly, in the word *restraint* there are three vowels—*e, a,* and *i*—and six consonants—*r, s, t, r, n,* and *t*.

Recognizing words as a whole can often lead to mispronunciation and later to misspelling. Sounding words out, on the other hand, can often improve spelling. **Every word is made up of units of sound called *syllables*.** Each syllable always contains at least one vowel. When you first pronounce a word, begin by saying each syllable separately.

In-scru-ta-ble
Pop-u-la-tion

Then say all of the syllables together.

Inscrutable
Population

Make sure that you do not add a syllable that is not there or skip one that is. Such errors in pronunciation can often lead to spelling mistakes. For instance, a commonly misspelled word is *athlete*. Although the word has only two syllables, *ath-lete*, many people tend to pronounce the word with an extra syllable, *ath-e-lete*, which is incorrect. Those who add the extra syllable are misreading and mispronouncing the word and will probably misspell it later.

Every dictionary uses symbols to show how the various letters in a word should sound and which syllable in a word should be stressed. You will find a list of these symbols in the front of your dictionary. Two of the most common symbols are ˘ and ¯. They are used to indicate some of the sounds for vowels. A ˘ above a vowel means that its sound should be short.

    Ăpple Lĕt Lĭttle Ŏn Ŭp

A bar above a vowel means that the sound of that vowel should be long.

    Āpe Mēēt Īce Nō Ūse

Another common symbol is the stress, or accent, mark ('). It indicates which syllable in a word should receive the most stress.

    Re-tire'   Glit'-ter

Thus, in the word *retire* the second syllable should be stressed, whereas the first syllable should be stressed in *glitter*.

Although correct pronunciation can be very helpful, you must be careful not to rely on it to too great an extent. Sometimes spelling a word according to the way it is pronounced can get you into trouble. For instance, the last syllable of the word *proceed* is pronounced exactly as is the last syllable of both *supersede* and *precede*, but the spelling of the sound is different for each word. Similarly, English has many letter combinations that are pronounced differently in different words. For example, the *ai* in *said* is not pronounced the same as the *ai* in *paid*. Therefore, as good a guideline as pronunciation can be, it is a guideline that must be used with caution.

LEARN THE NINE MAJOR SPELLING RULES

There are many different spelling rules, and each rule has a number of exceptions. It would be nearly impossible to memorize all of them. For this reason, only the nine major rules are given here. They cover the spelling problems that most frequently bother the largest number of writers. You should learn these rules well. It would even be a good idea to memorize the first four along with their exceptions. Learning these rules may not solve all of your spelling problems but, once you know them, you will be well on your way to becoming a good speller.

I before E

When *I* and *E* appear together in a word, the *I* normally comes before the *E*. The *E* comes before the *I*, however, when the combination is sounded like a long *A* or when it follows a *C*. The *IE* and *EI* rule can be mastered by learning the following jingle.

I before *E*
Except after *C*
Or when sounded like *A*
As in *neighbor* and *weigh*.

Examples:

| Sleigh | Weight | Receive | Receipt |
| Neighbor | Feign | Conceit | Conceive |

Exceptions:

| Either | Height | Seize | Seizure | Financier |
| Neither | Leisure | Weird | Counterfeit | Species |

Doubling the Final Consonant When Adding a Suffix

Double the final consonant before adding a suffix beginning with a vowel when the final consonant is preceded by a vowel and the word is accented on the last syllable or is composed of only one syllable.

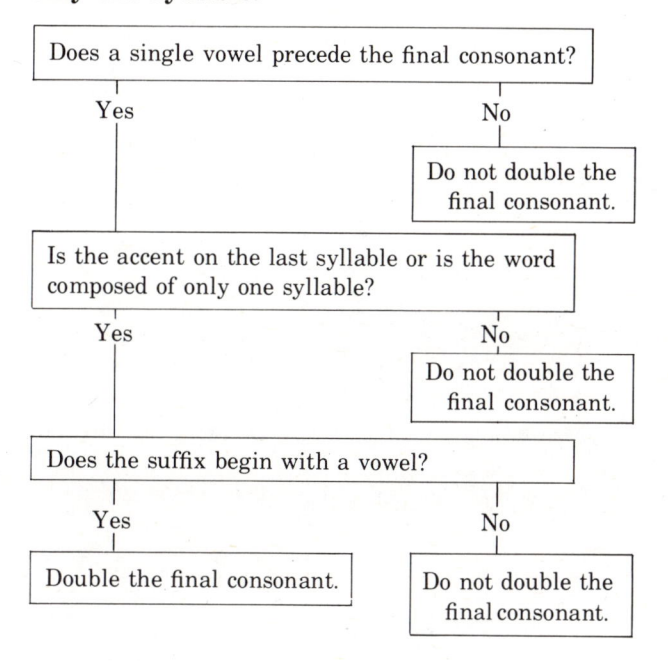

Does a single vowel precede the final consonant?
- Yes ↓
- No → Do not double the final consonant.

Is the accent on the last syllable or is the word composed of only one syllable?
- Yes ↓
- No → Do not double the final consonant.

Does the suffix begin with a vowel?
- Yes → Double the final consonant.
- No → Do not double the final consonant.

Examples:

| Occurred | Omitted | Occurrence | Recurring |
| Batter | Stopped | Madden | Running |

Exceptions:
  There are no exceptions to this rule.

Adding a Suffix to Words Ending with an Unpronounced E

Leave out the final unpronounced *E* before adding a suffix beginning with a vowel, but keep the *E* before adding a suffix beginning with a consonant.

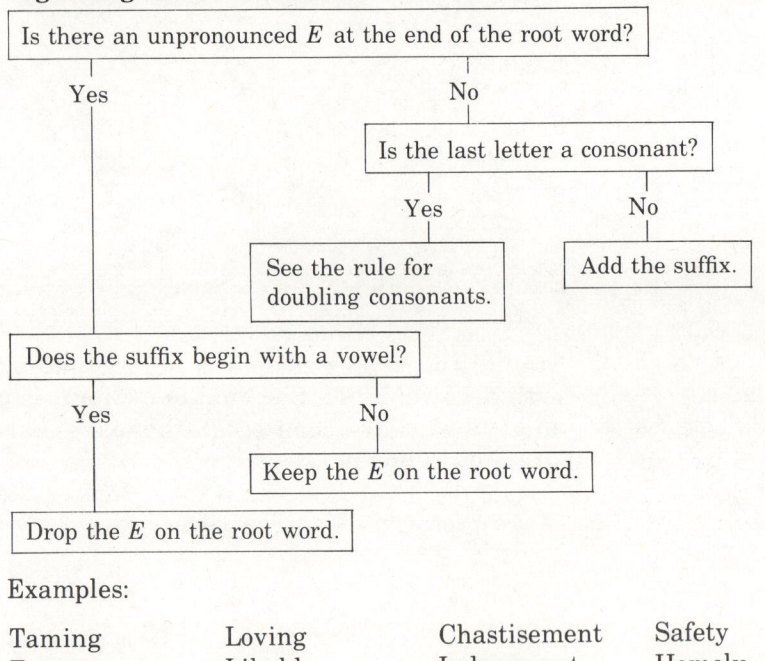

```
Is there an unpronounced E at the end of the root word?
         │
    ┌────┴────┐
   Yes        No
               │
               Is the last letter a consonant?
                    │
               ┌────┴────┐
              Yes        No
               │          │
          See the rule for    Add the suffix.
          doubling consonants.

Does the suffix begin with a vowel?
    │
┌───┴───┐
Yes     No
         │
         Keep the E on the root word.

Drop the E on the root word.
```

Examples:

Taming	Loving	Chastisement	Safety
Famous	Likable	Inducement	Homely
Advisable	Writing	Namely	
Smoking	Smoker	Timely	

Exceptions:

Mileage Dyeing Wholly Awful Judgment

Many of the exceptions to this rule have their own rule.

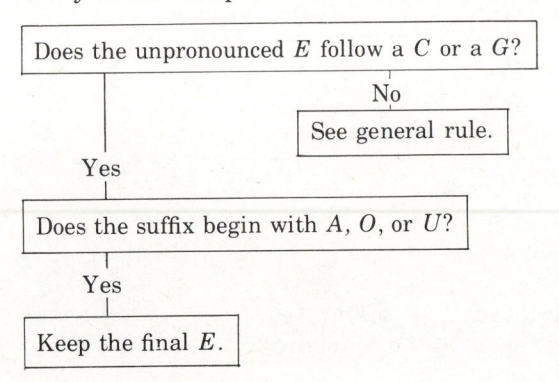

```
Does the unpronounced E follow a C or a G?
    │
    │           No
    │           See general rule.
   Yes
    │
Does the suffix begin with A, O, or U?
    │
   Yes
    │
Keep the final E.
```

Examples:

Changeable   Arrangeable   Courageous   Replaceable

A Review of Grammar and Spelling

Changing Y to I When Adding a Suffix

If the root word ends in a *Y* that is preceded by a consonant, change the *Y* to *I* before adding any suffix that does not begin with *I*.

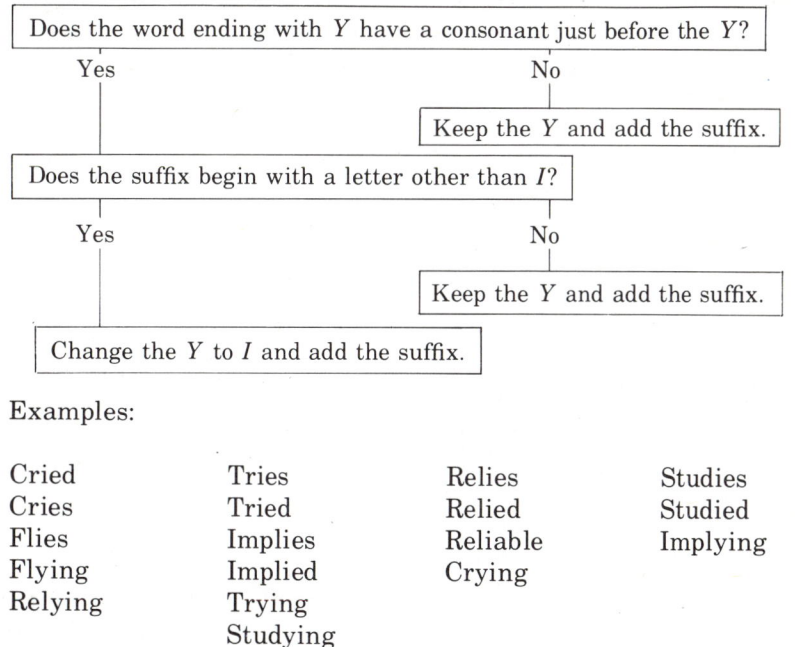

Does the word ending with *Y* have a consonant just before the *Y*?

- Yes
- No → Keep the *Y* and add the suffix.

Does the suffix begin with a letter other than *I*?

- Yes
- No → Keep the *Y* and add the suffix.

Change the *Y* to *I* and add the suffix.

Examples:

Cried	Tries	Relies	Studies
Cries	Tried	Relied	Studied
Flies	Implies	Reliable	Implying
Flying	Implied	Crying	
Relying	Trying		
	Studying		

Exceptions:
There are no exceptions to this rule.

Forming Plurals of Words Ending in O

Add *ES* to form the plural of words ending in *O* when a consonant precedes the *O*.

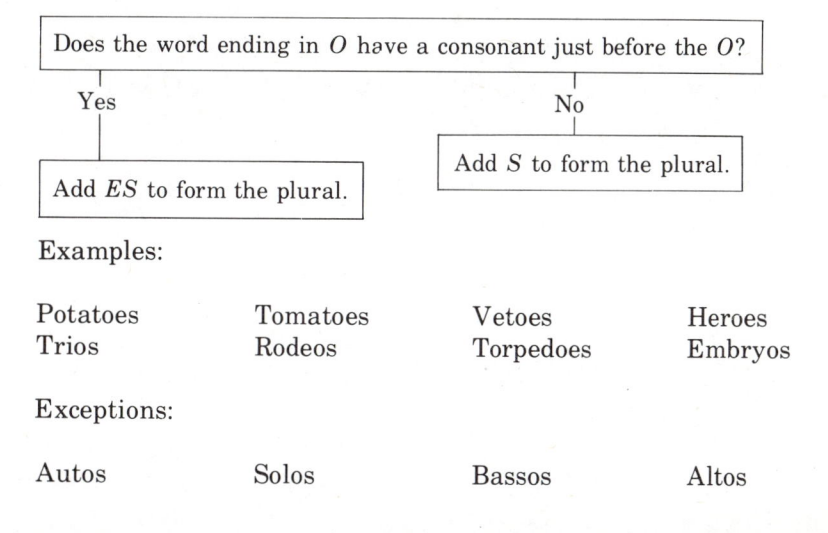

Does the word ending in *O* have a consonant just before the *O*?

- Yes → Add *ES* to form the plural.
- No → Add *S* to form the plural.

Examples:

Potatoes	Tomatoes	Vetoes	Heroes
Trios	Rodeos	Torpedoes	Embryos

Exceptions:

Autos	Solos	Bassos	Altos

Changing C to CK When Adding ED, Y, or ING as a Suffix

When a word ends with a *C* that is pronounced as a *K*, change the *C* to *CK* before adding *ED, Y,* or *ING* as a suffix.

> Is the *C* at the end of the root word pronounced like a *K*, as in *picnic*?

Yes → Change the *C* to *CK* before adding the suffix.

No → Do not change the *C* before adding the suffix.

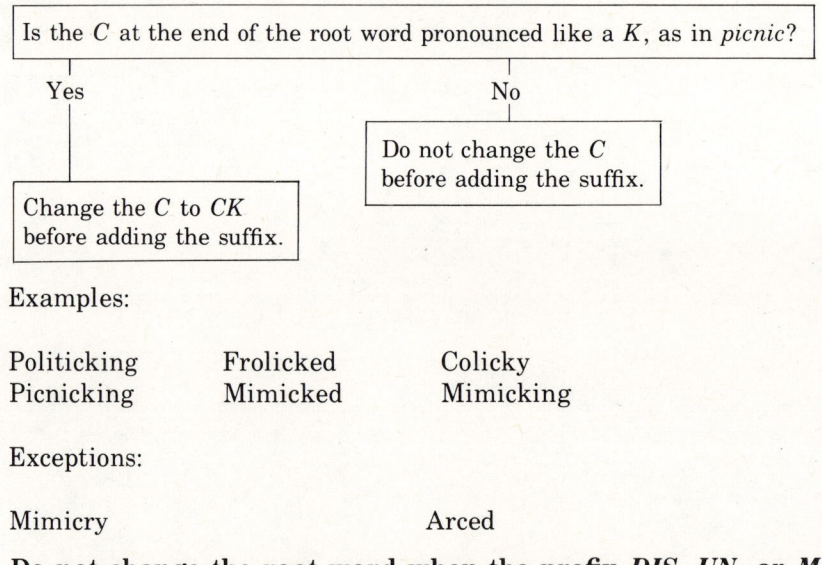

Examples:

Politicking	Frolicked	Colicky
Picnicking	Mimicked	Mimicking

Exceptions:

Mimicry   Arced

Adding DIS, UN, or MIS as a Prefix

Do not change the root word when the prefix *DIS, UN,* or *MIS* is added to it. This rule applies even if the root begins with the same letter that the prefix ends with.

Examples:

Disappoint	Unnecessary	Dissuade
Misrelated	Unnatural	Dissatisfy
Misspell	Unnerve	Dissolve

Exceptions:
  There are no exceptions to this rule.

Adding LY to Words Ending in L

When adding the suffix *LY* to a root word ending in *L*, keep the *L* on the root.

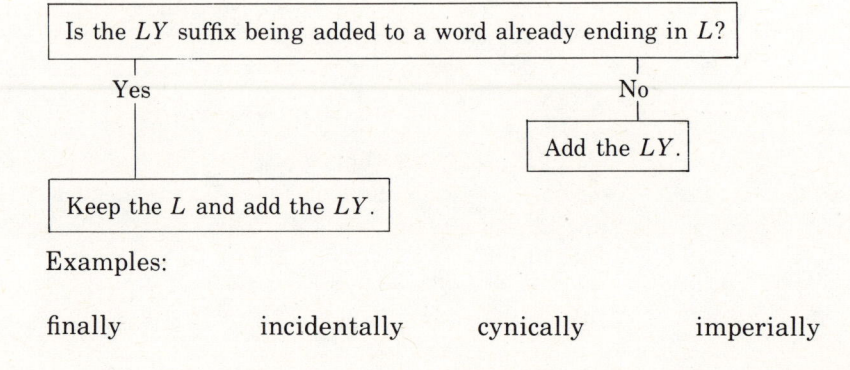

> Is the *LY* suffix being added to a word already ending in *L*?

Yes → Keep the *L* and add the *LY*.

No → Add the *LY*.

Examples:

finally   incidentally   cynically   imperially

Exceptions:
There are no exceptions to this rule.

Words Ending in CEDE, CEED, and SEDE

Use the ending *CEDE* for most English words ending with the sound "seed."

Examples:
   concede   precede   secede   intercede   recede

Exceptions:
Three words end in *CEED*:   succeed   proceed   exceed
One word ends in *SEDE*:   supersede

LEARN TO PROOFREAD EFFECTIVELY

Effective proofreading can save you a number of spelling errors on each paper. Unfortunately, proofreading is not always as easy as it may first appear. Frequently, writers are too familiar with what they have written. They become blind to mistakes they may have made. When reading over their papers, they tend to see what they meant to write rather than what actually appears on the page. For this reason, it is always a good idea to let a paper or essay "cool" before checking it for errors.

    When you proofread, try to concentrate on the individual words. Depending on sight recognition alone will seldom be effective. Instead, actually spell out each word to yourself. One way to help focus your efforts is to keep in mind the types of errors you most often make. As you proofread, try to find a set number of these errors, say three or four, on each page. You may also find that it helps to read aloud. Some writers find it easier to concentrate on the spelling of each word if they read each line of their papers backward, from right to left. Although the context is missing, you can easily note any words for which this might cause a problem and quickly check them by reading normally.

    Becoming a good proofreader takes practice. As you gain experience, you will discover the various methods that work best for you. Whenever possible, however, have someone else proofread your writing also. Talk a friend into trading papers. The fresh eye can almost always detect errors that the overworked eye would miss. In addition, proofreading one another's work will allow both of you to practice your skills on unfamiliar material. Frequently, finding errors in someone else's writing will actually help you to find similar errors in your own.

COMMONLY MISSPELLED AND CONFUSED WORDS

The following is a list of words that students and writers often misspell or confuse. Although a dictionary is always the best place to check the spelling of a word, some writers prefer word lists because they are so easy to refer to. The problem is that the lists usually do not include definitions. Therefore, anyone using a list must be very careful not to choose the wrong word simply because it looks like or sounds like another word. If you decide to use the following list, be sure that you do not make mistakes such as using *accept* for *except* or *device* for *devise*.

Abbreviate	Beneficial	Controversial
Absence	Biscuit	Convenient
Absorption	Breathe/breath	Correspondence
Absurd	Britannica	Courageous
Accept/except	Bulletin	Crises/crisis
Access/excess	Burglar	Criticism
Accidentally	Bureaucracy	Curriculum
Accommodate	Calendar	Decimal
Accumulate	Camouflage	Defense
Achievement	Candidate	Definite
Across	Carburetor	Delicious
Actually	Careful	Dependence
Address	Category	Descent
Adequately	Caucus	Describe
Adolescence	Cautious	Desert/dessert
Adopt	Cellar/seller	Desirable
Advise/advice	Cemetery	Desperate
Aggressive	Choose/chose	Destroy
Alleys/allies	Circuit	Deterrence
All right/alright	Circular	Develop
A lot/allot	Circumference	Development
Alter/altar	Clause	Device/devise
Amateur	Coarse/course	Dictionary
Analyze	Coincidence	Difference
Angle	College/collage	Dilemma
Annual	Coming	Disappoint
Apparatus	Commission	Disdain
Appropriate	Committee	Dissent
Arctic	Competent	Divine
Article	Compliment/	Dominance
Ascent	complement	Dropped
Assassinate	Compromise	Dying/dyeing
Athlete	Conceit	Echoes
Attendance	Conceive	Eighth
Audience	Condemn	Eligible
Awkward	Conference	Embarrass
Bankruptcy	Confidence	Eminence
Bargain	Conscience/conscious	Environment
Basically	Conscientious	Equivalent
Becoming	Considerably	Etc.
Beginning	Consistent	Exaggerate
Believe	Controlling	Exceed/accede

Excellent
Excess/access
Exercise
Existence
Expense
Extremely
Exuberance
Facetious
Fantasies
Fascinate
Feasible
February
Fictitious
Finally
Flexible
Foreign
Formally/formerly
Frantically
Friend
Frolicking
Fulfill/fulfil
Fundamentally
Further/farther
Goddess
Grammar
Grievous
Guarantee
Harass
Hear/here
Height
Hereditary
Heroes
Hindrance
Holiness
Hoping
Humorous
Hypocrisy
Illegible
Illogical
Incidentally
Incredible
Independent
Indict
Inherent
Inoculate
Insistent

Instance
Intelligible
Interruptions
Irrelevance
Irresistible
Irreverent
Jam/jamb
Judicial
Knead/need
Knot
Laboratory
Leisure
Library
License
Likely
Literature
Loneliness
Lose/loose
Maneuver
Marriage
Medieval
Mediocre
Merely
Mimicking
Miniature
Misspell
Muscle
Naturalization
Negroes
Nickel
Ninety
Observance
Occasion
Occurred
Omission
Opportunity
Panicked
Paragraph
Parallel
Parentheses/
 parenthesis
Passed/past
Peculiar
Pedal/peddle
Perceive
Permanent

Permissible
Perseverance
Personnel/personal
Pertain
Physical
Physician
Pickle
Piece/peace
Plagiarize
Playwright
Polar
Politician
Poll/pole
Possess
Practical
Presence/presents
Principle/principal
Privilege
Probably
Proceed
Professor
Pronunciation
Psychology
Purl/pearl
Quantity
Quiet/quite/quit
Quotation
Radioactive
Receipt
Receive
Recognize
Recommend
Reference
Relief
Reminisce
Repetition
Representative
Residence
Responsible
Rhythm
Scarcity
Schedule
Scissors
Secede
Seize
Sentence

Separate	Success	Usually
September	Summary/summery	Vacuum
Sergeant	Superfluous	Vetoes
Severely	Supersede	Villain
Shepherd	Supplement	Vinegar
Siege	Symbolize	Violence
Silence	Tawdry	Visibility
Simultaneous	Technique	Volume
Sincerely	Temperament	Waste/waist
Slimy	Tenant	Watt
Solemn	Tendency	Weather/whether
Sonnet	Than/then	Wednesday
Sophomore	Theses/thesis	Weight
Souvenir	Thorough/through	Weird
Species	Though/thought	Where/wear
Stationary/stationery	To/too/two	Wholly/holy
Statue/stature	Toeing	Whose/who's
Straight/strait	Tragedy	Wintry
Strength	Tried	Woman/women
Studying	Truly	Wondrous
Subsequent	Twelfth	Writing
Subtle	Tyranny	Written
Suburbia	Unanimous	
Succeed	Unnecessary	

13

Correcting Common Errors

When you write, it is normal to make a few grammatical errors. After all, you are concentrating on the content of your paper. However, you will want to find these errors before you turn your paper in. The best way to do this is to sift through your paper several times, directing your attention toward each potential error in turn. In effect, you want to treat your writing as if it were an exercise. By going quickly through your paper five times, you can cover the seven most common trouble spots.

As thorough as this method is, there is no doubt that it is also time consuming. Of course, the amount of time needed will depend on the length of the paper. Because you will not always have as long as you would like to correct your writing, two plans are included here. The first is for those times when you have thirty minutes to an hour to check for errors. The second is a briefer plan for those occasions when you have less than half an hour.

ADOPTING A PLAN

This section is designed to be of use both before you submit a paper and after the paper is returned. Before handing a paper in, you should use the section to edit your writing for any grammatical inconsistencies. As doctors say, prevention is the best medicine. After the paper is returned, you should review any errors that may have slipped by you but were caught by your teacher. Try to analyze your own errors by figuring out why you made them. This will help you to make sure that you do not make the same ones the next time. On the inside front cover is a list of questions that cover the major areas in the text.

The Writers Practical Rhetoric

PLAN ONE Sift through your paper once for each of the following questions, making sure that you correct any errors you discover.

1. Do your subjects agree with their verbs? Do your predicates match their subjects?
2. Are there any sentence fragments or run-on sentences?
3. Are all your verbs and verbals formed accurately?
4. Do all your pronouns fit their references and functions?
5. Is your syntax correct?

PLAN TWO The second plan, designed for when the amount of time you have to look over your writing is brief, is an abbreviated version of the first. It makes use of the most recent paper returned by your teacher.

1. Identify the three grammatical errors that occurred the most frequently in the last essay you wrote.
2. Categorize these errors according to the following numbers.

Verb agreement—1	Run-on sentences—2
Sentence fragments—2	Verb tenses—3
Pronoun agreement—4	Subjunctive verbs—3
Pronoun case—4	Predication—1
Pronoun reference—4	Syntax—5
Modifiers—5	Irregular verbs—3
Parallelism—5	Confusing modifiers—5

3. Follow the steps in Plan One for those numbers you are having the most trouble with. If many of your errors were in word choice, check "A Glossary of Usage." For errors in punctuation or spelling, see the next two chapters of this handbook.

HOW TO SIFT FOR ERRORS

STEP ONE: DO YOUR SUBJECTS AGREE WITH THEIR VERBS? DO YOUR PREDICATES MATCH THEIR SUBJECTS?

If you already know how to pick out a singular verb and a singular noun, you may want to skip to the section called "Check Verbs and Subjects for Number" on page 408. If you sometimes have trouble identifying singulars and plurals, you will want to study this section carefully.

Distinguish Singular from Plural

Recognizing whether your simple predicates (also called verbs) and subjects are singular or plural is not complicated. The same endings mean different things on nouns and verbs.

NOUNS

Most singular nouns do *not* end in *s: car, dog, tomato.*
Most plural nouns end in *s* or *es: cars, dogs, tomatoes.*

VERBS

Most singular verbs end in *s* or *es: says, runs, takes, smokes.*
Most plural verbs do not end in *s: say, run, take, smoke.*

Usually, then, both the subject—when it is a noun—and the verb will not end in *s.*

IRREGULAR NOUNS AND VERBS

Of course, there are a few exceptions to forming both the plurals of nouns and the plurals of verbs. Keep in mind the following irregular nouns.

Words like *people* and *children*:
Some nouns become plural by changing their forms, not by adding an *s* or *es* ending. *Person* becomes *people; child* becomes *children.*
Words like *species* and *deer* and names:
Some nouns have the same forms for their singular and plural meanings. Also, a person's name may end in *s*, but the *s* ending does not mean the noun is plural. *Charles* and *James* are singular, despite their last letter.

Simple predicates that include helping verbs reflect the number of the simple predicate only by the helping verb, and the other verb never ends in *s.* Thus, just looking at a verb that has a helper, you cannot expect to see an *s* ending, which would ordinarily reveal at a glance that the verb is singular.

GUIDELINES

Several general guidelines follow. Usually, a present tense verb will not end in *s* if any of the following conditions exist:

1. The verb has a helper (might *go*).
2. The subject ends in *s*, except for names or special words that have the same form in the singular and plural.
3. The subject of the clause has been made plural by changing the form of the word instead of by adding *s.*
4. The subject of the clause is *I* or *you.*
5. The verb is a form of *to be.*

When pronouns are the subjects of clauses, you can figure out if they are singular or plural very easily. Only with indefinite pronouns like *everyone* and *none* should you even question the number. Otherwise, the number for pronouns is consistently as the following chart points out.

Singular	Plural
I	We
You (ask yourself: Do I mean one person?)	You (ask yourself: Do I mean more than one person?)
He, she, it	They

Check Verbs and Subjects for Number

The point of checking the number of subjects and verbs is to make sure they agree: a singular subject should go with a singular verb and a plural subject with a plural verb. For example, in the following sentence the subject, *authorities,* is plural. Therefore, the verb for this subject should be plural also.

The *authorities consider* all the evidence before suspending a student.

But if the subject is singular, the verb must be singular.

The final *authority is* the President.

This rule may seem almost too easy. With most subjects and verbs, agreement is just as clear cut as in these examples. However, in some sentences, the rules are more complicated, and it is harder to tell whether the subject is singular or plural.

A prepositional phrase coming between the subject and the verb does not influence the number of the verb. In the following examples, the prepositional phrases are indicated by parentheses.

One (of the interviewers) *knows* just the right questions to ask.

The *impact* (of all the meetings) (with the leaders) (of the labor union) *was* hardly *felt* (by the employees).

The *flu* (as well as the common cold) *is* a threat (to every student).

When the word *it* begins a sentence, the verb following is always singular.

It sometimes *seems* as if I will never be able to get an "A" in French.

It is the three girls over there who have volunteered to serve on the screening committee.

When the word *there* begins a sentence, the verb depends on what comes next. If what follows is plural, the verb should be *are* or some other plural verb. If what follows is singular, the verb should be singular.

There are ways of adjusting an overdrawn checking account.

There is one *type* of woman I cannot tolerate—a girlish one.

When a sentence begins with a verbal, the subject sometimes comes after the verb. Nevertheless, the subject and the verb should still agree in number.

Splashed on the ground was the *blood* of the defeated men.

Wandering around the golf course were two *children* who had run away from the orphanage after being punished.

When a sentence contains a linking verb and a complement, the subject, not the complement, determines the number of the verb.

Mothers are a wonderful breed.

It is my grades that will suffer from all my frivolity.

Two subjects joined by *and* usually take a plural verb.

Scrabble and Hearts are my favorite games.

Exception: When two subjects connected by *and* really represent parts of the same unit—when they are actually inseparable—the verb is singular.

Bacon and eggs is a satisfying meal anytime.

There *is time and money enough* for an extensive study.

When *each* or *every* comes before singular subjects joined by *and*, the verb is singular.

Every man and woman has a vote.

Each owner and renter receives a different tax credit.

If *who, which,* or *that* is the subject, the only way to determine the correct number of the verb is to discover what the subject modifies. The simple predicate should take the singular form if the word that *who, which,* or *that* modifies is singular and the plural form if the modified word is plural.

The *person who sells* pretzels in the shopping plaza is not here today.

Sometimes the modified word is found in a prepositional phrase. Nevertheless, the rule remains the same.

I admire the type of *people who go* to midnight horror movies.

When *or* or *nor* separates two subjects, the number of the verb should agree with the number of the subject closest to it.

Jim *or* his *parents walk* and *feed* our dog when we are on vacation.

Either Eddie *or* his *sisters are* responsible for the debt.

Tomorrow is the anniversary of the day neither the unions *nor labor wants* to remember.

With indefinite pronouns such as *each, everyone, anybody, nobody, none, either,* and *neither* as subjects, use singular verbs.

Each of us *is* doing his or her share to clean up the air.

Anybody who *comes* late to a surprise party *is* inconsiderate.

Everyone has a vote.

Collective nouns such as *family, class, number, public,* and *orchestra* may be considered either singular or plural in a particular context. If the collective noun refers to the whole, a singular verb should be used.

The *committee votes* at noon.
   The *committee* is treated as a whole group who will vote together.

"The *public wants* more for its tax dollars than run-down and poorly staffed hospitals," said the president of the nurses' association.
   The *public* is one whole group who wants more.

However, if the collective noun emphasizes the parts of the whole, a plural verb should be used.

A *number* of my friends *have expressed* interest in joining the Peace Corps.
   The number is made up of several individuals, each expressing interest.

Half of the people in the afternoon crew *want* to work for overtime.
   The *half* is made up of several individuals, each wanting to work overtime.

Some words indicating quantities take singular verbs to show a lump sum and plural verbs to emphasize the individual units.

Fifty years of marriage *were* not easy.

Four blocks was not too far to walk.

Three hundred words is a short essay.

Four hundred words are on each page.

Sometimes an entire phrase is treated as a unit. When such phrases serve as a subject, they take singular verbs.

All men are created equal is a statement much in question.

Down and Out in Paris and London is a good book, but *Dubliners* is my favorite.

"The American people" is a common term in speeches.

When words end in *s*, they usually take plural verbs, but there are some special cases.

When a word ends in *ics*, apply a special test: ask yourself if the word in context describes a field of study. If it does, the verb is usually singular. Otherwise, it's plural.

Athletics is a required activity. *Athletics are* good for people.

Mathematics is hard for some people. My *mathematics are* incorrect.

Certain words such as *scissors, riches, pants,* or *hopes* are always considered as plural even though they seem to convey singular concepts.

These *pants do* not fit.

The *scissors are* in the drawer.

Some words ending in *s* take singular verbs.

The *news is* all happy.

Mumps is a childhood disease.

EXERCISES   A. In the following sentences, correct any errors in subject-verb agreement.
1. The buildings with red painted panels along their sides seems to fit an elementary school better than they fit a college.
2. If a pair of pants cost more than ten dollars, someone is making too much profit.
3. Nineteen of the windows in the house was blown out by the high winds.
4. The scissors has always been kept in one place, under a blanket, in the hallway closet.
5. If, as they say, there are not one place—much less two places—to stay in the town, then why is it called a tourist spot?
6. Neither Joseph nor the authorities knows why he speaks as he does.
7. Both the fishing and the skiing is excellent on Lake Isabella.
8. One among many are required to do extra work for no extra pay.
9. Either worldwide starvation of poor people or the redistribution of wealth are in store for us in the next thirty years.
10. The United States of America are a great place for people who have drive.
11. Because every one of the Bengals play as if his life depends on the game, I must conclude that the coach instills in his players a sense of competition and the knowledge of what it means to succeed.
12. The members of that group is so different from each other that I'm amazed to find them all still friendly.
13. People's style of talking is individualistic because no two people think alike.
14. Whether one person or a dozen people tells me to do something, I will refuse if I do not want to do it.
15. The mass media is not very responsible, surely not as responsible as the intellectuals are.

B. Correct any errors in subject-verb agreement found in the following sentences and state the rule that you apply to correct each error.
1. Either a refund or four new tires is in order for the customer whose new car had defective tires.

2. One of the many reasons a person should not suddenly undertake a strenuous program of exercise is that the heart cannot adjust to the excessive activity and must build up to it slowly.
3. There are a wealth of opportunities awaiting any adult who wishes to return to school.
4. The failure of the drug rehabilitation programs make current problems in the inner city seem even more difficult to overcome.
5. E.S.P. are, surprisingly enough, to be found in everyday experiences.
6. The depiction of ethnic groups on television shows are misleading.
7. It isn't easy to cook for six people who has different tastes from one another.
8. There are no reason a man and a woman cannot get along if they really try.
9. All the setbacks in a person's life adds up to nothing if that person succeeds at the one thing that matters to him or her.
10. On top of the dead man's dresser was found a woman's wedding ring, two tickets to a Ram's game, and a note addressed to Suzanne.
11. Near the train tracks live a group of tramps who survives on the heat of the sun and the food distributed by the mission on Main Street.
12. According to some sociologists, rivalry between gangs are expected and provide reinforcement of identity for urban youths.
13. White collar workers who use their heads to keep the "system" going are just as dehumanized as blue collar workers who are tied to the master slave relationship of assembly line work.
14. The only troublemaker in the group of children attending the concert is David.
15. The lack of concentration among poorly fed children are to be expected because their bodies cannot stop telling their minds how hungry they feel.
16. The delicate, restrained, and collected manner in which some women like to think of themselves are not in keeping with the sensibilities of today's liberated women.
17. The ability to understand and react to other people and their ideas are essential to personal happiness.
18. There are usually a combination of reasons for any war.

C. In the following paragraph, correct any subjects and verbs that do not agree.

Financial aids is not fairly given out to students whose parents are in certain income brackets. The government look at the money going into the homes of the students, but they fail to see how much of it must leave the homes because of special financial circumstances. A student with parents who earn over $10,000 a year may find it harder to get a job or a loan for school than will a student whose parents makes $7,000. I would seem that the parents who earn $10,000 have a lot more money than the ones earning only $7,000. But suppose that the family earning $10,000 supports a sick relative or has to pay for the college education of three children, whereas the family who earns $7,000 has only one child to support. If both students are applying for college, the $10,000 family is actually in worse financial condition to bear the burden of a college education.

D. When a sentence begins with the word *there,* what is the special rule for deciding if the verb is singular or plural? Write three sentences beginning with *there* and explain why the verbs you use are singular or plural.

E. Write four sentences that contain collective nouns as the subjects. What is the general rule for subject-verb agreement with collective nouns, and how does it apply to each sentence wrote?

F. Do you think that informal conversation should require strict adherence to rules of subject-verb agreement? Why or why not? Write a paragraph that explains your view and gives at least two examples of how the rules should be used in conversation.

G. Correct any errors in subject-verb agreement found in the following brief paragraph.

Descending from the sky high above, a sea gull swoop down for a piece of bread left on the ground by a sixth grader. Trees swaying left and right from the force of the north wind, flowers adding their sweet smell to the air, and children rushing to play on the swings also makes up this pleasant environment. These are just a few of the beautiful scenes one might see. Riding a bicycle is one of the best ways to feel and enjoy a lovely environment.

H. Which sentences below contain errors in subject-verb agreement? What caused the writer to make whatever errors you find?
  1. Even the best of people forget the social graces taught them in childhood.
  2. Either administrative priorities or concern for individuals seems to be the most important consideration of many of our current leaders.
  3. Neither I nor my neighbors are in a position to buy fencing, so their dog continues to run freely about my yard.
  4. Yesterday the neighbor's dog, along with another mangy stray I'd never noticed before, knocked over my trash cans; today I, with all my gumption, are in an argumentative mood.
  5. Pages of clean paper and a pencil are things I always seem to forget.

6. Strings tied in bows around index fingers is a clumsy and foolish technique for remembering something.
7. The first thing I was told was that the barracks are no place to keep private property.
8. Dickens, Melville, and Shakespeare, the greats of literature, are the writers I choose from when I want to enjoy a story.
9. The drivers who travels on our highways has a responsibility to drive safely.
10. The assembly were not clear whether one position or the other was best, so the vote was split.
11. Posters on walls are funny when they are inappropriate to the setting, when they are as out of place as Stan Laurel would be at a dieters' convention.
12. A pack of dogs don't have animosity toward each other unless food or mating are involved.
13. The alumni from this college is very successful.
14. Without being too harsh, I had to say that the kind of ideas he had were not those I'd care to share.
15. They sometimes play at those nightclubs in the area that gives them all the free food they want.

I. Write a paragraph that explains the main ideas of one of your beliefs. After you write the paragraph, underline all the verbs and circle their subjects. Are there any errors in agreement?

J. Circle all subjects and underline all verbs and correct any errors in agreement in the following paragraphs.

1. The American Dream of success supposedly held out the promise to all men that through industry, self-reliance, and individual talent the limitless vista of opportunity were theirs. Black men wanted to believe that this "good life" was promised to them, also. They felt that it was morally and legally owed to them. It might well have been said, however, that the American Dream was not for them. All the promises of the future seemed to pass them by. The real issues for black men was whether the American Dream included them or not.

2. Going to college are a waste of time and money according to a recent article appearing in *Psychology Today*. In this article, the author maintains that attending college is useless because it no longer guarantee the graduate good job opportunities. Furthermore, the educational benefits is minimal because the standardization of most programs don't help individuals learn all they should learn. Everybody study the same basic program, most learning just enough to get by. The emphasis is on getting a degree and not on the process of learning. College have become factories, turning out poor products that are not finding their way into the job market.

Check Your Predication

While checking your sentences for subject-verb agreement, make sure that the predicates of your sentences actually say something about their subjects. An equation is set up in sentences, especially when the simple predicate is a form of *to be*. It is easy to slip into the habit of faulty predication. The result is that your sentences do not say what you intended although, with a little trouble, the reader can sometimes untangle the mess. Look at the following sentence.

> Seven doctors on the staff of Rivers Hospital refused to use radiation to treat acne.

The predicate—*refused to use radiation to treat acne*—does say something about the subject—*seven doctors on the staff of Rivers Hospital*. The sentence is clear and correct. But now take a look at this sentence.

> Whatever the cause, the cure for bad behavior has to be patient, kind, and responsive.

The predicate—*has to be patient, kind, and responsive*—does not say something about the subject—*the cure for bad behavior*. How can a cure be patient or kind? The writer has lost sight of what the sentence was originally supposed to say. Patience can be attributed to a person or an animal, but not to a thing like a cure. Probably the writer means that *parents* need to be patient and kind in order to cure their children of bad behavior.

When you check the predicates of your sentences, you are really asking yourself, "What did I set out to say here, and what did I actually end up saying?" If you haven't said what you mean, you need to reword the sentence.

EXERCISE

Directions: Check each predicate in the sentences below, making sure that it says something about the subject. Make any necessary corrections by rewording sentences with faulty predication. Which sentences are made especially confusing by the faulty predication?

1. Love is patient and kind and never turns its back on its mate.
2. Fluorocarbons are a bad effect on our atmosphere because they decrease the ozone layer.
3. The life of a professional swimmer gets very little time off to relax.
4. The food served in most college snack bars is not a wide enough selection to satisfy discriminating eaters.
5. His restraint failed to answer the teacher's questions quickly enough.
6. A tragic man's mind must be a paradox, his pride must be strong, and his suffering must be without reason.
7. My roommate, Rosemary, was a prime example of wish fulfillment the other day.

8. Senator Price has been a man of many positions, including the power of secretary of state.
9. Friendship between men and women can be an uncomfortable role.
10. The drinks would be a small donation.
11. The Anglo ideal of beauty is fashion and femininity.
12. Since I was a child, the most disagreeable place for me was in the waiting room of a hospital.
13. Detachment was his ideal man in society.
14. Drugs are an escape from reality.
15. A comparison of the bike would be the car.
16. The child may interpret failure in class as lacking what most students have mentally.
17. The main function of a mixed bar is the transition from straight to gay and back to straight.
18. Conversations at a dance can range from gossip to pickups.
19. An early morning class is hard to get out of bed.
20. For the insecure person, the role of rebellion and its cause are a chance to find a place in the world and identity.

STEP TWO: ARE THERE ANY SENTENCE FRAGMENTS OR RUN-ON SENTENCES?

Fragments are incomplete sentences. The following are some common examples.

When we go shopping.

Being in the insurance business.

Of course.

How to Identify and Correct Fragments

Although they may have subjects and verbs, fragments are not complete thoughts that can stand alone. In most writing, they should be carefully avoided.

Look for Fragments

There are several patterns, phrases and clauses that begin with certain words, that writers tend to mistake for complete sentences. Once you familiarize yourself with these fragment patterns, you will be on your way to distinguishing incomplete sentences from complete ones. Then you can correct many of the fragments simply by incorporating them into adjacent sentences. Others will require, as you will see, converting the fragment into a complete sentence in its own right. First things first—let's take a look at some common fragment patterns.

Helping Verbs

A fragment can occur because a helping verb is needed to complete the main verb in a sentence. Check page 364 if you do not know the functions of helping verbs. The following is a list of helping verbs.

Am	Does	Were	Should be
Are	Had	Was	Will be
Can	Has	Will	Can be
Could	Have	Must	Might have been
Did	Is	Have been	

Of the following sentence pairs, one is complete and the other is a fragment. Looking at them closely, you will notice that the only difference between the two is the addition of a helping verb. The fragment (italicized) lacks the helping verb. In the complete sentence the helping verb is underlined.

1. *Jose counting the votes.* Jose <u>will be</u> counting the votes.
2. *The dogs barking because they feel hungry.* The dogs <u>are</u> barking because they feel hungry.
3. *Aunt Hilda gone to work early today.* Aunt Hilda <u>has</u> gone to work early today.

Words That Often Begin Fragments

A fragment may simply be a phrase, or it may be a clause. A clause, although it has both a subject and a verb, still may not be a complete thought. The following words often begin clauses that are fragments.

That   Who   To whom   Where   Whose

Of course, all sentences starting with these words are not fragments; the clause may be already connected to a main clause. When a clause beginning with the words just listed is connected to a main clause, the result is a complete sentence.

In each of the following examples, one sentence is only a clause that cannot stand on its own. The other sentence is a main clause. The clause beginning with *that, who, to whom, where,* or *whose* is italicized—it is a fragment that must depend on the main clause.

1. It was the Superintendent of Schools in the Lakeland District. *Who voted against the new program for school integration.*
2. The two girls were arrested at the Turkish border. *Where they were found to have in their possession fifty pounds of hashish.*
3. Americans who were able to escape Mexican prisons have exposed the truth. *That in Mexican jails physical abuse and substandard living conditions are the norm for those who are not willing to pay for a better life.*

More Words That Often Begin Fragments

Here is another group of words that often indicate fragments.

Because	As if	Though	If
Although	By	Even though	Unless
As	Since	In order to	So that

In each of the following examples, one sentence (italicized) is a fragment and could not stand alone. The other sentence is a main clause and could stand on its own. The fragment could be attached to the main clause to create one complete sentence.

1. Irene explained that she needed help with writing. *Because she had never studied grammar in high school.*

2. *Although she was tired of his excuses.* She listened to one last explanation.
3. You can come to dinner with us. *If you want to study for the psychohistory test too.*

Words Indicating Time and Place

Some fragments begin with certain words that indicate time and place.

Before	When	Whenever	While
After	Until	Wherever	

In the following examples, one sentence is a fragment beginning with a word that indicates time or place. The other is a main clause. The italicized fragment could be attached to the main clause to create one complete sentence.

1. *Before I knew that communists were considered "left wing."* I thought that they were at the far right.
2. She learned that her husband was blind in one eye. *After living with him for fourteen years.*
3. It is not rare to be in a room full of smokers. *Whenever you are in the waiting room of a doctor's office.*

PREPOSITIONAL PHRASES

Prepositional phrases are often mistaken for complete sentences. (See p. 367 for a list of prepositions.) Just think of how often this type of fragment appears in advertising.

In the following examples, the fragments are all prepositional phrases. Each fragment is italicized. Attached to the main clauses adjacent to them, they would be correct. They cannot, however, stand alone as complete sentences.

1. Felt tip pens are impractical. *For taking class notes.*
2. The three lost campers were found wandering in the woods. *Near Pike's Peak.*
3. *Between the unions' demands for better conditions and the employers' demands for greater productivity.* Very little change can occur.

PARTICIPLES

Verbals that act as adjectives often end in *ing*, *en*, and *ed*. As you recall, these verbals are called participles. A sentence having a participle but no verb is always a fragment.

In the following examples, the incomplete sentences begin with participles, and the phrases that contain the participles have no other verbs. These phrases (italicized) are, therefore, fragments. Connected to the main clauses that stand next to them, the participles would begin phrases that help to make up complete sentences. Still, you can see how incomplete the phrases are alone.

1. Late last night three girls saw two young men. *Running stark naked across campus.*
2. *Requiring so much discipline.* The freshman year at college is a difficult adjustment for many students right out of high school.
3. *Laden with bags of groceries.* She managed to make it to her front door.
4. *Called to jury duty.* I complained that it was a waste of time.
5. Three members of the collegiate basketball team found twenty dollar bills. *Hidden under the clothes in their lockers.*

INFINITIVES

If the only verb in a sentence is an infinitive with *to,* the sentence is a fragment. Infinitives cannot function as sentence verbs. Remember that all sentences must have both subjects and verbs. The fragment pattern beginning with an infinitive is easily recognized.

In the following examples, the fragments are introduced by infinitives. Each fragment is italicized. You will notice that there is no other verb form in the fragments. The fragments could be incorporated into the main clauses that come before or after them to make complete sentences. But as they stand you can see why the phrases beginning with infinitives are not complete sentences.

1. Ramos worked in a drug rehabilitation program. *To learn more about problems in the inner city.*
2. Ms. Corman tried to do her best. *To motivate her students, but with little effect.*
3. Returning to school after many years challenged my mother. *To define her present and to plan her future.*

APPOSITIVES

Appositives are words or groups of words that rename a noun. They are usually set off by commas. Take a look at the following sentence.

Jim Drugel, a baker at the Seventh Street Bakery, is coming to dinner.

The words *a baker at the Seventh Street Bakery* are an appositive renaming the noun *Jim Drugel.* An appositive used by itself is a fragment. Such fragments are particularly common when the appositive comes before or after the main clause containing the noun it renames.

In the following examples, appositives alone (italicized) are mistaken for complete sentences when, in fact, they are only fragments. Incorporating the appositives into main clauses would create complete sentences. But you can see that the appositives, as they stand, are incomplete.

1. My father gave Hilda a fascinating book for Christmas. *A study of Russian Jews who came to the United States during the 1920s.*
2. It is difficult to explain all the meaning Cesar Chavez holds for the Chicano people. *A group who had little to look forward to until he raised their pride and self-esteem.*
3. Since I constantly made long-distance telephone calls and got tired of feeding quarters to the black box on the wall, I decided to get my own telephone. *A convenience I have learned to regret.*

The types of fragments named in this section on "Looking for Fragments" are the most common. You may find others, too. However, if you can isolate all the fragments that fit the patterns discussed there, you are able to make great improvements in your writing. Up until now we have been looking at pairs of sentences so that the relationships between fragment patterns and main clauses could be shown. Now let's look at a paragraph from a student's paper. As you read along, try to identify the type of fragment pattern each of the italicized clauses and phrases represents. Also notice how the meaning of many of the fragments seems incomplete or confusing without the meaning of an adjacent main clause.

> A tarantula is an easy pet to get to know as long as you know how to handle one. Once your pet is settled in its new environment in your home and seems calm, move your hand slowly. *Across the line of vision.* If it remains calm, it is ready to be handled. If you are unsure of yourself or of your spider, you may feel better wearing close-fitting gloves. *Like a snake.* A tarantula cannot bite through cloth. Slowly try to put your hand into your spider's box. *In front of its head. Resting your hand there for a few minutes.* Gives the spider a chance to take the initiative and climb onto your hand. *If after a short time it hasn't moved toward you.* Reach over with one hand slowly. Pick it up. *Gently grasping the body of the spider and placing it in the palm of your hand. If it puts itself in a squatting position with its stomach making contact with your skin or gloves.* It is trying to bite. Its mouth is located on its stomach. If you find instead that it sits quietly, leave it for a minute, and then pet its back softly. *Whenever it acts jumpy.* Leave it alone for a few minutes. *To let it get better acquainted with his environment.* Once your spider will sit quietly. *In your hand.* You can do anything with it. The key words to remember are "calm," "careful," and "slow." *Which is how you should act with it.*

Correcting Fragments

There are two reliable ways to correct fragments. The best method to use depends on the particular sentences you are trying to correct.

The first method is to incorporate the fragment pattern into a main clause that comes before or after the fragment. This method often works very smoothly because in your own mind it is possible that many of the sentences you broke up into fragments and main clauses, when you put them down on paper, were actually linked. The result is a kind of postscript fragment, one that tags along with the idea just stated. No matter how the fragment became one, it is important to correct it. The combination of a main clause and one or more fragments makes one complete sentence. Once you have found a fragment, look at the closest main clauses that come before and after it. You may want to connect the fragment to one of these complete sentences, either at one end or at some appropriate point inside the sentence. Let's take a look at how the process works.

> Fragment: Like a snake
> Main Clause: A tarantula cannot bite through cloth.
> Complete Sentence: A tarantula, like a snake, cannot bite through cloth.

How about another?

> Main Clause: To June, a husband must be a perfect person.
> Fragment: Understanding in every way.
> Complete Sentence: To June, a husband must be a perfect person, understanding in every way.

Of course, each time you want to combine a fragment with a main clause, you must really think through what you are trying to say. What is the best possible way to get across what you mean? Haphazardly combining a fragment and main clause just because they seem related and are close to one another may cause you to write awkward, wordy, and even confusing sentences. Keep in mind that when you combine, you are combining ideas, not just words. You may need to change a word here and there to avoid repetition or add clarity. For instance, in the following combination the pronoun *he* is substituted for the name *Winston* in order to avoid repetition of the name.

> Main Clause: Winston tried his best in all sports, including baseball.
> Fragment: Which Winston had never played very well.
> Complete Sentence: Winston tried his best in all sports, including baseball, which he had never played very well.

The second method of correcting fragments is to remove the fragment pattern by changing a word or creating a complete subject and verb sequence. The point of these changes is to leave the sentence able to stand on its own. Perhaps this method is easiest for sentences lacking helping verbs.

> Fragment: Jim having a hard time with calculus but doing well in geology.
>
> Complete Sentence: Jim is having a hard time with calculus but is doing well in geology.

How about another kind of sentence fragment?

> Main Clause: Jinny knew she would be elected to serve as the chairperson of the finance committee.
>
> Fragment: Being the most experienced fundraiser in the group.
>
> Complete Sentence: Jinny knew she would be elected to serve as the chairperson of the finance committee. She was the most experienced fundraiser in the group.

Of course, the fragment could also be incorporated according to the first method: *Jinny, being the most experienced fundraiser in the group, knew she would be elected to serve as the chairperson of the finance committee.* In this group of sentences about Jinny, it was impossible to leave the two sentences and simply drop the fragment pattern "being"; you would not be left with a complete clear sentence since the result, *the most experienced fundraiser in the group*, is also a fragment. But adding a subject (*she*) and changing the participle to a verb (*being* to *was*) worked well. In other sentences dropping the key word in the fragment pattern is an easy way to make the fragment into a sentence in its own right.

> Main Clause: Everyone was surprised to hear the news.
>
> Fragment: That Bottleneck had been awarded the first prize.
>
> Complete Sentence: Everyone was surprised to hear the news. Bottleneck had been awarded the first prize.

Of course, a less wordy version would be *Everyone was surprised to learn that Bottleneck had been awarded the first prize*. The first method would have worked well here, too: *Everyone was surprised to learn the news that Bottleneck had been awarded the first prize*. The method you choose to correct fragments will be influenced by your personal writing style and the effectiveness of the possible combinations.

How to Detect and Correct Run-On Sentences

Run-on sentences are main clauses connected with a comma or simply run together without any punctuation. Instead, the sentences could be separated by a period and a capital letter. The following examples contain two main clauses incorrectly joined by commas.

> Making scrambled eggs is harder than most people think, it takes careful planning and a lot of concentration.

The kitchen in our new apartment was old and dingy, however, we have brightened it up with red-checked curtains and a new coat of paint.

The following example is a run-together type of run-on sentence, the kind containing two main clauses without any punctuation between them.

The sales personnel at Grandy's is very efficient they always know where to find the item a customer wants.

Two sentences may be closely linked in meaning. However, if each is a main clause, it generally must stand alone as a complete thought. Occasionally, however, you may find run-on sentences that are deliberately used for effect in a piece of writing. Generally, the main clauses are short and connected by commas. The point of connecting the sentences instead of leaving them separate is to show how one idea quickly leads to the next.

The stream gushed down the gulley, it whooshed through the fallen trees.

It is quite a different story to connect complete sentences unknowingly. Only experienced writers who can tell the difference between an effective run-on and an ineffective one should even try to use run-on sentences for effect. In most of your writing, you will want to avoid run-on sentences and stick to the more conventional structures instead.

Looking for Run-On Sentences

Many writers who tend to run their sentences together have trouble telling a correct sentence from a run-on. The most common way of trying to do it, reading their sentences aloud, often doesn't help because most readers normally pause for commas, just as they do for periods. As a result, a sentence that actually requires a period or semicolon may *sound* just fine when read with a comma. If you have a tendency to write run-on sentences, the best way to find them is to study your sentences carefully, one by one, after you have completed the first draft of a paper.

As you read through your paper, you can quickly eliminate any sentence that is a single main clause.

Today is hot.

You should also be able to bypass those sentences composed of two main clauses joined by a comma and a coordinating conjunction (*and, or, for, but, yet,* or *so*) or by a semicolon.

Today is hot, but last night was cool.

Today is hot; last night was cool.

You should then check the rest of your sentences one at a time, looking at them part by part. Let's use an example. Suppose you have the following sentence.

In the darkness, the two men saw the gunfighter, his face tensing with expectation.

Consider the first part, up to the comma. By itself, does this look like a complete sentence, or would it be a fragment? If it would be a fragment, place an *F* above it.

    F
In the darkness.

The second part of the sentence, which in this case is a main clause, would obviously be a complete sentence were it to appear alone. Therefore, put an *S* above it.

    S
the two men saw the gunfighter,

Now, what about the last part of the sentence? Since it has only an *ing* form of a verb and no actual verb, it is another fragment. Put an *F* above it also.

    F
his face tensing with expectation.

The final sentence should look like this.

    F   S   F
In the darkness, the two men saw the gunfighter, his face tensing with expectation.

Here are two more examples of sentences that have been analyzed using this procedure.

    F   S
When the swimming season is in full swing, there is hardly a spot to be found on a local beach.

    S   F
Harold, who is the most businesslike person I have ever met, keeps his room a mess.

Notice that in the second example, the subject and verb are split up by the fragment. When the subject and verb are united, the clause stands as a complete thought.

Each time you reach the end of a sentence, look back over it to check the combination of its parts. If the combination is a main clause with one or more fragments, the sentence is probably correct and complete. If the combination is two main clauses connected by a comma or having no punctuation, you have a run-on. All of the examples so far have been composed of a main clause plus a fragment. This combination is typical. Let's look at two more examples, one a correct sentence and one a run-on.

                             F
Correct: Whenever there is a gathering of students over some cause, there
             S   F
are bound to be those who call the protestors "dirty hippies."

         Fragments + Main Clause = Sentence

                        S
Run-on: People have little choice about what they pay for groceries, they
         S
just go shopping and pay the prices.

         Main Clause + Main Clause = Run-On

TRANSITIONAL EXPRESSION

One kind of run-on that occurs frequently is caused by the confusion of transitional expressions such as *however, consequently,* or *therefore* with coordinating conjunctions such as *and* or *but.* When preceded by commas, coordinating conjunctions can connect main clauses. Transitional expressions between main clauses, however, must be preceded by a semicolon, not a comma. They may also begin new sentences.

                   S   +   S
I cannot stay in town all day, nevertheless, it has been a pleasant afternoon.
A run-on sentence

                   S   +   S
I cannot stay in town all day; nevertheless, it has been a pleasant afternoon.
A correct sentence

                   S   +   S
I cannot stay in town all day. Nevertheless, it has been a pleasant afternoon.
Two correct sentences

The following list includes most of the common transitional expressions you should look for when checking for run-on sentences.

Therefore	Consequently	Indeed
However	For example	Still
Thus	Nevertheless	Of course
Instead	Besides	Next
For instance	Then	On the other hand

Some of the examples below are run-on sentences and some are correct. Note how the transitional word (italicized) comes between the two main clauses. The examples that are main clauses connected by commas or that are run together without punctuation are run-on sentences. The main clauses connected by semicolons or made into two separate sentences are correct.

                                              S   +

Apartment managers should not have the right to maintain adults-only

                                           S

buildings, *instead* they should screen all applicants equally.

A run-on sentence

                                S   +   S

Many fish are hard to see in the water, *for instance,* the brown trout hides itself among the rocks at the bottom of streams.

A run-on sentence

                                       S   +

The government should not treat minorities unfairly merely because they

                                                 S

have little power *nevertheless,* the rights of the majority must not be forgotten.

A run-together sentence

                                 S   +   F

There are no longer any heroes in baseball because baseball players have

                                                      +

become businessmen concerned only with money; *besides,* modern players

          S

are not as skillful as were the old-timers.

A correct sentence

                                           S   +   S

The president spent the afternoon with his cabinet. Then he took a walk on the White House lawn.

Two correct sentences

RELATED IDEAS

Many run-on sentences occur because a writer merges two related ideas improperly, not realizing that each idea forms a complete sentence on its own. In the following examples, some of the related ideas are joined correctly and some are joined incorrectly. Note that both halves of each sentence are main clauses, meaning that they should either stand alone as separate sentences or be joined with a semicolon. They should never be joined with a comma. The main clauses connected by commas are run-on sentences.

                                         F   +   S

In the early days of New England settlements, the life of Americans would

                                                   +

have been considered rough by modern standards, it was "rough" in more

                             S

than the sense that pioneers had no electric blankets, toasters, or televisions.

A run-on sentence

                                    S   +

Jobs that had been done by hand were taken over by machines, this revo-
                                                       S

lution drastically altered the life-styles of those Americans who lived in cities.

A run-on sentence

                                        S   +

Parents give up much of their own lives for their children; this is the way
                                   S

parenthood has always been and always will be.

A correct sentence

                                           S   +

The depiction of figures on Russian icons was a serious matter; the icon-
                                     S

ographers had very strict rules about the poses of figures and the surroundings used for each scene.

A correct sentence

                         F   +   S   +

In the schools of Peyrane, children are taught never to express their feel-
                          S

ings; they are told to keep what is inside them constantly under control

A correct sentence

Correcting Run-On Sentences

Once you have isolated the run-on sentences in the essay, there are several ways to correct them. For each method, a corrected version of the following run-on sentence is given.

There is a difference in the relationships.
Jeanie is your friend, Susan is only your neighbor.

1. Place a period at the end of one main clause and capitalize the first word of the second main clause.

    There is a difference in the relationships.
    Jeanie is your friend. Susan is only your neighbor.

2. Place a semicolon between the main clauses. Semicolons are not interchangeable with commas. In order to use a semicolon correctly, each main clause must be able to stand on its own as a complete sentence. The semicolon indicates a close connection between the two ideas.

    There is a difference in the relationships.
    Jeanie is your friend; Susan is only your neighbor.

3. Connect the two main clauses with a comma and a coordinating conjunction.

    There is a difference in the relationships.
    Jeanie is your friend, but Susan is only your neighbor.

4. Subordinate one of the main clauses. This can often be done by adding *because, since, while,* or some other subordinating conjunction (see p. 369). Notice that the subordinating conjunction makes the main clause it is added to a fragment, which can no longer stand alone as a separate sentence.

There is a difference in the relationships.
Although Jeanie is your friend, Susan is only your neighbor.

EXERCISES   A. Mark each sentence in the following pairs with an *F* for a fragment or an *S* for a main clause. Make any fragments into complete sentences.
1. The Puerto Rican is subjected to the unfortunate racial discriminations against two groups of people. Which he is often mistaken for, blacks and Chicanos.
2. Many students are so relieved to finish final exams that all they want to do is either go out and celebrate or fall into bed and sleep. Because finally the pressure on them has been lifted and there is a chance to breathe.
3. The Forest Service was formed due to concern over the devastation of forests. Because of the movement west, the railroads, and the timber industries.
4. Politics attracts people who desire power and popularity. Who at heart do not really care about serving the public.
5. Enhancing the parent-teenager relationship through better communication can help a great deal. In eliminating some of the reasons teenagers want to run away from home.
6. America wants the Supreme Court to maintain the principles our government operates on. Perceiving the court in idealistic terms.
7. People who plan to marry have to think about their future. Where they plan to live. Whether they will have children.
8. The feeling of alienation known to anyone who grows up on the streets. He or she just doesn't seem to fit in like other guests at a party.
9. In South Africa, blacks are refused many of the rights and freedoms of citizenship. Despite their being natives by birth.
10. The main concern of the Truman administration was to achieve a smooth transition from a wartime to a peacetime economy. With the immediate objective being to insure full employment.
11. Based on the careful observation of two distinct populations of sparrows. The study lasted for ten years.
12. In 1884, William LeBaron Jenney designed the first ten-story "skyscraper." The Home Insurance Company of Chicago.

13. *De facto* segregation occurs even in schools that have busing. Counteracting the value of busing and making it seem only an expensive worry to the taxpayer.
14. Due to the constant threat of urban renewal and other possible government projects. We are losing the sense of neighborhood that once united the community.
15. If I agree to protect you and you agree to protect me. We will not need police everywhere on campus.

B. In the following paragraph there are six sentence fragments. Find and correct them by writing the correct sentence on a piece of paper.

Do you think that any of the fragments is effective as a fragment? Which ones and why?

A runaway teenager can be symptomatic of deep family problems. Some parents, for instance, are overly intent on their children's success in school. Often, the children are under such pressure to get good grades that they do just the opposite. Fail. Failure in school is a way to get back at parents. The children cannot stand the parents' pressure. Nor the prospect of failure. Which makes them feel inferior to other students. One answer to the frustrations of either route is to avoid everything. To run away from what seems to be the source of the problem—home. Other family problems are apparent in the runaway who has been abused or neglected. Parents sometimes cannot cope with their own problems and may take them out on the children. Who at these times seem nothing but a burden to them. Perhaps deep inside they resent the children for limiting what they wanted to do in life. No matter what the reason is, the child who is abused over a period of years gets to the point where he or she can't take any more mistreatment or indifference. The child develops an emotional wound. That may never heal, one that seems especially painful when the parents are around. For many, the only answer to the problems of home is immediate.

C. Indicate which of the following sentences are run-on sentences. Give two possible ways of correcting each run-on.
1. We are arriving at the time when human beings will no longer have to be able to analyze, they will only have to learn to program computers.
2. This question is disturbing, will people survive all this industrialization?
3. My first unpleasant encounter with vending machines occurred during my freshman year of high school, I put in a quarter and nothing came out.
4. One major obstacle in changing from single sex to coed dorms is the fear that it might encourage a decline in students' morality, however several studies have shown this fear to be unjustified.

5. An important question must be asked, has technology caused people to lose their individuality?
6. Today more and more people are disregarding the need for marriage, many people are just living together.
7. There are two factors that help explain why so many young people begin to smoke, one is the desire to imitate adults and peers.
8. About one-half of all persons living in the United States die of arteriosclerosis, consequently, concerned physicians are recommending that adults minimize milk and dairy products in their diets.
9. It is people's nature to create, creativity comes from a desire to communicate.
10. The beginning of the scientific revolution occurred during the seventeenth century; for this reason the period is known as the "dawn of modern science."
11. Culture is not static, to cling to the ideas of the distant past does not preserve it.
12. Filling in the "personal questions" on my registration computer cards, I came to the question of race, as usual I checked the box marked "other."
13. The parent is the key to a child's development, that parent can mold the child into either a criminal or an angel.
14. One of Manet's most controversial paintings was banned in Solano until 1863. People thought its subject matter was immoral.
15. The young should not take jobs from the aged; the elderly may lack the physical energy and productiveness of youth, but they often offer more dedication and knowledge.
16. Many people conclude that those who speak a different dialect are less educated or less intelligent than themselves, this attitude is a product of ignorance.
17. Over-the-counter and prescription drugs are abused just as often as those drugs that are considered "dangerous," therefore even people who are not using illegal drugs may have a drug problem.
18. Gang members who leave the community may not have the chance to change their roles completely, back in the old neighborhood everyone remembers them as they were.

D. Correct any fragments or run-on sentences in the following paragraphs.
1. In starting your search for a job. You will probably want to rely more on personal contacts than on the classified section of a newspaper. Thousands of people begin by looking at the want ads; that is why the odds are against you right away.

There is too much competition. Seeking interviews through personal contacts; you will already have an "in." Whereas applying for jobs as a total stranger puts you in a more difficult position. Sometimes you can learn of possibilities while in your present job by speaking with other employees, they may have information about openings at other firms. Openings that may not even be advertised. Of course, you have to be discreet so you do not offend your present employer. Always remember that the more personal contacts you cultivate, the better chance you have of hearing about good opportunities.

2. Being considerate of one's spouse is a vital part of marriage, the awareness of each other's needs and feelings makes for a close relationship. Also helping in the raising of children. The opportunities to explain situations or problems and to settle them fairly become easier to find. The couple enjoy one another more than do people in relationships that are full of pent-up feelings. All people should try to be honest with their mates. Not an easy task but it can be done.

E. There are several fragments or run-on sentences in the following paragraph. Find and correct each of them.

Why do well-mannered house pets suddenly begin to chew pillows and upholstery, steal shoes, and wet the carpet? The problem may be physical, that possibility should always be considered. More likely, though, the problem is an emotional disturbance. A problem you should look into. There are certain things that might have happened, in such circumstances, what was going on in the house when the behavior first started? Did an unfamiliar visitor upset your house pets? For example, a strange pet in the house or a newly born child? Maybe a piling up of many events caused this bad behavior. Not necessarily one recognizable incident. Such as you moved, left your pets at a kennel, and then took them to a new home. Retraining pets will not work. If all you want to do is scold them. You should calm yourself down, try to understand their emotional environment, then you can attempt to get your pets to respond properly. Without doing things behind your back.

STEP THREE: ARE ALL YOUR VERBS AND VERBALS FORMED ACCURATELY?

Read through your paper once to check all verbs and verbals for accuracy and consistency.

Verbs

You will recall that verbs change their form to show tense and mood. Because the forms of verbs are so essential to communicating exactly what you mean, you will want to double check to make sure you have selected the most accurate tense and mood. Tense shows time. The interaction of verbs creates a sequence of time frames within each sentence and between sentences. Mood shows how close your meaning is to being a simple statement. The mood of a particular verb shows whether it makes a statement of assertion, sets forth an idea to ponder, or presents a condition or consequences. A more thorough discussion of the basics of verb forms is in Chapter 12. If you feel unfamiliar with the concepts of tense or mood, you will probably want to review the basics before you continue reading this section.

Use the Right Tense You should use the verb tenses that convey the exact meaning you want.

THE PERFECT TENSES

The perfect tenses are used to show the relationships of verbs in time. *The past perfect tense expresses an action that occurred before the action expressed by another verb in the past tense.* It uses the helping verb *had*. For instance, study the following sentence.

    The judge *asked* the defendant if he *had wanted* to confess.

There are two actions in the sentence: *asked* and *had wanted*. Which action occurred first? Using the past perfect tense shows that the wanting came first. It puts the verb *wanted* into its proper relation to the verb *asked*. Suppose this had been the sentence:

    The judge *had asked* the defendant if he *wanted* to confess.

Here, the sequence is reversed. Had the writer wanted both actions to occur at the same time, the past perfect tense would have been omitted.

    The judge *asked* the defendant if he *wanted* to confess.

Let's look at another example.

    Sarah had known Joe for two years before she realized he was a liar.

The two actions are *had known* and *realized*. Which happened first? She knew him and *then* she realized. The first action to occur is always the one placed in the perfect tense.

    The *present perfect* tense is used to express an action that occurred just before the present. It uses *have* or *has* as a helper. Here is an example.

    Although Sarah *has known* Joe for two years, she now *realizes* he is a liar.

Sarah realizes right now (present tense), after knowing Joe for a while (present perfect tense), that he is a liar. Observe the similar sequences in the following sentences.

    Unless the group *has* already *decided* otherwise, *we can* go to Florida for a vacation.

    Once he *has apologized* to her, she *wants* nothing more than to be his friend.

Another use of the present perfect tense is to indicate something that happens *up until now*. *Always* and *never* may serve as clues that *has* or *have* may be needed as a helper.

> Norbert has always been a tolerant individual.
>
> I never have drawn such a large check on my account.
>
> His life has been full of disappointments.

The future perfect tense is used to express the completion of some future action. The tense is formed by using *will have* along with the past participle of a verb. Take a look at the time expressed in the following sentence.

> By the time we will have graduated, there may be many more teaching jobs available.

Which is the action that already will have been completed? The clause *we will have graduated* expresses what will already have been done before *there may be many more teaching jobs available*. Here is another example.

> How many criminals *will have been* rehabilitated when they are released from prison?

Using the future perfect tense, the writer questions whether a completed action will have occurred (the rehabilitation) by the time another future action (release from prison) occurs. Thus, the future perfect tense tells the reader to look ahead to a time when a future action will have been completed.

USE OF *WOULD* TO EXPRESS THE FUTURE CONDITIONAL

If the verb is in the past tense and you want to express an action in the future, use the helper *would* with your verb.

> As a new employee, Pat understood that he *would* not *be* permitted to have keys to the locked jewelry cases.
>
> Linda Davett knew that she *would have* to act hurt in order to convince her employer to give her a raise.

DISCUSSING LITERATURE

The present tense is used to write about the actions that occur in literature. Although you may have read a particular book a month ago, and although it may have been written over two hundred years ago, the work is still considered to be alive. In a sense, it remains living forever. Consistency with the rest of your essay is most easily achieved if all discussion of the work is placed in the present. Below is a sample from a student's literary discussion. Note the careful attention to tenses.

In Henry V, Shakespeare portrays King Henry as an ideal Christian king. Through his every action, Henry rules according to the guidelines for a Christian king as set forth in Erasmus' Institutio Principis. When he is contemplating war on France, Henry checks with the Church to be sure England has the right to the French throne, and he proceeds to France only after being assured that England can remain safe in his absence. Once in France, he maintains his unspotted conduct, tolerating no abuse of the French or of their countryside. Henry judiciously hangs Bardolph and Nym for violating a French church.

Even when quoting passages written in the past tense, your own tenses should be in the present.

In "The Princess," by D. H. Lawrence, the descent from mountainous heights to cavernous depths becomes a journey into Dollie's unconscious. It is a descent that she, in the ebb and flow of her consciousness, is able to make when Romero unveils "some unrealized part of her wish which she never wished to realize."

Because it is part of a quotation, *wished* remains in the past tense while the rest of the discussion is in the present tense.

Make Tenses Consistent

Events that occur at the same time should be written about in the same tense. A common error, especially when telling about a sequence of events, is to slip back and forth between the past tense and the present. This error is demonstrated by the following passage from a student's essay.

I was walking down Laurel Canyon one day when a strange looking man crossed my path. He said, "Howdy," and I respond with a hello. But I am quite reserved and suspicious of his motives. What is this guy all about, I wonder. Then, before I can resist, he pushed me down on the sidewalk, grabbed my purse, and ran away. The whole incident changed my opinion of taking an afternoon stroll in my own neighborhood.

The writer first goes wrong in the middle of the second sentence. Up to that point, all the verbs have been in the past tense. *Respond* begins the use of the present tense but then, in the middle of the fifth sentence, the writer shifts back to the past tense with the word *pushed*. Since all of these events happened in a sequence, there is no reason to shift tenses. The writer probably wanted to use the present tense, as many story tellers do, to make the events sound immediate. This method would have been effective if it had been employed throughout the passage.

I am walking down Laurel Canyon one day when a strange looking man crosses my path. He says, "Howdy," and I respond with a hello. But I am quite reserved and suspicious of his motives. What is this guy all about, I wonder. Then, before I can resist, he pushes me down on the sidewalk, grabs my purse, and runs away. The whole incident changed my opinion of taking an afternoon stroll in my own neighborhood.

Of course, the passage could also have been written completely in the past tense.

Being consistent does not mean that you must always use the same tense throughout an essay, a paragraph, or even a sentence. Sometimes you will want to express two or more different time frames, and the only way to do so is to use different tenses. In many of these cases, you will also use the other words as clues to the various time frames in your sentences.

> Thirteen years ago he *embezzled* one hundred thousand dollars from the company, and now he *is asking* the same firm for a job.

Besides the verbs, there are two clues to time in this sentence. *Thirteen years ago* obviously refers to the past, and *now* just as obviously refers to the present.

> They *were* good friends a long time ago, but these days they never *speak* to one another.

In this sentence, there are again two clues in addition to the verbs. The past is indicated by *a long time ago*, and the present is indicated by *these days*. As helpful as these types of clues can be, they are not always present, nor are they always needed.

> I *used* to like mathematics, but the more I *study* the humanities, the more I *am* impressed with them.

Although this sentence includes no extra clues, the tenses of the verbs make the meaning clear.

Clear writing makes understandable connections between the time sequences. Because the reader can comprehend any time shifts built into the sentences and because each verb represents an accurate time frame, the writing is meaningful and still considered consistent when you shift tenses deliberately.

Use the Subjunctive Correctly

The subjunctive mood is used either to show conditions when they are contrary to fact or to show requests or demands.

CONDITIONS

A *conditional* statement is a sentence stating that something would happen *if* something else were to occur first. The conditional word *would* is used in one part of the sentence, and the subjunctive form of the verb is used in the other part. The subjunctive verb often follows the word *if*. Present tense subjunctives seem to give writers the most problems.

> If tea *were* as expensive as coffee, most Americans, a recent survey shows, *would select* coffee as their morning beverage. (Present.)
>
> If New Yorkers *had been* more prepared than they were for the 1977 blackout, they *would have suffered* less than they did. (Past.)
>
> *Were* we the referees, the Reds *would* not *have won,* since there was too much fouling at the free-throw line. (Past.)

Be careful, however, not to place would in both parts of the sentence.

> Incorrect: If he *would* have asked, he would have found out the answer.
>
> Correct: *Had* he *asked,* he *would* have found out the answer. (*If he had asked* is also correct.)

A statement including a subjunctive verb is often described as being *contrary to fact.* In the previous examples, for instance, tea is not as expensive as coffee, New Yorkers were not prepared, and *we* were not the referees. *Conditional statements that are not contrary to fact are not in the subjunctive mood,* even when the word *if* is used in the sentence. You should never substitute *would* for *will* or *can* in statements such as the following.

> If we take umbrellas, we will not care whether it rains.
>
> If we arrive at six-thirty, we can be on time for dinner.

REQUESTS OR DEMANDS

The subjunctive is used with requests or demands introduced by the word *that.* Regular uses of *that,* without the tone of demand or request, do not take the subjunctive.

> I saw a car *that* reminds me of yours.

The following sentences, which are requests or demands, do require the subjunctive.

> The airlines require that travelers *make* reservations thirty days in advance in order to get the reduced rates.
>
> I only ask that you *understand* the position I am in.

The subjunctive is also used for a few commands that are common expressions.

> Heaven *forbid.*
>
> Let it *be* known.
>
> God *bless* you.

FORM THE SUBJUNCTIVE CORRECTLY

For conditional statements that are contrary to fact, the present tense subjunctive for all verbs with the exception of *to be* is the same as the past tense of that verb.

If he *asked* me, I would feel flattered to accept the invitation.

The present tense subjunctive for requests or demands introduced by *that* for all verbs, including *to be,* is formed by using the infinitive without the *to.*

He only asks that I *act* with understanding.

He only asks that you *act* with understanding.

He only asks that she *act* with understanding.

He only asks that we *act* with understanding.

He only asks that they *act* with understanding.

The past tense of the subjunctive takes the same form as the past perfect tense.

Had he *asked* me, I would have accepted.

If he *had asked* me, I would have accepted.

The subjunctive forms of the verb *to be* are especially puzzling to many writers. In the present tense, *were* and *be* are used. With *if,* you should use *were.* Never use *was.*

If he *were* my friend, I would help his mother fix her car.

Be should be used with *that.*

I demand that he *be* fired.

In the past tense, the subjunctive form of *to be* is *had been.*

If I *had been* there, the accident would not have happened.
Had I *been* there, the accident would not have happened.

Form Irregular Verbs Correctly

Basically, *a verb is irregular if its past tense is not formed by simply adding d or ed.* Variations in forming the present participle, the *ing* form used with *is* or *was* as an adjective, and the past participle, used with *has, have,* or *had,* also make a verb irregular. Whenever you are unsure of the correct form for a particular verb, you should check in your dictionary. The listings for verbs always include the infinitive, the past tense, and the past participle. You can also refer to the following partial list of irregular verbs. It gives the correct forms for most of the troublesome verbs you are likely to run across.

COMMON IRREGULAR VERBS

INFINITIVE	PRESENT PARTICIPLE	PAST TENSE	PAST PARTICIPLE
Be	Being	Was, were	Been
Bear	Bearing	Bore	Borne
Beat	Beating	Beat	Beaten
Become	Becoming	Became	Become

INFINITIVE	PRESENT PARTICIPLE	PAST TENSE	PAST PARTICIPLE
Begin	Beginning	Began	Begun
Bend	Bending	Bent	Bent
Break	Breaking	Broke	Broken
Bring	Bringing	Brought	Brought
Build	Building	Built	Built
Burst (never bust)	Bursting	Burst	Burst
Choose	Choosing	Chose	Chosen
Cling	Clinging	Clung	Clung
Dive	Diving	Dived, dove	Dived
Do	Doing	Did	Done
Draw	Drawing	Drew	Drawn
Dream	Dreaming	Dreamed, dreamt	Dreamed, dreamt
Drink	Drinking	Drank	Drunk
Eat	Eating	Ate	Eaten
Fall	Falling	Fell	Fallen
Fling	Flinging	Flung	Flung
Fly	Flying	Flew	Flown
Freeze	Freezing	Froze	Frozen
Get	Getting	Got	Gotten, got
Give	Giving	Gave	Given
Go	Going	Went	Gone
Grow	Growing	Grew	Grown
Hang (on the wall)	Hanging	Hung	Hung
Have	Having	Had	Had
Keep	Keeping	Kept	Kept
Know	Knowing	Knew	Knew
Lay (to place)	Laying	Laid	Laid
Lead	Leading	Led	Led
Lie (to recline)	Lying	Lay	Lain
Make	Making	Made	Made
Put	Putting	Put	Put
Raise (to lift up)	Raising	Raised	Raised
Ride	Riding	Rode	Ridden
Ring	Ringing	Rang	Rung
Rise (to go up)	Rising	Rose	Risen
Run	Running	Ran	Run
Set	Setting	Set	Set
Sew	Sewing	Sewed	Sewed, sewn
Shine (to glow)	Shining	Shone	Shone
Shine (to polish)	Shining	Shined	Shined
Show	Showing	Showed	Shown
Shrink	Shrinking	Shrank, shrunk	Shrunk, shrunken

INFINITIVE	PRESENT PARTICIPLE	PAST TENSE	PAST PARTICIPLE
Sink	Sinking	Sank, sunk	Sunk, sunken
Sing	Singing	Sang	Sung
Sit	Sitting	Sat	Sat
Slay	Slaying	Slew	Slain
Speak	Speaking	Spoke	Spoken
Steal	Stealing	Stole	Stolen
Strive	Striving	Strove	Striven
Swim	Swimming	Swam	Swum
Take	Taking	Took	Taken
Wake	Waking	Waked, woke	Waked, woken
Wear	Wearing	Wore	Worn
Weave	Weaving	Wove	Woven
Weep	Weeping	Wept	Wept
Write	Writing	Wrote	Written

Special Problem Verbs

Are you always sure when to use *lay* and when to use *lie*? What about *set* or *sit*, *raised* or *rose*, and *hanged* or *hung*? These irregular verbs are often confused by writers, who use one when they mean the other.

LAY-LIE

Lay means to place.

> You *lay* down the glass.
>
> Yesterday, you *laid* down the glass.
>
> You *have laid* down the glass.

Notice that lay is always a transitive verb. Each time you use it, *lay* must have a direct object.

Lie means to recline.

> I *lie* down every afternoon.
>
> I *lay* down yesterday afternoon.
>
> I *have lain* down today already.
>
> *Lie* down right now.

The past tense of *lie* can be tricky. It is spelled the same as the present tense of *lay*. A good way not to mistake the two is to remember that *lie* is always intransitive. It *never* takes a direct object.

RAISE-RISE

Raise means to lift up.

> I *raise* my hand in class.
>
> I *raised* my hand in class yesterday.

I *have raised* my hand several times this week.

Raise is a transitive verb and always takes a direct object.
Rise means to go up or to get up.

The prices *rise* every week.

The prices *rose* last week.

The prices *have risen* constantly for a month now.

Rise is an intransitive verb and never takes a direct object.

Many things—prices, grades, people (she *rose* from her chair)—can either *rise* or *be raised*. The important clue is whether or not the verb takes a direct object.

SET-SIT

Set means to place or arrange.

The students *set* their books on the table every afternoon before they go to recess.

The children *set* the table for their mother.

Anyone who *has set* his or her hopes on becoming wealthy eventually becomes disenchanted.

Set is usually transitive and takes a direct object. The only exceptions are when it means "is situated" or makes reference to the sun.

The house *is set* high on a hill overlooking the city.

The sun *set* at 5:05 today.

Sit means to occupy a seat.

The people who work at the bank *sit* all day.

The student who *sat* in this chair last week is absent.

I *have sat* here long enough.

Sit is intransitive and never takes a direct object.

A common mistake is to write something like "It's so hot. Let's just set awhile." The correct form is *sit*.

HANGED-HUNG

The past tense of the verb to hang, meaning to execute, is hanged.

They *hanged* Tom Dooley.

The past tense of the verb to hang, meaning to put up on the wall or to attach to a line, is hung.

We *hung* out the wash yesterday because it was sunny.

Verbals Verbals function as parts of verbs (with helpers) and as other parts of speech: nouns, adjectives, and adverbs. They are not the verbs that distinguish main clauses, being in themselves only half-verbs. In fact, as you recall, any sentence having only a verbal and no other sentence verb is incomplete, a fragment (see p. 416). The verbals are infinitives, gerunds, and participles. Each verbal has tense and voice as the following table shows.

INFINITIVES

TENSE	PRESENT	PRESENT PERFECT	ONGOING PRESENT	ONGOING PRESENT PERFECT
Active Voice	to show	to have shown	to be showing	to have been shown
Passive Voice	to be shown	to have been shown		

GERUNDS AND PARTICIPLES

TENSE	PRESENT	PAST	PRESENT PERFECT	ONGOING PRESENT PERFECT
Active Voice	showing		have shown	having been shown
Passive Voice	being shown	shown (participles only)		having been shown

More information on the basics of verbals can be found in Chapter 12. You may wish to review that section before continuing to read the section at hand.

INFINITIVES

If the time expressed by the infinitive is not before the time expressed by the main verb, use the simple infinitive—*to go, to sew, to speak, to shun*—for all tenses of the main verb.

    I want *to know* when you're free for lunch.

    It has been nice *to meet* you.

    He needed *to say* what he felt

    We will need *to make* airline reservations before Sunday.

If the infinitive expresses a time *before* the time of the main verb, insert *have* after the *to* and use the past participle to form the infinitive.

    For them *to have begun* on time is unusual.

    We believed that they had *to have been* licensed physicians since they were listed in the phone book.

Often it is clearer to shift to main verb to another tense in order to keep the simple infinitive.

> It is nice *to have met* you.
>
> It has been nice *to meet* you.
>
> There is no reason *to have gone* to so much trouble.
>
> There was no reason *to go* to so much trouble.

VERBALS ENDING IN *ing*: GERUNDS AND PARTICIPLES

If the time expressed by the verbal is not before the time expressed by the main verb, use the simple verbal, no matter what the tense of the main verb is.

> *Needing* attention from everyone around him is Norman's problem, not mine.
>
> *Knowing* that Marvin would be pleased, his wife chose a simple gray dress to wear to his parents' house.

If the action of the verbal expresses a time before that of the main verb, use *having* plus the past participle to form the verbal.

> *Having worked* for a lawyer for the past two years was not enough to get Lydia a position on the District Attorney's staff.
>
> *Having known* David for five years, Marcia could guess what he would say on most subjects.

VERBALS ENDING IN *ed, t,* OR *n* PARTICIPLES

If the participle follows a linking verb (is, are, was, were, seem, seems, appear, appears, become, becomes, etc.), the past participle is used. You will recall that complements after linking verbs often act as adjectives that describe the subject of the clause. In such constructions, the participle, not the infinitive without the *to*, is used.

> Ineffective: He is *prejudice* against tall people.
>
> Effective: He is *prejudiced* against tall people.
>
> Ineffective: He is *use* to being successful.
>
> Effective: He is *used* to being successful.

Similar guidelines might be set up for verbs with forms of *be* or *have* as helpers. Even though the past participle ending is often hard to hear in speaking the words, the *be* or *have* helper must be joined by the verb with its *ed, en, t,* or *n* ending if the simple predicate is to be formed properly. Do not use the infinitive without *to* instead.

> Ineffective: She *has listen* to this recording before.
>
> Effective: She *has listened* to this recording before.

Ineffective: The canvas *is wash* and laid out to dry.

Effective: The canvas *is washed* and laid out to dry.

Even without the helping verb, a participle (a verbal used as an adjective) often takes the *ed, en, t,* or *n* ending.

Ineffective: *Stretch* out on the couch, Bob fell asleep.

Effective: *Stretched* out on the couch, Bob fell asleep.

Ineffective: *Bias* in favor of the team, Jill expected them to win.

Effective: *Biased* in favor of the team, JIll expected them to win.

EXERCISES A. Correct any errors in the tenses of the verbs found in the following sentences.
1. Traveling in a car brings me closer to scenery and is better for distinguishing details, but the plane gave me a new perspective of the landscape.
2. I always had a negative view of my marriage, but yesterday my encounter group made me realize how much my marriage really means to me.
3. I develop a fear of writing what I think, so I wrote what I thought my teacher wanted to hear.
4. Every night I turn on my television to hear the news, and every night I heard the same thing with only the names and the statistics slightly changed.
5. It was not until Ricardo telephone me to say he learned of my mother's remarriage that I really had to tell anyone my feelings about the event.
6. Many Americans are so disgusted with politics that they wanted to never vote again.
7. Living in the city all my life, I didn't have the opportunity to see many of the country's natural wonders.
8. In the novel, the minister suddenly decides early in his career that there is no supernatural being, so he left the church.
9. This community is integrated. It was integrated for as long as I can remember.
10. Admitting his tendency to get angry at the smallest disturbance, my father told my boyfriend Charles that he was not welcome in our house because Charles had slammed the front door.
11. The most embarrassing moment I can remember is the time I planned a meeting for the Student Committee on Equality and forget to attend.
12. Before I told my parents the truth, I had hoped they would discover it by themselves.

13. A big problem in the last presidential election is voter apathy.
14. Up until this year, I played on the women's volleyball team and served as manager for the men's track team, but now I must quit and concentrate more on my studies.
15. As the over-the-counter drug industry grows, so did our reliance on it; we began to take nonprescription pills for the slightest discomfort, telling ourselves that they can't harm us since they are weak enough to get without prescriptions.

B. Identify the tense of each underlined verb and check its accuracy.
1. It has always been difficult for me to speak with strangers.
2. Although the term "senior citizen" somehow did not seem appropriate to me, I prefer it to "old man."
3. Before I knew a real actor, I think their lives were charmed.
4. Last on my list of chores for today was washing the windows of my room.
5. The high cost of food has practically assured malnutrition for the nation's poor.
6. Racial and ethnic jokes can promote stereotyped thinking.
7. Platonic friendships between the sexes can be more fulfilling than friendships between members of the same sex.
8. In <u>Lady Chatterley's Lover</u> Connie's values conflict with the values of most aristocrats, yet her relationships with others seem to be healthy.
9. The conquest of Mexico was accomplished by Spaniards from many different social classes.
10. Unless the legislature does decide to give the residents in our area a tax break, many will have been forced to sell their homes.

C. Correct the verbs that have inaccurate endings or confusing shifts in tense.
1. When students look back at all the years they spend in high school, they sometimes wonder why they learn so much faster in college.
2. I wanted to have understood everything we studied by the time I took the examination, so I got a tutor.
3. During my years as a student, art classes were always a relaxing way to end the otherwise hectic days.
4. If the three of us had more sense, we would have shopped around for a place to live instead of taking the first apartment we saw.
5. The state capital was where I had to sent the letter for my teaching credentials.
6. Unless I am marry, I will remain in a "single's only" apartment complex because it offers enjoyable activities and facilities.

7. In our culture, there is a constant battle between the sexes for who gets the upper hand. Neither men nor women can be happy as long as they have allowed this battle to continue.
8. At first glance, this group of college students may seem to have nothing in common. One was from as far away as Egypt or Iran, and another could be from the all-American San Fernando Valley. Some spoke in foreign tongues, and others speak in English.
9. Restrictive policies against ethnic minorities have been illegal for a long time and should be, but the law could not stop private clubs from skirting the issue through cleverly worded phrases on contracts and brochures.
10. A common type of date is the "joking session." I found this type of constant teasing and kidding very frustrating because it gets nowhere. All the fooling around makes it impossible to have an honest conversation or get to know each other.

D. Correct any tense errors in the following paragraphs.

The other day, when my sisters and I were in a department store looking for a gift for my mother, we discovered how it feels to be subjected to racial prejudice. After a long search, we finally found what we thought would be a nice present. Then we went to stand in line to pay for it. The line seems especially long, and forty-five minutes pass before we reach the cashier. As we stand in line, we happen to notice how nice and pleasant the cashier is to all the customers. She always smiles and offers a friendly hello to each one. I finally get up to the counter and placed the present on it. I said hello to the cashier, but she did not answer. At first I thought she did not hear me. I want an answer, so I waited a minute until I got her attention and repeat my hello. Still she doesn't answer. In fact, she looked and yelled, "Is there anyone else?" It was as if I did not exist. I tried to show her that I was next, but she continued to ignore me.

The realization of the clerk's motives made me so hurt and angry that I knew I had to insist. When I still did not get service, my sisters moved to another line, but I stayed put. Finally, after helping a few customers who had been behind me, the clerk turned to me impatiently and said, "Yes?" I looked her straight in the eye and smiled. Somehow, I expected my insistence to feel more rewarding than it did, and I still wish I had the nerve to give that woman a piece of my mind.

E. Identify which of the conditional statements below are contrary to fact and require the subjunctive.
1. If I were a Martian, I would find the marriage ceremony on Earth a very strange celebration.
2. If two and two are four, what is two squared?
3. Were you a patron in the days of the Renaissance, what type of art would you support?

4. If young ghetto children want to succeed, they have to overcome their fear of failure.
5. If a man and a woman are compatible, they still are not necessarily in love and should think twice before getting married.
6. Television would be better if the shows were about people like you and me and not about stereotyped characters.
7. The need for relaxation away from the pressures of the office would be less apparent if a shorter work week were the rule instead of the exception.
8. What is the safest method to use if you have to jump from the sixth floor of a burning building?
9. I thought I would make my demands only if my boss did not offer me a big raise.
10. When times are difficult, I always say to myself, "You are really lucky. What if you were in a situation like Jim's or Mary's?" I always pick a situation that is much worse than my own, so I don't feel so bad.

F. Correct any errors in the use of the subjunctive in the following sentences.
1. If I were in his situation, not wanting to insult an important client but feeling unable to accept a valuable gift, I would simply explain my policy about such matters.
2. The coach asks that all members of the track team work out every day if they are serious about running.
3. If it were Molly who just telephoned, we can leave now.
4. His attitude that all men be equal is admirable, but he doesn't practice what he preaches.
5. If we are supposed to be your best friends, why must you ask that we leave?
6. Students who attend a college near home often want to stay close to their parents.
7. If interracial marriages were more accepted in our society, there is no doubt that I would date members of other races.
8. If I would always have all the money I would need, my values would be less developed than they are now.
9. Were the voters to demand an explanation for our President's actions with regard to foreign policy, the country would be in a lot better shape today.
10. When Jeffrey Thomas was three years old, his mother taught him how to read, and now, in third grade, Jeffrey has an eighth-grade reading level.

G. Correct any mistakes in verb usage in the following sentences.
1. Before long it became apparent that everyone at the party had drank more than anyone who wants to drive home should.
2. The self-hypnosis class offered by Balley College begin last Thursday in Bunglow 32, and the turnout was enormous.

3. The crew should have took the day off if the weather report said it would rain.
4. Despite studies that have show a trend toward equality in the distribution of family income, we still have many people who are poor.
5. A machine can get things did faster than a person can.
6. We have build entire cities that could not function without the automobile.
7. My roommate's telephone had just rang when someone knocked at our door.
8. My sister wrote a long letter to the Hilton Hotel in which she complimented their services, but few people ever do this kind of thing.
9. Whenever I really need to lay down, my eyes begin to feel heavy.
10. Knowing that most species had flew south already, we wondered what a little bluebird was doing on our snow covered lawn.
11. They hanged criminals in France in those days for the same things we fine people for today.

H. In the following paragraph, identify all the irregular verbs and tell the tense of each.

After completing our swimming drills, we swam back to shore, shook the water from our bodies in the cold morning air, and set out to find waters more suited for skin diving. During the short drive to the other shore, the sun shone brightly and the temperature rose. By the time we found a good place, the day had become lovely. I looked across the glistening lagoon at the many sailing boats, and I prepared to dive.

STEP FOUR: DO ALL YOUR PRONOUNS FIT THEIR REFERENCES AND FUNCTIONS?

The fourth time you sift through your paper, if you're using the first plan, you should concentrate on the pronouns. For each one you find, ask yourself the following questions.

Have I used the proper *case*?

Is the pronoun's *reference* obvious?

Does the pronoun *agree* with its reference?

Checking these areas will insure that every pronoun does exactly what you want it to. For a review of pronouns, see Chapter 12.

Case *The case of a pronoun is determined by the way it is used in a sentence.* There are three cases—subjective, objective, and possessive. Each one has its own group of pronouns.

SUBJECTIVE PRONOUNS

A pronoun that acts as the subject of the verb or as a subject complement

(except for possessive pronouns like *his, hers,* and *ours*) *is in the subjective case.*
The following is a list of the subjective pronouns.

I	We
You	You
He, she, it	They

The following sentences include subjective pronouns used correctly.

He and *I* are best friends.
  He and *I* are the subjects of the sentence.
They asked the minister for advice.
  They is the subject of the sentence.
It is *she* who borrowed my typewriter.
  She is the subject complement.
If I were *he*, *I*'d be honest about the situation.
  He is the subject complement. *I* is the subject of the main clause.

In informal writing and speaking, the use of the subjective pronoun for the subject complement is no longer popular. For instance, in the last sentence, most people would use *him*, not *he*. If you were to answer the telephone, would you say "This is me"? Or would you say "This is I"? Usage seems to call for the *me*, even though strict grammarians say it should be *I*. In formal assignments, it is best to stick to the subjective case of the pronoun.

OBJECTIVE PRONOUNS

A pronoun that serves as the direct or indirect object of a verb or as the object of a preposition is in the objective case. The object of a preposition, you will remember, is the end word or words of a prepositional phrase. Here is a list of objective pronouns.

Me	Us
You	You
Him, her, it	Them

Learning about the objective case can help you with some very common problems. For instance, many writers have trouble deciding whether to use *I* or *me* in the phrase *between you and me*. *Between* is a preposition, so the final word in the phrase is the object of a preposition. As you have just seen, the object of a preposition is always in the objective case. Therefore, *me* is the pronoun that should be used. You might also find it interesting to note that *you* and *it* can be used in both the objective and the subjective cases.

In the following sentences, the underlined pronouns are all in the objective case.

Mr. Brown gave John and _me_ the highest grades in all of his intermediate Spanish classes.
  _Me_ is one of the indirect objects.

The solution to the problem I had been thinking about for days finally struck _me_.
  _Me_ is the direct object.

My father lent Joe and _her_ the car for the evening.
  Her is an indirect object.

The police officer told _them_ which traffic laws were and were not enforced.
  Them is the indirect object.

Campus security officers explained the misunderstanding to _us_ students.
  _Us_ modifies the object of the preposition to.

To Joe and _her_, nothing could be more pleasant than a quiet evening at home.
  Her is one of the objects of the preposition.

POSSESSIVE PRONOUNS

A pronoun that shows ownership or that modifies a word ending in _ing_ is in the _possessive case_. The following is a list of possessive pronouns.

My, mine	Our, ours
Your, yours	Your, yours
His, her, hers, its	Their, theirs

Notice that possessive pronouns do not have apostrophes. Apostrophes are unnecessary since the words are possessive to begin with.

All of the possessive pronouns in the following sentences are underlined.

The book is _ours_.
  The pronoun _ours_ shows ownership. Therefore, even though it is a subject complement, it is possessive.

Your studying late may disturb your roommate.
  It is _your_ studying, not you studying, that might be disturbing.

His ability to win tennis matches arouses envy in us all.

Their constant nagging about the money they lent me makes we want to scream.

Our knowing Bill influenced the company's decision to hire him.

In sentences such as the following, however, you should not use possessive pronouns.

I could hardly stand to watch _you_ fawning all over the professor.
  It was _you_ that the writer could hardly stand to watch, not the fawning.

We wanted to see _him_ doing his act at the Bitters Box.
  They wanted to see _him_, not the doing of the act.

Special Problem Pronouns

WHO AND WHOM

Many writers have problems when trying to decide whether to use *who* or *whom* in a sentence. Knowing the following rules can help you to avoid this difficulty in your own writing.

Who is a subjective pronoun. It should be used as the subject of a verb. The same rule applies to *whoever*.

> *Who* asked President Carter if he really believed in the Equal Rights Amendment?
> *Who* is the subject of the verb *asked*.

> *Who* is it?
> *Who* is the subject of the verb *is*.

Whom is an objective pronoun. It should be used as a direct or indirect object of a verb or as the object of a preposition. The same rule applies to *whomever*.

> He is the person with *whom* Dr. Sabin travels.
> *Whom* is part of the object of the preposition *with*.

> *Whom* did you speak with?
> *Whom* is again the object of the preposition *with*.

Who and *whom* or *whoever* and *whomever* can also cause what may appear to be another type of problem. Take a look at the following sentence.

> You may give a check to *whoever* needs the money.

At first glance, you might think that *whomever* should be used because the pronoun seems to be the object of the preposition *to*. Notice, however, that there is a verb following the pronoun. Every verb must have a subject. Therefore, *whoever* has to be the subject of the verb *needs*, and the entire clause, *whoever needs the money*, acts as the object of the preposition *to*. As you can see, situations such as this may be a bit more difficult to figure out, but the rules still apply.

WHOSE

Whose is a possessive pronoun.

> *Whose* handwriting is this?

Be careful not to confuse *whose* with *who's*. *Who's* is the contraction for *who is*.

REFLEXIVES AND INTENSIFIERS

A reflexive pronoun is an objective pronoun that renames the subject of the clause. A list of reflexives follows:

Myself　　　　　　　　　　　Ourselves
Yourself　　　　　　　　　　 Yourselves
Himself, herself, itself　　　　Themselves

Note that there are not such words as *ourself, themself, theirself,* or *theirselves*. Correct formation of words that end with *self* or *selves* requires that both halves of the word be either singular or plural.

Singular	+	Singular	=	Singular
him	+	self	=	himself
Plural	+	Plural	=	Plural
them	+	selves	=	themselves

Reflexives should never be used as the subject of a sentence. They never, in the subject position, make the writer seem polite or modest. If you slip into putting a reflexive into a subject position, your sentence can easily be corrected by replacing the reflexive with a subject pronoun.

Incorrect: *Joseph and myself* have done our art project together.

Correct: *Joseph and I* have done our art project together.

Incorrect: It was *myself and Judy* who were responsible.

Correct: It was *Judy and I* who were responsible.
　　　　　or
　　　Judy and I were responsible.

Reflexives should only be used if the subject of the clause is the same as the object. Otherwise, substitute the correct objective pronoun.

Incorrect: I was surprised that they voted for *myself* on both occasions.

Correct: I was surprised that they voted for *me* on both occasions.
　　　　　They is the subject of the clause. The object *me* does not refer to the same person.

Incorrect: We knew *us* better than anybody did.

Correct: We knew *ourselves* better than anybody did.
　　　　　We is the subject of the clause. The object *ourselves* refers to the same people.

Incorrect: I asked them to give their donations to Henry or *myself*.

Correct: I asked them to give their donations to Henry or *me*.
　　　　　The object, *Henry or me*, is not identical to the subject of the clause; *I* is the subject of the clause, not *Henry and I*.

Try not to confuse the functions of reflexives with the functions of intensifiers, which look exactly like them. An intensive pronoun emphasizes the word it reflects, whether the word is a subject or object in the sentence.

Correct: The Pope *himself* will speak on television this evening.

Note that there is no such word as *hiself* or *hisself*. The word is *himself*.

Correct: I want to write this essay *myself*.

Reference Personal, possessive, relative, and demonstrative pronouns all stand for nouns or other pronouns. The word that a pronoun stands for is called the pronoun reference. Just what this word is should always be clear to your reader. As you check over your paper, make sure that the reference for every pronoun that needs one is easy to find.

Look at the following sentence.

They tell us that the solar system is several billion years old.

How many times have you said something like this, only to be asked, "Who is they?" You were asked this question because you had not provided a pronoun reference. In your writing, take extra care not to make the same mistake. Try to ensure that all of your pronoun references are obvious, whether they refer to a noun or to another pronoun. Most of your pronouns should appear in the same sentence as their reference or in the one immediately following. Even the clearest reference should never be separated from the pronoun by more than two or three sentences. If you find that you have used a number of pronouns in a row, it is probably time to repeat the reference. Also, when you use two or more pronouns having different references, make sure that it is clear which reference belongs to which pronoun. Finally, you should avoid starting a paragraph with a pronoun. References are hard to carry from paragraph to paragraph.

In the following sentences, the pronouns that require references and the words that they refer to are both italicized.

People who smoke should make sure that *their* smoking does not bother others.

Frozen yogurt *parlors* are currently making huge profits because *their* product is rare and *they* can charge high prices.

Everyone who had intended to go to the concert should return *his* or *her* ticket for a refund.

Most private *colleges* in the United States are restructuring *their programs* to make *them* more responsive to the needs of today.

Sentences having pronouns with no references may sound correct, but often they do not communicate exactly what the writer intends.

Ineffective: In restaurants I often order fish dinners, but sometimes I wonder whether *it* is fresh.

The writer wants *it* to refer to *fish*. Fish, however, serves as an adjective in this sentence. Since pronouns should refer to nouns or other pronouns, the sentence would work better if expressed in either of the following ways.

Effective: In restaurants I often order fish dinners, but sometimes I wonder whether the fish is fresh.

Effective: In restaurants I often order fish for dinner, but sometimes I wonder whether it is fresh.

Here is another example:

Ineffective: Robert's arms were a mess of grease and suds by the time *he* finished cleaning the oven.

The writer wants *he* to refer to *Robert*. But in this sentence, the word *Robert's* acts to describe *arms*. The word Robert is not even in the sentence. The word *Robert's* is there, but it would be imprecise if it were used to replace *he*. The writer could correct the sentence easily in either of the following ways.

Effective: Robert's arms were a mess of grease and suds by the time Robert finished cleaning the oven.

Effective: By the time Robert finished cleaning the oven, his arms were a mess of grease and suds.

CONFUSING REFERENCE

In some sentences, it is difficult to tell to which reference a pronoun refers. Even if the meaning can be figured out from the context, it is best to avoid any possibility of confusing your reader. If a pronoun can possibly refer to more than one noun or pronoun, you should repeat the reference or reword the sentence rather than leave the sentence ambiguous. Let's look at an example.

Candy and Joyce talked for a long time about the trip *she* was planning to take.

Who was planning to take a trip? Was it Candy, Joyce, or maybe even someone else? The way the sentence is worded, these questions cannot be answered. Repeating the appropriate name, however, makes the sentence clear.

Candy and Joyce talked for a long time about the trip Candy was planning to take.

References for pronouns should be explicit whenever possible. The pronouns *that, which, it*, and *this* are often used to refer to a complete statement that precedes them. The result of this practice is that sometimes the connection between the pronoun and its reference is too subtle. Some statements are perfectly clear, and you can use one of these pronouns to refer to them. Others, especially those that contain other nouns that could be possible references, are confusing. Let's take a look at a few examples.

Effective: Human beings reason. *This* is the difference between them and other animals.

Ineffective: My brother always has liked reading, but I am different. *This* annoys me.

What annoys the person in the second example? Is it that his brother likes to read, is it reading itself, or is it that he and his brother are different and that is the source of annoyance? The *this* does not specify. How about another example?

    Ineffective: We often go for a drive in the city late at night. *It* is so interesting.

What exactly is interesting? The late hour? The city? The whole idea—going for a drive in the city late at night? The *it* confuses the reader.

The best solution to avoiding ambiguity is to try, as often as possible, to use clear, distinct references. Whenever you want to use a *this*, a *which*, an *it*, or a *that* to stand for an entire preceding statement, be prepared to defend the usage on the grounds of absolute clarity, or recast the sentence as did the writer of the following sentences.

    Original Sentences: Many artists' work is so entwined with values that there is no separation between the artists' life and their work. *This* almost makes art into a religion.

    Recast Sentences: Many artists' work is so entwined with values that there is no separation between the artists' life and their work. *This intense involvement* with their artwork almost makes art into a religion.

    Original Sentences: Last week my friend won a raffle with a $1000 prize. *It* has changed his attitude about entering contests.

    Recast Sentences: Last week my friend won a raffle with a $1000 prize. *This stroke of luck* has changed his attitude about entering contests.

Agreement   In your writing, you should make sure that every pronoun agrees with its reference. *Agreement simply means that a pronoun and the word it stands for have the same gender, number, and person.* The following sentences are all examples of correct pronoun agreement.

Anita was upset with *her* mother.
    Her is correct because it is a feminine singular third person pronoun and therefore agrees with *Anita*.

You should receive *your* grades tomorrow.
    Your is correct because it is a second person pronoun and therefore agrees with *you*. It is impossible to tell whether *you* is singular or plural from its form alone. Context provides the number of the reference.

Everybody has *his or her* own way of telling a story, and the same story told by two separate people will seem very different.
    His or her is correct because it is a singular third person pronoun and therefore agrees with *everybody*. Note that the expression *his or her* indicates no gender, and its use avoids the sexist connotations of using only *his*.

The *chickens* ran around in the yard, never knowing that any minute the butcher would chop off *their* heads.

Their is correct because it is a plural third person pronoun and therefore agrees with *chickens*.

Many of the errors in pronoun agreement (and in reference) are simply caused by writers' becoming too rushed to pay enough attention to what they are putting on paper. These errors are usually very easy to find and correct when you look specifically for them. There are a few specific areas, in fact, that you will want to watch for because problems in agreement seem to occur there with some frequency.

EITHER . . . OR AND NEITHER . . . NOR

When *either . . . or* or *neither . . . nor* serves to connect the words that are references for a pronoun, use the noun or pronoun closest to the verb of the sentence to determine the number of the pronoun. The following sentences are correct.

> Neither Ms. Karr nor her *students* could simply explain *their* school's policies on attendance.
> *Their* is correct because it is a plural third person pronoun that agrees with *students*.

EACH

Use the singular pronoun to refer to *each*.

> *Each* of the members of the class has completed *his or her* assignment.
> *His* or *her* is correct because it is a singular third person pronoun that agrees with *each*. See page 177 for a discussion on how to avoid sexist language.

EVERYONE, EVERYBODY, NOBODY, ANYONE

Use the singular pronoun to refer to *one, everyone, everybody, nobody, no one, anybody, anyone, somebody,* and *someone*. The word *one* or *body* contained within each word is the indication that references to these words should, as much as possible, retain the singular meaning. In current informal usage, people often ignore the rule, preferring the plural *their* or *they*; the main point of avoiding the singular in speaking is to avoid sexist language. But the use of the singular expression *his or her* or the avoidance of singular concepts such as those expressed by *someone* and *anybody* are desirable alternatives to mixing plural pronouns with singular references. The sentences below illustrate informal and formal usage.

> Informal: *Everybody* believes that *they* have the right answers.
> Informal: *Everybody* believes that *he or she* has the right answers.
> Formal: *Everybody* believes that *he or she* has the right answers.
> Formal: *Everybody* believes that *he* has the right answers.

If the meaning you are trying to convey is clearly plural and could not be singular, the plural pronoun is appropriate.

> Formal: *Everybody* thanked me for the gift, which meant so much to *them*. (Clearly not singular.)

A PERSON

Use the singular to refer to the word *person*. The sentences below are formal and correct.

> A *person* should investigate for *himself or herself* what jobs seem most rewarding.
>
> or
>
> *People* should investigate for *themselves* what jobs seem most rewarding.

COLLECTIVE NOUNS

Use the singular to refer to a collective noun treated as one whole unit and the plural to refer to a collective noun emphasizing the separate but many individuals that make up the unit. The sentences below are correct.

> The *team* plays *its* best when feeling confident.
> *Its* is correct because it is a third person singular pronoun that agrees with *team*, treated as a unit.
>
> The *committee* did *their* best to convince the governor to reconsider the antiquated law.
> *Their* is correct because it is a plural third person pronoun referring to *committee*; the meaning of the sentence emphasizes the many individuals who make up the committee.

REFERENCES JOINED BY *AND*

Use the plural pronoun for most references joined by *and*. If the words joined by *and*, however, are treated as a unit, the singular pronoun seems more appropriate. The following sentences are correct.

> *Karen and Martin* do their calculus homework together.
> *Their* is correct because Karen *and* Martin are two separate people.
>
> *Love and affection* brings its own rewards.
> *Its* is correct because *love and affection* are not intended to be separate, as far as the meaning of the sentence shows.

ANY, NONE, ALL, SOME

Use either the singular or plural pronoun to refer to *any, none, all, some, most,* and *more*. The pronoun should reflect the meaning. Examine the following sentences.

> If *any* of the turkey is left, *it* should be frozen.
> *Most* of the story is as good as *it* can be.

None, which contains the word *one*, should be singular when its meaning in the sentence is *not one*. You should be careful to use the singular pronoun with *none* whenever possible, reserving the plural pronoun only for instances in which you can clearly justify it. Both of the following sentences are correct.

> *None* of the wild animal parks in California is as scenic as it is described in the advertisements.

> The writer is stressing that not one is as scenic as the advertisements promise. *It* is correct because *none* emphasizes the singular.

> *None* of us have even thirty cents in our pockets.

WHO, WHICH, WHAT

Use the singular pronoun if the word that *who, which,* or *that* refers to is singular, and use the plural if the reference is plural.

> Senator Miles is the kind of *person who* makes up *her* own mind on issues. *Her* is correct because it is a third person singular pronoun that refers to *who*. And *who* refers to the singular word *person*.

> Senator Miles is one of those *people who* make up *their* own minds on issues. *Their* is correct because it is a third person plural pronoun that refers to *who*. And *who* refers to the plural word *people*.

EXERCISES
A. Correct any pronoun errors in the following sentences.
1. There are very few secrets between my boyfriend and I.
2. Orwell's *1984* is a book that predicts what we will do to ourself if we continue to be apathetic to our surroundings.
3. Knowing that my grandfather was happy when he died helped myself accept the loss more easily.
4. Only a pessimist like he would say that a glass is half-empty when it's obvious that it is half-full.
5. The grades the students gave theirself were surprisingly fair.
6. Natural philosophy comes from looking around you and finding the truths in your own existence.
7. For most students, final exams are the natural completion to a semester; it sums up all the information studied during the term.
8. Myself and many other economics majors protested the question on the midterm because we felt it was sexist.
9. When we were children, the smell of freshly baked cookies was enough to drive we children wild.
10. John asked whether him or me will do the work.

B. Correct any errors in pronoun usage in the following sentences.
1. A light bar, which is a deluxe feature in many cars, is a bar of lights that will light to different sounds from the car's stereo. They are placed on the dash on the passenger side.
2. What makes the adult student special is that they are often

very motivated and have many life experiences to bring to what they study.
3. A car club provides a cruiser with a common group of friends and provides him or her with social events in which they are able to participate: dances, parties, and picnics.
4. The average person thinks that they can derive increased pleasure from life by depending on time-saving devices.
5. Anybody who wants to increase their tolerance should practice sharpening a pencil with broken lead in it.
6. It is common for the college graduate to be hired for jobs requiring specialized skills because they feel a college graduate can quickly be trained in almost any field.
7. For some people, low carbohydrate diets are dangerous because it drastically reduces the amount of sugar the body gets, though sugar still may be needed by the body.
8. It is hard enough for a freshman to decide what courses to take for the term during the first few days of the semester, but for them to decide courses for a whole year is an unreasonable demand.
9. Confucianism sets out to reform people, for they believe change and discipline to be very important.
10. Two areas of concern to psychology majors are physiology and mathematics. It is an important course for a psychology major because of all the computations required in surveys and experiments.

C. Correct any errors in pronoun references in the following sentences.
1. Once you are in a car club, they care for their own people.
2. In California, repeated attempts by public officials to ease traffic problems by setting up special lanes for car poolers have failed. Most of them want "the other guy" to give up his car.
3. The world is evolving to a point where thinking is less important than it used to be. They have computers to do thinking of all kinds.
4. Many times, a dieter consumes too much of one food. This results in an unbalanced diet and is just as fattening as eating small amounts of very fattening food.
5. Although I knew my friends were behind me, I could not get up enough nerve to invite the President to dinner. It didn't seem my place.
6. For the first time in my life I realized that if I wanted to play football I would have to work for it.
7. In the book about the theologian Lao Tzu, it explains the way the sage is to conduct his government.
8. In the selection from Whitman's "Passage to India," he describes the terrifying search for satisfaction that most Americans experience at some time in their lives.

D. Correct any mistakes in pronoun agreement or reference in the following paragraph.

Some members of the "cruiser" culture belong to car clubs. There are many car clubs in Los Angeles, and it serves a social and political function for this subculture. The car clubs provide cruisers with a group of common friends that are all interested in cars. It also provides him or her with social events in which they are able to participate: dances, parties, and picnics. Politically, the car club is a source of prestige, demanding respect within the cruiser subculture. The cruiser who is a member has no worries about trouble from others. In a way, the cruiser subculture could be viewed as a clan and the different clubs as a lineage. Once you are in, they care for their own people.

E. Correct any errors in the use of pronouns in the following sentences.
1. Anyone who could prove something was wrong with them was excluded from service in the Army.
2. The lecture hall looks like a long and narrow tunnel. This makes for too great a distance between the speaker and their audience.
3. Since my roommate's mother lives nearby, she goes home more often than I can.
4. I do not like to study in the library, though it is fine for locating books I need for classes.
5. Many companies make electric heaters, but most of them are small.
6. Even though love involves a longer involvement with other people than infatuation does, they seem to occur at the same time.
7. Christmas is a joyous time in a child's life. The thought of getting a present makes them all excited. I can remember times when my brother and I would be awake all night waiting for Santa Claus. It wasn't that Santa was a special figure in our life. We knew Mom and Dad put presents under the tree for us. We just couldn't wait for morning to celebrate the holiday in all their warm spirit.

F. Correct the pronoun usage in the following paragraph. The writer has used the very informal "you." Would the type of audience for whom the paragraph is intended make a difference as to whether the use of "you" is acceptable?

Hypnotizing yourself is a simple routine of progressive relaxation. The first step is physical. Start with your feet. Stretch them and relax them two or three times. Next, move up to your calves. Tense and relax them. Progressing up the body to your thighs, do the same tensing and relaxing, tensing and relaxing. Then one must continue to move upward until you have relaxed every part of your body. The second step requires you to use your imagination. Picture yourself slowly walking down a flight of stairs. It helps if one can think of a specific staircase. You see yourself stepping down with one foot, then the other, then the first again, until you reach the bottom of the stairs. At the bottom, you imagine that you have come to a beautiful, peaceful place. This is an ideal spot that has whatever environment you consider most desirable. In fact, thinking of a real place oneself has been helps to make the experience vivid. You want to linger at that place until you feel worry-free and wonderfully relaxed. Then you are ready to place positive suggestions into your mind.

STEP FIVE: IS YOUR SYNTAX CORRECT? Syntax is the arrangements of words and groups of words in sentences. You should read through your essay to make sure that sentence parts are arranged in the best possible way so that they do not sound awkward. Although keeping your reader interested is also important, the best arrangement is, of course, the one that produces the clearest statements. Because most errors in syntax sound wrong when you hear them, it is helpful to read your paper aloud as you listen for placement of modifiers, parallel statements, use of negatives and comparisons, and positions of emphasis.

Modifiers Modifiers are words or groups of words that describe nouns, pronouns, verbs, or other modifiers. They may function, as you recall, as adjectives that answer the questions *what, which*, or *what kind* about a noun, or as adverbs that answer the questions *how, why, when*, or *to what extent* about a verb, adjective, or other adverb. Modifiers should be placed as close as possible to what they modify. Sometimes no special effort is needed to make clear the connections between modifiers and what they describe, but some structures can be a bit tricky. Knowing what to look out for will help you to recognize and correct errors in the placement of modifiers.

Misplaced Modifiers In good sentences, the proper placement of modifiers is very important. Misplaced modifiers can make what you intend to say hard to understand. Sometimes, they may even cause the sentence to seem nonsensical. *Whenever possible, a modifier should come immediately before or after the word or phrase it modifies.* When this close relationship is not practical, you should take extra care to ensure that it is perfectly clear which modifier is associated with which word or phrase.

One of the best ways to detect misplaced modifiers is to read what you have written aloud. *Misplaced modifiers usually sound misplaced.* Try this procedure on the following sentence.

Weak: The *young girl* skipped down the street and bumped into an elderly gentlemen *with bells on her shoes.*

Did the phrase *with bells on her shoes* surprise you? You probably expected it to tell you something about the elderly gentleman. Then you ran into the pronoun *her,* so you knew the phrase had to refer to the young girl. The momentary confusion you likely experienced could have been avoided if the writer had put the phrase next to *young girl* where it belongs.

Here are two more examples of sentences with misplaced modifiers, each followed by a corrected version. Notice how much better the sentences sound when the modifiers come where they are supposed to.

Weak: Next week my cousin whom I haven't seen in eight years will be visiting our family from Oregon.

Effective: Next week my cousin from Oregon whom I haven't seen in eight years will be visiting our family.

Weak: I made a beautiful blanket for my bed that was made of wool.

Effective: I made a beautiful wool blanket for my bed.

A slightly different problem occurs when a modifier could modify either of two different words or phrases. If the writer is careless in the placement of such a modifier, the intended meaning may be unclear.

Weak: Her ability to dance *quickly* affected her career.

Does *quickly* refer to the way she dances or to the way her career was affected? Logically, *quickly* would be more likely to modify *affected*. See how much clearer this would have been if the writer had been more careful.

Effective: Her ability to dance affected her career *quickly*.

Effective: Her career was *quickly* affected by her ability to dance.

Dangling Modifiers

A dangling modifier is a modifier that has no word or phrase to modify. It is an error that often occurs because a writer begins a sentence with one idea in mind and then has another idea before the sentence is completed. Check over writing to make sure that you have not allowed any dangling modifiers to creep into your sentences. Pay special attention to participle phrases that begin sentences. This type of modifier tends to dangle the most often.

Being almost eighteen, my little brother was born.

This sentence does not make much sense, does it? The phrase *being almost eighteen* has nothing to modify. It obviously does not refer to *brother*. The following might be what the writer meant to say.

Being almost eighteen, I was surprised when my little brother was born.

When you find a dangling modifier in your writing, the best way to correct it is to rewrite the sentence so that the word meant to be modified is included. Check your understanding of dangling modifiers and how they should be corrected by looking over the following examples.

Incorrect: Tired and looking forward to a rest, the day dragged on.
Correct: Tired and looking forward to a rest, he felt that the day dragged on.

or

Because he was tired and looking forward to a rest, the day seemed to drag on.

Incorrect: Speaking for the committee, the President's decision is appropriate and fair.
Correct: Speaking for the committee, I think that the President's decision is appropriate and fair.

or

I speak for the committee in saying that the President's decision is appropriate and fair.

Parallelism In a sentence, words or groups of words that express similar thoughts should be similar in their form. This similarity in form is called *parallelism*. Elements in a series should be parallel. So should words joined by *and, or, but, as well as,* and sometimes *is*. Grammatical structures used with comparative pairs of words such as *neither . . . nor, not only . . . but also,* and *if . . . then* should be paralleled. A lack of parallelism is shown in the following sentence.

Incorrect: I like not only swimming but also to run and to jump rope.

The use of *not only . . . but also* should serve as a clue that the elements being compared should be similar. Rewording the sentence in either of the following ways makes the structures parallel.

Effective: I like not only swimming but also running and jumping rope.
Effective: I like not only to swim but also to run and to jump rope.

The lack of parallelism occurs most frequently with verbs and verbals. Nouns, prepositions, and adjectives, however, can all cause problems as well. The best way to detect elements that do not have parallel structures is to read sentences aloud. You should try this method with the following examples.

Incorrect: Eating well, exercising, and enough sleep are part of healthy living.
Correct: Eating well, exercising, and getting enough sleep are part of healthy living.
Incorrect: My math teacher makes every effort to encourage, instruct, and to praise her students.
Correct: My math teacher makes every effort to encourage, to instruct, and to praise her students.

or

My math teacher makes every effort to encourage, instruct, and praise her students.

Incorrect: All my work paid off, not only because I learned a lot about a subject I was interested in, but also got an "A" on the paper.

Correct: All my efforts paid off, not only because I learned a lot about a subject I was interested in, but also because I got an "A" on the paper.

See how much better the sentences sound when the elements are parallel? Here are some more examples of effective parallelism that are taken from students' papers.

> Other proposals by gun control advocates include a *ban on handguns, registration of all firearms,* and *control over the manufacture of guns.*

> Alexander Phillips maintained his contract labor force by a yearly recruitment of poor whites from nearby *towns and villages*. On roads that were too far from towns for anyone to commute there, he not only *set up work camps* but also *provided wholesome food* for these people.

> If a *forest is cut down, earth is removed, coal is extracted,* and *earth is replenished* with new plants, in about fifty years the location will look the same as it did before strip-mining.

> *Mourning* is *dying. To mourn* is *to express* the death wish.

Comparisons

Comparisons are used to show differences or similarities. They tell how things are alike or how they are not alike. Many writers run into difficulties when making comparisons. Their mistakes generally fall into two categories: *incomplete comparisons* and *inappropriate comparisons*. As you read through your paper, make sure that all your comparisons are complete and accurate.

INCOMPLETE COMPARISONS

A comparison may be incomplete because only part of it is given. Such incomplete comparisons are particularly common in advertising.

> Learning to read with Eve Woodhue is *more* fun.

> Smoke Choker's 100's, a *longer* low tar cigarette.

These advertisements promise a comparison, but only one thing is mentioned. What is "learning to read with Eve" more fun than? What are Choker's longer than? The advertisements are incomplete. The thing the product is compared to is left to the imagination. Although such comparisons may serve the purposes of ad agencies, they should be carefully avoided in your own writing. At best, they can only lead to confusion.

Even when all of the things being compared are included, *a comparison may still be incomplete because necessary words or punctuation is missing*. In some cases, the omissions simply cause confusion. In others, the sentences may be nonsensical.

> Chicago has a skyscraper that is taller than any building in the world.

> My mother is kinder than any woman.

According to the wording of the first example, a skyscraper is not a building. In the second, a mother is not considered to be a woman. The addition of the word *other* to both makes the intended meaning of the sentences clear.

> Chicago has a skyscraper that is taller than any *other* building in the world.
>
> My mother is kinder than any *other* woman.

A word you should be particularly careful to include when it is needed is *as*.

> Weak: Rosa is as strong, if not stronger than, Mike.
>
> Effective: Rosa is as strong as, if not stronger than, Mike.

Perhaps an even better way of writing this sentence is the following.

> Rosa is as strong as Mike, if not stronger.

Here are some more examples in which missing words make the comparisons incomplete.

> Weak: John has lived in the building longer than anyone.
>
> Effective: John has lived in the building longer than anyone *else*.
>
> Weak: I like Fred more than Mary.
>
> Effective: I like Fred more than *I like* Mary.
>
> or
>
> Effective: I like Fred more than Mary *does*.
>
> Weak: Larry used to seem much younger.
>
> Effective: Larry used to seem much younger *than he was*.
>
> or
>
> Effective: Larry used to seem much younger *than Margaret*.

INAPPROPRIATE COMPARISONS

An inappropriate comparison has no sound basis and reflects a problem in thinking. A comparison may be inappropriate because either a form of the word "compare" is used too loosely or the two or more ideas being related are not expressed in a form that makes them comparable. Inappropriate comparisons always sound awkward when read aloud. They also make no sense when they are analyzed. The following sentence illustrates the first kind.

> *In comparison to people,* the song shows people's inability to cope with social problems.

Such statements promise a comparison, but no comparison is made. The writer probably does not understand the exact meaning of the word *comparison*. In the example above there are no similarities and differences to discuss. It is likely that the writer wanted to lead into the point with a sentence like those following:

> The song reflects people's struggles with social problems.
>
> or
>
> The song is about people's struggles.

After one of these sentences, the writer could have expanded on the point. But, actually, the best revision would simply involve the deletion of the italicized phrase, leaving a straightforward sentence.

> The song shows people's inability to cope with social problems.

Even when two ideas or things are present in a sentence and they are to be compared, the comparison may be inappropriate because the basis for it is not clearly stated or thought out. You cannot compare the incomparable. All comparisons and contrasts are based on some likeness between ideas or things. For instance, you could show comparisons and contrasts between two chairs, one modern and constructed of aluminum with simple, sleek lines, and the other old fashioned with curved and carved wood. Clearly, the chairs are different. They are still both chairs, however, so there is a logical basis for comparison. The same would be true of a comparison of two writers from the same period who were influenced by the same people and had similar ideas but radically different styles. The form of a sound comparison, then, makes clear the basis of the comparison or contrast. In the following comparative statements, the basis for comparison is italicized.

> The *personality* of my French teacher is similar to the *personality* of my Aunt Essie.
>> The statement is correct because the basis of comparison is the personality of each person.
>
> The color of her eyes is similar to the *color* of mine.
>> The statement is correct because the basis of comparison is the color of each person's eyes.

You can see why the following sentence winds up trying to compare the incomparable simply because the writer fails to state the basis for comparison.

> The embarrassment I felt when I realized that I was wearing two completely different shoes was like the time I mistakenly wore my pajamas to school in fourth grade.

According to the wording of the above example, embarrassment can be compared to a time. Of course, such a statement is nonsense. What the writer probably means to compare is the embarrassment she felt on both occasions. An effective revision would be written as follows.

The *embarrassment* I felt when I realized that I was wearing two completely different shoes was like the *embarrassment* I had experienced back in the fourth grade when I mistakenly wore my pajamas to school.

Some inappropriate comparisons are less obvious than the one above. They may even sound correct if you aren't listening closely. Here are two examples.

My hat is bigger than Jan.

Their old VW is in better condition than Alec.

The bases for comparison, *hats* in the first sentence and *old VWs* in the second, are not stated. The result is that the first sentence compares a hat to Jan and the second sentence compares an old VW to Alec. It doesn't make much sense to compare hats or cars to people. The following sentences are correct.

My hat is bigger than Jan's hat.

or

My hat is bigger than Jan's.

Their old VW is in better condition than Alec's old VW.

or

Their old VW is in better condition than Alec's.

Let's look at one more example. The following comparison is incorrect.

In France, like the United States, and unlike Sweden, any driver can refuse to take a test for drunk driving.

On a quick reading, you might think the sentence sounds correct. But the basis for comparison is not stated. The writer is not comparing France, the United States, and Sweden with each other generally— but is, instead, comparing *the drunk driving laws in the three countries*. The writer could rework the sentence as follows:

In France, like in the United States, and *unlike in Sweden,* any driver can refuse to take a test for drunk driving.

Double Negatives

Negative words such as *no, not,* and *nothing,* are very useful for making negative statements.

This relationship is *nothing* like my last.

I do *not* like him.

She has *no* friends.

Nevertheless, these simple little words often cause problems when more than one is used for the same idea. This usage is called a *double negative. All double negatives should be avoided.* Their use is a case of two not being more emphatic than one. If you wish to be technical, two negatives actually cancel one another out and make the statement positive. Suppose someone has written the following.

I can't do nothing about it.

What the writer probably meant to say was

I cannot do anything about it.

But what the sentence actually states is

I can do something about it.

As you read through your paper, make sure that any time you have used a negative you have used only one. Remembering that the following words should usually be used together may help you to avoid double negatives in your own writing.

Not . . . anything
Not . . . anybody
Do not . . . any
Does not . . . any
Hardly . . . any
Scarcely . . . any

Another good thing to remember about *hardly* and *scarcely* is that they should never be preceded by a negative.

Incorrect: He cannot hardly realize how rich he has become.
Correct: He can hardly realize how rich he has become.

Special Negative Expressions

There are several types of negative expressions that seem to cause problems for many writers. If you use any expressions such as the following in your writing, be sure that you do not accidently make them double negatives.

Incorrect: I should not wonder if he did not make a fool of himself.
Correct: I should not wonder if he made a fool of himself.
Incorrect: I cannot help but wonder whether the fuel crisis will get worse.
Correct: I cannot help wondering whether the fuel crisis will get worse.
Incorrect: I doubt but what the team will win.
Correct: I doubt that the team will win.

Mixed Syntax

As you read through your paper, make sure that you do not have any sentences in which the syntax is mixed. *Mixed syntax is the blurring together of two related but distinctly different sentence patterns.* These mistakes are often hard to spot. The beginning sounds right and the ending sounds right, but the two parts together sound awkward and are incorrect.

Incorrect: The reason for the general's anger is because some young officers did not behave properly at his garden party.

The writer of this sentence probably had both of the following sentence patterns in mind and allowed them to become mixed.

Correct: The reason for the general's anger is that some young officers did not behave properly at his garden party.

Correct: The general is angry because some young officers did not behave properly at his garden party.

Either sentence is fine, but mixing the two is incorrect. Here is another example.

Incorrect: Janie has serious learning disabilities, but she tries her best as she can.

Again, the writer was probably thinking of two different sentence patterns.

Correct: Janie has serious learning disabilities, but she tries her best.

Correct: Janie has serious learning disabilities, but she tries as hard as she can.

Just as before, either pattern is acceptable, but a mixture is not.

There are generally two causes for mixed syntax. Frequently a writer may begin a sentence and then get a related idea but forget to go back and change the first part accordingly. Such errors are easily eliminated by carefully rereading what you have written. The other cause of mixed syntax is a lack of familiarity with particular expressions. You can avoid mistakes of this type by noticing how these expressions are used in what you read and by looking closely at any sentences that might seem strange. Writing sentences in imitation of good prose, as covered on page 154, can also be helpful. In addition, you should take special care when using any expressions with which you are not totally at ease.

EXERCISES

A. Correct any confusing or misplaced modifiers in the following sentences.
1. She'd be the one to recognize the house, as a native of the area and a friend of the past owners.
2. The decision to give up my future for her which was so promising was a difficult one.
3. Not pretty and no conversationalist, I still cared more for her than I did for any model or social jabberer.
4. Steaming so comfortingly in the mug, I sometimes think that hot chocolate offers even more companionship than a friendly dog.
5. Schools and prisons, which are both institutions, are often similarly designed.

6. It is where the road narrows that cars speed through the curves like lightning.
7. So that no one would get them confused, large signs were placed on the machines made of cardboard.
8. Given the open classroom approach to education, I think there could be some improvement made by teachers of most subject areas.
9. My car was returned after a few days by the police all dirty and scratched.
10. I should mention now that some people will be given more time than others so that there will be no confusion.

B. Underline all the modifiers and draw arrows to the words they modify in the following sentences. Correct any dangling or misplaced modifiers.
1. When young, the id is the dominant part of the personality.
2. As a child, all needs are felt intensely.
3. Sitting in the classroom, the time to give my speech grew near.
4. Looking at the boring art exhibit, each minute went by so slowly I thought the tour would never end.
5. Trying to be friendly but assertive, the subject of conversation was a bad one.
6. Full of thoughts of winning, the game seemed to pass quickly.
7. Knowing that Evel Knievel was not too happy about his record, the successful jump was a surprise to the audience.
8. Being an advocate of preserving endangered species, lions and tigers should be kept on animal reserves.
9. Glued to the counter, they laughed at him as he tried to hide what he was doing.
10. Without a cent, traveling would be difficult but not impossible.

C. Correct any dangling or misplaced modifiers in the following sentences.
1. Moving on to the days of Malcolm X, young blacks at that time had very little to do.
2. Eating only a few bites, my lunch was unfinished.
3. When looking at the pencil's diameter, lead forms a circle about half the way across the instrument.
4. The unique vocabulary and syntax of the Old Testament helps to disprove the theory of cultism.
5. After a year of frequent use, I found myself unable to do certain math problems without a calculator.
6. Out of habit, I waited in the long line at the bank until the teller recognized me.
7. Speaking to an expert on teaching reading to young children, he told me that using phonetics is the best method.
8. As an example of the Swiss franc's potential, if you converted $1,000 into Swiss francs in 1971 and reconverted it today, you would have $1,640.

9. In speaking to a successful motion picture director, the movie industry is losing hundreds of thousands of dollars each year.
10. In keeping with the cosmic cycles of the universe, the Chinese thought that the human body had 365 parts, corresponding to the number of days in a year.

D. Underline the parallel structures in the following sentences.
1. Although nobody knew it then, we were ashamed of ourselves and our families.
2. He said that I was usually cheerful and always trying to see the best in a situation.
3. People without mates, without self-respect, and without foundation are also without happiness.
4. A life spent with well-defined goals will be a life that brings clearly defined successes.
5. Going out on the town results often in the same sort of fatigue one feels after reading from a book for a long time.
6. In case of a fire, or in the event of an earthquake, a person should not worry about saving a few bits of clothing or a handful of jewelry.
7. Working on a farm, one learns much about the land on which one labors and the seasons that change the land.
8. "If there isn't a pail by the door or a basin in the farm house, I'll let the cow's milk soak into the ground," he said.
9. Even though the senator is an important political figure, she is not a popular one.
10. I never met a person who enjoyed eating, fishing, and sleeping more than my brother does.

E. Correct any errors in parallelism in the following sentences.
1. I enjoy arguing and yelling, but I don't like to fight.
2. There was a building that I thought would look good in New York City and cause a stir there, too.
3. If, as is sometimes the case, a bride hasn't met the father of her fiancé or his mother, a meeting of them all during the wedding will be very emotional, to say the least.
4. But it's true that a day with a friend's company seems brief and full.
5. Although there are many attaché cases on the market, there is none I would like to have, to use, or even enjoy carrying as much as I did the one I lost.
6. Summer is a time for swimming and to relax.
7. Right now I want rest and to stop working so hard.
8. Everyone is invited to an evening of singing, to dance, and to feast.
9. The house is too stilted, cold, and without any grace.
10. I am looking for a man who is intelligent, understanding, and a good friend in times of stress.

F. Underline all the parallel elements in the following introductory paragraph from a student's essay.

Dull, lifeless, and metallic, the machine may one day replace people's best friends. People will have robot friends to talk to and to confide in. It will be perfectly acceptable to invite a robot home for dinner. Every robot, just like every person, will have an address and telephone number and maybe even a social security card. If all these possibilities seem farfetched or undesirable, one has only to consider the advantages of an automated relationship. First, robots can be turned off whenever he or she desires peace and quiet. Robots tend to be servile and are willing to do anything to please. Also, many people will program their robot's topics for conversation in order to assure themselves that they will never be bored. Having a robot as a companion might be a little hard to get used to, but in the end it might offer more privacy, better schedules, and more stimulating talk than the conventional, person-to-person relationship.

G. Correct any faulty comparisons in the following sentences.
1. The chief of the Navaho tribe is more powerful than any Navaho.
2. Having a better English teacher in college helped me improve my writing skills.
3. A beginning police officer has to undertake fewer risks.
4. A raquetball player has a faster response to the ball than in tennis.
5. When I was younger, people used to think I looked older.
6. In a competitive situation, the runner is much more nervous.
7. The writer's role in making a film is not as demanding as the producer.
8. Drawing inferences from the stories a person tells can make them more interesting.
9. The President's response to the bill was more like a child.
10. Eating TV dinners instead of home-cooked meals is like single people.

14

A Glossary of Punctuation and Mechanics

As a writer, you have an obligation to assist your reader in every way possible to get the intended meaning from what you write. One way that you accomplish this goal is through the use of generally accepted practices regarding punctuation and mechanics. Because most writers have agreed on basic concepts of usage, your own ability to use punctuation and mechanics correctly will bring your own writing into line with other writing with which your reader is probably familiar. For instance, your reader is already accustomed to other writers helping him or her through a passage by marking off units of thought into sentences. Certainly, then, you should also punctuate your sentences to provide this same assistance.

Standard guidelines for mechanics, if applied, will also help you to make certain that your essay will be properly received and interpreted by your reader. After all, a reader who finds "individualized" mechanics in an essay is likely to find his or her attention drawn not to what the writer intends but to the nonstandard method of presentation.

Entries in this glossary are arranged alphabetically so that information regarding particular topics can be easily located. Although this chapter is intended as an easy reference, a source of answers to questions that occur as you write, you can benefit from a close reading from start to finish. By reading all entries carefully, you can discover new ways to present your ideas. You might also discover that some of your old habits should be broken.

ABBREVIATIONS

Abbreviations are space-saving devices. They are especially helpful in footnotes, bibliographic entries, inside parentheses, and on charts or graphs. There are a few abbreviations that are acceptable in all forms of writing. Most, however, should be avoided in papers and essays.

FORMS OF ADDRESS Titles or forms of address such as *Ms., Mrs., Mmes.* (plural of Mrs.), *Mr., Messrs.* (plural of Mr.), *St.* (Saint), *Jr., Sr., Dr., Ph.D., and M.D.* should be abbreviated only when they come before or after names. Otherwise, they should be spelled out.

> Ramon R. Alba, Ph.D., and Mr. James S. Wright are the junior members of the committee.

Mr., Ms., Mrs., and *Dr.* are dropped if *Ph.D., M.D.* or *D.D.S.* follows the name.

TIME Indicators of time such as *B.C., A.D., P.M.* (or *p.m.*), and *A.M.* (or *a.m.*) are used with dates and times. *A.D.* precedes the date, but *B.C.* comes after it.

> The manuscripts dated A.D. 900 were an amazing find.

> Aristotle wrote the *Poetics* in the fourth century B.C.

ORGANIZATIONS AND AGENCIES The abbreviations for well-known organizations and agencies such as UNESCO, NATO, the CIA, the VFW, and NOW are often written without periods, but they may also be written with them. It is a good practice to spell out the full name of an organization the first time it is used in your essay and to place the abbreviations next to the name in parentheses. Doing so will assure that the reader recognizes what the abbreviation stands for when it appears again.

> National Organization for Women (NOW) is becoming well known in our town.

MONEY Symbols for dollars and cents may be used if spelling out the figure would take several words, if the figure is to be compared to several other figures in the sentence or paragraph, or if you think that using them lends special clarity to what you are saying. Otherwise, spell out the figures.

> Last summer my brother earned twelve hundred dollars working for a moving company.

> Including tax and license the car cost $4,026.37.

> A dinner that cost two dollars a few years ago now costs four.

> I paid $57 for the stove, $40 for the refrigerator, $400 for the first and last months' rent, and $35 for a cleaning fee. That means I have exactly $47.29 left to live on this month.

TECHNICAL TERMS In technical papers, terms such as *mpg* or *BTUS* are common and correct. Note that these terms are used with figures, not alone.

> How many miles per gallon does your car get? The estimated consumption by the energy-saving devices was 1,000 BTUS.

PERCENT Spell out the word *percent* unless it is used in a comparison. Most comparative uses of percent symbols are obvious because the percents are used frequently throughout a sentence or paragraph. Using the symbol in these instances not only saves space but makes for consistency. Always spell out *percent* or *percentage* when the term is not preceded by a figure.

> The percentage of smokers in the crowd was unusually high.
>
> I am not talking about 10% cutbacks in hospitalization payments or even 20%—I'm talking about a whole 60%.

MEASUREMENTS Standard abbreviations such as the following should be used in technical or scientific writing only. In your other writing, spell out the word.

in.	inch or inches
ft.	foot or feet
cm.	centimeter or centimeters
lb.	pound or pounds
yd.	yard or yards

Except in tables, you should avoid using the symbol " to mean inches or ' to mean feet, since it is easily confused with punctuation.

LATIN TERMS Latin terms are sometimes abbreviated in footnotes, bibliographies, and parenthetical references. Terms such as *i.e.* (that is), *e.g.* (for example), *c.* (circa, means *about* and is always used with a specific year), *cf.* (compare), *etc.* (and so forth), and *et al.* (and others, always referring to people) are most effectively saved for places in a paper where space is at a premium. To use them in the text of the paper, where an everyday English word would serve just as well or better, is unnecessary, not to mention a bit pretentious.

PUBLICATION DATA Publication data are also abbreviated in notes, bibliographies, and parentheses. Terms such as *vol., ed., trans., col., p.,* and *pp.* are commonly used instead of the full words.

> Azuela, Mariano. The Underdogs. Trans. E. Munguia, Jr. New York: New American Library, 1962.

BUSINESS TERMS Abbreviations of business terms such as *Co., Inc., Corp.,* and *Ltd.* are used in notes and bibliographies to conserve space.

Wagner, Kenneth A., Paul C. Bailey, and Glenn H. Campbell. *Under Siege*. New York: Abelard Schuman Ltd., 1973.

Our findings coincide with those of other environmental investigators (see *Report to the Consumer*, Ballard Corp., January, 1978).

ABBREVIATIONS INAPPROPRIATE TO THE TEXT OF A PAPER

Many abbreviations should not be used in the running text of your papers. There are two reasons for this rule of thumb. First, in the text of the paper there is plenty of room to spell out the words you mean; you are not cramped into a few inches as you are in writing footnotes. Second, the tone of abbreviations in the text may conflict with the tone you want to maintain. Abbreviations seem out of place because they are too casual. The most common mistakes in this area occur because the etiquette of writing letters permits the use of many of the following abbreviations. Since most of them are fine to use in the addresses of letters, continue to use them there. For your essays, however, either use the following suggested rewordings or make up your own.

Place Names

Weak: She lives on Macapa *Dr*. in a huge house.

Effective: She lives on Macapa *Drive* in a huge house.

On envelopes this abbreviation in acceptable. The same is true on the following: St., Ave., Blvd., Ct., Pl., Ln., Rd., and so forth.

Ampersand

Weak: Crankson & his undefeated team play our team next week.

Effective: Crankson *and* his undefeated team play our team next week.

Ranks

Weak: My *prof*. had already assigned us fifty pages of reading when he decided to add a thousand-word essay for next week too.

Effective: My professor had already assigned us fifty pages of reading when he decided to add a thousand-word essay for next week too.

Places

Weak: After attending college in *N.Y. City* for one term, I decided to transfer to a university in *L.A.*

Effective: After attending college in *New York City* for one term, I decided to transfer to a university in *Los Angeles*.

Names

Weak: The letter of recommendation was sent to *Jas*. Mitchell on Thompson Street.

Effective: The letter of recommendation was sent to *James* Mitchell on Thompson Street.

Days or Months

Weak: Last *Mon*. the Senate met to discuss funding for the proposed energy plan.

Effective: Last *Monday* the Senate met to discuss funding for the proposed energy plan.

Weak: Is *Sept*. or April the beginning of the new fiscal year?

Effective: Is *September* or April the beginning of the new fiscal year?

EXERCISES Directions: Correct any abbreviation errors in the following sentences. Assume that the sentences are from an informal essay you might write for a class.

A. Never has there been a President of the U.S. of A. who was younger than J. F. K. when he was president.
B. All the pp. in the novel are filled with witty dialogue, fast action, pathos, etc.
C. Stat. and econ. are courses worth taking even though one's major makes it unnecessary to do so.
D. Nobody around here ever believes me when I say that I do not own a t.v.
E. By the time I reach my Jr. year, I will be taking only those classes I need for my major.
F. When she looked at me that way, I said, "Well, how many lbs. do you think I've gained?"
G. Pretense is not respected where I come from: Chicago, Ill.
H. There's no place like Frisco for a night out on the town.
I. Outpost Dr. is so steep that bike riders have to push their ten speeds up it.
J. I never get upset by anything anyone over six ft. tall says to me, even though I'm only four ft. tall. We've, both groups, had a hard time with ribbings from other people.

THE APOSTROPHE '

The apostrophe is used to form possessives, contractions, and certain plurals.

POSSESSIVES Possession indicates that a thing or person belongs to or is closely associated with another. There is a simple test that usually shows if a word will require an apostrophe because it is possessive. Can you say "the _____ of (a *or* the) _____ "? In this test you insert in the blanks any combination of the nouns or indefinite pronouns that come next to each other in your sentence. If the word following "of" or "of the" needs an apostrophe, the phrase will make perfect sense. Otherwise, it usually will not make sense. Let's look at an example.

   A person's life is what he or she makes of it.

Suppose you wanted to check the relationship between *person* and *life*. You would insert it in the test phrase:

   the *life* of a *person*.

The phrase makes sense; it says what you mean. Therefore, you should write, just as you had written in the above sentence, *person's life*. Similarly, you could say that the phrase *Mary's hat* can be thought "the *hat* of *Mary*" or that *anyone's guess* could be thought of as "the *guess* of *anyone*." Every now and then, however, you will find a phrase that sounds better with the "of." Follow your ear in such cases. Here are some examples.

The roar of the crowd sounds better than *the crowd's roar*.

The height of the bookcase sounds better than *the bookcase's height*.

Placement of apostrophes becomes automatic once you get the hang of it. One of the main distinctions you have to make is whether the possessive word is singular or plural. Regular singular words take *'s*, and regular plural words take *s'*.

Singular	Plural
The girl's grades	The girls' grades
The student's attitude	The students' attitude

If the singular noun ends in *s*, the singular possessive usually adds *'s*. It is true that whether to add the apostrophe alone or to add the apostrophe and the *s* is up to the writer. However, most people form the possessive according to how they say the word. Since they would pronounce the possessive of *Jones* as *Jonesus*, they would write *Jones's*. Plural possessives that end in *s* take the *es'* ending. Take a look at the following examples of how nouns ending in *s* form the possessive.

Singular	Plural
Mr. Jones's cat	The Joneses' cat
One boss's orders	The bosses' orders
Camus' novels	

When a noun has a special plural form, such as when man becomes men, the possessive of the plural is formed by adding *'s*.

Singular	Plural
A woman's liberation	Women's liberation
The child's toy	Children's toys

When a word ends in *z*, the singular form of the possessive is *z's* and the plural is *zes'*.

Singular	Plural
Mr. Gonzalez's son	The Gonzalezes' house
Chavez's campaign	The Chavezes' dedication

Compound words or groups of words take the *'s* on the last word only.

my father-in-law's house

the Secretary of Defense's office

someone else's paper

Individual ownership is shown by placing the 's at the end of each person's name.

Jane's and Mary's business venture

Joint ownership may be shown either in the same form as individual ownership or it may be shown by adding the 's only to the last name.

Jack's and Jill's dog Spot

or

Jack and Jill's dog Spot

Double possessives use both the 's and the *of* phrase. Using them is perfectly correct; they serve to indicate one possessive relationship among many. Note how the possessives are formed in the following examples.

A remark of my Aunt Esther's
   This phrase refers to one remark of Aunt Esther's, among many other such remarks.

A friend of my sister's
   This phrase refers to one friend among my sister's many friends.

CONTRACTIONS

A contraction is a word, number, or group of words that has been shortened by omitting certain letters or numbers. The apostrophe is used to indicate the omission and is placed where the original letters or numbers occurred. Contractions tend to be informal and should be used when you wish to give a conversational tone to your writing. Adding a few contractions to your essays when you would naturally use them in speaking increases the flow and makes the writing lively. For instance, the following sentence would be rather stiff.

Do they not realize the important implications of this decision?

It would be much more natural to use the contracted form of *do not*.

Don't they realize the important implications of this decision?

Other commonly used contractions and their full forms are listed as follows.

Would not	may be contracted to	wouldn't
Could not	may be contracted to	couldn't
You would	may be contracted to	you'd
I would	may be contracted to	I'd

A Glossary of Punctuation and Mechanics

It is	may be contracted to	it's
Are not	may be contracted to	aren't
They are	may be contracted to	they're
Will not	may be contracted to	won't

Do not confuse the contractions *who's* (who is), *they're* (they are), and *it's* (it is) with the possessive pronouns *whose, their,* and *its.*

Contractions of numbers are treated in the same way: the apostrophe is placed where numbers are left out. Here are some examples.

| 1955 | may be contracted to | '55 |
| 1977 | may be contracted to | '77 |

Contracted numbers are commonly used in phrases such as *the class of '81* or *back in '74.*

PLURALS An apostrophe and *s* ('s) may be used to form the plurals of certain letters, numbers, symbols, abbreviations, and words used as words. But it is also correct to form the plurals of these words by adding a simple *s*, as long as no confusion results. Here are examples that could be written either way.

> I asked my little brother if he had studied the three Rs yet.
>
> I asked my little brother, if he had studied the three R's yet.
>
> In the late 1970s natural foods became an established part of the food industry.
>
> In the late 1970's natural foods became an established part of the food industry.

Now, here are examples that require the apostrophe to avoid confusion.

> The first paragraph of my essay had seven I's in it.
>> The apostrophe prevents any confusion between the plural of I (I's) and the word *Is*.
>
> I have always figured out problems in terms of x's and y's.
>> The apostrophe clearly shows that the plurals of x and y are to be treated as nouns.
>
> How many M.A.'s and how many Ph.D.'s applied for the job?
>> The apostrophe clarifies that the abbreviations end with a period.

EXERCISES Directions: Correct any mistakes in the use of apostrophes or formation of possessives and contractions by rewriting the incorrect words.
- A. There a'rent any good old beer halls anymore where people can laugh, sing, and generally have a good time.
- B. A cat is considered a calico only if it's fur is of three or more colors.

C. The room's air seemed unusually stuffy, and one look at the tightly locked windows revealed why.
D. Most people's impressions of the lives led by Hollywood stars are very naive.
E. A woman's need for companionship is no greater than a man's.
F. We were surprised to find so many old toy's still in the attic, abandoned so many years ago when we stopped playing there.
G. With as many colds' as I have suffered through in my life, I really don't believe vitamin C helps very much.
H. The surface of the plants' leaves was tinged with brown spots which indicated a fungus.
I. Even though my cousin childrens' are not of elementary school age yet, they often go with her to activities held at the school where she is a teacher.
J. Wonderful opportunities' present themselves at the parties' held by the Martinez family.

BRACKETS [ ]

Square brackets are used when a writer wishes to clarify or comment on certain parts of a quotation. They are used to set apart the writer's words from the material being quoted. You will generally find that you will want to use brackets in one of four ways.

FURTHER IDENTIFICATION

Brackets are used to clarify or explain words or ideas that may not be perfectly clear from the quoted material given. Here are a few examples.

> They [the existential psychologists] were willing to respond directly and humanely to people's problems; for example, rocking a frightened child to sleep was considered part of therapy.

> According to Jones, "That man [D. H. Lawrence] was simply childish."

ADDITION OF A PERSONAL COMMENT

A personal comment may be added when it shows your interpretation of the quotation and can help to lend support to the thesis at hand. Personal comments should be used sparingly, however. An example follows.

> A typical example of glossing over the problem came from Smithson's report to the State Referral Board: "We are not aware of [that is, they never investigate] any mistreatment of mental patients in California's hospitals."

EDITORIAL CORRECTION

Occasionally you will find an error in spelling, tense, pronoun reference, or word choice in the quotation you wish to use. The usual way to note that the error is not your fault is to use the Latin term *sic* which means "*thus or so*." The *sic*, in brackets and underlined, [*sic*], is placed next to the incorrect word. Note how the *sic* is placed in the following example.

A Glossary of Punctuation and Mechanics

The group complained that "protestors were siezed [sic] by police without first being asked to leave the site."

PARENTHESES WITHIN PARENTHESES

Parentheses that come within parentheses are marked with brackets.

A thorough discussion of problems with syntax may be found in one of the best new books on the subject (see Mina P. Shaughnessy, *Errors and Expectations* [New York: Oxford University Press, 1977], pp. 49–50).

Most typewriters do not have keys for brackets. The parentheses, which are on most typewriters, can not be substituted for brackets. Therefore, the most practical alternative is to leave space for the brackets and draw them in after you have typed the page on which they appear.

CAPITALS

Capitalization is one of those areas in which we all know some rules, but it is also an area in which we have all probably been puzzled at one time or another. Most people would agree that capitalization is a matter of some importance. After all, it helps readers to see the point of what they read. For example, the message the brain receives differs when the eye sees *Turkey* and when it sees *turkey*. Also, the eye refocuses itself on the signal of a capital letter at the beginning of the sentence. Even though there is agreement about the value of capitalizing words, there is controversy as to exactly what should be capitalized. Modern publishers in the United States would like writers to use the lowercase instead of capitals whenever a controversial word is clear and unchanged by doing so. They feel that, basically, nothing is lost.

The rules here are drawn from those in *A Manual of Style*, Twelfth Edition, published by the University of Chicago Press. That source may be turned to for further assistance with any rule included in the following section on capitalization.

BEGINNING OF A SENTENCE

Capitalize the first letter of the first word of every sentence. This rule also applies to the first letter of the first word of a direct quotation that could stand alone as a sentence within a sentence.

Connors asked, "Why in the world should I be accused of murder?"

Oscar Wilde once commented, "Divorces are made in heaven."

BEGINNINGS OF LINES OF POETRY

Capitalize the first letter of the first word of each line of poetry if the original is capitalized.

Let me not to the marriage of true minds
Admit impediments; love is not love

Which alters when it alteration finds,
Or bends with the remover to remove.

TITLES OF BOOKS, RECORDS, STORIES, ESSAYS, PLAYS, AND POEMS

Always capitalize the first and last word of a title or subtitle. Articles (*the, an,* and *a*) and *to* infinitives are usually not capitalized when they appear inside a title. Prepositions, regardless of length, should not be capitalized. Coordinating conjunctions (*and, or, nor, for, but, yet,* and *so*) are not capitalized, but subordinating conjunctions such as *because, since,* and *after* are.

An American Dream
You Know I Can't Hear You When the Water's Running
"Ode on a Grecian Urn"
"A Tent That Families Can Live In"

Do not capitalize references to any of the following: *introduction, preface, forward, contents, appendix, glossary, bibliography, index, chapter* (when used with an arabic numeral); the same rule applies to the words *edition* and *series* when not part of a title.

The introduction to the novel is an essay by Lionel Trilling.

In chapter 4 of *Secret Agent*, Conrad introduces a new symbol.

The hardcover Modern Library edition is usually more attractive than the paperback copy.

NAMES

Capitalize the names of specific people, places, monuments, artworks, organizations, schools, buildings, companies, and movements in history.

The Lovers by Picasso
Watson Hall
Kennedy Airport
Statue of Liberty
the Arts Division of
the Russian Revolution
Rutgers University
the Industrial Revolution
Mexico
Johnson and Johnson

Do not capitalize words such as university, college, or company when they appear alone unless they are used as a proper name.

My college is highly thought of.
I go to the University of Texas.

Do not capitalize nouns and adjectives derived from names but used to refer to common objects.

chinaware
roman numerals

baked alaska
dutch oven

Capitalize the names of people and countries and the nouns and adjectives derived from those names.

Freud	Freudians	Freudian
Orient	Orientals	Oriental
New York	New Yorkers	New Yorkish
		New Yorkese

GROUPS OF PEOPLE Capitalize the names of most racial, linguistic, religious, and tribal groups of people.

Magyar
Mormon
Nordic

Afro-American
Indo-European
Caucasian

However, do not capitalize groupings by color, size, or common expressions.

redneck
black
white

pygmy
small people
gays

TITLES OF PEOPLE Capitalize a title or an office if it precedes a person's name.

President Gilman

General Eisenhower

Pope John

Titles following a name or used alone in place of a name are not capitalized. The following examples show how to treat some common titles.

Earl Warren, chief justice of the United States

but

Chief Justice Warren

and

the chief justice

>   Jimmy Carter, president of the United States
>
> but
>
> President Carter
>
> and
>
> the president

In England certain high offices and forms of address are still capitalized.

> Queen Mother   Your Royal Highness
> the Prince of Wales   His Majesty

Do not capitalize epithets that indicate a role.

> The homemaker and mother, Elda Simpson
> the brilliant new comedian, Jim Wise

Do not capitalize terms that indicate a person's year in school.

> freshman   sophomore   junior   senior

RELATIVES Capitalize a relationship when it is used as a name or when the person is spoken to directly.

> It was fun to go fishing with Grandpa.
> Mother, why did you marry Dad?

Likewise, you should capitalize a relationship when it is used as a part of a person's name.

> Ask Aunt Emma whether she wants to go out to dinner tonight.

Do not capitalize a relationship when it is preceded by *my*.

> my uncle   my uncle Al   my brother Bill

TIME Capitalize the days of the week, months, and the names of holidays (except for any prepositions, articles, or conjunctions). Never capitalize the names of the seasons.

> Monday   July   Memorial Day   spring
> Mother's Day   the Fourth of July

Do not capitalize words that refer to general periods of time.

the nineteenth century   the space age
the fifties   the romantic age

Many established historical periods, however, should be capitalized.

the Middle Ages   the Industrial Revolution
the Roaring Twenties   the Stone Age
the Christian Era   the Age of Reason

Do not capitalize most philosophical or artistic schools or movements unless derived from proper nouns.

Aristotelian   Stoic
jazz   romanticism
naturalism   pop art

PLACES Capitalize the abbreviated forms of time and time zones, but do not capitalize the words when they are spelled out.

daylight saving time   (DST)
eastern standard time   (EST)
central daylight time   (CDT)

Capitalize words that show political divisions such as *empire, state, county, city,* and *territory* when they are part of a name.

New York City is fun to visit.

The District of Columbia is about sixty-nine square miles in area.

Do not capitalize such divisions when they are alone in a sentence or come before the name.

The city of New York has many exciting museums.

The whole province was colorful.

Capitalize geographical terms such as *lake, stream, river, delta, mountain,* or *valley* if they are used as part of a name.

Vassar Mountain is a good place to ski.

The Channel Islands are not as isolated as they seem.

The White Hills are lovely in summer.

Do not capitalize the terms when they are not part of a name.

I love the mountains in the deep of winter.

My father has moved to the desert.

Do not capitalize the plural form of the terms unless they are part of a name.

Between Blue and Carson Lakes is a vast mountain range.

SCHOOL COURSES Capitalize the names of specific courses, but do not capitalize general subject areas. Exception: Capitalize the names of language courses.

I liked Math 91, but that isn't surprising since I usually like math classes.
My *physics* class has a two-hour lab each week.
We study short stories in *English*.

DIRECTIONS Capitalize directions only when they are generally considered to be the name or a part of the name of a specific geographical area.

    the East   the South
    the West Coast   Southeast Asia

Words that indicate directions or points of the compass should not be capitalized.

    Turn left at Cahuenga Boulevard and then travel *east*.

Do not capitalize words such as northward, southward, eastward, or westward.

RELIGIOUS WORDS Capitalize the names of religions and their derivatives.

Christianity	Christian	Christian
Seventh-day Adventists	Adventist	Adventist
	Buddhist	Buddhist
Buddhism	Shintoist	Shintoistic
Shinto, Shintoism	Islamic	Muslim
Islam		

Capitalize sects, orders, and movements along with their derivatives.

the Baptist church	Baptists
Christian Science	a Christian Scientist
Gnosticism	a Gnostic
Jehovah's Witnesses	a Jehovah's Witness

Religious contexts often contain the capitalized forms of ideals.

Truth	Goodness
Beauty	Charity

Do not capitalize words like *church*, *synagogue*, or *temple* unless they are part of a name.

    the Church of England
    the Universal Church of Love
    the church on the corner
    the beautiful temple

Capitalize the titles of religious books.

    the Koran   the Bible   the Talmud

Do not capitalize the word *god* if referring to other than the one God of Judeo-Christian religions.

    The Greek *gods* often interfered in the lives of humans.

DISEASES   Unless the name of the disease is based on a person's name, do not capitalize it.

mumps	diabetes
influenza	Parkinson's disease
Asian flu	

PRODUCTS   Unless known by a brand name, do not capitalize the names of food products or cosmetics.

Bond's ice cream	pizza
Cocoa-Cola	Magic Eyes makeup
cantaloupe	Chanel No. 5 perfume

PROFESSIONS   Do not capitalize the names of professions unless they are a person's title coming before or after a name.

    attorney   surgeon
    professor   Doctor Jimenez
    Joseph Campbell, Attorney at Law

EARTH   Do not capitalize the word earth unless it is listed along with the other planets, which are always capitalized.

    On this earth, is there any place without air pollution?
    The Earth, Mars, and Venus are relatively small planets.

ABBREVIATIONS   Do not capitalize abbreviations of words that are not normally capitalized when spelled out.

    mph   Fri.

EXERCISES   A. Add capital letters to any words that require them and remove capitals from those that do not. State the rule for every capital letter you add or delete.
    1. The government official said that he had to spend more time with his family.

2. When archbishop frandee decides to do something, he usually does it.
3. Some would say that politics is filled with fawning lobbyists and snooty senators.
4. I was surprised to discover that the lady biscuit, my friend's yacht, has been to the galapogos islands.
5. Her vacation in the east was uneventful, but the united airlines flight was, at least, a pleasant one.
6. father tried to stop smoking; my sister, at the same time, was trying to learn how.
7. a black I know said he had no patience with "jive artists" of any race.
8. the capital gains tax does not help the "common Man" put bread on the table or braces on his children's teeth.
9. The Moon has always intrigued Dreamers; it is a symbol of the quest for a new life in a new eden.
10. I wanted to take an english class, but the counselor insisted that a mathematics course would be more useful.

B. The paragraph below, from a student's essay, is missing some essential capital letters. Change any incorrect lowercase letters to capitals. Also correct any capitals that should be lower case.

Mexicans are the second largest Group of illegal aliens in the united states for understandable reasons. Because of the united state's curtailment of the bracero program for migrant workers in 1964, there has been a sharp increase in the number of Illegal Aliens coming from mexico. Figures show that 800,000 to 1 million illegal aliens are now in the United States; 500,000 of these are mexicans. Many come from mexico because they are looking for a Better Life in the united states, where a week's salary is equivalent to a month's salary in Mexico.

THE COLON :

In a sentence, the colon normally follows some sort of introductory main clause. The colon is also used as a separator.

THE COLON AS INTRODUCER

Introducing a List or Series

The colon frequently signals that a list or series of items, ideas, or explanations that illustrate the clause preceding it will follow.

General McNally was divorced by his wife for three reasons: his affair with an associate's sister, his violent manner, and his disturbing habit of gnashing his teeth while sleeping.

The results of this year's election are the following: 17 votes for Grand, 117 for Connelly, and 84 for Bogden.

There could have been any number of elements in the list as long as there were at least two. A colon is not usually used after "for example."

The colon should follow only after a main clause, never between a "to be" verb and the complement or the verb and direct object.

Introducing a Related Statement

The colon prepares the reader for an expansion on the idea in the main clause that precedes it. What follows the colon may be either a grammatically complete or incomplete clause.

> Helene possesses a fine gift for music: she has won many awards for her performance.

Note that the main clause that follows the colon is not necessarily capitalized. It would also be correct, and more common today, to place a semicolon between the two closely related main clauses.

> Helene possesses a fine gift for music; she has won many awards for her performances.

The colon may also expand on the introductory clause by explaining a word or phrase that comes at the end of the clause.

> We have only one concern: your safety.
> The information after the colon explains the word *concern*.

Introducing a Quotation

The colon should be used to introduce long quotations. It may also be used in place of a comma to introduce short quotations. The colon is simply a little more formal than the comma. It creates more distance between the statement that leads up to the quotation and the quotation than the comma does.

> It was Buddha who stated the idea best: "The thoughtless are dead already. The thoughtful live forever."
>
> Chan restated his position on open admissions: "Everyone should have a chance to get an education, even though some will prove unworthy."

Use a comma to set off a direct quotation when the introduction could not stand alone as a complete sentence.

> Jim Constance asserted, "Any adult interested in learning should not be kept away from a college's doors."

THE COLON AS SEPARATOR

Openings of Formal Letters

Dear Mr. Simpson:
   Dear Ms. Jones:

Expressions of Time

10:30
11:00

Separation of Titles from Subtitles

The Way of the Land: Our Last Domain
The Doll: The Mystery of Childhood

Using a colon now and then can add sparkle to your style. Be careful to add the colon only in places that would require a stop in the reading. The mechanics of the colon are simple. In most cases two spaces should be left after a colon. With expressions of time, no space is left between the colon and the numbers on either side. When a colon is used with other punctuation, such as parentheses and quotation marks, the colon comes outside the other punctuation.

> When students are unsure of a term their teacher uses, there is only one thing to do (no matter how silly they may feel): raise their hand and ask about it.
>
> There are at least two possible interpretations of the phrase "personal relations": one stressing "personal" and the other stressing "relations."

EXERCISES Directions: Correct the misused colons in the following sentences. Write the correct punctuation, if any, in place of the errors.

A. Jorge had only one complaint to direct to the teacher: two hours is not enough time to answer all the questions on the exam.
B. His only response was: that two hours is not sufficient time to finish the exam.
C. By tomorrow or Friday, there will be initiated industry-wide controls on waste seepage which will include: dumping schedules, use of improved filtering systems, and independent pollution surveillance.
D. English 255, Introduction to Literature, has recently become popular with students since it: introduces students to famous literary works, teaches students how to read critically, and is relevant to the cultural interests so prevalent at most colleges.
E. Cultural anthropologists use the results of studies made by: sociologists, psychologists, and linguists.
F. Variety in the growth patterns of vegetables is considerable: radishes grow quickly in observable spurts, tomatoes develop gradually, and squash starts slow but suddenly races out in all directions.
G. He believed that children were a plague on adults: and that dogs were even worse.
H. Listen to me: you're the ones who are being taken advantage of.
I. She recently told me that most men are: selfish, insecure, spoiled, and crude.
J. She recently told me that she thought men were sad creatures: selfish, insecure, spoiled, and crude.

THE COMMA ,

Commas make reading easy. The comma interrupts a sentence to clarify its grammatical structure and its meaning. When deciding whether to use a comma in a certain spot, you should try to keep your reader in mind. Breathing pauses, although they are not always a reliable guide, can be a helpful aid in the placement of commas. However, everyone has to take a breath at some point, and not all those points require commas. It is therefore important to familiarize yourself with the established rules for comma usage. Combining a knowledge of the rules with your own common sense will give you a feel for those places where the use of commas will make your writing easily readable.

MAIN CLAUSES JOINED BY COORDINATING CONJUNCTIONS

Use commas to separate most main clauses that could stand as individual sentences but are connected by *and, or, for, nor, but, yet,* or *so*. The comma should precede the coordinating conjunction. If the clause or phrase on one side of the conjunction is a subordinate clause, do not connect the two parts of the sentence with a comma. Note the effective use of commas in the following sentences.

> There are times when fights are unavoidable, but to go out looking for them is quite another matter.
>
> The political climate in most Mid-Western towns has been solidly conservative for a long time, and it does not look as if it will change.
>
> We were perplexed by the finding that nearly all the subjects in the sociology experiment had very low incomes, but the people involved had high self-esteem and considered themselves successful.
>
> Only a few of the students in our class are taking photography for credit, so our teacher is very relaxed about attendance.

When the main clauses are brief, the comma may be omitted.

> I may be hungry but I can't eat.
>
> He left and she stayed.

INTRODUCTORY GROUPS OF WORDS

Many introductory groups of words are followed by commas. Some contemporary writers omit the comma if the clause or phrase is brief and is clear without it. However, it is wise to include a comma if you are not sure how clear a particular sentence might be without the comma.

Clauses

Introductory subordinate clauses are usually followed by a comma.

> When our basketball team concentrates on teamwork, we usually win.
>
> If the weather is as cold this January as it was last year, I will need warmer clothes.

Even when introduced by a short clause, some sentences might be misread if the comma after the clause were left out.

> If he tells, somebody might feel hurt.

Without the comma, a reader might perceive the beginning of the sentence as *If he tells somebody*. The comma makes the reading clear. If even for a moment a sentence might be confusing to the reader because you have left off the comma after the introductory clause, you should put the comma in.

Phrases Introductory phrases are usually followed by a comma, unless they are immediately followed by a verb.

> After hearing the news, everybody celebrated.
>
> To surprise her parents, neighbors, and friends, Karen had not told anyone that she was coming home for vacation.
>
> Knowing his own motives had become important.
>
> Going to school at night is stimulating.

Even a short phrase sometimes needs to be set off from the rest of the sentence so that the meaning will be clear.

> To help, his friends pooled their money and lent it to him.

Without the comma, a reader might perceive the beginning of the sentence as *To help his friends*. Use commas in any sentence that could cause a reader even momentary confusion.

Also use commas with short phrases to indicate a distinct pause.

> Before today, I never realized how much I like the rain.
>
> Without a doubt, my dog is bigger than your dog.

TRANSITIONS Transitional words and phrases such as *nevertheless, however, therefore, besides,* and *on the other hand* are usually followed by a comma when they appear in a sentence, set off by commas when they occur in the middle of a sentence, and preceded by a comma when they are at the end of a sentence.

> He did not succeed in business. On the other hand, he did not succeed in life either.
>
> Herman doesn't like formal occasions. He felt very pleased, however, to be at my wedding.
>
> Judy wants to wait until tomorrow morning, but we are leaving tonight, nevertheless.

The comma should be omitted, however, when the transitional word is obviously a part of the sentence, not an addition to it, and requires no breath pause.

> The best qualified applicant was therefore Montoya.

INTERJECTIONS Interjections and short phrases inserted in a sentence to create a conversational tone are set off by commas.

> Well, there doesn't seem to be any complaint.

I think, by George, that the time has come!
You realize, of course, that the situation isn't serious.

ELEMENTS IN A SERIES Use commas to separate the elements in a series. A series is a listing of three or more words, phrases, or clauses in a row, such as *apples, bananas,* and *peaches*.

Close to the surface of the water, bees, mosquitoes, and flies are plentiful food for jumping fish.

Most of the salesmen, all of the managers, and a few of the clerical staff came to work early today to attend a meeting.

I wanted to please my mother, I wanted to shock my father, and I wanted to convince myself.

Although some authorities say the comma before the conjunction in a series is optional, you should develop the habit of putting it in, simply for clarity. You never know when you might be writing a sentence that would be ambiguous without it.

Boredom, jealousy, anger, guilt, a need for reward, and fatigue are some of the psychological reasons for overeating.

If the last comma had been left out, the final element would have read "a need for reward and fatigue." This is not what the writer had in mind, we can be sure.

ADJECTIVES BEFORE NOUNS Use commas to separate two or more coordinate adjectives. Coordinate adjectives independently modify the same noun. The order of these adjectives is reversible without changing the meaning of the sentence. A reliable test for this type of adjective group is to insert the word *and* between the adjectives. If you still have a fluent sentence and the adjectives still say what you mean, the adjectives are coordinate.

The *tarnished, worn-thin* fork gave the food a metallic taste.
The fork has two qualities. It is *tarnished* and *worn-thin*.

A *dedicated, humane, concerned* veterinarian from Denver saved my dog's life.
The veterinarian has three qualities. He is *dedicated, humane,* and *concerned*.

A *wealthy, friendly, too-attractive* woman met my uncle for what he called a "business lunch."
The woman has three qualities. She is *wealthy, friendly,* and *too-attractive*.

Do not use commas between two or more cumulative adjectives. Cumulative adjectives do not modify their noun independently. Adjectives indicating number, color, size, and age are often closely linked to the noun that follows them. In such cases, the preceding adjective often modifies the combination of the second adjective and the noun, and the order of the two adjectives is not reversible.

The old brick house was well kept.
>This sentence describes a *brick house* that was *old*, not an *old* and *brick* house. The sentence would not mean the same thing if the adjectives were reversed.

UNESSENTIAL ELEMENTS Use commas to set off unessential modifiers and appositives in a sentence. A modifier and appositive is unessential if what it modifies is fully identified without it. A modifier is essential if it limits the scope or meaning of what it modifies.

Note the function of modifiers and appositives in the following sentences.

Unessential (requires commas): Commander Michilen, *who conducted the inspection of the barracks*, found no unauthorized weapons.
>Place commas around unessential elements. In this sentence there is only one Commander Michilen. The title and the name fully identify him for the reader

Essential (requires no commas): The commander *who conducted the inspection of the barracks* found no unauthorized weapons.
>Since a reader can identify which commander is meant only by the information in the *who* clause, that clause is essential to the sentence and therefore is not set off by commas.

Unessential (requires commas): His attention to detail, *it is known*, was compulsive and undesirable.
>The underlined phrase could be removed without changing the meaning of the sentence.

Essential (requires no commas): The Spanish poet *Lorca* wrote a lovely piece of verse about his guitarra.
>*Lorca* is not set off with commas because it distinguishes the subject, a poet named Lorca, from other Spanish poets.

CONTRASTS Use commas to set off contrasted elements.

>Their grandmother, not mine, is standing on the porch.
>
>I want to proceed toward, rather than away from, my intended goal.

DIRECT ADDRESS When people are directly addressed by their names, the names are set off from the rest of the sentence by commas.

>I wonder, John, when your dental appointment is.
>
>Ladies and Gentlemen, may I present Mr. Rhodes?
>
>It's later than you think, Sally.

OMISSIONS Use commas to show omissions from parallel statements.

>Mary got an "A"; John, a "B."
>
>To err is human; to forgive, divine.

A Glossary of Punctuation and Mechanics

QUOTATIONS Use commas to set off a quotation from the rest of the sentence, unless the quotation is integrated into the grammar of your own sentence.

> My best friend looked at my girlfriend and said, "Glad to meet you."
> Mark said, "Can you tell me where to find Mr. Johnson?"
> According to my mother, my fiance is "one girl in a million."

CUMULATIVE SENTENCES In a cumulative sentence, the main clause comes first and is followed by additional modifiers, expanding the base idea. Commas should separate the modifiers from each other and from the initial clause.

> People streaked down Main Street, trying with all their might to escape the flames from the burning buildings, their legs flying in front of them, their arms propelling them.
>
> No woman should apply for a job she is incapable of doing, hungry, liberated, and adaptable as she might be.

NUMERALS Commas are used to set off every three digits of a number.

> 42,319   2,350   1,275,500

They are not used, however, when writing years or zip codes.

> 1979   77011

For telephone numbers, parentheses and hyphens are used.

> (213) 555-1212

DATES Dates are usually written in one of two ways.

> July 7, 1969   7 July 1969

Notice that in the second example, no comma is used. The form chosen also determines whether a comma should follow the year when a date is used in a sentence.

> May 30, 1980 is the last day on which applications will be accepted.
> On 7 December 1945 Japan attacked Pearl Harbor.

If the day of the week is included, it should be set off from the date by a comma.

> She was born on Monday, January 17, 1977.

When just the month and the year are used, the comma is optional.

> August 1977 was the hottest month I can remember.
> January, 1978 was a dreary month.

ADDRESSES Commas are used to separate the elements of an address when it is included in a sentence.

> His address is Daniel Speigelman, Attorney, 24 Drury Lane, Oswego, Illinois 54041.

Notice that no comma is used between the state and the zip code. When written as it would appear on an envelope, no commas are used between the elements.

> Daniel Speigelman
> Attorney
> 24 Drury Lane
> Oswego, Illinois 54041

STATISTICS Commas are used to set off statistics.

> Her mother is five feet, eleven inches tall.
> Read page 26, line 5 aloud.
> Act IV, scene 3 is the climax.

AVOID THE EXCESSIVE USE OF COMMAS If an extra comma seems necessary to clarify your meaning, you should not hesitate to put it in. At the same time, you should be aware that most established writers today avoid using a lot of commas. Using commas only where they are needed makes for the most clarity. A sentence with too many commas in it confuses readers more than it helps them. There are a few places in sentences where you might tend to overuse commas. As you read through the following guidelines, note how the use of excessive commas actually obscures the meaning of the sentences. Each incorrect sentence that follows would be correct if the comma were left out.

Commas never come between the subject of the sentence and the verb, unless they are setting off unessential elements.

> Incorrect: The issue I have been trying to get on the June ballot, is property tax relief.
>> Do not confuse a pause in this particular sentence with the need for a comma. No comma is needed.
>
> Incorrect: "To teach in a public school, is a difficult position," admitted the Superintendent of Schools.
>> Naturally, a pause comes after a long subject with modifiers, but no comma is needed.

Commas should never come between the verb and the direct object or the subject complement except to separate unessential elements from the rest of the sentence.

Incorrect: The reason the power company has been waiting so long to begin construction is, that the people of the town requested a hearing on the project.

Incorrect: The three ingredients of old-fashioned ice cream as we knew it were, cream, butter, and sweetener.
Note that a colon after *were* would also be incorrect.

Incorrect: I told the officer, that, had she come an hour earlier, we might have been able to contribute to the fireman's ball.

EXERCISES Directions: Remove any unnecessary *commas* and insert any that are missing.

A. A man, who told neighbors that he saw the murder committed, later was too frightened to testify.
B. Having many sisters and brothers living with you in your youth, makes you feel secure.
C. Even, if I had studied for that math test I wouldn't have known the answers to the questions the teacher asked.
D. The last person in the world I thought would show up on graduation day was, my uncle.
E. Intramural sports are fun, but not as much fun as intermural.
F. The reason over half my friends wanted to watch the movie on television, was, it was filmed in our neighborhood.
G. Neighborhood parties brighten up the block, and can even make friends of enemies.
H. My youngest brother, who was elected president of his eighth-grade class, lost all his popularity when he started to associate with the wrong crowd in high school.
I. The Roberts who introduced my wife to her current employer were at our party on Christmas Day.
J. Registration to vote is a necessary system, because, otherwise, everybody would show up at the same polling place and other places would be left empty.
K. I lost my place in the book I was reading, when the telephone rang.
L. Street violence is at its height, in the hot, summer months.
M. Unless we try to change the new law that allows adult book stores to open, in any neighborhood, we could find our children bringing home copies of *Hustler* and *Oui*. Maybe that's an exaggeration but the situation could get serious.
N. On the one hand we expect political candidates to be honest. On the other hand we want them to be shrewd.
O. Therefore we have concluded that young children are not harmed by television violence. But are we right?

THE DASH   — —

Writers use the dash to indicate a break in the thought expressed in a sentence. The dash, like commas and parentheses, separates part of a sentence from the main clause. The dash is different from these other marks of punctuation, however, because the break in thought that it creates is greater than the break introduced by the comma and less than the break introduced by the parentheses. Furthermore, the dash creates a sudden shift of thought. In other words, what dashes set apart is more important to the sense of the sentence than what the parentheses set apart, and less important—though more dramatically presented—than what commas set apart. When what is to be set off has punctuation within itself—as does the series "Fred, Mary, and Jorge," for instance—dashes rather than commas work well.

Dashes may set off a word, a phrase, or a clause and may do so at the beginning, middle, or end of a sentence.

Try to add liveliness to your writing by using dashes, but remember that you should use them sparingly. An essay sprinkled with dashes is like a highway with too many stop signs—annoying. The overuse of dashes makes them ineffective. Note the effective use of dashes in the following sentences.

> The phenomenon of "precognition"—perhaps the most often reported extrasensory perceptual experience—offers an explanation for many dreams.

> All the men—William, James, Arthur, and Ted—arrived at ten in order to get a volleyball court by eleven.

Be careful when you use dashes in the middle of a sentence. The rest of the sentence must be grammatically complete without the portion set off by dashes. The tendency to fit the end of the sentence to the part of the sentence in dashes leads many to writing incorrect sentences.

> Ineffective: Although she hoped for her children to attend the best possible school—she wanted one with excellent teachers and supplies—but she did not want to live in an expensive neighborhood to buy the privilege of education.

The writer goes wrong by inserting the *but*, which shows she has lost sight of the first word in her sentence. Make sure you do not slip into this error. Read over the sentence without the portion in dashes to make sure it could stand alone grammatically.

The dash is effectively used in certain specific situations.

SETTING OFF A CLIMACTIC PHRASE

The dash can be used to emphasize a phrase or word at the end of a sentence.

> Swimming was the best event of the day—the only event that was really fun.

At the end of the day, there was only one thing left to do—sleep.

SETTING OFF A SUMMARY

The dash can focus the meaning of an involved sentence.

People who will give you their last dollar, who will comfort you, even when they are depressed, who will listen to your plans and dreams as if they were their own, who will dare to criticize you to help you, who will remain loyal at all cost—these are the ideal friends we carry around in our minds.

EXPANSION ON THE MAIN CLAUSE

Use the dash to expand on a word or phrase in the main clause.

Shelley's moods—happiness one moment, depression the next—were difficult to judge.

Harriet had decided to leave early—why, no one knew.

The high school diploma—that essential piece of paper—was worth studying for at night.

INSERTING AN APPOSITIVE OR PARENTHETICAL ELEMENT

The man—the one at the bakery—must have been more than seventy, but he arrived on a bicycle.

Before we knew it, Alicia—that sensitive girl!—had phoned the chaplain.

INSERTING ONE SENTENCE INTO ANOTHER

A dash may be used to insert a complete sentence next to the word it explains or expands on.

Maria—she was the second person to arrive—slowly pressed the door buzzer.

The mission was to be a difficult one—three men would have to travel on foot across the frozen lake—and not many were willing to take the chance.

SETTING OFF MODIFIERS WITH INTERNAL PUNCTUATION

Use a dash to make the separation from the rest of the sentence clear when the phrase enclosed in dashes has its own special punctuation.

All the volunteers—Rita, Ted, Linda, Carole, and Jack—had grown up in the inner city and were used to many of the problems faced by the people in the county program.

SETTING OFF A LIST FROM A CONCLUSION

Games, dolls, puzzles—these are the effects of an affluent childhood. But are they good for the child?

The dash is made on the typewriter by connecting with two unspaced hyphens the last letter of the last word you typed to the first letter of the next word:

the old dog—the poor old dog

In handwriting draw a line twice as long as that for a hyphen. Elements set off by dashes should be separated grammatically from the rest of the sentence. When the idea set off in dashes occurs in the middle of the sentence, be sure to place dashes on both sides of it—at the beginning and at the end. When a dash is used where a comma would normally fall, the comma is omitted.

> When I reported the incident—the burning car, the bolt of flames, the odd visitor—the police looked at me as if they thought I had dreamed it.

EXERCISES Directions: Insert dashes where appropriate into the sentences below.

A. The people who attended our party, Mike, Joe, and Christopher, were considerate enough to help us clean up.
B. Dogs, cats, goldfish: they would all be a drain on my schedule, and that is why I have no pets.
C. My aunt bought me the pair of boots, a sturdy pair that look like the kind cowboys wear that I had wanted for months.
D. There is one thing I demand from every friend: consideration for the feelings of others.
E. During the filming of the movie *Some Prefer Nettles* an earthquake struck, but much to everyone's relief, nothing was damaged.
F. The train, the last one to leave Oakland this year, departs from the terminal at 11:15.
G. The medical supplies, desperately needed to keep the victims of the accident alive, arrived by helicopter before they were expected.
H. The best kind of hero, the only kind I can take seriously, is the hero who does not try to be one.
I. It wasn't his life he ended up fighting for in that war; it was his philosophy of living.
J. Preferring to be known as Dr. Stone, Ellaine Doople, daughter of the man who invented carrot peelers, was hired as Chief of Nutrition for our local hospital.

ELLIPSES . . .

Ellipses, or ellipsis points, are used to indicate omissions from quoted material. They are handy for removing those parts of a quotation that do not add to the point you wish to make. These omissions may range from a single word to entire paragraphs.

When using ellipses, you should keep several things in mind. First, make sure that your omissions do not change the meaning or intent of the quoted passage. Second, all of the sentences in the quotation must still be grammatically correct even though you have left out some of the original words. The same guidelines apply to sentences that are a combination of your own words and quoted material. Finally, ellipses should be used only when quoting the work of others. You should not use them in your own writing.

PROSE
Midsentence

Three spaced periods can be used to note omissions in the middle of a sentence of a quotation. Compare the original quotation with the student's use of it in the example that follows.

> That budget can be drawn up in no time with everyone in mind, not with just a few top officials in the company getting all the benefits.

> Michael Conrad, the union leader, disapproves of the proposed budget: "That budget can be drawn up . . . with everyone in mind, not with just a few top officials in the company getting all the benefits.

Ends and Beginnings of Sentences

Four spaced periods—the period marking the end of the sentence added to the three ellipsis points—show that the end of a sentence in a quotation has been omitted. Again, note the original quotation and the student's use of it.

> It can be disastrous to continue our operation before a thorough investigation of each department's safety standards, before an agreement upon the part of all of us that safety on the job is what counts. Unless we agree to carry this procedure forward, we might as well expect to be closed down by the county.

> Mr. Cohen says, "It can be disastrous to continue our operation before a thorough investigation of each department's safety standards. . . . Unless we agree to carry this procedure forward, we might as well expect to be closed down by the county."

Ellipsis points are rarely used at the beginning of a quotation. Most quoted material is extracted from a passage, and it is therefore already obvious to most readers that passages often begin before the section extracted for quotation. In the rare instances in which the use of ellipses will clarify the meaning of the quoted passage, you may use three spaced periods before the first word of the quotation. The quotation marks, if needed, would come before the ellipsis points.

Other Punctuation

Punctuation may be retained from the original quoted passage and placed on either side of the ellipses if doing so will help retain the meaning of the passage.

POETRY

A line or more omitted from poetry is shown by an entire line of spaced periods.

THE EXCLAMATION POINT !

The exclamation point is used with strong imperatives or to show intense emotion.

> Watch out!
> Help!
> She loves me!

Exclamation points should rarely be used in essays written for classes. Rather than relying on them, you should try to make sure that your choice of words reveals any emotion you wish to convey.

QUOTING, DIALOGUE, AND APPEALS

When quoting, writing dialogue, or trying to move an audience through an appeal to action, you may find that an exclamation point is either required or appropriate. Remember, however, that exclamation points should always be used sparingly. Using too many of them lessens their effect. You should avoid exclamation points in sentences such as the following.

> Weak: If abortion is not paid for by welfare, mothers and children will starve, and the populace will be overrun by poor, unhealthy children!
>
> > No exclamation point is needed. The language is emotive enough, perhaps too emotive for expository writing (see p. 101).
>
> Effective: Women of the United States, get off your rump roasts!
>
> Effective: "I can't believe it. All my money—gone!" screamed Hillary.

INTERJECTIONS

Interjections, expressions such as *well, ah, oh, whew, too bad,* and *darn it all*, are used to interrupt the normal flow of sentences in order to express emotion. An interjection is usually set off from the main clause by commas (see p. 374). If the sentence is meant to convey strong emotion, an exclamation point may be used for the entire sentence.

> I am late again, darn it all!
>
> Ah, look at that view!

Milder interjections, of course, take a period at the end.

> Oh, that's too bad.

In some rare cases, where the emotion is particularly strong, both the interjection and the sentence will take an exclamation point.

> Whew! That was a close one!

Again, with sentences having interjections as well as all other kinds of sentences, you should be very sparing in your use of exclamation points.

THE HYPHEN   -

The hyphen is used to divide words at the end of a line, to separate some prefixes from their base words, and to form compound words.

DIVIDING WORDS AT THE END OF A LINE

You may wish to avoid the problem of hyphenating words at the end of a line by always taking care to end lines with complete words. But most writers, at one time or another, wish to hyphenate words out of convenience—they have already begun to type or write a word before they realize they are at the right-hand margin. In order to maintain the margin, they choose to divide the word. Words must be divided between their syllables. Some words are easier to divide than others because the syllabication is obvious. Words with prefixes or suffixes are usually divided between the prefix or suffix and the base word.

Pre-fix   Com-fort-ing-ly
Pro-vide   Use-ful
Re-tire   In-spir-ing

Words with double consonants usually are divided between the two consonants.

Bab-ble   Em-bel-lish   Cun-ning

Syllable divisions can often be guessed at by the pronunciation of a word, but whenever you are in doubt of the proper place to divide a word, the best bet is to look up the word in the dictionary. There are a few rules for dividing words at the end of a line, even when you already know the syllables.

One-syllable words can never be broken.
Proper names of people, places, or things should not be broken.
A one-letter syllable should not be used either at the end of one line or the beginning of the next.
Two-letter syllables should not begin a line.
Words should not be divided in a way that causes even momentary confusion.
Hyphenated words should be divided at the hyphen only.
The last word on a page should not be divided.

HYPHENATING WORDS IN THE TEXT

Prefixes

The hyphenation of prefixes from their base words is a tricky area in the mechanics of grammar. Some words are hyphenated and some are not. To make matters even more confusing, some words used to be hyphenated that are now written without the hyphen. The following general rules can serve as good guidelines, but for specific words you may be unsure about, you should always check in your dictionary.

When the last letter of the prefix and the first letter of the base word are the same, the prefix is normally hyphenated from the base word.

Pre-existing   Anti-intellectual
De-emphasize

Sometimes, however, the word is not hyphenated when the consonants are the same.

Unnecessary   Nonnegotiable

There are also those words like *cooperation*, where the hyphenation has been dropped as a result of the trend to reduce the number of words joined by hyphens. Again, when in doubt, check your dictionary.

The prefix *ex*, meaning former, is usually hyphenated.

Ex-officio   Ex-ball player
Ex-husband

The prefix *self* is usually hyphenated.

Self-starting   Self-involved

However, be careful not to confuse the prefix *self* with the base *self*. *Selfish* and *selfless*, for example, are both composed of the base *self* plus a suffix. There is no prefix in either word, and there are no hyphens.

When confusion would occur from combining a prefix with the base word, the word is usually hyphenated.

Re-collect (to pick up again)
Recollect (to remember)
Co-op (a cooperative)
Coop (a home for chickens)

Hyphenate when joining a prefix to a proper noun.

Un-American   Anti-Darwinism
Anti-Marxist

Sometimes, however, the words are not hyphenated in current usage.

Unchristian
Antichrist

Prefixes such as *ultra, pseudo,* and *co* should be checked in the dictionary; their usage varies greatly. Most dictionaries will use a dot between syllables and a hyphen between hyphenated parts of a word.

Compound Words

Sometimes words are used together to act as a single noun or adjective. Such words are often hyphenated.

Nouns

When two or more words act as a single noun, the way they are written varies greatly. Some that were originally hyphenated are now combined.

Bookkeeper   Basketball

In other cases, the words remain separate.

Boot camp   Problem solving

In still others, the words are hyphenated.

Vice-president   Mother-in-law
Mayor-elect   Know-it-all

Unless you are familiar with the particular words, the only way you can be sure whether or not they should be hyphenated, remain separate, or be combined is to look them up in your dictionary.

Adjectives When two or more words act as a single adjective, they are connected by a hyphen if they precede the noun they modify.

> A soft-spoken person
> The all-in-one automatic cooker
> The well-designed house
> A mass-produced toy

When the words follow the noun, they are not hyphenated.

> The man was soft spoken.
> The house was well designed.

Also, if one of the words ends in -ly, the combination of words is not hyphenated.

> A firmly drawn decision
> The perfectly executed crime

A special rule operates with compound adjectives that include the word *all*. Words formed using *all* are hyphenated wherever they appear in a sentence.

> All-purpose paragraph
> All-around fellow

Sometimes you want to join two separate prefixes or words to the same noun. Normally, you would hyphenate each prefix. In combination, they are still hyphenated. Remember to place a hyphen after the prefix that precedes the conjunction.

> Second- and third-grade students

A fast- and sure-footed hiker

Numbers Numbers between twenty and one hundred are hyphenated when written out no matter where they appear in a sentence. Fractions are also always hyphenated.

Seventy-nine   One-third
Thirty-four   One-half

EXERCISES A. From the dictionary, copy out the following words, showing the syllable breaks where each might be divided. If the word is only one syllable, write "one."

1. Loosely
2. Apparent
3. Infinite
4. Tryst
5. Caution
6. Apologetic
7. Knowledge
8. Recently
9. International
10. Reclusive
11. Reputation
12. Accidental
13. Restoration
14. Opportunity
15. Reforestation
16. Pliant
17. Pronunciation
18. Children
19. Anxious
20. Deliberate

B. Add hyphens where needed in the italicized words in the following sentences.

1. The *infant mortality rate* has decreased greatly in the past ten years among children born to mothers in their thirties.
2. Julia was a *self reliant woman* who did not need others to make her life complete.
3. That *pseudo intellectual* is not worth considering as a candidate for office.
4. She is the most *self centered* person I have ever known.
5. One of her *co workers* is married to an actor who makes a lot of money.
6. *Try as you will* to get there on time, the stores always seem to close just before you arrive.
7. Suzanne was an outgoing individual, but she was *nevertheless* often lonely.
8. Their *ex football coach* left teaching to become an advertising executive.
9. His views are strongly *anti business and taxes*.
10. My *ex boyfriend and employee* recently got a new job.
11. A *by product* of inflation is *unemployment*.
12. As part of a sociological experiment, three people on Market Street were stopped by a *passerby* and each was given a thousand dollar bill.

13. The *tenth and eleventh grade* students at Hoover High were instructed in self-defense measures.
14. The *who done it movie* playing around the corner is worth seeing.
15. This is the *eighth or ninth time* I have seen *Gone with the Wind,* and I would still go again.

ITALICS

See entry under Underlining.

MULTIPLE END PUNCTUATION

Avoid the use of multiple punctuation for the purpose of emphasis. Instead decide which mark of punctuation is most fitting.

Weak:	The conditions in Mexican prisons are terrible!.
Effective:	The conditions in Mexican prisons are terrible.
Weak:	And just why should women accept lower salaries than men for the same work?!
Effective:	And just why should women accept lower salaries than men for the same work?

Of course, it is correct to use parentheses, quotation marks, and ellipses along with other punctuation without violating the rules.

NUMBERS

NUMBERS WITHIN SENTENCES

As a general rule, numbers that do not require more than two words should be spelled out in a sentence.

Twenty-four   Three thousand   One-half

When Jeremy was *thirty-three*, he was married for the *third* time.

My grandmother lived to be *one hundred* years old.

Numbers that would require more than two words should be written in figures.

154   5,423   22,324

Numbers in short lists should be spelled out, but figures should be used for long lists or for comparisons among several numbers.

My uncle has *three* dogs, *four* cats, and *one* parakeet.

The stock for the Johnson and Meyers Corporation has fluctuated quite a bit over the past *three* months: starting at *18½*, it dropped to *11*, rose again to *17*, and is now back down to *16¼*.

However, if any number in a paragraph referring to a particular category is written in figures, all of the numbers referring to that category should also be placed in figures, even though some of them could be spelled out in one or two words.

My grandfather has *5* horses and *125* cows.

Of the *three* buildings built in the past *two* years, one has *60* stories, one has *75*, and the tallest has *105*.

NUMBERS BEGINNING SENTENCES Numbers at the beginning of sentences should always be spelled out, even if other numbers in the same category are written in figures. If spelling out the number would be awkward or if you wish to avoid spelling out one number and writing another in figures, the sentence should be rearranged so that the number does not come first.

Incorrect: 125 men and 132 women were in my graduating class.
Effective: There were 125 men and 132 women in my graduating class.

TIME The time of day should usually be spelled out.

My biology class begins at eight in the morning.
Some people eat supper as early as five o'clock.
We should be finished by half past three.

However, figures should be used when you wish to emphasize the exact moment or when using a.m or p.m.

The movie starts at 6:25.
We got home at 5:30 a.m.
There are two buses a day to Cincinnati, one at 10:00 a.m. and the other at 4:36 p.m.
Last night, I studied from 8 p.m. until 2 a.m.

You should never use *morning* after a.m. or *evening* after p.m. Also, you should never use *o'clock* with a.m., p.m., or with figures.

DATES The year should always be placed in figures unless it comes at the beginning of a sentence.

The first award was made in 1978.
Nineteen seventy-five was not so very long ago.

There are several ways to write dates, all of them acceptable.

May 6, 1978
6 May 1978
the sixth of May
May sixth

According to *A Manual of Style*, The University of Chicago Press—an authoritative source widely used by publishers—*st, d,* and *th* should not be used with figures.

May 6   not   *May 6th*

Ordinarily, you should spell out the names of centuries in the text of a paper. The names of decades are also spelled out.

> twentieth century
> the thirties and forties

ROADS Use arabic numerals with highways.

> Interstate 90   Route 66
> Texas 291

However, spell out the numbers of street names.

> Fifth Avenue   Eighty-fourth Street

PARTS OF BOOKS Always use arabic figures to refer to pages.

> page 55
> page 77

Chapter numbers may be indicated either with an arabic figure and a small letter "c" in the word chapter or with the number spelled out and capitalized along with the capitalized word Chapter. The guidelines are the same for *part* and *exercise*. You should, however, decide on one way and use it consistently within a particular paper.

> Chapter Seven   part 4
> chapter 7   Exercise Eleven
> Part Four   exercise 11

VERY LARGE ROUND NUMBERS Figures may be used for emphasis or for comparison with other figures, but they should be avoided if the number of zeros becomes cumbersome. All the following usages are correct.

> Two million people
> 2 million people
> 2,000,000 people

There seems to be a trend toward using the plural for *millions* and *billions* when the words are used as nouns. All the following usages are correct.

>two billions
>
>>or
>
>two billion
>
>>but
>
>two billion people

CURRENCY Most units of currency including whole dollar amounts should be spelled out.

>My gloves cost eight dollars.
>
>Bus fare has gone up to thirty-five cents.

Fractional amounts should be placed in figures.

>They are on sale for $4.99.

When whole dollar amounts appear in the same sentence as fractional amounts, you should place all the amounts in figures.

>One usually costs $4.00, but you can buy three for $10.25.

There are various forms for very large amounts of money. All are correct, and you should pick the one you like. Then use that form throughout the paper.

>three million dollars
>$3 million
>$3,000,000

FRACTIONS AND PERCENTS Fractions should be spelled out when they require no more than two words.

>The man was able to pay only a third of the costs incurred in his accident.
>
>Two-thirds of the group arrived early.

Whole numbers mixed with fractions should usually be written as figures.

>Of the couple's assets, only 66 and ⅔ percent could be used as collateral on the loan for the new building.

However, certain commonly used mixed numbers are spelled out.

>My bill was one and a half times as much as yours.
>
>Five and a quarter percent interest on savings adds up.

Except in common usages, as in the above example, percentages should usually be written in arabic numerals. They should only be expressed with the percent symbol, %, in technical or scientific writing. In other types of writing, the word *percent* should be spelled out.

NUMBERS IN PARENTHESES In legal documents and commercial writing, numbers are sometimes spelled out and then repeated as an arabic numeral in parentheses.

The fee should not exceed seventy-five (75) dollars.

In all other types of writing, this usage should be avoided.

PLURALS OF NUMBERS You may form the plurals of arabic numerals either by adding an *'s* or by simply adding an *s*. Either way is correct, but make sure that you are consistent throughout the paper.

| 5's | 10's | 40's |
| 5s | 10s | 40s |

When numbers are spelled out, their plurals are formed just as they would be for any other nouns.

| Fives | Tens | Forties |

EXERCISES A. Assuming that the following phrases appear in a paragraph without any other numbers in it, indicate which of the numbers and symbols should be spelled out.
1. 153 couples
2. 97 days
3. $200
4. 1,000 people
5. 84 percent
6. 666 letters
7. 308 books
8. $100,000
9. 32 guests
10. 21 months
11. 18 men
12. 454 dollars
13. ⅓ of the pie
14. 10.2%
15. 75%
16. 40 individuals
17. 4,024 contestants
18. 12 p.m.
19. 20 women
20. 3.44 liters

B. Correct any errors in the writing of numbers in the following sentences.
1. When my uncle was 37, he married a countess in Spain.
2. The year 1984 is expected to raise eyebrows.
3. 19½ percent of the company's revenue went to charity last year.
4. Joseph is 3, his sister Marce is 12, and little Karen is two months old.
5. As corny as it may sound, I love films from the 40's.
6. If 15 or more people sign up for the class, it will not be dropped.

7. 3 of our guests were from Montana.
8. 1.333 was the answer to the math problem.
9. The budget was for nearly 1,000,000 dollars.
10. Chapter 5 is the hardest one in my math book.

PARENTHESES ( )

Parentheses are used to include extra information, such as explanations, amplifications, or digressions that you consider important but not quite important enough to interrupt the flow of your writing. The material inside parentheses, then, is a sort of aside that adds meaning to your discussion but does not exactly fit into it.

> The entire family (Mary, Karen, Bob, I, Mom, and Dad) are the token intellectuals on our block.
>
> H. G. Wells (1866–1946) was more than a simple science fiction writer.
>
> I told her that I was unsure (I actually did know) and that I would find out the answer to her question the next morning.

CROSS REFERENCES

Cross references are often enclosed in parentheses and placed next to the word or phrase that the cross reference expands on.

> The predicate adjective (see Chapter 13) should take the participle form of the verb.

ENCLOSING LETTERS OR NUMBERS

Parentheses should be used to enclose letters or numbers in the running text of a paper. This type of enumeration is most common in papers written for the sciences, social sciences, and other technical fields such as mathematics.

> The main types of wooden joints are (a) dovetail, (b) mortise and tenon, (c) miter, (d) oblique, (e) square butt, (f) housed, or (g) rabbet.
>
> Before a juvenile is placed behind bars, he or she is screened closely by the staff of the Kirkby Institute and the case is judged (1) approved, (2) approved with reservation, (3) approved with strong reservation, or (4) rejected.

Be sure not to confuse parentheses with brackets. Brackets are used for interior comments in quotations or for parentheses within parentheses.

Parentheses, dashes, and commas can all be effectively used to set off parenthetical expressions. Commas are used when the parenthetical elements are closely knit to the rest of the sentence. Dashes usually emphasize the elements, but parentheses de-emphasize them. Used sparingly, parentheses are interesting and lively. Overused, they are constant interruptions in the flow of thought and thus annoying to the reader.

PUNCTUATION WITH PARENTHESES

A sentence containing parenthetical elements must be grammatically correct even when the parenthetical elements are excluded. This requirement makes the use of punctuation with parentheses a bit tricky at times. There are a few cases that require special use of punctuation. If a remark in parentheses is independent of other sentences and is a full sentence on its own, the period is contained *within* the end parenthesis.

> When it was ready, Laura refused to eat the lasagne I had just spent an hour and a half preparing because she had said she was in the mood for it. (This annoying habit of changing her mind was nothing new.)

If the parentheses contain a complete sentence that is inserted into another sentence, the remark in parentheses neither begins with a capital letter (unless the word is always capitalized), nor ends with a period. The period comes at the end of the sentence into which the parenthetical remarks have been inserted.

> Sheilah Graham depicts F. Scott Fitzgerald (he was a close friend) as a person full of tenderness. She tells about the time he steps into the bathroom while she is bathing to set a pillow gently beneath her head.

A comma should never precede a remark in parentheses; if a comma would normally have followed what comes before the parentheses, place it after the closing parenthesis.

> If students can get as far as their junior year in college (six out of ten can), they have already mastered the academic formula and should have no trouble with the last two years of college.

Often no punctuation is needed after the parentheses.

> Did you ever wonder what draws people (men, women, and children) to nude beaches?

EXERCISES

Directions: Correct any errors in the use of parentheses and correct the punctuation used with them in the following sentences.

A. The act of writing an essay, (a short expository piece), is as creative as writing fiction.
B. Their astonishment at the beauty of the snowy mountain roads reminded us that they were from sunny (and warm) California.
C. Most of the members of the band had rehearsed all week for the one-evening performance, (only a few had missed rehearsals because this was the really big night for the troupe) and they were tense and exhilarated as the curtain was drawn.
D. The security officers were too worn out (they had been working all day) to help us carry our parcels, but it was nice to have their company.

E. Mary knew her way around Memphis (a point of pride with someone like her); she led us up alleys, using all sorts of shortcuts, so that we would get to the restaurant in time for our reservations.
F. Louise Acker (my great aunt) was a suffragist.
G. Guinea pigs, (I was surprised to learn,) are intelligent pets, considering how little they are and how people always laugh at them.
H. In the end, no knowledge can hurt. (Even when it is the painful truth, knowing is better than not knowing). The doctors are morally obligated to tell people what their conditions really are so that they can plan their lives accordingly.

THE PERIOD

END PUNCTUATION

Declarative and Imperative Sentences

Of the three types of end punctuation—the period, the question mark, and the exclamation point—the period is the most common. It is used to indicate the end of many sentences.

> I hope to go to Florida on my vacation.
> Wait a minute.

Sentence fragments used deliberately for effect are also usually followed by a period.

> Ice and snow. Freezing cold. Will winter ever be over?

You should remember, however, to be very careful when using sentence fragments. For the most part, they should be avoided.

Indirect Questions

A period is used to mark the end of an indirect question, which is a statement about a question.

> She asked me if I would go with her.
> The senator wondered whether he would be re-elected.

Sometimes one can use either a period or a question mark.

> Would you try to be on time tomorrow.

Although this statement is worded as a question, it is actually more of a command than it is a request, so the period is appropriate. However, a question mark would also be correct.

WITH OTHER PUNCTUATION

The period is used in conjunction with only three other types of punctuation: quotation marks, parentheses, and brackets.

Quotation Marks

The period should be placed inside both quotation marks and double quotation marks.

> My favorite short story is "The Dead."
> She said, "My mother told me there would be days like this."

John complained, "I have always had trouble defining words like 'love.'"

Parentheses and Brackets

The period is used in the same way with both parentheses and brackets. If the enclosed expression comes at the end of a sentence, the period goes on the outside.

Jackie was there (as usual).

One of the protesters carried a sign that read: "Save Amerika [sic]. Leave now."

If the expression is a complete and independent sentence, the period is placed inside the parentheses or brackets.

Every fifteen minutes or so, I checked the locks on the doors and windows. (I have never liked being alone.)

The president stated: "Our most important possessions are *freedom* and *dignity*. [The italics are mine.] Without them, we can never be happy."

However, if a complete sentence is inserted as a parenthetical expression into another sentence, the period should be omitted.

Once upon a time (I hope this does not sound too familiar), two young children were playing in the park.

ABBREVIATIONS

A period often follows abbreviations.

e.g.   a.m.   m.p.h.
N.A.S.A.   p.m.
N.O.W.

Some of the words on the list above could also have been abbreviated without the periods.

NASA
NOW
mph

Neither method is more correct than the other, but you should try to be consistent in a particular paper. Scientific and technical writing usually calls for the use of certain abbreviations without the periods. Good indicators of the appropriate form are the sources you use for the papers you write. For instance, you may wish to check if journals in the field use or leave off periods.

When an abbreviation comes at the end of a sentence, the period for the abbreviation also stands as end punctuation. When the abbreviation is the last word in the parenthesis, the period may also stand as the end punctuation.

AS A DECIMAL POINT   Periods are used as decimal points in figures.

 11.25%   2.5 acres
 $25.95

AS AN ELLIPSIS POINT   Three spaced periods are used to signal that something has been left out of a quotation.

THE QUESTION MARK   ?

DIRECT QUESTIONS   All direct questions should end with question marks.

 Why would a doctor become a politician?
 Is it possible to learn how to spell in ten days?
 I read that the bank was defrauded for a million dollars—is it true?

Many questions begin with interrogative words such as *what, which, who, when,* and so forth.

INDIRECT QUESTIONS   Indirect questions are statements about questions. They are not actually questions themselves. Therefore, an indirect question should end with a period instead of a question mark.

 He kept asking himself what he had done wrong.

The preceding sentence is not a question even though the word *asking* appears. However, notice how easily the statement may be turned into a question.

 He kept asking himself, "What have I done wrong?"

One of the best ways to tell whether a sentence is a direct question or an indirect question is to figure out if it asks for a response. If it does, it is probably a direct question. If it does not, you can be almost sure that it is an indirect question. Here are some more examples of indirect questions.

 I wonder if it will rain today.
 They asked me how they might find the library.
 The committee wanted to know whether the motion had been passed.
 I asked him when the assignment was due.

For some more information about indirect questions, see page 514.

INTERIOR QUESTIONS   Direct questions that are inserted into a sentence and are set off from the rest of it usually take question marks. Basically, the question is set into a statement and the end punctuation for the sentence is usually a period or another question mark standing for the entire statement.

It was only two weeks ago—wasn't it?—that I met you?

George Chapman (1559?–1634) was a British poet, translator, and dramatist.

The question mark should not be used to indicate sarcasm. Instead, the diction and discussion should show your attitude.

Incorrect: Ms. Baker's beauty (?) was only skin deep.
Correct: Ms. Baker's beauty was only skin deep.

WITH OTHER PUNCTUATION

Question marks with quotations are a little tricky. If the entire statement is a question, place the question mark outside the quotation mark at the end of the sentence.

Do you like the sound of the word "iconographic"?

If just the quotation is a question, place the question mark inside before the quotation mark.

Last night my boyfriend asked me to sing "What Now, My Love?"

Because the quotation ends the sentence and the quotation requires the question mark at the end, the sentence period is dropped.

There are also special rules for the use of question marks with parentheses. If the whole question is in parentheses and is independent of other sentences, place the question mark inside the parenthesis.

We could attempt to solve the problem by May. (But do we dare?)

EXERCISES

Directions: In the following sentences, correct any flaws in the position or use of periods and question marks.

A. We all tried not to laugh, but we couldn't hold back when my grandfather said in his Russian accent, "So vat".
B. Last New Year's Eve, I went to see a movie by Woody Allen.
C. The policemen who were helping us find our way were very kind, and one of them suggested, "You both ought to get some sleep before you drive much farther."
D. We had a flat just after we passed a sign that said, "Seven miles to Stuckeys."
E. Stores that accept food stamps are very cautious about what products they allow to be purchased with them. No wonder. They are audited by the federal government.
F. I have often questioned myself about my own motives when I do something excessively honest, such as tell a checker at a store that he or she has given me too much change.
G. Many Americans are beginning to question whether living together is as popular as some advocates of common law marriage claim?

H. Why would the President want to change his energy policy in midstream?
I. Have you ever known a person who thinks everything is "beautiful?"
J. I have gone to see *To Have and Have Not* so many times that I know Bogart's lines by heart.
K. If there are any questions concerning the homework, we are supposed to ask our professor before we do it, not guess at what she means. But I often wonder if she will think we are "dumb" if we ask her.
L. What should we do if we can't get in to see *The Crying of Lot 49?* asked the leader of our group.
M. Sometimes it is hard to determine what people are thinking if they do not want to communicate with you; at other times, they are very easy to "read."
N. "Isn't this the same restaurant we ate at on the day we were married" asked his wife?
O. The dieffenbachia, a common house plant, contains a white liquid which, if it is ingested, affects the vocal apparatus and "can make a person temporarily mute even if only a few drops are eaten". says an article in a weekly magazine.

QUOTATION MARKS " "

There are two kinds of quotation marks: the double quotation mark (") and the single quotation mark ('). Although you may sometimes come across books, particularly novels, that use only single quotation marks, you should avoid this usage in the papers you write. Single quotation marks should be used when quotation marks are needed inside of other quotation marks. In all other situations where quotation marks are required, you should use double quotation marks.

DIRECT QUOTATIONS

Words taken from another source and dialogue should be placed in quotation marks.

> Dr. Johnson sums up his argument by stating that "far too many individuals are not aware of the almost limitless possibilities for self-improvement."
>
> The professor asked, "How many people have not read the assignment?"

When you are quoting dialogue, only the words actually spoken should be placed in quotation marks. For material from a source, only the words actually taken from that source should be placed in quotation marks. Remember, though, that sometimes even one word taken from someone else can require quotation marks.

> The article deals with the "sexploitation" present in many television commercials.

QUOTATIONS WITHIN QUOTATIONS

When quotation marks are needed inside of other quotation marks, single quotation marks should be used.

> Professor Peterson explained, "The line 'And sawdust restaurants with oyster-shells' is not a reference to Cape Cod resorts."
>
> Jane Shahan, literary critic for Channel Seven, said, "A close look at Comrack's newest short story, 'Daddy's Mother,' reveals it to be just another sentimental love story."

WORDS AS WORDS

When a word is used as a word instead of for its meaning, it may be placed in quotation marks.

> Try not to have too many "and's" in your sentences.
>
> In the jargon, "cherry" means "fantastic."
>
> For me, all those "if's" hindered growth in our relationship.

However, underlining is more often used for this purpose than are quotation marks (see p. 527).

TITLES

Titles of short stories, essays, articles, parts of books, short poems, songs, and television shows are placed in quotation marks. The titles of long poems, published separately, are usually underlined.

> In the story "The Peaches," Dylan Thomas mixes autobiography with fantasy.
>
> Ciancio's article, "The Sweetness of the Twisted Apples," explains Sherwood Anderson's view of the grotesque.

You should not put quotation marks around your own title for a paper or essay. If that title happens to include the name of a poem, short story, or some other work that would normally require quotation marks, place quotation marks around those words only.

> Fantasy and Fact in Dylan Thomas's Poetry
>
> "The Peaches": An Autobiographical Sketch

SPECIAL USES

Quotation marks are an effective way to call attention to an uncommon use of a word or phrase. This usage is particularly appropriate when you are using a technical term in a nontechnical context. For instance, in the following example terms from computer science are applied to the field of writing.

> Your "hardware" is a pen and a piece of paper, and your "software" is everything you know about good writing.

Writers sometimes use quotation marks to show that they know that a particular word or expression they are using is slang or a cliché. Although this usage may occasionally be effective, most often it should be avoided. The quotation marks are unnecessary if the word or expression works well in your sentence. If it does not work well, you should find a better way of expressing the thought instead of using quotation marks.

Some writers also use quotation marks to add a note of disparagement or to indicate irony. This usage should almost always be avoided.

Weak: The Queen's address was typically "proper" and boring.
Effective: The Queen's address was typically proper and boring.

PLACEMENT OF QUOTATION MARKS

Placement of quotation marks follows certain standards established by American printers. The rules differ slightly in England, and you may have learned the British method from a teacher schooled by others who have learned the British way. The American method, which is a bit less complicated than the British, is the one you should use.

For Direct Quotation

Fit the quotation into your sentence. Punctuate the sentence as your own. Usually, periods from the original passage are dropped unless the quotation also ends your sentence.

"There's a type of intense personality that drives me wild," Senator Wilard has been quoted as saying.

When footnote numbers are used they always follow the closing quotation marks.

Johnson said, "The man before you, MacArthur, is the the last of the true heroes."[2]

With Parenthetical References

When you use a parenthetical reference for a quotation, omit the end punctuation for the quotation unless it is a question mark or an exclamation point. The parenthetical reference, which is considered to be a part of the sentence, should follow the closing quotation mark and should in turn be followed by a period.

"During the sixties, protest was at such a height that often five or six prisoners a day in a single cell block would go on starvation diets" (*Daily Newsletter*, p. 17, col. 2).

H. L. Mencken, talking about his experience as a reporter, said that though he had never covered a lynching, he "had rather better luck with revolutions" (*The Vintage Mencken*, p. 57).

Parenthetical references for block quotations are slightly different. The reference is placed on the line after the quotation, which retains its own end punctuation. Remember that quotation marks are not used with block quotations.

My mistress' eyes are nothing like the sun;
Coral is far more red than her lips' red;
If snow be white, why then her breasts are dun;

> If hair be wires, black wires grow on her head.
> I have seen roses damasked red and white,
> But no such roses see I in her cheeks;
> And in some perfumes is there more delight
> Than in the breath that from my mistress reeks.
>   (Sonnet 130, p. 184)

WITH OTHER PUNCTUATION

Periods and Commas

This rule couldn't be simpler. Periods and commas always go inside quotation marks.

> His reserved nature made us nickname him "Mole."
>
> The officer remarked, "Hot days like this one can bring out the anger and violence in people."
>
> "These hot days can bring out the anger and violence in people," remarked the officer.

Semicolons and Colons

Semicolons and colons always go outside quotation marks.

> There is one thing I have always liked about reading "Dover Beach": the mood it puts me in.
>
> It is not unusual for a consumer to argue with a store manager that an item he or she purchased was advertised as complete, "not a bunch of rubber and plastic scraps with a few washers"; the important question raised by such complaints is whether a manufacturer should be required to advertise items as "unassembled."

ALL OTHER MARKS OF PUNCTUATION

Other marks of punctuation are sometimes placed inside and sometimes placed outside quotation marks. You must determine how the other punctuation relates to the group of words enclosed in quotation marks. Question marks, exclamation points, and dashes go inside quotation marks when they are part of the quotation. Otherwise, they go outside the quotation marks.

> Did he say, "Your teeth are like pearls"?
>   The whole sentence is a question.
> I was the one who asked, "What time is it?"
>   Only the quotation is a question. Note that the period for this writer's sentence is dropped because the question mark acts as ending punctuation.

EXERCISES

Directions: Make any needed corrections in the use of quotation marks or in the punctuation used with them.

A. Yesterday three men, according to a local report, 'were herded into a pick-up truck on Vineland Avenue, abducted to a beautiful forest, and given the time of their lives.' This is a new kind of "personsnatching" that is spreading across the country.

B. It is "the American Way" to try to outdo your neighbors.
C. According to Fromm's essay, "Where Are We Now and Where Are We Headed?" we can have a 'humane technological society!.
D. Even in ordinary conversation, some people cannot resist the temptation to quote what they are reading or to drop lines from their favorite authors, a practice that can get rather foolish: "You look beautiful today, my dear, and 'that is all ye know on earth and all ye need to know' ".
E. Many people get into the annoying habit of saying "you know" after almost every other word.
F. If writers get "hung up" on personal experiences, they may not be able to relate to a broad audience.
G. Phrases like "the fact that" and "in my opinion" make sentences wordy and can be chopped off without changing the meaning.
H. In my contract for automobile insurance is a line I had not noticed before that says, "Only the undersigned is protected under the aforesaid conditions".
I. The best essay I ever read by Joan Didion is "Some Dreamers of the Golden Dream".
J. When I read Twain's "The Storm", I was struck by how he uses the senses in his descriptions.

THE SEMICOLON ;

The functions of the semicolon are less like those of the colon than they are like those of a combination of a period and a comma. The semicolon has three uses.

THE USES OF THE SEMICOLON

Joining Main Clauses

Semicolons can join two related main clauses. A grammatical balance is set up between the clauses. Sometimes the second clause expands on the first; sometimes it does not.

> Farmworkers often do not demand their rights; the fear of deportation makes them afraid to speak up.
>
> She is hasty when making decisions; he takes too long.
>
> The Supreme Court unites and transcends the separate denominational religions and groups; the Court is far more powerful than any of these sects and can serve as an impartial judge.

With Transitional Words

Semicolons are used before words like *however* and *therefore* when they join main clauses. Other transitional words include *nevertheless, consequently, thus, instead,* and *on the other hand.* Note that the use of a comma instead of a semicolon would create an incorrect sentence.

> Energy supplies are not getting any more plentiful; therefore, Americans

will probably have to give up many of the luxuries they have become so used to.

For Clarity Semicolons can help to clarify the meaning of a sentence. They may be used in place of commas to join the elements of a series when the elements themselves contain commas.

> Some people picture a rural school as a one-room schoolhouse with a fatherly principal who caters to every student's needs; a motherly teacher, who knows all the answers and imparts them with tact and grace; and sisterly and brotherly students, who teach each other important values in life. Those who picture this heavenly family scene have obviously never gone to school in a small town.

The semicolons make the sentence easier to read than if commas had been used between the elements of the series.

The semicolon can also be used in place of the comma when a coordinating conjunction (*and, or, but, nor, for, yet,* or *so*) is used to join two long or complex independent clauses that contain a number of commas.

> Leash laws must be drawn up, enforced, and respected by all citizens; and everyone must realize, once and for all, that the problems the city faces with stray animals are serious and not merely "hogwash," as one councilman has called them.

Notice that, even for the sake of clarity, the semicolon is still only used between elements that are grammatically equal.

THE SEMICOLON WITH OTHER PUNCTUATION Semicolons always come outside quotation marks and parentheses.

> Mr. James suggests that if in one week we could attend all the movies shown in New York City, we would become "saturated with a mish-mash of mediocre entertainment"; the chances are, however, that nobody will prove James to be right or wrong. The argument is academic.

> The meeting was rescheduled for the noon hour (it had originally been set for 10 a.m.); the chairperson realized that the turnout would be better on everyone's lunch hour.

EXERCISES Directions: Correct any errors in the use of semicolons or commas in the following sentences by writing out each sentence correctly.
   A. I have tried all my life to overcome my fear of water; and in the past two years I have made progress.
   B. New artwork for one's house is always fun to frame and hang up; even if finding a place for it can be frustrating.
   C. It is often not easy for people who have grown up in the city to adapt to country life; rural lifestyles seem slow to them.
   D. When we first moved to the city from a small town in Iowa; we were shocked at how impersonal the people in the stores were.

E. The need to find approval for everything he does makes Jeffrey very frustrating to deal with; at the same time, we people at the clinic understand his needs and do our best to help him.
F. Scientists who have studied the causes for earthquakes claim; within twenty years we will be able to predict them well enough to avoid fatalities.
G. Tea is supposedly as bad for one's health as coffee if it is consumed in very large quantities; nevertheless, I can drink tea all day without it upsetting my stomach, while just a little coffee bothers me a lot.
H. Its coat is like a rabbit's its voice is like a cat's; so it's called a "rabicat."
I. I am not the kind of person who wants to work all her life; neither do I want to stay at home and have children.
J. I love to build furniture from oak, its hard texture is a challenge to work with.

SLASH /

The slash has five basic uses. Only two of these are commonly found in essays, but the others are often seen in technical writing and scientific reports.

POETRY QUOTATIONS The slash is used to mark the separation between lines of poetry when they are quoted in the text of an essay or paper. This is the use of the slash that most frequently occurs in essays.

> Erica Jong may be describing the feelings of women dissatisfied with their roles as mothers and wives; alienated "by quarrels, baby bottles, charge accounts of guilt/ & the sour smell of money," they want a way out of the marriage trap.

> The common theme that the world is a stage and life is a mere play can be found in "What is our life?" by Sir Walter Raleigh: "What is our life? A play of passion,/ Our mirth the music of division."

The slash is necessary only for short poetry quotations. Longer quotations are normally put in block form. The slash is not necessary in blocked quotations because the lines of poetry appear as they do in the original.

INDICATING ALTERNATIVES The slash is used to show options. It is rarely used in essays except in cases such as the following.

The that/who controversy
The male/female roles

The legalistic term and/or should be avoided in essay writing (see p. 533).

STANDING FOR PER The slash is used to stand for *per*. *Per* means "each" and is commonly used in technical and scientific writing.

20 mi./hr.   (miles per hour)
33 mi./gal.   (miles per gallon)
30 min./person   (minutes per person)

LINE FRACTIONS The slash separates the numerator and denominator of line fractions, which are commonly used in technical papers.

Two-thirds   ⅔
Three-fourths   ¾

Line fractions are also used in essays when a fraction would have to be written out in more than two words.

> Because I kept track of distances, I knew that 21/62 of the trip had not yet been completed.

ABBREVIATING DATES The slash may be used to abbreviate dates in much the same way as the hyphen. Usually abbreviations of this sort are not used in essays. Instead, the date is normally spelled out.

April 11, 1980   4-11-80   4/11/80

It may also be used to indicate that a period spans parts of two consecutive years.

The 1979/80 school year
Fiscal year 1980/81

UNDERLINING (ITALICS)

In print, italics (*this kind of print*) are commonly used to distinguish certain words. These include titles, foreign words, and words used as words. Italics are also used for emphasis. In your papers, indicate that a word should be italicized by underlining it. When underlining several words that come together, each word may be underlined individually or the entire group may be underlined together. The rules for when to use italics are fairly simple and straightforward. Notice that in a few cases you may either italicize a word or place it within quotation marks.

TITLES Italics are used for the titles of independently published words. These include books, plays, long poems, musical compositions, newspapers, and periodicals. The titles of movies are italicized, as are the names of ships, aircraft, trains, and works of art. Here are some examples.

My Life As a Man (a novel)
Hamlet (a play)
The Waste Land (a long poem)
The Planets (a musical composition)
the *Los Angeles Times* or the Los Angeles *Times* (a newspaper)
    For periodicals, the initial article in the title is usually not italicized. Sometimes, the name of the city is not italicized for newspapers.
Newsweek (a periodical)
Grease (a movie)
the *Amsterdam* (a ship)
the *Spirit of St. Louis* (an aircraft)
the *Orient Express* (a train)
    Notice that with the names of ships, aircraft, and trains, the initial article is not italicized.
Brancusi's *The Kiss* (a work of art)

Common usage requires that some titles not be italicized. These include holy books as well as a few other well-known works. You should not italicize titles such as the following. Notice that when an article is used with the title, it is not capitalized.

the Bible
the New Testament
the Koran
the Book of Common Prayer
the Declaration of Independence
the Gettysburg Address
the Constitution (of the United States)

FOREIGN WORDS Foreign words and abbreviations that are not commonly used in English are usually italicized. Foreign words and abbreviations that are common in English writing need not be italicized. Dictionaries may indicate that particular words have become sufficiently common so as not to require italicizing. A general rule, though, is that when you are in doubt, do not italicize foreign words or abbreviations.

Following are two short lists of foreign words and abbreviations. Those on the first list do not require italics and those on the second list do.

Foreign Words or Abbreviations That Require No Italics

Alter ego	Barette	Status quo
Apropos	Berserk	vice versa
Aria	Bourgeoisie	et al.
Baccarat	Fiancée	etc.
Baguette	Petite	e.g.
Ballerina	Placebo	i.e.
Barrage	Pimento	ibid.
	Salon	op. cit.
		ad hoc

Foreign Terms That Require Italics

Ad infinitum (to infinity)

Ars poetica (art of poetry)

A posteriori (inductive argument)

Intelligentsia (intellectual elites)

Pièce de résistance (the main dish, item, or event)

Pince nez (special eyeglasses)

WORDS AS WORDS

Words used as words instead of for their meaning are generally italicized.

Is *fitted* the past tense of *fit*?

Love and *happiness* are both hard words to define.

You may also use quotation marks instead of italics to indicate that a word is used as a word, although italics are used the most often. Whichever form you decide on, make sure that you are consistent throughout the essay.

EMPHASIS

Italics are also used in prose to emphasize words or ideas. This practice is very helpful in textbooks for pointing out those words or phrases you should be sure to take note of. As a general rule, however, the use of italics in papers and essays should be kept to a minimum. There are times when using italics can be very effective, particularly when they help to clarify what you are trying to say. At such times, do not hesitate to use them. Make sure, though, that you are not using them simply to prop up ineffective prose. You should depend on your choice of words for your meaning and emphasis. To rely on italics not only diverts your reader's attention, but it also lessens the effectiveness of italics when they are appropriate.

EXERCISES

Directions: In the following sentences, underline any words that should be italicized.

A. The textbook used in our reading class has a funny name: Topics for the Restless.

B. My favorite poem, "Ode on a Grecian Urn," was read at the art festival last week.
C. It is surprising how accurate Ibsen was in A Doll's House, a play about women's frustrations with the role of the perfect little wife.
D. The Wizard of Oz is a movie that I simply cannot forget.
E. Every year Esquire Magazine puts out an anniversary issue with many literary articles in it.
F. Before I took an introduction to literature class, I didn't know how to find the symbols in a novel or short story, but now I can read a book as hard as Moby Dick and see beyond the basic adventure story.
G. Georgia O'Keefe's paintings are full of mysteries, especially the Ladder to the Moon.
H. When my dad goes to Las Vegas, he likes to stand around and watch the wealthy people play baccarat.
I. Because of their political connections, the Smiths were asked to serve as ad hoc members of the book selection committee at our school.
J. The Bible is one work of literature I have never studied as carefully as I should have.

15

A Glossary of Usage

Good writing is made up of those words that convey the writer's message to the intended audience as clearly and concisely as possible. Sometimes, however, the best words are not easy to find. A word or phrase that means one thing to one person may mean something entirely different to someone else. This difficulty is partly overcome through the use of standard English, which you will remember is that form of English accepted and used by the largest number of educated people. But standard English is not frozen. Its usages are mostly habits, not hard and fast rules, and these habits are constantly changing. Words and phrases that were frowned upon in the past are now accepted, and many current usages will undoubtedly become obsolete in the future. Still, the standards of the times determine what is good writing. For this reason, every writer should learn what is presently acceptable and what is not.

Good usage is also determined by the intended audience and the level of formality of what is being written. An expression that is well suited to a specialized paper may be jargonistic in something aimed at a general audience. Similarly, a phrase that is perfect for a formal essay may be stuffy or obscure in one that is informal. It is up to you, the writer, to decide what works in each specific case. To help you make the best possible choice, certain key words are used frequently in this chapter. *Nonstandard* means that a usage should be avoided in relatively formal speaking and writing. *Colloquial* indicates that a usage is fine for speaking, but it should usually be avoided when writing. *Formal* and *informal* mean just what they say. The one to use depends on the needs of the paper, and only you can decide which is best suited for your purposes.

Of course, every writer has questions about different words and phrases. A Glossary of Usage has been designed to present those usages that most often cause problems for writers. Some of the usages will already be familiar, but others may answer questions that have long bothered you. A number of them are controversial. Whereas liberal experts allow certain expressions, purists condemn them. Neither group is absolutely right or wrong. When you encounter such disagreement, however, you are usually safest if you side with the conservative viewpoint. You will offend the least number of potential readers.

Unfortunately, there is only room enough here to present the most common problem areas. If you have a question about a word or expression that is not listed in this guide, a good place to look for further information is Roy H. Copperud's *American Usage: The Consensus*.

A, AN Use *a* before words that begin with consonant sounds and *an* before words that begin with vowel sounds.

A doctor *An* idea
A lion *An* opinion
A waste *An* unusual opportunity

When a word begins with a vowel that sounds like a consonant, use *a*.

A one-year guarantee
A useful gadget

Use *a* before words beginning with *h* when the *h* is pronounced, but use *an* when the *h* is silent.

A hurt finger *An* hour
A happy occasion *An* honor

Be careful not to inject an unnecessary *a* into a sentence.

Weak: This is no kind of *a* way to act.
Effective: This is no kind of way to act.

Also, do not invert the natural order of *a* or *an*.

Weak: He is even less known *a* figure than Smith.
Effective: He is *an* even less known figure than Smith.

After *so* or *too*, however, an *a* is often included.

I was surprised I felt so strong *a* dislike for the movie.
That was too spicy *a* meal.

A Glossary of Usage

ABSOLUTELY NO   The phrase *absolutely no* is wordy (see circumlocution, p. 173) and should be avoided.

ACQUIESCE IN   Use *acquiesce in* instead of *acquiesce to*.

> Jim *acquiesced in* his parents' demands.

AD   The word *ad* is a shortened form of the word *advertisement*. *Ad* should be used only informally and is best avoided in papers.

> An *advertisement* in the *Times* led to my current job.

The word *exam* is a shortened form of the word *examination*. *Exam* should be used only informally and is best avoided in papers.

> To become certified by the state, one has to take an *examination*.

ADVICE, ADVISE   *Advice* is a noun.

> His mother's *advice* was to finish college before getting married.

Advise is a verb.

> His mother *advised* him to finish college before getting married.

AFFECT, EFFECT   Except in psychology, where it has a specialized meaning, *affect* is always a verb meaning "to influence" or "to put on or pretend."

> He *affected* sophistication.

Effect is usually a noun meaning "a result."

> The law did not have the *effect* that was intended.

But *effect* can also be used as a verb meaning "to bring about."

> The employer *effected* many changes that angered her employees.

AFTEREFFECT   The phrase *aftereffect* is wordy, since an effect always comes after its cause. The word *effect*, by itself, is all that is necessary.

AGGRAVATE   *Aggravate* means "to make worse."

> Her insistence *aggravated* his bad mood.

The colloquial use of the word, meaning "to bother or annoy," is acceptable in informal writing but should be avoided in most papers or essays.

> Weak: You *aggravate* me.
> Effective: You *annoy* me.

ALL READY, ALREADY   *All ready* and *already* mean two different things. *All ready* means either "completely prepared" or that "all are prepared."

If we are *all ready,* we can leave.

Is the equipment *all ready?*

Already is an adverb that means "before an indicated time" or "previously."

Since I have *already* completed the requirements for basic Spanish classes, I will now take a more advanced class.

ALL RIGHT   *All right* is correct. *Alright* is a misspelling.

ALL TOGETHER, ALTOGETHER   *All together* and *altogether* mean two different things. *All together* means "physically or spiritually close together."

This Christmas, my family will be *all together* for the first time in over three years.

Altogether means "completely, thoroughly, or when all is said and done."

The evening seemed *altogether* too brief.

Altogether, it was the best show to open this year.

ALMOST ALWAYS, MOST ALWAYS   *Almost always* is more acceptable than *most always,* which is generally considered to be nonstandard English. However, you are probably better off using *usually* instead of either of these expressions.

ALSO   *Also* should not be used as a coordinating conjunction. It cannot be used in place of *and. Also* may occur at the beginning of a sentence as a transitional word or may follow a semicolon that separates two main clauses. Most often, however, if what follows the *also* is a main clause and what precedes it is also a main clause, you will want to replace the *also* with a coordinating conjunction from the following list: *and, or, nor, for, but, yet,* or *so.* Make sure that the one you choose fits the context of your sentence.

    Weak: I like painting, *also* singing is fun.
    Effective: I like painting; *also,* singing is fun.
    Effective: I like painting, *and* singing is fun.

When there is not a main clause before and after the *also,* you should change the *also* to *and.*

    Weak: Ted needs new shoes, *also* socks.
    Effective: Ted needs new shoes *and* socks.

ALTHOUGH THOUGH   *Although* and *though* can be used interchangeably.

A Glossary of Usage

ALUMNUS, ALUMNA — An *alumnus* is a male graduate. *Alumni* is the plural of *alumnus*, but it is also generally used when referring to groups that include both male and female graduates. An *alumna* is a female graduate. The plural of *alumna* is *alumnae*.

AMBIANCE — Avoid using *ambiance* to mean "atmosphere." This usage sounds pretentious.

> Weak: The *ambiance* of luxury at the hotel suited the Queen's tastes.

Use *atmosphere* instead.

AMONG, BETWEEN — See *between, among*.

AMOUNT, NUMBER — *Amount* refers to a quantity.

> He left a small *amount* of milk in his glass.

Number refers to items that are countable.

> The *number* of people who demand the right to free speech is increasing every year.

AN, A — See *a, an*.

ANALYZATION — *Analyzation* is not a word. It is a mistake some writers make when what they mean to say is *analysis*.

'AND ETC. — See *etc*.

AND/OR — Although sometimes effective in legal or commercial writing, *and/or* is distracting to readers and should be avoided in most papers and essays.

ANYWAYS — *Anyways* is a colloquial usage that should be avoided in papers and essays. Use *anyway* instead.

APROPOS OF — Be careful not to write *apropos to*. *Apropos of* is the correct usage.

> My point is apropos of the remark you made a few minutes ago.

ASPECT — Although it actually refers to "a particular side or view of something," *aspect* is too often used to mean *part* or *element*. When you use the word, be careful to retain the original meaning.

> She views the problem from a different *aspect* than does her father.

ASSURE, ENSURE, INSURE — *Assure*, *ensure*, and *insure* are similar in pronunciation, but different in usage. *Assure*, means "to engender trust in a person by encouraging him or her to believe in the truth of something."

Ivan *assured* us that the party could not go on without us.

Ensure means "to make certain."

Getting a real estate license does not *ensure* a successful career.

Insure means the same thing as *ensure,* but is most often used in the context of the insurance business.

I was insured for $100,000 if my car had gotten into an accident.

AT THIS POINT IN TIME
Always wordy for "now."

A WHILE, AWHILE
A while and *awhile* sound alike, but they are quite different. *A while* is made up of the noun *while* and the adjective *a*.

I told him I would see him in *a while*.

Awhile, on the other hand, is an adverb meaning "for a time."

We walked *awhile* instead of going right home after dinner.

BASICALLY
Even though it is sometimes appropriate, the adverb *basically* is often overused. Be careful not to allow it to become deadwood in your sentences.

Weak: He is *basically* six feet tall.
Effective: He is six feet tall.

BETWEEN, AMONG
Generally, *between* is used when referring to two people or things and *among* is used with more than two.

Saturday's game was *between* the Sea Hawks and the Brass Bells.

Is there anyone *among* us who will stand up to the mayor?

BETWEEN YOU AND I
The usage should be *between you and me* because *me* is the object of the preposition *between* (see p. 448).

BROKE
The word *broke* meaning "out of money" is colloquial and should not be used in papers.

Weak: Martin was *broke,* and he couldn't afford to buy a hamburger.
Effective: Martin was *without any money,* and he couldn't afford to buy a hamburger.

CAN, MAY
Often used interchangeably, *can* and *may* have different meanings. *Can* indicates the ability to do something.

I *can* touch my toes.

May indicates the permission to do something.

May I go with you?

CANNOT, CAN NOT Either *cannot* or *can not* is acceptable. The form *can not* emphasizes the *not*.

CLIMACTIC, CLIMATIC *Climactic* is an adjective that means "referring to or constituting a climax."

The story ends following the *climactic* meeting between the two brothers.

Climatic is an adjective that means "referring to the weather or climate."

Scientists are studying the *climatic* effects of sunspots.

COMPOSE, COMPRISE The words *compose* and *comprise* are often used to mean the same thing, but they are actually opposites. *Compose* means "to form by putting together." The parts *compose* the whole.

The organization is *composed* of hard-working men and women.

Comprise means "to be made up of" or "to consist of." The whole *comprises* the parts.

My chemistry course *comprises* both class meetings and laboratory sessions.

Keep this in mind; the phrase *is comprised of* should be avoided.

CONSIST OF, CONSIST IN *Consist of* means the same thing as *comprise*—"to be made up of." The whole *consists of* the parts.

The play *consists of* three acts.

Consist in means "to exist in" or "to have a basis in."

Their relationship *consists in* mutual dependency.

CONTEMPORARY The word *contemporary* occasionally causes problems because some writers think that it always refers to the present. Actually, *contemporary* refers to the period being discussed. For example, if a writer is speaking of the late eighteenth century in one sentence and uses the word *contemporary* in the next, then *contemporary* refers to the late eighteenth century. In the same way, if the writer is talking about the 1960s, *contemporary* would refer to that period.

CORRESPOND TO, CORRESPOND WITH *Correspond to* means "to be in close agreement with" or "to match."

The line on the right of the graph *corresponds to* the number of heartbeats per minute.

Correspond with means "to communicate with through an exchange of letters."

I *correspond with* my aunt who lives in Connecticut.

COULD OF See *should of, could of, might of.*

COUNCIL, COUNSEL, CONSUL A *council* is a group of people, usually formed to give advice.

The students formed a *council* to consider student-faculty relations.

Counsel is advice or, particularly in a legal sense, a person who gives advice.

My friend's *counsel* was sound, so I followed it.

A *consul* is a government official who lives in a foreign city.

Her uncle is the American *consul* in Sidney.

CREDIBLE, CREDULOUS *Credible* means "believable" or "worthy of belief."

Some stories about flying saucers are surprisingly *credible*.

Credulous means "gullible" or "believing too readily."

The man was *credulous* in his dealings with the pawnbroker.

CRITERIA, CRITERION *Criteria* is always plural. It should be followed by *are* or another plural verb.

The *criteria* for the proper evaluation of each new product are many.

Criterion is the singular form of the word. It should be followed by *is* or some other singular verb.

The only *criterion* Ms. Gage has set for hiring a new secretary *is* the ability to type well.

DILEMMA *Dilemma* should not be used interchangeably with *problem*. A *dilemma* is a special kind of problem, one for which there seems to be no satisfactory solution or one having two solutions that are equally unattractive.

The city faced the *dilemma* of raising taxes or going without adequate garbage collection.

DISCREET, DISCRETE *Discreet* and *discrete* sound the same but mean two different things. *Discreet* means "acting in good taste" or "tactful."

Senator Corey had to be *discreet* about the information he had received that afternoon.

Discrete means "entirely separate."

The scene has two *discrete* functions in the play.

DISINTERESTED, UNINTERESTED   In recent years, *disinterested* and *uninterested* have come to be used interchangeably. Their original meanings, however, supplied useful distinctions, and to some extent the words still have the following connotations. *Disinterested* implies an unbiased attitude or a lack of selfishness.

> A *disinterested* person is usually the best judge.

Uninterested implies a lack of interest.

> Irene is *uninterested* in the sciences.

DRINK, DRANK, DRUNK   The forms of *drink* that give the most trouble are the past tense and those with *have, has,* or *had.* The correct usage of these forms is as follows:

> She *drank* too much wine.
> She *has (had) drunk* too much wine.
> They *have drunk* too much wine.

Have drank, a common mistake, is a nonstandard usage.

DUE TO   *Due to* is always acceptable after "to be" verbs.

> His poor writing was partly *due to* his lack of reading experience.

In most other cases, it is better to use *because of.*

> Weak: *Due to* his negligence, we had to pay a lot of money to fix the car.
> Effective: *Because of* his negligence, we had to pay a lot of money to fix the car.

DUE TO THE FACT THAT   The phrase *due to the fact that* is overworked. Try to do without it or replace it with "because."

> Weak: I was late for work *due to the fact that* I missed my bus.
> Effective: I was late for work *because* I missed my bus.

DURING THE COURSE OF   The phrase *during the course of* is wordy. Leave out *the course of.*

EFFECT, AFFECT   See *affect, effect.*

e.g.   See *i.e., e.g.*

EMPHASIS, EMPHASIZE   *Emphasis* and *emphasize* are similar in meaning, but they are different parts of speech. *Emphasis* is a noun.

The main *emphasis* in most writing should be the orderly arrangement of ideas.

Emphasize is a verb.

Many women feel that there is a need to *emphasize* equality between the sexes.

ENSURE, INSURE, ASSURE See *assure, ensure, insure*.

ENTER INTO *Enter into* should be used only when referring to nonphysical things such as agreements, contracts, and discussions.

He finally *entered into* the discussion.

They *entered into* a partnership.

Enter should not be followed by *into* when referring to a physical structure.

She *entered* the room.

EQUALLY AS *Equally as* is a nonstandard usage that mixes *equally* with terms such as *as good as*. In your writing, use one term or the other, but not the combination.

John's essay is *as good as* Marsha's.

John's and Marsha's essays are *equally* good.

ET AL., ETC. *Et al.* and *etc.* are abbreviations for Latin words meaning "and others." *Et al.* is used for people; *etc.* is used for things. These abbreviations should be used in footnotes, bibliographic entries, and other places where space is at a premium. Normally, they are not italicized. In the text of a paper, such abbreviations should usually be avoided and words such as *and others* used instead.

Weak: Many poets of the period—Wordsworth, Keats Shelley, et al.—wrote about nature.

Effective: Many poets of the period—Wordsworth, Keats, Shelley, *and others*—wrote about nature.

ETC. Omit *and* before *etc.*
See *et al.*

ETHICS, MORALS The two words are not interchangeable. *Ethics* means "a system of moral principles" and is theoretical.

Effective: His business *ethics* were questionable.

Morals refer to behavior based on ethics. *Moral code* usually refers to sexual behavior.

	Effective: The closed-minded young man believed that anyone who dated more than one woman was *immoral*.
EXAM, AD	See *ad, exam*.
EXCESS VERBIAGE	Using *excess* with *verbiage* is redundant. *Verbiage* by itself means "wordiness" or "an excess of words." Thus, you could say that the phrase *excess verbiage* is verbiage.
FACET	The word *facet* is often misused. It is not interchangeable with the word *part*. A facet is technically the plane surface of a cut gem. Try as much as possible to retain the original meaning by using the word only in reference to a new or unexpected consideration or aspect of a subject. Otherwise use *part*.
	Weak: There are four *facets* to doing original research.
	Effective: The most shocking *facet* of the testimony by Ms. Conroy was her involvement with mass hypnosis.
FACTOR	The word *factor* is greatly overused. Try to do without it.
	Weak: Good eating habits are an important *factor* for good health.
	Effective: Good eating habits are important for good health.
FARTHER, FURTHER	Although the words are often used interchangeably, *farther* is generally used to refer to physical distance.
	He lived *farther* away than we thought.
	Further is used to refer to a greater degree or extent in a more abstract sense.
	Taking his argument a step *further* shows why it is illogical.
FELLOW	The word *fellow* is colloquial. *Man* or *person* should be substituted in your papers.
	Weak: He is a *fellow* who likes to win arguments.
	Effective: He is a *person* who likes to win arguments.
FEWER, LESS	*Fewer* refers to items that can be counted.
	Fewer dignitaries than ever attended the convention this year.
	In the fraternity, *fewer* men like to play cards than like to play backgammon.
	Less refers to quantities or amounts.
	There is *less* time left to register for voting than I had thought.
	Less money was found in the old box than had been expected.

FICTITIOUS NOVEL   Novels are a type of fiction. Therefore, the phrase *fictitious novel* is redundant. Use only the word *novel*. Works that are not fiction are called *nonfiction*. An historical novel is a fictionalized account of an event in history.

FLAUNT, FLOUT   *Flaunt* and *flout* sound similar and are sometimes used in the same context, but they mean different things. *Flaunt* means "to show off" or "to display oneself."

> He *flaunted* his wealth.

Flout, however, means "to condemn" or "to scorn."

> He *flouted* the convention of removing one's hat in public.

Both words could be used to describe someone's behavior, but the words are not synonymous.

> Must they *flaunt* their immorality and *flout* the upstanding values of the respectable citizens in this town?

FLUNK   *Flunk* meaning "to fail" is colloquial. Do not use it in papers.

> Weak: He *flunked* the eye test for his driver's license.
> Effective: He *failed* the eye test for his driver's license.

FORMER, LATTER   See *latter, former*.

FUN   *Fun* is sometimes used informally as an adjective before a noun. In papers, however, this usage is inappropriate. *Fun* should be considered a noun.

> Weak: My friend Tom is a *fun* person to be with.
> Effective: My friend Tom is a lot of *fun* to be with.

FUNNY   You should use *funny* only when referring to something that is humorous. Avoid using it to mean "strange" or "unusual."

> Weak: A *funny* feeling came over me.
> Effective: A *strange* feeling came over me.

FURTHER, FARTHER   See *farther, further*.

GENERALLY, IN GENERAL, OBVIOUSLY   Try to do without these words. They are overworked. Nevertheless, they may be valuable to you in one way. In your rough draft, they may be clues that you are tending to think in too general a way or are making obvious statements. In such cases, you will want to omit, or at least revise, the sentences and ideas these words point out.

GENERAL PUBLIC *General public* is wordy and overused. *Public,* alone, will serve the purpose.

GEOGRAPHICAL LOCATION The term *geographical location* is wordy (see *circumlocution,* p. 173) and should be avoided. Instead, use *location.*

GOOD, WELL *Good* should always be used as an adjective. Notice that it frequently follows linking verbs (see p. 364) such as *to be* and *to feel.*

> He feels unusually *good* today.
> She looks *good* in brown.
> Carla is a *good* driver

Well is used as an adjective only when referring to physical health.

> Michael is not *well.*

Otherwise, *well* should be used as an adverb that tells "how" about a verb.

> Carla drives *well.*
> Most college students do not write as *well* on in-class exams as on take-home papers.

GREAT DEAL The phrase *a great deal* is often a wordy way of writing *much* or *many.*

HE/SHE, HIS/HER You should avoid using constructions such as *he/she* and *his/her.* Instead, use *he or she, his or her.*

> Each student was asked to write about a subject *he or she* found interesting.
> Each of us was expected to do *his or her* own laundry.

Some writers feel that using *he or she* is awkward, yet they do not like the implications of using *he* by itself. An easy way to avoid this problem is to make the noun referred to plural.

> The *students* were asked to write about subjects *they* found interesting.
> *We* were expected to do *our* own laundry.

HEALTHFUL, HEALTHY *Healthful* and *healthy* are both adjectives, but they have different meanings. *Healthful* means "good for the health."

> Jogging is a *healthful* exercise.

Healthy means "in good health."

> Jacques is a *healthy* man.

HEAP OF, HEAPS OF Although they are frequently heard, the words *heap of* or *heaps of* are too informal for most essays. In papers, use either *a great deal* of or *a large number of.*

HEIGHT, HEIGHTH *Height* is the correct spelling. Be careful not to confuse the spelling of *height* with that of *length,* which should end in *th*.

HISSELF, THEIRSELVES *Hisself* and *theirselves* are not standard usages. *Himself* and *themselves* are the accepted forms.

HOPEFULLY Literally, *hopefully* means "full of hope."

> Janice looked at her doctor *hopefully* as he told her the results of her laboratory tests.

In conversation, *hopefully* is often used to mean "it is hoped." In papers and essays, however, it is best to avoid this usage unless you are writing informally.

IDEA, IDEAL The two words are confused because they sound similar. An *idea* is a thought in the mind.

> His *idea* is worth considering if it can save time.

An *ideal* is a state of perfection to be striven for. The same word acts as an adjective meaning "perfect."

> His *ideal* of a good parent is a good friend.

> An *ideal* arrangement would be driving to work together.

i.e., e.g. An abbreviation of a Latin term, *i.e.* means "that is." It is used to explain or restate a preceding word or phrase. The abbreviation should not normally be italicized and should be used primarily in places where space is at a premium, such as in footnotes and bibliography entries. You should usually avoid using it in the text of an essay. An abbreviation of a Latin term, *e.g.,* means "for example" and is used to introduce one or several examples of a preceding word or phrase. It should normally not be italicized. The abbreviation is frequently used in footnotes and other places where space is at a premium but should usually be avoided in the text of a paper.

IF, WHETHER *If* and *whether* both convey the sense of something conditional, doubtful, or uncertain. Each word is used differently. *If* is generally used to show general uncertainty.

> I wonder *if* we will have to wait on line.

If is sometimes used with *then*. This usage, however, is not effective, since the sentence the expression is contained in makes perfect sense without the *then*.

> Weak: *If* my intentions appear good, *then* you must trust me.
> Effective: *If* my intentions appear good, you must trust me.

Likewise, it is not effective to write *if and when*. In speaking, some people feel that the combination of the words emphasizes their point. Actually, the combination, at least in writing, would weaken the point, since either *if* or *when* alone would do the job. *If* may also be used to express alternatives along with conditions, doubts, or uncertainties.

> I wonder *if* we will go to the movies or stay home and watch television.

The word *whether* could have been used in the preceding sentence instead of *if*. *Whether* is used only when alternatives are expressed.

> Weak: They did not know *whether* they would stay for the night.
> Effective: They did not know *if* they would stay for the night.
> Effective: They did not know *whether* they would stay for the night or leave early in the evening.
> Effective: They did not know *if* they would stay for the night or leave early in the evening.

IMPLY, INFER *Imply* and *infer* are often confused. In a sense, these two words can be thought of as the opposite sides of a single coin. *Imply* means "to indicate without stating" or "to express indirectly." *Infer* means "to draw a conclusion." Thus, what a writer may *imply*, a reader may *infer*.

> The writer of the article *implies* that the mayor is incompetent.
> I *infer* from the article that the author believes the mayor to be incompetent.

IN TERMS OF *In terms of* is a vague phrase that is seldom necessary. Usually, a sentence is more effective without it.

> Weak: *In terms of* money, Terry is very frugal.
> Effective: Terry is very frugal.

INCIDENT, INCIDENCE The words *incident* and *incidence* are often confused because of the similarity in their pronunciation. An *incident* is an occurrence or happening.

> One senator has been involved in a number of embarrassing *incidents*.

Incidence means "the rate of occurrence."

> Surprisingly, the *incidence* of polio in the United States is once again increasing.

INCREDIBLE *Incredible* is a word that is frequently misused. Too often, writers use it as a catchall intensifier. Actually, *incredible* means "too improbable or extraordinary to be readily believed." Use of the word should be reserved for this meaning.

Weak:	Nuclear accidents represent an *incredible* hazard to human life.
Weak:	He is an *incredible* person.
Effective:	Her story about the ordeals of the survivors of the airplane crash was *incredible,* but true.
Effective:	The jury felt that his testimony was *incredible.*

INSURE, ASSURE, ENSURE See *assure, ensure, insure.*

IRONIC, IRONY The words *ironic* and *irony* are often used imprecisely. You should not use these words to point out just any contrast or change of events. For something to be *ironic,* what is said must contrast dramatically with what the reader would normally expect.

Weak:	The *irony* is that to get fresh green beans she went to a market that carried no produce.
Effective:	It is *ironic* that many bank tellers are unable to balance their own checkbooks.

IRREGARDLESS *Irregardless* is nonstandard. This form of the word is redundant as both the prefix *ir* and the suffix *less* mean "without." Use *regardless* instead.

IT MUST BE NOTED HERE Phrases such as *it must be noted here* are usually deadwood and should be avoided.

ITS, IT'S The words its and it's are often confused because one is a possessive and one is a contraction. What confuses people is that the possessive does not take an apostrophe.

> The cat played with *its* tail.

It's is the contraction for "it is" or "it has." The omitted letters are marked by an apostrophe.

> *It's* been years since I have gone to a baseball game.
>
> *It's* not fair to the rest of the team if you always show up late.

KIDS *Kids* is a colloquial term. It should be avoided in formal writing. Use *children* or a similar word instead.

KIND OF *Kind of* is colloquial. In most papers, the word *somewhat* would be more appropriate. Either expression should be avoided if it does not add information to your sentence but is, instead, used as a catchall.

Weak:	Herman Core is *kind of* outspoken for somebody who calls himself a "diplomat."
Weak:	Herman Core is *somewhat* outspoken for somebody who calls himself a "diplomat."
Effective:	Herman Core is *outspoken* for somebody who calls himself a "diplomat."
Effective:	My father is not angry but *somewhat* disturbed by my decision.

LATTER, FORMER *Latter* or *former* should be used only to single out one of two previously mentioned items. These terms sound very formal. Instead of using them, it is often more effective to repeat the particular word you are referring to.

LAY, LIE Confusion between *lay* and *lie* is the cause of a large number of errors in speaking and writing. Most of the difficulty seems to stem from the forms of these words in the past tense.

Yesterday I *laid* the magazine right here, and now I can't find it.

Yesterday I *lay* down at around the same time as I did today.

See pages 437 to 439 for a complete discussion of these two verbs.

LEND, LOAN Lend is always a verb.

Please *lend* me a cup of sugar.

Loan is normally used as a noun, but it can also be used as a verb.

I am going to the bank to ask for a *loan*.

James *loaned* Elizabeth his class notes.

LESS, FEWER See *fewer, less.*

LESS, LEAST *Less* and *least* are both comparative words. *Less* means "not as much" or "smaller" and is used when comparing two things. It is usually followed by *than*. *Least* means "smallest" or "the minimum amount" and is used when comparing more than two things.

He is *less* friendly than she is.

Burt is the *least* interesting person I know.

MAY, CAN See *can, may.*

MORE When using the word *more,* be careful that you do not form an incomplete comparison. *More* should usually be followed by *than*.

Weak: He is *more* willing to work.
Effective: He is *more* willing to work *than* we expected.

MORE PREFERABLE
When you state that one thing is *preferable* to another, you have made an appropriate comparison. Adding the word *more* is therefore redundant and should be avoided.

MOST ALWAYS, ALMOST ALWAYS
See *almost always, most always*.

NEITHER . . . NOR
Neither should always be followed by *nor,* never by *or.*

Neither Jan *nor* David was in class today.

NICE
The word *nice* is greatly overused. It is also a very imprecise word. How can your reader know exactly what you mean by *nice*? Whenever possible, you should replace *nice* with a more specific word or phrase.

Weak: Marsha is a *nice* person.
Effective: Marsha is a *friendly and considerate* person.

NOWHERE NEAR, NOT NEARLY
Nowhere near is colloquial. For essays, *not nearly* is preferred.

Weak: He was *nowhere near* as strong as Atlas, but sometimes he felt that the whole world was on his shoulders.
Effective: He was *not nearly* as strong as Atlas, but sometimes he felt that the whole world was on his shoulders.

NUMBER, AMOUNT
See *amount, number*.

OFF, OFF FROM, OFF OF OUT, OUT FROM, OUT OF
Avoid using either *from* or *of* with *off* or *out*.
They jumped *off* the wagon.
The Robbins put the cat *out* the door before going to bed.

ONE, YOU
See *you, one*.

ON THE BASIS OF
The phrase *on the basis of* is greatly overworked. It is seldom necessary and should usually be eliminated from your sentences.

ORIENTED, ORIENTATED
Orientated is usually a mistake for *oriented*.
The Puritans were a God-*oriented* society.

Orientation is the noun form of the word.

OWING TO THE FACT THAT
Phrases such as *owing to the fact* that are almost always wordy. Use *because* or *since* instead.

PECUNIARY REIMBURSEMENT, REMUNERATION Avoid these highly formal phrases for *pay*.

PHENOMENA, PHENOMENON *Phenomenon* is the singular form of the word.

> An eclipse of the moon is an impressive *phenomenon*.

Phenomena is always plural.

> Many *phenomena* in nature are sill unexplained.

POTENTIAL Potential is often used ineffectively as a noun when it is, in fact, an adjective. The incorrect usage is jargon from the social sciences.

> Weak: The man's *potential* was not evident in his work.
> Effective: The young man was a *potential* genius, but his work did not show his ability.

PREFER . . . TO *Prefer* should be followed by *to,* never by *than*.

> Weak: I *prefer* talking on the telephone *than* writing letters.
> Effective: I *prefer* talking on the telephone *to* writing letters.

Prefer may also be followed by *instead of*.

> I *prefer* talking on the telephone *instead of* writing letters.

PREJUDICE, PREJUDICED *Prejudice* can be either a noun or a verb.

> His *prejudice* against foreigners is a sign of his immaturity.
> The judge was accused of trying to prejudice the jury in favor of the defendant.

Prejudice, however, should never be used as an adjective. The correct adjective form of the word is *prejudiced*.

> Jim is a prejudiced man.

Of course, *prejudiced* can also be used as a verb.

> Betty Jo's attitude *prejudiced* the committee against her.

Notice that *prejudice* and *prejudiced* can be used in either a positive or a negative sense.

PRETTY *Pretty* is sometimes used colloquially to mean "rather" or "quite." This usage should be avoided in papers or essays.

> Weak: She reads Spanish *pretty* well.
> Effective: She reads Spanish *rather* well.

PRIOR TO In most cases, it is better to use *before* instead of *prior to*.

PSEUDO-INTELLECTUALS Do not use this term for people who you think are lacking intellect. Call them *nonintellectuals*. *Pseudo-intellectuals* applies to people who pretend to be more intellectual than they actually are.

PUT ACROSS *Put across* is a wordy and often confusing phrase. More appropriate are either *expressed* or simply *said*.

QUOTE, UNQUOTE It has become a habit of speech to include *quote unquote* (or *endquote*) at the opening and closing of quoted information, but the habit should be broken. A good speaker shows the beginnings and end of quoted material by raising and lowering his or her voice. In writing, the expression is, of course, not needed.

RAISE, RISE *Raise* and *rise* are often confused, especially in the past tense. *Raise* (raised, raised) means "to lift up."

The girl *raised* her hand.

Rise (rose, risen) means "to lift up."

The girl *raised* her hand.

Rise (rose, risen) means "to go up" or "to get up."

The company's stock *rose* over eight points last Thursday.

He *rises* before seven every morning.

RARE, SCARCE Both *rare* and *scarce* mean "infrequently found." *Rare*, however, usually connotes a permanent lack of availability.

The prize of my collection is a *rare* Egyptian gold piece.

Scarce, on the other hand, usually connotes a temporary lack of availability.

When commodities are *scarce*, their prices rise.

REAL, REALLY, VERY *Real* is often used colloquially to mean *very*. Unless you are writing informally, you should avoid this usage in papers and essays. *Really* will work, but *very* or a word that is even more descriptive is better.

Weak:	Mary is *real* happy about her new job.
Effective:	Mary is *really* happy about her new job.
Effective:	Mary is *very* happy about her new job.
Effective:	Mary is *ecstatic* about her new job.

REASON, RATIONALIZE To *reason* is to think rationally.

Her *reasoning* led her to the correct solution of the complex math problem.

To *rationalize,* however, has the connotation of providing reasons for conduct that are plausible but untrue.

> He *rationalized* his mother's drinking problem by telling himself that she had lived a difficult life.

REGARDS, IN REGARD TO It is never acceptable to say *in regards to* or *with regards to.* Correct idioms for the phrase include *in regard to, with regard to, regarding,* and *concerning.*

The word *regards* means *good wishes* and is used as in the following sentence.

> Give my regards to Emma.

Regard is also a verb used to mean *refer to.*

> Effective: My concern *regards* a disturbance you initiated in class the other day, Jim.

SELF-CONCEPT Adding words such as *of herself* to the term *self-concept* is redundant. You should use either *her concept of herself* or *her self-concept,* but be careful not to combine the two.

SENSUAL, SENSUOUS *Sensual* and *sensuous* both refer to satisfaction of the senses. However, the two words are usually used with different connotations. *Sensual* implies indulgence in one's appetites for pleasure and often suggests sexuality.

> Lord Byron was known as a *sensual* man.

Sensuous, on the other hand, implies taking enjoyment from more esthetic delights such as those of nature or the arts.

> Concerts under the stars appealed to her *sensuous* nature.

SET, SIT *Set* and *sit* are often confused. To *set* means "to place."

> She *set* her glasses down on the table.

To *sit* means "to rest the body upright" or "to be situated."

> They *sit* in the same seats at every concert.
>
> Our house *sits* on a hill overlooking a golf course.

For a more detailed coverage of these words, see pages 437–440.

SHOULD OF, COULD OF, WOULD OF *Should of, could of,* and *would of* are sometimes incorrectly written for *should have, could have,* and *would have.* The confusion probably arises from what is heard when someone speaks quickly. A good way to avoid this mistake is to remember that in the contractions of these words—*should've, could've,* and *would've*—the *ve* is a shortened form of *have.*

SIGHT, SITE, CITE *Sight, site,* and *cite* all sound the same, but their meanings are very different. Sight is a noun meaning "something seen."

The *sight* of my grandmother working in her garden lives in my memory.

Site is a noun meaning "the location of something."

The *site* of their next film is a small ranch in Mexico.

Cite is a verb meaning "to refer to" or "to quote in order to offer an example, establish authority, or provide proof."

To back up her argument, she *cited* the opinions of several noted experts.

SO Using *so* as the first word of a sentence is highly informal. Use a transitional word such as *therefore* instead in papers.

Weak: Our new neighborhood was well integrated. So, our high school offered all the advantages of multicultural experiences.

Effective: Our new neighborhood was well integrated. Thus our high school offered all the advantages of multicultural experiences.

SOME TIME, SOMETIME, SOMETIMES *Some time, sometime,* and *sometimes* have different meanings and are often confused. Some time is made up of an adjective and a noun. *Some time* means "an amount of time."

Whenever you have *some time* to chat, feel free to visit me.

Some time has passed since our last conversation.

Sometime is quite different from *some time.* First of all, *sometime* is an adverb. It means "an unspecified time."

No one is sure when, but the dog will have to eat *sometime.*

Sometimes is also an adverb, but it means "now and then."

Sometimes I feel so clever that I could do anything.

STATIONARY, STATIONERY *Stationary* is an adjective meaning "not moving" or "not changing in condition."

The flight was so smooth that the airplane seemed to be *stationary.*

Stationery is a noun meaning "paper used for writing letters."

John writes his letters in dark brown ink on light brown *stationery.*

A good way to avoid confusing these two words is to remember that *stationery* and *paper* both contain *er.*

A Glossary of Usage

SUCH AS When you introduce a list or series with the term *such as,* be sure that you do not use the phrase *to name a few* to conclude the list or series.

>   Weak: At the party there were many refreshments *such as* fruit, cheese, homemade candies, ice cream, soft drinks, and coffee *to name a few.*
>
>   Effective: At the party there were many refreshments such as fruit, cheese, homemade candies, ice cream, soft drinks, and coffee.

SUCH THAT *Such that* is a term that usually introduces a formal description. It often follows a linking verb, usually a form of *to be.* What comes after the *that* is a further explanation or description of the *subject* under discussion in the sentence.

>   The behavior of the two men was *such that* none of the rest of us wanted to admit to knowing them.

SUMMARY, SUMMATION A *summary* is an abstract or a concise condensation used by writers to present the substance of something they do not wish to quote directly.

>   Our teacher warned us not to give a *summary* of the plot in our book reviews.

A *summation* is the final part of an argument that reviews the points previously made and offers conclusions.

>   The prosecuting attorney presented an emotional *summation* of the state's case.

SUPER The use of *super* as an intensifier is colloquial and should be avoided in most papers and essays.

>   Weak: She is *super* intelligent.
>
>   Effective: She is *very* intelligent.

SUSPECT, SUPPOSE *Suspect* usually has negative connotations. Avoid using it when what you really mean is *suppose.*

>   Weak: We *suspect* that all the members of the committee will attend the luncheon.
>
>   Effective: We *suppose* that all the members of the committee will attend the luncheon.

TERRIFIC *Terrific* is overused. Try to substitute a more specific word for it.

>   Weak: All in all, he was a *terrific* friend.
>   Effective: All in all, he was a *loyal* friend.

THAT *That* should be used to connect a subordinate clause to a main clause if you feel the word sounds natural. Keep in mind that it is acceptable and correct to omit the *that* whenever the subordinate clause following it is clearly subordinate. Both of the following sentences are acceptable.

> I felt he was less qualified than I was.
>
> I felt *that* he was less qualified than I was.

However, when the clause introduced by *that* comes before the main verb in the sentence, be sure to use the *that*.

> *That* I had run the mile in record time was a surprise to me.
>
> *That* she could be fooled I had to question.

THAT THAT Sometimes the phrase *that that* is present in a sentence. Even though the two *that*'s appear next to each other, they are not redundant and are acceptable. They each have different functions. If you wish, you may leave out the first that, which acts as a subordinate conjunction (see entry for *that*). Either of the following sentences would be acceptable.

> It would surprise me to learn *that that* house down the block is for sale.
>
> It would surprise me to learn *that* house down the block is for sale.

THAT, WHICH, WHO Although the preferred usage of *that, which,* and *who* is less rigid than it once was, *that* is normally used to refer to people, animals, and things. *Which* usually refers to things or animals, and *who* generally refers only to people. *That* is used to introduce essential clauses. Remember that essential clauses are never set off by commas. *Who* and *which* can introduce either essential or unessential clauses, but many writers use *which* only for unessential clauses. Unessential clauses should be set off by commas. (See Chapter 14 for more information on the use of commas.)

THEIRSELF, THEIRSELVES *Theirself* and *theirselves* are nonstandard. You should avoid using them in papers. The correct form is *themselves*.

> Weak: They did the work *theirself*.
> Effective: They did the work *themselves*.
> Weak: The team did *theirselves* a favor by cooperating with the coach.
> Effective: The team did *themselves* a favor by cooperating with the coach.

THIS When the word *this* is used, the word that follows it usually should have been mentioned before. The exact reference word or a synonym for it may come after the *this*.

Weak:	It was three in the morning when *this* knock came at my door.
Effective:	A man with a white hat and cowboy boots came into the room. It was *this man* who later married my sister.
Effective:	A man with a white hat and cowboy boots came into the room. It was *this person* who later married my sister.

THOUGH, ALTHOUGH — Though and although can be used interchangeably.

THUSLY — The word *thusly* is not used by careful speakers or writers. Use *thus* instead. *Thus* is already an adverb and does not benefit by the *ly* ending. The *ly* is thus unnecessary and a bit pretentious.

TO, TWO, TOO — *To*, *two*, and *too* are often confused. Each is set into a different context. *To* is used as part of an infinitive or a prepositional phrase.

> I want *to* know the answer.
> They went *to* college.

Two is the number.

> *Two* hours is hardly enough time to study for a final examination.

Too means "also" or "excessive."

> John played very well. I did well *too*.
> Labor unions require *too* much dues of their members.

Be careful to use intensifiers like *too, very,* and *really* only when they add meaning to your statements.

Weak:	I was too thrilled when I found a letter from my sister in the mailbox.
Effective:	I was thrilled when I found a letter from my sister in the mailbox.

TODAY'S SOCIETY — The expression *today's society* is trite and should be avoided, especially in the introduction to an essay.

Weak:	Prejudice against minorities is surprisingly widespread in *today's society*.
Effective:	Prejudice against minorities is surprisingly widespread.

TOWARD, TOWARDS — *Toward* is more common in the United States while *towards* is more common in England. However, either form is acceptable.

TRY AND, TRY TO — *Try and* is colloquial. Most often, *try to* should be used instead. The phrase "to try and learn" actually indicates two distinct actions—trying and learning. Avoid the *and* unless you really mean it.

> Weak: I always *try and* help my friends when I can.
> Effective: I always *try to* help my friends when I can.

TWO, TOO, TO See *to, two, too*.

TYPE When the word *type* is used as a noun, it should usually be followed by *of*.

> Weak: This *type* person should not be trusted.
> Effective: This *type of* person should not be trusted.

UNCONSCIOUS, SUBCONSCIOUS The two adjectives *unconscious* and *subconscious* are often confused. *Unconscious,* in popular usage, means "lacking awareness" or "not intentional."

> His *unconscious* slip of the tongue was funny.
>
> He was *unconscious* for a few seconds after the fight.

Subconscious, in popular usage, means "not fully aware of" or "working in the mind beneath the level of consciousness."

> Luckily, some *subconscious* conservatism in my nature told me to return to my home town instead of venturing into strange places.

Each of these words has slightly different meanings in psychology than in popular usage.

UNINTERESTED, DISINTERESTED See *disinterested, uninterested*.

UNIQUE Technically, *unique* means "one of a kind." The use of *unique* to mean "rare" has become generally accepted, but you should be very careful when using the word for this purpose. Avoid using *unique* to mean "appealing" or "not very common." You should also avoid using adverbs such as *more, very* or *most* with *unique*. Such intensifiers corrupt the meaning of the word.

> Weak: He has a *unique* personality.
> Effective: He has a *warm and outgoing* personality.
> Effective: Gerald Wilson's photography is *uniquely* displayed.

USE TO, USED TO *Use to* is a mistake for *used to*. Confusion between the two occurs because of the way words are frequently pronounced together. When you are writing, make sure you include the *d*.

> He *used to* be my friend
>
> She is *used to* getting "A's."

VARIANCE The term *at variance* should always be followed by *with*, not by *from*.

The majority of the committee is *at variance with* the mayor's ideas about how to curb street violence.

VESTED INTEREST The term *vested interest* does not automatically have a negative connotation. The use of the term in each of the following sentences can be negative or positive, depending on the context.

An executive has a *vested interest* in every project the company undertakes.

The gardener has a *vested interest* in keeping the yard in order.

WAIT ON, WAIT FOR Although it is sometimes used colloquially to mean *wait for, wait on* should be used only when you mean "to serve."

The Young man who *waited on* us at the restaurant was studying to be an actor.

We had to *wait for* John almost an hour.

WANDER, WONDER *Wander* means "to travel about without a fixed course" or "to stray in thought."

I like to *wander* around the country.

During the spring, my mind often *wanders,* and I find it difficult to concentrate.

Wonder means "to feel curiosity or doubt about something."

I *wonder* what Jim is doing.

Since *to wonder* is a mental activity, the expression *wonder in my mind* is redundant.

WELL, GOOD See *good, well*.

WHERE *Where* should be used only to refer to location. Using *where* in place of *that* is colloquial and should be avoided in most papers and essays.

Weak: I read in a report *where* many high school stu-ents have trouble doing simple math problems.

Effective: I read in a report *that* many high school students have trouble doing simple math problems.

WHERE ... AT, WHERE ... TO You should avoid adding *at* or *to* to the end of sentences or phrases beginning with *where*.

Weak: Where do you suppose John is *at*?
Effective: Where do you suppose John is?
Weak: Where are you going *to*?
Effective: Where are you going?

WHETHER, IF See *if, whether*.

WHICH, THAT See *that, which, who.*

WHILE Technically, *while* refers to a span of time and is used to indicate that two or more things occur at the same time.

While I recite the poem, you read along in the book.

While is also used in two other ways, although they are not as generally accepted and can sometimes lead to confusion. Often, *while* is used to mean *even though.*

While he is my best friend, I will not lie to help him.

Less frequently, *while* is used to mean *and.*

I like coffee, *while* she prefers tea.

This usage is not accepted by some in formal writing, and it should definitely be avoided if there is any chance that it will cause ambiguity.

Weak: I fixed dinner, *while* she washed the dishes.

The use of *while* is confusing. It seems to indicate that the two actions—fixing dinner and washing dishes—take place at the same time. Since dishes are usually washed after the dinner is fixed and eaten, *and* would be more effective.

Effective: I fixed dinner, *and* she washed the dishes.

WHO'S, WHOSE *Who's* and *whose* sound alike, but they are quite different. *Who's* is a contraction for "who is" or "who has."

Who's responsible for this mess?
It is Jim *who's* pulling his car into the driveway.

Whose is a possessive pronoun.

The parents *whose* children acted in the play were proud.
Whose book is it?

WISE Coining new words by adding *wise* as a suffix to existing words has become a fad in recent years. These manufactured words—*contrarywise, friendshipwise,* and *selectionwise,* for example—are nonstandard and should be avoided.

Weak: Overeating is dangerous *healthwise.*
Effective: Overeating is dangerous to the health.

Established words, such as *otherwise* and *likewise,* are another matter, of course.

WOULD OF See *should of.*

YOU, ONE   Both *you* and *one* can be used to refer to people in general. *You* is more informal than *one*. In an informal situation it would be fine to write the following:

> The Grand Canyon and the Carlsbad Caverns are two of the most impressive creations of nature *you* could ever hope to see.

However, in formal papers, *one* is most often used to refer to people in general and *you* is reserved for occasions when the writer wishes to speak directly to the audience.

> The Grand Canyon and the Carlsbad Caverns are two of the most impressive creations of nature *one* could ever hope to see.
>
> *You,* the students at this school, must speak up to make the educational needs in our community clear to the school board.
>
> Did *you* ever wonder what caused *you* to forget something?

Whichever level of formality you choose, be sure to remain consistent throughout a particular essay.

Index

Abbreviations, 473–475
  in addressing people, 473
  inappropriate, 475
  of Latin terms, 474
  of measurements, 474
  of money, 473
  of organizations, 473
  of percents, 474
  periods in, 515–516
  of publication data, 474
  of technical terms, 474
  of time, 473
Abstractions, 101–103, 175–176
Abstracts of English Studies, 237
Active and Passive, 144–146, 192, 365, 372–373
Adjective, 366
Adjectives-adverbs, contrasts in nonstandard/standard, 387–388
  contrasts in Spanish/English, 390–391
Adverb, 366
Afro-American Encyclopedia, 250
Almanac, The World, 230
Analogies, in conclusions, 80
  in introductions, 61
  logic of, 105–106
Angry/Delighted Chart, 38
Annotated bibliography, 341–344, 632–636
  Antecedent, *see* Pronoun, agreement of; Pronoun, reference
Anthropology research, 242–243
Appositives, 143–144, 419–420
Apostrophe, 476–480
  for contraction, 478–479
  for plurals, 479–480, 511
  for possession, 476–478
Argumentation, 9–10. *See also* Logic
Arrangement, *see* Middles

Article, contrasts in nonstandard/standard, 388
  contrasts in Spanish/English, 391–392
  defined, 366
Art research, 232–234
Audience, 2–5
  and building paragraphs, 127
  defined, 2
  of peers, 4
  of popular magazines, 4
  in selecting subject, 49
  and sentence patterns, 150–151
  of teachers, 3
Audience Survey, 5–6

Bartlett's Familiar Quotations, 226
Beginnings, *see* Introductions
Bibliography, *see* Research paper
Bibliography, annotated, 341–344
Biography indexes, 229
Biology research, 263–264
Black English, *see* Nonstandard/Standard English
Blurred syntax, 467–468
Book Review Digest, 227
Book reviews, 227, 337–338
Brackets, 480–481, 515
Brainstorming, 42–45
Business and economics research, 243–244
Business letters, 353–356

Cambridge History of English Literature, 236
Capitalization, 481–487
  of abbreviations, 487
  of directions, 486
  of diseases, 487
  of first word in sentence, 481
  of names, 482–483
  of places, 485

  of planets, 487
  of poetry, 481–482
  of products, 487
  of professions, 487
  of races, 483
  of relatives, 484
  of religious words, 486–487
  of school classes, 486
  of times, 484–485
  of titles, 482, 483–484
Cause and effect reasoning, 104–105
Chemistry research, 264–265
Chicano Bibliography, A Comprehensive, 251
Christensen, Francis, 128
Chronological arrangement, 68
Circumlocutions, 173
Classification, 69–70
Clause, 374–377
  adverb/adjective, 375–377
  commas with introductory, 491–492
  defined, 374
  main/subordinate, 374, 427
  modifiers in, 376
  noun, 374–375
Cliché, 170–171, 194
Colon, 488–490
  as introducer, 488–489
  with other punctuation, 490
  with quoatations, 489
  as separator, 489
  in titles, 489
Comma, 490–497
  with adjectives, 493–494
  with appositives, 494
  with conjunctions, 491
  with contrasts, 494
  in cumulative sentence, 495
  with direct address, 494
  excessive use of, 496–497
  with interjections, 492

with introductory phrases and
   clauses, 491–492
in numerals, 495
with quotations, 495
in a series, 493
to set off modifiers, 494
to show omissions, 494
between subject and verb,
   496–497
with transitions, 492
between verb and object, 496
Community dialect, *see*
   Nonstandard/Standard English
Comparison, arrangement by,
   71–74
Comparisons, 463–466
   inappropriate, 464–466
   incomplete, 463–464
Complement, 373
Complete predicate, 374
Complex sentence, 379–380
Compound-complex sentence,
   379–380
Compound sentence, 379–380
Computer science research,
   262–263
Conclusions, 77–84
   basic patterns, 79
   effective strategies, 79–82
   function of, 77–78
   ineffective strategies, 83–84
Congressional Record, 255
Conjunction, 368–369
Coordinating conjunction, 369
Coordination, in the outline, 88–89
   in the paragraph, 128–129
   in the sentence, 141–142
"CR," 348–353
Critical analyses, 337–338
Critical reading, 331–337

Dangling modifier, 461–462
Dash, 148, 498–500
"A Degree," 16–19
Demonstrative pronoun, 362
Description, 7–8, 131–134
Development of ideas, 15–19
   in "A Degree," 16–19
   and evidence, 16
   and prewriting, 17
   from thesis, 16
Dialect, 380–388
   defined, 381
   and grammar, 381–382, 383
   and language, 382
   and pronunciation, 381

standard English, 382–383
and vocabulary, 381
Diction, 158–188
Dictionaries and encyclopedias,
   225–226
Dictionary of American Slang, 226
Dictionary definition, as
   denotation, 164–165
   in introduction, 63
Dictionary, use of, 181–184
Direct object, 372
Double negatives, 466–467

Economics and business research,
   243–244
*Educational Resources Information
   Center* (ERIC), 245–246
Education Index, 245
Education research, 244–245
Ellipses, 285–286, 500–501
Encyclopedia Americana, 225
*Encyclopedia of the American
   Indian,* 251
Encyclopedia Britannica, 225
Encyclopedias and dictionaries,
   224–226
Endings, *see* Conclusions
Engineering research, 261–262
English as a second language,
   388–394
Environment Abstracts, 260
Essay evaluation, 331–337
Essay examinations, 326–331
*Essay and General Literature
   Index,* 226, 245
"ESP and Skepticism," 199–215
Ethnic studies and minority
   research, 250–252
Euphemisms, 176
Evaluating nonfiction, 331–337
Examination essays, 326–331
Exclamation point, 501–502
Expository essays, 7

Facts on File, 230
Film Literature Index, 238
Folklore, Abstracts of, 242
Footnotes, *see* Research paper
Foreign phrases, 279–280,
   290–291, 473, 526–527
Forster, E. M., 1
Fragment, sentence, 416–422

"Garbage by Any Other Name,"
   297–325
Geography research, 246–248, 265

Geology research, 264–265
Gerund, 370, 442
Gerund phrase, 377–378
Government documents, 230
Grammar defined, 380, 383
Great Gatsby, The, 3–4
Grove's Dictionary of Music, 234

Hanged, hung, 440
Hemingway, Ernest, 158
History research, 248–250
Home economics research, 262
Humanities Index, 232
Hyphen, 502–506
   in compound words, 504–506
   at end of line, 502–503
   with numbers, 506
   with prefixes, 503–505

I, use of, 166–167
Idiomatic expressions, 392–394
Illustration arrangement, 70
Imperative mood, 365
Impromptu theme, 326–331
Indefinite pronoun, 179, 363
Indicative mood, 365
Indirect object, 372
Inference, drawn from reading,
   331–337
Infinitive, 370, 441–442
Infinitive phrase, 377–379, 419
Interjection, 369
International relations
   research, 256
Introductions, 57–65
   basic patterns, 58–59
   effective strategies, 59–62
   ineffective strategies, 62–65
   purpose of, 56–57
   in research paper, 294
Invention (see Prewriting)
Irregular verbs, 437–440
Italics, 525–527

Journal, 39–42, 357–358

Laboratory report, 346–347
Language, *see* Words
Language research, 235–236
Lay, lie, 439
Letters, business, 353–356
Library research, 219–266
   use of *Bibliographic Index* in, 223
   use of card catalogue in,
      219–221, 222–223
   use of *A Guide to Reference
      Books* in, 224

use of *National Union Catalog* in, 223
use of *Subject Heading Guide* in, 221–222
see also particular fields: anthropology, biology, geology, psychology, physics
Limiting the subject, *see* Prewriting
Literature research, 236
Logic, 93–110
 in abstractions, 101–103
 in analogies, 105–106
 in assumptions, 99–100
 in causes-effects, 104–105
 inductive and deductive, 93–95
 and objectivity, 100–101
 of opposing views, 104–105
 progression of, 99
 of representative information, 107
 and sources, 107
 of statistics, 108–109, 231
 of stereotypes, 106–107
 in supports, 96–99
 in thesis, 95–96

Manuscript form, *see* Typing
Mathematics research, 264–265
Medicine research, 263–264
Metaphor, mixed, 171
Middles, 56–57, 67–77
 chronological, 68
 classification, 69–70
 comparison, 71–73
 function of, 56
 illustration, 70
 patterns, 67
 process, 67–68
 spatial, 68–69
Minority and ethnic studies research, 250–252
Misplaced modifier, 146, 460–461
MLA International Bibliography, 235–236, 237
Modes, 7–10
 argumentation, 9–10
 defined, 7
 description, 7–8
 narration, 9
Modifiers, 376, 460–462
Mood, 365, 435–437
Multiple end punctuation, 507
Music research, 234–235

Narration, 9

Negatives, contrasts in nonstandard/standard, 388
 contrasts in Spanish/English, 391
 double, 466–468
 as idioms, 467–468
Newspaper indexes, 229
Nonstandard/Standard English, 384–388
 adjectives and adverbs in, 387–388
 articles in, 388
 conjunctions in, 388
 negatives in, 388
 nouns in, 385–386
 plurals in, 384–385
 possessives in, 386
 pronouns in, 386–388
 verbs in, 384–385
 see also Spanish/English contrasts
Noun, 362
 contrasts in nonstandard/ standard, 385–387
 constrasts in Spanish/English, 389–390
 defined, 362
 formation of plurals, 35
 possessives of, 362
Numbers, 507
 beginning sentences, 508
 in books, 509
 in currency, 510
 in dates, 508
 in fractions/percents, 510
 large round, 509–510
 with parentheses, 511
 plurals of, 511
 of roads, 509
 within sentences, 507–508
 in time expressions, 508
Nutrition Abstracts, 262

Observation report, 348–353
Oliver, Kenneth, 380
One, use of, 167
Opinions, 16
Opposition, 53, 62, 103–104
Orwell, George, 103
Outlines, 85–93
 checking logic in, 95
 conventions of, 86–87
 developing, 87–92
 faulty and corrected, 90–92
 for research paper, 281
 scratch, 85

topic or sentence, 85–86
 see also Logic
Oxford Companion to American Literature, 236
Oxford English Dictionary, 226

Paragraph, 114–137
 coherence in, 121–123
 coordination in, 128–129
 development of, 124–125
 division in, 127
 and essay, 114–116
 subordination in, 128, 129–130.
  See also Paragraph models
 topic sentence in, 116–118
 top sentence in, 118–119
 unity in, 119
Paragraph models, 130–135
 for comparing, 134–135
 for describing, 131–134
 for explaining, 130–131
Parallelism, 462–463
Paraphrasing a source, 275, 277, 296
Parentheses, 512–513
 with cross references, 512
 for extra information, 512
 with letters/numbers, 512
 with other punctuation, 513
Participial phrase, 377–378
Participle, 370, 442–443
Parts of speech, 362–370
Passive voice, 144–146, 192, 365, 373
"Peanuts," 6
Performing arts research, 237–238
Period, 514–516
 in abbreviations, 515
 as an ellipsis point, 500–501, 516
 at end of sentence, 514
 with indirect question, 514
 with parentheses, 515
 with quotation marks, 514
 with sentence fragment, 514
Periodical indexes, 227–229
Personal pronoun, 362–363
Persuasive writing, *see* Argumentation
"The Phenomenon of Death," 74–76
Philosopher's Index, 239
Philosophy and religion research, 238–239
Phrase, 376
 absolute, 377
 commas with introductory, 491–492

defined, 376
functions of, 377
prepositional, 367, 378
verbal, 377–379
Physical science research, 264–265
Physics research, 265
Plagiarism, 282–286
Plural noun, 362, 406
Point of view, 12–13
consistent, 12–13
defined, 12
Polishing the draft, 189–218
for clichés, 170–171, 194
for deadwood, 192
for noun pile-ups, 192–193
for organization, 191–192
for repetition, 194
for research paper, 292
a sample of, 198, 200, 202, 204, 206, 208, 210
steps in, 194–195
for "to be" verbs, 193
for transitions, 194
Political science research, 253–256
Poole's Index to Periodical Literature, 249
Possessive noun, 362, 476–478
Poverty and Human Resources Abstracts, 257
Predicate, in sentence structure, 371–372
in topic sentence, 117
Predicate noun, 373
Predication, faulty, 415
Preposition, 367–368
contrasts in Spanish/English, 392
in idioms, 392–394
Prepositional phrase, 367, 378
Prewriting, audience, writer, subject in, 48
brainstorming in, 42–45
charting in, 45–48
defined, 24–25, 36–37
journals in, 39–42, 357–358
need for, 36–37
and procrastination, 35–36
for research paper, 267–268, 270–271, 281
sources of invention in, 37–38
subject selection in, 48
in "The Value of College," 26–27
Primary sources, 249
Process arrangement, 67–68
Process of writing, 24–34

prewriting in, 24–25
proofreading in, 34
rewriting in, 25, 27
typing in, 33–34
in "The Value of College Today," 26–34
writing in, 25, 27
Pronoun, 362–364
agreement of, 454–457
case of, 447–450
constrasts in nonstandard/standard, 386–388
contrasts in Spanish/English, 390–391
defined, 362–364
demonstrative, 362
indefinite, 179, 363
intensive, 451–452
personal, 363–364
reference of, 452–454
reflexive, 364, 450–451
relative, 143–144, 363
Psychoanalytical Writings, Index to, 253
Psychology research, 252–253
Public Affairs Information Services (PAIS), 241

Question, contrasts in Spanish/English, 389
indirect, 514, 516
within a quotation, 517, 521
Question mark, 516–517
with direct question, 516
with indirect question, 516
with interior questions, 517
with other punctuation, 517
Quotation mark, 518–521
with dashes/questions/exclamations, 521
with direct quoting, 518, 520
formation of, 518
with periods/commas, 521
for quotations in quotations, 519
with semicolons/colons, 521
for special tone, 519–520
in titles, 519–520
for words as words, 519; 519–520
Quoting a source, 274, 277, 283–286, 296–297, 495

Raise, rise, 439–440
Reader's Guide to Periodical Literature, 228–229
Reasoning, *see* Logic

Redundancy, *see* Words
Reflexive pronoun, 363
Religion and philosophy research, 238–239
Repetition, in outlines, 96–97
in paragraphs, 121–122, 127
in sentences, 194
Reports, 344–346, 346–347, 348–353
Research paper, 267–325
bibliography cards for, 271–272, 275
bibliography forms for, 272–274, 294–295
choosing topic for, 268–269
footnoting in, 287–288, 291–292, 294–295, 295–296
footnote forms for, 288–290, 290–291, 520
materials for, 268
notetaking for, 275–277, 279–280
outline for, 281
paraphrase in, 275, 277
plagiarism in, 282–283, 294, 295
questions/answers about, 294–297
quotations in, 274, 277, 283, 296–297
research strategy for, 268–270. *See also* Library research
sample, 297–325
sample notecard for, 280–281, 320
summary in, 275, 277
title page for, 297, 309
typing and proofreading the, 292–294, 297
Résumé, 338–341
Retained object, 373
Revision (see Polishing the draft)
Rewriting, 25, 27, 189–191, 212–216. *See also* Polishing the draft
Run-on sentence, 422–428

Scientific reports, 344–346, 346–347
Secondary sources, 249
Semicolon, 522–523
for clarity, 523
for joining related ideas, 148–149, 380, 427, 522
with other punctuation, 523
with transitions, 522

see also Run-on sentence
Sentence, 138–157
  emphatic punctuation in, 148–149
  incomplete, 416–422
  length of, 147
  parallelism in, 147–148
  the passive, 144–146, 192, 365, 373
  periodic and cumulative, 149–151
  reordering of, 146–147
Sentence combining, 138–147
  by coordination, 141–142
  for maturity, 138–140
  of relative clauses, 143–144, 375
  by subordination, 142–143
  for texture, 138
Sentence mimicry, 154–157
Sentence structure, 371–380
  clause in, 374–376
  complement in, 373
  completeness in, 371
  complex, 379–380
  compound, 379–380
  compound-complex, 379–380
  direct object in, 372
  indirect object in, 372
  phrases in, 376–379
  predicate noun in, 373
  retained object in, 373
  simple, 372–374, 379
  subject/predicate of, 371–372
Set, sit, 440
Sexist language, 177–180, 455
Shuy, Roger, 381
Slang, 174–175
Slash, 524–525
Social science research, 240–242
Social Sciences Index, 241
Sociology research, 256–258
Spanish/English contrasts, 388–393
  in adjectives and adverbs, 391
  in articles, 391
  idiomatic, 393–394
  in negatives, 391
  in nouns, 390
  in prepositions, 392
  in pronouns, 390–391
  in questions, 389
  in verbs, 389–390
Spatial arrangement, 68–69
Spelling, 395–404
  checking dictionary for, 395

  list of correct, 401–404
  pronunciation and, 395–396
  and proofreading, 401
  by rules, 396–401
Standard English dialect, 382–383. See also Nonstandard/Standard English
Statistical Abstracts, 231
Statistics, 230–231
Statistics Sources, 231
Subject chart, 45–48
Subjunctive mood, 366, 435–437
Subordinating conjunction, 368–369, 428
Subordination, in the outline, 136–137
  in the paragraph, 128, 129–130
  in the sentence, 142–143
Summarizing a source, 275, 277
Syntax, 460–468
  comparisons and, 463–466
  mixed, 467–468
  modifiers and, 460–462
  parallelism and, 462–463

Tenses, contrasts in Spanish/English, 389–390
  correct use of, 432–435
  in nonstandard/standard English, 384–385
  of verbals, 440–443
Term paper, *see* Research paper
Thesaurus, use of, 184
Thesis, 50–54
  defined, 50, 50–52
  in "A Degree," 17
  development of, 52–54
  and development of ideas, 15
  in introduction, 58–59
  and opposition, 53
  reasonableness of, 95–96
  in research paper, 267–268, 270–271, 281, 296
  restatement of, 79
  in "The Value of College," 27
  versus intention, 50, 51
Thinking, *see* Logic
Titles, 64–65
"To be" verbs, 158–159
Tone, 19–22
  consistent, 22
  defined, 19
  flowery, 21
  in introduction, 56, 58, 64
  ironic, 21

  objective, 19–20
  preaching, 20
"Toward a Humanistic Society," 342–344
Transitions, 122–123, 425, 492
Trite expressions, 170–171, 194
Typing, 196, 292–294, 297

Underlining, 525–528
  for emphasis, 527–528
  foreign words, 526–527
  titles, 526
  words as words, 527

"The Value of College," 28–33
Verb, 364–366
  agreement with subject, 406–411
  conditional, 435–436
  contrasts in nonstandard/standard, 384–385
  contrasts in Spanish/English, 389
  irregular, 437–440
  linking, 364
  mood, 365
  number, 364–365
  passive/active, 365, 372–373
  tense, 364–365, 432–435
  transitive/intransitive, 364
Verbal, 370–371, 440–443
Virgule, 524–525
Vita, 338–341
Vocabulary development, 180–184
Voice, 5–6, 159–160

Webster's Third New International Dictionary, 225
Which, who, that, 457
Whose/who's, 450
Women's Studies Abstracts, 251
Word List, 44–45
Words, 158–188
  abstract, 175–176
  as circumlocutions, 173
  connotation of, 164–165
  contractions of, 169
  as euphemisms, 176
  jargon, 173
  levels of, 160–161
  origins of, 184
  sexist, 177–180
  slang, 174–175
  trite, 170–171
Writer's Notebook, 39–42, 357–358

You, use of, 168

THE LIBRARY
ST. MARY'S COLLEGE OF MARYLAND
ST. MARY'S CITY, MARYLAND 20686